STORYBOOK PUB

STORYBOOK PUB

A CONTEMPORARY ROMANCE COLLECTION

LOVE & DEVOTION AUTHOR SERVICES, INC.

Storybook Pub, A Contemporary Romance Collection
Copyright © 2020 Love & Devotion Author Services, Inc.
Published by Love & Devotion Author Services, Inc.
All rights reserved
Print Edition ISBN 978-1-7347960-1-8
Storybook Pub, A Contemporary Romance Collection is a work of fiction and does not in any way advocate irresponsible behavior. This book contains content that is not suitable for readers 17 and under. Please store your files where they cannot be accessed by minors. Any resemblance to actual things, events, locales, or persons living or dead is entirely coincidental. Names, characters, places, brands, products, media, and incidents are either the product of the author's imagination or are used fictitiously. The author acknowledges the trademark status and ownership of any location names or products mentioned in this book. The author received no compensation for any mention of said trademark.
Cover Photographer: Tonya Clark - All About the Cover Photography
Cover Model: Matt Carothers
Graphic Designer: Irene Johnson johnsoni@mac.com

Welcome to the Storybook Pub. I'm Kole O'Shea, proprietor of the pubs around the world. I invite you to join us and watch wishes come true —maybe yours will, too.

CONTENTS

DENISE WELLS	BREEZY LIKE SUNDAY MORNING	1
KRISTINE DUGGER	LOVE AT FIRST BREW	49
HALO ROBERTS	LONELY HEARTS	85
ZN WILLETT	ART LIFE	127
DC RENEE	A GREAT LOVE STORY	153
JESSALYN JAMESON	WISHED FOR YOU	189
MAYRA STATHAM	TAKING CHANCES	233
TONYA CLARK	HIDDEN WINGS	269
NAOMI SPRINGTHORP	FOR ONE LASS	309
TESSA MCFIONN	WISHES AND WHISKEY	345
EMBER-RAINE WINTERS	HIDDEN FATE	387
RAYNE ELIZABETH	BEWITCHED BY THE BARTENDER	419
TERI KAY	COMING HOME	455
MARY DEAN	TRADING LIVES	497
MARY ROGERS	THE SHOW'S NOT OVER	527
TARRAH ANDERS	SPEAKEASY	561
FAITH RYAN	LOVE IS BLIND	599
KENZIE ROSE	HEARTS COLLIDE	637
PEPPER NORTH	THE SCENT OF HER	675
LANE MARTIN	IRISH TWINS	715
C. J. CORBIN	A MORNING KISS	749

About the Author 783

BREEZY LIKE SUNDAY MORNING

DENISE WELLS

**One secret fantasy.
Two changed realities.**

Sub-genre: Romantic Comedy
Relationship: Male/Female

1

BREEZY

JAY: Dude. They're interested. You HAVE to take this one.
JAY: Don't back out on me again.
JAY: It's Reckless X. You don't say no to Reckless X.

What does Jay mean *again*?
My boyfriend is a musician. Jay's managed Levi's career for years now. And from this text it becomes apparent Levi's been rejecting gigs, fucking with his future, just so he can stay behind for me.

Yeah, yeah, don't start on the whole "privacy" thing with me—the incessant buzzing made me think there was an emergency. Levi accidentally left his phone behind for his quick trip to the corner store to pick up the coffee creamer I love. He's perfect like that, always doing things to make me happy, like running out first thing on a Sunday morning to replace the creamer he ran out of so I can have some in my coffee.

My heart suddenly feels weighted down with the guilt that maybe I'm holding Levi back. Which is the last thing I want. So, I do that thing that is even worse than reading your guy's messages. I fake answer the text.

LEVI: Again?
JAY: Don't play dumb.
JAY: You reneged on Brad Plaid Band 6 months ago.
JAY: Because you didn't want to leave Breezy.

He could have gone on tour with Brad Plaid Band and he didn't because of me? They are only one of the top rock-country-fusion groups around. Ohmigod, that's got to be the sweetest thing he's ever done for me. That's a huge opportunity that he gave up.

Shit.

That's a huge opportunity that he gave up.

Double shit.

LEVI: I won't pass this up. Tell them I'm in.
JAY: And that's how we get it done, son!
JAY: We leave in a week.
JAY: Emailing you deets and contract we looked at last week.
LEVI: **thumbs up emoji**

I set Levi's phone down in a daze. He didn't even tell me he was approached by Brad Plaid Band. That was six months ago. What would he have done this time with Reckless X?

He *has* to do this.

Reckless X is just as big, if not bigger than, Brad Plaid Band. But Reckless X is more rock, like Levi is. Their single, "Satin Sheets," is number one right now. Levi would be stupid to pass this up.

How do I get him to understand that?

Why didn't he talk to me about Brad Plaid Band? Touring, playing in front of a live audience is what every musician strives for. Living his dream for a couple months is something I would totally understand. And I could visit him on the road, maybe even become a groupie or a roadie.

I can't believe he hasn't said anything.

Who am I kidding?

Levi is exactly the kind of guy who would lie to me again just to stay here and not damage our relationship. He's always wanted a relationship like his parents. They have an amazing marriage and have been together for over thirty years. It's incredible if you think about it.

Shit. He's going to be back any minute.

How do I do this?

I flop back on the bed, holding my stuffed Siberian Husky for inspiration. I have one at each of our apartments, since neither of our leases allow for live pets. Levi bought me the next best thing for each place because I love them that much.

Speak of the devil. . .

"Hey, beautiful, I'm back," he calls out. "Want me to bring you coffee?"

Because he's the kind of guy who not only goes out first thing in the morning to get you coffee creamer, he also brings you coffee in bed, with two fingers of cream mixed in, exactly the way you like it.

Levi appears in the doorway, a mug of coffee in each hand. Brown hair still tousled from sleep, already having taken his T-shirt back off and removed his shoes. He saunters toward me in low slung jeans that curve to his body in all the right places. With his sexy smile that makes the dimple on his left cheek pop; the one I like to stick my tongue in it when he's not paying attention.

"Z?"

"In here," I call back. I like that he calls me "Z." With a first name like Breezy I'm used to taunts and nicknames, but his for me is my favorite.

"Mmm, you're still in bed, just the way I like it." He wiggles his eyebrows, almost making me giggle in the brief second that I forget I'm upset about this whole touring thing.

He leans in to kiss me as he settles by my side on the bed, careful not to spill the coffee. I smile softly and look down into the caramel colored liquid he's just handed me. Warming my hands around the bowl. I'm still trying to piece together how I'm going to broach the subject.

"I got us a Sunday paper." He pulls it from behind him where it must have been stuck in the back of his jeans.

"Great," I say flatly.

"You okay, babe?" he asks, settling back further against the headboard, his coffee in one hand, the other separating the news sections that we each like to read first.

Him: sports, entertainment, local news.

Me: cooking, comics, travel.

I take a deep breath and feign nonchalance. "I haven't heard you talk about Jay in a while. How's everything going with the band and stuff?"

"Huh?" He glances up at me distractedly. "Oh, yeah, it's good. Everything is good."

"Any new gigs?" I sip my coffee and turn the page, slowly perusing the featured recipes of the week.

"Nah. It's slow right now."

"You'd think he'd be able to get you guys a small tour just around the Pacific Northwest or something. I mean, that is what he's paid for, right?"

"Small tour?" He hides a smile behind his coffee cup as he takes a drink.

I watch his face for any hint at going on the road. But he's blanked it.

"You trying to get rid of me, baby?" He reaches over and squeezes my knee, then pats it almost absently. Not turning to meet my eyes.

"No, not at all. I just like to stay on top of what's happening with the band."

"That's sweet. Believe me, if there was something exciting to share with you, I'd be sharing it."

I study his profile, but his expression gives nothing away.

"Has Jay ever gotten you guys a tour?" I ask.

Levi sets his coffee down on the nightstand beside his bed and turns to me. "Where's all this coming from, Z? You aren't usually this inquisitive about the music stuff."

"Yes, I am. I always want to know what's going on," I argue. "You didn't answer my question."

"What question was that?" He turns back to his paper.

"Has Jay ever booked you a tour?"

"Have we gone on tour?"

"No."

"Well." He waves his hand as though that completes his sentence. "But I'm right in that his job is to book you gigs, right?"

"I guess. Yeah."

"So, he sucks at his job."

"I wouldn't say that," he hedges.

"He's not doing the job you've hired him to do."

"We play gigs all the time," Levi defends.

"Sure, gigs here in Seattle."

"Well." He pulls me into a one arm hug. "I happen to love Seattle gigs."

"What about the guys? Would they rather have gigs outside of the greater Seattle area?"

"Why, you got a gig for us, babe?" He smiles and leans in the other direction, snagging his coffee from the nightstand and taking a large drink.

"No. I just want to make sure you guys get all the opportunities you've got coming to you."

"I assure you, Jay is great at his job." He's back to looking at his paper and not me. Attempting to stifle this discussion, I'm sure.

"If you had the opportunity to go on tour, would you?"

He winces. It's slight, but I see it before he has a chance to mask his face completely. "Of course, I would."

"Really? You'd leave me and your family for months on end to go play in a different city every night."

"I would talk to you about it first." He looks at me finally. "But, Z, that's part of being a professional musician. Touring and concerts. I would hate being away from you. I'd miss my family, but it would be temporary. So, yes, as long as you were okay with it, I'd probably go."

"Probably?"

"It would depend on the type of tour, if we were headlining or opening. If it was bar gigs or arenas, that sort of thing."

"Let's say you got the opportunity to tour with a big-name band. A nationwide tour, would you do it?"

"Are you worried I'm going to leave you or something?"

"Just answer the question, Levi."

"I'll always talk to you about anything that could take me away from you before making a decision."

"So, how come you didn't tell me about Brad Plaid Band?" I ask.

And there it is. The guilt floods his face. My only question now is, is it guilt because he really wants to go, but thinks I can't handle the separation? Or is it guilt because he lied just now?

"How do you know about that?"

"It doesn't matter how I know. Tell me why you failed to mention it."

He takes my coffee from me and sets both mugs on the nightstand, then folds his paper up and sets it aside. Turning to face me, he takes my hands in his. "I . . ." His mouth opens and closes, like a fish. Lips trying to form words, but no sounds coming out.

"And while you're articulating your excuses so well, how about Reckless X? Were you going to say anything about that?"

"How did you . . . Breezy, it wasn't . . . I mean . . . I didn't . . . Shit." He runs his hands through his hair, tousling it further, making the front stand straight up. He looks sexy as hell. So much so, I almost forget that he's a fucking liar.

"It's not how it looks," he says, finally getting a complete sentence out.

"How do you think it looks, Levi?"

"I think it looks like I'm keeping information from you."

I raise my brow, waiting for him to continue.

"And that I lied about it just now," he finishes, looking down into his lap. "It's my fault. I didn't want to leave you, didn't want to mess up what we have. I mean, Breeze, I love you so much. You are *the most* important thing in the world to me. I would pass up any and every opportunity for you."

His words warm my heart as much as they infuriate me. How dare he put this on me. Make it about me, and then lie about it?

"Why lie about it?"

"Because I didn't want you to try and talk me into it."

"Why not, Levi? This is what you've been working toward, for years. If this isn't the benchmark for success, what is?"

How could he possibly *not* want to go? If we weren't together would he go?

"How come it's not enough to just play local gigs and make a decent living? Stay here with you and be happy? Why does it have to be all about the fame and recognition?"

"Because that's kind of the point, isn't it?" I ask.

"No, the point is love and family."

"And I'm someone you love?"

"With all my heart."

"Yet you lied to me—before and just now. Outright lied."

"Yes." His chin lowers to his chest, eyes downcast.

I get off the bed and gather my clothes, then slam the bathroom door after me. It takes all my strength not to break down right then. Instead I dress to leave without another word. Holding my palm up to Levi as I go in response to his attempts to get me to stay.

I'm not even to the parking lot of his complex before he's calling after me. Shoeless, shirtless, running down the front steps yelling my name.

"No!" I yell, pointing my finger. "I need time and you need to give it to me. You lied to me, lied right to my face. I don't know if I can trust you anymore." I let the tears pool now, because on some level I know this is the beginning of the end. If I can't trust him, I can't be with him.

Because if he'll lie about something this huge, what else will he lie about? And if he does really want to go on this tour, I don't need to be the reason to stop him. Despite what he says. Because as much as I love this man, as much as I see my future with him, I also see what he could be. I don't want to be the reason he doesn't live the life he's destined to lead, living a lie with me instead.

Which is why I block his number when I get home and try to pretend today never happened.

2

LEVI'S FIRST HIT

Breezy Like Sunday Morning

There ain't nothing I loved more
Than our lazy Sunday mornings.
Till the time you slammed the door
Left me broken with no warning.

I put you up on that perch so high,
Loved you harder than I know how.
But then you're gone with no goodbye,
Looks like we're all over now.

You're Breezy like Sunday morning.
Just comes on without a warning.
Make me love you, make me hate you.
Threw away my heart just like you do.

Don't matter what you want,
I gladly give it to you.
But you're lovin' was a taunt,

BREEZY LIKE SUNDAY MORNING

Now you're onto someone new.

You're Breezy like Sunday morning.
Just comes on without a warning.
Make me love you, make me hate you.
Threw away my heart just like you do.

You left me standing there,
Not even one look back.
Woman, did you ever care?
Now you've turned my heart to black.

I brought you coffee in my bed
Gave my shoulder for your head
Thought you made my life complete
You fucking thought I was a liar and a cheat.

Breezy like Sunday morning
Comes on without a warning
Make me love you, make me hate you
Threw away my heart just like you do.

3

BREEZY, TWO YEARS LATER

I look up toward the ceiling of the café where Susan and I are having brunch. Levi's first hit of many, "Breezy Like Sunday Morning," is playing on the overhead speakers.

The hit I hate the most.

Because, yes, the Breezy in the song title is a reference to me.

"At least he has other hits now," Susan says to console me. "It's not the only song of his people are singing anymore."

"Yeah, but it's still the most popular one," I grumble.

"No, it's not." She's lying and I love her for it. "Everything he writes now becomes popular."

She has a point.

Since the last time I saw him, Levi Miller has become a near household name. You can't go anywhere without hearing his music playing or seeing his handsome face plastered on something. T-shirts, posters, endorsements, you name it. Case in point, his music is playing at the very freaking café where we're brunching. Taunting me.

After I broke it off with Levi, he went on tour with Reckless X and immediately released a new single about his ex-girlfriend breaking his heart. The song became a hit, almost overnight, and Levi and his band worldwide sensations. Going on that tour changed Levi's life. And while I cannot stand that I'm the subject of an international hate anthem for men after a breakup, I'm happy that he finally has the recognition he deserves.

It's taken me until now to be mature enough to admit that.

I'm not one hundred percent sure I believe it, but at least I say it aloud.

Or in my head.

"So, you know how you said you're ready to move on?"

"I did?"

"Yeah, and that you thought you might start dating again."

She's right, I did say that. After the last time the tabloids pictured Levi with some bimbo hanging all over him on the front cover, declaring love is in the air and wedding bells are ringing.

For someone so hurt, he sure got over it quickly.

I mean, it's only been two years.

"You know," Susan says. "It's been two years."

"That's what I was just—"

"It's a long time to be alone."

"—Not thinking."

How can she think that two years is so long when I feel like just yesterday Levi and I were still together and happy? Would we still be happy now if we'd stayed together? Maybe married with kids?

As it is, once he released that song, Levi became an instant hero with millions of women offering themselves up as salve for his broken heart. I, on the other hand, was hated instantly by women and men alike. Women calling me a heartless bitch, and men . . . well, men said the same. Let me tell you, there is nothing more humbling than becoming a social pariah.

And even though Levi issued a statement asking the public not to judge me for his words written in the heat of the moment, during a personal and private time. He still released the song and didn't keep any of it personal or private.

I turn my attention back to Susan when I notice she's still talking.

"Well, I did something for you," she says. "And I think you're going to like it."

She uses *that* tone—the one that guarantees I'm not going to like it at all. Then she keeps right on talking as though her idea *is* a good one.

"I didn't even really think it would work out when I started. But it has and well, now, you're in. And I, for one, am so excited about it. I mean, it's truly the opportunity of a lifetime."

An endorsement that rings true for many things over the past couple years.

"And since you're already in—"

"In what?" I ask.

"Have you been listening to me at all?"

I shrug.

"You're going to be on Storybook Pub."

"The reality dating show?"

"Yes!"

"The one where someone in your life nominates you and sends in your entire life story and all the reasons why you should be picked. Then the main guy narrows it down and selects a few who then go on television and pair up with all sorts of other people until they find the one?"

"Well, ideally you're just pairing up with one person, but yes, that's the show."

"Why would you do that?"

"Because you love reality TV and you need to start dating again."

"Just because I love reality TV does not mean I want my own reality on TV."

"Come on, you'll have fun. When are you ever going to get a chance like this again?"

"Uh, I don't know, next season? Or the next reality dating show to become popular? Or how about never, because it's a stupid idea."

She looks at me, eyes wide and blinking. She's been my friend since we were kids, yet I still fall for her little puppy dog expression every fucking time.

"I don't want to be in the public eye again, Suze." I'm whining. I know I'm doing it; she knows I'm doing it, we both hate it, but I still do it. Because after Levi wrote that song about me, and every freakin' person in the world decided to love it, all I heard from then on when someone found out my name, was: oh, are you the girl that song is about?

"You don't even go by the name Breezy anymore. You're Bree now, and she's a whole new person. Not the subject of a number one worldwide hit song."

"You're not helping," I grumble. "Plus, the second someone hears my real name, they'll know it's me and then all the questions will start."

"You've always wanted to be on a reality show," Susan says.

"No, I haven't," I lie.

"Um, Ultimate Cooking Championship? You tried out but didn't get on. And don't forget you signed up to be on The World Legit in college, didn't get on. And I'm sure there's at least one you've never told me about. Not to mention all the ones you watch. For real, how many shows do you have recorded on your DVR?"

"I refuse to answer that on the grounds it may incriminate me." I smile.

"Okay, well, did I mention that it's fifty thousand dollars to the charity of your choice this time around? Think of all the little Siberian Huskies you could feed at the rescue with that."

"That is a lot," I agree.

"Yeah, that's what I thought." She smiles and bounces in her chair a bit. Like she's just said something that's amazing and is going to make me feel better. Since she did.

"I hate you."

"I love you."

She preens. She sits across the table and preens. Because she knows I'll do this. Because she's right, it's been a secret fantasy of mine *forever* to go on a reality show. And she's not lying when she says I love them. I do. I'm obsessed. Something about seeing what people do in their everyday lives, but still in front of a camera, fascinates me.

I know there's the whole school of thought that everything is scripted, I prefer to believe otherwise for the sake of entertainment. But, even if it is scripted, that doesn't discount the fact that you've then, as someone on the show, allowed your life to be scripted by another person. And then you put it in front of a camera. *Still* fascinating to me.

"Fine," I tell her. "What do I have to do?"

4

BREEZY

I may be a reality show junkie, but I'm not a put-my-life-in-front-of-the-camera-for-real kind of person. Which is why I'm standing on the street corner in front of the Storybook Pub debating changing my life by going inside.

I suppose there's always the chance it *won't* change my life. I may not even make it through this final selection process. I've gone over it in my head a million times. What will happen if I'm chosen. And what will happen if I'm not. Susan says I'm perfect for this. That I will have the time of my life. But she has to say that. It's in the best friend contract.

Not to mention this whole thing was her idea to begin with.

But Kole O'Shea, the creator of the show, always says there's love out there for everyone. It's practically his catch phrase. Plus, *out there* is a big place. And I'm included in *everyone*. So, really, what have I got to lose? Not to mention, I said I'd be here so I can't back out now.

Pull up your big girl panties, Bree. Let's do this.

Squaring my shoulders, and taking a deep breath, I tug open the heavy wooden door to the Storybook Pub and make my way into the colorful interior. If you ignore the cameras, makeup station, and staged interview area, it looks just like a spacious, super eclectic Victorian-age living room. Except for the large half-moon bar just off to the right.

The Kelly green painted wood paneling on the bottom half of the bar matches the color of the walls. It sounds like it should be hideous, but instead it's inviting and friendly. I take a moment to glance around the rest of the massive room. Mismatched chairs and tables make up a large part of the main space, with several large couches and chairs surrounding a fireplace off to the left. An attention-grabbing sign near the back announces a spirit station and facilities upstairs.

Large crystal chandeliers hang sporadically from the ceiling, modern paintings decorate the walls, and two small dogs—so still I mistake them for statues—lounge on a red leather chaise near a window. Wood floors melding with brick walls, ship lap and wood paneling, what should be a hodge-podge mess is oddly beautiful. An incredibly welcoming space.

It's good I feel that way, because if I stay on the show, the bulk of my dates will be here at the Storybook Pub, and in this very room. I'm tempted to tour the upstairs before I check in, but a thin, hawkish-looking man stops me from going any further.

"Name?" he asks brusquely.

"Bree Winter."

He looks down at his clipboard, flipping from one page to another.

"No Bree here." He turns to walk away.

"It's short for Breezy," I call after him.

When he faces me again, it's with an odd smile on his face and I know exactly what he's going to say: *Oh, aren't you that girl who—*

"Your parents named you Breezy Winter?" he asks.

Okay, that's not what I thought he was going to say.

"Yes." I feel my face burn as the red creeps up my neck. I'm not sure if I'm embarrassed because of just my name, or the song, or the fact he obviously doesn't know about the song. Or he does know about the song but is just being nice. Because, really, how many girls are there named Breezy in the Pacific Northwest? Just one. Me. I checked on social media.

You'd think that after twenty-seven years I'd be used to the teasing about my name.

But I'm not.

And I don't think I'll ever get used to the teasing from the song. Nope. No way. No how.

"Did they hate you?" he asks.

I scoff and look up to meet his eyes again. This time the smile on his face is warm and friendly. It changes everything about him. What originally looked standoffish and cold is now supportive.

"I get it," he says, leaning in closer to me. "Harold Johnson." He points to his chest and then holds a hand out to me. I return the gesture. "Nice to meet you. Do you prefer Harold or—" That's when it hits me, and I can't stop the giggles from erupting.

"Oh no!" I say, slapping my hand over my mouth to stifle further mirth.

"Oh yes." He nods grimly. "My parents are proper and English; the idea of my entire life being surmised by one big penile joke never occurred to them. Pun intended."

I laugh so hard at this, I snort. He winks in return.

"It is big, but I keep the hairy under control."

I can't contain myself once he says that. Huge, unladylike guffaws come spilling out of my mouth, which turns to coughing. He pats my back indelicately.

"There, there cold and windy. It gets a little less funny after about twenty years."

I pull myself together and wipe at the tears under my eyes. "It's awful, isn't it?"

He nods in response.

"And mine is nowhere near as bad as yours," I commiserate.

He shakes his head.

If he doesn't know about the song already, and he's nice enough not to say anything if he does, I'm not going to be the one to bring it up.

"I don't often tell people my full name. I go by Rye in the real world."

"Rye, like the whiskey?"

"Exactly."

"I like it."

"Thanks." He claps his palm against the back of his clipboard. "Okay, you want to head over to the makeup station, have them give you a looksie, and when they're ready you'll be called over to the interview station."

I look in the direction he's pointing and see there are a couple girls at the makeup station, and another being interviewed.

"How many people were called in? Am I allowed to ask that?"

"Forty-two total. But five have already been sent home."

"Oh, wow. Why?"

"We didn't like the looks of them."

My heart sinks into my stomach. He must see it in my expression because he grabs my shoulder in a reassuring manner and says, "Don't worry. I like the looks of you."

I smile up at him. Deciding at once that even if this doesn't work out, Harold Johnson is exactly the kind of person I'd want as a friend. And I would make sure to never call him Harry.

5

BREEZY

The instructions had said to dress casually for the first day, as though hanging out with close friends. Which is exactly what I did: boyfriend jeans cuffed at the bottom, Converse low tops, white T-shirt under an oversized navy-blue cardigan, and a bright pink beanie, because it's cold out this morning.

As I glance around, I see that a couple of the other women must hang out with close friends while at a formal luncheon, because with the exception of the staff, I'm one of the most casually dressed people here.

"Didn't the instructions say to dress casually?" I ask the makeup artist in a low voice as I sink into the chair at her station and pull the beanie from my head. My hair sticks out in all directions on top due to the static electricity.

"There's always a few girls like that. Wouldn't let me touch their makeup either. They gravitated right to each other when they got here. Probably high maintenance pains in the ass, if you ask me." She shrugs as she says it.

"What time must they have to get up to look like that this early? And why?" I ask, not really expecting an answer. Well, maybe an answer about the time they'd have to get up because those two girls put some serious hours into their appearances this morning.

"Good first impression, I suppose," she says neutrally and begins wiping at my face with what feels like a baby wipe. "Okay, you want flirty, vampy, or girl next door?"

"Uh, I guess girl next door."

"Okay, sit still." She leans in close to my face and begins her ministrations with what must be fifteen different brushes and wands.

"So, we're actually on camera today?"

"Pretty sure you're on camera right now." She gestures with her chin over her left shoulder. Sure enough, there's a camera on a tripod pointing right at us. If I could move, I'd roll my eyes at myself.

You know better than this, Bree!

First, I know not to take the instructions literally; especially with how much reality TV I've watched. Second, of course we are going to be on camera the entire time, otherwise how would there be a show? The only unbreakable barrier is the bathroom, and even then, they can still listen if they want to.

Shit. Shit. Shit.

But there are scenes on the show, *The Last Single Guy*, where all the girls vying for his attention are in sweats and glasses and are still on camera. And every reality show has first thing in the morning shots, it's like the new thing to try and catch contestants as off guard as possible. So, maybe what I'm wearing won't be so bad.

Per the instructions, I also brought a selection of different outfits with me, so maybe there will be time to change as well.

After five minutes of the makeup girl poking, painting, prodding, and plucking at my face, I'm absolutely convinced she's got me looking like Ursula the Sea Witch from *The Little Mermaid*. But she spins me around to face the mirror, points to the left with her finger and says, "Okay, off to hair. That way."

I glance at my reflection, barely noticing the girl in the mirror. In a good way. My idea of makeup most days is mascara and a soft pink lip gloss. If it's fancy and I'm going out, I'll do a deep red lipstick. But that's about it. I'm lucky enough to have good skin and a fair complexion. Green eyes that contrast with my blond hair, so the need for a lot of makeup isn't there. At least not as far as I'm concerned.

My mother calls me "naturally cute."

But this woman staring back at me is gorgeous. Like me, only better.

"Ohmigod," I say as I touch my cheek in wonder. "You're amazing."

"You're a good canvas," the girl says in return.

"Can you do my makeup every time?"

"Not sure they've got us here the entire shoot but stop by later and I'll give you some tips for when you do it yourself."

"Thank you so much." It's all I can do to tear my eyes away from myself. It's like she took everything about me and just made it flawless. I shake my head to clear it and wander over to the hair stations.

"Straight? Up-do? Curls?" the man asks as I take a seat.

"Straight, please," I say since that's how I usually wear it.

He takes a step back and studies me in the mirror, then runs both hands through my hair and says, "I think we'll go beachy waves."

I nod, wanting to ask him why he asked me if he was just going to make the decision anyway, but I refrain. It's important for me to remember that I'm not in charge here, they are. And what they say goes. So, I settle back in the chair and let him go at it. Twenty minutes later I face the mirror to find my head is full of softly tousled waves.

God, these people are good.

I reach up to stroke it.

"No touch!" He slaps my hand away and glares at me.

I lower my hand slowly. "I won't touch, I promise."

He dismisses me with a wave of his hand, and I head toward what I think is the interview area. There's a director's style chair placed in front of a camera, with a huge light shining on it, up-lit background behind it, and a large umbrella shaped light diffuser above it. I move to take a seat in the chair and almost hit my head on the hanging microphone I hadn't seen before now. All I can think is, thank god it didn't mess up my hair.

"Name?" one of the women behind the camera asks.

"Bree Winter."

She smiles. "Okay, Bree, why don't you tell us a bit about yourself."

"Okay," I take a deep breath and let it out slowly. I don't really know what I want to say even though I'm fairly sure I know what they want to hear. "I'm twenty-seven years old. I love reading, kayaking, working in my garden, and volunteering at the local dog rescue. Huge football fan—go Seahawks! I'm close with my family and friends, and I love creating new experiences. I'm at a point in my life where I want to create those experiences together with a partner."

And that right there, my friends, is what I like to call the perfect reality dating show answer.

"That's fantastic," the interviewer says as though on cue. "And what are you looking for in a partner?"

"Oh, same as every girl, I suppose. Loyal, funny, charming, smart, generous, happy."

"Do you think you can meet your partner on a show such as Storybook Pub?"

"It's as good a place as any, right?" I smile. They smile. And I'm through to the next round.

6

BREEZY

After my brief interview, I'm sent to my room to drop off my things and take a few minutes to unpack. They have us housed in a converted hostel two doors down from the pub. Girls on one side of the building and boys on the other. The only way between the two sides is through the lobby downstairs.

Unlike some reality shows, *Storybook Pub* has a fast turnaround time from filming to airing. Even though there's a camera on you at all times, they know what they want to air and what they don't, and if something unique comes up, they've been known to throw it in raw and unedited. And the entire thing is broadcast over eight nights in two-week's time, so the viewing audience doesn't have to wait long to find out what happens.

Also unlike other shows, we are not cut off from the outside world and have access to social media, the internet, phones, and print media. I'll be able to keep Susan apprised of everything that happens as it does. I know from watching the show that they will keep us busy, but there will be some down time.

I jump in surprise as my TV turns on—by itself—and Kole O'Shea's handsome face appears on the screen.

"Hello, everyone, welcome to Storybook Pub. My name is Kole

O'Shea, proprietor, and this idea is my baby. My goal is to bring love to everyone who wants it."

I can't help but shiver as I watch him give his speech. One, he's hot, but not on the market according to what I've heard and read. Two, he's got that urban, gritty, sexy, Irish vibe that makes a girl want to steal away with him and never come back.

Well, it makes *me* want to do that.

"You're all here under the pretense of wanting to find love. But not all of you mean it. I know it, and you know it. Soon, America will know it too. I don't mean for that to sound as malicious as it may appear. Just that Storybook Pub has a way of digging in deep and finding your truth, whether you want it to or not."

He hops down from the coffee table he'd been standing on and begins his stroll through the front room of the pub. "Today marks your first chance to begin that exploration. Because the introduction mixer starts now. What are you waiting for? Get over to the Storybook Pub."

I change out of my cardigan and into a fitted navy blazer and substitute my Converse for a pair of heeled ankle boots. Still casual, but a little nicer than what I arrived looking like; I'm excited to get to the Pub. While I know that Kole won't be there, he rarely is featured on the show, there have been reported sightings of him popping in on set. And if I get a chance to meet him, I want to take full advantage.

Kole O'Shea is my reality TV hero. I know we've established that he's good looking with a voice and accent to die for. But he also has a purpose for his show, and it's not just the money he makes. He really believes in what he says. That everyone deserves love if they genuinely want it. I've seen some of the most amazing stories come out of his efforts.

I walk in the front door and Rye immediately catches my eye from across the room. He's talking to a camera guy stationed near the main bar. Rye winks and I wave in return. Then he twirls his finger to indicate he wants me to turn, so I do, giving him a three hundred sixty-degree view of my outfit update and the miraculous results of my face and hair. He gives me a thumbs up, which makes me happy.

And empowered.

He sees women every day in environments like this. If I have a thumbs up from him, I must be doing something right. Contestants/guests are still trickling in the front door, so I step up onto one of the empty barstools at the main bar to get a drink and scope things out.

I order a white wine because I like the way it looks on TV and if I spill, it won't stain. I can't even tell you how many white T-shirts I have at home with red wine stains on them. Actually, I *can* tell you. This one I'm wearing is the only one without one. I might like my wine a bit too much.

Someone takes the stool next to me, I turn to see a girl also dressed in jeans, but with a sequined top and silver strappy stiletto heels. "Skinny margarita, please."

She leans toward me before speaking next. "Rumor has it they are about to pair us up using a questionnaire of all things. Got your eye on anyone yet?"

"No. I've barely had a chance to look around let alone talk to anyone. You?"

"Maybe a few. Definitely beige sweater and black button-down." She nods in the direction of the two men she's speaking of and I turn discreetly to check them out. Beige sweater smiles and raises his glass in my direction. I look away quickly and pretend I wasn't just checking him out. Then realize how stupid that is, given this is a dating show. So, I glance back, but he's moved on.

The TV's around the room come alive, and Kole's face looks down at us from their high perches.

"Hello again, contestants."

"Hello," I murmur back, along with a few others.

"We're doing things a bit differently this time around. Producers are coming around with pen and paper. I ask five questions designed to tap into what you are looking for in a mate, whether you realize it or not. You have five minutes to answer all five questions, don't worry they are multiple choice. Then we'll feed your answers into our very own analysis program and soon you'll be introduced to the one here best suited for you statistically."

I look down at the questionnaire. It seems easy enough with basic questions and answers but knowing that it could dictate my entire future weighs heavily.

    1. How do you spend your free time?
    2. What is your attachment type?
    3. What is your sexual drive and style?
    4. What do you spend extra money on?
    5. How spiritual are you?

That's it. Yet it covers everything: interests, commitment, sex, money, religion. I can't believe my entire romantic future can be narrowed to and mandated by five things.

I answer them as quickly and truthfully as I can, then drop mine in the box as the producer comes around to collect them. We were each assigned a number which will help identify us in the pairing off process. The bartender refills my wine glass I hadn't even realized I'd emptied, and I wait impatiently for my future to be determined.

7
BREEZY

Dear Susan,

Okay, you were right. This show was a great idea. You can't lord it over me forever that you were right. And this is the only time I'll say it. But you've got it in writing so you can refer to it whenever you'd like. Just don't be a bitch about it.

Anyway, we were paired off last night based on results from the worlds simplest questionnaire ever. But it obviously worked because I have so much in common with the guy I was matched with—funny enough, his name is Guy. He loves to rescue dogs too but doesn't have any right now because of where he lives. How are my fur-babies, btw?

Okay, so, Guy, dark hair, dark eyes, tall, lean, muscular but not all gym rat about it, great smile, nice teeth, loves to read, but not a football fan. I'm not worried, I think I can convert him easily enough. We've had two mini dates already. Drinks last night and breakfast this morning. I would say it's going . . . well. There is potential there. I'm not bowled over or anything, but I can see where the questionnaire is effective.

In a few minutes I have to report back to the pub for the challenges this afternoon, designed to demonstrate how well we work together and communicate to get something accomplished. I've heard rumors of everything from an escape room to a two-person straight jacket. I'll keep you posted. And we have a dance contest tonight. Word is we're in for a real treat.

I love you. I miss you. Talk soon!
Love, Bree

8

BREEZY

Guy and I make it through the first round of challenges without an issue. Simple logic games that both of us were good at. In this second round, they have us dressed in body suits—leaving little to the imagination—and mummy wrapped together face to face.

I can't remember the last time I've been so physically close to a man.

Oh wait, yes, I can.

Levi Miller.

Abort! Abort Levi thoughts! This is Operation Moving On, and this guy, Guy, is nice.

I giggle at my thoughts: *this guy, Guy*.

The challenge is to either get unwrapped and walk across the room or stay wrapped and worm our way across the floor from one end to the other. Since a way to unwrap isn't apparent, we choose to try and make our way across the room on the floor.

Right now we're halfway through and he has yet to get a boner. Even though I've been undulating against him for a good twenty minutes. Couple that with, even if he had a boner, I don't think I'd be trying to rub up on it. I mean, his thigh is rubbing between my legs as we speak, pushing against my center as he tries to get traction on the floor.

And nothing. No shiver of excitement. No wave of lust. No wet panties.

It could just be that he's more a competitor than a lover, and so he won't let himself think about sex until after we win, but then what would my reasoning be? And he hasn't tried to kiss me yet and this is technically our third date. Though in his defense, I haven't tried to kiss him either.

So, while he's fun, funny, and easy to be around, I can't be with someone who doesn't light my fire. I don't think that lack of spark between us is just on my end. Otherwise we'd have ourselves a full bigstick popsicle right about now instead of soft-serve in a soggy cone.

What started as ten couples has been narrowed down to seven in just three dates. For some reason when the show is being broadcast it seems to take much longer than that to begin whittling them down. But whichever couple finishes last in this challenge will be the next to go home.

Guy and I finish second.

And we are down to just five couples. I'm not sure how two got sent home, so I stop to ask Rye on my way back to my room.

I tap him the shoulder to get his attention away from whatever he's examining on his cell phone screen.

"Hey, cold and windy, how's it hanging?" He smiles.

"I'm good"—I try to come up with something snappy to call him that's a play on his name, like he's done with me, but I'm just not quick under pressure like that—"Rye."

"You're doing good out there. What do you think of Guy?"

"He's nice. We're a good match."

"Using words like nice and good, huh? So, no fireworks?"

I shake my head.

"Well, I've been guaranteed there will be fireworks tonight, so get ready."

"Okay, I will," I laugh. "Hey, why did two couples get sent home during the challenges?"

"One lost, and one was disqualified."

"What did they do? Can you tell me?"

"No, but let's just say that if you're going to cheat, make sure you aren't on camera when you do it."

I gasp, my hand over my mouth, eyes wide. He nods solemnly.

We're interrupted by another of Kole's television appearances, this one to congratulate us winners and tell us to go back to our rooms to get ready for tonight's big event. A dance contest. Couples need to be in coordinated outfits and the remaining rules will be given to us at the beginning of the dancing. The last couple standing wins.

I tell Guy that most of my clothes are either navy blue or green, with some black thrown in for variety. We agree on green as our color for the evening. What I don't tell him is that green is my ex's favorite color and that I still think of him whenever I wear it.

I REALIZE—TOO late— that Guy and I didn't discuss shades of green. So, while everything that I have is more of a Kelly green like the bar, what he has is more pastel. We still coordinate a little, in that we're in the same family, but not as well as some of the other couples.

The rules are simple: stay on beat and stay moving.

Slow songs, we can kind of clutch and sway. More up-tempo will require originality. I don't know any technical dances like the tango, jitterbug, or waltz, so Guy and I agree to just make sure our joined hands are bobbing and our feet are tapping.

We head out onto the dance floor and the lights dim. The long black curtains surrounding the stage begin to part and a spotlight centers between them.

"Ladies and gentlemen, please welcome Levi Miller and the Swayeds."

What?

Wait, what?

Did I hear that right?

It can't be?

My head swivels back and forth trying to get a glimpse of him. I know there aren't two bands called Levi Miller and the Swayeds. Logically I know it's him. Also logically I know if I am patient, he'll appear on the stage and I'll see him. But I want to and don't want to see him with equal fervor.

We've not talked since I broke it off with him and blocked his number. Then, of course, he wrote the song. After *that,* I was done. Over the years the sting of the song has faded, and I've tried to remember him more with fondness instead of hatred.

Unfortunately, my heart interprets fondness as soul-crushing, gut-wrenching, world-spinning, all-encompassing love. At least when it comes to Levi. So, you can see why it's easier to just slide into that hate zone—a shared hatred of one another, him for me over the breakup. Me for him over the song.

Fuck.

There he is.

My eyes are drawn to him like magnet to steel and I can't look away.

"You a fan also?" Guy asks.

"Huh?" I force myself to look at Guy instead.

"A Levi Miller fan? I love the guy. He's fantastic," Guy enthuses.

Making me wonder if Guy would've gotten a boner had he been worming his way across the floor with Levi instead of me.

I snort laugh softly. "Yeah, I'm a fan of sorts."

I recognize the song Levi's singing; it's one of loss and heartache. The girl has died, and the man remains by her grave singing to her ghost. He refuses to leave until she comes back to life. Which, of course, doesn't happen, so he ends up dying there too and they bury him beside her.

Ugh.

Does he know I'm here?

I let my gaze travel back in his direction. Where it stays for god knows how long. Because I could look at Levi Miller forever and never tire. Especially in person. For over twenty-four months I've not been able to drink my fill from the well that is this beautiful man. I've had to get by with online images and tabloid spreads.

And none of those are even as close to as good as this. Long legs encased in worn jeans, vintage T-shirt spread across his broad chest, right foot tapping softly next to the mic stand, soft brown hair shorn close to his scalp with the front sticking up slightly from his forehead. Brown eyes filled with softness and feeling.

Oh, and that scruff of his whiskers on his cheeks and down his neck. That used to pull at my hair when he and I would dance, or hug, or embrace. In contrast, Guy is smooth shaved. Even now at the end of the day. Not that it's a competition.

Levi finishes the song and looks out toward his small audience, dimple flashing as his cheeks move into a smile. This must be the smallest crowd he's played for in years. How can they afford him?

"Hello." His deep voice resonates through the room. I hear the girl next to me sigh. Or maybe that was Guy.

"My name is Levi Miller, these guys are the Swayeds, and we're here tonight to help y'all along with your dance competition. What do you say?"

Everyone, I'm sure, except for me yells back at him. He's got us pumped. Them with the adrenaline only a celebrity and live music can cause. Me with the adrenaline only an ex can cause.

I don't know what he's doing here. Or what the fuck I'm going to do if he sees me, but I guess I have twenty songs or so to figure it out.

9

LEVI

I find her in the crowd right away. She's dancing with some guy that I'm sure is gay. I can tell by the way he looks at me and the way he doesn't hold her. If I had Breezy in my arms, we'd be toe to toe, hip to hip, chest to chest with my face buried in her hair. Her fantastic smelling hair that always reminded me of cherry pie with vanilla ice cream.

She didn't know I'd be here.

I knew she'd be here.

It took me a long time to get to the point where I could even think about Breezy without it gutting me. It didn't help that I wrote that fucking song, it became an instant hit, and the world decided to hate her for it. I regretted it at once. Still do.

But I was upset when I wrote it and I didn't realize the reach it could have; I was expressing my feeling through lyrics, the same way I always have. Just that time I made the mistake of using her name in the song.

Dumb.

Really fucking dumb.

Then a couple of weeks ago I was flipping through social media and I saw a post Susan was tagged in. A public post that linked back to her. And just for fun, I clicked on it and sent her a message. She responded. Shocked the shit out of me. I figured I was the last person she'd ever want to hear from.

We made small talk for a while, via messaging, then she asked if she could call me. That call changed everything.

Breezy, my beautiful, loving, caring Breezy, was upset over the lies about touring opportunities, and rightfully so. I should have talked it out with her, gotten her opinion and trusted in our relationship. According to Susan, Breezy hasn't moved on and she misses me. This show is her first attempt at getting some semblance of a dating life back.

Back when it first happened, I assumed I was drunk when I answered Jay's texts about the tour. That it'd happened after Breezy left me, not before. It never occurred to me that she might have seen his texts. And he and I never really talked about the timing. It all happened on the same day as far as I was concerned. Breezy left me, Jay convinced me to go on tour. My world got rocked. Literally.

For a while I was so angry all I could do was accept it by way of avoidance. I was too mad to meet it head on, so I just left the whole situation alone and tried my best to calm down. When that didn't work, I threw myself into the tour. Writing song after song, getting my band together, perfecting my craft.

Despite how it looked in the tabloids, I've not been with anyone since Breezy. I knew when I first met her that she was the one. It was foolishness and folly that prevented me from proposing. I worried that I couldn't provide for her, and I figured we had time.

There's never extra time.

So, when Susan admitted she'd signed Breezy up for this show, I contacted the producers and offered to come on for free. Telling them that it was a favorite of mine and that it would be fun for me to do it. Kole O'Shea called me shortly after and we had a brief talk. He told me he knew it was more than that, but that it was okay. I deserved love and he wanted to help me find it.

How he knew, I'll never know. But I'm not questioning it.

And it takes all my willpower right now not to jump off this stage, pull my girl from that guy's arms, and whisk her away from here. Now that I know the truth, I'll stop at nothing to get my Z back. The only problem is, convincing her that she's not holding back my career in any way. And, of course, making sure her feelings haven't changed.

I wrote a new song for tonight, that will hopefully explain it all to her. If that doesn't work, Kole has agreed to figure out a way for us to get some time together without her being to suspicious.

I watch her now, in that green dress that makes her eyes pop and her hair glisten as she tries her hardest not to stare at me, and I know, still, that she's it for me. There will never be another woman that I love as much, want as much, as I do Breezy Winter.

And judging by the expression on her face, she's uncomfortable as hell with me being here.

Which I like.

It means I still have an impact on her. Which also means I still have a chance. If she didn't care, I wouldn't matter. And no way is this guy going to be my replacement.

10

BREEZY

I'm not sure if he's seen me yet. If he has, it doesn't show on his face. Hopefully, it's difficult to see into the audience when a bright spotlight is shining on your face. I'm going to assume it is and just roll with that. And each time Guy tries to dance us closer to the stage, I dance us further away.

"You know the man leads, right?" he asks every so often. Passive aggressively making his dissatisfaction known. I don't care. If I could, I'd be off the stage right now and hiding in the bathroom until the contest was over and Levi was gone.

But the producers would notice if I left suddenly. And I want to win the fifty thousand dollars for the rescue. So, Guy can just suck it up and dance in the background with me.

I can't get over how good Levi looks and how comfortable he looks on a stage, in front of a crowd. It's like he was born to do this. Which makes me all the happier for him. All the sadder for me.

He moves from hit to hit seamlessly, not stopping for an hour. Thankfully, he leaves "Breezy Like Sunday Morning" out of the lineup. At least so far.

"Okay, I'm going to play a new one now." His deep, husky voice sends shivers down my spine. I remember when he used to sing to me at night until I fell asleep. Either on the phone or in person. I still can't fall asleep without music playing. We'll just pretend that it's not Levi Miller and the Swayeds that I usually listen to.

I tune back into Levi, who is still talking. "We've never played this one live, never even rehearsed it, so bear with us. It's written for someone incredibly special to me. I hope when she hears it, she listens to the words."

My heart sinks.

He's moved on.

Of course, he has.

Why wouldn't he?

I'm sure he's fallen in love with over half the skanks the tabloids have featured him with. Not that we had a chance to getting back together. I mean, how could we? He'll never forgive me for leaving him. I still can't believe he didn't tell me about the tour opportunities. Besides, there's no way he could know that I'm on the show. The first episode doesn't air until tonight. The contestants are kept a secret until then.

So, at the very least my identity is safe. I would be absolutely mortified if he knew that I was here dancing to a song he wrote for someone else. It doesn't get more pathetic than that.

"I wonder if this song is for Breezy too," Guy murmurs.

"It's not. I guarantee it," I tell him.

11

THE BALLAD OF BREEZY WINTER

The Ballad of Breezy Winter

Girl with you, I never knew,
that I could feel, a love so real
Got in my mind, changed its state
Filled my heart, gave it weight

Took my walls, tore them down
Created smiles from all my frowns.
Reached deep inside, got what's me
Girl, in your arms, is where I'll be

You been shakin' up perceptions
Destroyin' expectations
Promise me, we'll last forever

Miss your lips rubbed raw,
Want my whiskers on your thighs
This is the last of my resolve
Won't be telling no more lies.

You walked in, and blew my mind
Knew I needed you, for all my time
All my minutes, all my hours
I give you all, my every power

You been shakin' up perceptions
Destroyin' expectations
Promise me, we'll last forever

Want your reflection in my mirror
Your voice the only one I hear.
All my cracks, your love will seal.
Girl, I like the way you feel.

When I whisper you're beautiful
My love for you is plentiful
This is my vow, my aim is true
Give you the world, and all you're due.

You been shakin' up perceptions
Destroyin' expectations
Promise me, we'll last forever

12

BREEZY

I have tears in my eyes as Levi finishes the song. I think Guy does as well. It's the most beautiful thing I've ever heard. What makes it worse is that I know he's capable of those feelings. I've been on the receiving end of them. He makes a girl feel like she the only woman in the world. Like she's a treasure that he cherishes.

His sultry voice along with the slow tempo of the song makes it a perfect testament to love.

I sigh.

Long.

One of the producers taps me on the shoulder. "Bree?"

I turn toward her but keep dancing.

"They want to see you in the back."

"They?" I ask.

"I think it's Kole," she says, her eyes wide.

"Oh!" I start to step away, but then remember the contest. "Am I going to lose if I stop?"

"I don't know," the producer says honestly. "But if Kole O'Shea is asking for you. . ."

True.

"Sorry, Guy." I pat him on the shoulder then turn to follow the producer to one of the back rooms. She opens the door and steps aside so I can step in, then closes it behind me. There, staring out a window in this small room that looks more like a living room than anything, is the man himself.

Kole O'Shea.

"Mr. O'Shea?"

He turns to me and smiles. It's a beautiful smile. But unlike before, it does nothing for me. Not after seeing Levi again.

"Ah, Bree, come in, sit down. I thought we could chat a moment."

I love that everything he says in that brilliant accent of his sounds like more fun than it would had I said it.

I take a seat opposite him.

"How is your journey to love going so far? Have you made a connection?"

I think of Guy, and how I like him, but there's no spark. And how much I want to win for my charity. And how much I want to move on from Levi. Especially now that he's so publicly moving on from me. Or from whoever came after me. But I can't lie to this man. He seems to see through my soul somehow.

So, instead of nodding, I shake my head.

He nods solemnly in return. "That's too bad."

"It really is," I say. "Because I really wanted to win the contest tonight for my charity. And I really want to move on from my ex. He's moved on. I don't see why I can't do the same."

"Your ex? Is this a recent break-up?"

I nod. "Two years ago."

"A significant amount of time. Not so much that it's irrelevant, but not so recent that it still burns."

"It does still burn though. That's what I can't stand."

"Why did the relationship end?"

I take a deep breath. I'm never going to be able to move on until I acknowledge my part in breaking it up. I'm convinced of that. "I found out he had a chance to further his career, but it would have meant leaving me for a while, and he didn't do. Didn't even talk to me about it. Then he lied when I asked him if it happened."

He brings his steepled palms up to his mouth and studies me. "So, he made a decision about his own career, one that benefitted you, then spared your feelings when you asked about it, and that upset you?"

"You make it sound like I did something wrong."

"Did you?"

"No. I just, I wanted to be a part of the decision."

"Would you have wanted him to make a different one?" he asks.

"Yes, I wanted him to take advantage of every opportunity."

"I see. So, this was commonplace for the two of you, to discuss career changes before making decisions?"

"Not exactly," I admit. "No. But this wasn't just a career change."

"Wasn't it?"

"No, it was the chance of a lifetime," I say, using the words I hate that keep resonating in my life.

He frowns and nods as though considering what I've told him. "Did it work? Did he take the chance of a lifetime?"

"He did. And now he's extremely successful. So, it was worth it."

"Except it still burns."

I look down, feeling slightly ashamed suddenly. "It does."

"Oddly enough, I know someone in a comparable situation," he says. "I'll be right back."

You've got to be kidding me.

He leaves me alone in the room and I take a moment to appreciate the decor. It's much like the rest of the pub, eclectic, comfortable furnishings and bright inviting colors. I want whoever decorated this place to come and redo my apartment. That would be a good prize for the winner.

It's fortuitous that Kole wanted to see me, since it ensures that I'll avoid Levi for the rest of the night. For all I know his special person is here with him and I'd have to watch the two of them being in love.

Gross.

I hear the door opening and turn toward the sound.

But instead of Kole, it's Levi who enters the room.

13

LEVI

The expression on her face is the perfect blend of terror, nausea, and joy. I cling to the joy and try to ignore the other two. Kole already told me she is still in love with me, but I need to see it for myself. Hear it from her.

Musicians have successful relationships all the time. And if I can stay celibate on the road with no woman waiting at home for me, for sure I can do it if Breezy is my prize.

"Hey," I say softly.

"Hey."

I hold my hands up in surrender. "I just want five minutes of your time. Is that okay?"

She shrugs as though indifferent, but her eyes tell another story. "I guess."

"Before you say anything, let me say thank you."

Her brow furrows in confusion.

"You're right in that I wouldn't have left you. But you're wrong in that I lied because I didn't want to live my dream."

"I—"

I hold a hand up to stop her. "If anyone could have made it work, it was me and you. *Is* me and you. I wouldn't have left you, but that's because you're more important to me than anything. Especially any of this." I wave my hand toward the direction of the stage in gesture to my career.

"But—"

"Which doesn't mean I don't appreciate it. I do. I fucking love being on stage and singing for people. Writing songs and making money doing it. But, Breezy, I still love you more. Two years later, I still love you more."

Tears pool in her eyes and threaten to fall down her cheeks.

"I know you did what you thought was right, I'm pissed as hell you cut me off, didn't give me any opportunity to explain. But I'm also grateful because I've had the opportunity of a lifetime. But can we please go back to you and me?"

"You don't hate me?" she asks.

"I could never hate you. I would love to hear your rationale, in your own words. And I want your promise you won't ever do anything like that again. And I want to make sure you understand that song out there, that last one, it was for you. And I'm here tonight for you. I asked to come on the show because I knew you'd be here."

"You did?"

I nod. I walk a little closer to her. Not wanting to spook her, but at the same time liking my chances right now of getting her in my arms in a matter of seconds.

"I love you. I want us to try again. I want to know that you want that too. You are more important to me than anything else."

"I love you." She rushes toward me and I take her in my arms. Capturing the lips I've only been able to fantasize about for the last two years.

I kiss her until we can't breathe. Until our lips are numb. Until I'm so hard for her, I can barely see straight. Only then do I pull my head away.

Her eyes are at half-mast and she looks as dazed as I feel.

"I missed this," she says dreamily.

"Me too." My head buried in her hair, breathing in that scent so unique to Breezy.

"Wait." She raises her eyes to meet mine. "You aren't going to quit, are you?"

"Hell, no. But I am probably going to write a million or so more songs about how much I love you."

"You'd better not mention my name in them this time."

"So, I shouldn't tell you that song tonight was called 'The Ballad of Breezy Winter'?"

She buries her face in my chest. "Oh god, no. I feel like I just got over everyone knowing my name from a damn song."

"But this one is a good song," I protest.

She nods. "It is. I agree. But it's got to be the last one."

"Hmm. No peaceful, Breezy feeling?"

"No!"

"What about 'Take it Breezy'?"

"No!"

"Lovin' you is Breezy?"

"Ohmigod, I hate you right now!"

"It ain't Breezy? Breezy Love? Breezy Lover?"

She covers her hands over her ears and starts chanting, "La la la la la la la la la. I can't hear you. La la la la la."

I make a mental note to donate twice what her winnings would have been to the dog rescue that she loves. And buy Susan whatever she wants for helping me get my girl back to me.

"Okay, I got one more," I tell her. "What about . . ."

LEARN MORE ABOUT DENISE WELLS AT:
HTTP://WWW.DENISEWELLS.COM

ALSO BY DENISE WELLS:
HOW TO RUIN YOUR EX'S WEDDING
LOVE UNDECIDED
DIRTY DARLA

LOVE AT FIRST BREW

KRISTINE DUGGER

Beer me, baby.
Oh, just like that.
Beer me.

Sub-genre: Contemporary Romance
Relationship: Male/Female

PROLOGUE

Logan

Looking back...

Craft beer is exactly that, a craft. After running my father's pub for ten years, we closed the door to his beloved bar. It was a sign of the times. Neighborhood bars weren't lasting. I hated closing the doors. But I wasn't making a profit. The only way to make a profit was to sell. It was extremely hard, not only on me but the few regulars that were left. Most of the regulars were deceased, or were too old to walk themselves to the bar. My father passed away of lung cancer five years ago. The year he was diagnosed was the year I agreed to help him with the business. I left my stable accountant position to help continue my father's dream. Now, that dream has become a memory. However, with that door closing, a new dream began.

In the last few years, I have adapted a taste and appreciation for craft beer. My cousin and roommate, Barry, started experimenting with the brewing process in our garage. Barry went on a bucket list vacation to Ireland to learn about their brewing process. When he came back, he brought his friend, Kole, back with him. They were college rugby teammates. The two of them had this crazy idea that Barry should open his own brewery. I thought they were both insane. But Kole has experience with brewing and owning several pubs. With his guidance, Barry felt this was the right move.

Barry's beer is great but I wasn't sure it was spectacular enough to open up a brewery and sell. Kole expressed that craft beer is becoming more and more prevalent in the beer market. Then the big question came after the decision to brew craft beer; if I wanted in.

Barry says, "Dude, with your business and financial background, my beer making skills, and Kole's input on taste and combinations, we are like the trifecta. We can't go wrong."

I answer, "I don't know, man. I'm not sure if I want to jump in – and possibly fail – another business."

He says, "You didn't fail. You tried to keep your father's business afloat. You knew when it was time to let go."

Kole interrupts, "You won't fail. Trust me, I know what I'm doing. I'm like Joe Tappa for new businesses. This will be a win-win for all of us. I'm investing in you guys. We will need more investors, but this is a start."

My hands start to fidget. It was just three months ago that I closed the doors on Henry's Place. I'm dreading the day when funds run low and I have to find a typical 9-5 job. I'm not sure I want to go back to that. I have everything to lose but maybe this is the journey I'm supposed to take.

Kole and Barry are both looking at me. I smile, "What are we going to name our pub? We need a name."

They raise their hands to hive five me while saying, "Yes!"

Here we go.

Let the adventures begin.

1
LOGAN

It has been a successful year for Barry, Kole and myself. We are officially out of the red and making a profit on our pub. Pint Niner has exceeded every goal we could imagine. Yeah, it is still a lot of long hours of brewing and working behind the bar, but it is so worth it. Tonight is another Saturday night, with a food truck out front. The joys of local Omaha businesses coming together and supporting one another. People drink great-tasting beer while eating spectacular food.

Barry and Kole come out from the back of the brewery and sit down at the bar. They both nod at me, signaling for a beer. Kole is a big fan of our coffee stout and Barry enjoys our spicy IPA. After a long day of brewing, this is their pattern.

I don't get to brew much. That is all Barry and Kole. I run the pub as a bartender, manager and accountant. According to some, I have the personality to pour great-tasting beer.

I set their beer in front of them. They each take a sip and, in unison, they say, "Mmm. That's good."

I ask, "When will the new brew be done?"

Before they can answer, a drunk patron slams up next to Barry, spilling his beer all over him.

The cute, little blonde with way too much to drink giggles, "Oh my God, I'm so sorry."

Barry turns around, looks at her and says, "It's fine."

Then, a brunette beauty comes to rescue her friend. She looks at Barry and rolls her eyes. She apologizes, "I'm so sorry for my friend. It's her birthday, and yeah, you know how that goes. Let me buy you a drink."

He smirks, "It's fine." Barry nods at me and I pour him another.

She comments, "Seriously, let me buy that for you."

"Doll face, it's fine."

"Doll face? Are you serious?" she replies snotty.

I shake my head and quickly distract her. "What would you like to drink?"

Her crystal blue eyes glance at me. I set a bottle of water on the bar and say, "This is for your friend."

She smiles, "Thanks. What do you suggest? I have never been here before."

Barry and Kole shake their heads at me. This is what I'm also good at, diverting my patron's attention.

I reply, "In my opinion, they're all good. It all depends on what your taste buds are."

She grins, "Well, I'm not a beer connoisseur but I do enjoy dark beers. Surprise me."

"One more question. Rich and smooth?"

She purrs, "Smooth; not too rich."

"I have the perfect beer for you."

Her blues sparkle in anticipation.

I turn to the beer taps and pore her one of my favorite porters. Most porters are very rich yet smooth. Our peanut butter porter tends to be smooth but light. It is a crowd pleaser. I haven't yet to craft a beer but the peanut butter porter was my suggestion.

I set the beer in front of her. She picks it up and looks at the glass.

She laughs, "Well, this looks like a porter." She takes a sip. "Nice choice. Smooth, nutty taste with a hint of chocolate. You gave me a peanut butter porter. My absolute favorite."

Confused as to how she knew the flavors, I ask, "I thought you weren't a beer connoisseur."

She smirks, "I lied." She grabs her beer and walks away.

Holy shit. Her curves shake with confidence as she walks toward her group of friends. I continue to watch her as she sits down on the plushy red couch nestled in the corner of the pub. Her crystal blues glance up and our eyes lock. She brings her beer to her lips and takes another sip. All while staring back at me.

"Hey! Bro," says Barry as he interrupts my fixation on the gorgeous brunette that shook her plump ass away from me.

I shake my head and look at Barry and Kole. They laugh. They knew.

2

IRIS

My friend, Bailey, is an absolute mess. I guess you only turn thirty-five once. Bailey is divorced and now living the 'single let's mingle' life. Being single in your thirties isn't all the hype she thinks it is. She will quickly realize men at our age are either baby daddy's, momma's boys or someone's ex-husband. I know this from experience. The numerous combustions of relationships I have had makes me wonder if I'm destined to be single for the rest of my life. I figured, by now, I would be either married with a family or divorced with a family. I got neither.

Oh well. I don't need a man to make me feel like my life is complete. I'm a successful woman. I have my own place. I pay my own bills. I have a successful career as a columnist and blogger. My Thirty and Flirty column has been called the next Sex and the City. I discuss dating and living in your thirties. It's a lot of fun, but I'm worried that, one day, the material will be redundant. My back-up life is my blog, where I write about everything from reviews of books to restaurants to the latest fashions and even sports. I like to keep myself diverse and busy.

Tonight is definitely one of those nights that I'm keeping myself busy. Busy as in babysitting my lovely friend. I set the bottle of water in front of her and say, "You need to drink this or you will be sick."

Bailey rolls her eyes and muffles, "Okay, Miss Party Pooper."

Our friends, Clarissa and Sydney, just shake their heads and laugh at Bailey. Clarissa is happily married with five children. It was great that she was able to take some time away from the family life to have a girl's night out. Sydney, on the other hand, is living her best life as a single mom who lives with her mother. We all live very different lives but we have been friends since college.

I take a sip of my nutty, delicious beer. The smoothness drips down my throat, leaving me completely satisfied. I glance toward the bar to check out the sexy man behind it. It was fun letting him think I had no clue about beer. It is one of my favorite topics on my blog. But you know how it is; let a guy think he's teaching you something. It's all part of the game. I take another sip, thinking of his recommendation. His dark, chocolate-brown eyes gleamed with excitement when I stated I needed help. Then, a look of surprise when he realized I knew beer. This time, I smile while I look at him. This time is different; he notices me. I play it cool, lifting my beer and nodding my head. He smirks.

Sydney starts laughing, "You are so eye-fucking the bartender."

"What are you talking about?" I ask as she grabs my attention.

Bailey slurs, "He's super-hot."

Clarissa says, "Bailey, are you serious? Are we sixteen?"

Sydney and I laugh.

Bailey continues, "I'm just saying. Look at him. His slender build, tatted up arms, combed-back brown hair and then, there is the scruff. Good Lord Almighty, he looks delicious."

Clarissa, Sydney and I have the same bug-eyed expression at hearing our friend describe him.

"Whoa, Nelly. Calm down, girl," comments Sydney.

"What? He's hot. But I don't want him. I want the fiery red-head with the legit long beard," Bailey continues.

I laugh, "The one you bumped into and spilled his beer all over?"

She smirks, "That's the one. I want to talk to him."

Clarissa jokes, "Sure you do."

Bailey again, "Watch me. He will be my next victim."

Sydney laughs, "Who the hell is she tonight?"

I laugh, "I have no clue. But she is hilarious tonight. She is cut off for the night."

Clarissa stands up and says, "I'm too old and too tired for this. I'm out for the night." She looks at Bailey and continues, "Have a great night." Her attention goes to Sydney and me, "You two got her taken care of, right?"

I nod but Sydney doesn't. My attention goes to Sydney, I ask, "Are you leaving too?"

She smiles, "Yeah, this girl I've been seeing just texted me. My mom is watching Tyson. I need to take advantage of this situation while I can. I'm out too."

This is just great. I get why they want to leave, they have other lives. I know Bailey is not ready to leave and I can't leave her alone. So, I down my beer and say goodbye to my other friends.

After the hugs and comments about getting together soon – which is never soon – I notice Bailey is no longer sitting on the red velvet couch. I know exactly where she is. I glance up at the bar and there she is. I take a deep breath, grab our purses and head to the bar. Bailey is twirling her hair while talking with the red-head. He is entertaining her drunk ass.

When I reach the bar, I pull out the stool and sit down. Sexy bartender is pouring a beer for another customer. He glances over at me and smiles. I return the smile. He hands the beer to the customer and heads my way.

He asks, "What can I get you?"

I answer, "Any more recommendations?"

He smirks, "You tell me."

I squint my eyes, reading the blackboard of beer listed. I see one that captures my attention. I ask, "Please tell me about Joe Mama?" I start to laugh.

He chuckles, "That is our coffee stout."

"Clever name."

"Yeah, we thought so too."

"I'll try that one."

He winks and smirks, "Okay, doll face."

I shake my head at his reference. This gorgeous, mysterious bartender has drawn my interest. I watch as he grabs a tulip beer glass and fills it with thick, almost black, coffee-like beer. My mouth starts to water in anticipation of the first sip. Or maybe it's the bartender causing my lips to dampen with moisture. A grin appears on his face as he notices me watching him intently.

He sets the beer on a cardboard coaster in front of me and questions, "You like what you see."

I bite down on my lip. He has no idea that I am totally drawn to, not only, the beer in front of me but the person serving me. Time to flirt. Looking into his deep, brown eyes, I reply, "You have no idea how much I like what I see in front of me."

He smirks, "Is that so?"

"I cannot wait to put my mouth around the opening and take a sip. Soon, feeling the smoothness slowly glide down my throat." I pick up the tulip glass and take my first sip. Staring at him, staring at me. Our eyes lock on one another. I continue to drink, tasting the notes of chocolate mixed with coffee beans. My heart begins to pound against its chambers. Whatever this is, it is like an orgasm in a mug.

My other hand rests on the bar. Our eyes never part. A rough, worker's hand touches mine. I gulp down one more sip and nearly choke.

He starts to chuckle, "That good, huh?"

I set my drink down and cough, "You have no idea."

"It was good for me too" He winks as he lets go of my hand.

Oh, fuck me. I have no clue what that was, but it was more than just good beer. I grab my beer again and take another sip.

3

LOGAN

The end of the night is approaching. The beautiful brunette whose been eye-fucking me all night has been caught up with her friend for the last hour. Barry had me cut her off. The girl is beyond drunk. She comes out of the restroom, with her friend draped over her. She is practically carrying her. She guides her to the red velvet couch and lays her down. Once she steadies her passed out friend, she heads my way. She glances back at her friend. She shakes her head, "Well, this has been a night."

Barry comments, "Is your friend going to be okay?"

"Yeah, she should be fine. Her brother is on his way to pick her up."

I ask, "You're not taking her home?"

"Nah, I love her but I have had enough of her," she answers.

Barry laughs, "Aren't you a nice friend?"

She glares at Barry and says, "I am. She lives twenty minutes the other direction. Her brother is sober and just getting off of work. It's a win-win."

Barry laughs, "Okay."

Brunette looks at me and asks, "Is it too late for me to have another beer?"

I look at Barry, and he nods. I answer, "What do you want?"

She examines the chalkboard and responds, "Can I try the Lucky Charm?" She pauses, "Wait. Is it sweet?"

"No, it's our Amber ale."

"Another clever name. You guys have something going on here. Catchy names to go with great beer."

"You're funny," I laugh.

"Well, I try."

I set her beer in front of her and ask, "What's your name?"

Before she answers, her plump lips touch the Pilsner glass. Her eyes close as she enjoys another taste of one of our craft beers. My cock pulsates once more. Earlier, I almost busted a nut watching her drink our coffee stout. She sets the glass down and licks the foam off her lips. I don't know this woman but she clearly has an effect on me.

She answers, "Iris." She bites down on her lip. Again with my cock. Iris asks, "Yours?"

"Logan."

She raises her drink toward me. "Thanks for pouring me great beer tonight."

"Hold that for a minute." I grab a glass and pour me the same beer.

She laughs, "My arm is getting tired waiting."

With my beer in hand, I raise my hand and say, "Great beer. Great company."

"Aww. I'm great company. Why thank you, kind sir."

Clink goes our beer glasses. We both take a drink.

She sets her beer down and says, "You know what would be awesome?"

"What's that?"

"Y'all should design a beer after me."

Barry starts to laugh, "Like we haven't heard that before."

She continues, "I'm serious. I could seriously promote the hell out of that. My local readers would be all about it."

Confused at what she is saying, I ask, "Your readers?"

"Oh, I didn't tell you because we just met. But I'm a local and nationwide columnist. I'm kind of a big deal."

"What do you mean?"

"Have you heard of Iris McIntyre?"

"Fuccckkkk," grunts Barry.

She giggles, "He has."

Barry comments, "My ex read your column religiously." He snaps his fingers and says, "It was something like Dirty and Flirty."

Iris giggles again, "Thirty and Flirty."

I examine, "Is that so?"

"They say, I'm the next Sex and the City. Since Carrie had cosmopolitans, I should have craft beer as my signature drink. Get to it."

I laugh, "Just like that? Barry and I should craft you a beer?"

"Yessss. Ohhh, wait. You can call it the Nut Smut."

"Nut Smut?"

Barry chimes in, "She discusses sex a lot in her column."

"Yeah, I kinda do. I could imagine describing my beer. Nutty flavor with a salty aftertaste. Oh, it's perfect. When can we get started?"

I look at Barry, who looks at me. I reply, "I don't know about that."

"Why not? Just think, me writing about the gorgeous bartender and his hot red-headed friend who crafted a local celebrity her signature drink. Just imagine the business y'all would acquire."

Barry scratches his beard and asks, "Where did this come from?"

Iris laughs, "My creative mind. Let's do it. I'm excited. I can be here tomorrow to discuss more. Noon okay? Great, see you then."

Before we can say more, she finishes her drink and out the door she goes.

I look at Barry and ask, "What just happened there?"

Perplexed, he says, "That one is all yours. You let me know what she wants, and we'll do it. I'm heading out."

"Are you serious?"

"Yep, see you later. Let me know how it goes with your girl."

I'm not one-hundred-percent sure how I'm going to craft her beer. I'm the face of the place and the business-side guy of Pint Niner, not the brewer. That's Barry and Kole's thing. Yeah, I have helped them out in the back but I prefer tasting and recommending. But here is my chance to formulate a recipe and have Barry and Kole to show me the ropes. I take a sip of my end-of-shift beer and invisibly cheer for the brunette who volun-told me to design her drink. Here goes nothing.

4

IRIS

Last night was interesting, to say the least. It is going to make for a great story. I can picture him behind the bar, showing off his slender, tatted arms, drinking my beer. The title will say, *Local Bartender Crafts the Perfect Nut Smut for Local Sex Columnist.* I can see so many of my readers heading out to the bar, trying my beer and enjoying the scenery. I wonder if they would donate a portion of sales to a local charity, like Omaha's Autism Speaks chapter. This is going to be fun.

Today is the day Logan and I chat. Do I go professional or fun and flirty? I was fun and flirty last night. My column is Thirty and Flirty. Cute and sassy it is. I rummage through my closet of clothes. The weather man said it is going to be a damp morning, with dew on the blooms. The high sitting around 69 degrees. This is the perfect day for an oversized sweater, jeggings and knee-high brown boots. I search and find a royal blue, pullover sweater with the tags still on it. *This will work.*

After getting dressed, it is time to apply makeup and figure out what the hell I'm doing with my hair. Looking in the mirror, I scrunch up my nose. Do I let my wavy, wannabe curls flow or do a high pony-tail? Hmmmm. I pull my hair into a high pony-tail and meh. Maybe, a messy bun would do the trick. Quickly, I wrap my hair tie around my long brown hair and finish it off with a knot. A few strands fall loosely to the side. Jackpot! I look cute. Messy bun intact, my blues popping with the help of my sweater, and solid curves for days. This is 'thirty and flirty' for sure.

∼

I WALK into the brew pub and Logan is sitting at the bar with a pen and paper. He is scratching his scruffy chin.

I say, "Knock, knock."

Logan glances up and greets me with a boyish smile, practically knocking me back a few steps. He is more than just easy on the eyes; he has a kindred spirit about him. I blush, returning the smile. I walk up next to him and grab a whiff of his clean shower and mainly musk combo. Can we say that I'm knocked down once more? I inhale, then exhale. My body becomes flush. What the hell is going on here? A simple smile, wet. A simple smell, wetter. What is next? Him touching me and me combusting from that touch? Stay away. No touchy.

Logan grins, "What's going on in that head of yours?"

I laugh, "You don't want to know."

"Impure thoughts?"

"Say what?" I'm shocked by his response.

"I looked you up last night."

"Shut up, you did not." I playfully hit him.

"I can't believe you get away with writing that. You're pretty open about your *adventures*."

I nod, "Yeah, it's what I'm good at. I'm the next Carrie Bradshaw."

He tilts his head, "So, does that make me Big or Aiden?"

And, floored. Let's pick my mouth up off the tile floor.

He chuckles, "I have two older sisters. They made me watch it with them."

"Well, that explains it. But...you asked if you were Aiden or Big? I was not expecting that response."

He laughs, "Iris, I was just playing around. Don't look too much into it."

"I'm not."

He smirks, "You're a female. That's what you do."

"Ugh, we do not." I lightly push him this time. Changing the topic, I question, "What's the verdict on my beer? What's the process?"

Scratching his scruff once again, he responds, "It takes a few weeks for the brewing process. After reading about you, I have an idea for your recipe."

"Okay, let's hear it."

"We don't give our recipes out."

"It's my recipe."

"No! Our recipe, your idea."

I roll my eyes. "Fine. But can I claim the name?"

That boyish smile appears across his face once more. "That's what we are hoping for."

"Yay!" My hands clap together.

"You're really excited about this."

"Duh, who wouldn't be?"

His big, brown eyes look up into mine. My heart begins to thump, thump. Breathing becomes asthmatic. What the hell is going on here? This isn't me. I don't get all flustered over a man like this.

He smiles, "You okay?"

I fan myself. "Is it hot in here?"

A gruff voice speaks, "Actually, no."

Logan and I look toward the brewery doors. Logan comments, "I figured you would come."

The red-headed beard man comes walking in, saying, "You have no idea what you are doing."

What? Wait?

My attention goes back to Logan. I interrogate, "What does he mean, you don't know what you are doing?"

Red continues, "He's the bartender, not the master brewer."

Logan comments, "I'm more than the bartender here."

Red again, "Well, you're the pretty face of the business."

Logan runs his hand through his luscious brown hair and says, "Fuck you, Barry."

I interrupt, "I'm confused. Logan, I thought you were one of the brewers. Are you not?"

Logan sighs, "Actually, I'm not a brewer. Barry and Kole are the brewers. I'm the business/marketing guy who enjoys working behind the bar."

"Well, I feel like an idiot."

Barry comments, "Why?"

I answer, "Um, because I gave my idea to the bartender. So, all of this was just to appease me. Make me think I'm getting a beer crafted for me, but I'm really not. Not cool."

Logan speaks, "No, it's not like that at all. I'm going to craft you a beer."

I roll my eyes. "I want it to be good. If you have never brewed before, how do I know it's going to be good. I will not promote something shitty."

"Damn, woman. He's not doing this by himself. I'll be there teaching him," states Barry.

I look at both of them and feel like a complete idiot. I know they are saying they are going to craft me a beer, but this does not sit well with me. "You know what, just forget it," I say as I grab my purse off the bar. I start to walk to the door. This is a joke. Here goes a funny story. *Sex Columnist Lets Her Loins Get to Her Head and Falls for the Bartender Pretending to Brew*. Here's to lessons learned.

"Iris, wait," Logan says as he grabs my arm, turning me around to face him. BAM, my face plants into his broad chest. Then, the smell again. Fuck me. Weak sauce.

I give in. "What?"

"I have an idea."

"Okay, spill it."

"How about you learn with me?"

In unison, Barry and I say, "What?"

Logan continues, "It would be a great opportunity for you to showcase your talent, Barry. And Iris, your readers would love to hear that you were involved in the process."

Barry laughs, "You know her readers read her stuff because she talks sex, right?"

I interrupt, "I like the idea. When can we start?"

Logan looks at Barry and then back at me and says, "Tomorrow morning good?"

I sigh, "I'll be here at eight."

Both men nod. I turn around and leave. I'm not sure how I can angle this experience into something my readers would want to read. I know I can use the hot guy approach but let's be serious here. This is an opportunity to display something fun and out of the ordinary for me. *Thirty and Flirty Meets Mid-Life Adventure*. I smirk just thinking about it.

5

LOGAN

"What the hell were you thinking? You know the brewery is like my man cave," Barry says angrily.

I know I should have discussed it with him before offering his assistance to teach us both. The brewing process is an art for him. I just didn't want her to leave and not come back. This is my opportunity to see if I can brew. And I want to do this for her. Plus, the exposure she will provide for the brewery will boost business with a different audience, female audience. It's a win-win situation. I do want to do this for her. She is excited about it. The look of disappointment on her face was demoralizing. I hate not being 100% confident that I can provide the product she is dreaming of. But with Barry's help and skills, we will craft her dream beer. I just don't want to disappoint her.

I reply, "I know but I didn't want her to walk out."

"So, allowing her to brew with us was the plan you went with."

"You know this is free publicity for us."

"I get that. You were thinking with your dick though."

"You fucking serious?"

"Yeah."

"It's not that."

"Then, what is it?"

I look at my cousin who is like a brother to me. I can't answer the question. I would be nuts to say I'm not attracted to her, because I am. But I want to do this for her. I want to see her again. There is something about her.

I answer, "I don't know, man."

Barry sighs, "Well, figure it out. Now, let's look at this recipe and get started."

I present Barry with the recipe I created. He looks over my notes and pulls on his beard. Barry takes my pen and scratches out some of my calculations. He scribbles some new numbers to the concoction. I look over the changes. He increased the salted peanut butter amount and withdrew a little of the chocolate malt. We kept the hoppiness to a subtle amount. From what I remember, Iris tends to like her darker beers. Then it comes to me. I ask, "Barry, what if we added a little coffee to this recipe."

He smirks, "That's good."

Barry goes back to tweaking the amounts to add in the coffee flavor. Once he is done, his smirk tells me, we have the perfect beer for Iris. Her Nut Smut.

I return the grin, "Tomorrow is going to be a busy day of brewing."

Barry replies, "Yeah, wear a pair of old jeans and a good pair of shoes. We will be busy."

"Time to open shop for Sunday Funday."

Barry shakes his head at me and walks back toward the brewery. He likes to prep for the upcoming week. It's his ritual. This place is his dream. If it wasn't for Kole convincing him to pursue his dream, he would be stuck in a job he hated and had no passion for. Now, his passion is beer making. With my business sense, we can do it. Fuck, we are doing it.

6

LOGAN

Monday morning, and I need a double shot of espresso with my cold brew. Because it is a brew pub, we are busy with football Sundays. It was mostly regulars who enjoy coming in and watching their games in a quieter, more intimate setting.

I'm a bit uneasy this morning. It is because of her. I meet a lot of women who come into the bar. Not to sound arrogant, I'm a good-looking man, and they all like to flirt, even the married ones. Sometimes, I flirt back. Most of the time, I grin at them. But something about Iris is different. She is a smart ass. The banter between us is natural. She is someone I could see myself having a lot of fun with. With all of that, she is beautiful. When she walked in yesterday, her baby blues bounced off her blue sweater. Her jeans hugged in the right places, emphasizing her curves. I was a bit lost for a minute or two. One could say, I was mesmerized by her. I want to know more about her. Starting today, I'm going to seize the opportunity to get to know her.

∼

BARRY, Kole and myself meet at the brewery before she is supposed to arrive. Kole and Barry are getting the supplies together for our latest creations. I walk over to help them out.

Barry states, "Hey man, we are going to start mashing the grain."

I answer, "All right. Do we want to wait for Iris?" I look at my watch and notice it is after eight. I wonder where she is.

Kole responds, "We have a lot to do. It's best if we get started. Her beer isn't the only one on the list to brew today."

I nod in agreement and walk over to start the process. I'm slightly bothered that she isn't here right now. Who knows if something came up. We don't have each other's numbers, so she wouldn't be able to let me know. Oh well, work needs to begin.

AFTER TWO HOURS OF MASHING, Iris is still not here. We continue the lautering process before we boil. I'm annoyed now. No word from her. Barry and Kole are not bothered one bit. They just keep doing their jobs. It must be just another beer creation for them. The recipe we created is a solid one and our patrons will enjoy it.

In the background, the office phone is ringing. I let Barry and Kole know I am going to answer it. I walk into the office and pick up the phone and say, "Hello."

"Oh my goodness, I'm so sorry," says the soft, feminine voice.

I ask, "Who is this?"

"Is this Logan? This is Iris."

"Where are you?"

"It's a long story. You remember my friend, Bailey?"

"Yeah."

"Well, she was admitted last night for a psychiatric evaluation."

"Shit. Is she okay?"

"Yeah, she's fine. She's just going through some shit and cracked. I'm so sorry I was a no show this morning. I've been at the hospital since three this morning, and she just got a bed. I can come now, if that is okay?"

Now, I feel like a total d-bag. Iris had a legit reason for not showing up. She was helping a friend. I respond, "Hey. Don't worry about it. We got the brewing process started. It sounds like you had a long night. Go home and get some rest."

"Are you sure? I want to know all about this process."

"Iris, it's fine. You can just be surprised when you taste it in a few weeks."

"I still want to come by. Will you be there this afternoon?"

"I can be."

"Great. Maybe, I can tour the brewery?"

"I think I can arrange that."

"Awesome. Thank you, Logan. I appreciate you being so understanding."

"Iris, take care of yourself."

"Bye, Logan."

I hang up the phone and go back to the brewery to let the boys know she is not coming until later. They don't seem to mind. But this is Barry and Kole's man cave, no females allowed during the brew process.

7
IRIS

It is two in the afternoon when I wake up. Clearly, I needed some sleep. I hate the fact that I missed some of the crucial steps of brewing. Before I got the call that Bailey was having a meltdown, I researched the complicated process. It requires a lot of prep and time. I had no idea what I was getting them into. I figured it was a simple process. I was wrong. All I know about beers is that I know what I like and what I don't like. That's it.

AFTER PARKING MY CAR, I walk up to my favorite new place, Pint Niner. I'm a wee bit excited about the tour. It's another opportunity to learn. I plan to take some pictures for my column. I want to showcase these guys. My readers will love to know these entrepreneurial men are more than just some yummy eye candy. I am ecstatic just thinking of the new business they are going to get from my publicity. I should get free beer for life. But that's not how a business runs.

When I walk in, I see Logan sitting next to a dirty blonde. The fiery red-head is behind the bar, pouring himself a beer. They hear me walk in and all greet me, saying, "Hey." Logan stands up from the bar stool and walks behind the bar.

I acknowledge, "Hi, guys. Sorry about earlier. I really wanted to be here."

Barry comments, "No worries. How's your friend doing?"

I answer, "As best as she can be. She's just under a lot of stress."

The dirty blonde asks, "Is this the drunk woman from the other night?"

I nod, "Yeah, she's going through a nasty divorce."

Barry replies, "That explains everything. Divorce sucks."

I answer, "I wouldn't know. Happily single."

Logan sets a pint of dark goodness in front of me. Excitedly, I say, "Yay, Joe Mama."

All three men laugh at me.

I ask, "How about that brew tour while explaining the process that went into my delicious drinky-drink?"

Kole and Barry look at Logan. He replies, "I got this. You two, enjoy your beer before we open." He looks at me and says, "You ready?"

"I got my beer. I'm ready," I answer, smiling.

He walks around the bar and grabs hold of my hand. Holy shit, zingers race through my veins. My heart accelerates. What the fuck is going on here? Again, with feeling all the warm and fuzzies inside. This is not me.

I follow Logan toward the back of the pub, heading to the brewery. He is still holding my hand. I am giddy. There are several ginormous metal kegs. "What are those thingamajigs?" I ask while pointing.

Logan laughs, "Thingamajigs?"

"Yeah, what are they?"

He chuckles, "Those are the mush tuns. We brew the beer in them. And those are the fermentation funnels."

I giggle, "One step ahead of my questions."

He smirks, "Yeah, something like that."

He continues to walk me around the brewery, explaining the

brewing process as we go. They have been working on my brew all day, along with others. Logan lets me know my beer is in the fermentation process. I ask, "How much longer after that will it be done?"

Logan answers, "It will be about three to four weeks before we can keg it."

"Meh. What are we going to do in the process?"

He laughs, "Work."

I look down at my beer, gently shake it and say, "Well, my beer is empty. Time for another one."

Logan smirks, "I can help you with that."

That smile. It's so cute. He's so cute.

He grabs my hand again. Zingy, zingers. We walk out to the pub area. A young, strawberry blonde is behind the bar, serving many delicious beers. Logan's partners are sitting at the bar chatting with some of the patrons. Everyone is having a good time. I smile.

"What are you smiling about?" Logan notices.

"Just that everyone is having a great time. It's refreshing."

"This is our place."

"Like Cheers?"

"Where everybody knows your name?"

"You had to go there." I smile while I nudge him with my elbow. He leads me to the bar and hollers at the bartender for two more beers. I set my empty glass on the counter. She hollers back, asking him what we wanted. Logan says, "Dealer's choice."

She smirks and grabs two pints and starts to pour.

I shake my head at him.

He winks, "What?"

"You just ordered for me. You know, I'm an independent woman."

"I have a secret for you."

"What's that?"

"Sometimes, you just gotta let a man order you a drink," he winks, again. There goes that charm again. He continues, "How about you go find a seat?"

"Sure. Is this turning into a date or something?"

"Nope. Just two people having a conversation over beer."

"Okay," I say while rolling my eyes. He's playing coy, for sure. I walk over to the infamous red velvet couch. This is where it all started. Me going all goo-goo over him. My friend, Bailey, wanted to puke while I eye-fucked him, numerous times. There is something about him. I need to know more about him. I want to know everything. He and his friends are being so nice by crafting a beer for someone they don't know. Well, Barry knew *of* me. Logan had no clue. Now, he does.

Logan walks over to me with two frothy, golden brews. I examine them closely. Maybe, they are Hefeweizens. I really hope so. One of my favorite lighter, bitter beers. Logan hands me my beer and watches as I take my first sip. Gotta love the taste of spicy cloves and banana. Nom. Nom. Nom. "Mmmm, beer."

Logan laughs, "Did you just quote Homer Simpson."

"Duh!! It was a Homer Simpson moment."

"You're funny."

"I have been called worse."

"Like how? Tell me more about you."

"Oh, look at you. You're intrigued by the mysterious woman that I am."

"Mayyybbbeee. Just a little."

"What do you want to know?"

"How does one become a sex columnist?"

"I write more than just sex. Granted, it's my readers' favorite topic."

"Is it all experience or are you just making stuff up?"

"Do you really want to know?"

"I asked."

Such a loaded question. I sigh, "I started writing for the column about five years ago. I was thirty and newly single. My fiancé at the time was sleeping around with a former friend and college roommate. I was demolished. Unfortunately, this story is quite common. But I was pissed. The article started off being thirty and starting over. I went on numerous dates and talked about all the men I saw. Trust me when I tell you this, I went on a lot of first and only dates with a bunch of winners. Then, there was the 'I'm going to fuck who I want' phase. That's when the readers really started to bloom. I was criticized for being a woman who was so open about her sexual adventures. I didn't care. Still don't. Yeah, the dates were fun but nothing like the dates that turned into hitting the sheets. This story could go on and on. But as I got older, I started to realize who I am and what I want."

Logan runs his hand through his chestnut brown hair. I shiver with delight. He asks, "I read a lot of your articles the night I met you. I was curious about you. You really don't hold back. Why?"

"Full transparency. I want to relate. And in order to do that, you have to put it all out there," I pause. "Enough about what I do. Tell me about you. You have a story, I know."

He laughs, "No story here. Just enjoying life, working behind the bar and crafting beer with my cousin."

"Fiery red-head is your cousin?"

I laugh, "That nickname you gave him. But yes, he's my best friend and cousin. Our fathers were brothers. My father passed away five years ago."

"I'm sorry to hear that."

"Thanks." He picks up his beer and looks at it. "He would've been proud of this place."

"Yeah, he would. This place is amazing. What made you decide to get into craft beer?"

He takes another sip. "It was all Barry. I thoroughly enjoy craft beer but I didn't want to run another business. I was considering going back to a more stable job. But his big green eyes lured me in, and here I am. I take care of the business side of the brew."

"You ran a business?"

"Yeah. When my dad got sick, he asked me to help him with his bar. Henry's Place. I took over everything. When he passed, I continued, but neighborhood bars were struggling. Our regulars were dying off or just couldn't make it to the bar. I wanted to close while I was ahead. It was hard, though."

"Wow. You've been through a lot."

"We all have."

"Thank you for sharing that with me. Do you care if I spotlight that in my story?"

"How about you just focus on two cousins and their friend brewing a tasty beer for a local writer."

My face becomes flush. The way he grumble-purred those words makes my body electric.

And here it comes, I blurt, "Damn, you're hot."

"Well, you're not bad yourself," he laughs.

Being embarrassed is an understatement; mortified is more like it.

He continues, "Well, that answers my question."

"What's that?"

"Would you like to have dinner tonight?"

"Now, the date?"

He grins, "Yeah, the date."

"Hmm. I dunno," I say while tilting my head to one side.

He stands up, grabs my hand and demands, "Finish the beer and let's do this."

Playfully, I say, "Look at you, getting all demanding."

That beautiful grin appears on his face. I just can't get enough of that smile. "Let's get going. I have the perfect place."

We finish our beers and leave his brewery. I can't believe I'm about to experience another first date. This is a different kind of first date, though. We started off touring his brewery and then, the whole getting to know each other thing. All while playfully flirting. It's been some time since I have been excited about a date with someone. I keep saying this but… he's different. I like him, like, a lot. This is day three. Good Lord, not sure how I feel about this.

8
LOGAN

To be honest, I have no clue where I am taking her. I just like seeing the excitement and fluster appear across her face. It makes her more beautiful. Our conversations are so natural. The banter she dishes, makes me laugh. Then, there is the no filter. She just comes out and says it, even when she is not meaning too. It's cute. She's cute. I like her.

I open my truck door for her. She looks at the truck, then at me, then back at the truck. I smile again. I'm only six foot but my truck is made for someone taller. I like to have a clear view of my surroundings. I point to the step rail. She rolls those blues at me and steps on the rail to climb in. Once she is in and settled, I shut the door behind her. Quickly, I run to the driver's side and hop in.

Those mesmerizing eyes stare at me. She says, "Where are you taking me?"

I answer, "Do you want me to be honest?"

"Yeah."

"I have no clue."

"Are you serious? Didn't you just say you had the perfect place?"

"Yeah, I did. I just wanted to leave the bar and be with you."

"Well, that's sweet."

This time, I'm the one who is flustered.

She leans in and whispers, "I kind of don't want our day to end. It's weird."

I laugh, "Why is it weird?"

"I don't know. It's like I don't know you but don't want to keep anything from you."

"Do you have some secrets you need to share?"

"Actually, yes. Will you be my sub? You would be perfect as my next slave."

I snort, "You're a dominatrix, huh?"

"Whips and chains excite me."

"You make me laugh."

"I have succeeded in life then."

"Iris." I look into her eyes.

"Logan." She gazes back.

We lean in toward each other and our lips meet. She tastes of sweetness and hops. It's an unusual combination but mixes well on her. Our tongues interlock. She leans in more and climbs over the center counsel. Our lips are still smashed together. Her curvy legs straddle me. We continue to kiss. Her hands run through my hair. She purrs, "This damn hair."

We go back to kissing. I grab a hold of her long, luscious hair and tug. This time, she moans. Our kissing starts to become uncontrollable. Her hands reach for my belt buckle. My cock has been hard for a hot minute. Fucking her would be fun and ideal, but not yet.

Then she stops and jumps back to her seat. She apologizes, "I'm sorry."

Confused, I ask, "Why are you sorry?"

"I need to go." She opens the door and jumps out. I have no clue what just happened there. One thing I know for sure, I'm not letting her leave like this. I get out of my truck and run in her direction. She's quick and is at her car already. My speed picks up. She's not going anywhere.

Before she opens the door, I grab hold of her arm and turn her around. I question, "What's wrong? Did I do something?"

She sighs, "No, it's not that. I just… I don't know. I really like you. Yet, I don't know you."

I cup her face. "I really like you too. I want to get to know you more."

"I practically jumped you. I don't want to come off as easy."

I look into her gorgeous, blue eyes. "I don't think you're easy. There is an attraction between us that is undeniable."

"You know who I am. You know that I'm promiscuous. I want to do this the normal way."

I laugh, "What's normal? I met you three days ago. You are trusting me to brew your signature drink for your column. We can go as fast or slow as you want. But for the time being, you are kind of stuck with me, for at least another three to four weeks. You have no choice but to get to know me. I'm holding your beer hostage."

She smirks, "Hostage, really?"

"Yeah!" I nod in agreement.

She sighs, "You totally chased after me."

"Yeah, I did. I would do it all over again, if that meant stopping you from leaving me. I told you, I want to be with you. What do you want to do?"

Her crystal blues gaze up at me. A big, goofy smile appears across her face. She grins, "Beer me, baby."

"What?"

"Oh yeah, just like that. Beer me, baby."

And stumped. Did she just change the words to Freak Me by Silk? I rest my head against hers. "Really?"

"Let me brew with you until you say stop."

I laugh, "You're crazy." My lips slam against hers. She wraps her arms around my waist and brings me close. My arms swaddle her. This is the start of something; not sure what it is yet. I don't care. All I know is, I need to know more and be with her more. Simple as that.

The END ... for right now.

Let me guess, you want more. Me too. Trust me, me too. But this is

good for right now. There will be more to Iris and Logan. This is just the beginning for them.
Love is a *brewing* between these two.

Learn more about Kristine Dugger:
https://www.amazon.com/Kristine-Dugger/e/B01DTT7KME

Also by Kristine Dugger:
  All I Wanna Do
  The Last Check
  Turn The Page

LONELY HEARTS

HALO ROBERTS

Stormy seas hit the Lovely Hearts Cruise

Sub-genre: Romantic Comedy
Relationship: Male/Female

1

KAYLA

"You can't be serious." Staring into her brown eyes, identical to my own, I can't even find the words to express how ridiculous this idea is, no words at all.

"I am, and you are going." With an unmistakable note of finality, Doris raises her hand to call for the check. We're sitting in the middle of a busy diner, yet my mother raises her hand like she's in a five-star restaurant.

"I've got a job and a *life,* you can't just decide that I'm going to walk away from everything for a week to satisfy your, your, your...I don't even know what this is," throwing up my hands in frustration, I begin an angry shimmy out of the booth, *this is destroying my dramatic exit.* "Is this how bad you want grandchildren? Is that what you want Mom?" It's insulting how fast she throws her head back in gales of laughter to the amused, *and in one older man's case, annoyed,* glances of our fellow patrons.

"Darling, be serious, it's only three days." Pulling a small lace handkerchief, *who even carries those anymore,* out of her purse, she dabs at her eyes, still smiling. Tucking it away, she sighs. "If you would just come to your senses and work for your father, you'd be dating David within a week, married in six months and I'd have a grandbaby in my arms within a year." Holding up a finger, she wags it at me firmly. "Don't spout any math at me right now, Kayla, I know how these things work." Reaching out she puts a hand on my arm as I'm rendered motionless in disbelief.

"In spite of the fact that you are *killing* your father with all of the work he has to do *by himself* because of your selfishness, I just want you to get *out*, darling, live a little! After all, you are 27 years old! I *hardly* believe you can call your little web-netter hobby and one fat, spoiled cat a *life.*" She stares at me earnestly as if she didn't just lay on the 'killing your father' guilt, followed by condensing my life into one sad little sentence and barfing it on my chest.

"Wow, Mom, that wasn't at *all* an awful thing to say," with the eye-roll to end all eye-rolls, I shake off her hand and stand up. "For the record, David and I tried dating. It was a disaster. Also, I am a web designer, and just because I work from home in my pajamas, *should have left that out, dammit,* does not make it less of a job. Also, I have *two* cats," *crap, I'm now making her case for her,* "and they are *not*...uh, very...fat." *And with that super-lame retort, I'm going on a fucking lonely hearts cruise.*

2

ETHAN

"Let me get this straight." *This is not happening.* "You *sold* our company." I stare at the man across the desk. Paul's gaze doesn't waver as he watches me over steepled fingers. We're both silent for a moment and then he sighs, pushing his chair back and surreptitiously checking his watch. "Well damn," I sneer, noticing, "is ruining my life bumping up too close to tee time? Sorry to be such an inconvenience, Dad."

My father huffs in annoyance, standing. Smoothing his dark hair into place and adjusting the cuffs of his shirt, he sighs once more and looks at me again.

"Ethan, here's what *you* need to get *straight*," his voice is cold, he's done with this conversation. "This company was *mine*. *You* did not start it from ground zero, *you* did not ruin three marriages and waste the best years of *your* life building it into a successful venture." His voice has gotten louder with every word, and he stops, visibly calming himself before continuing softly.

"It wasn't as if I had a choice anyway, Montgomery has all the leverage, his fucking second-in-command made sure of that," my father claps his hands together angrily. "What's done is done, and selling set me up for the rest of my life. Your severance pay will set you up for a good year. Time to stand on your own two feet, Son." He nods, matter closed, and walks out of his office.

Standing there for a moment, I try to order my thoughts and fail. Slowly, I walk out of the office. My father's receptionist, Pamela, is watching me closely over the gossip magazine she's reading.

"So he told you the news?" Her fakely sweet voice grates on my last intact nerve.

"Yes." I don't have the energy for our usual verbal sparring match.

"Well," she pops her ever-present chewing gum and smiles, "you're a cutie and all Ethan, so anything I can do for you? Your father said the transition is going to be pretty quick, no need for you to come into the office tomorrow." *Of course not, why would I need to tie up any loose ends? This wasn't my company, I wasn't working towards owning the family business. Nope, this was a cash cow to fund my dad's early retirement and I've got a generous severance package coming to me. Super.*

"You know what, Pamela? There is something, actually," the words fall out of my mouth on impulse. "With all this change, I think I need to regroup, figure out my next move. Could you book something? I need to get away, somewhere warm."

"Somewhere warm…I bet I can find something, a little sun, a little booze, maybe a little romance?" Pamela smirks at me, cracking her gum again.

"Let's start with sun, I'd like to leave as soon as possible. Email me the details?" Waiting only to hear the affirmative, I stride out the door, a weird feeling of freedom creeping into my chest.

3

KAYLA

I am in hell. It is too sunny, everyone smiles too much and the music is too loud. I'm on the Lido deck with what feels like everyone else on the planet. The staff won't let us into our rooms yet, they have to get all the bags delivered and everyone has to wave off the deck when we leave the pier. In the meantime, I'm actively trying to avoid the first of many ice-breaking mixers by claiming a lounge chair and burying my nose in a book.

"Hey y'all I'm Chet-ski!", the cruise director, who is carrying *a bullhorn*, arrives on the scene. Inexplicably, everyone goes wild, cheering and hooting. "Take a peeky-peek at your boat passes y'all, we're going to divide up into groups for a little speed-date to start things off!" Everyone cheers again and begins chatting excitedly as they gather around Chet.

"Lady in the red sundress hiding behind that book, come on over and join us!" The bullhorn honks and I glance down at my sundress-covered legs. *Yep, red, I hate my mother...* When the ship doesn't conveniently spring a leak, I tuck my book away, paste a smile on my face, and get up to join the group. As soon as Chet turns his gaze on a different unfortunate soul, I bail to a bathroom around the corner.

Staring at myself in the mirror, I pull off my sunglasses. I don't look happy. This just isn't my thing...I like my crazy-cat-lady-in-training life. Mixers are not my thing, too much sun and loud music is not my thing.

I'll enjoy this trip my way. Resolving to stay off Chet's radar, find a quiet corner and enjoy my book, I smile at myself in the mirror. Pulling my hair up, in an effort to control the curls that are getting fluffier by the second in this humidity, I put my sunglasses back on, and peek out into the hall to see if the coast is clear.

Chet has effectively corralled everyone and the speed dating is going full tilt. I walk away from the noise, along a mid-deck balcony, and spy a group of double loungers with sunshades on the deck below. *Perfect.* It takes me a few minutes to find my way, and as I gleefully prepare to take my pick of all the unoccupied loungers, I hear music. Not the dance party chaos from the deck above, something lighter.

Glancing around, I'm surprised to see what looks like a tiny Irish pub tucked between the piano bar and the entrance to the buffet. The music is coming from there, gilt script lettering on the dark wooden door glimmers as I walk closer. Without giving another thought to my abandoned lounger, I open the door and enter The Storybook Pub.

They've really gone for theme with warm lighting, green leather cushions on the bar stools and a polished wood bar with a brass rail that takes up one entire side, curving at the corner to continue along the back wall. A shelf full of books covers the other side wall, surrounding a fireplace. It's too hot for a regular fire, the air conditioning is running constantly, but they've filled the fireplace grate with twinkle lights and the effect is pretty. Cozy little tables for two dot the rest of the open space, and as I take it in slowly, movement at the back of the bar catches my eye.

"Didn't fancy the speed-dating?" The man behind the bar also looks the part with a striped button-down shirt, sleeves rolled to the elbows, under a dark vest. He's got dark blonde hair, green eyes and a friendly smile. He carefully sets the glass he's been polishing on the shelf behind him and picks up the next one, waiting for my reply.

"No, speed-dating is a hard pass for me," I smile back, walking up to the bar, glancing at the taps over his shoulder. No brands, just styles, interesting.

"Can I get a pint of the porter, and I guess I should ask if you're open or if you're supposed to chase me back to the mixer?" I'm relieved when he laughs.

"A porter it is, and you can stay as long as you like, Chet gets pretty aggressive when he's spearheading the Lonely Hearts cruises." The bartender holds out a hand over the bar and I accept a warm handshake.

"I'm Kole, I'll be here for the duration of your cruise, ready to provide a hide-out," he smiles, turning to pour my beer.

"Kayla, and I think I'll be taking full advantage of your kindness, and beer." I pick up the glass Kole sets on the bar before me and toast him before taking a sip. *Delicious.* I'm about to nerd-out and ask which brewery supplies the bar when I hear a jingle as the door to the pub opens.

Glancing over my shoulder, I see a good-looking man quickly step inside, scanning the room as if he's being hunted. Light brown hair and blue eyes, he's dressed casually in cargo shorts and a green t-shirt. I'm immediately a little obsessed with his shoulders, they're broad and stretch the t-shirt just right, his arms are muscular and tan. *He doesn't skip leg day either, turn around and stop drooling Kayla.* Kole turns and walks along the bar to meet the newcomer.

"Another speed dating avoider?" Kole wipes off the bar in front of Super-Hot Guy, who laughs and shrugs.

"Not my thing, I did the first two rounds, it was insanity out there."

I take my beer and slide off my stool, heading for a cozy chair in front of the twinkle light fire, listening intently. *I would have risked speed dating if I'd known that guy might sit down across from me, wow.*

"Well you're in good company," Kole says, and my cheeks flame as I glance up to see that Kole has pointed at me and Super-Hot Guy is now looking at me as well. *Ohmygod.*

4

ETHAN

The dark-haired woman sitting by the fireplace has a beautiful smile as she blushes and nods at me. I already feel better knowing that there are places outside of my cabin to hide from the 'Lonely Hearts' aspect of the cruise. *Well played Pamela, I knew your gum-popping smarmy-ass hated me.* The bartender sets a cold beer in front of me, I didn't think I'd ordered, but it's got a beautiful clear red color, so I must have.

"I'm Kole, and welcome to the Storybook Pub," the bartender leans against the counter behind him, crossing his arms. "As I told Miss Kayla, this place is open anytime you need to hide from the increasingly-aggressive matchmaking mixers." We both laugh and I hear Kayla join in quietly. Nodding at Kole, I turn and smile at Kayla.

"Ethan, nice to meet you." Taking another drink of my beer, I think about what he just said and turn back to look at Kole. "Increasingly aggressive? That sounds a little worrisome."

"Oh, you don't know the half of it," Kole pulls a face and then laughs. "Chet makes it his mission to play matchmaker to every person on this boat. He takes it as a personal affront if he can't get the majority of you paired up and snogging in the corners by day three." Kole continues to wipe down the bar, moving away from me. "Don't worry though, it's all in good fun, and who would come on a Lonely Hearts cruise if they weren't looking for a little company?"

Glancing back at me, Kole gives me a hard look, not at all in keeping with the lightness of his comment. His gaze turns to Kayla, who seems immersed in her book, and then he glances at me again.

"Let me know if you need anything, I'll just be prepping snacks in the back." Disappearing through the door to the back of the bar, Kole leaves me alone with Kayla. I'm sitting here, nursing a beer, near a beautiful woman who thinks I *chose* to come on a lonely hearts cruise...*shoot me now*. Except...she came on the cruise too...

Taking another drink of my beer, I glance at the mirror behind the bar, and I see Kayla peeking at me over the top of her book. She jerks her eyes back down, a blush creeping up her cheeks. She really is lovely, masses of dark curly hair pulled up in some kind of knot at the back of her head, pale skin, brown eyes that are now studiously ignoring me. *You know what, Pamela? Fuck it, maybe I do need a little romance to go with the sun and booze.*

Sliding off my bar stool, I walk over and sit in one of the comfortable chairs near a fireplace full of Christmas lights, across from Kayla. The blush on her cheeks deepens, but she looks at me and a small smile plays across her lips as she closes her book. I hold out a hand and she shakes it playfully, her hand is cool and soft.

"Hi, how's the...is it a porter or a stout?" *Okay, that was safe, now shut up.* Her eyes widen in surprise. *If this pub dropped a fellow beer-nerd in my lap...*

"Kayla," she replies softly, "and yes, porter, it's perfect, nice and smooth, chocolate and coffee..." she trails off, blushing again.

"So, Kayla, what made you come on a Lonely Hearts cruise only to skip the mixers?" *That was stupid, I'm skipping the mixer too, I'm an idiot.* She grimaces and rolls her eyes.

"Well, I could probably ask you the same question, you're also avoiding the mixers." Her tone is teasing, and she's right.

"Too true, although I'll admit, I'm the victim of a spiteful secretary, I just asked her to book me a vacation." Taking another sip of beer, I join in when Kayla laughs.

"I can match that," she giggles, "I work from home and my

mother doesn't think my social life is exotic enough...she booked this and guilted me into coming." Raising her glass in a toast, Kayla finishes off her beer. As if on cue, Kole appears from the back, pulling two more beers and delivering them with a smile.

Several people enter the bar, chatting and laughing as they take seats. Kole moves away to greet them, and another man arrives from the back of the bar, setting up on a tiny stage I hadn't noticed in the corner and tuning a guitar. Leaning forward to be heard over the noise of the bar, I continue the conversation.

5

KAYLA

The Storybook Pub is a popular spot. Ethan has scooted his chair closer and our heads are together so that we can hear each other over the music and the noise of the crowd. We've been talking for hours, and I've lost track of the beers Kole has delivered with a smile. Glancing at the clock over the bar, I realize that my window for eating in the dining room is quickly closing.

"So maybe this is weird, but I've really enjoyed talking to you and I'd like to continue," *my mother would die if she heard me rolling out my mad-skills right now, I am incapable of flirting.* "Um...so I was wondering if you'd like to go to dinner...with me?" My heart flips when he smiles, his blue eyes lighting up.

"Yes, I'd like that," he stands, holding out his elbow in a grand gesture. Giggling, I stand and link my arm with his as we find our way through the crowd and leave the pub.

Now that I'm standing, my head registers that I've had a couple more beers than is probably a good idea, and I'm glad he offered me his arm. As the wooden door closes behind us, I realize that the beer sloshing around in my otherwise empty stomach, and the motion of the boat are combining into a potentially vomitous situation.

Breathing in deep, I look around, mentally begging my stomach to stop trying to offer up everything I've ever eaten. *No, no, no, no, no, not right now, no, ohmygod.*

"Excuse me," I gasp out, letting go of Ethan's arm as he glances down at me, startled. Turning away, I fast walk across the deck. There's not a bathroom in sight, and my situation is getting worse by the second as my gut chimes in with a gurgle. *OHMYGOD, no, no, no, no, no.*

"Kayla, what can I do, are you okay?" *God his voice is sexy, and this is the worst thing that has ever happened to me. Ohmygod please don't let me barf in front of this man.*

"I'm going to be sick," I panic-whisper, clapping both hands over my mouth as my stomach gives a little practice heave. I dart around the corner, hoping he won't follow, because me, barfing, is *definitely* happening.

Time's up, I spot a nearby planter and stumble to it just in time to seriously traumatize a philodendron. I feel a gentle hand rubbing my back, and while my heart insists on doing a cartwheel because he is seriously *so nice* right now, I would give up coffee for a month if I could wish for him to be *anywhere* else. Adding insult to injury, I feel another gurgle in my gut and I hear the tiniest squeak. Tears of mortification fill my eyes and I turn away from him, breathing carefully. *OHMYGOD I just farted.*

His hand stops moving for just a second, and I hear him give a tiny snort of laughter before it resumes. *Yep, he heard me fart, awesome.*

Standing shakily, I glance at his chest, unable to look at his face. I'm blushing so hard I'm dizzy, and I wipe my mouth with a shaky hand.

"So, um, I'm just going to go hurl myself in the ocean," I whisper, and a burst of laughter escapes his lips. His arms wrap around me carefully and he pulls me in close, gently rubbing my back.

"For the record, that was the cutest fart ever," his laugh rumbles through his chest into my ear and I can't help the startled giggle that escapes my own lips, breaking off in an embarrassed little sob. His arms squeeze gently and I feel his lips brush across my forehead.

"I'm just sorry I was too stupid to feed you," he rumbles, leaning back to look at my face. "Come on, let's go get you something to eat, soak up any beer that might be left in there." *Wow, how drunk is he that he's not bailing? I literally just horked in a plant.*

6

ETHAN

"Would you like to take a walk on the deck? The moon is full tonight." I know Kayla is still bothered by what happened earlier, but she slowly relaxed over dinner, and the conversation was easy. It's kind of ridiculous how much we have in common, right down to living in the same city. I think Chet snuck something in the water to aid his matchmaking efforts, because all I can think about is spending more time with Kayla.

"Yes, that would be nice," she says softly.

Standing, I take a last drink of my water and hold out my hand. She smiles and takes it, standing gracefully. We walk along until she stops at the railing at the front of the ship. A breeze kicks up and I see her give a tiny shiver. Being in a t-shirt and shorts myself, I have nothing to offer, but I lean on the rail next to her and put an arm around her, sharing body heat.

"Mmmhm you're toasty warm," she murmurs, turning so that her back is against my chest. Encouraged, I put my other arm around her, and we stand without talking for a few minutes, just watching the sky. Eventually, she sighs, one hand coming up to trail along my forearm, back and forth, I feel her nails playing along my skin, the barest of tickles.

"I feel like I've known you forever," I lean down and say the words quietly by her ear. Her lips quirk up the tiniest bit in a smile and her eyes close as she leans her head back on my shoulder.

"Same," she whispers, and I tighten my arms around her slightly as her fingers dance up and down my arm again. I would stay here forever if it weren't for the breeze that continues to flutter her hair. When she shivers again, I sigh and link our fingers together, leading her to the stairs.

"This is my stop," Kayla pauses as we reach the landing at the third deck. "Will I see you tomorrow?"

"I'd like that, want to carb-load some brunch?" *For fuckssake I may as well have just asked if I could get her drunk again, that was stupid.* "I mean, do you want to hit the pastry aisle so your stomach doesn't freak again?" WHAT IS WRONG WITH ME, NOW I'M REMINDING HER THAT SHE THREW UP?! I'm relieved when Kayla laughs.

"Yeah, pastries because I'm such a lightweight make sense."

"Shit, I didn't mean that," *mayday, mayday.* Kayla laughs again softly.

"I know Ethan, I'm teasing, but honestly, pastries are my kryptonite, so...Lido deck at ten?" *She's awesome, and I feel like I'm fifteen again, I don't know what to do with my hands and I'm sweating.*

"Lido deck at ten, it's a date." *Ugh, that was lame.* Kayla smiles and waves as she turns and walks down the hall. I roll my eyes at myself and head for deck two, smiling. *Lido deck at ten.*

7

KAYLA

Waking up the next morning, I feel amazing. My stomach is fine, I must have barfed enough to skip a hangover, and Ethan wants to carb-load with me at ten. *That was so cute, usually I'm the blushing, tongue-tied one in a conversation.* Standing up and stretching, I see a piece of paper on the floor near my cabin door. Picking it up, it's part of the day's agenda with writing on the back.

Meet me for mimosas at the Captain's Lounge, 9:30?

That's weird, I wonder what made him change his mind? Shrugging it off, I shower and try to tame my curls into some semblance of controlled chaos. Skimming through the outfits in the closet, I settle on a short blue t-shirt dress and sandals. Checking the mirror, I grab my cabin key and head for the Captain's Lounge.

It takes me a little while to find my way, it's at the other end of the ship two decks above mine. Giving my name at the host stand, a very pretentious waiter takes me to a small alcove overlooking the ocean. Ethan hasn't arrived yet, so I scoot into the booth and enjoy the view.

"Surprise! Sorry I'm late!" *That's not Ethan.* Turning to the familiar voice, I see a man with blonde hair strolling towards my table.

"David? What are you doing here?" *Ohmygod, my mother.* "Did my mother send you on this cruise?" His smile wavers a tiny bit, but he slides into the booth next to me, dropping a kiss on my cheek.

"Of course she did," he laughs, "why would she send you on a cruise like this otherwise? She just figured everything would be geared to couples, and she wants us to give things another shot." I'm gaping like a fish at his words.

"And this was all just *okay* with you? Seriously? I'm sure you remember that we tried dating?" I scootch away from him a tiny bit, turning to look at him directly. "Also it's weird that we're sitting on the same side of this booth, go over there." David laughs, but stands up and moves to the other side of the booth, immediately reaching out and capturing one of my hands in his, it feels nice, familiar.

"Kayla, I know we tried, but I think there was just too much pressure and too many other things going on...can we just take this week and give *us* a chance?" His blue eyes are so earnest, and he squeezes my hand.

"This is too much for me to think about right now, David," I whisper. This is so confusing, David and I broke up for the simple reasons that he was too busy working for my father, and my mother was *way* too involved in pushing us towards the altar.

"Then don't think, let's just have some fun, see what happens," David shrugs, with a hopeful smile, "are you hungry? The pastries here look amazing." *Ohmygod, Ethan.*

"I'm sorry, I can't, I made plans to meet someone." I stand up quickly, looking around for a clock. "I'll see you later, David." Quickly walking out of the dining room, I ignore his startled response.

By the time I find my way to the Lido deck, I'm at least twenty minutes late. Ethan isn't in any of the lounge chairs or at the cabana bar. I head into the dining room and look around, happy and nervous when I see him sitting alone at a table overlooking the deck below. He sees me approaching and smiles broadly, standing up.

"I wasn't sure which kind you'd like, so I ordered one of everything," he laughs, pulling out my chair. He drops a quick kiss on my cheek before taking his own chair. "Did you sleep well?" I can feel where his lips touched me, and I just nod, taking a quick sip of orange juice. *He's so hot it scrambles my brains.* He reaches for a donut, taking a large bite.

"Yes, sorry I'm late, it was the strangest thing, I got a note to meet for mimosas at the Captain's Lounge, and I thought it was from you, so I went there first." I feel suddenly shy, which is silly considering he's here after arguably seeing me at my worst yesterday. Reaching for a muffin, I meet his eyes, alight with curiosity.

"Another knight enters the fray? Do tell!" He takes another bite as I laugh at the reference to the medieval fiction books we discovered we both like to read last night.

"Well, um, it's a little more complicated than that actually. It's an ex-boyfriend," Ethan's eyes widen, but he waits for me to continue. "My mother sent him on the cruise too…she's kind of the original helicopter parent." He chokes a little on the donut and then his cough turns into a laugh.

"So if I'm understanding this right, your mother sent you on this cruise, hopefully to meet people and live a little…and then she also sent along your ex?" His tone is incredulous, and I really hope he doesn't just walk away.

"Yes, and I'm only telling you this because, well, I like you," my cheeks predictably flame right up, "and if you meet him, which I hope does not happen, he will probably do something ridiculous like call me his fiancee." *That might have been too weird of an example.*

"I don't want to step in the middle of anything," Ethan's eyes meet mine, searching.

"No! Sorry, *no*, you're not. I just didn't want it to be weird, *too late*. It's just that he's on the boat, and…he and my parents have decided that everything tied up in a neat little bow, with us *married*, would be an ideal situation."

"And what do *you* think would be an ideal situation?" Ethan says softly.

"I don't know…but I know that I don't want to quit a job that I love, so I can jump into the family business for a few years before I have to quit and become a baby-factory." I realize I've picked the muffin to crumbs, so I set it on a little plate and scoot it away, embarrassed. Taking an eclair from the plate between us, I wait for him to respond.

"I don't blame you, and it's funny that I'm almost in an opposite scenario," Ethan muses, "my father sold the business I thought I would take over someday. I'm free to find my own way, start fresh, and I have no idea what I want to do." He shrugs, glancing at the deck below before meeting my eyes again. "I like you too."

His eyes are so blue and sincere. I don't want to think about David anymore. I smile at him and take a bite of the eclair. Cream shoots out the other end, landing on the table cloth. We stare at it in startled silence, *because, yeah, my eclair just splooged on the table,* and burst out laughing.

8

ETHAN

As Kayla and I are leaving the dining room, we hear the honk of Chet's bullhorn from the pool area.

"Hey y'all! It's Chet-ski! Get on over here double-time! The biggest game of Twister you've ever seen will be happening in T-minus three minutes!" Immediately a crowd begins to gather, and Kayla looks at me in mock horror.

"He found us!" I grab her hand and pull her to the back of the deck. Finding the stairs, I head for the loungers I saw yesterday. Basically a circular bed with a domed sunshade covering, they're the perfect place to hide. Kayla runs with me, giggling, and I dive into one in the far corner, pointing towards the ocean. I've still got hold of her hand, and instead of letting go, I accidentally pull, and she lands in a heap on my lap.

"Sorry, are you okay?" She's warm and her skin is smooth, and I realize that I know this because her dress rode up and my hand is on her thigh. *Really high up on her thigh.* At some point while we ran, her hair popped free of the clip she had containing it, and she puts her hands on my chest, sitting up slightly as she pushes the curls out of her face. Her eyes are dancing and her breath is fast, and before she moves away from me, I slide my other arm around her waist.

"Very okay," she whispers. I feel her breath on my cheek and turn my head, pausing just before our lips touch. Kayla closes her eyes and kisses me. Her kiss is sweet and hot, her lips molding to mine and opening as I feel the flick of her tongue. She moves, letting out a sigh and I feel one of her hands slide up my chest and around my neck.

Holding her tight to me, I roll us so that she's on her back. She hums with pleasure as I kiss my way along her jaw to that sweet spot on the side of her neck. I let her feel my teeth and she gives a tiny gasp, pulling my hair to bring my face back to hers as she kisses me, hungrily this time. Pushing up to hold my weight off her, I deepen the kiss and feel her shift, one of her legs moving up and around my waist. *Fuck, I want her.*

I feel her hips roll, forward, back, grinding us closer together and I badly want to get rid of the layers of clothing between us and drive in deep. Ending the kiss with a gasp, we're both breathing hard, and I'm sure she can feel me, hard and ready. As I lean down to kiss her again, we're interrupted.

"Kayla?" It's a man's voice, and we both startle, glancing around. No one is in view of the opening of the lounger, but I hear someone moving behind. Kayla pushes against my chest, and I shift to lay beside her as she jerks her dress down to cover what looked like a tiny bikini. *Note to self, take Kayla swimming.*

"You've found me, David, I'm busy though," her voice is clearly annoyed, and I narrow my eyes at the man who walks over and leans on the rail between us and the ocean. He's very clean cut, and he's got a spoiled look to him that screams money. His lip curls slightly as he glances at me, and I swear I've seen him somewhere before, but I turn to look at Kayla instead.

"Busy?" The newcomer repeats.

"Yes, David, fairly obviously Ethan and I were enjoying some time alone," Kayla sighs, sitting up, but keeping a hand on my knee. I stay leaned back and put my hands behind my head, smirking at David from behind Kayla.

"When we met this morning for drinks," David gives me a glance, hoping I'm not aware that they were together, *no such luck Davey,* "I thought we decided to talk about our engagement, work things out?" Kayla gives a little snort of laughter, glancing at me.

"Dude, she told me you left her a note and met for drinks, she also mentioned that you would say you're engaged," I smile at Kayla, resting one hand on her back and rubbing gently.

"When she mentioned me did she mention that once we're married, she'll be the wife of the CEO of Montgomery Financial?" David looks proud to be dropping this little bomb, and Kayla gasps at the same time that it clicks where I've seen him before.

"He's making *you* CEO?" she whispers. At the same time, I sit up, looking at him hard.

"Montgomery?" I look at Kayla. "Your father is Carlton Montgomery?"

"Yes," she whispers, confused. "Ethan, what-"

"*This* man, and *your* father, drove my father's company into the ground," I grate out, unable to keep the anger out of my voice. I stand and walk away.

9

KAYLA

"Is that true, David?" As I watch Ethan walk away, I can still feel his lips on mine, his hands on my skin. I look up at David, and his handsome face is serious, his eyes meeting mine.

"It could be, Kayla, business isn't all tee times and cocktails. I don't know him, but it could be." David sighs, sitting down next to me on the edge of the lounger. "Sometimes people make bad business moves and that makes them vulnerable, it happens." He picks up my hand, linking our fingers together, but I pull away.

"I'm going back to my cabin," standing up, I take a step away from David as he reaches for me, "alone."

"Have dinner with me tonight," he stares down at his hands and then looks up at me, "please?" My head is all over the place and my heart aches to go find Ethan, but I look at David. He's safe, and familiar, and watching me with eyes that really, really want me.

"Okay." I turn quickly and walk to my cabin. I need to think.

I'm hurt that Ethan walked away without another word. The look in his eyes sticks with me as I stand under the spray of the shower, letting it pound my shoulders and the back of my neck. Full of anger and disgust, it's not fair that he looked at me like that, I didn't buy his father's stupid company.

It's still a couple of hours until dinner, but I've got too much nervous energy to stay in my cabin. Getting ready quickly, I slip into a short lace dress with a v-neck and thin straps. I like the way the silvery gray glimmers, it looks pretty with my dark hair. Walking the decks aimlessly, I admit to myself that I'm hoping to see Ethan. I just met him, but I felt like something was really there, we just clicked. *And holy-moly can that man kiss, my lady-bits clenched up so hard I bet it registered on a Richter scale somewhere.*

Turning a corner, I hear familiar music, and see the burnished wooden door of The Storybook Pub. The oldest trick in the book is to lay all of my problems out for the bartender, but I think that's exactly what I'm going to do. Pulling open the door, I step inside.

"Good evening Miss Kayla, a porter for you?" Kole's welcoming smile makes me feel better as I take a seat on one of the stools.

"Yes please, it's been kind of a day." I sigh and take a sip of the beer he sets before me, thinking about Ethan, and David.

"What kind of a day has it been, might I ask?" Kole's voice is friendly, so I spill my guts.

"...so I'm not sure what to do," I end my story, and my beer, and look expectantly at Kole. For whatever reason, I'm pretty sure he can give me a solution.

"David is the man your parents feel would be a good match for you, yes?" Kole asks directly.

"Yes, but-"

"David is safe and wealthy and handsome, and a host of other things that many women are looking for in a mate, yes?"

"Yes, but-"

"David came on this cruise for you, it doesn't matter if your mother planted the idea in his head, he is here for you, yes?"

"No."

"No?" Kole glances at me in surprise.

"No. I think he is here because my father is going to make him the acting CEO if he manages to settle me down." I whisper.

"Then in spite of their wishes, David is not the man for you. But is Ethan?" Kole's voice is understanding, but firm. "There are other fish in the sea, Kayla."

"I know, but why does it feel like Ethan was *my* fish?" I barely squeeze the words out, my throat feels tight.

"I think you have your answer," Kole smiles, turning away to pull a beer for another patron.

Feeling strangely resolved, I slip off the stool and pull my wrap around my shoulders to ward off the night air. Leaving the pub, I head for the dining room. I need to talk to David, it's only fair. Whether Ethan wants to talk to me or not, I need to end things with David.

10

ETHAN

I decide to grab a burger at one of the little restaurants mixed in with the duty free shops in the center of the ship. I don't want to risk seeing Kayla in the dining room, I'm feeling like a complete asshole for blowing up at her earlier.

Wandering along one of the side decks, it seems easiest just to call it an early night. Heading for the stairs, I see The Storybook Pub. Change of plans, a beer seems like just what the doctor ordered.

"You look like a man in need of a nice IPA," Kole smiles, pulling the beer before I even sit down.

"That I am, how'd you guess?" Taking the beer he offers, I sit down on one of the bar stools and take a drink.

"Oh, I've been doing this for a while, Ethan, you kind of get good at guessing," Kole laughs, clearing a glass from the space next to me and wiping down the bar. "I'll admit I'm a little surprised not to see you with Miss Kayla this fine evening."

"I haven't seen her since earlier this afternoon. I'd imagine she's with David," my voice is short, it hurts to think about her with him.

"David, eh? She might be with him, but I'd imagine not in the way that you think," Kole gives me a hard look. "You need to go find her and give her a chance to talk to you."

"Was she here?" *Did we both dump the same problem on the same bartender?*

"No, I'm psychic." Kole laughs at my startled look, "Of course she was here, and I told her there were other fish in the sea, seeing how she'd respond," he turns and starts pulling clean glasses from a tray, stacking them neatly on the shelves.

"And?" *He's killing me here.* Kole puts away the rest of the glasses before he turns back to me.

"And if you want to know what she said, you'll be asking her yourself." Kole taps the bar with the flat of his hand. "Goodnight sir."

11

KAYLA

David is the perfect gentleman at dinner, and I have the tiniest nervous flutter in my belly that this is a mistake and I'm going to be alone forever.

"Why do you want to marry me, David?" *There were about a million better ways to get around to that, but whatever, I'm handing the elephant in the room a peanut.*

"What do you mean? We're great together, Kayla." David's smile is comfortable.

"I mean, I feel like you just want to marry me because you feel like it's the right move for the company." I blurt the words out, watching his face. He glances at me assessingly, taking a drink of his wine.

"It *is* the right move for the company," his tone is so matter-of-fact, my heart shrivels a little.

"What about love?" I whisper, afraid of his answer.

"Well of course I love you," he tosses the comment out there with a shrug, "from the standpoint that you and I are a smart match, we make sense. I love making sense, and therefore, I love you." He takes a bite of his food, unaware that he's just revealed the chasm that's been between us all along.

"I'm going to tell my father that I support you being the CEO," I say softly, looking at his face, "but we're not going to get married. I need to marry for love, real love, and I don't want to be part of a company that behaves like a shark smelling blood. You and Dad can do what you like." Standing, I look down at him, watching the emotions playing across his face. Initially he looks angry. As my words sink in, I watch David realize that I'm giving him what he wants without the burden of being saddled with me as his wife.

I don't know what else to say when he looks up at me, his face solemn. Standing, he pulls me into a gentle hug.

"I would like us to be friends," he whispers.

"I would like that too."

12

ETHAN

I head for the dining room, hoping Kayla is there alone. She's not, and my heart sinks to see her standing up from the table, wrapped in a hug with David. I'm about to cut my losses and turn away, when she nods at David, and turns to walk out of the dining room, alone. David sits back down at the table, waving at the waiter for more wine and continuing his meal. She sees me when she's almost to the door.

"Hello, Kayla."

"Good evening, Ethan...I'm surprised to see you." Her voice is soft, uncertain.

"I'm so sorry I walked away from you this afternoon, my father's bad business decisions have nothing to do with you."

"I'm sorry my father is a cutthroat asshole," as our words tumble over each other, Kayla's eyes meet mine, shining.

"Can we go somewhere and talk?" I reach for her, and I'm ridiculously relieved when she puts her hand in mine.

We walk the deck and find ourselves back at the covered loungers, now providing shelter from the breeze. A neatly folded blanket is placed at the end of each, and the stars are bright in the sky. Sitting on the edge, I watch Kayla as she walks to the rail, looking out at the water.

"You're beautiful," it's true, the moon glows off her shoulders and her hair shines. Kayla turns her head and looks over her shoulder a small smile on her lips. She walks to me, takes my face in her hands, and kisses me.

Clearly the time for talking has passed, and Kayla's kiss isn't playful or sweet. Kayla kisses me like she owns me. Her lips explore mine and her fingers wind into my hair, pulling lightly.

When we break the kiss to breathe, a groan escapes my lips and I kiss her shoulder where the strap has fallen down her arm. I kiss the top of her breast, her collar bone, her neck, smiling at her hum of pleasure. My arms around her waist, I hold her close and lay back, taking her with me, our lips locked together. I would happily give up breathing if it meant I could kiss this woman forever.

Sliding her other strap off her shoulder, I kiss her skin, letting her feel my teeth, lost in Kayla. Her hands pull at my shirt, untucking it and moving to the buttons. Sitting up, I pull it off completely, lowering myself beside her on one elbow.

"That's fucking hot," she moans softly. She reaches for me, kissing me again and then my eyes slide closed and I lay back as I feel her lips move down my neck. She sets her teeth in my chest, nipping the skin gently as her fingers play across my stomach and reach for my belt. Reluctantly, I reach down and hold her hand still.

"You have no idea how bad I don't want to kill the mood, but I don't have a condom."

"Hold that thought," Kayla whispers, sitting up on her knees and tugging her dress into place, she quickly climbs out of the lounger.

13

KAYLA

Darting quickly across the deck, I find the nearest bathroom and rip open the door, smiling when I see my target. Someone, *most likely Matchmaker Chet-ski*, has left the bathrooms fully stocked with everything from sample-size lip gloss and perfumes to lube...and condoms.

Catching a glimpse of myself in the mirror, I stop and really look. The woman in the mirror is sparkling with happiness. My eyes are excited, my color is high, my hair is tousled. I'm not blushing, and I'm not embarrassed, not a nerve in sight really, and that more than anything else, makes me run back out there. Ethan makes me feel right.

He's laying on his back, shirt still off, looking at the sky when I walk back into view. He smiles and sits up, his eyes widening when I toss my haul off to the side on the cushion.

"Chet-ski stocked the bathrooms," I whisper, smiling when he laughs. "Also...the deck is empty, I think most of the passengers are at the dance party on the main." The idea of having sex with Ethan under the stars flips every switch I've got. His eyes immediately darken with lust, and when he reaches for me, I let him pull me on top of him.

His lips are everywhere, and I let my fingers explore the planes of his abs until they find their way to his belt. Unbuckling him and popping open the button, he obligingly arches up off the cushion as I push his pants and shorts off his hips. Pulling them off his feet, I throw them to the side and reach down for the blanket, bringing it over us as I straddle his thighs.

Ethan's hard and ready, and he reaches up, sliding the straps off my shoulders and then shoving my dress up over my hips. It's basically a belt now, and the night air tickles my exposed breasts. My nipples harden to points until his warm hands close over them, pinching softly.

"Ethan," I gasp, looking down at him, rolling my hips over him with need. His hands slide down my ribs, over my belt-dress, and find the sides of my thong. With a quick pull, he snaps one side, and then the other, tossing the lace aside as my clit bursts into flames.

Reaching to the side, he grabs a condom and I take it from his hand, tearing it open. Flexing his abs, he arches up on his elbows, claiming my lips for a searing kiss and then watching as I roll the condom down his length.

"Fuckkk." His hips jerk once and his eyes slide shut as he fights for control. I run my fingers up and down, teasing, and his eyes snap back open. I let out a tiny squeal as his arms wrap around me, rolling us. He kisses me once and then trails his lips down my belly and buries his face between my thighs.

"*Ohmygod, yessss*," I hiss, fighting not to orgasm immediately as his tongue teases me. He turns his head and I feel him laying a kiss on the inside of each thigh before he sucks in hard, marking me. Hoping there's still no one around, but way too far gone to give a shit, I moan softly, humming my pleasure as he kisses his way up my belly. His lips find mine, and in the same motion his hips surge forward, and he drives in deep.

He holds still for just a moment as I get used to the stretch, and I prop up on my elbows, watching as he starts to piston his hips, kissing his neck and his shoulders. He speeds up, pounding hard, and suddenly I'm riding that fine line. I feel the swirl building in my belly and echoed in my head, and start to drop my head back.

"Not yet," he groans, slowing his hips as my eyes open with dismay.

"Oh Ethan, I need to," I wiggle my hips and he smiles. Leaning down, he kisses me and rolls us over. Putting my hands on his chest, I push up, riding him, and my hips immediately start rolling. Over and over, he hits that sweet spot deep inside and I feel the swirl building again, bigger this time.

"Yesss," I gasp, and this time he doesn't stop me. I watch his eyes flutter shut, his jaw tight. As I let my head drop back, I fall off the cliff. I feel his hands on my hips, holding me tight as he pumps his hips hard, coming with me.

14

ETHAN

Pulling the blanket up over us, we talk until we fall asleep, waking to watch the sun come up. Kayla's head is on my chest, our legs tangled together, and I'm lazily running my fingers up and down her back.

"Mmmm, feels so good," she murmurs sleepily.

BE-OOP! The bullhorn honk comes from directly behind our lounger, followed by Chet at high volume.

"Good morrrr-ning campers! For our final day together we've got something special planned, so gather round and pair up! We'll be assigning lounge pods in just a few minutes!"

Kayla's eyes find mine in horror, and she dives under the blanket, frantically shimmying into her dress. I pull on my shorts quickly, but there's no way pants are happening.

"Ohmygod, ohmygod, karma is such a bitch," Kayla whispers, quietly giggling hysterically. I find the rest of my clothes, pulling on my shirt and kissing her quickly.

"Okay honey, two options." I lean close to her ear, speaking softly. She stills, waiting for my amazing plan.

"Neither of them are good, but either we do a walk/run of fame right now, or we play it cool and pretend we got paired off in here."

Kayla's eyes are wide, and she's on her back, her dress is on backwards. She sits up and I can't help the gasp that pops out of my lips.

Her hair has gone beyond tousled, and Kayla is now sporting a full-on lion's mane of dark curls. She sees my face, and her hands fly up to her hair.

"Shit, shit, shit I lost my hair tie," she whispers.

"Walk of fame it is," I whisper back, rolling the rest of our things in a ball, and holding out my hand. The bullhorn honks again and Chet begins to pair off couples. Kayla blushes deeply, but gamely takes my hand and holds her head high as we stand up, still out of view. She looks down and realizes her dress is on backwards, and now that she's standing her boobs are dangerously close to freedom.

"Ohmygod," she whispers, yanking her dress up in a futile effort to find more fabric, and we both start laughing.

"Run!" I whisper yell, pulling her into motion. I hear a dramatic pause in Chet's bullhorn augmented instructions as all of the other passengers watch us bolt to the stairs, startled laughter squawking through the bullhorn.

We hole up in Kayla's room for the rest of the day and night, ordering room service, showering, and using up the rest of the condom stash she brought from the bathroom supply. Early the next morning, I wake up and regretfully gather my things. She stirs as I get out of bed.

"Morning," she whispers. I lean down and kiss her lips.

"Morning," I whisper back, "I've got to go back to my own cabin, they'll be pulling into port in about an hour and I haven't packed anything."

"Okay," she murmurs sleepily, "do you want to share a cab when we get off the boat?"

"I'd like that," I kiss her again, "I'll meet you at the deck one ramp."

"I'll be there," she yawns, stretching like a cat.

15

KAYLA

After Ethan leaves, I shower and slowly start packing, smiling at the delicious little aches and pains that remind me of last night, *and this morning*. Shoving everything into my suitcase and taking a last look around the room, I find myself nervous to meet Ethan in the 'real world'.

On one hand, we've been together on a boat for three days, we've spent a lot of time talking, getting to know each other, sharing our hopes for the future. On the other, it seems pretty easy to get to know someone in the controlled environment of a cruise. We've got no responsibilities, nothing else vying for our time.

I hope the magic doesn't wear off when we leave the boat. I hope Ethan still wants to be with me, form an 'us'. Leaving my cabin, I slowly close the door behind me, and it sounds so final.

The chaos of departing the ship quickly sweeps me up, and I follow the flow of passengers to deck one. Ethan is there, standing off to the side, scanning the crowd. My heart lifts when I see him and we smile at each other.

"Ready?" He reaches out and takes the larger of my bags, lifting it easily.

"Ready," I nod, ignoring the little rush I get when he flexes like that, *down girl, you've had enough for today, cripes.*

We hold hands during the ride home, stopping at my apartment first. He asks the driver to wait, and carries my things to my door.

"Oh hello babies!" I coo and then laugh as my pair of angry Siamese cats storm the door. Rubbing all over my calves, they paw my knees, investigate Ethan, and yowl loudly to express their displeasure at being left behind.

"Pedro, and Bianca," I point at each by way of introduction.

"They're gorgeous," Ethan kneels, ruffling Pedro's fur behind the ears as the cat pushes into his hand purring. He stands, reaching for me, and pulls me into a hug.

"I need to go, honey," he whispers into my hair. We programmed numbers into each other's phones during the cab ride, so there's not much left to say, and the cab is waiting. I nod into his chest, hating that my eyes fill with tears. Blinking them away fast, I look up at him with a smile.

"See you soon." *I hope.* I walk him out the door, he kisses me hard, and then I watch him walk down the hall and out the main door. Turning back into my apartment, I sit down on the couch, feeling a little lost. I play with Pedro and Bianca a while and then they wander away, curling up for a nap together in the window seat.

I unpack, and start some laundry. Several hours later, a knock at my door surprises me, and my heart flutters when I look through the peephole and get a fish-eye view of Ethan. Yanking the door open, he's holding two milkshakes and an orange kitten.

"Ethan, what's going on? Hi! Who is this lovely?" I coo at the kitten, tapping its nose as it swats at me with baby paws.

"I walked out your door without asking you to be my girlfriend," he mutters, trying to juggle the kitten who is now very interested in the milkshakes. He holds her out to me, and I take her, rubbing little ears as she purrs. What he just said registers in my brain and I look up to see him smiling.

"Oh! Well, yes, I'd...like that, yes," *considering how much sex we had over the past day and night it's funny that I'm shy, but there you go, that's me in a nutshell.* I smile back.

"And this little lady has been hiding out by the dumpster at my apartment for a week. My landlord has a super strict no cats policy, so I can't have her sitting in my window...do you think Pedro and Bianca might want to adopt?" He boops the orange kitten on the nose and looks at me.

"I'm sure they'll get used to the idea, she's adorable," setting the kitten down, it immediately runs over to touch noses with Pedro, who yawns widely and goes back to sleep.

"That looks like a yes to me," I sigh, smiling as he hands me a milkshake and wraps an arm around my waist.

"I already named her though."

"Oh yeah?" I look up at him and he winks, smiling.

"Yep. Kayla, meet Tootie."

Ohmygod. My new cat is a fart joke. This man is my fish.

The End

LEARN MORE ABOUT HALO ROBERTS:
WWW.HALOROBERTS.COM

ALSO BY HALO ROBERTS:
FINDING MY NIGHT
FINDING MY ONE
FINDING MY SAFE

ART LIFE

ZN WILLETT

**Does art imitate life
or is it the other way around?**

Sub-genre: Contemporary Romance
Relationship: Male/Female

1

"Hey, my little guy. We're going to let your mom sleep. We don't want her cranky. Tonight, is her big night."

Collin spit up, as Tony took off his diaper.

"Oh, man, where do you keep all this hidden?"

I watched from outside the door as Tony grabbed a towel off the changing table. He was getting good with the late-night feedings. I was with Collin all day, so my husband tried to give me a break at night.

"You're going to have to control this dribbling for the ladies because there will be a lot of them. You'll learn quickly what they like and don't like, but you won't have any problem," he cooed at Collin as he bounced him in the air. "I'll show you all my moves, and one day, I'll tell you how they worked on Mommy."

I covered my mouth, holding in laughter as I watched my son's pee fire across the air, hitting his daddy in the chest.

"Damn it, again, Collin? Come on, buddy, give me a break." He laid Collin down on the changing table. "What is Mommy feeding you?" he said, grabbing a fresh diaper. "There you go. Let's put this stuff on that Mommy uses." He smelled it, then slathered it on Collin's bum. "There, nice and fresh."

Tony lifted him off the table and rocked him back to sleep.

Watching my two boys swelled my heart, and tears rolled down my cheeks. I couldn't blame it on the hormones. Tony was an incredible father. The love in his eyes every time he looked at Collin was palatable. There was something there I had never seen in him.

Our world now revolved around our son, and I knew I could not love anyone more. The love I have for Tony was magnified tenfold the moment Collin came into our world.

The memory of his birth came to mind.

The delivery was quicker than I had expected. The moment the contractions started, Collin was there. This was a gift for both of us. Tony was a train wreck and felt helpless as he tried to make me as comfortable as one could be in labor.

When it was time for Collin to be born, he paced around the room, mumbling to himself about being a father and everything it meant.

"Rebecca, what if I missed something?"

"Tony, you have read every parenting book there is. Oh no, here's another... ahh!" He ran over to me, taking my hand.

"Baby, breathe."

I looked into his eyes as he mimicked my breathing technique. When the contraction eased, I released his hand and grabbed his face.

"Tony, you are going to be an incredible father. Now, get the damn doctor. This baby is coming out!"

I WAS NERVOUS, leaving Collin at home. It was the first time we were away from him, but tonight was a big night for me. Tonight was the night the world would see the pages of my first book on screen.

I was glad filming was over. Standing behind the camera my husband stood in front of, made me appreciate his job more and I realized being a movie star wasn't as easy as I had thought.

Most of the time, I could still walk down the street by myself. Whereas, my husband was always recognized. We're waiting for the day it all settles down—be able to go to the mall undisturbed, have dinner anywhere we wanted, or just take a nice stroll without having our picture posted in a magazine.

Tony hoped in the next year or two, things would be better, now that he had taken a step back to be with Collin. He said he was happy being a boring dad, doing dad things versus a Hollywood actor. No one would care anymore, he said. 'Mr. Boring Dad' was just voted the hottest dad of the year, which he deserved. Tony, as a dad, was hot. It's sad when changing a diaper or feeding our little guy, made me want to jump him.

∽

WE ARRIVED FASHIONABLY LATE to my premiere.

Everything was in full swing, fans and photographers busy screaming and snapping away at the next generation of superstars.

When Tony stepped out of the car, the volume of screams became deafening. The man still had it. This time, I didn't feel overwhelmed or anxious like when we went to his premier. I took everything in, knowing this moment would be cherished for a lifetime. Surreal... but beyond that, I felt like I was floating, watching myself as I answered a multitude of questions as countless pictures were taken.

∽

TONY and I separated on the red carpet, participating in individual interviews. I would glance his way, beaming when I heard him speak about our son. After a while, I took a break, stepping to the side to let the celebrity guests take over the interview.

I stood back, remembering the first time I met Tony at The Pub before his premier. That night changed my life forever, and it all started with a beer. I laughed to myself. I still had the beer stained blouse. I kept it as a memento.

I stared and watched Tony finish up his interview. He looked over at me as his tongue moistened his lips...

Visions of what that tongue could do rippled straight to my core.

The smirk that spread across his face as his eyes darkened and locked to mine caused my breasts to ache.

At midnight, it would be six weeks, to the day, since Collin was born, and we were counting down the seconds. The moment the clock turned twelve, it was game on, and Tony wasn't playing fair. He had done better than I had expected. The first three weeks, he did well, but the sex ban was felt week four.

Tony winked at me, then poked that tongue out again. I knew he'd done it on purpose, but the look on his face when I slid mine out before biting my bottom lip was priceless payback.

His smirk was wiped clean off his face.

However, when he walked up to me, he turned the tables.

Tony leaned in and whispered. "I know what you're doing. If you don't stop looking at me as if my cock is already down your throat, you'll miss the rest of your premier while I fuck you in the bathroom." He pinched my butt, kissed me, and slapped my ass before he strutted back on the red carpet.

EVERYONE SAID a few words before the movie started. I thanked my husband, of course. There wouldn't have been a book without him. I kept the part that he was my muse to myself, but Tony knew the truth about how I stalked him, and he loved me in spite of it.

At the end of my speech, I mouthed, "It was always you," staring into his eyes. He walked over and passionately planted a very public kiss on me.

THE FEEL of him felt somewhat foreign as my body molded into his. Our hips were joined, and Tony was going too slowly.

"More," I begged.

"I need to feel you. All of you," he groaned.

His movements were excruciatingly slow. I could feel every inch of him as he stretched me open. As much as I wanted to yell, "faster," my body reveled in the pleasure. These past six weeks, we had found other ways to satisfy each other, each one better than the last. The things Tony could do with his mouth... His hands and fingers could make me bow down to his will. His touch alone raised the hairs on my sensitive flesh.

"Tony, please..."

He had been counting down to this moment, and several times, I thought he was going to lose it. But now that he could finally have his way with me, he took his time.

Tony's hands caressed my breasts as his fingers gently rolled over my swollen nipples. Lowering his head, the tip of his tongue flicked my right bud before sucking it into his mouth.

"I need you, Tony."

"Shhh," he whispered, looking up. "Let me love you."

My eyes rolled back as he lifted my arms above my head. They stayed there as he continued to shower my breasts with affection. His mouth alone caused me to shiver, and I was close to the point of exploding. His eyes grew darker, and he seemed pleased with himself.

The air around us grew heavier with each touch, the moans more carnal. Tony's movements were in sync with mine as I writhed and twisted. He licked slowly down my quivering body, grabbing behind my knees as his lips trailed down my inner thigh.

When he blew on my swollen clit, I had enough of his teasing.

"Fuck, Tony!"

Grabbing his hair, I pushed his face down.

His control started to waiver, and I felt the rumble from his mouth as I continued to plead. The warmth of his breath saturated my swollen pussy, and for a moment, there was no movement.

It felt like our first time, and the anticipation was maddening.

Tony was finally losing control.

I felt the sheets moving underneath me.

"No touching," I bellowed, feeling his hand moving along his shaft.

He chuckled, moving over me, showing exactly what I already knew. His hand was wrapped around his thick cock.

"Baby, if I have you now, it won't last long."

I held back the satisfaction that *I* did that to him.

We stared at each other for a moment, then I took what was mine. I lifted myself up and shoved Tony onto his back. Before he could protest, I straddled him and began to glide myself up and down his cock.

He hissed at the contact, and I purred from the feel of him.

"Mine," I moaned, lifting myself up before reconnecting with my husband.

Tony closed his eyes, humming in satisfaction, then looked back into mine. "Always," he said, before thrusting upward.

"I love you, Tony."

"And I couldn't love anyone more."

THE NEXT MORNING, Tony found the copy of my first book I had left on the nightstand and read the inscription.

It's always been you.

The End.

2

REAL LIFE

I sat, staring at the words *The End*, a sense of melancholy fell over me. I was sad to say goodbye to my characters, Tony and Rebecca.

I had drunk the last sip of my now cold tea and found myself standing in the jetted shower while the water tried to cleanse away the feeling of loss.

I had finished my story.

There was a bottle of champagne chilling in the refrigerator with a glass ready to be filled, but I wasn't in the mood for celebrating. These characters had been my life for over six months. I had told my editor, Sara, I was going to find a cottage somewhere in the U.K. and finish before the deadline. She didn't care where I was as long as I had another best seller.

The idea for the story had taken on a life of its own. I couldn't stop writing, tuning out the world around me. It all coincided with the time I had seen *him* for the first time.

There was something about him that spoke to me. At first, his sexy, dark, fuck-me hair and those green eyes… but there was more to the man than the physical attraction. The more I read about him and his kindness, the more story ideas flooded into my mind.

When I pitched my idea to my editor, she smelled a winner. I wasn't sure what she actually was smelling, but I knew he had something to do with it.

Six months later, I was finished, but I wasn't quite ready to step back into reality.

THE NEXT WEEK, I moped around the cottage, knowing my time had come to an end. My editor was calling every day to get her greedy hands on the manuscript, and my friends and my mother were ready for me to come home.

I packed my things, loaded the rental car, and was ready to head back to the states. When my stomach growled, I thought food was in order to fuel the long drive back to London.

I had patronized The Storybook Pub, the name fitting for my little adventure. The quaint pub had been recommended by my best friend, Vivian, who had eaten there when she was working as a costume designer on a movie set. She talked with high regard about the young owner, Kole and his now deceased wife, Rebecca and told me to try Rebecca's pie and mash. The recipe had been passed down by her family. The owner still had it on the menu, and it was as good as she said it would be.

The pub was special to Viv; she met her husband there. She always said there was something special about the place.

I loved my dear friend, but she could be a bit much. She was in love and wanted everyone around her to be as happy as she was, but that wasn't reality. I was better at writing about love than the actual relationship part.

She couldn't understand why I was content with who I was and my relationship status. That's why I caved and found this place when I first arrived. Every time I spoke to Viv, she would ask me if I had been to the pub. I thought about lying but had to eat, so I tried it.

I fell in love with the quaint pub, but to her dismay, there was nothing to report other than the pie was delicious. Whatever she hoped for in the relationship area didn't happen.

Just like I told her.

ART LIFE

~

THE PUB WAS NEARLY empty with only a few locals sitting at the bar. The decor was typical English pub with wood tables, mix-matched chairs, and stained-glass chandeliers. I was going to miss the place, especially the owner, Kole.

"Leann, you're leaving today," he said when I stepped up to the bar. "You'll be back." He ran his hand through his dirty blonde hair.

I was a bit taken aback how he could have known I was leaving. I must have mentioned it another time.

"On the house," he said as he slid a shandy toward me, his green eyes shining brightly. He was handsome and always respectful, but you could tell he'd loved his wife and he enjoyed sharing stories about her.

"Thank you, I am going to miss this place."

Vivian said it was special, and it had been a great place to relax and have a beer.

"I'll have another pint waiting for you."

I smiled and tilted my glass with cheers, then walked over to an empty booth. I usually only drank one pint, which he knew, but maybe he thought with me leaving...

I knew the menu by heart, but for some reason, wanted to peruse it one last time. I didn't want to tell Kole, but it was doubtful I would return.

The bell over the door rang a few times as more people came in. Again, I heard the door open and felt a chill, but ignored the feeling of déjà vu.

Whatever it was, it had to be nothing.

I decided to get my order in before they ran out of Rebecca's pie.

I walked back to the bar, and Kole looked up with a dimpled smile and said, "Your order's already in, and it's on the house."

"I can't let you do that."

"Yes, you can. It's a pleasure and specially for my VIP guests." He nodded to the guy sitting on the stool by me.

His back was turned, and I could see a glimpse of his wild dark hair sticking out from under his baseball cap. *I'll get a better look at him later*, I thought and added pie to my order.

A few people were picking up their orders, and I didn't want to be in their way, so I moved to the side. Kole handed me another beer, and before I could say I hadn't finished my first one, two things happened at once—I turned and my elbow knocked the beer over the stranger in the hat, and I stopped breathing.

It couldn't be him.

The words in my books didn't compare to the feelings that flooded my body.

It was him—the inspiration for my six-month obsession—in the flesh. Seeing those green eyes in person made me mute. Kole snapped me out of it.

"Let me go get something to clean that up," he said chipperly.

I nervously leaned over the counter and grabbed some napkins. The contents of the beer mug were all over the side of my shirt and in his lap. He sat there as I wiped up and down his leg. When he reached for my hand, awkwardly close to his cock, I was mortified. I apologized profusely and offered to pay for his dry cleaning.

The moment those words came out, I think I lost all sense of reality. There I stood, bending over, laughing at what had just occurred—the first scene of my book, when the hero's brother-in-law spilled a beer on the heroine.

That was how my characters first met.

This was not happening. Evidently, I didn't realize I'd said it out loud.

"My wet pants wouldn't agree," he said.

I stared into his eyes, and his signature smirk, more powerful in person than on screen, captured me. Suddenly, his eyes narrowed in thought.

"Hey, you're *that* author."

I smiled. "And you're *that* movie star."

Who says life doesn't imitate art?

Kole came around with a towel and cleaned up my mess.

"Steven, I'm sure you've heard of this pretty lady. Leann, a big-time author in the states, was staying at Liam's cottage half the year."

He smiled at me, extending his hand, and my limp hand took his.

"I heard about your books. Nice to meet you."

I was proud of being an erotic author, but the way he was looking at me made me self-conscious.

"N-nice meeting you as well."

Get it together!

Living in L.A., I often met famous people, and I knew how to act around them. It was not like this.

I took a deep breath and remembered to let go of his hand, but for a moment, I felt a squeeze and looked down at our locked hands.

What was happening?

My inner goddess was spazzing, and for a second, I wanted to feel the connection, but I couldn't. It had to be one-sided. I had been writing about the guy for six months. He just happened to jump out of my pages and manifest himself in this pub, that's all.

"Can I ask why you're here?"

He chuckled.

"I mean, this place isn't... London, and I didn't realize anyone like..."

"*Me* or *you* would be here?" His brow arched. He had a point. The town was small, rural, and far from touristy. I'd only found it because of Vivian.

"My parents live in town, and you're right, it's not London. It's home for me, one I try to visit when I'm back in the country."

How did I miss that information? I quickly thought about the articles I had read but had never come across his family.

"It must be nice to have a place like this to get away to."

"Very few people know about it. I was born in Essex, and that's what is published as my hometown. However, my dad worked in Essex, and my mum raised me here while she took care of my grandpa and the farm. After he died, my parents took over the farm."

The man was voted the sexiest man alive. I couldn't picture him farming but would love to see him do it.

"Why don't you both head over to the table? I'll mop up this sticky floor and bring your pies in a few," Kole said.

"Kole, please let me help with that." I reached for the mop.

He swung it out of my reach. "Leann, it's your last day here. Go, enjoy yourself." He winked.

I looked at him, now more confused, but Steven got up, and I walked back to my table.

"Is it alright if I join you?" he asked.

"Of course, I would love the company. I've been in isolation for a while."

He slid in beside me. The booth was round, and I wondered why he didn't take the other end.

"Were you working on a new story?"

"Yes, and I am very happy it's finished, even though it's hard to get out of that mindset."

"What you do is amazing. Reviewing my scripts, I know my talent is reciting the words, not writing them."

He was great at reciting them.

"I have always enjoyed writing. What about you? You've obviously done a great job in your career."

His smile lit up the room and caused a stirring in my stomach.

"I have always enjoyed acting for art's sake. I've been lucky to pick films people enjoy."

"You've had a lot of luck."

He leaned in. "I'm assuming you've seen my movies?"

"I've been in isolation for half a year, not eternity."

He laughed.

I grinned like a schoolgirl, looking at him as I grabbed the beer for my parched mouth.

"I have to apologize. I haven't read one of your books *yet*, but I plan to rectify that soon. I've been curious about BDSM."

Unladylike, I choked on my beer, thinking that had been the worst time to take a sip.

"For the record, I'm not in the lifestyle."

His brows furrowed as he stared at me.

"I researched and visited a few clubs, but that's the extent of it."

"I need to get the books *today*." He laughed. "I heard your sex scenes were pretty… well written."

I smiled, not touching that. It felt like he was flirting, but he was as kind as I had read. He made me feel comfortable, even after rubbing up and down his cock.

Okay, why did I think about rubbing his leg and feeling said cock?

"Are you okay?" He looked concerned. "I didn't mean to make you uncomfortable."

I took another sip of my beer.

"No, I'm comfortable talking about my books. What I'm embarrassed about is accosting you with napkins."

"I'm already dried, and please, it was an accident. One I'm thankful for." He chuckled.

We stared at each other, and I now believed he was flirting with me. I wasn't ugly, but I wasn't a model like his last girlfriend or the ones before her. I mean, I was petite with wavy brown hair, but in normal circles, I was just cute.

"Seriously, it's fine," he said, staring at me.

Leann, get out of your head.

I took two deep breaths and willed myself to focus.

"You must have a few stories about growing up here?" I asked.

That broke the ice, and he began to tell me about the town and his family. As we ate, we laughed over the stories, some of his and a lot of mine. He wanted to know about my childhood, my family, and what made me start writing erotica. We had a few more beers and laughed. We sat there for hours, talking as the pub filled up with patrons.

The locals were done with work, and people stopped by to say hello to Steven, then left him alone. They all knew who he was, but not one cell phone was seen or autograph asked for. He was at home, and I understood why he loved it here.

"You're leaving tonight?" he asked.

"I was supposed to have left this morning but have been dreading the drive back to London. My flight is in the morning."

"That's a long drive. If I had known, I wouldn't have kept you."

"The pleasure was all mine. Besides, I couldn't feel you up then bail. How rude."

He leaned over closer. "I'm glad you did."

We looked at one another, and I smiled.

"Why don't I drive you to London?"

I sat back, shocked. "No, you just arrived, I couldn't. Plus, you're here to see your family."

"I insist. We can keep talking if that's okay with you?" He turned around. "Henry, I need to go to London. Have George drive Leann's car and follow us."

"Yes, sir." The large man stood and walked over from the bar. "I'll take your keys." Another man came to his side.

I stared at the two men and handed the large one my keys, and they left.

"Really, Steve, this isn't necessary."

"Like I said, I've enjoyed talking to you, and you'll need company to stay awake. We can talk while Henry drives to London."

I didn't even notice he had been sitting next to another man, one who had been at the bar the entire time. I should have assumed he had a bodyguard.

His eyes looked eager as he waited for my response.

"I would like that very much."

"Perfect, I'll go settle the bill while you show my driver your car."

As we walked to the bar, he placed his hand on my lower back, and a giggle escaped. I actually giggled at his touch.

Kole was staring at us with a warm smile when we walked up.

"Kole, thank you for everything," I said.

"No thanks needed, and I told you, you'll be back." He winked.

I looked at Steven and smiled.

"Yes, I think you may be right."

3

I had been dreading the drive back to London, other than enjoying the driving mix I made on Spotify. However, my brain wouldn't have come up with the romance novel I had entered.

I relaxed on the soft leather seats as Steven handed me another cocktail from the bar we had been enjoying the last two hours.

"Glad I'm not driving," I giggled.

Giggled—something I rarely did… until now.

"Cheers to that," he said, as he clinked the edge of my glass with his beer.

He checked his cell, sent a text, then looked back at me. It had been buzzing the entire night, and I wondered if I had kept him away from something or someone. I had been out of the loop with celebrity news and assumed he was seeing someone but hoped he wasn't.

"Your life has to be amazing. I would love to have a driver at my beck and call. They say you get used to the traffic in LA, but that hasn't happened."

"You aren't from there?"

"I was raised in Louisiana, moved to Seattle for College, then settled in California."

His arm rested along the back of the seat, and I imagined his fingers stroking my neck. I was strangely obsessed with his long fingers… and his berry colored lips.

Watching him talk was the highlight of my night. It was also going to get me the stalker of the evening award. Several times, I had to ask him to repeat what he said, too busy watching his tongue.

I had to shake myself out of the hormone induced fog. Live in the moment was my motto, one I wasn't following.

"Are you happy with what you do?"

His brow arched, and he smiled in that million-dollar way.

"I enjoy the work. Of course, there are parts of the job I could live without. People think acting is a cake walk, but what we have to do for roles isn't talked about. I had to lose fifty pounds for one role and walked around like a human skeleton. After that picture, I had to bulk up for a gladiator film. I had a scare with my heart because of the extreme dieting."

"I heard about that," I said as I sat up.

"You did? For some reason, I don't see you as a celebrity follower."

I polished off the rest of my drink and turned to face him.

"I have to come clean about something."

He leaned back and laughed. "Please, don't tell me your side job is reporting?"

"No, nothing like that. I use muses for my writing, someone I can picture for my characters."

He nodded to continue.

I wasn't sure how to explain without sounding strange, but I felt I should tell him. The alcohol seemed to help.

"I've used you as a muse for a book or two."

He stared at me for a moment, then the biggest smile appeared on his face.

"I am ordering every book you have."

I looked away, flushed and relieved.

"I'm honored," he said as he reached under my chin, lifting my eyes to his. "Really honored."

"I'm glad you feel that way. I wasn't sure what you would think."

"That you're a stalker?"

"Okay…"

"Joking." He laughed. "You heard of Keith Blow? I'm his muse for his collection of sunglasses. You know the best part? I get them for free."

It was my turn to laugh. "My apologies. I'll send you my latest book as payment for your motivational skills."

"I may want more than that."

All humor was gone, and he had a sexy smirk on his face.

I was thankful the interior was dark, so he couldn't see the blush I knew was present—I could feel the heat in my face *and* between my legs.

He scooted closer, his arm falling behind me, and I could feel those fingers stroking my shoulder. I closed my eyes, willing myself to behave. His touch was electrifying, and each stroke of his fingers sparked and burned my skin.

FOR THE REST of the drive, we talked about his current filming experience and my latest book. With each hour that passed, I felt more comfortable.

Steven was as charming and funny as everyone said. The kindness he showed me proved his heart was as big as his reputation stated.

"THANK YOU FOR THE RIDE, well, the out of your way ride. This has been the highlight of my journey."

He picked up his cell, sent the usual text, then looked back at me.

"It's my pleasure, but if I'm honest, I did this for selfish reasons."

"Oh, really?"

He leaned in and whispered. "I wanted to spend more time with you."

Chills ran down my spine as he nuzzled through my hair.

I turned my head, and we were face to face. "Well, I'm glad you did."

The interior filled with our heavy breathing and felt like a pressure cooker about to blow. When his hand cupped my face and he leaned his soft lips to mine, I held my breath. Even with my eyes open, it all felt unreal.

I had to be dreaming.

If so, I never wanted to wake up.

He pressed his lips gently, and when I opened my mouth for a breath, he invited himself in.

The kiss was everything and more—gentle, passionate, sexy, and sweet. His hands moved through my hair, and he tilted me to his will.

We kissed like teenagers, making out in the backseat of a car, and I didn't want it to stop. When I thought it would, he laid me back on the seat and continued igniting the scorching fire.

What seemed like hours had to end when we felt the car slow down. We had entered the city, and London was asleep around us. Steven reached for my arm and lifted me up as his thumb ran across his swollen lips.

"I've been thinking about kissing you all night."

"I'm glad you did." I smiled. "That was…"

"Yeah," he said with a huge grin.

"So, I see we're almost at my hotel."

He looked out the window behind me.

"I'm not ready to let you go yet. Do you mind if we drive around for a while?"

"I'm not sleepy if you aren't."

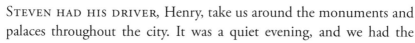

Steven had his driver, Henry, take us around the monuments and palaces throughout the city. It was a quiet evening, and we had the roads mostly to ourselves.

"Want to take a walk?" His green eyes looked hopeful.

"Yes, I would love to."

We were dropped off along the Thames and could see the London Eye from a distance. Steven took my hand, and we strolled along the Riverwalk.

"Have you always wanted to be a writer?"

"I wanted to be a preschool teacher."

"Preschool to erotica?" He looked shocked.

"Didn't you know teachers are freaks?" I laughed.

"Teachers have always amazed me. They're undervalued and underpaid."

"My favorite award to give out is Teacher of the Year," he added.

Stopping at a bench, we sat down. He placed his arm around me, and I snuggled against him.

"This is nice," he said.

"I have never seen this area so quiet."

He looked at his watch. "I should get you back to the hotel."

I looked at him. "Or we could grab breakfast."

He stared across the street behind me with a furrowed brow.

"Why don't I cook for you? My flat is close by."

"That's not necessary, we can grab something at the diner across the street."

His eyes shifted, and I wondered if he had a change of heart. I had my answer when he leaned in for a kiss.

"Are you afraid of my cooking?"

"Not at all. I just don't want to inconvenience you. You've done so much already."

"I wanted to, and now, I'm going to feed you," he said, standing. He reached out his hand, and I placed mine in his.

I didn't want the night to end, but there was a tugging in my gut that I was missing something.

As we got into the car, there was a flash of light, I assumed from another car, but by his jerk reaction, I wondered if it was a passerby who took a picture of him. Whatever it was caused him to hurry us into the car as he told Henry to take him home.

4

By the time we arrived at his place, it was two in the morning. I was too wound-up to be tired, but I was hungry. Steven gave me a quick tour of his home. He had a place in the city to conduct business and said his parents used it often when they were in town. It was bright and airy and extremely clean. If he saw my place, he would think I was a hoarder. He put on the bacon, and the aroma caused my stomach to growl.

"Breakfast will be ready shortly. I figured a traditional English breakfast unless you want waffles or crepes?"

"Crepes, huh, that sounds amazing."

"I'll have them ready."

"I'm joking. What you have planned is perfect."

His smile made my stomach flip, then its growl made us both laugh.

He placed toast in front of me as I sat on the bar stool.

"Start with this," he said, putting a piece of toast in his mouth, then handing me one.

He even chewed sexy. How was that possible? I was starving, and as much as I tried to take small bites, that wasn't going to happen. I tore into the toast and grabbed another piece. When he placed a small fruit salad in front of me, I dug in.

"I thought you said you weren't coming back to London for a while?" I asked.

He turned around as he scrambled the eggs. "I wasn't planning to."

"How is it you have fresh produce?" I waved to my bowl of fruit.

Grabbing two plates, he divided the eggs between them, then dished out the beans and placed a slice of tomato on it as he garnished with bacon. He placed the plates in front of me and stood.

"My housekeeper keeps the place stocked. Between me, family, and friends, someone is usually here."

He grabbed his fork and started in, and I followed.

"This is really good."

"Next time, I'll make you those crepes."

I choked on my bacon, and he handed me some water.

"Thanks," I said, taking a few sips. "Next time?"

He chuckled. "Unless I'm reading this wrong?"

His cell buzzed, he looked at it, then placed it back down.

I took a few more bites, then asked, "I wasn't sure with your busy schedule." I nodded at his cell. "If I'm keeping you away from someone..."

"There is no other place I need to be." His face pinched up, and he cocked his right brow. "The studio has been sending rewrites and discussing if they are going to reshoot. But I'm assuming you thought the interruptions were more of a personal nature?"

"Of course, I did. I'm sure you're dating someone... or someones."

"Plural, huh?" He laughed. Wiping his mouth, he leaned closer to me.

"You think I'm the type to fuck around?"

I dropped my fork. "No! I'm... you have options, a lot of them. I didn't mean to assume. I just like to know what I'm getting into."

He walked around the bar, settled himself between my legs, and put his arms on top of my shoulders.

"I'm not seeing anyone, Leann, but I would like to see you again."

"I would like that."

"Good." He leaned down and kissed me. "Glad that's settled." He pulled his plate over and took a bite, not moving from between my legs.

I wasn't hungry anymore, very aware of being spread open and having him that close. I wanted to close my legs to calm the pulsating ripple between my thighs.

We watched each other as we ate, and it was incredibly erotic. The swipe of his tongue and the moan on his lips when he ate the bacon was too much. I was no longer hungry for food.

"Can I have ice for my water?" I asked.

He went to get it, and I took that moment to breathe. I needed to cool off. I wasn't the kind of woman to jump into bed with a man on the first date or whatever this was. Even though my characters did just that, and often, I wanted to get to know him better before taking it to another level.

"Here's your water," he said in a deeper tone.

He could feel it too, and I needed to be honest.

"Steven, even though I write erotica, I still believe in the romance part if that makes sense?"

He took a sip of my water and said, "I want you. *Very much.*"

Well, hell.

"But I want to get to know you better, too. We can go at our own pace and see what happens. Is that good for you?"

"I would like that."

"Great. Now that's settled, I need a stronger drink if we're only going to talk."

I stood, wrapping my hands around his t-shirt, and pulled him close.

"First, I need a kiss."

I tasted every part of him, and he was delicious.

"Damn," he breathed out when he pulled back, then pushed me against the counter and pinned me in as he kissed up and down my neck.

I was about to let it all go to hell when he released me with a smile.

"I think I need that drink."

"Make it two," I added.

ART LIFE

∽

STEVEN and I sat on his sofa, talking for the few hours we had left. When it was time, Henry collected us, and we headed to the airport.

"Well, this is it," I said, letting go of his hand. "Thank you for the ride and a night I will never forget."

"Ditto."

He kissed me one last time before Henry opened the door.

Steven threw on his baseball hat and glasses, then got out of the car.

"You don't have to…"

"I want to give you a proper goodbye. It's too early for the paparazzi assholes. I saw one by the diner in the city, but he must have been stalking someone else."

"Ah, the flash we saw…"

"My life is *crazy*, Leann. It's nice when I can keep something to myself, even if it's only for a short time."

"I understand."

He had no clue how much. The new novel was about the hero keeping his new girlfriend to himself and the turmoil they had to endure when their relationship was made public.

Steven walked around to give me a bear hug and a final kiss goodbye.

"Have a great flight."

"Thank you," I said, photographing the moment to memory one last time.

I just met the man, but it felt like I'd known him all of my life. He was nothing like I had imagined, and I felt lost with each step I took away from him. I was sure we would keep in touch, but we lived on two different continents.

"Leann," he yelled from behind me.

Looking back would sting, but I was ready for the pain of another goodbye.

"I'll see you in two days when I'm in LA." He smiled.

My heart pounded in surprise. The ass had kept that information from me.

"I'll drive," I yelled back.

The End, End.

Learn more about ZN Willett:
https://linktr.ee/zn.willett

Also by ZN Willett:
The Devil has a British Accent Series
Acquired Asset
The Trouble with Dating a Movie Star Series

A GREAT LOVE STORY

DC RENEE

My heart was no longer mine.
I hadn't realized that until this moment.
That it belonged to Zach,
and it would go with him,
be with him,
follow him wherever he went.

Sub-genre: Contemporary Romance
Relationship: Male/Female

PROLOGUE

There's a reason that people have been getting lost in stories for as long as time. Before the written word, people would gather around and listen to the tales that others weaved of gods, of men, of war, of love, and everything in between. Nowadays, novels, short stories, and even anthologies and the like are the story platforms of choice.

Why? Because everyone wants a little magic, everyone wants a little escape, everyone wants to believe in the power of a good story.

It's not just about romance and love, it's also about mystery and fantasy. Any story will do.

That's where the pub comes in. That's where *I* come in. Don't get me wrong, I don't make all stories come to life. It's just the ones that happen to stumble into my pub, especially the ones needing a little push.

I help those who need helping, mostly in the romantic sense. I'm not a participant; I just move some things around, nudge where a nudge needs to be, and shove if that nudge isn't working. I make the stories into reality.

So who am I? That's a story for another time, another place … another book.

All you need to know is that I just made another story come to life ... a romance. And the happy couple will never know I was part of their great love story.

1

HAYDEN

"That's it. Enough is enough," Mina said as soon as she walked through my door. "You're not going to let that good-for-nothing, piece-of-shit cheater ruin your life any more than he already has."

"What are you talking about?" I asked, confused as to how he could possibly screw things up for me any more than he already had. My story was one as old as time.

Girl meets player at a bar. Player attempts to pick up said girl. Girl tells player to take a hike, but he doesn't, manages to charm the girl, steals her phone to get her number, then wears her down with cute text messages until she gives him a chance. Next thing you know, he's sworn off other women, or so the girl thinks. The couple is deliriously happy, time goes by, engagement ensues, wedding approaches, and then bam.

It took me a full minute to actually process what I was staring at. Just long enough for Justin to finally notice me, effectively pushing the big-breasted redhead currently riding his cock like she was starring in a fake-ass porno right off, causing her to fall off the bed with a loud thud. It would have been comedic if it wasn't happening to me. If I hadn't come to my boyfriend's place, one that was soon to be our *place as soon as my lease was up next month. Guess I was renewing, I shockingly had the presence of mind to think at that moment. If only I hadn't wanted to surprise him after getting off work early and was ironically donning a new set of lingerie under my pencil skirt and blouse. If I hadn't caught my soon-to-be husband fucking another woman ...*

Lots of ifs. But no good reasons.

"Hayden." *He yelped out my name as he jumped up and slipped on a pair of running shorts that had been on the floor by his bed, not bothering to discard the condom still wrapped around him, covered in another woman.*

"What the fuck?" *the redhead said after popping up off the ground.* "We were in the middle of something." *Oh, she was bright too. Real step up from me, Justin.*

That snapped me out of my frozen place. I pivoted on my heel and stormed out. At least Justin chased me. That would have been an even worse blow to my ego if he had let me walk out. He caught up long enough to apologize, tell me it was a one-time thing, explain how he was just scared with the wedding approaching, knowing he was going to spend the rest of his life with only me, and needed one last hurrah. I'm pretty sure he even used those words, but things were a bit fuzzy, so I can't be sure. Way to make a girl feel good about herself, huh?

Needless to say, the engagement was over, the wedding was called off, I definitely didn't move into his place, and I'd found the strength to block his number and ignore his attempts to contact me.

That was a month ago.

"What I'm talking about is that loser doesn't get any more of your wallowing, any more of your moping. He was a charmer, that's practically his living. So he charmed you? Big deal. Lucky for you, you found out before the number of legal hoops to jump through to separate yourself from him would have been a pain in the ass."

"Yeah," I mumbled an agreement.

"Good. Now get dressed. We're going out."

"I don't feel like it," I told her, to which I was met with a stare that could melt ice. Clearly, I *was* going out. It took me a few minutes to put on a cute pair of jeans and a shirt that was a cross between sexy and understated. Then I did my hair and makeup. What? You think I *wanted* to be heartbroken and single? Hell no. That was why I bought into Justin's charm in the first place. We all wanted to believe in fairy tales. I was hoping I'd be another book in real life, the one where the player found "the one" he was willing to change for. Guess I was just real life with no romance book involved at all.

"That's what I'm talking about," Mina said as soon as I walked out of my room. When she whistled, I actually felt better about myself. "Alright, let's go. I heard of this pub just ten minutes away. It's supposed to be a quaint little place, something right out of a storybook. I have a feeling it's right up our alley."

We grabbed an Uber so that we could both drink. Mina said I needed it, and she was right there with me in solidarity. I think she just needed an excuse to let loose. She'd been stressed at work lately, and I felt sort of bad that I hadn't been a better friend to her in the past month, lending her my ear or even my shoulder. Especially since she'd done that for me.

We made it to the pub in just under ten minutes, and the minute I laid eyes on it, I was in love. There was indeed something special about the place. Like straight out of one of my favorite little fantasy novels. I could imagine witches and warlocks gathering there. And then we walked in, and I almost salivated. Picture a bar from the 1700s like something you would see on a movie set. Add a touch of Harry Potter magic and you had The Storybook Pub. I didn't even catch the name, but that's what I'd forever refer to this bar as.

We sat at the bar and ordered a couple of drinks. Oh, who am I kidding? We ordered two double shots of tequila each.

"I'm sorry, Mina," I said after we'd seemed to settle in.

"What for?" she asked, taking in the cuteness of the pub herself. She was a book buff just like me. That's actually how we became friends. We met in the library in high school when we were both looking at the same book. We got to chatting, found out we had the same taste, and the next thing you know, we were the best of friends. We'd been through high school drama, college drama, boyfriend drama, and now fiancé drama together. Mina had just started dating a co-worker, and although it was new, I could see them making it for the long haul. But working together posed quite several challenges. Add that to her workload, and I knew she was worried.

"You've been there for me through it all, especially through this Justin crap, but I haven't been supportive these past couple of months. I know you're freaking out, and I haven't been there for you."

"You've had a lot going on."

"I know, but it doesn't excuse it. You have a lot going on, but you're still listening to me bitch and getting me out of the house, finding this place."

"You got cheated on by your fiancé; I think your 'lot going on' trumps mine," she said with a bit of a chuckle.

"Gee, thanks," I said with a wry smile. "I love you, Meen," I told her, calling her the nickname only her closest friends were permitted to use. "I'm lucky to have you as my friend."

"Damn right, you are."

"Okay, now tell me about work, about Harris."

"What's there to tell? We're just starting out."

"But you like him a lot."

"I do," she said with a goofy smile. "But we work together."

"Different departments, different floors, different everything. And you said you checked the policy three times. You're okay to date, to even marry and live happily ever after as long as you don't report to each other."

"I know. It's just that I've heard it's not good to work together because you need time apart."

"And you see him every day, huh?"

"No … I mean, sometimes we stop by to say hi to each other, but we're both busy, and we're on different floors," she said, echoing my words.

"Okay, so that's settled. What about work?"

"Oh God, don't get me started. I've been working crazy hours the past three weeks."

"But that's going to be over at the end of this month, right? It's like this every year."

"Yep," she responded with a nod.

"Okay, so just two more weeks to go. You got this. You're a kick-ass, badass, hard-ass woman."

"So much ass," Mina said, chuckling.

"Yes, indeed," I said with a smirk as I tried to jokingly check out her butt.

"Oh, please, I'm sitting. You can't see anything."

"You forget I know what you're working with," I pointed out. "Lucky Harris."

"Yeah, yeah, lucky Harris," she said, brushing me off. "Now it's time for *you* to get lucky."

"Uh, yeah, no."

"You've had serious, and serious got you burned. Now it's time for some fun. Besides," she said, "the best way to get over someone is to get under someone else."

2

ZACH

"Dude," James said from beside me, "she wasn't even worth your time in the first place. None of us liked her."

"What?" I asked, turning to look at my best friend. "You never said anything. Neither did anyone else," I added, referring to our other two friends. Mike was at home with his wife and newborn, and Rick was supposed to join us in a bit for a quick drink before heading home to his longtime girlfriend.

"You thought you were in love," James said with a shrug. "We weren't going to kill your buzz."

"I wish you would have," I mumbled into my beer.

"She was a materialistic bitch, always looking over her shoulder for something bigger and better."

"Going for the gusto, huh?" I said sarcastically. "Way to bury my ego even further when it's already six feet under."

"Fuck that. You need a dose of reality, Zach. You need to stop moping about the she-devil and realize you just won the fucking lottery with her leaving you."

"Doesn't feel like it," I mumbled yet again.

James ignored that statement. "Besides, your ego could take the hit," he said with a chuckle. "That fucker had its own zip code." That actually got a smile from me.

Before Trish, I'll admit there was a line of broken hearts out the door. Not my fault. I was up front with what I wanted. No commitments. No strings. It wasn't on me that every girl threw themselves at me, assuming they'd be the one to change me. I knew I was lucky in the looks department, and I used that wholeheartedly to my advantage, but I never *took* advantage of anyone.

They came willingly, including Trish. We'd met at a bar, and of course, I noticed her. With legs for days, her killer curves, and her wicked smile that promised both pleasure and maybe even a bit of pain, I was the one to approach her.

"Hi," I said. And before I had a chance to say anything else, she asked if I wanted to get out of there.

I did, *we* did, and it was one of the best nights I'd ever had. Trish had me wanting more. In retrospect, I knew what James said was right. I also knew that she knew exactly who I was, exactly how much money I was worth, and was skilled at manipulation, among other things. For the first time, I wanted a repeat performance, but she said *she* didn't do more than once. *Fuck me.* That had never happened. Lo and behold, I found myself chasing her. The next thing I knew, I was dating her, and bam, we were a couple. She played me, making me think I fell for her.

I think, deep down, I was upset by the entire experience more so than I was by the fact that Trish had left me. But I was too prideful to admit that out loud.

She'd found a bigger fish in a much bigger pond to con and left me. I was the CEO of my family's small winery. When I say "small," I mean compared to other companies. We made good wine, held tastings and tours, sold quite a bit of merchandise, and did plenty well for ourselves. My parents were retired but on the board, and my younger brother was the CFO. My family and I didn't have to hold back if we wanted to live a decent life of luxury, not that any of us splurged too often. We worked hard and were raised to appreciate the value of money. Something Trish didn't understand and was always complaining about how "frugal" I was. Trust me, I wasn't frugal, I just clearly wasn't up to her standards in frivolity.

"Forget her," James said right as Rick walked into the door.

"Fuck, I love this place. It makes me feel like I'm in another time and place," Rick said as he sat down next to us before ordering a drink. "I should bring Liz here one day," he mused out loud, talking about his girlfriend. "Who are we forgetting?" he asked before understanding dawned on him. "Oh God, not that bitch."

"You never said anything," I pointed out.

"You were a lost cause," he said with a shrug similar to the one James had given me. "But now you're free. Let's toast, and then let's find you someone to fuck and forget."

"I don't need any help in that department, thank you very much."

"Then why haven't you picked up anyone else since Trish?" he asked.

"It's only been two weeks," I told him.

"Before her, you didn't go more than two *days*." The truth was complicated. It was a mixture of me actually having enjoyed spending time with just one person and thinking about a future, all the things that hadn't come to mind before. I was getting older, and two out of three friends were settled or settling. Mike was my wingman, but he was never a player like me. He'd actually wanted to do the whole girlfriend thing a while back; he just hadn't found that someone special yet. The other part was that even if I did partake in some fun and done, I was scared I'd be played yet again. That shit didn't feel good. It didn't feel good *at all*. But I clearly hadn't seen the signs. What if it happened again, and I missed the signs once more?

"Well, well, well, looks like Zach is back," Rick said with a smirk.

"What the fuck are you talking about? And why the hell are you rhyming?" I asked.

"The rhyme was unintentional but very fucking good, if I do say so myself. What I'm talking about is right there," he said as he tilted his head to indicate I look over my shoulder.

I knew exactly who he was talking about without having to turn around. I'd noticed her. Of course, I noticed her ... the minute I'd walked through the door. I think any red-blooded man would notice her. She made Trish look like a fucking hag. Brunette but with a golden sheen when she turned her head and the light hit it, full, pouty lips, big innocent-looking hazel eyes, a full rack I could tell was natural —something Trish could *never* claim even when she tried—and even sitting down, I could tell she had an hourglass shape to her body that was the stuff of many, many, many spank banks. She was definitely going into mine.

But the biggest difference between her and Trish? She hadn't even once looked around the room in any of the glances I'd spared her way. She was absorbed in a conversation with her friend, focusing her attention on her. She wasn't looking to see who was available. I doubt she even knew she was in a bar full of guys begging her to look their way.

I turned anyway, wanting another look, if only to add another image of her to my collection for later, thinking nothing else, knowing I wasn't going to get a night with her.

But the minute I did, a slow smile spread over my face. *Well, what do you know ... maybe Zach* was *back.*

3

HAYDEN

"From the gentleman on the end," the bartender said as he placed a tequila sunrise in front of me before turning to leave.

"Wait, what?" I asked, stopping him.

I had ordered drinks from him, but I hadn't paid attention to him. Now though, as he stared intently at me, almost like he was deciphering my question, I took a moment to take him in. Kole, I'd heard him called, was attractive in his own right with dirty blond hair and green eyes. There was something mysterious about him, but I couldn't put my finger on it.

He spoke before I could think about it more. "The guy currently turned away in the blue sweater over there," he said as he tilted his head in the direction of three guys. I'd been so engrossed in conversation with Mina, specifically her trying to convince me to go have some fun with random guys, that I hadn't even noticed any other patrons around, nevertheless any specific guy. "Said something about a pretty girl like you not being allowed to look down," Kole said. "Asked me what kind of drink you were drinking. When I told him straight tequila, he said that wouldn't do since he couldn't very well get to know you while you were drunk, then asked for a weaker tequila-based drink. So you wouldn't mix drinks, of course. The tequila sunrise was my idea. The rest was him," he said with a shrug before turning away, dismissing any further conversation.

"Huh," Mina mused beside me.

"Huh, what?"

"Oh, nothing. But if this isn't the sign you need to listen to my advice, I don't know what."

"How is this a sign?" I asked.

"He's hot, he's interested, he's clearly got game," she said with a nod toward my drink, "and he's apparently a gentleman too. 'So you wouldn't mix drinks, of course,'" she repeated Kole's paraphrase of what the mystery guy had told him.

"How do you even know he's hot?" I asked.

"Because I saw him when he walked in," she told me. "Come on, Hayd, what do you have to lose? A night of potentially steamy, hot sex, a way to get that cheating loser off your mind, and the bonus of sticking it to him that now you're fucking someone way hotter? Sounds perfect to me. At least say, 'thank you' to the man," she added.

I nodded before holding up the drink, looking in the guys' direction, and getting his friend's attention. The friend smiled and said something to my secret admirer, which had him turning around. And *fuck*, Mina was wrong. He wasn't hot. He was beyond. Shaggy brown hair a similar color to mine, a touch on the long side, with a bit falling over his forehead made him seem younger than he probably was, considering the age his friends looked. Piercing green eyes that rivaled those of evergreen trees, a seductive smile with a light stubble, and a jawline made of sharp edges completed his god-like features. And that tight-fitting long-sleeve shirt he was wearing? Even sitting down, it proved eight-pack abs existed.

I truly had absolutely no intention of following through with Mina's advice. I was simply saying thank you like she'd instructed. But right now, with a smile on mystery man's face directed at me as I held my drink up to him as my gesture of "thanks," I wholeheartedly thought Mina was a genius.

There was something about him that promised hot sex, *great* sex, naughty, dirty, *satisfying* sex. I'd definitely take him home to find out.

He lifted his own drink up as if we were toasting through the air before downing what looked like beer. He then stood without saying a word to his friends and strode my way.

"Zach," he said, holding out his hand as he reached us.

"Oh, um, hi, I'm Hayden, and this is Mina," I told him, taking his hand and pointing out my friend.

"Nice to meet you both," he said, but his eyes were trained on me.

"What do you know, my seat is suddenly free," Mina said with obvious exaggeration. "I have to head home, but Zach, you should really keep this seat warm," she said as she nodded vigorously.

She gave me a quick goodbye, told me to call her tomorrow, and then headed out, allowing Zach to sit down in her vacated spot.

"Interesting friend you got there," he said with a smile.

"She's special, but she's the best friend anyone could ask for," I told him honestly.

"I have a few of those," he said as he looked back at his friends, both of whom were blatantly watching our exchange.

"Thank you," I told him when he looked back at me.

"For?" he asked.

"The drink," I told him.

"Uh, sure?" he responded like he still wasn't sure what I was thanking him for. I shrugged. "I've never seen you here before."

"It's my first time. My friend, who just skittered away, found this place. I think she thought this place would get me more willing to get out and about."

"I guess she was right," he said with a charming smile.

"I guess so," I agreed.

"Are you usually a homebody?" he asked. I could have lied and said that was it, but what was the point? Figured I might as well be honest, and maybe assuage any fears he might have that I wasn't up for a one-night stand, not that I knew that's what he wanted. But come on … he screamed player.

"Not generally, no. I guess I've been the past few weeks. Found my fiancé cheating on me, so that kind of killed my desire to go out and have fun."

"Ouch," he responded. "My girlfriend left me for a richer man a few weeks ago," he told me.

"Ouch," I echoed.

"Kind of killed it for me too," he admitted. "Until I saw you pointing your drink at me."

"Thanks to you," I told him. He furrowed his eyebrows in what seemed like confusion, but I didn't know what there was to be confused about. It was the second time he did that, though, but I brushed it off. I wasn't there to seek the answers to any questions. I was there to see if he'd get me to forget Justin ever existed, and I had a feeling he would.

"To asshole exes," he said, grabbing a beer I hadn't even noticed had somehow landed in front of him.

"To asshole exes," I repeated, picking up my drink. We clinked glasses, then sipped our respective drinks, both of us looking over the rim, staring at each other.

"For the first time in my life, I'm going to be bold," I told him. "Want to get out of here and get acquainted with my bed?"

He froze, and for a minute, I thought it was the shock of my forwardness, but I realized shortly after that, he looked panicked. Did he think I wanted something serious? I mean, what part of what I'd said screamed, "relationship?"

"I'm not looking for a relationship," I assured him. "It's just that my friend told me the best way to get over someone was to get under someone else."

If I thought he looked panicked before, he looked downright scared then. I was instantly embarrassed, and I also knew how to take a hint. Wasn't good for my confidence, either. "I, uh, better go," I said. Tossing some bills on the bar to cover my drinks, I scooped up my purse and rushed out. Once I ran out the door, I leaned my back against the side of the bar as I allowed myself to cry big, fat rejection tears. Justin had burned me, and the mystery man hadn't wanted me. What next?

4

ZACH

"Wow." I heard the incredulous voice and turned to the resident bartender, Kole. "That was tough to watch," he said with a shake of his head. *It was tough to be a part of too, buddy.* But I didn't say that out loud, still just staring at him, too numb to speak. I'd been transported back to shittier times the minute Hayden had offered to go back to her place. Her same boldness, her same assertiveness, was exactly what had transpired with Trish. And then she threw in that she wasn't looking for anything else. Exactly what had drawn me to Trish.

I locked up. And the next thing I knew, Hayden had run off, her embarrassment at my unintended rejection apparent even in my frozen state.

"You really going to just let her run off like that? Idiot," Kole said with another shake of his head.

That snapped me out of whatever funk I'd been in. In reality, for all I knew, Hayden was an even better manipulator than Trish was, and this was a part of her game. But something told me she wasn't. Trish wouldn't have let my rejection get to her. She would have just brushed me off and found her next target.

"I have to go," I told Kole, not that he cared.

"Yeah, you do," he responded with a smirk.

I ran out of there, not bothering to say anything to my friends or even pay for my drinks. I knew they'd have me covered.

I didn't know the first thing about Hayden, and she could have been long gone, but I still went looking for her. Luckily, I didn't have to look far. I found her just outside the pub. Her back was against the wall, her face was buried in her hands, and her shoulders were shaking as she cried quiet tears. *Nothing like Trish.*

"Hayden?" I asked, causing her to snap her head up and look at me, her eyes wide. She began furiously wiping at her face, trying to get rid of the evidence of her tears. I didn't want her to. It made her human, made her beauty that much more striking because it wasn't just on the surface. She had a bleeding heart, and I liked that. "I'm sorry for what happened in there," I told her. "Your words took me to another place and time, but it had nothing to do with you."

"Thank you," she whispered, then opened her mouth to say something else, but I'd had enough of the words from those lips. I wanted something more from them. I *needed* something more from them. I stood directly in front of her, holding her face in my hands, and crashed my lips against hers before she could utter another word.

She was shocked for just a moment, but then her lips began to move with mine. Parting them on instinct, she allowed my tongue to delve into her mouth and taste the salt of her tears, the bite of the alcohol, and the sweetness of *her*. It was a kiss I'd never experienced before. Something hot, something sexy, but also something more. Something mixed with emotions.

I'd needed this after Trish, and I'm guessing Hayden needed this after her ex. We were two peas in a pod, and right now, the only pod we needed to get to was either my bed or hers. Or anywhere where we could be just us, just two bodies experiencing release, experiencing passion, experiencing pleasure by letting go of the pain.

"Is your bed still on the table?" I asked after pulling away.

"Yes," she said breathlessly, and I couldn't help the smug smile that graced my lips.

"My car's this way," I told her and then led her to where I'd parked. She didn't live far away, and aside from her directing me where to go, we didn't speak. The anticipation was its own special foreplay.

But the minute we were through her apartment door, I pinned her against her own door as I ravaged her mouth, making our kiss from before seem like child's play. She moaned into my mouth as her hands roamed across my back, her nails digging in just enough for me to feel her urgency.

I let her go, and she grabbed my arm before pulling me to her bedroom. "I can give you a tour later," she said with a cheeky smile, but I couldn't give a flying fuck about a tour unless it was a tour of her body.

When she led me to her bedroom, she pushed me down on the bed and stood in front of me as she undressed. The only giveaway that she wasn't as bold as she let on was the slight uncertainty in her eyes. I smiled wide, showing her that I liked what was happening, hoping to give her the last bit of courage she needed to show me everything, to show me *her*. She did. She undressed for me slowly, allowing each article of clothing to fall off her body naturally until she stood before me wearing nothing. Absolutely nothing, and I'd never feasted my eyes on a more perfect woman. Fuck, the statues in all the museums had nothing on her. I'd never been harder either.

"Fuck," I said out loud. "Hayden, fuck." I tried to be more eloquent, but words escaped me as I took her in, savoring every inch of her creamy skin. Soon I'd be doing more than looking.

"Your turn," she whispered as a satisfied smile played on her lips. I stood faster than possible and took my clothes off before she could blink. I stood there, letting her soak me in as well. I was proud of my body, proud of the hours at the gym I put in, proud of the lust-filled look in her eyes.

And then I cursed out loud again. "Oh fuck," I said as she knelt in front of me. I'd wanted nothing more than to taste her, fill her. But when she was down on her knees—her innocent eyes looking up at me through her lashes, and her mouth just a breath away from my dick—all those thoughts went out the window. Then I was in her mouth, her lips gripping me tightly as her tongue swirled up and down, her hand on the base of my shaft, moving with perfect rhythm to her mouth. It was like nothing I'd ever experienced. She put all other women to shame.

"No," I said as I felt myself reaching my climax. This wasn't how it was supposed to be, but damn Hayden and her mouth. I reached down, grabbing her under her arms, and forced her to release my dick with a pop of her mouth.

"What the-?" she started to ask, but I cut her off.

"That mouth, God, woman, best fucking blowjob I've ever had, hands down, but I'm not coming that way. I'm going to be in you, deep, hard, hitting every one of your fucking senses, squeezing an orgasm out of you when I come."

"Oh," she said, and the dazed look in her eyes was enough to tell me I'd made the right decision.

I sat her on the bed, pressing lightly against her chest, indicating for her to lie back.

"I thought we weren't doing that," she said when she realized where I was headed.

"I said that's not how *I'm* coming, but you're coming like this first, and then again when I'm in you."

"Oh," she said again, this time more breathily as I flicked my tongue across her nipple and trailed my hand across her thigh, inching toward her core before moving away again, teasing her, tempting her, making her want more. I continued this, my tongue trailing slowly down her body until it connected my fingers, one sliding inside her slowly while my tongue flicked her clit. Then it was two fingers, finally three, in and out, in and out, slowly, torturously as she moaned, her back arching off the bed from the pleasure I was giving her. I knew when she was close, and I began to lick faster and pump harder until she was crying out my name, her juices coating my fingers, smearing my lips.

I licked them as she stared at me, tasting her sweetness. I could come like that, from her sated look, but still full of hunger as she took in what I was doing. Her awe coming off her in waves. I'd bet anything she never experienced anything like this, and I felt like a fucking victorious caveman. I quickly found my jeans, grabbing the condom I had in my wallet and placing it on before I covered her body with mine.

"I told you deep and hard," I said as I hovered over her, my cock aligned perfectly with her entrance. "Are you ready?" I asked.

"Please," she whimpered, and I pushed in ... deep and hard, a cross between a groan and a moan escaping her lips. "More," she said as I moved inside her, giving her everything I had. Capturing her lips, I crushed them, bruising them with the same ferocity I was using on her body.

It wasn't long before I felt her climbing toward euphoria, felt her walls begin to squeeze me, and I'd been right. When she came, she clamped down on me so tightly, I couldn't help but come as well.

I collapsed half on top of her, half on the bed, staying like that for a moment, gathering my bearings before I heard her say, "Wow."

"Me too," I told her, so she'd know it wasn't just her that had experienced something out of this world.

"My God, that was something else," she said, and damn if she wasn't good for my ego. "Mina was right. I needed that." Then she began to climb out from under me.

"Where are you going?" I asked.

"To clean up," she said with a shrug.

"Then I guess we're cleaning up together."

"Something tells me I'm about to get dirtier instead," she said with a smirk.

"But I promise you'll be clean at some point," I told her with a matching smirk.

And I'd kept my promise. At some point ... close to morning, we'd actually taken a real shower, no sex involved. Then I broke my cardinal one-night stand rule ... I'd crashed out, only I didn't know it yet ...

5

HAYDEN

I didn't know when it happened, but Zach and I fell asleep. I didn't mind it so much, the cuddling, the feeling of being in someone's arms, the security I got from it. Those were all great. It was the fact that you usually slept with a guy you were at least dating, not someone you were going to wham-bam-thank-you-ma'am.

I woke up just a moment before Zach did to realize what had transpired, but I didn't have enough time to process or to freak out before he woke up.

"Oh, um, hi," I said awkwardly as he turned to face me.

"I conked out," he said out loud as if he needed to justify why he was still there. "I'll, uh, I'll just grab my things and head out," he added after I stayed quiet. Everything felt surreal. I'd never been one for one-night stands, but if they were anything like Zach, I was clearly missing out. I had a feeling it was all him, though. And then I realized I hadn't said anything to him after his "conked out" comment and wondered if I was being rude. But what the heck was the appropriate response to something like that? I was new to this. I figured honesty was the best policy.

"Zach, wait. I've never … I haven't ever had a one-night stand before," I admitted. "So, I'm not sure what the right etiquette is. I was serious when I said I wasn't looking for anything more than sex last night, and I still mean it, but you don't have to go. Last night ... it was great," I told him with a bit of a goofy smile, and that brought a smile to his lips as well. "I wouldn't mind a repeat if you're up for it. And then maybe we could grab some breakfast or something. Or not. Like I said, I'm not sure if we part after this, or we stay friends."

He seemed to contemplate my words for a minute before he spoke. "I would have been long gone by now," he told me, and I felt a tinge of disappointment. "But I don't think I want this to end. I don't even know your last name," he said with a wry chuckle. "Yet I think there's something here. Even if it's temporary. Breakfast sounds good," he said with a huge smile. "And then maybe a proper date tonight? If you're free. I can learn your last name, and then we can come back and repeat last night." He waggled his eyebrows, and I laughed out loud.

Just minutes before, things were weird between us. Just minutes before, I couldn't even imagine going on a date. And suddenly, with just a few sentences from this man who had rocked my world just hours before, I wanted nothing more than to get to know him better. And not like that ... I was pretty sure I knew his body pretty damn well. I wanted to know *him* better.

I couldn't hide the giant smile that consumed my entire face. "Yeah," I said with a nod. "I'd like that. I'd like that a lot. Just give me a few minutes to get ready."

He nodded with a smile of his own.

"Funny," I said as I slipped a shirt over my head before heading to the bathroom. "If you would have asked me last night if I wanted a date with you, the answer would have been no. Now, even with you still in my bedroom, I'm already looking forward to tonight."

"Same here, Hayden. Exactly the same for me."

It took me fifteen minutes to take a quick shower, brush my teeth, and put some mascara and lip gloss on. I found Zach looking at pictures in my living room. I gave him a quick tour and explained the family and friends in the pictures he was looking at before we headed out to breakfast.

We walked to a little diner a couple of blocks away from my place, sat down, and ordered without saying much to each other. I'm not sure if we were both trying to figure out how to navigate this new territory we seemed to both want but weren't sure how to handle, if things were suddenly awkward, or if we were enjoying the quiet comfort we magically had. Or maybe a little of all three.

"So who are you, Hayden ..." he trailed off, clearly waiting for me to fill in the missing last name.

"Gendry," I told him. "Hayden Gendry. Nice to meet you, Zach ..." I trailed off just like him with a quirk of my eyebrow.

"Zach Straus. It was *very* nice meeting you," he said with a raised eyebrow of his own and a smirk. I blushed, and he smiled wider. "Alright, Hayden Gendry. Now that I can finally put a face to your very, very lovely body," he told me while his eyes roamed up and down, "tell me about yourself. Age, career, hobbies, the works. You know, first date basics." I chuckled at that, and so did he. And then I told him everything I could think of after that. He listened, he asked questions, and he was genuinely interested. I found myself smiling like a love-struck teenager the entire time, even when he managed to wrangle some embarrassing stories out of me that had us both laughing so hard we were in tears.

After I was done, I had him do the same. He told me about his family, his childhood, some very interesting college stories, and more. By the end of breakfast, we were laughing and bantering as though we'd known each other forever instead of only half a day.

I didn't even have this instant level of comfort and chemistry with Justin. Was it just because Zach had been burned by his ex-girlfriend recently, which made him sympathetic to me? Did being in a similar boat add a level of intimacy? And let's not forget the small voice inside my head that was spitting out all sorts of observations about whether I truly loved Justin if I didn't have this with him. Unless there was just something special about Zach. Hell, I wouldn't be surprised if that was it.

Breakfast was over too quickly, but after he walked me back to my place and gave me a scorching hot kiss, he reminded me the day wasn't over. "Until tonight," he said.

Until tonight indeed.

6

ZACH

I didn't know what it was about Hayden, but there was something indescribable about her. She was sexy as hell, but there was also an underlying innocence about her. The sex … my God, the sex had been spectacular, but as much as it pained me to admit this because I was a red-blooded male, the getting-to-know-her was high up there too.

After the bit of awkwardness in the morning that made me want her infinitely more, especially with her shyness, our breakfast date was so easy, as though we had known each other forever. When I dropped her off, I actually couldn't wait to get back to her. That hadn't happened to me before. Even with Trish. I had desired her, had wanted to "catch" her, but I hadn't wanted *her*. I thought I did at first, but I realized now that it was the chase that was what I had craved. Now, I just craved Hayden.

When I picked her up later that day, I immediately grabbed her, wrapped my arms around her, and pulled her into a kiss. Bruising her lips, I snaked my tongue into her mouth, hearing her moan against my lips. I had to remember I wanted to spend time with her before I dragged her back into her place and mauled her.

I took her to dinner at a restaurant near her house, and much like breakfast, we talked, we got along, but more importantly, we laughed.

I could spend hours listening to her laughter, and I knew then that if this continued, I could see myself falling for her. I wasn't romantic enough to believe in love at first sight, but I definitely believed in chemistry at first conversation, at least I did now. And we had it in spades.

"Hey," Hayden said after dinner. "Isn't the pub nearby?" she asked.

"Yeah," I said with a nod, realizing she was right.

"Want to stop in for a quick drink? Seems fitting, right?"

"Yeah, actually, it does."

We walked the couple of blocks, hand-in-hand to what she'd dubbed "The Storybook Pub," I learned during our walk, and then took the same seats at the bar.

"Hey, the lovebirds are back," said Kole as he dropped off two drinks without even asking what we wanted. "Glad to see things are working out between you two," he said with a big smile.

"Me too," I answered with a smile of my own.

"And it started with you buying me a drink," Hayden said beside me.

"I bought you a drink?" I questioned, not sure what she meant.

"Best drink I've ever had," she said as she took a sip of her fruity-looking concoction.

"I … uh … huh," I said, completely confused. I could have questioned her on it, but some inexplicable force kept my tongue tied in knots. Maybe she meant this one now, or maybe it was some sort of slang, but whatever it was, it made things happen between us, so I kept my mouth shut because I was eternally grateful for it.

"Drinks are on the house," Kole called out as I tried to leave money on the bar after we'd finished. Our stares had turned heated sometime in the few minutes we were there, and without words, I knew we were both on the same page. Time to make chemistry not just in conversation but also between the sheets.

And we did, colliding like two magnets forced together the minute we entered her place. Clothes went flying, arms tangled, and bodies intertwined. It was magic, and I knew I was already addicted.

"This is … It's never …" Hayden couldn't get the words out, but I knew what she meant.

"Me too," I told her. "Me too," I repeated, and then once again, I fell asleep in her arms, and even though it was too soon—*way* too soon—I knew I wanted to stay there for as long as she'd let me.

"Morning," I told her when we woke up the next day.

"Morning," she said groggily but with a shy smile ghosting her lips. "This is nice," she added after I gave her a quick peck on the lips.

"Yeah," I said with a nod. "It really is. So, let's keep doing it."

"Mmm," she responded with a throaty moan. I laughed.

"Yeah, Hayden, that too, but I meant, this, us."

"Are you ... are you asking me to date you?" she asked with hesitancy.

"Yeah," I said assuredly. "I guess I am. I like you. I know it's quick, and I should be cautious, but there's something special here. I know you feel it too."

"Like we were hit with cupid's arrow," she chimed in.

"Exactly. And the thought of not having you ... or worse, sharing you ... it's driving me crazy even though it's only been a little over twenty-four hours. So, what do you say? You and me? Let's make it happen."

"I ... I don't know," she responded. "I feel the same way you do, but I just got out of a serious relationship. I was engaged, Zach. And not just engaged. The invites were sent, the place was booked, and my dress was ready. It feels like I'm jumping from one thing to another so quickly."

"I get that," I told her. "I do. But when it feels right, it's right."

"I need to think about it," she said. At what I imagine was a disappointed look on my face, she was quick to add, "But I don't want to stop this, and I don't want to go find anyone else. I just ... I just don't know how comfortable I am with calling this something official."

"I can work with that," I told her. "I can make you feel comfortable enough. And I can prove to you I'm not your ex. I'm not going to hurt you, but more importantly, I'm going to show you that we're worth something official."

"Okay," she said after a beat, and I found myself smiling.

I *could* work with this. I just had to figure out how I'd accomplish all I promised.

7

HAYDEN

Zach was ... Zach was ... I couldn't even put into words all that Zach was. He was gorgeous, and he was smart, incredibly caring, and damn near perfect. We'd been seeing each other now for about two months, and it was better than anything I could imagine. Which is why I didn't believe it.

Things with Justin had seemed great in the beginning too. They were even great all along, minus the usual arguments and things that annoyed each other. And look how that turned out.

And Zach, in just two months, was *better* than Justin. When I'd caught a cold and had to cancel a date with him, he showed up with soup and didn't leave my side, hugging me to him as we watched a movie in bed. Justin never did that. When I was running late to work one day and complaining to Zach that I forgot my lunch and probably wouldn't have time to run out and grab anything because I was too busy, a delivery from the local deli showed up at eleven thirty. When something similar like this happened while I was with Justin, he'd said, "Keep some Cup O'Noodles at your desk."

And those were just a few examples of how Zach had been too good to be true. And I'd learned that before his ex, he was a player, just like Justin. He'd changed his tune for Trish but look how that worked out for him. He said he was thankful for that because it made him realize that he had actually wanted to settle down after all, just "thank God not with her." His words. I knew he was implying he wanted to settle with me, but it had only been two months. How did I know he wasn't going to get bored of me after six? He'd only lasted with Trish for five. Maybe he would have been bored of her after six too?

"You're driving yourself crazy for no reason," Mina had told me when I voiced my concerns. "He's obviously into you. He's given you no reason to doubt it."

"Neither did Justin?"

"Oh, really?" she asked with a quirked eyebrow. "He didn't? All those late nights? All those boys' trips, the times he didn't like to talk on the phone? He didn't give you a reason, or you were too blind to see them?"

She was right, of course, but it didn't do anything to chip away at the wall around my heart.

That was why I couldn't label what Zach and I were. In theory, we were dating—exclusively. You could even call us boyfriend and girlfriend with the way we were. But I *couldn't* call it that. There was some force preventing me from doing so. I knew Zach was getting restless, and I was helpless to stop it.

And of course, that was when it happened … when the shit hit the fan, for lack of a better way to say it.

We'd been about to head out to dinner when Zach casually brought up going out with his friends and maybe even with Mina. He'd met Mina briefly the first night we had met, and I'd seen his friends from a distance, but we hadn't actually hung out together with any of them. Mina knew all about Zach, and I knew his friends knew all about me, so meeting the friends seemed like the natural next step. But that's the thing, that was the *natural* next step for boyfriends and girlfriends, and we weren't there.

I didn't say anything, which had him turning to look at me, and I knew he saw the panic written across my face, the hesitancy, even the doubt.

"I don't mean today," he said with a teasing smile.

"Oh, yeah, of course not," I said with a shake of my head, trying to joke back but failing miserably, my words stilted.

"They're great guys," he added. "Jokesters, sure, but they're good people. If you're worried about how they'll be around you, don't. I promise they'll be on their best behavior."

"Yeah, yeah, sounds good," I said halfheartedly.

"Are you okay?" Zach asked.

"Yeah, I'm fine," I told him. I was *not* fine.

"Do you ... do you not want to get together with my friends?" he asked. His vulnerability rang loud and clear with his words, and it made me feel like an asshole.

"It's just that ... it's a big step, and I thought we were taking things slow," I told him.

"I'm not asking you to marry me, Hayd," he said, using the nickname he'd started calling me about a week into whatever this was. "I'm just asking to get together with friends."

"I know, I know," I said but didn't know what else to follow up with.

"Fuck," he said out loud, but it felt like he had said it to himself. "Fuck," he repeated and hung his head as if he'd been defeated. And now I felt like an even bigger asshole. "I can't," he said after he'd lifted his head, staring directly at me. "I can't, Hayden. I can't do this."

"What are you saying?" I asked, panicked again but for a very different reason.

"I like you, Hayden. I more than like you. And I thought I could be your little fuck buddy until you realized we were more than that. I thought I'd show you what we were until you knew it yourself. And I've been showing you, and I've been proving it to you, but you're not seeing it. I can't keep doing this. I've been hurt before by someone I didn't give a damn about. But with you ... If I keep doing this with you, I'm bound to be ruined."

"You're right," I told him. "You have been there for me, more than Justin ever was, and we were together for a long time. We were set to be married. If things went south with him, and we were so serious ... I'm just ... I'm waiting for the other shoe to drop here."

"You think I'm not scared?" he responded. "I didn't even want a relationship before Trish.

She manipulated me into one, then dumped me for a fatter wallet. I sure as hell wasn't looking for anything serious after her, but you … you were inevitable. There was a spark there from the very beginning, and I was drawn to the damn fire, hoping I wouldn't get burned. Stupid me … should have brought a fucking fire extinguisher." He shook his head sadly. "I'm not your ex. I'll never be him, and I can't keep competing with that asshole. I will spend every single day of my life proving to you I'm worthy of you if that's what I need to do, but I can't spend every day proving I'm not him. And right now, it feels like I am."

"You're not!" I shouted at him, but even I knew the words weren't true. I'd literally just compared him moments before.

"I know it, and you know it, but you just don't believe it. And until you do, I don't think I can do this anymore." He grabbed his few belongings that he had at my place before stepping toward me. "I'm sorry, Hayd. I just … I deserve more." He kissed me quickly, too quickly, but not before I got a taste of his lips, and they tasted like goodbye. He turned to leave, and I suddenly couldn't breathe. I felt my heart beating so hard it felt like it was trying to escape my chest … probably because it was. Because its owner was currently leaving me, walking away, and it wanted to go with him.

My heart was no longer mine. I hadn't realized that until this moment. That it belonged to Zach, and it would go with him, be with him, follow him wherever he went.

I'd been scared, I'd been insecure, and I'd been letting my past dictate my future, but that was on me, not on Zach. He'd said and done everything just as he'd promised.

"You're right," I blurted out, causing him to turn back to me. "You're right," I repeated. "I've been comparing you to Justin because I was hurt by him, and I didn't feel a tenth in all the years I was with him that I do for you in just two short months. He hurt me," I told Zach. "But you have the potential to destroy me. I was just guarding my heart."

"I believe you," he said. "I believe you mean it. But I haven't given you a reason to doubt me. But you have. I think … maybe you need some time to think about all this. Maybe you need to understand that I am not your ex, and I'm not going to hurt you. Not intentionally, at least. That's not why I'm here. I'm here for the long haul. I'll be waiting," he told me, "until you understand that." He turned again, giving me his back.

"I love you," I said, no hesitancy, no vulnerability. Loud and clear.

He hadn't had a chance to move when I'd said the words, but after I did, he turned slowly back to me. "What did you say?"

"I love you," I said again, a tad bit louder, with a smile on my face and my eyes staring intently into his. "I'm not saying it because I'm afraid to lose you. I'm not saying it because I'm backed into a corner. I'm saying it because I mean it, and because I want you to know, even if you choose to walk out that door. You deserve to know how I feel. I'm just sorry it took me this long, and it took all this for me to realize it, but I do. I love you, Zach."

He closed the distance between us in seconds. "Say it again," he demanded while cradling my head in his hands.

"I love you," I repeated happily before he captured my lips with his own. I tasted them once more, but this time, they tasted like love.

"I love you, too," Zach told me against my lips. "I've loved you probably from the minute you ran out of the pub and made me see you were something special. I didn't realize it then, but I realized it a hell of a lot faster than you did. And I knew you loved me too. You just needed to know it also."

"I do," I said with a vigorous nod. "I love you."

"I love you too, Hayden. I love you so much."

"Oh?" I said with a mischievous little grin. "Show me."

"Happily," he said. "Today, tomorrow, and every day for the rest of our lives."

And he did. Not with his body, although, let's just say that dinner wasn't entirely forgotten that night, it was just of a different kind—the naked, bedroom kind—but rather, with his actions, with his words … with his love.

EPILOGUE

HAYDEN

Ten months later...

"Happy one-year anniversary," I read the sign that was behind the bar out loud, and I couldn't help the wide smile that overtook my face. That night that we admitted our love for each other was the turning point in our lives. It was a bigger step than any I was afraid of having, but it was the one I needed to realize Zach was my future. We met up with all of our friends that weekend, and things were perfect. We even met each other's parents the following month, and both of those meetings went smoother than butter. My parents adored him and even made it a point to tell me that they never liked Justin, and it was clear Zach was a better man than Justin would ever be. I know Zach overheard that. He walked around like a proud peacock after that, and then after we got back to his place, he admitted he'd heard that.

His parents were older versions of him. Sweet, caring, and definitely had a teasing side. "They fucking loved you," he said triumphantly afterward. "I mean, I knew they would, but it feels damn good to hear them praise the hell out of my woman." It sure as hell did.

He tried to convince me to move in with him shortly after those meet-and-greets, but my lease wasn't up for a few months. When it was, though, you can bet your ass that Zach pounced on me to give it up and move in with him. I did. We were at each other's places every single night, so it only made sense to merge it into one place.

That took a bit of adjustment, but Zach gave me a wide berth at his place. He said I could do anything, buy anything, throw out anything ... you get the point. And he meant it because he didn't say a single word when I did just that. In fact, he smiled like a Cheshire cat. "I'm just so fucking happy you're here to stay every night that I couldn't care less if you wanted the damn walls a pink cheetah print." I'd gotten so very lucky with him.

And now it was our one-year anniversary, and we thought it would be only fitting to celebrate at the place that started it all. It wasn't fancy, but the sentiment was romantic, and I absolutely loved that Zach had suggested it. He knew me so well. He knew I loved that place for more reasons than one and would appreciate it.

I didn't realize he could make it even better, though, until I walked in to see the sign, a smiling Kole, who seemed to always be there whenever we were there, and our two favorite drinks sitting on the bar beside the two stools where we'd met, complete with a little sign that said "Reserved." I chuckled at that.

I even noticed two fancy looking pasta dishes by our seats.

I turned to Zach with a question on my face.

"We can't not have dinner for our anniversary," he said with a shrug. "And they don't have much here, considering it's a bar. I ordered from our favorite Italian place, and Kole put it out for me," he said as if it wasn't a big deal. It *was* a big deal. He'd taken a perfect night and made it a proverbial unicorn. There was no way any night after this could top this. He smiled at Kole before giving him a head nod in "thanks," assuming for his help in all this. Kole nodded right back.

When we made our way to our seats at the bar, Zach pulled out my chair, and I sat down, turning to face him in his chair. But he didn't sit down next to me. I had lied. He topped this night, and this night wasn't even over yet.

He was beside my chair, down on one knee holding an open ring box with a beautiful solitaire diamond ring nestled safely inside. I was a crier, I can admit that, but the tears that instantly fell down my cheeks were one-hundred percent worthy.

"Yes," I blurted out before he'd even had a chance to say anything.

He laughed, and I think I heard a few people laughing around us too. "Wait, I have a speech," he said, and I nodded through tears. "Exactly a year ago today, we met here, this very spot," he started. "Two people not looking for each other, but there was something bigger than us; some force, fate, destiny, magic, whatever you want to call it, brought us together because the universe knew we were perfect for each other. You're perfect for me, Hayden. From the way you treat others to the way you treat me. From your self-deprecating laugh to your beautiful smile, from your charity to your kindness, and your beauty, inside and out. I've loved you since the moment we met here, and I'll love you for the rest of my life and even after. I can't imagine a world without you by my side. This is just another step, one of many more to come, but please, Hayd, take this step with me. Please say you'll be my wife. Please marry me."

"Yes," I said again. "Yes to it all, yes, yes, yes," I chanted through my happy tears as Zach slid the ring on my finger and stood just as I got out of the chair and wrapped my arms around him, kissing him to cheers, whistles, and clapping around us.

But at that moment, it was only Zach and me, and the magic surrounding us ... from day one ... that would be there for us until our last days. At that moment, and I knew many, many moments after, life was good, our love was good, hell, our love *story* was good. No, as Zach would say, it wasn't a good love story, it was a fucking great love story. And I couldn't wait to live the rest.

LEARN MORE ABOUT DC RENEE:
HTTPS://LINKTR.EE/DCRENEE

> ALSO BY DC RENEE:
> LOVE'S DECEPTION
> SAVE MY HEART
> SCARS OF MY PAST

WISHED FOR YOU

JESSALYN JAMESON

**One night.
One wish.
One sexy blast from the past.
At the Storybook Pub, wishes come true…
and reality isn't always as it seems.**

Sub-genre: Contemporary Romance with a Twist
Relationship: Male/Female

1

Be gone when I get home. With his words on repeat in my mind, I take one last glance at the room I shared with Richard for the past ten years, inhale a deep breath, then raise my hand and open my fist to expose a mound of glitter shimmering in my palm. The end of an era, punctuated by the herpes of the crafting world.

Noemi's an evil genius; I'm so glad I get her in the divorce.

I pull in a deep breath, pucker my lips for one final kiss off, then blow. Sparkles fly in an iridescent arc, floating down to the chaise, dusting the bed, and sinking into the plush carpet.

"Ooo," Noemi squeals from the doorway behind me. "Now there's a blowy for ya, *Dick*." She steps into the bedroom and sidles up beside me, then extends her arms in front of her, palms up, matching piles of glitter in each hand. "My turn. Grab your suitcase and get your hot little ass out front."

As Noemi finishes glitter-bombing the master suite, I pull my suitcase through the bedroom doorway and down the long corridor, the wheels echoing loudly as they slide over the pristine white Italian tile. Glitter decorates every surface of our home—sorry, *his* home—in every shade of the rainbow… a petty victory over a miserable man who's caused me nothing but heartache, but a victory nonetheless.

"Consider me gone, asshole." Richard will find sparkly reminders of me for years to come.

"Did you just call me an asshole?" Noemi starts down the stairs behind me.

"Asshole? Never. Evil mastermind, however…"

"I'll have you know that being an evil mastermind is just one of my many *stellar* qualities." Noemi wraps her arm around my shoulders and leads me out the massive front door, slamming it loudly behind us.

The moving truck is already gone, on its way to my new house.

"I'm also an incredible divorce party planner."

I blink. "What? Divorce party?"

Noemi nods. "Mhmm."

"Dare I ask where we're headed?"

"Vegas, baby. Vegas. We're going to fill their slots with money, and your slot with—"

I nearly choke on my intake of breath. "Jesus, Noe."

"What? You don't want to get your slot filled?" She blinks innocently.

"I'm just… I'm not dignifying that with a response." I knew she was up to something the way she was oh-so-particular about what I packed in this suitcase versus what went into the moving boxes, but Vegas wasn't even on my radar. I assumed we'd do one of our usual self-care weekends at The Montage, or a day trip to—

"Let me guess… you were picturing mud baths and massages."

I laugh. "Guilty."

"Those six-inch stilettos would have been a bit out of place at Glen Ivy, don't you think?"

She has a point.

Noemi grins, her dark eyes disappearing slightly in her cheeks. "You still underestimate me. Where better to sow your wild oats than the city that *created* sin?"

Shaking my head, I pull my sunnies down against the brightness of the setting sun. "You know what happened the last time I sowed my wild oats in Las Vegas."

Noemi rolls her eyes. "You don't *know* that."

She's right; I *don't* know. I never wanted to find out. Or, maybe I just never had the balls to find out. Richard and I had been separated when I met Tristan. It was a one-night stand, nothing more. I didn't know his last name and he didn't know mine. I certainly didn't know how to find him again. Plus, Richard and I got back together soon after that Vegas trip and… well, when I found out I was pregnant, I convinced myself that the twins were Richard's.

When it came time to write their father's name on the birth certificates, how could I write anyone's name but my husband's?

So I put the past behind me. I protected my marriage, my daughters…

And the memory of that mind-blowing night with that beautiful stranger. A memory that had since become a sanctuary, a port to return to when the storms inside my marriage grew too strong.

A smile pulls at my lips as anticipation blooms warm in my chest, and I meet Noemi's gaze again. "Fine. Just the two of us?"

Noemi scoffs. "Hell no. You know Cassie and Bridge would kill us." She shakes her head, waving her hands in the air. "I'm too young to die. I haven't even boinked someone famous yet."

"Noemi!"

"What? It's true."

"You're married."

"That's why I said *yet*."

"To someone famous, FYI."

"Details, details."

Frowning, I scan the driveway. "Wait. Where's your car?"

"That hot famous guy I'm married to just came and grabbed it."

I look at her over the top of my sunglasses. "I'm all for exercise, Noe, but Newport to Vegas is a bit of a trek."

Noemi grins and nods behind me, so I turn toward the street. A black party bus creeps up the steep driveway, then stops in front of the house.

"You didn't."

Noemi shrugs as Cass and Bridgette climb out of the bus. "We couldn't agree on who would drive. And you know Cassie hates flying…"

"I like to be the one in control," Cass adds, waggling her eyebrows.

A party bus, though? "Isn't this a little bit… bachelorette party-ish?"

Bridgette places a sash over my head, positioning it on my chest, then kisses my cheek. "Good friends throw bachelorette parties, Gracie; *best* friends whisk you off to Vegas to celebrate your divorce."

"And get you laid."

I nearly choke on my own spit.

"What?" Noe deadpans. "The best way to get *over* Richard is by getting *under* someone else."

With a groan, I look down at my chest. *I do, I did, I don't!* is emblazoned in hot pink letters on a black satin sash. Good grief, this is really happening, isn't it? I look up at the three of them and can't help but laugh at their matching grins.

If you can't beat 'em, join 'em. "Come on, then. Let's get this shit-show on the road."

"Chugga-chugga!" Noemi's train imitation could use some work. "All aboard the Hot Mess Express!"

I sit in the far back as my besties crowd around the bar upfront, and as they pop champagne bottles and we pull away from the curb, excitement stirs in my chest.

My phone vibrates in my purse, so I grab it quickly. Before Richard's face on the screen even registers in my mind, I've pressed *talk*.

Old damn habits die hard.

"Are you fucking kidding, Grace?"

I close my eyes and breathe deeply through my nose.

"You have some goddamned nerve. Do you have any idea the cleaning bill I'm going to have? I ought to press charges for vandalism!"

"Vandalism?" I shriek, opening my eyes as Noemi grabs the phone from my hand, giving me a bottle of champagne in its place.

"Hi, Dick!" Noemi's voice is saccharine sweet. "Bye, Dick!" She presses *end* on the call, then spends a few seconds pressing buttons before handing the phone back to me. "There, hon. Blocked."

My chest tightens, but that instant flash of panic is stupid. Tallulah and Jaymes aren't with him this weekend, so he has no reason to call me other than to bitch and moan and ruin my first weekend of freedom. And, with the divorce finally final and the house emptied of anything that was mine, I really don't see a need to talk to Richard until it's his weekend with the girls. I'll unblock his number then.

"Thanks, Noe." I lift the champagne bottle into the air, then pause. How do I appropriately toast the end of my marriage? Hmm... "To no more Dick for the rest of my life."

"Grace," Bridgette whispers, eyes wide. "Don't put that kind of thing into the universe."

Cass clears her throat and raises her glass. "To *plenty* of dick... but no *Richards*."

2

Four hours fly by if you drink enough champagne.

And sleep for half of the ride.

Waking up beneath the bright lights of the strip, I stretch, then nudge Noemi with my foot to wake her up.

She opens her eyes, then squeals and jumps to her feet. "It's time, bitches!"

Bridgette puts down her book, stretching her long arms as she sits up, and Cass pulls her ear buds out, then tucks her cropped blonde hair behind her ears, grinning as she looks out onto the strip.

I'm afraid to ask, but... "What's first on the list?"

"There's this new club we're going to." Noemi pulls tickets out of her purse and distributes them to us. Each pass is on a lanyard and laminated.

"VIP?" Bridgette asks.

"As it should be." Noemi winks. "Supposedly the employees are all hot as hell, and the theme is, like, fairytales and fantasies, so everyone who works there is dressed up."

Storybook Pub is bright green across the top of the pass and almost glowing against the black background.

"So, it's a pub?" I ask.

"No, Grace, it's a *club*. But, like, different. I met the owner, Kole something"—Noemi waves her hand in the air, trying to remember—"It's Irish. O'Rourke... Oh! O'Shea! Kole O'Shea. Anyway, I met him at that charity gala Geoffrey dragged me to last month. This *club* is based on some pub in Ireland, so it looks all old and dark inside, and there's a lot of dark wood, and ivy climbing the walls... Excuse me, lady, why the long face?" She pushes a fresh glass of champagne toward me. "This is supposed to be a fun trip, remember?"

"I'm just not sure I'm up for a nightclub."

"You'll be up for this one. Trust me." Noemi walks to the front to instruct the driver where to go next.

"You know she's not going to let you stay in the room all weekend." Bridgette pats my knee. "And you need a night out with your crew after all this shit."

She's not wrong. I also need a strong set of hands to work this divorce and the ten years preceding it out of my shoulders. "Can we get massages tomorrow?"

Bridgette laughs. "Like your girl up there hasn't already planned that." She shakes her head. "Knowing her, tomorrow is a full day of pampering, and our massage therapists will be of the happy ending variety."

"Did someone say happy ending?" Noemi looks back at us, wiggling her eyebrows, then narrows her eyes at Bridgette. "Shush, you."

"Oh, Jesus. I was only joking." Bridgette's eyes widen. "You didn't actually schedule *that* kind of massage, did you?"

Noemi laughs. "Time will tell."

We look at each other in horror.

"Is that even legal?" Bridgette whispers.

"Okay, girls, this is our stop. We have a penthouse suite—no need to thank me. Food and booze will be delivered in twenty minutes. Shower, shit, shave... whatever you have to do, then be ready to go at ten, sharp." She looks at me pointedly. "You. Wear that hot little lace bodysuit with the black leather pants."

I nod, taking a sip of—

"And clean up your undercarriage."

I nearly choke on my champagne. "Yes, ma'am."

Two hours and three more bottles of bubbles later, our party bus pulls up outside the club, and before we even roll to a stop, the bass melts into my body, calling to me with a steady rhythm.

I'm ready to dance the stress away.

Noe lines up four shots of Fireball whiskey on the little bar, then hands them out and raises hers in the air. "Gracie, you've been through hell and back this past year—"

"Ten years," Cass interrupts with a sympathetic smile.

Noemi nods in deference. "Ten years. And, well, I hope tonight's surprise makes up for that just a little bit."

"Surprise?" I narrow my eyes. "What have you done?"

Noemi feigns offense. "I don't know what you're talking about."

I groan and shoot the whiskey back, then hold the shot glass out in front of me. "Might as well pour another. I have a feeling I'm going to need it."

Noemi glances at the shot glass warily, then fills it. "We want you loose, but not *too* loose."

The last ten years have increased my tolerance for alcohol. I shoot the second shot. "Whatever that means."

"After you." Bridgette motions toward the door.

The girls giggle behind me as I step down off the bus, but I ignore them. Whatever they have planned, I'm sure I'll enjoy, but my stomach's a bit uneasy now that I know something is lurking around the corner.

The question is, which corner?

I pick up my pace down the plush carpet—green, not red—lined with matching green velvet ropes.

My heart sinks as I realize my new emerald velvet blazer matches the freaking nightclub.

I turn around to my friends and extend my arms out from my sides. "I dressed like a waiter and you let it happen."

Cass looks away from me, laughing, the asshole, but Bridgette has the courtesy to shake her head in an attempt to at least *try* to lie.

Noemi tilts her head, assessing. "Lose the jacket. Show some skin. It's Vegas."

"It's cold."

"Drink more." Noemi waves toward the door, so I resume walking as I strip off my jacket. Cold air hits my bare skin, and I instantly regret the thin lace bodysuit.

I dig in my purse for my license, but the dude at the door glances at the badge hanging around my neck and waves me through.

"He didn't even card me," I whine as Noemi joins me inside.

"I would have. You don't look a day over nineteen, babe." She winks, then scans the room as we wait for the other two. "Ooh, look at that hot piece of man meat." Noemi nods to our left. "Is that a…" She groans. "It is. It's a leather loincloth. Well, hello, Tarzan. Me Jane." She leans closer to me. "I'd swing from his vine."

"Jesus, Noe." My cheeks heat up out of embarrassment for my friend.

Bridgette and Cass join us and Cass elbows me. "Check out He-Man."

"Tarzan," Noe says on a cough as he turns toward us. "Oh shit. Now you've done it." She tilts her head back to shake her golden ringlets off her back, then flashes her megawatt smile.

Tarzan returns her smile and inclines his head. "Ladies, welcome to Storybook Pub, where your dreams become reality, and your wish is our command."

"Ooh," Bridgette whispers. "Mama like."

He leads us to a half-moon booth, right in front of the stage, like, front and center, all eyes on us as he motions for us to slide in.

I raise an eyebrow at Noemi. "How did you swing this?"

"A girl never reveals her secrets."

Cass snorts. "A girl is married to Geoffrey Black, head of Blackrock Records."

"Shush, you."

The girls all slide into the booth, and I follow, sitting on the outer edge. It's probably the comfiest chair I've ever sat in, with high-backed tufted emerald velvet so deep it's almost black, and a seat that you sink into, but not so much that it makes your back hurt almost instantly. Welcome to your thirties, where the wrong chair could make your neck not work right for a week. The table itself is polished dark wood, complete with knots and grooves that resemble an actual tree.

"You think this is really part of a tree, or just made to look like it?" I ask over the music.

"*That's* what you're looking at?" Noemi's focused on something above, so I look up.

Tarzan has climbed a rope in front of our table, and dangles almost on top of us, the muscles in his legs taut and delicious.

I suck in a breath. Noe's right: forget the décor.

While hanging upside down, Tarzan fills our glasses with champagne. If an Irish Pub and Cirque du Soleil had a baby—

Noemi elbows me as another server walks past our table, his olive skin taut over hard muscles. He wears a chain mesh shirt, a sword on his hip, and a half-skirt made of thin metal. "He reminds me of you-know-who," Noe whispers. "Remember that one skit he had? Rawr." She laughs, raising her eyebrows. "Maybe he's here."

Ha. Right. Like I'll ever see Tristan again. Just because the guy was in Vegas ten years ago, doesn't mean he's here now. And, even if he is, this isn't some small town where you can just look up a guy knowing only his first name and where he worked ten years ago. Besides, that gig was a kicking off point for him—Tristan's plan wasn't to dance forever. He wanted to start his own business and…

Wait.

I couldn't just put *Tristan* and *PR companies* into the Google search bar, could I?

I laugh, shaking my head. No, that's silly. He's probably married to some knockout goddess of a woman, has three little dark-haired babies running around and, let's be honest, I'm not that carefree little sexpot he met ten years ago—

"Everything okay over there?" Noemi asks, pulling me out of my thoughts. "Care to share with the class?"

I shrug as embarrassment heats my cheeks. "Sorry. Just thinking."

"About…?"

I sigh, looking into her big hazel eyes, then shake my head. "Never mind. There's no way I could ever bump into him again."

Her lips twitch, but she nods like she knows something I don't know.

This can't be good.

3

A man approaches our table, wearing a black top hat with two playing cards sticking out of the hat band, a white shirt collar with a black bowtie, and white cuffs decorating each wrist. His black slacks look like they were custom made for him and sit high on his waist, giving off some serious Patrick Swayze vibes. And, bonus, he's built like every other guy working here: Greek gods would be green with envy.

"Ladies, welcome to Storybook Pub." He grins and my stomach flutters stupidly, like his friendly smile was somehow a direct flirtation.

Maybe Noemi's right. Maybe the best way to get *over* Richard is by getting *under* someone else.

My cheeks heat with embarrassment. Thank God this dude's not a damn mind-reader.

I give my head a subtle shake then try to focus on what he's saying.

He's looking right at me, eyebrows up expectantly.

Oh. Shit. "I'm sorry?"

"Your name?" His lips curl into a seductive smile.

"Oh. Sorry. Grace. Grace Michaels. I mean, no. Not Grace Michaels." I groan, shaking my head. "Never mind. Just Grace is fine."

Noemi giggles beside me. "Breathe, babe. He's lookin' like a snack, sure, but he's not your main course."

I turn toward her, about to ask what the hell *that* means, but Hot Magician extends his hand, drawing my attention back to him.

He hands me a card, leaning forward to be heard over the din of the club. A black permanent marker appears in his other hand. "Write down your one wish, Grace. Your deepest desire."

"Ooh, I know!" Noemi raises her hand.

"Wait your turn," I tease, taking the marker and flipping the card over to its face. The Queen of Hearts. I look up at him and raise an eyebrow.

"Your wish is within your grasp. You only have to write it down." He smiles, and his light eyes sparkle with mischief.

"Please wish Richard away."

I scoff, turning my head. Noemi's eyes are closed and her head is tilted toward the heavens, hands clasped in prayer.

"You're so ridiculous." But I write down my wish anyway and, though I can't say what my wish is—because *rules*—I'm sure Noe would be pleased.

I turn the card back over and hand it to the magician, a tiny flutter in my stomach as he meets my gaze. His fingertips graze mine and my skin tingles.

"Watch." He takes the card in one hand, crumples it, then uncurls his fingers to reveal a tiny paper airplane made from my playing card. My eyes widen and I look around at my friends, who all wear equally astonished expressions. I return my attention to the magician and he smiles, slowly, playfully, then his fingers guide the tiny card airplane to his thumb and middle finger, and he flicks it up into the air.

I look up quickly, searching for my card, but so many others are up there, sticking out of the ceiling tiles that I'll never know which one is mine.

"How'd you make it stick?" Cass asks. "That's at least twenty feet up…"

"Same way I make the wish stick." He raises his arms and turns his hands back and forth, then smiles and gives me a wink. "With magic."

And then he's onto the next table.

"You better not have wasted that wish."

Laughing, I shake my head at Noemi.

"I'm serious, Gracie. That better have been something about Dick's dick falling off."

I tilt my head. Hmm. *Did* I waste my wish?

The music slowly dies down, so I focus on the stage as the lights of the club dim even lower and spotlights illuminate the stage with a pale green glow.

I lean toward Noemi. "What's going on?"

"Oh, you'll see." She smiles like the evil mastermind she is. "Sometimes wishes really do come true."

Sometimes I don't trust her as far as I can throw her. I keep a straight face and ask, "My ex-husband's dick fell off?"

"One can hope." She nudges me with her elbow. "Now, shush. Watch."

A soft green glow illuminates the back curtains, then the music changes to a slower song. The bass is heavy and low, vibrating deep in my belly, adding to the anticipation blooming in my chest.

"Ladies and Gentlemen," an announcer says as he steps onto the stage. It's the hot magician. "Welcome to Storybook Pub, where wishes aren't just empty prayers on the backs of coins cast into fountains."

The crowd cheers, and the announcer takes off his hat. His ears are pointed, matching the theme of this place, and he now has an open tuxedo jacket on over his little shirt collar.

"My name is Kole O'Shea, and I am the owner of the Storybook Pub. What started out as a small family-owned pub in Ireland, has now grown to an empire of Storybook Pubs spanning the globe. You never know where we might pop up next." He winks, then pauses as the crowd applauds. "And this, my latest baby, this was my wife's dream. She always wanted a massive Storybook in Vegas because, in her words, 'only the best dreams come true in Las Vegas'." His voice cracks, so he pauses. "I couldn't have done it without you: my friends, family, and"—he presses a hand to his heart—"my gracious investors."

Noemi runs her hand over my long hair, smoothing it, and I turn toward her, eyebrows raised.

"Sorry."

I frown. Did I miss a spot with the flat iron or something?

"Here." She hands me a lip gloss.

"I'm good."

"Put on the lip gloss, Grace."

She's acting weird, but… I put on the lip gloss.

"There. Perfect." She nods at the stage. "Pay attention."

"Oh my god, you just—"

She motions for me to pay attention.

I run my tongue over my teeth and turn toward the stage.

"Thank you," Kole continues. "Thank you from the bottom of my heart." He looks up at the ceiling. "This is for you, Rebecca." Then he extends his hand toward the curtains at the back of the stage. "Now, without further ado, back on stage for a very special"—he looks pointedly at the audience—"*very rare* performance, my dear friend, Tristan Slade."

I blink. Repeatedly.

My breath stalls in my chest.

I can feel my friends' eyes on me, but I can't take my gaze off the stage. I never knew his last name, and I probably still don't, since Slade is likely a stage name, but… could this be *my* Tristan?

There's no way.

The dark green velvet curtains pull aside and a man steps out onto the stage, draped in shadow. His upper half is bare, his chest glistening in the spotlight, all hard lines and ridges, and that well-defined v muscle bulging out over either hip and dipping down into his pants.

I suck in a shaky breath.

The man lifts his head and everything else stops. The announcer. The music. My heart.

His eyes scan the crowd, though I'm sure he can't see anything past the glow of the spotlights.

But I'd know those eyes anywhere. Dark, captivating eyes.

I can't breathe.

Ten years, and he's only gotten better with age.

"Wow," Bridgette whisper-yells. "Who's that?"

"Gracie's wish," Noemi replies.

Dressed like some fairytale hunter, he carries a bow and arrow and he's naked from the waist up, wearing ruddy brown, leather-style pants with brown boots that wrap up his calves, and matching leather cuffs circle each bicep.

Each large, muscular bicep. I remember those biceps.

Sunk my teeth into them a time or two.

My stomach tightens as more memories rush to the surface, just as vivid as ever except now with an added dose of clarity. Because, as much as I held onto the memory of Tristan all these years, the man is even better in person. Or, maybe he's just gotten better with age.

Don't know, don't care.

He dances as well as I remember, slow and sensual as he works the stage, confident and sexy as hell with a rhythm not all men possess. He's not just shaking his ass and flexing his muscles for the audience like most male strippers, he glides languidly across the stage, each movement calculated and precise. He can dance, he knows it, and he uses it to seduce every single person in the room.

Consider me seduced.

There's a decent amount of beard stubble lining his jaw now, smattered with a bit of salt and pepper that wasn't there ten years ago, and a dusting of neatly-trimmed chest hair accentuating his pecs. I imagine running my fingers over that patch of hair, then roll my eyes. Look at me getting all carried away when he probably won't even remember who the hell I am.

He jumps down from the stage, continuing his dance closer to the tables arcing around the front of the room.

I breathe deeply, trying to calm my nerves, fighting against a wild grin that threatens to break free any second. I'm a kid at Christmas and Tristan's the tricycle under the tree.

Can I ride it?

Noemi squeals beside me, squeezing my thigh as Tristan dances for the table beside ours.

I watch him, my body tense. In a matter of seconds, he'll be at our table.

Will he recognize me?

He stops in front of me and I look up into eyes so full of recognition I'm instantly transported back to that night, back to laying beneath him, back to the way those eyes broke down every wall and stared straight into my soul.

"Grace," he mouths.

I pull in a sharp breath. He remembers me.

His lips quirk up to one side and he shakes his head, then leans forward and circles his hand around my neck, and just like that, my body recalls how much it loved being touched by this man. He brings his mouth to my ear and sends a delicious shiver down my spine. "You're even more beautiful than I remember."

Heat shoots south and I clench my thighs together, his gravelly voice causing a reaction in my body that I can't ignore. I don't *want* to ignore it.

What I *want*, is to climb him like Tarzan's vine and never let my feet hit the ground again.

Tristan drags his lips along my jaw and I shiver, then he pulls back, eyes focused on my mouth. He smirks and desire burns between my legs, so I quickly cross them, trying to play it cool.

It's fine. I'm *fine*.

He runs his thumb over my bottom lip. "To be continued." Then he inclines his head and moves on to the next table.

"Holy shit," Noemi whispers a bit too loudly. "I think I just came."

4

When Tristan's performance ends, he walks to the end of the stage and bows without taking his eyes off me. Then he jumps down and stalks toward me with so much lust in his eyes I wish we were alone, not in the middle of a nightclub full of people.

Watching us, I'm sure, but I can't bring myself to care.

If he asked me to leave with him right now, I don't think I could say no even if I wanted to.

But who would want to?

He extends his hand and I slide mine into his, then he pulls me up into his arms. He's sweaty and musky, and I breathe in deeply as he embraces me, letting his scent twist down through my body, claiming me, awakening me. His hard body is hot fire against my skin, and my stomach tightens as desire pools low in my belly.

"Can you leave with me?" His lips tickle the skin just below my ear, and his velvety voice sends a message south.

"Yes." The word comes out breathless, but at least I didn't scream my response with barely-controlled excitement.

He releases me, sliding his hand into mine, then inclines his head toward Noemi, Cass, and Bridgette. "Enjoy the rest of the show, ladies."

Noe shoves my jacket and purse into my free hand then dismisses me with the flick of her wrist. "Shoo, shoo. See you... whenever." Her grin is wicked and my cheeks heat in response, but then Tristan begins leading me out of the club and all I can do is follow behind him on weak, baby deer legs.

The last ten minutes have been a whirlwind, everything happening so quickly I can barely make sense of it in my mind. Tristan on stage. Tristan seeing me, remembering me, saying my name like he'd said it a million times, not just a word or a name, but...

A prayer.

He pulls me down a long hallway and into a dressing room, closes the door, then leads me to the chair in front of the vanity. His nostrils flare as he points to the chair. "I'll be quick." He unties the armband on his left arm, then struggles with the one on his right arm, so I walk over to him, stilling his fingers with my hand.

"Here." I slowly untie the armband, then place it in his hand.

He closes his fist over mine. "What are you doing here?" he whispers reverently. "I've looked for you in every face, in every crowd."

My breath catches. "What?"

"Grace, you... I've never gotten over you." He shakes his head, then lifts his fingertips to my cheeks. "I can't believe you're real."

I lean into his palm, his warmth. "I can't believe you are either."

His thumb grazes my bottom lip and my lips part.

He drops his hand and takes a quick step back. "Not here." He searches my gaze, then shakes his head. "Sit. Please. My self-control is slipping."

I pull my lips into my teeth to fight my smile and give a curt nod, then cross my arms to keep from touching him again. "Why not here?" *Whoa, girl. Slow your roll.*

Tristan's eyes darken with desire. "I have ten years to make up for. This is not the place."

His words send a rush of anticipation through my veins.

He starts unbuttoning his soft leather pants and I turn away as heat rushes up my chest and neck.

"Grace."

I clear my throat. "Yes?"

"It's nothing you haven't seen before."

I close my eyes as the memory of him rushes to the forefront of my mind, naked, all hard lines and olive skin. "That was ten years ago." God, am I always so breathy?

He steps up behind me, the warmth of his body enveloping me, then pulls my long hair aside, sending a shiver down my spine. He leans his head over my shoulder. "Tell me you haven't thought of that night every day since."

I pull in a shaky breath, then swallow the thickness in my throat. "I can't."

"Turn around."

I turn slowly and look up into his eyes.

"You have consumed me for ten long years."

I shake my head; this can't be real.

"Are you saying no?" He gently tilts my face up so I'll meet his gaze again.

"I'm not." I slide my hands over his chest. "I just… I didn't even think you'd remember me."

He laughs, and the sound is like velvet, sliding over me, then he cups the base of my head and searches my gaze. "I couldn't forget you if I tried. And believe me, Grace, I *tried*." He holds up his left hand, showing me a faded tan line on his ring finger.

I raise my left hand. "Me too."

He shakes his head. "What a pair." His thumb slides back and forth over the soft skin below my ear. "Divorced?"

I nod.

"Good." He drops his hand, then starts on his pants again. "Me too."

I don't look away this time.

He watches me watch him, and, somehow, this moment does more to turn me on than any sexual experience I've had since those twenty-four hours ten years ago.

And he's not even touching me.

I sit down heavily in the chair, crossing my legs.

He smirks, then slides his pants down slowly, tediously, and, thank god for his years of stripping because just the act of undressing is an art form with Tristan.

Beneath the pants he wears boxer-briefs that are… well, brief. They leave little to the imagination, and his imagination must be working as overtime as mine is right now because his cock presses against the black fabric.

My clit throbs.

I swallow hard and look up at him.

He holds my gaze, then adjusts himself, and the pressure between my legs builds, so I press them together tighter. Pretty soon I'll lose circulation in my lower limbs.

"Tristan, I…" I swallow, shaking my head, then lean back in the chair and press my lips into a fine line to fight the way they keep trying to curl into a maniacal grin. I close my eyes and breathe deeply through my nose, then wait for him to finish getting dressed without watching because I don't know how much more I can take.

Minutes tick by slowly, but soon he clears his throat and I open my eyes.

He stands by the door dressed in faded gray jeans, a snug black t-shirt, and a black peacoat.

"Oh my god." I shake my head. "Really?" He's even sexier in this outfit than he was in his goddamn boxers. Well, maybe not, but damn close.

"Ready?" Is that amusement in his voice?

I uncross my legs and focus on my feet. "I don't think I can stand."

He growls. "Well, Grace, that's sexy as hell."

I finally meet his gaze and he stalks toward me.

He places his hands on my knees and opens my legs, then kneels between them and pulls me to the edge of the chair. The heat of his body so close to the apex between my legs makes me whimper. He slides his hands up my sides, trailing his fingers over the delicate lace of my bodysuit, then wraps his arms around my waist and, in one quick movement, lifts me into his arms and rises to his feet.

I shriek in surprise.

"See? No need to walk." He grabs my jacket and purse off the vanity, then turns and exits the dressing room.

I study his face as he looks past me to watch where he's going—from that gorgeous scattering of salt and pepper in his beard stubble, to those dark, mesmerizing eyes and the way his lips are so full they'd be feminine if they weren't set into that rugged jawline and sitting beneath that strong nose. He walks us past people I don't know and I'll probably never see again. Somewhere deep down, a voice tells me I should be embarrassed by this, I shouldn't be acting like this with someone I barely know. Sure, we had a one-night stand ten years ago, but I'm a different person now.

A mom, that voice reminds me.

But then Tristan's eyes flick to mine, and the raw hunger there makes me push that voice away. Yes, I'm a mom, but I'm also a woman, and this is a man who knows what to do with one.

I tighten my legs around his waist and his nostrils flare, but he doesn't meet my gaze, just keeps on walking.

"Careful, Grace."

I run my nails over the back of his head and constrict my legs again, pressing against his erection.

He groans and his jaw tightens.

"Are you going to be able to drive like this?"

"Let's fucking hope so."

5

He lives an excruciating forty-five minutes from the strip. Forty-five minutes that feel like hours, no, *days*, because all I want is to reacquaint myself with this beautiful, sexy man, and teasing him while he carried me to the car might have been fun at the time, but now I'm the tortured one, a mess of hormones about to combust.

Mistakes were made.

"Are we there yet?" Borderline whining.

Tristan chuckles, squeezing my thigh. That hand has sat there, at a safe, *torturous* distance from the bundle of nerves between my legs for this entire ride. Even though I've moved, adjusted my position multiple times in hopes that he'll slide his hand up a bit further. Just a few more inches up my thigh and we're dancing in the end zone, baby, but nope. Every time I move, he readjusts his hand, keeping the same —safe—distance.

"How do you like it?"

"What?" I uncross then re-cross my legs and he settles his hand right back above my kneecap. I'm gonna kill him.

"I asked how you like it." He side-eyes me, then squeezes my thigh. "You had no problem teasing me when I was trying to get you out of that club."

"I'm fine." *Lies.*

He chuckles.

"Seriously, though, are we there yet?"

He slides his hand up my thigh and I suck in a breath. Finally!

Then he stops, just a smidgen away from the part of me that begs for his touch. "Patience, Grace. We've waited ten years for this."

"Exactly," I say too loudly. "Ten *long* years."

"What's a few more minutes?" He reaches up and trails his fingertip over the edge of the lace cupping my breast, sending a shiver down my spine.

I clench my teeth.

We pull up to a large gate and he presses a button on the visor above his head, then waits for the gate to open and guides the Maybach inside, then up a long driveway.

When he rolls to a stop in front of a white house that makes even Noemi's look like a shack, I raise my eyebrows and turn to him, unsnapping my seatbelt. "Yours?"

His gaze narrows playfully. "No, this is my mom's place. You good with that?"

"Cute."

"I know." He smiles, then shrugs one shoulder. "I do all right."

"All right?" I look up at the house again, then back at him, pride warming my chest. "You started your business."

A flash of surprise dances across his features. "You remember."

Smiling, I lean over the console and trail my fingertip down his cheek, then softly caress his earlobe. "I remember everything from that night." I bring my nose to his throat and inhale. "Your scent." I pull back and trail my finger over his bottom lip. "Your mouth." I pause, watching his eyes close, then place my hand between his legs.

He hisses in a breath.

"The way you say my name when you come."

He groans, slamming his hand over mine and squeezing my palm around his hard cock.

I smile. "How do *you* like it?"

"Too fucking much. Come on." He gets out of the car abruptly and I follow, laughing softly as he strides to my side of the car. He shakes his head. "You're even better than I remember." He picks me up again, and I wrap my legs around his waist as he makes his way to the front door.

I bring my lips to his throat, kissing him gently as he carries me inside his home, then starts up the stairs.

I run my fingernails over the short hair at the back of his head. "You know, I've always come back to that night."

"What do you mean?" He meets my gaze, then his eyes flick to my mouth.

"When I'm... when I fantasize."

"Good God, woman." He groans as he kicks the door to his room open and picks up the pace, then sets me gently on his bed. I start to look around, but then his hands are at my waist, and he's working at the button of my leather pants, and all I can focus on is this gorgeous man in front of me.

Giving up on my pants, he leans over me and I run my hands through his hair. He holds my gaze for a long time, both of us stuck in this moment, this still, silent moment, drinking each other in, reacquainting ourselves, our eyes saying more than words ever could.

Hello. I've missed you. I love you.

Love. I know it can't be love, but... I don't have any other word for the way he makes me feel. I don't think there is one.

"Grace," he whispers. Then his lips are on mine, crushing, claiming, tasting, and I can't get my pants off fast enough, but soon they're off, and I start working on his, but he pulls back, letting his gaze travel over the lace bodysuit slowly, and before I can finish his button-fly, his hands are on my sides, sliding down to my hips, my thighs. He stands up and reaches back to pull his shirt over his head, then he finishes his button-fly and pushes his jeans down—

My gasp is audible.

No boxers stand between me and that rock-hard cock.

He chuckles. "You seemed so interested back at the club, I figured one less thing in your way."

I nod, reluctantly dragging my gaze up to his face. "So thoughtful."

He smirks.

"That smirk." I shake my head.

He tears into a foil packet with his teeth, then steps between my legs. My mouth goes dry as he slides a condom over his length. "What about it?"

I blink. "What?"

"What about my smirk?" Amusement laces his tone.

I look up into his eyes. "I can feel it."

"My smirk?"

"Yes." I pull in a deep breath, trying to focus on words when *naked* Tristan is so close but still too far away. "When you smirk, it's… my body reacts."

"Show me where." He nods toward the head of the bed and I scoot back, then he climbs on top of me and settles between my legs.

"Where…?"

"Where does your body react, Grace?"

I bring my hand between my legs. "Here."

He moans, pressing his cock against me. "My body reacts to you, too, Grace." He presses harder and I gasp, then reach up and pull his head down to mine and wrap my legs around his waist.

When we kiss this time, it's slow, deliberate, fucking tantalizing. My lips tingle with every brush of his; every gentle nudge of his tongue sends a message to my clit. A reminder. A promise.

My hips move against him and he slides a hand between us, then guides his fingers over the lace between my legs. I moan, then reach down and undo the snaps of the bodysuit. He pulls back, eyes wide, then slides his fingertips over the wetness, massaging me gently. "Fun feature."

I nod, because I can't speak when his fingers move over my skin like that.

"Grace." My name on his lips… heaven.

"Mhmm."

He slides his fingers inside me and I gasp.

"Look at me."

I open my eyes and look up into his.

"I'm going to fuck you now."

My body shudders with anticipation as his words and his fingers combine to create the start of a beautiful orgasm, then he smirks again and pulls his fingers away, replacing them with the head of his penis. I open my legs wider, biting down on my lip in anticipation, and then he slowly edges his way in.

I tilt my head back as my body stretches around him, taking everything he gives, just a hint of pain in a sea of pleasure. He grips my hip as he starts to thrust, then slides the other hand behind my neck, tilting my face toward him once more. He holds my gaze as he thrusts harder, faster, then, already so close to the brink, he claims my mouth with his, kissing me hard as my body starts to clench around him, and he starts to twitch inside me.

I kiss him like he's the first, the last, the only kiss I'll ever need, and he fucks me with just as much desperation. I grip him tightly as we come, then he breaks the kiss, breathing heavily in my ear, my name a whispered prayer on his lips with each final thrust.

"*Grace, Grace, Grace.*"

6

I wake a little while later, tangled in Tristan's sheets. I'm surrounded by the scent of him; it lingers in his bed, on my skin. I stretch, smiling as a soft ache between my legs reminds me of the incredible sex we had earlier. It was hurried and hungry, ten years in the making, and... only the beginning of what I'm going to do with Tristan tonight.

A shower is running nearby, so I get up from the bed and tiptoe toward the sound. The master bathroom is massive, with a large closet on either side of me, then a set of double sinks on each wall leading into the main bathroom area. The shower is a giant viewing box, with floor to ceiling glass on three sides, and a stone tile wall in back. The glass is steamed up, but I can still see the shape of him. The curve of his ass, the thickness of his thighs, the strong arms reaching up to run his hands through his hair.

My stomach tightens and I bite my lip. I don't *really* know him... what if shared showers aren't his thing? What if he's one of those guys who hopes I'll be gone by the time he comes back to bed?

The water stops and my stomach sinks, and I quickly look around the room for an escape.

"Are you going to join me or just gawk all day?"

I grin, then walk to the shower. He opens the door and—

Yep. He's just as sexy dripping wet as I imagined he'd be.

"That lace thing is…" He shakes his head, licking his lips as his gaze travels down my body.

I forgot I was still wearing my bodysuit, which must look ridiculous unsnapped and just hanging there. I start to pull a strap down my shoulder, but Tristan clicks his tongue.

"Come here." He pulls me in, guiding me against his body, then starts the shower and positions me beneath the warm stream. "I hope it can get wet."

"Well, *I* certainly can."

Tristan growls, then his hand is between my legs, testing my words. He pulls my bottom lip into his mouth gently, then releases it and smirks. "Be right back."

My mouth drops open, but he lowers into a squat, and I realize what he meant.

"Oh," I say, a bit embarrassed.

His mouth closes over me and—

"*Oh*." I gasp as he plunges his tongue inside me.

If I thought he could do amazing things with his mouth while kissing, this is another thing entirely. His tongue massages me, and he grips my ass with his hands, holding me to him. My knees weaken, so I look around for anything to grab onto. As if reading my mind, he lifts first one leg, then the other until I'm straddling his shoulders, and I grip his hair as he pushes my back into the stone wall, balancing me between the wall and his strong shoulders. I'll have bruises for sure, but—

He swirls his tongue in a circle and all thoughts leave my mind. "Ohhh…"

He chuckles, sending vibration into my clit.

I gasp.

He increases the pressure, flicking his tongue back and forth firmly until my legs start to tremble, then he tightens one hand on my ass and slides the fingers of his free hand inside me, massaging my inner wall.

"Tristan," I groan, and he moans over my clit, sending me right over the edge. I grip his hair harder, holding onto him while I shake and quiver around him, my second orgasm of the night rocking me even harder than the first. Stars burst behind my eyes and the tingle of tears mixes with the euphoric desire to laugh, a roar of sensations and emotions claiming my body as Tristan claims my pussy.

When I can think straight again, I open my eyes and look down at him, and he slowly lowers my feet, holding onto me in case my legs give out, then he doesn't say a word, just smirks in that sexy, knowing way of his as he grabs the soap and starts gently soaping my body.

I lean my head on his chest for strength and he washes my hair, then rinses it and rubs some conditioner through the long strands. I moan as he massages my scalp, then his cock twitches against my stomach and I open my eyes to look up into his.

They're dark, heavily lidded. Lustful.

He licks his lips, then turns off the water and leans down to brush a soft kiss against my lips.

He leads me out of the shower, and I reach for a towel on the wall, but he pulls me into a small room to the right of the glass enclosure.

The heat of the sauna hits me immediately. The room is lined in red cedar, with two long wooden benches along either wall and a stove in the back. The scent of eucalyptus fills the hot air.

Tristan places a towel on the bench, then sits down and motions for me to sit beside him.

Instead, I step between his legs, then push him back and straddle him, settling on top of him so his hard cock is between us.

He groans, bringing his hands to my waist.

I lean forward and press my lips to his, then he opens his mouth and our tongues meet, tangling gently as the kiss intensifies. His fingers tighten and he starts to move my hips, so I take over, sliding up and down over his length. He leans back, resting his head against the wall and closing his eyes as I rock my hips.

"Grace," he growls, tightening his fingers; I'll have perfect little fingertip bruises spread over each hip. "I don't have a condom in here."

I'm not sure I care. I should, but...

I lean forward and pull his earlobe into my mouth, sucking gently, then he wraps his arms around my waist and stands, claiming my mouth with his. In this new position, his dick presses into the apex of my legs, and it takes all of my self-control not to just slide down onto it.

He pulls back and our eyes lock as he pushes the door open and steps back into his bathroom. The cold air hits my back and I tighten my hold on him reflexively.

Bad idea. His cock inches inside, and he groans loudly, slamming his eyes shut and holding completely still.

Fuck it. I press down slowly, letting our bodies do what they so badly want to do, caution to the wind.

His eyes fly open, searching mine.

Using my thighs and arms as leverage, I push up, then down again, taking more of him this time, taking control.

He takes a struggling step forward, then shakes his head. "Grace. Fuck." He claims my mouth, kissing me hard, then walks. Hopefully toward the bed.

He bumps into something, then bends over, placing me on the bed.

He grips my hips.

Thrusts.

Fills me with his length until I whimper.

He's passion, and pain, and raw fucking pleasure, and he's real. He's mine… at least for tonight. And I'm his.

I've *always* been his.

7

The soft light of dawn trickles in behind his dark curtains, making his room glow a soft violet. We've dozed off and on, made love more times than I can count, and, frankly, I never want to leave this man's bed.

Tristan lies beside me, propped up on one elbow, trailing circles over and around my breasts with his fingertips, making my skin jump beneath his touch.

His hair is mussed from my hands. Faint scratches line his shoulders.

My body aches in delicious ways I never knew possible.

"I can't believe you're here." He leans forward and claims my breast, pulling my nipple between his teeth and sending a rush of pleasured pain into my toes. I gasp, clamping my hand into his hair. He laughs softly, his mouth vibrating against my breast, then releases my nipple and moves to straddle me, pulling the sheet away as he does so. He focuses on my lower belly, then runs his thumb across my c-section scar. "You're a mom."

My body goes rigid as ice floods my veins. I was hoping to avoid this conversation a little while longer.

He looks up at me. "I'm sorry. You don't have to…" His dark

eyebrows bunch together. "That's too personal."

I shake my head. "No, it's..." I close my eyes and lean back into the pillows. "It's not too personal, Tristan, I just... I don't know where to start."

Repositioning himself beside me once more, he stretches his hard body along mine, then nudges my face toward him. "You don't have to tell me. We barely know each other."

"It doesn't feel like we barely know each other."

He shakes his head. "No. It never has."

I sigh, then roll my body so I can face him and push up on my elbow. "I don't know how to tell you this."

His smile falls. "You're still married."

"No, no." I shake my head. "But." I swallow, my stomach twisting into knots. "I was."

Tristan frowns. "I know, we went over that last night." He raises his left hand. "Me too, remember?"

"No, you're not..." I meet his gaze. "I was married when we met ten years ago."

He rocks back slightly, like my words are a physical blow. His hand freezes on my waist.

"We were separated at the time, and still so new... we'd only been married a month when we separated; I didn't think we'd get back together, honestly." I sigh. "I wish we hadn't. Richard was... is..." I lie back, throwing my arm over my eyes. "He's an asshole. I was young. He said all the right things, made me believe..." I brace myself for these words. "I cheated on him with you, but, when we got back together, I was faithful." I look up at Tristan. "I need you to know that about me. I don't cheat. I don't take vows lightly." My throat tightens. "He, however..."

"He cheated?"

"Only every chance he got." I snort. "I guess I deserve it for what I did."

"Whoa." He moves my hand away from my face. "No one deserves that, Grace."

I look up into his eyes and shake my head. "How are you so good?"

He smirks. "Who says I'm good?"

I run my thumb over his lips. "Don't smirk at me like that."

He cocks an eyebrow. "Why not?"

"Because I can't concentrate when you do, and I have more to tell you."

He licks his lips, dropping his gaze to my mouth, then nods. "Fine. I'll behave."

"Thank you." I breathe deeply, trying to figure out how to tell him what comes next.

They have his eyes. Tallulah has his nose. There's no doubt in my mind.

If there ever was one.

"I have two daughters."

He smiles. "I bet they're beautiful."

"They are." I swallow hard. "They're nine."

"Both of them?" A muscle works overtime in his jaw as he connects the dots. "They're twins?"

I nod.

"Do twins run in your family?"

I shake my head.

His brows furrow. "Your husband's?"

"No."

"My mom is a twin."

And with that, any lingering doubts are gone.

"How old are they?" A muscle in his jaw works overtime.

"Nine." The word comes out barely a whisper.

"They're mine?"

I close my eyes against the tingle of tears. Not only have I kept him from his daughters for nine years, but I've kept my daughters from knowing this beautiful man.

"Were you ever going to tell me?"

A tear drips down my cheek.

"Grace. Look at me." He searches my gaze, then shakes his head. "No. You weren't."

"Tristan, please understand." I reach for him. But he pushes away from me, quickly leaving the bed.

"Understand what, Grace? I have *daughters* I don't know anything about? I have two fucking kids, Grace? Two?" His voice cracks on the word and he runs his hand over his head as he paces. "How? How could you…" He looks at me, then shakes his head and resumes pacing.

"I didn't know what to do—"

He scoffs loudly.

"I was so young. And married. To this horrible man. And, when he found out I was pregnant, he… he was so excited, so…"

He rounds on me, his eyes wild. "I would have been excited, too, Grace. You ever think of that?"

Only every day of my life. I swipe at the tears on my cheeks. "I didn't know how to find you."

"Bull fucking shit." He grabs his wallet from the nightstand, then whips a thick business card at me. "I own the largest fucking P.R. firm this side of the Colorado River, Grace. You Google *Tristan* and *Las Vegas*, and guess what pops up? My fucking face." He points to his face, his nostrils flaring. "I'm on a goddamn billboard!" He huffs out a harsh breath. "You never even *tried* to find me."

I close my eyes, releasing a fresh rush of tears. "I wanted to."

"Did you?" His voice is so close my eyes fly open. He's bent over the bed, his gaze flicking all over my face. "I've been in love with you since the moment you walked into that bar ten years ago. I've done everything I can to forget you, Grace, but you got under my skin with that fucking smile, the way you watch me when you think I'm not looking. The way you listen when I talk, memorizing each word the way your eyes memorize my face. No one has ever looked at me the way you do, Grace, like you actually see me. Twenty-four hours with you and I was ruined for every other woman who came after you."

My chest constricts, his words everything I've wanted to hear from him, more than I even dared to imagine, but now, laced with so much anger, so much pain.

Pain that I caused.

"Tristan," I whisper. His name is a prayer. I can't lose him now.

"I'm fucking pissed at you right now."

I look up into his eyes. "I deserve that."

"Stop telling me what you deserve, Grace."

I swallow hard and nod.

Tristan grips the back of my head tightly, then searches my gaze. "I'm fucking pissed," he growls, "and I have every right to be. Every right. But if I've learned anything in the past ten years without you it's that I swore if I ever found you again, I wouldn't lose you twice." He backs away from me, shaking his head. "Fuck, Grace. I can't believe you…" His throat bobs as he swallows. "Get some sleep. I need a minute." He stomps to the door, then looks back at me over his shoulder. "What did you wish for?"

I blink. "What?"

"You heard me. When Kole came to your table last night, what did you wish for?"

"How did you know?"

"He went to every table, Grace. Answer the damn question."

I flinch at the harshness in his tone and more tears fill my eyes. "I wished for you."

He winces, then gives a curt nod and closes the door.

I curl up into a ball as a wave of anguish claims my body.

HOURS LATER, with the sun high in the sky, and my mind still drifting between chaotic and comatose, the bed moves, pulling me from my interrupted slumber as Tristan crawls into bed. He curls around my body, his warmth bringing a new rush of tears to eyes I thought had long ago dried out.

He pulls me close, holding me tightly to him, then presses his nose into my hair. "I wished for you, too, Grace. Every damn day for the past ten years."

My shoulders shake on a sob and he tightens his arm around me. I have a lot of work to do to earn this man's trust, but I'm determined to do just that.

I fall asleep in his arms, full of regret. If only a magician's magic trick could erase the last ten years of my life.

If only wishes were real.

8

"Mommy! Daddy! Wake uuuuuup," Jaymes calls.

My eyes fly open. My pulse speeds. An arm tightens around me and I look down in horror; the last arm around me was—

Wait.

Hard muscle moves beneath dark olive skin.

Tristan moans, snuggling closer to me. "It's too early," he murmurs in that gravelly voice I love. "Tell them to go back to bed."

I search the ceiling as if an answer lies there, but all I confirm is that I'm looking up from Tristan's four-poster bed, and somehow, my daughter is outside his door.

"Tristan…" What do I even say right now? How is Jaymes at his house?

Maybe I was dreaming about her. Yeah. That makes sense. I dreamed of my girls, and woke up in the middle of—

"Good morning, wife."

My eyes widen. *Wife?*

He pushes up on his elbow to look down at me. "You're especially beautiful today."

He trails his finger across my cheek, then leans down to start a trail of kisses on my arm.

"Helloooo," Jaymes whines.

My body goes rigid. Just what the hell is happening here?

"She's persistent, I'll give her that." Tristan nips my shoulder with his teeth. "Password?" he calls loudly.

"Fart," Jaymes answers.

Tristan makes a loud buzzer noise. "Wrong. That was last week's." His brow furrows as he watches me. "What's wrong?" he asks softly.

I open my mouth, but no words come out. What's wrong? How about this *Sliding Doors* shit happening right now, for starters? Who did I switch places with? What is happening here?

"Butthead!" Jaymes yells triumphantly.

Tristan flashes a wicked smile. "To be continued," he whispers. "Come in, butthead!"

"I'm not a butthead. That's the password." The bed shakes as Jaymes jumps onto it, and Tristan sits up quickly to catch her as she flies into his arms, then he steamrolls to the side, placing her between us. His eyes are wild and playful as he tickles her.

My mouth falls open. He's so… paternal, so gentle with my girl, so playful. This is all so… natural?

I've lost my mind. That's all. Maybe I'm dreaming. Dreaming about a life with Tristan. It wouldn't be the first time I've dreamt of this impossible scenario.

"How's my spunky monkey today?" he asks, tickling under her chin.

Jaymes squeals. "Stop, Dad, stop!"

Dad? My heart stutters in my chest.

"White flag?" He tickles her harder, eliciting more squeals.

"Yes!" She laughs in that deep, belly way only a kid can. "White flag!"

"Okay, okay." Tristan raises his hands. "I'll accept your surrender. Where's your sister?"

Jaymes shrugs. "Being emo in her room. Where else?"

He looks at me and shakes his head. "She gets that from you, you know."

I offer him a weak smile because *what the actual fuck.*

Tristan's eyes settle on my lips for a beat too long. He drags his gaze away and looks at Jaymes, but the heat from his stare remains.

"All right," he says to my daughter. "Go start getting the stuff for pancakes going."

"Yes!" Jaymes pumps her fist in the air.

"We'll be down in a bit. I want to talk to Mom about something."

Jaymes tilts her head, her eyes flicking back and forth between us. "About what?"

"Nunya." Tristan nods toward the bedroom door. "Go. Or I won't add chocolate chips."

"Ugh, fine." Jaymes scoots to the edge of the bed, jumps down, then calls over her shoulder, "Your breath stinks!"

Tristan whips a pillow at her, but she's too quick and it just hits the closed door.

He looks back down at me and smiles. "Where was I? Oh. Here." He resumes kissing his way down my arm. His hand snakes across my lower belly, then his fingers dance down between my thighs. He growls low in his throat and my stomach clenches with desire.

My sharp intake of breath draws his gaze to mine. His lips quirk up on one side.

I shake my head as heat rushes to my cheeks. "That smirk…"

"You're blushing, Mrs. Rutledge."

Mrs. Rutledge?

He pulls the sheet down my body, slowly revealing my breasts. "Yep. Blushing clear down to your perfect tits. I love these tits." He leans forward and pulls one into his mouth, twirling his tongue over the tip until it's a hard peak.

God*damn*, I can feel that clear down into my toes.

I pull in a shaky breath and he lifts his head to look at me. "Hold that thought." He climbs out of bed, strides to the door and locks it, then turns to face me. "Come brush your teeth. I think she was talking to you."

"You ass." I don't know what the hell is going on here, but he looks damn delicious in those gray sweatpants hanging low on his hips, and I'm not one to look a gift horse in the mouth, so I follow Tristan into his bathroom.

He puts toothpaste on a toothbrush and hands it to me, then leans against the opposite double sink and shoves his toothbrush into his mouth, grinning.

Watching him warily, I start brushing my teeth. "What?"

"You're even more beautiful than the day I married you," he says around a mouthful of toothpaste foam.

I spit toothpaste into the sink, then look back up at him. "When was that?"

He frowns. "You're acting weird."

"Am I?"

"Yeah, Grace. Just a bit."

I raise an eyebrow. "And… I'm… your wife."

He chuckles. "Best decision you ever made." He twists at the waist, swinging his cock back and forth like a pendulum.

"Oh my God."

He turns away from me and leans over his sink, spits, then rinses his mouth and watches me in the mirror as he wipes his face off on the towel. He turns and strides toward me, his eyes dark, the playfulness replaced with desire.

My stomach tightens in response to that gaze.

Maybe that Kole guy was an actual magician.

God, that's so dumb. I'm just dreaming.

But… I look up into Tristan's eyes. Touch the counter. Taste the toothpaste.

Everything *feels* very vivid. Very real.

Maybe I should have wished for Richard's dick to fall off, after all

"Spit."

I do as he says, quickly rinsing my mouth and wiping it with the closest towel.

He pulls me toward him, claiming my mouth with his. This kiss is hungry, powerful. He claims me with his mouth, his hands, his hard body. I moan as his cock hardens between us, teasing me with the promise of what's to come.

Nope. This was the right wish.

I pull back, pressing my hands against his chest, which only causes a distraction, drawing my focus to the pectoral muscles filling my palms. "Good grief, you're perfect."

He growls, low in his throat. "If you keep looking at me like that..."

I look up at him, my lips twitching on a smile. "Like what?"

"Like you want to fuck me right here on our bathroom rug."

Our bathroom rug. I look down, contemplating. It's not a bad idea.

He tightens his grip on my hips and I look back up into those dark eyes. He slides his hands into my panties, reaching around to cup my cheeks, then tugs the fabric down until I can step out of my underwear. He slides his hands back up my legs slowly as he rises, sending my eyes back into my head with his firm, but somehow gentle, touch. He grips my neck and tilts my head back, then runs his teeth along my jaw until he reaches my ear. "Ten years together and I still can't get enough of you, Grace."

I open my mouth to respond, but he slides his fingers between my legs, and all I can muster is a gasp because words fail me. I whimper and he chuckles, a soft, velvety sound low in his throat.

He pulls his fingers back and quickly lifts me onto the vanity, then kneels between my legs.

I look down at him, take a deep breath to steady myself, then whisper, "What did I do to deserve you?"

He smirks. "You must have been a very good girl in a past life."

"Mm. Indeed." I slip down from the vanity and push his shoulders back until he lies down on the plush white rug. Then I step over him, giving him an unobstructed view between my legs. "This life, not so much."

His nostrils flare as he looks up at me.

"Naughty, even."

Tristan groans, then grips my calves. "Come here, wife."

He slides his hands up my legs as I lower myself down over him.

I straddle him, a mess of desire and confusion, but as he pulls his pants down and reminds me how we fit together so, so perfectly, all thoughts leave my mind except him.

Tristan Rutledge.

My *husband*.
He thrusts hard and my head falls back.
"Grace," he growls.
I don't know how. But with one wish, I changed my life. Our life.
I erased my past and filled it with Tristan. Only Tristan.
It's *always* been Tristan.

Learn more about Jessalyn Jameson:
https://linktr.ee/JessalynJameson

Also by Jessalyn Jameson:
    Chlorine & Chaos
    Whiskey Burned
    Claiming Atlas

TAKING CHANCES

MAYRA STATHAM

**How do two awful first dates turn into the best night ever?
With the magic of Storybook Pub of course!**

Sub-genre: Contemporary Romance
Relationship: Male/Female

1

SARA

The man sitting across from me was not six-two.

Not even close.

Don't get me wrong. I knew people lied online and on dating apps. But the man in front of me was missing an entire foot of height. Did he think I wouldn't notice? Not that I had any room to talk—hey, I myself was vertically challenged, but I owned it. I didn't lie. I am a shorty and a half, but the man across the table from me was only about two inches taller than my own five feet.

He'd lied about a whole foot!

Bob Desmond's nasally voice droned on and on about his career in real estate. How his mother had decided that route for him. His mother. Not his mom, but *mother*. I could have looked past that and the lying, probably. But he hadn't just mentioned his career choice once and moved on like a normal person.

Nope.

He had brought it up eleven times. Eleven! I'd counted. As I looked around while Bob muttered on and on about what his mother thought, and all the advice she had given him, the guy across the restaurant caught my eye.

Not only was he handsome with shaggy brown hair that slightly fell over his eyes. Broad shoulders I knew were muscular and strong beneath the crisp black dress shirt he was wearing. The sleeves were rolled up his forearms, which only highlighted the colorful artwork. Bright and beautiful artwork down one arm. There was an air about him. Something sexy and dangerous.

What would it be like to go on a date with a man like that? Would he be sweet? Or a jerk like my date tonight?

"So, you eat steak?" my date asked, and I shook away my thoughts of the tattooed stranger. There was no point in daydreaming over a man like that. Men like that didn't date women like me. "I'm sorry?" I cleared my throat and looked at the man sitting across from me.

"You eat red meat," he repeated with a curl to his lip like he was disgusted, and I forced a smile.

"Yeah," I simply answered because I wasn't sure what else to say.

"You really shouldn't. Red meat is terrible on the digestive system," he shared, catching me off guard. I wasn't sure how to respond.

One side of me wanted to pick up my water glass and throw it in his face. Who did he think he was? The guy himself had ordered a fifteen-ounce ribeye!

But I wasn't the type. Not like the leggy redhead with the tattooed stranger. I could totally see her being the type not to take any shit.

"Do you know how much they mark up meat at places like this?" he asked, the irritation with me crystal clear.

Why was I still sitting with him? His voice grated my patience. He wasn't nice. He was a condescending ass with little man syndrome. *Strike two*, I thought with a tight smile. You would think the first had been the fact he'd lied, but I wasn't shallow.

Strike one had been set when he had honked from across the street of my place and texted Hurry up. I'm here. It's not that I was wishing for Prince Charming or a back-in-the-day gentleman who opened doors and stood when I stood. I was more than capable of opening my own doors. I just didn't want a jackass. Life is too short to share your life with someone like that.

"I could change the order for you," he suggested, and I opened my mouth to say what I ordered was just fine, but he didn't notice. "A salad would probably do you better, don't you think?" he asked just as the sexy tattooed stranger passed our table, and I cringed.

Embarrassment flooded over me. I looked up and the tatted strangers' eyes met mine. By the look on his face, there was no way sexy Adonis missed what Bob had said.

Could this night get any worse?

"I'm fine with—"

"No. Don't stress. Waiter!" he shouted, and all I wanted to do was hide. *Worst date ever!*

The waiter came over and looked as uncomfortable as I felt as my date changed my order. *Loudly.* Adding in how he thought it would be better for me. Especially a woman with hips my size.

My hips are just fine, I thought with a pout.

The waiter left, but not before giving me a sympathetic glance.

This was a disaster. I was never going to look for a date online again.

"Welp. I better go to the bathroom… you know, make space," he shared arrogantly, and I forced myself from not grimacing.

Did he really think it was charming to share his bowel movements? Did he think I would fawn over him taking a poop?

I shouldn't have been shocked, but it was all I could do to keep from not throwing up.

He stood and left, and that was my chance.

I was done with online dating and everything that came with it. I really wished I had met him at the restaurant instead of letting him pick me up like he had insisted. I really didn't want to spend the extra money on a Lyft, but this was an emergency. I was going to get home and delete all my dating apps.

The sound of glass shattering and a commotion followed, grabbing all my attention and distracting me from getting the hell out.

The tattooed guy was back at his table and the leggy redhead was yelling at the waiter who had just run off. Glass shards were strewn over the floor.

"You idiot! No wonder all you can do for a living is bring people their drinks!" she hissed, dramatically flailing her arms in the air, my eyes wide as I watched the show. "Obviously, you can't even do that right!" she shrieked. My eyes moved over to her before I glanced at the tattooed hottie, who was now gritting his teeth, his huge hands in a tight fist on the table.

Our eyes met again, and something warm washed over me. His state was intense, and it felt like he was pulling me in. So much I had to look away.

Was he okay with her temper tantrum and abusive behavior? It was a shame she was so pretty yet ugly where it counted.

I had always wondered if outside beauty was enough for some hot guys, enough for them to overlook everything else.

Taking a sip of my water, I glanced up again, and my glass almost slipped from my hands. The stranger's eyes weren't on his leggy date, but oddly enough, right on mine. Again. Like he was trying to say something. I almost wanted to giggle. What would I do if he came over and like some scene in a romantic comedy stretched his arm out a silent request to get the hell out of this pretentious restaurant?

I would run off with him. I closed my eyes and shook my head. I definitely needed something to eat; my imagination was running wilder than usual.

I opened my eyes and looked down at my hands, my head filled with the inked hottie. Was he embarrassed by his date's behavior like I was? Was he used to it? Did he even care? Was he just as bad?

I peeked through my lashes. His eyes were still on mine, and I watched from the distance as he blinked once and then twice before he looked away and up at the waiter. He mouthed an apology as his date stormed off toward the bathroom. And something about the small gesture restored my faith in men.

Unfortunately, Bob returned a little too quickly, and I gave him a tight smile as he sat back down in front of me. My chance to leave had slipped through my fingers. *Damn.*

"Our food's not here yet?" he whined.

"No." *Obviously*, I was dying to say but didn't. I wasn't rude, even if he really deserved it.

Not that I was particularly looking forward to eating a side salad, but I was starving. I'd skipped lunch because I'd been running around at the soccer park with my twin nieces.

"Maybe you should eat your salad without dressing?" What was it with this guy and his high concern about the food I was about to consume? "We could ask for a wedge of lemon."

"Excuse me?" I asked, dumbfounded by what he was saying.

"You could do without the extra calories." I'd had enough of Bob Desmond. I was done. The audacity of the man... no, not man, the *imbecile* in front of me.

My eye twitched. I'd tried to be nice and polite. I was a firm believer of treating others the way you want to be treated and projecting the energy you want to attract.

But I was no one's doormat.

Time for me to excuse myself and get the hell out of here was now. I didn't care if it made me look like a horrible bitch. I was going to excuse myself and call for a ride home.

I opened my mouth, but he spoke first.

"Oh man." His stomach rumbled. Loudly. My eyes widened in horror. "I should go to the bathroom again. Mother always warns me about milk products. I really shouldn't have had that milkshake on the way to your place," he overshared. Again. But this time there was no masking my disgust.

My date stood up again, now pale and sweaty as he rushed back towards the bathroom.

This was my chance to escape and make a run for it. No getting distracted by the dramatic and beautiful couple.

I made eye contact with my waiter, and he quickly made it over to me. I asked if I could pay for my side salad as quickly as possible, so I could slip out of there before my date returned.

Thankfully, the waiter patted my shoulder and told me not to worry. He would cancel it right away. I thanked him and slipped him a twenty in gratitude and because I was almost positive Bob Desmond was not a huge tipper.

I grabbed my purse and cardigan from the back of my chair and quickly walked off.

The temptation to glance at the tattooed stranger was huge, but I resisted.

What would be the point anyway? He was with his own obnoxious date. Not that he would give someone like me a second glance. He was way out of my league. He was what normal everyday girls like me used as eye candy, and nothing more.

Stepping out into the chilly air, I seriously wished I had thought ahead and checked the weather. That way I would have brought a coat instead of a flimsy cardigan, but you dealt with things and moved on. Thankfully, the restaurant from my date from hell was on a very well-lit street. I walked a block down and happened to look up.

The sleek modern building was pretty and bright. I smiled at the name of the place.

Storybook Pub.

Now that was a place for a bookworm like me. *Maybe they serve food?* I thought to myself.

Searching through my phone, I brought up the Lyft app and found a driver about 20 minutes out. Maybe that would be enough time to grab something to go? I could always order something first and then order a ride? I mean, after my night, I deserved a moment to myself.

With a plan in mind, I stepped in, directly heading to the bar, and sat down.

One drink? *Why not?* My hips and I deserved it after that asshole of a date.

"I'll be right with you, beautiful," the green-eyed, dirty-blond bartender said, and I glanced behind me wondering if he was talking to someone else. "Come on over, take a seat." He winked, setting a coaster in front of the stool he'd pointed to and a glass of water.

My face was probably beet red. I wasn't used to being called that.

"You okay?" he asked, beautiful calm stare on mine, and I pointed at myself.

"Me?"

"Yeah." He smiled, a flirty boyish smile that made the temperature rise a couple of degrees in the bar, and I nodded.

"Yeah. I'm okay." I said, taking the seat he'd offered.

"Hmm." He studied me.

"What?"

"I don't know. Let me guess?" He stood in front of me with a studious stare, his hands at the bottom of his chin. "Bad date?"

"You have no idea," I said softly.

"Oh. I don't know. I've heard a lot of bad dates."

"I bet." As a bartender I was sure he could write a book about the stories he heard.

"You never know. The night's still young."

"Young?" I chuckled and shook my head. "It's after eight." I shrugged and inwardly cringed. I was such a grandma! Eight o'clock and ready for a drink and bed.

"Exactly. It's just getting started. You never know. I have a feeling about you and tonight."

"You do, huh?" Was he flirting with me? Because apps or not, I was done with men.

"I do. Do me a favor, will you?" He leaned in closer, and I found myself matching him to hear what he wanted.

"What's that?"

"Whatever the night brings, take a chance on it."

"A chance?"

"The night might take a turn for the better. Don't miss out, take a chance." His green eyes almost sparkled when a little bell over the door chimed, but I was too intrigued by the charming bartender to look behind me.

"Here's a menu. Look it over. I'll be back in a sec, okay?"

"Thanks," I whispered, taking the menu from him, and he walked to the far end of the bar to help out other patrons.

I opened it, my eyes zeroing in on the cocktails, when something changed.

The air and energy seemed to crackle and pop. Almost sizzle.

"Hey," a deep voice said behind me, and I jumped in my seat. I turned to look, and my brows were probably in my hairline with surprise.

Holy crap! It was him!

Tattooed stranger.

Standing behind me!

"Hello," I politely answered, and his eyes dropped to my lips. I could feel his gaze on them. They tingled for a kiss, and I pressed them together to take away the feeling. His eyes moved back up to mine.

"Seat taken?" he asked, and I shook my head. "Thanks," he rasped and took the seat.

Right next to me.

There were a couple of other empty stools, but he sat next to me. Close to me. So close, I felt like every nerve ending was on full alert to feel anything from him.

His body heat.

His scent.

"Bad night?" he asked as he settled his tall frame into the seat, his elbows brushing up against mine as his scent seemed to waft around me. I wanted to take in a deep breath of him so I wouldn't miss one note, but I didn't want to get into a catfight with his date. My luck, she was around somewhere.

"One of the worst, actually," I admitted. I mean, the guy had heard my date call me fat, for goodness sakes. "You?" I asked, and he gave me a manly shrug.

"You can say that," he simply answered.

Huh? Maybe exterior beauty wasn't enough for some men.

"I'm sorry," I said genuinely, our gazes meeting, and something warm and silky flashed behind his beautiful hazel eyes.

Eyes that hadn't looked away from my brown ones.

God, I was a complete idiot!

Staring like total love-torn nerd, without anything witty to say. Breaking eye contact, I looked towards the bartender, but I could still feel the tatted stranger's eyes on me.

That didn't mean anything though.

He would probably order something for him and his date. She was probably in a booth or in the bathroom right now and he was being a gentleman as he waited. He would leave soon.

Join her to make out in some dark corner of the bar. And I'd be nothing but a girl he chose to sit next to. For all I knew, he didn't even realize I was the same girl from the restaurant. I was plain.

That was fine. I didn't need a man.

I would sit here and order a Tequila Sunrise from the sexy blond waiter. I'd find the most sinfully delicious thing I could find and order a second drink. Something sweet but strong. I'd bring up a steamy romance on the kindle app of my phone and disappear in a world where book boyfriends existed. Alpha men who went after the woman they knew they wanted. Men who were strong and sweet like my drink would be.

I'd indulge and order a third drink and a dessert to go before calling for a Lyft and officially never dating again.

"Can I buy you a drink?" the tatted stranger asked, and I minded my own business. There was no way he was talking to me. No way, no how. "Sunshine?" His hand touched my shoulder, and I dropped my menu and met his gaze straight on. Looking into his eyes felt like looking into the sun. You couldn't look away from the sultry gaze.

"What?"

"Can I buy you a drink?"

"Why?" I asked without thinking and covered my mouth with my hand. Shit. That had been rude. But he was looking at me like he thought I was cute. He was sitting close enough that I could feel his body shake with silent laughter.

He probably felt bad for me, which was worse. He could keep his sympathy drink, thank you very much.

"Why not?" he answered, and I shook my head.

"Maybe next time," I answered, pretty proud of how confident I sounded as my attention went back to the menu in front of me.

"Does that mean we'll have another date?"

"Excuse me? What?" I dropped the menu, and his gaze glittered.

"If we go Dutch tonight—"

"Tonight? Umm, look, I don't know your game here, but you gotta know I'm just not that girl," I leaned in closer and said as gently as I could do.

"What girl?" he leaned in closer, and I made the stupid mistake of inhaling.

He smelled like a forest and citrus with something smoky. It was easily my new favorite smell of all time.

"The friend or side chick or whatever it is you're trying to do." *Stop talking, Sara!*

"Umm, I'm sorry?" His lips quirked upward, but I was on a roll and was not about to let the little lines at his eyes and the way they crinkled distract me.

"Look, I was at the other restaurant," I pointed out, hating how embarrassing this was.

"I know." He grinned, obviously thinking I was a lunatic.

"Look, your girlfriend is probably going to come out of the bathroom soon, and I don't do, umm, drama. I'm not that girl. Sorry." I winced at myself for apologizing.

Why was I apologizing? I had nothing to be sorry about.

"I'm actually not sorry," I added and shook my head. What was wrong with me today. "I deserve more than to be some hot bored guy's side piece."

"I agree."

"Good," I clipped and shook my head. What was wrong with guys nowadays?

"She's not my girlfriend," he said, and I froze, my eyes on the menu, but I wasn't reading, "My co-worker set us up. He thought we might hit it off. I'm not sure what he was thinking," he clarified, and I rested the menu on the bar top and looked at him.

"Saw you walk out."

"My date wasn't pleasant."

"You're too nice," he complimented, and I shrugged, "Took guts to walk out."

"Guts?"

"Hell yeah. You two came in together. You getting out of there said loud and clear that you aren't the kind of woman who wastes her time, and I liked that."

"Oh." Heat hit my face and chest.

"In pursuit of complete honesty here, I saw what you did, and I might sound like a stalker, but I followed you out."

"Followed me?" I hadn't noticed that. I really should pay closer attention to my surroundings.

"It's late and dark, and you're beautiful. I wanted to make sure you got wherever you were going safe and sound." *Whoosh.* If I had been standing, my knees would have gone weak at his words.

"What about your date?" I asked

"She drove herself, and I don't think she liked me very much."

"Sorry about that. You two—" The bartender interrupted, and I looked away, glad for the moment to gain my composure.

Had the tattooed hottie just said I was beautiful? That he'd followed me to make sure I made it somewhere safe?

"I'm Kole. What can I get you guys?"

"Tequila Sunrise for her and a beer, whatever you have on tap, for me. And can I get a menu too?" he shocked me by ordering, and he looked at me.

"What?"

"Why a Tequila Sunrise?"

"Because after that dick you were with you deserve something strong to wash that moment away. You're spunky and sweet. A combination I really freaking like and I hope you will let me get to know," he laid out, and I shivered.

I broke eye contact and met Kole's. His words about taking a chance echoed in my head. *Take a chance.* I smiled and nodded, silently accepting hot guy's offer to buy me a drink.

I didn't know it at the time, but my worst date became my last first date.

2

DILLION BROOKS

There are nights in your life that change the course of your path. I was usually good at spotting nights like that.

Nothing could have prepared me for tonight. My co-worker had set me up on a blind date and sure, Maggie had been gorgeous. Tall, not as tall as me but close, especially with those heels. With her thick red hair and pouty makeup, the woman was gorgeous, and she knew it. Not that I didn't like confidence. Confidence on a woman is like lingerie. I loved it. But Maggie was ruthless, rude, and not at all compatible with me. I'd known the moment we met at the front of the restaurant and watched her be rude to the valet attendant, but I would share a meal with her out of duty and leave.

Sitting at our table as she talked about her designer purse collection, I saw *her* walk in. A burst of sunshine. It was like my brained stilled, all the blood in my damn body rushing south.

Tiny and curvy. With silky jet-black hair, peaches and cream skin, and the most beautiful brown eyes I'd ever seen. I couldn't tear my eyes away from her, and out of respect for my date I tried.

Then I passed by her table and heard what that chump of a date said to her. I saw red. I had no idea how I didn't rip the asshole's eyes out. Didn't he know what a precious gift was sitting across from him?

When our waiter dropped a glass of wine, Maggie went from not interesting to psycho. Shrieking and yelling at the waiter, she made a huge unnecessary scene over a genuine mistake.

During her drama, I'd looked over and realized a woman like the one across the way wouldn't do shit like that.

She'd be sweet.

Understanding.

I didn't know her name, but I knew those two things in my gut, just like I knew the sun would rise the next day.

I knew what people thought about me when they looked at me, but they were usually wrong. I wasn't the kind of man who played the field. I hardly went out and when I did, ninety-eight percent of the time was with my buddies or family. The other two percent was when I got roped into stupid blind dates that went nowhere.

"I'm sorry! I just... I honestly can't do this today!" Maggie said, and I nodded, half standing as she stood and left.

I looked over to the sweet thing at the table only to see she was gone.

Gone.

"Excuse me," I asked the waiter who had been serving both tables,

"Yes, sir?"

"The girl from that table over there?"

"Oh, she just left," he said, and I reached for my wallet, dropping two hundred-dollar bills in his palm. "Thank you!" I said, and without thought or reason, I let my heart lead the way.

I stepped out and saw the soft green hue of her dress in the distance and followed her. She was too innocent and pure to be walking the streets alone, even if they were well lit. A primal caveman-like urge rushed through me. I wanted to be the one to keep her safe. I wanted her next to me. She stopped and looked up and smiled. *Fuck, that smile.* The soft, sweet smile was like the best kind of sunshine, and I wanted each and every one of them. I wanted her.

Mine.

She stepped into the building, and I found myself exhaling a breath I hadn't known I was holding.

She was safe.

I slowed my steps as I reached the pub she had entered. I had to come up with a way to approach her. To get her to talk to me. *Be yourself,* a voice that sounded a little too much like my annoying sister sounded in my head, and I frowned. Be myself. I could do that.

I approached, and I wasn't sure where the smoothness was coming from, but by the way she was peeking at me through her dark lashes and the light tint of pink adorning the apples of her cheeks, I wanted to high five myself. I was usually tongue tied around women who caught my eye. But from the moment I saw her walk in with that chump, I'd wanted to approach her. Mine.

"Sorry about that, you two," the bartender interrupted, but I kept my eyes on her despite her looking away. I missed her sweet chocolatey gaze right away. "I'm Kole. What can I get you guys?" the bartender asked.

"Tequila Sunrise for her and a beer, whatever you have on tap, for me." I had no idea what made me order what I did for her, but I had. "And can I get a menu too?" I spoke, and the surprised look on my innocent girl's face lit up. Curious interest piqued, and I smiled.

"What?"

"Why a Tequila Sunrise?" she asked. Her melodic tone made me lean in closer.

"Because after that dick you were with, you deserve something strong to wash that moment away. You're spunky and sweet. A combination I really freaking like and I hope you will let me get to know," I laid out honestly and held my breath.

"You want to get to know me?" she asked quietly, and I swallowed hard and gave a stiff nod. I wanted to get to know her more than breathe my next breath. Something told me the payoff was going to be huge. Her eyes were on my neck, watching my Adam's apple bob.

"Yes," I rasped, my voice hoarse in my own ears.

"And your date—"

"Gone."

"She wasn't your girlfriend?"

"No." I smiled and added, "I'm completely single. If I weren't, I wouldn't be talking to another woman. I'm not that kind of man." Her blush deepened, and I licked my lips. I wanted to chase that blush with my mouth and trace every single direction it went.

"I'm Sara."

"I'm Dillion." I winked and laced my hands together so I could fight from touching her.

"Dillion," she repeated. I liked the way my name sounded coming from her lips.

"Here's the menu," Kole said, handing it to me.

"Thanks, man."

"For the beautiful lady, a Tequila Sunrise. Beer on tap for you," he said, setting our drinks on two coasters in front of us. "Did you two want to start a tab?"

"Yes. Thank you." I tipped my head and moved my attention to Sara. Sara. I liked her name.

"What looks good?"

"I'm sorry." She shook her head, her hair swaying back and forth so much of a temptation, my hand had a mind of its own as it went and captured a strand, silky in my fingers, "What's going on?" she asked with wide eyes, and I smiled, dropping the strand and cupping her face.

"We're on a date," I clarified, and my heart fucking froze waiting to see what she would do. No way would I have been prepared for the true beauty of her smile.

Her genuine smile was stunning. She was beautiful without it, but with it, she was a knockout and then some. And as cheesy as it might make me sound, it felt like a gift when she flashed it in my direction.

Not some tight lip service I'd observed her give the idiot earlier. No. This was a true blue smile, and it was like a shot to the heart.

"A date, huh?" Her soft voice with that damn smile was killing me. I wanted to lean in and kiss her, but there was no way I was rushing this.

"Sunshine, I have a feeling this is our last first date." I didn't know where the Casanova talk was coming from. I wasn't a player. I didn't date. But she was bringing it out of me, and I didn't mind it at all when she was looking at me as if I was too good to be true.

"You're as smooth as you look."

"I'll take that as a compliment." I grinned. Her shyness was like candy to my sweet tooth. "So, what looks good?"

Her pink tongue peeked out, taking a swipe of her puffy lower lip, and damn, I wanted a taste.

"How do you feel about loaded fries?"

"Let's do it." I winked, dropping my hand from her face, I leaned in and kissed her cheek.

I couldn't help myself.

My lips touched her powdery soft skin, and I breathed her in and had to bite away a groan. So damn sweet. Like vanilla and brown sugar blended with chocolate chips.

I pulled away, and she looked away from me. I pulled her stool in closer. Yeah. There was no way I was going to let this beautiful girl slip through my fingers. I got Kole's attention and ordered us loaded fries and an order of chicken strips.

I lifted my beer and she did too.

"To terrible dates that turn into something more when you take a leap of faith."

"To leaps of faith," she repeated softly, and our glasses clinked.

3

SARA

Minutes ticked into hours, but it all went over my head. Time didn't exist after he toasted the way he had.

All that existed was Dillion and his deep voice and the way he looked at me. He made me feel like I was the only woman he could see. It was flattering, but more than that, I could tell it was real.

He was really interested in me.

Simple and plain me.

But talking to him, laughing, enjoying drinks over our meals and desserts had been easy. It'd felt like we had done it a million times before. I was comfortable with him. After our second drink, we had moved into a booth tucked into a dark corner of the pub.

Chemistry was thick and electric between us.

"Last call!" Kole called out, and it was like the bubble around us started to fall, but I wasn't ready for that.

"Wow. It's last call?" I asked, glancing at my phone. I'd never, not once in my twenty-six-years, been out at a pub or bar late enough to hear last call.

"Let me take you home," he said, his hand holding mine, and I nodded.

I wasn't the type to fall into one-night stands or even kiss on the first date, but there was an incredible energy and pull between us. There was no way I would turn him down. I was going to invite him in.

He paid the tab, refusing my offer to pitch in and split it. Instead, he brought my hand up to his lips and kissed it, and there was something incredible and sweet about the gesture. He was the first real life gentleman I had ever met.

A Prince Charming come to life.

We walked hand in hand to his car. He opened my door and closed it before rounding the car and taking me home. I had given him my address and phone number before he had taken care of the bill.

The ride was quiet but comfortable.

As much as I tried to get out of my own mind, I couldn't. I was a little freaked out. I knew I was going to invite him in, and I was trying to shake my mind awake to see if I could remember if my panties matched my bra. I tried to remember if it was Busch Gardens or a tame field downstairs. He parked his car, and I looked up. We were at my small two-bedroom bungalow.

"Let me open the door," he said, his voice raspy, and I nodded. I undid my seatbelt and quickly wiped my sweaty palms on the skirt of my dress.

He opened my door and extended his hand for me to take. His large powerful hand. I took it. A warmth like no other washed over me and any nerves I had just been fighting fell to the ground below us.

"Thank you for tonight," I said when we reached my front door.

"Sunshine, I think you're the one I need to thank," he said, tucking a hair behind my ear.

"Why's that?"

"For giving me a chance when you could have told me to go to hell after the date you'd had with that dirtbag."

"I'd given up on dating the moment I walked into Storybook Pub," I shared.

"I can't say I blame you. He was a real jerk." I laughed and leaned in closer, his hands taking hold of both of mine. "I want a chance, Sara."

"A chance?" There was that word again. Chance. *Take a chance*, Kole's words replayed in my mind.

"To see you again."

"Okay. I like that."

"Good. I'll call you in the morning." He would call? My smile faltered, but I tried to save face.

He was going to call? Had I misread the entire night of stolen heated glances and sweet touches?

"Sounds good." I smiled, and he kissed my cheek. My cheek! I'd definitely read the night wrong.

"Sweet dreams, Sunshine," he whispered against my cheek, and I held my breath.

Maybe this was his move?

Maybe he would move his lips just slightly and finally kiss me.

But he didn't.

He turned and stepped back. I quickly recovered, realizing he was waiting for me to open my door, and I did. I waved goodbye before stepping inside my place and closing the front door. I leaned against the cool wood and shut my eyes.

"Totally read the night wrong," I whispered to myself. The disappointment felt heavy.

I pushed off the door and walked through my house. It was almost two in the morning; I should have been exhausted. It being a Friday night, the work week earlier had been heavy.

I went into my nightly routine. I washed my face making sure to get rid of the little makeup I had put on and quickly brushed my teeth. Moving into my bedroom, I slipped out of my mint-green dress and into cozy pastel tie-dyed joggers and matching sweater.

Once all cozy, I tried to get comfortable in bed, but I couldn't get into a sweet spot. My head was filled with Dillion and the night we had shared. After tossing and turning, I lay in bed staring at the ceiling fan. I was wide awake trying to figure out what I'd done to scare off my tattooed gentleman.

4

DILLION

I had messed up and choked. Nerves getting the best of me, I'd fucked up. Kissed her cheek? I was an idiot!

It turned out, small world, we only lived about ten minutes away from one another. I tried to make my way home, but before I reached my street, something came over me.

I busted a U-turn and went back.

When you found the woman you wanted to spend a hell of a lot of tomorrows with, you didn't walk off like I had. You manned up and went after what you wanted.

And I wanted my Sunshine. My sweet, sweet Sara.

I parked in front of her house like some kind of fucking stalker and picked up my phone.

Me: I should have kissed you.

I texted my girl honestly. Because how fucking stupid had I been by walking away? Only kissing her cheek!

Whatever Casanova I had been channeling earlier had disappeared and my nerdy thirteen-year-old self had been left on that doorstep.

I'd choked, but I was going to fix it, goddamn it!

I smiled when I saw the little bubbles pop up letting me know she was responding.

Sunshine: You should have.

Fuck. I rubbed my face and grabbed a mint from my console.

Me: I messed up.
Sunshine: Wish you were here for a redo.

That was my opening, and I wasn't about to look a gift horse in the mouth.
I stepped out of my car and shot off one more text.

5

SARA

Dillion: Open the door.

Open the door!? He was here?

"Holy shit," I whispered to myself and rushed to the front door. I didn't think of anything, not about my hair looking like a mess or the fact I wasn't wearing a bra beneath my cozy but girly pajamas.

A deep but soft knock sounded, and I stopped in my tracks, my heart beating wildly.

"Sara?" his deep voice called, and my feet had a mind of their own. They moved me forward, and I opened the front door.

The soft porch light and silver from the moonlight behind him spilled over him. He looked larger than life and even more handsome than the moment I'd first laid eyes on him. His dress shirt sleeves had been rolled up over his elbows, his colorful tattoos seemed brighter. The buttons undone at his thick neck gave a small hint of dark chest hair. His hazel eyes were dark, and before I could think about saying hello, he kissed me.

One of his hands wrapped its way around my waist, making me feel tiny and delicate, and the other went to my face. His beautiful full lips fell over mine.

His kiss was dominant and passionate. There was no doubt he was in control. It was beautiful. Amazing. The most perfect first kiss ever!

I tried to give as good as I was being given. I clung on to him until neither of us could breathe. We pulled apart, but he didn't get too far. He rested his forehead against mine.

"I definitely should have kissed you earlier." He sighed, and my lips quirked upward.

"Want to come in?" I asked. I wasn't positive what was going on, but I was going to be damned if I didn't take a chance. Even if this ended up as a one-night stand or a booty call. Though something about the serious way he was looking at me made that hard to believe.

"Get that out of your head," he said, nuzzling his nose against mine, like he could hear my thoughts, and I exhaled slowly. "I want to come in," he said, his strong jaw clenched.

"But?" I could feel the word standing between us. This was where the proverbial shoe would drop.

"But I'm not that guy."

"What guy?" Would he say the commitment kind? He was too busy with his career?

"The one that gets in there deep with you one night and doesn't call the next." My brain was slow to process his words, but when they did, hope fluttered to life. "Sara, I'm not a player—"

"Dill—"

"Let me say this, beautiful. I know this is going to sound insane and it could scare you off, but I know what I want, and it's you. Only you."

Holy. Smokes.

Had he really just said that?

"Dillion…"

"I can be intense when I know what I want. I get that, and I know I'm not doing myself any favors letting it all hang out, but I have to be crystal clear with you. I'm a one-woman man, and I want to be your man."

"We just met," I giggled, and his arms wrapped me up tightly into his body.

"Tell me you don't feel it, and I'll back off."

"I feel it." What would be the point of lying? "Want to come in?"

"I'm only so strong, Sunshine," he warned, and I bit my lower lip and clenched my thighs together at the gruff tone. "You invite me in, I don't think I can keep my hands to myself."

"Who is asking you to?"

6

DILLION

Jesus Christ! She was going to kill me!

"I'm trying to be a good guy here."

"You don't have to try too hard. Dillion, I know you are. Just like I know if I invite you inside and we start to…"— her face turned an adorable shade of pink—"mess around and I don't feel comfortable with something, I trust you to stop."

"How would you know that? I could be a dick and—"

"You telling me you wouldn't stop? A man who opens every single door like you do and tries to be respectful and leave me with only a kiss on the cheek isn't about to push me into doing something I'm not comfortable with." She was stroking my chest, the light heat of her hand seeping through, making my body more than alive.

"Of course, I would," I groaned, and her eyes flared. She stood on the tips of her toes, and my Adam's apple bobbed.

"Come in, Dillion," she whispered against my mouth, her tongue skimming my lower lip before she stepped away and back into her home. I looked at the empty spot where she had just been standing, my dick throbbing and begging me to follow her.

So, I did.

7

SARA

Tonight was about taking chances. The bartender had struck a chord with me, and I was going to ride the wave.

I wasn't positive Dillion was going to take me up on my offer, but it didn't stop me from taking my clothes off. One piece at a time I let them fall to the floor as I walked through the house to my bedroom, leaving a trail like breadcrumbs for him to follow.

I wasn't shy about my body when I was alone, but this was completely different. Dillion Brooks was the kind of man I thought only existed in romance movies. Tall and tatted, powerful in his own way. A gentleman in every way, and I hoped when the doors closed, he'd turn into an animal. I was probably biting off way more than I could chew, but I wasn't going to back down. I wanted Dillion like I had never wanted anything in my entire life.

I only had one more thing to take off and I'd be completely bare. I hooked my thumbs beneath the sides of my white sheer thong and let gravity take over as they fell to the ground. I stood in my bedroom completely naked, facing my bed, my back to the door, and hoped to God Dillion would walk in soon.

My heart felt like it was going to leap out of my chest.

Thump-thump. Thump-thump. Thump-thump.

Would he come in?

Did he think I was being too forward?

Was I being kind of slutty?

Who was I tonight? Doing something so crazy?

So many thoughts piled over one another, it was almost overwhelming, but from one moment to another, my brain registered his touch. And just like that, every wild thought in my head cleared away.

I breathed out raggedly. A breath I hadn't realized I'd been holding. His firm, strong large hand was on my bare hip, and my head fell back to his shoulder.

"Do you have any idea what your body looks like?" he rasped by my ear before taking the lobe into his mouth and taking a nip. I whimpered, pushing my bottom against his front. I didn't miss the thick bulge bumping against me; it only made me wetter. Messier. His other hand wrapped around, falling over my belly open palmed, his thick thumb stroking above my belly button. "You're exquisite, Sara. My own ray of sunshine on earth. All for me."

"Yes," I hissed as his hand moved from my belly button up my torso to the underside of my left breast.

"You're all mine."

"Yours," I whispered, his fingers tugging my tightly wound up nipples. "More, Dillion. Please?" I begged. God, I needed his touch all over my body. I needed him.

"You're all mine, baby," he whispered into my ear as he rolled my nipple between his fingers harder than he had before.

"Dillion," I cried, and he turned me and picked me up and tossed me on my bed.

"I'm in charge, baby," he growled, and the wetness between my legs grew. "Fuck," he cursed, licking his lips, looking at me like he was about to devour me alive. "I'm going to have my way with you," he said roughly. I watched as he impatiently worked his black dress shirt buttons off one at a time, and I pulled my body up on my elbows for a better view.

And what a great sight it was.

His shirt fell right over my discarded panties, and it unveiled more ink over his chest. Bright and beautiful work I wanted to lick and trace with my tongue. His pant buttons were undone; he pulled them off in a hurry, along with his navy-blue boxer briefs. My mouth went dry. Holy shit.

"You're huge," I whispered honestly, my eyes fixated on his thick, long shaft. It jerked forward and looked like it was about to hit his belly button.

"I'll fit," he promised, and my eyes moved to his.

"Dillion…" The apprehension was clear in my voice, but he leaned in between my legs, his dick nestled in just the right spot. His strong body hovered over mine, and he kissed me. Sweet and soft, he took his time making the need and desire grow hotter. His tongue slid against mine, his taste addicting, making me forget about his size and only making me aware of how empty I felt. Reminding me of how badly I needed him. "Dillion," I panted, needing so much more.

"I won't hurt you. I'd fucking die first."

"I need you."

"You're going to get me, Sara. Every inch I have is going to be yours. Only yours from here on out, baby. I fucking promise. But I gotta get my woman nice and wet first." His mouth moved from mine to the crook of my neck. My nipples grazed against his chest, the tingles of scraping against his coarse chest hair incredible.

My body involuntarily arched into his, like I was fighting to get as close as possible to him. But Dillion wouldn't be distracted. He was a man on a mission. To get me nice and wet, and damn was he succeeding. His mouth moved deliciously slow down my body. My neck. My shoulders. My collarbone. My breasts. The way he peppered affection down my body made me feel drunk. Dizzy with lust and need. Until he got *there* and took his first swipe.

"Oh my god!" I cried out in a broken whimper and clenched the sheets beneath me.

He didn't stop.

He kept at me like he was enjoying every single moment. Like he couldn't get enough of me, and it was embarrassing how quickly he got me off. Never had I ever got off with anyone else, much less that fast. But even as I crashed from the high of my orgasm, his mouth didn't leave my pussy.

Nope.

He worked his thick finger inside of me, stretching me so damn good my toes curled, then worked in another digit. He was amazing with his hands and his mouth. I panted and cried out his name like a prayer. I'd never been so loud, but with him, it was like all my inhibitions were gone. I was safe with him to let it all out. Dillion was amazing. His attention was bringing my body up higher and higher. My thighs trembled, my body tight as an ache tightened in my belly. I was so close to another earth-shattering orgasm it was crazy! My skin was burning up and sweaty. So incredibly close to the edge, I mourned the loss of him when his mouth and fingers left me. His body moved and he hovered over me.

His muscles tight and strained, I felt the tip of his crown at my entrance. With our gazes connected, it felt like an out-of-body experience. We didn't need words. His thick shaft sunk in balls deep in one thick thrust. I was that wet!

"Yes!" I hissed, my hands holding on to his shoulders, nails digging into the granite-like muscle.

"Fuck, Sunshine!" he groaned, and I lost sight of his eyes. His face fell into the crook of my neck. He pulled out and back in, in a delicious rhythm. It was like our bodies were in sync as I met him thrust for thrust, taking everything he had to give and holding him tightly to me. I was going to go over the edge, but I didn't want to go alone.

"I'm so close, baby," I whispered, and his speed picked up.

It was rough and decadent and beyond my imagination. When it was time, I have no idea how, but we crashed at the same time. Blinding white lights burst behind my eyes as wave after wave of pleasure hit me and he emptied himself inside of me. I cried out his name so loud I was shocked if I didn't wake up my neighbors in the dead of the night. My own name on his own lips, even muffled, in my own ears at that moment had never sounded sweeter. The entire experience was cathartic and intimate. Primal. His body dropped on top of me, and I held him close. I enjoyed the weight of his body covering mine. We lay there with sweat-slicked skin as we caught our breath.

"You okay?" he asked, licking my neck, and I moaned softly.

"So much better than okay."

"I'm staying," he said, pulling his head back so he could look at me, and I brushed his hair out of his face and smiled.

"Good." His nose grazed mine before he rolled us over with him on his back and me pulled in close. We lay there quietly. The sweat quickly drying on our skin gave me a little bit of a chill despite the heat radiating off his body. Without me having to ask, he pulled my comforter over us and stroked my hair.

"Dillion?" I said his name softly, breaking the silence between us, and smiled when I heard him grunt.

"Hmm?"

"Thank you," I whispered, and he stilled. Quickly shifting our bodies so we were lying on our sides and looking into one another's eyes.

"For what?"

"For tonight. For following me to Storybook Pub. For coming back tonight. This has seriously been the best night of my life," I opened up and confessed. I was being vulnerable, but with Dillion, as crazy as it was since we'd only met hours earlier, I knew I was safe.

"Oh, Sunshine." He rolled my body over his with a smile. "It's only going to get better from here on out," he promised, and before I could say anything, he kissed me and just like that everything around us blurred. Only our bodies existed, and they did a damn great job communicating.

8

DILLION

I woke up with a smile on my face, my body refreshed and renewed despite the lack of sleep. Sara was tucked sweetly into me, softly snoring, looking like an angel in my arms. I had no idea how life could be so damn amazing, but I knew in the marrow of my bones this was the start of something incredible.

Beautiful beyond recognition.

I'd left my house to meet one woman and had chased after another. I couldn't believe what had happened, but I knew myself. I wasn't the player type, not even close. So, when a man like me knew who he wanted, come hell or high water, he would go after it and cherish it to the day he died. That's what I was going to do when it came to my sunshine. Staring at her sleeping, I couldn't believe how close I'd come to messing it up. How close to not having this moment I'd been. I had almost messed it up by not kissing her good night and leaving like I had.

I'd been an idiot.

"It's too early for you to think so hard," she groaned playfully, her voice still heavy with sleep.

Her eyes fluttered open, and fuck, I felt her gaze in my heart.

Those were the eyes I would look into every morning for the rest of my life. I was twenty-eight and in love for the first time. Head over ass in love with a woman I had just met. An angel who had let me in her bed. It was crazy. If my brother called and told me this had happened to him, I'd rush to get his head examined.

But staring at Sara, I knew everything I was feeling was right as rain. We were two puzzle pieces to live connected and next to one another for the rest of our days.

"Morning, Sunshine."

"Mmm, hello, handsome." She grinned, her hand moving to cup my face, and kissed me good morning. "Can I say something crazy?" she asked against my lips, and I nodded. "I loved that you came back last night to kiss me, but there is something incredible about kissing you good morning."

"Agreed," I rumbled. "I don't think I wanna wake up any other way from here on out, Sara," I said seriously, and her grin grew warm and sugary sweet.

"I don't either," she answered, her pretty dark brow lifting upward, and I pulled her into me even closer.

"We sound crazy," I chuckled, not giving a shit.

"Taking chances can sound like that," she said so damn wisely.

I liked that.

I liked it a hell of a lot.

But I didn't tell her that; I showed her.

I would show her that taking a chance on me was worth her time, day in and day out.

Over and over and over again.

The End... *for now*

LEARN MORE ABOUT MAYRA STATHAM:
HTTP://AMAZON.COM/AUTHOR/MAYRASTATHAM

ALSO BY MAYRA STATHAM:
 BURNING BRIDGES
 LIE (RIGHT MAN SERIES #1)
 SOMETHING WORTH SAVING

HIDDEN WINGS

TONYA CLARK

**Falling is just the beginning…
Her secret is going to change both their lives.**

Sub-genre: Shifters
Relationship: Male/Female

AYDIN

Secrets, everyone has them. Mine are only found in storybooks, though. I have learned to follow my instincts. That's how I ended up here in a very small little town in upstate Maine, in front of a bar called the Storybook Pub.

Today is my twenty-fifth birthday and I woke up from a very vivid dream and needed to drive. I had no idea where I was going, I just sensed I needed to go. I've been on the road for at least eight hours and my mom has called me at least forty times.

Make that forty-one times, as my phone lights up and my mom's picture flashes up on the screen. Pressing the green circle, I answer, "I'm all right, Mom."

"Are you still driving?" I hear the concern in her voice.

Her first call came at exactly 5:26 this morning, like it does every year on my birthday. She didn't sound surprised when I told her I was already on the road and had no idea where I was going, but again she has had twenty-five years now of my secrets.

"No, I'm parked in front of a place called the Storybook Pub, in Maine."

"Maine?! Why would you be up there and why does that sound like it's the name of a bar?"

"Well, Mom, I think it is a bar."

She takes a deep breath and lets it out slowly. I can only imagine what is going through her head. She doesn't question these "feelings" I get or ask many questions. We have both learned following them is a lot easier than trying to deny them. Ignoring them, I've found out, can attract attention that we've both worked very hard on making sure doesn't happen since I was a child.

"Aydin, please be careful."

It's been just my mom and me since I was born, and she never talks about my father. All I know is they were together for a few months and then he just took off one day. She found out she was pregnant with me shortly after he left. It's because of me she never dated when I was a child, though I have no idea why she hasn't now that I'm an adult. I think whoever my father is, he broke her heart and she just doesn't want to give it up again.

Looking at the clock on my dashboard, it's almost two in the afternoon and I've been on the road since five this morning. I made only one stop and that was for fuel, a bathroom break, and I grabbed a bottle of water and a bag of chips. I'm starving and hoping this place serves food.

"Mom, I'm all right. Let me call you back in a little while."

She sighs deeply and I know it's killing her to not ask the multiple questions flying through her head right now, or beg me to turn around and come home.

"Please be careful."

I almost laugh. Be careful, I have no issue taking care of myself and she knows it. I think that's the only reason she doesn't try and stop me when I leave on these little "Sense Adventures" I get.

"I promise, Mom, love you."

"Love you, too. Please don't forget to call me later."

Call her, right! She'll be calling me back probably within the hour.

"Promise." Hitting the end circle on my phone's screen, I turn the key to my car, shutting down the engine. It's time to find out why I'm so far away from home and in a town I have never heard of in Maine.

Opening the large, beautifully-carved wooden door, I step just inside and take in my surroundings. It has a very welcoming feel to it, decorated with Irish décor and music that hums through your head the moment you step inside. It's very clean, no smoke in the air, and void of the rowdy sounds of any bar I have been to. It's very calming and inviting. Taking a deep breath in relief, I feel very comfortable, sensing I belong here.

"Can I help you?" The voice comes from the direction of the bar at my right.

Looking over, I see a man I would say in his early to mid-thirties, dressed in a white button-up shirt and vest, blond hair and very green eyes.

"Do you guys by chance serve food here?"

He places a hand on the bar in front of him. "Have a seat," he pulls a menu out from under the bar and places it down as an answer to my question.

"Perfect." Walking over, I take the open bar stool.

"Can I grab you something to drink while you scan the menu?"

"Water, with lemon please, for right now."

He nods, "I'm Kole, if you need anything just ask. I'll be right back with your water." He pats the countertop and walks away.

Scanning the menu, everything looks amazing, which tells me I'm starving and would eat just about anything.

A tall glass of ice water with lemon is sat down on the counter. "Have you decided what you would like?"

"Yes, I'll have the club sandwich and fries, please."

He nods and takes the menu, "Good choice, it shouldn't take long."

I hear the door behind me open and a shiver runs up my spine then settles there in a low vibration. It's not fear, but almost an excitement that I'm sensing. I take a deep breath and try to settle the vibration rippling along my spine. I have never had a problem controlling this before, at least not since I was a child.

Looking over my shoulder, my eyes instantly make contact with a pair of light blue eyes that sends a shock of electricity shooting through my body. My back ripples a little stronger down my spine and the fear I'm sensing isn't from the new patrons but from losing my own control. I never lose control, ever!

I can't blink, our eyes are locked, I'm not even sure I'm breathing at the moment. I feel as though I should know who this guy is but I've never seen him before. The vibration is only getting stronger, it's almost painful, but I refuse to give in.

Just when I think I have no control left, he blinks and the contact between us is broken. My shoulders slump a little and I take a couple of deep breaths, willing the control back into my body. What the hell was that?

For the first time I see the other two guys who entered the bar with him. None of them are hard to look at, but the guy who first entered has me mesmerized. Dark wavy hair, a blue to his eyes so unique, they almost seem to change color, floating between a white blue and a bright sky blue. Dark jeans and black boots, with a t-shirt that hugs every muscle of his chest and abs to perfection. His arms flex and the evidence of his strength is proudly visible. My ability to control myself is back but I can't seem to look away from him.

The sound of a plate being placed in front of me and the smell of the fries makes my stomach rumble with the reminder of how hungry I am. As hard as it is to look away, the food wins out and my attention is finally brought back to what is in front of me and the knowing smile of Kole who is standing there on the other side of the bar.

"Something catch your eye, Aydin?"

Puzzled, I try to think back to if I told Kole my name. He just stands there smiling at me. I must have when he introduced himself to me, how else would he know it? Damn, I need to get some sleep or something, I'm losing my mind.

"Yes, this food," my stomach rumbles again as I look over my plate and the large sandwich and plate full of fries in front of me. "By chance do you have ranch?"

I keep my eyes averted down on my food, but I can tell Kole is still giving me that very knowing look. "Sure, let me go grab some for you." I don't have to look up to know he is smiling.

I'm relieved when he walks away. Grabbing a fry, I force myself to concentrate on my food and not look back over my shoulder again. I'm making a fool out of myself and it's embarrassing the hell out of me.

Kole places a bowl of ranch on the counter next to my plate and turns to leave.

"Is there a place where I can get a room for a couple of days?"

"Down the street is a bed and breakfast, great couple who runs it, Nick and Rebecca. I'll call and tell them you are headed that way after you finish here."

COLTON

"Man, you haven't stopped staring at that woman since we walked in, what's going on?"

Alexsander's question is the same one I have been asking myself since I walked through the door. She hasn't turned back around again, but I can't keep my eyes off of her and the vibration in my back has been intense since before we walked in the door. I felt it outside.

"How are you guys today?"

"Hey, Kole, who is the newbie over there?" Dagan's interest in the woman sends a need to punch him running through me. What the hell?

"That's Aydin, she just arrived in town and is staying for a couple of days." His eyes are directly on me as he answers Dagan's question.

"Has anyone else noticed the eye color on that woman? They are almost violet." Dagan's questions are starting to piss me off and I have to control the need to grab him by the shirt and throw him outside.

"It's impossible, right?" My question is directed straight to Kole.

Kole knows things that no one can explain. He isn't much older than us, if older at all, someone you would think of more like a buddy, but his knowledge sets him apart in age by years.

"I've definitely learned nothing is impossible, but he has never said anything to me about it and I'm guessing to you either. Maybe you should ask?" Kole isn't saying something and I can see that written all over his face.

"She is definitely a Falen and violet eyes are only for the head family, but it's impossible, she has never been mentioned. I would think Raidan would have mentioned having children. I know he has no siblings."

"Well, I think I'm going to go introduce myself to the new girl in town. Only one way to find out the questions we have and that is to ask." Dagan starts to get out of his chair.

My hand shoots out and grabs him, putting him back into his chair. He isn't going anywhere near this woman, not until we get some answers.

Dagan laughs, "Then maybe you should go over there and introduce yourself."

"I'm going to go and grab your drinks." Kole's smug smile is starting to get on my nerves as well. If he knows something he needs to just say it.

"Either you go over there, or I am." Dagan starts to get out of his chair once again. I'm going to beat the shit out of him.

"Sit your ass back in the chair. She doesn't need you trying to hit on her while she's eating, she will lose her appetite." Plus, I'm sure my friend will be leaving with a busted jaw. My hands are already twitching, I'm not quite understanding why, but I'm pretty sure I will punch him if he approaches her.

"Maybe you should go over there, man. It is a little strange," Alexsander speaks up.

Rolling my eyes, I get up from my chair. Walking over, my back vibrates more and more with each step taken. I have been around Falen women before, never have I had to control myself as much as I have to right now. I have a need to grab her and carry her out of this place, literally!

I notice her back stiffens as I approach. She doesn't turn around, but I know she knows I'm standing behind her. The bar stool next to her is empty, I look up and see Kole directing me to take a seat.

My arm brushes hers as I sit next to her. It's the slightest touch, and I feel myself starting to lose control again as my shirt is stretched tight against my back. What the hell?! She leans away from me and her head swivels to stare at me.

"Hi, I'm Colton."

The vibration in my back is intense and I'm about to get up and leave, but then she speaks.

"Hi, Colton."

"Are you not going to tell me your name?"

Her eyes move from me to Kole, "I overheard our dear bartender here telling you and your buddies my name already."

"That same bartender says you are staying for a couple days, are you visiting family?"

"Is this a small town thing, interrogate the new person in town? I've heard people in small towns can be pretty nosy, I guess it's true." She looks down at her plate and plays with a fry.

I should take the hint but I'm still curious as to who she is and why she is here. "You must be from the city."

She just nods.

"So being the nosy small town guy, what brings you to our town?" I try once again.

Aydin takes a deep breath and wipes her hands on a napkin, throwing it down onto her half-eaten plate of food. "Thank you so much, Kole, for the food and information on a place to stay. I'm sure I will be back, a girl needs to eat." She pulls her wallet out, taking out a twenty and placing it on the counter in front of her.

"Nice meeting you, Colton." No eye contact, she just gets up from her seat and heads out of the bar.

Kole grabs the twenty off the counter, turning to put it in the cash register behind him. "She is staying down the street at Nick and Rebecca's place," he informs me without turning around.

"All right, Kole, tell me what you know."

Turning, he leans back against the counter and crosses his arms over his chest. "She is staying for a couple of days, and will be down at Nick and Rebecca's," he repeats.

The vibration has almost disappeared now. I nod at Kole, understanding I'm getting no further information out of him. Maybe I should go and have a quick talk with Raidan first, maybe he will have a little more information than our dear bartender is giving out.

AYDIN

Plopping down in my driver's seat I instantly lock my door, for what reason I don't know. Taking a couple deep breaths, my body starts to relax. I had to get out of there, I wasn't sure how much longer I could sit there and keep control of myself with Colton sitting so close.

When his arm brushed against mine, I thought that was it. I felt the back of my shirt push away from my skin a couple of times and it took everything in me not to panic and run from that place and Colton. Who is this guy and why am I having this kind of reaction to him? Sure, he's good looking, but he's not the first hot guy to hit on me, and definitely not worth drawing unwanted attention to myself.

The hardest part about my secret is I have absolutely no one to talk to about it, I have no one like me. My mom knows but she doesn't have my situation, she just did what she could to keep me safe. The rest has been a self-taught program.

The door opens and Colton and his two friends exit the building. Colton instantly finds me sitting in my car and our eyes lock once again; a shock shoots up my back as I'm pushed slightly forward in my seat. I need to get away from here. As hard as it is, I find the ability to blink and gain a little control back. Starting my car quickly, I put it in reverse and back out of the parking spot, probably driving too fast out of the parking lot and in the direction Kole told me I could find a place to stay for a couple of nights.

Passing through the town, I feel myself calming down as I look at all the shops that line the street. A coffee shop, flower shop, book store, it's that perfect little town you see on Hallmark movies. The store fronts are all brick, trees lining the sidewalks, and everything is clean. Two old men are even sitting on a bench in front of the barber shop. I'm falling in love with this little town with every shop I pass.

At the end of the main street is a large, beautiful, white-painted Victorian style home, a big circular driveway in front. A sign out front announcing it as a bed and breakfast confirms this must be the place Kole was talking about.

Pulling up to the front, I start to get out when my phone lights up and my mom's image once again is up on the screen. I have to give it to her, she waited longer than I thought she would.

"Hello, Mom."

"I haven't heard from you and wanted to make sure no one kidnapped you at the bar."

Kidnapped, no, took my breath away, not up for conversation at this time. If I told her about my reaction to Colton, she would freak out and demand to know where I was, or for me to come back to the city.

"Actually the bar was like an Irish pub. Very clean, nice people, very welcoming and great food."

"You didn't call, and all you told me on our last call was you were sitting outside of a bar."

"I'm sorry, Mom, I had a bite to eat and I'm just pulling into this beautiful bed and breakfast to see about a room for a couple nights."

"Couple nights?! How long do you think you will be gone?"

"Not sure, I'm here for a reason and I need to figure out what it is. I will keep you updated, I promise. This town is very clean, the people are very welcoming and I promise you no one is going to kidnap me."

"All right, hon. Well, I wish I could have spent some of today with you for your birthday and all."

I feel bad, I'm all my mom has and I left without saying a word to her. "There will be more birthdays, Mom. I love you but I want to go and get a room, I will text you all the information as soon as I get settled."

"All right, I love you, please at least try to find a place where you can get a cupcake or maybe a birthday sundae. Everyone should have at least one of those two on their birthday."

I love this woman with everything in me. She has always said a person should always have a birthday cake and there hasn't been a year that has gone by that I haven't. I may need to see if that bakery I passed has something, it will give me an excuse to walk down to the town and explore a little more once I get settled in.

Walking up the stone steps, the front door opens before I even reach the top step.

"Hello, you must be Aydin, Kole called and said you would be stopping by." The woman standing at the door looks to be in her mid-forties, blonde hair about to her shoulders and very kind brown eyes.

"Yes, hello, I'm Aydin." I reach out my right hand to greet her.

"I'm Rebecca, let me help you with that." She reaches for my one bag that I'm carrying.

"Thank you, but it's not heavy. Do you by chance have a room for a couple of nights?"

"Absolutely," she stands off to the side of the door to allow me to enter.

The inside of the house is just as breathtaking as the outside. "Your home is beautiful." Looking around the updated home, everything is in place and very neat.

"Thank you, it's been in the family for years. Follow me and we will get you all set up."

By the time I get into my room and unpacked it is almost five o'clock. Sitting down for just a moment in a large wingback chair next to the window, I'm loving the view my room has overlooking the front of the house and a park across the street.

Rebecca had mentioned dinner at around six-thirty, but I'm still all right from the club sandwich I had over at the pub. Though, that cupcake is sounding amazing right now. I declined the dinner invitation, letting her know that I'm excited to walk around the town a little tonight. With the open window I can tell tonight will get a little chilly so I grab my lightweight jacket and head out in search of my birthday cupcake.

COLTON

"Raidan, didn't you say you were an only child?"

He only nods and keeps his eyes averted to the paperwork he is going over at his desk. I decided before I confronted Aydin again I wanted to talk to Raidan about our new guest in town. I know she is a Falen, I sensed her the moment I walked into the door, but the violet eyes are throwing me off. We have been taught only the head family have violet eyes.

"Do you have any children?"

This question brings his attention to me. Squinting at me, he stares me down for a moment. Raidan and I are close, I'm the first in command after him. He took me under his wings when my father passed away, leaving only my mother and me. Everyone in our community thought eventually the two of them would get together, but it never happened. I don't think I have ever seen Raidan with any woman.

I was twelve when my father died. Raidan said he saw a lot of potential in me so he taught me everything I would need to know so that I could stand next to him as a leader in our community. That happened on my twentieth birthday and for the past seven years I have been right by his side.

"Colton, you know I don't have any children."

"Only the bloodline from your family can have violet eyes, correct?"

Getting up from his chair, he walks around the large desk, resting back against it and crossing his arms over his large chest, "That's right, not all of the bloodline have violet eyes, those born with the eye color signifies that they are able to lead our clan."

"Do you have any cousins that were born with violet eyes?"

"No, I was the only one."

"Can a child be born of a family member who doesn't have violet eyes?"

"All right, what's with all of these questions all of a sudden?"

"If no one has the eyes, what happens when something happens to you?" The question is asked before I answer his.

He takes a deep breath and studies me for a moment. "That has been in discussion for a while now. Trust me, my father isn't happy about me not having any children. He can't think of a time when there hasn't been a legit heir to our kind. It has always seemed to be, this is the enigma the elders are trying to figure out. My father just points his finger at me, telling me it's hard to create the next in line if you aren't fulfilling the creating side of it."

I understand what he is implying with the "creating." Like I said, I have never seen this man with a woman. Something he said, though, has now officially piqued my interest in the new Falen in town.

"Again, Colton, I'm going to ask, what's up with all of these questions?"

"Today at the pub we met a visitor to our town."

Raidan shrugs his large shoulders, I get it that's nothing out of the ordinary. We get passersby all of the time.

"Raidan, she is a Falen."

"Not unheard of. Those from other regions have a tendency to find their way to our town. Falens don't only exist here, Colton, you know that."

"Raidan, she has violet eyes."

His violet eyes start to turn to a darker shade of purple—that's always tripped me out. Having violet eyes is one thing to get used to, but when they turn the dark purple it's unnatural.

"Are you sure?"

"Yes."

"They couldn't have been contacts? You know the young people these days, doing anything to change their appearance."

I get what he is saying and I can't say I really know this woman well, but Aydin didn't seem like the type that was worried about changing her appearance.

"I would say I'm almost a hundred percent sure that is not the case, Raidan."

He pushes his large frame away from the desk and starts for his office door. "Where are you going?"

"We are going back to town, I think we need to figure out who this young woman is and how she has come about having the eyes of my family."

Driving through town, I instantly spot Aydin as she is exiting the bakery. Pulling the Jeep over along the sidewalk, I look over at Raidan to see what he has planned.

"You have spoken to her already, correct?"

I only nod in response. I'm not sure if you can say our brief encounter was actually a conversation.

Looking out the window, I watch as she takes a seat at one of the outside tables alone. She turns in our direction.

"Damn." Raidan's words are low but I hear the disbelief in his tone.

"Do you know her?"

He shakes his head no, but his eyes are telling me something completely different.

"I'm going to stay here, you go see what she will tell you."

"Anything specific you want to know?"

"Just who she is." His eyes haven't left Aydin. He doesn't look mad, but upset.

Getting out of the Jeep, I head across the street and in the direction of where Aydin is sitting at an outside table eating a cupcake.

"Eating alone again?" I watch as Aydin dips her finger into the frosting and then into her mouth. My back shivers and the intense vibration is beginning again.

She doesn't respond to me, she doesn't even look up. She just continues to dip her finger into the frosting and then proceeds to lick it off.

Pulling out the chair across from her, I invite myself to join her. She licks her finger one last time then finally her eyes look up at mine. Her eyes deepen in color just like Raidan's. That answers that question. Eye color is definitely real.

"I was all right eating alone."

"No one should eat alone."

She studies me for a moment and that's when I notice her slight movement in the chair, almost like she is uncomfortable. She presses her back hard against the back of the chair and that's when I figure it out, she is just as affected as I am when we are in the vicinity of each other.

"Your senses are a little more intense than usual?"

Her eyes narrow and instantly she sits straight up in the chair again. She leans across the table and it takes every ounce of willpower to not grab her by the arm, haul her across the table into my arms, and fly away with her, but we are out in public and even though most of this town is some kind of shifter, there are humans as well, even if they're just passing through.

"My senses are on high alert but only because I have a strange guy who seems to be following me around in a town that I know nothing about. So like any typical woman, my senses are very normal right now."

She is lying and I can see it shining in her eyes. Falens have strength beyond most, we don't scare easily, female or male.

"You don't have to pretend with me, don't you sense me?"

The chair scrapes loudly on the sidewalk as she quickly stands and starts to walk away from me. I'm up and out of mine instantly, following her. It's unusual for a Falen to take flight from fear, but I saw it in her eyes for a small moment before she turned to walk away. None of this is making sense to me but I'm going to clear it all up.

I follow behind her. I know she knows I'm here, but she hasn't turned to look at me. Her back is still very rigid and I can tell it is taking everything in her to not run from me. We are in public right now and I'm not going to make a scene.

She rounds the corner of the building, which will put us out of sight. The sun is pretty low so it's casting a darkness. That is a sign she isn't scared for her safety, so something else is going on that she is trying to get away from me for.

"Are you done running yet?"

Her movements are so quick it's actually a little impressive. Controlled and to anyone else probably not noticeable, but to a Falen eye the control she expresses is amazing.

"Colton, right?" I nod to confirm that she has my name right. "I don't know what you want, and I'm sorry if I made any impression that I'm interested, but I'm going to put it very straightforward for you. I'm not interested."

"Most Falens don't have violet eyes."

Her eyes instantly drop, like that is going to change the fact that I have already noticed them. She starts shifting foot to foot and looking as though she is going to run, but there is also pain etched in her face and that is confusing to me.

My senses are in overload. I am fighting every impulse to extend my wings and more so not because I'm afraid of who will see, it's pretty dark and I could get out of sight pretty fast, but because I am in fact losing control of it. It's the very reason I refuse to allow it to happen, I never lose control.

"Where does your eye color come from?"

"What is a Falen?"

"I sensed you the moment I walked into the pub, you don't have to play dumb."

Her eyes shoot back up to mine, anger, definitely anger in them now. "Look, you are freaking me out and I would appreciate it if you just leave me alone."

"Falens don't freak out."

"All right, you are officially weird and I'm done." She turns and starts to quickly walk.

I have no idea why she won't admit it, but I have one sure way she can't hide from it. I pull my shirt off, tucking it into the back of my pants, and quickly catch up with her. Wrapping my arms around her waist, our feet leave the ground and within seconds we are high above the town.

There isn't much time for her to say anything or scream. I let her go and watch as she falls quickly back to the ground, this is how sure I am of her being a Falen. I watch as she falls, the sky is almost dark now and I'm about to lose sight of her. I'm not questioning my choice to drop her, but when she falls almost out of sight I start to descend, and that's when I see a white flash heading in the direction of the thick trees behind the town.

AYDIN

My mind is spinning in a million directions. I'm shocked at first when my feet leave the ground and before I can register what is really happening we are already high in the sky, heading straight up. I glance quickly over my shoulder right before he lets me go to fall just as quickly back to the ground. I see his brown wings and that is what almost causes my death. I'm so amazed that someone else has wings that I almost forget to open mine. I blink a couple of times before I realize the ground is quickly approaching.

I hear my jacket rip and fall from my body as my wings extend to their full width. Once they release, the sharp stabbing feeling in my spine finally disappears. Quickly making my way into the trees, hoping no one sees me, I finally find ground and slump back against one of the large trees trying to catch my breath.

Colton has wings! How is that possible? Honestly I didn't think I could be the only one, but then again I have never met anyone else, or now I think maybe I have and didn't know it.

"Again, I'm going to ask, who are you?"

Colton's voice makes me jump and then anger boils up and I completely lose it. "You dropped me! Are you insane?" Marching up to him, I stop only inches away from him as the intense vibration down my spine shakes my entire body once again.

"You wouldn't admit who you are, so I decided to show your hand for you."

"What made you so sure I could fly?"

"Like I said, I sensed you the moment I walked into the pub. I knew you were a Falen. Trust me, I don't just drop women out of the sky for pleasure."

"A Falen?" He has used that word a lot and I'm starting to think that should mean something to me.

"You are kidding, right?"

"Obviously my largest secret is out, that's my wings, why would I be kidding about not knowing what a Falen is?"

"You are a shifter and you don't know what kind?"

I found out very young that I had wings and nothing since then has made me really freak out until today when this man walked into the pub and I almost lost complete control of something I have hidden my entire life. Now not only am I still wanting to lose complete control with this man standing in front of me, but he is talking about Falens and shifters. I'm starting to freak out again.

"Humor me and start explaining." I take a couple steps back, hoping the vibration in my body will relax a little.

"Falen, half human, half falcon. Have you seriously never known what you are?"

I had done some research on the type of wings I have and I did find out they most resemble a falcon, but with no one to ask, how the hell am I supposed to know what I'm considered? I just figured I was a freak all of my life. No one until now has ever approached me and said, "Hey, you are a Falen, too."

"Aydin, one of your parents has to be a Falen."

"Well, it isn't my mom."

"Then who is your father?"

"Good question, he left my mom before I was born. I…"

"What is your mother's name?"

The deep voice that interrupts me comes from our left and I feel like I should know who it is. I turn just as a large figure, wings proudly extended out to full width, walks out from the trees. Once he walks a little closer a humming starts in my chest and a sense of calm and protectiveness washes over me. The man has to be in his early fifties, well built, but what catches my attention over everything is the violet eyes. No one has ever had my eye color and here I am in this strange, cute little town, with one guy who dropped me out of the sky and one with violet eyes like mine.

"Aydin, how old are you?" The man's voice is deep, but soothing.

"Twenty-five today, actually."

"Who is your mother?" he asks me again.

I knew it! He knows, I can read it in his eyes, and all I want to do is get away. I thought if I ever had the chance to meet the man that left my mom alone and broken-hearted I would have so much to say, but now that he is standing in front of me all I want to do is take flight.

I don't realize I'm crying until I feel the cold chill of the tear running down my cheek. Colton takes a couple steps toward me and I have to fight the need to walk into his arms. What the hell is going on with me?

"Kristine." Her name echoes through the trees in his deep voice.

Just hearing her name on his lips, that's all it takes and I lose it. Before I know it, I'm in the air and trying to get away from the pull Colton has on me and the man who left us twenty-five years ago.

COLTON

"You need to go after her, Colton."

My wings have had a mind of their own since I walked into the Storybook Pub and I laid eyes on the violet-eyed visitor to our small town. They are fully extended and I'm fighting the need to go after Aydin.

"Why do I need to go after her? With the exception of our two very brief encounters, and of course dropping her out of the sky, I'm sure I'm not what she needs right now. Did you not know that she existed?"

Raidan doesn't answer, but he doesn't have to. I can see it written all over his face. His surprise is just as genuine as Aydin's was moments before she took off and left. Even more strange is that right now I have to ball my fist to keep from walking over to the man that has raised me since my father's death and punching him in the face. It has been an impulse I have had to hold back since the first tear fell from Aydin's eyes.

Raidan pointed down at my fist, "That reason right there is why you need to be the one to go to her. Is it hard to control your wings when she is near you? Do you feel such an intense vibration down your spine that it's almost painful? Is the need to protect her so strong that right now you want to beat the hell out of me for hurting her?"

The reason these questions are being asked is confirmation that something stronger is happening here than I am prepared for or have been taught, and Raidan seems like he may have the answers.

"Why do I have these feelings, the loss of control, the need to punch you?"

Raidan's sad laugh is surprising. Something deeper is going on inside of him as well. "She is your mate."

"What?"

"In my family, our mates are basically picked for us by destiny. It's the way it assures our control at the top. We are the only family that is encouraged to take another Falen as a mate. The purity of the bloodline of our species, for example the violet eyes, to ensure our next leader. The percentage of human/Falen relationships that will not produce a violet-eyed leader is about ninety-nine percent. I met Kristine, Aydin's mom, and I fell head over heels, she was the one. Strangely I had all the same instant reactions to her that I should have had with my mate. I tried everything to find out if she was a Falen and somehow the sense was being hidden, but she was human. My father called, it was time for me to step up and it was forbidden for me to bring her back. I needed to find a woman who could assure the next leader. I have never felt for another woman, human or Falen, the same that I have for Kristine."

My head is spinning. I am hearing Raidan's words but they are in the background of my mind, trying to settle on the fact that Aydin is my mate. I am the chosen one to mate with the next leader of our kind. How can that be love, though?

"Colton, finding your mate is beyond anything most of our kind can even imagine. Everyone in any species hopes to find their perfect match. When you are chosen, it is led right to you when the time is right. That's one reason I have never found another, I knew no one would make me feel like Kristine did and it was my way of getting back at my father for making me leave her the way I had to."

"I think this is what you need to explain to Aydin, Raidan. She is your daughter. She just found her father. I don't think she even knew what kind of world she was a part of and has had to hide her whole life. Now you want me to go to her and tell her we are meant to be together? I think that may be a little bit of an overload for anyone. My mind is whirling and I'm just finding out the simple part of it all."

"Colton, falling in love slowly isn't simple, having it smack you like a train head-on is anything but simple. She doesn't want to talk to me, she feels the same pull to you that you feel to her. She will want to take comfort with you."

The pull is intense right now. Usually after we have a little distance between us, the vibration settles, but right now it is actually more severe than any other time we have been close.

"Colton, she needs you just as much as you need to go to her right now. Trust me, go to her."

I can't deny the pull any longer, it's painful and I feel like I'm being ripped apart. My wings take action of their own and before I know it, I'm high above the ground.

AYDIN

I try not to draw too much attention when I enter the house and head to my room. I don't want to talk to anyone except my mom, but how am I supposed to tell my mom what just happened? I just met my father. The man that captured my mother's heart and then just threw it away. I'm still working on registering everything in my mind, I think it's best if I hold off on calling her right now.

The vibration up my spine is more intense than it has been all day. The room feels stuffy and I feel like I can't take in a solid breath. Walking over the window, I open it and welcome the cold breeze that instantly washes over my body. Taking a couple deep breaths of the cool air, I try to will my wings to settle. Colton is nowhere near me. Maybe the vibration wasn't because he was near, maybe I read that wrong. It's different this time. I don't feel like they are going to burst from my back, but I feel like my body is pleading for something it isn't getting.

Lying down on the bed I curl up in a ball, the cool air against my back. I want to hate the man that I met today, I want to leave this town and act like I never met him, but there is something stopping me from both. I saw the sadness in his eyes. He wasn't cocky, didn't act like my mom was no big deal. It was the same sadness I see in my mom's eyes.

Twenty-five years I have wondered how it could be that I am like I am. I didn't know what caused it, if I was the only one. I'm a Falen. Colton said he could sense me when we met earlier today. He knew I was a Falen. Half human, half falcon. This only happens in books written by an imaginative writer. I have always known the truth that everyone else believed to be the imagination.

Tears spring to my eyes once again as the pain along my spine is becoming unbearable. Maybe I shouldn't have flown away so quickly. The only ones who can answer why this is happening would be Colton or my father, and I have no idea where to find either.

Air rushes into the room and against my back, blanketing me in comfort right when I think I can't take any more of the pain. I feel the bed dip and strong arms wrap around me. You would think this would be an instant fight or flight moment, but all I want to do is curl deeper into his warmth.

"I've got you, Aydin," Colton's deep voice whispers in my ear.

"I don't understand what's happening to me."

"Take a couple of deep breaths, let me hold you for a few minutes and then we'll talk."

This man is a complete stranger to me and yet I have never felt more comfortable around someone in my life. His arms instantly soothe me, but I want more, I just don't know what.

Turning, I bury my face in his chest and that's when I feel his wings surround the two of us almost cocoon-like; it's a very intimate feeling. I'm not sure how long we lay like this and I don't care. The vibration along my spine is gone and I'm afraid if I move away from him it will return.

His hands are slowly running up and down my back and creating a different sensation along my spine. My wings feel like they are following each movement of his hands. I no longer feel the need to scream from pain and frustration, but now I need more. I need Colton!

His warm chest is an invitation to my lips and I can no longer hold back the need to kiss him. Right above one strong pec, I lightly brush my lips across his warm skin. I hear his deep intake of breath and a very low rumble vibrates under my lips. This encourages me to keep exploring. With his wings wrapped tightly around us I can't move much, but my hands have the freedom to trace his back and along his wings. With the first touch of my hand against his wings, they shiver around me and the groan that escapes Colton is very animalistic. This just drives the need in me to continue and ask for more.

I don't feel shy, which I thought I would. Instead I feel empowered, like I hold all the control with this immaculately-built man wrapped around me. This feels right and the warm sensation flowing through me is foreign. I don't understand what it means, but I know I want it to continue.

His hands begin to move against my body and the temperature in the room instantly triples. He wastes no time with small foreplay, his hands are under my shirt and capturing both of my breasts. I didn't even notice that his wings had moved from around us but he now has me under him, pressed deep into the soft bed.

Our eyes lock and there is no amount of strength in me to look away from them, it's like I'm in a trance. My back arches, begging for more of his touch. Nothing could have prepared me for when his lips touch mine. Bolts of energy shoot through my body and a need so strong hums in my core.

This should be scaring the hell out of me, but it feels so right that all I want is more. "Please, Colton," I hear myself beg.

"Aydin, I don't know what's happening between the two of us," his voice is very low and husky.

"Me either, but please don't stop."

The speed that my clothes are removed is almost comical and I hear a small giggle bubble out of my own throat.

I watch as Colton's eyes literally worship my body, it makes me feel beautiful. I can't stop running my hands over his body, feeling the contour of his muscles and feeling them flex under my hand each time I touch him.

His head dips and his tongue circles one nipple; my body arches, begging him for more. My hands bury into his hair and press him tighter to me, giving him full permission to take more. He sucks hard and my hips flex up toward his.

He kisses my neck and then claims my lips, his tongue finding mine, his hardness teasing me, his hand working some kind of magic on each of my nipples.

I run my hand down the length of his back, over his backside and then around to wrap around his hard length. Stroking my hand up the full size of him only excites me more. Running my thumb over his tip, I feel the proof and need he has for me and I can't wait any longer. I guide him to me, letting him know what I want.

His hand wraps around my wrist and he pulls my hand away from him and above my head. I'm about to complain when I feel the tip of him, just outside the most heated part of my body. My hips thrust up, begging. He begins to enter me and then stops.

I look into his puzzled eyes, "Aydin, you haven't..."

No, I haven't! This is my first time and I thought I would be scared, but there isn't an ounce of fear anywhere in my body. This feels the opposite. It feels right. This is where I'm supposed to be and it's supposed to be with Colton. I may not have known I was a Falen and I may not understand everything about what that means or what it makes me, but there's one thing I have learned in twenty-five years—my senses are never wrong.

I believe my next move surprises both of us the same. With strength I didn't even know I possessed, I flip the two of us over, my wings springing out of my back, and I am now straddling Colton. Before he can stop me again I take him deep inside of me with one thrust. There is a moment of pain as I feel myself give to his fullness, but nothing is more amazing than having him deep inside of me. My wings are fluttering and there isn't a moment to think. Colton's hands are on my hips, controlling the movement. I may have taken charge, but I'm new at all of this and he seems to know exactly what I need and the pace.

The vibration is back but this time it just intensifies the need in my core. Colton's hands are pulling hard at my nipples now, my hands are behind me grabbing his thighs and helping me thrust my hips harder against his.

"Aydin, I need to know you are close."

Colton sits up, his wings are now fully extended with mine, the tips almost touching. His mouth captures one breast and his teeth catch my nipple between them. His hands are once again on my hips as he uses his strength to drive deeper into me.

That's when it happens, nothing could have prepared me for the bolts of electricity. His wings' tips touch mine at the same time he thrusts one last time deep inside of me and that's it, the room explodes in color, my body shakes with electrical shock and all I can do is begin to rock harder against him once again as I feel his warmth fill me. I'm not sure how I am doing this, my nails are deep into his back and my release is almost painful, but I need more of him.

I'm once again under him and without missing a moment in our movement, Colton is now using his strength to fulfill the need I'm feeling. His hands are wrapped tight in my long hair, his mouth is in full control of mine. The deeper his tongue goes the harder his hips thrust. I thought the first release was insane, but it is nothing compared to the intensity of the power shaking through my body at this moment. If not for his mouth on mine, this whole house would hear what is happening. His hips pull back one last time and with the final thrust, we meet together in an explosive fire as my release rocks my body and sends me into a black void.

THE MORNING LIGHT shining bright through the window is what wakes me. The heavy arm around my waist and the warm body behind me, holding on like I'm his life line, reminds me of what happened last night. His breathing is light and in a steady rhythm, a sign that he is still asleep. I have so many questions and how I feel right now just adds to the list. I'm not sorry last night happened. There are no regrets, quite the opposite, my body has a constant hum of wanting him again. This feels right, this is where I'm supposed to be.

I just slept with a man for the first time and I only knew him for a day, and right now I can't get over the feeling that this was supposed to happen. We were meant to find each other, I was meant to wait for him.

The only unsettling feeling I have right now is how I feel about meeting my father last night. Now that I have settled down and think back to last night, I remember seeing pain and sadness in his eyes when he spoke my mother's name. I was too angry last night to pay attention or ask more questions.

COLTON

"You are going to have to talk to him."

She has been awake for a little while now. This mate thing is a little insane. I knew the moment she woke up. The feelings she has gone through in the last fifteen minutes I have felt as well.

The silence stretches throughout the room. "Aydin, he is the only one who can answer all the questions you have regarding him and your mom."

"You are right and I know you are. I'm just trying to register everything from the past twenty-four hours and my mind is in overload."

I can only imagine what's going through her mind. I grew up knowing what I was and who my parents were. I even had a man take me under his wing after my father's death. That same man who should have been a part of this woman's life.

"Have you really never known what you are?"

She tries to pull out of my arms, but I'm not ready to let her go so I tighten my arms around her. She takes a deep breath and relaxes in my arms again.

"I obviously knew I was different, I mean I have wings that spring from my back, and then to add to that I have purple eyes. No one else has any of that. I've grown up alone, no friends really. Mom homeschooled me until I was in high school and we were sure I had control over them. I can only imagine what my mom has gone through, trying to keep me safe but wondering why her child has wings. This stuff only happens in books, right? Growing up, I pushed myself to see what I could and couldn't do."

She twists her body to look over her shoulder at me and I finally release my hold on her enough so that she can twist around and face me fully.

"You asked me yesterday if I sensed you, that I should have known who you were because you knew what I was. I had a sensation, I just had no idea what it all meant. You walked through that door and I've never been that scared that I was going to expose myself, it was like I had no control over my wings. I have never wanted to run out of a building so fast, but I don't have a take-flight personality, I refuse to have to hide so I learn to control everything."

This woman is amazing to me. I don't think I would have handled the situation the same. Her eyes are searching mine, she is struggling to ask me something.

"Aydin, I will answer any questions you have. Remember, fight not flight." I remind her of her words.

"Why is this all right?" Her hand comes up and rests on my chest right above my heart, "Why are we so right?"

I was expecting her to wake up this morning and freak out, but she didn't. Instead her body has rubbed against me slightly at times in a teasing fashion.

"This is a little new to me as well, and I definitely have a few more questions for Raidan, your dad, about it. He explained it very briefly to me last night. I guess we are mates. There was an instant connection between the two of us that brought us together. This is so natural because you and I are supposed to be together, we are the other's half."

Her eyes squint as I see her trying to decide if she is going to believe me or if I just handed her a pile of crap since she slept with me last night.

"I think it's time to go and have a talk with my dad."

WE SHOWER TOGETHER, which again Aydin surprises me by how responsive she is to me. Shower time isn't rushed and this time I'm able to appreciate her fully and in the light. For someone who hasn't done anything with a man before, her natural instincts can't be questioned.

If you would have asked me yesterday morning if I was ready to settle down with one woman, I probably would have laughed at you while walking away shaking my head in disbelief. I walked into the Storybook Pub and my life has shifted completely. I don't want to be far enough away that I can't touch her and the closer we get to Raidan's house, an instinct to protect her is so powerful I want to convince her to wait and talk to him later. I don't want her to hurt. This needs to be done, though, and I know that. It should be done between the two of them, but I'm not leaving her alone.

This house is like my second home, so I don't even knock, I just open the front door and stand back as Aydin enters before me.

"You and Raidan must be pretty close?" She looks at me with a questioning look as she steps around me and enters the house.

"I owe Raidan a lot, but we can talk about that later."

She follows me through the house and up to his office. I don't even knock, he knows we are here. Opening the door, this time I lead the way into the large room, Aydin holding my hand and following right after me.

"Hello, Colton, Aydin. Colton, why don't you give Aydin and me a little time."

Aydin's hand tightens around mine, she doesn't want me to leave. Looking at Raidan, he smiles and nods. He understands I'm not going anywhere.

AYDIN

I'm not sure I'm ready to face this man alone and right now Colton seems to be my anchor. There are questions that I need answered, but my anger from last night is starting to return. Colton's touch is soothing that anger enough to keep me here.

"Your connection is strong. I couldn't have picked a better man for you, Aydin."

Picked a better man? Who in the hell does this man think he is to me? His blood may run through my veins but that doesn't mean he gets to play the father role with me.

"I'm not sure what makes you think you have anything to say about the matter."

Raidan rounds the large desk and leans his large frame against the front, pointing at the two large chairs in front of him, "Please, have a seat. I know you both have questions and I won't be hiding anything from you. Both of your lives are about to change drastically."

I'm not sure if I'm prepared to be that close to this man, but Colton moves forward and I follow, might as well get this over with.

"What question would you like answers to first?" He directs his question straight at me.

"I think you should explain why you left my mom without a word."

"Leaving Kristine was one of the hardest things I have ever done in my life. Just for the record, I had no idea she was pregnant."

"My mom has said that, she told me she found out shortly after you left. She had no way to get ahold of you to tell you, though."

"Our family has been in the highest power of the Falen community since the beginning. Only the ones with violet eyes are born leaders. In order for a Falen to have a violet-eyed Falen is to mate with another Falen. Most Falens mate with humans, except the head of the community, we are the ones who take another Falen. Your mate is matched by destiny, you are led to each other." He moves a hand between Colton and I.

"You are saying Colton and I are put together by destiny?"

"Yes, the two of you can't be apart now that you have found each other. Don't think of it like an arranged marriage, but more destiny brought your love together as a gift."

This should be freaking me out. I have just been told a man I have known for only a day is going to be my mate for life, but something tells me it's right. That's why last night I gave myself to him and why this morning we blended together as one.

Colton isn't bolting for the door either. Instead, he grabs my hand and squeezes it. It all just feels right.

"So you are saying you are the leader of this Falen community?"

"No, Aydin, I'm saying I'm the leader of all Falens."

"How was I born with violet eyes, if it only happens when you mate with another Falen? My mother isn't a Falen."

"That need for Colton you feel, that vibration of excitement you have when he is around, the pain you feel when you are hurting and he isn't around, that is what happens when you find your mate. Not everyone senses all of that and it's only supposed to happen between two Falens. I had all of that with your mom. I fought with the idea that she was a Falen and I just didn't sense her, but she wasn't. We were in love, she was my world. One night I received a call from my father, it was time for me to take his spot and he was forbidding me to bring your mom back. She couldn't give our family the next leader. The hardest thing I have ever done in my life was walk out of your mother's life, but since birth it has been pounded into me that I was going to take over and it was bigger than anything I may want."

I'm trying to understand, but I could never imagine leaving the ones I loved. "I would have fought for love."

"I don't doubt it, Aydin, you are very strong, stronger than myself I am learning. You should not exist as the next leader, you are half human, but again destiny is making the plans. I just wish I would have known years ago, it would have stopped all the pain."

"Pain?" I think back to the pain I felt last night, it was something I couldn't explain and hope to never feel again.

"When a Falen is away from their mate their pain is physical. I have learned to live with that pain for the past twenty-five years."

My heart breaks. If this man has had the pain that I felt last night for twenty-five years and has had to learn to live with it, that speaks volumes for the love he has for my mom.

"Why have you never found another mate?"

"One reason was to get back at my dad, he isn't very happy that I haven't mated, he is worried the leadership of our kind will be moved to another family. He pulled me away from the one I loved, I pulled what he loved away from him. Most of all, though, it's because I mated with your mom, my heart belongs to her. Once you mate it's meant to be that way, I didn't want to settle for something with no meaning."

Looking over at Colton, he smiles at me, "Looks like you are stuck with me."

Shrugging, I smile back, "Could be worse I guess."

Raidan closes the space between us and squats down in front of me. "Aydin, please believe me when I say if I would have known about you I would have been in your life. I can't imagine what it was like growing up a Falen and having no one to teach you. I am very proud to be your father and I will not be walking out of your life from this moment on."

As much as I want to be mad at him I can't. He didn't know, and I don't quite understand everything related to my family and where they stand in this world. He left my mom, but I think he has suffered enough pain because of that action. Sitting forward in my chair, I wrap my arms around the giant of a man in front of me, and hug my father for the first time.

I don't know how long we sit like this, but I'm afraid if I let go I am going to wake up and find this all to be a dream. My life has never been normal, I think that's why none of this scares me. The opposite actually.

"I have so many more questions, but I'm starving as well. How about we head back to the pub and grab some lunch, we can talk some more there," I suggest.

Walking into the Storybook Pub, I look around and smile. What a difference twenty-four hours can make. I walked into this place yesterday at about the same time as now and had no idea why I was led to this location. Looking over at the bar, I see Kole standing there with a knowing smile. Soon, someone is going to have to explain his part in everything to me as well, he isn't just a bartender.

"Kole," Colton acknowledges him as we walk to a table.

"And their story begins." I hear Kole's words as we walk past.

Learn more about Tonya Clark:
https://Linktr.ee/AuthorTonyaClark

Also by Tonya Clark:
    Sign of Love Series
    Shift
    Retake

FOR ONE LASS

NAOMI SPRINGTHORP

**One night changed my life.
His darkness became my light.**

Sub-genre: Contemporary Romance
Relationship: Male/Female

A RAINY NIGHT

When you take a vacation, you should vacate. Sometimes I think I take it a bit too far, but what would life be without experience? For some, the getaway may be a tropical island or an exotic rainforest. For others, a ritzy hotel surrounded by culture. For me, it was simply walking into the Storybook Pub.

I don't know what I was doing there. I had to get out and went for a walk. My life had become mundane. I was bored with it and my circumstances weren't going to change. I'd never been one to run from my responsibilities and commitments, simply vacate them temporarily. Nobody needed to know.

It was a dreary night and the rain began to pour. I didn't turn back. I moved forward and ducked under an awning to escape the rain. I stood there watching the rain fall heavier from the sky when the clouds opened with a roar of thunder. Chilled by the dark wet night that continued to get wetter, warmth and light from the establishment lending me its awning was inviting. I tucked myself into a dry corner and gazed through the window observing the patrons of the Irish pub. I was drawn in by the warmth shining through the window of the Storybook Pub. Odd that I'd walked here hundreds of times yet never saw the establishment before. It's as if it appeared out of nowhere to invite me in for the night, and I didn't turn it down.

The patrons were all in groups, partying to their hearts content. The servers were everyone's friends yet moved with clockwork efficiency. The barkeep was telling a never-ending story to whoever would listen, as he filled glasses up and down the bar. I sat off to the side and watched it all over the top of my menu. Chilled, I reviewed the drink menu with house cocktails, Irish beer, and ciders. The servers were all young ladies wearing tight jeans and dress shirts unbuttoned to show off their cleavage. I'd seen worse and imagined it helped with their tips.

THE DARK

I'd started to read the storybook left on the table when he walked up to me and spoke in his Irish accent, "Welcome. Would you like to order or just getting out of the rain tonight?" Where the gorgeous man came from, I have no idea. He simply appeared like the pub in the first place. His presence made my belly flutter before he said a single word. His sexy unkempt jet-black hair hung into his face like a shield for his eyes. But, not enough to hide his piercing ice blues. He was tall and slender with very little fat on his body, if any at all. The closer I looked the more I saw and my intrigue grew. Tentacles of tattoos reached out of his long sleeves, as well as up his neck to the underside of his chin. I wondered where else they went and if he was completely covered.

"I'd love a drink."

"I suggest a house cocktail. They all tell you a different story."

"Pick the story for me, please."

"I'd love to, lass," he nodded and walked away. I watched, enjoying the view of his tight buttocks and swift steps.

I sat in my alcove waiting for the server to return with my drink, anxious to try the drink he chose for me and to hear him speak to me again with his wonderful sexy accent. What is it about an accent? Is it simply how much it stands out compared to the general population of men? It wouldn't stand out if I were visiting Ireland. Then again I might find many men attractive there if they spoke to me like my waiter did. There's always something exotic and tempting about things that are different.

The bar and walls are solid dark woods. The walls are covered with a mixture of plaques featuring Irish blessings, and ads for Guinness, Magners, Jamesons and Paddy. Dimly lit throughout, but brighter in the very back of the pub where I can hear a band running through their sound check. My alcove is fairly private with its black cushioned curved booth bench and tufted high back with brass accents. Perfect for a couple to rendezvous.

I watched my waiter standing at the bar, talking to the bartender. The bartender was a well-built, average-sized man with short light-brown hair that was long on the top, kind of standing with a mind of it's own. The barkeep had a mischievous look in his green eyes and they gleamed when he was mixing up a drink. He turned and examined me boldly, then made a drink and passed it off to my waiter.

I wonder what my waiter's name is. I didn't notice a name tag or anything. He didn't introduce himself using a name. Something extremely proper and Irish that was given to him by his mother. I'll bet he hates it. It's not appropriate for his shadowed persona and ominous tattoos. I wonder how his tentacled appendages connect, what was hiding under his black clothes. I need his name.

"Paddy is here to tell your story," he leans in and says lightly.

"Thank you, Paddy," I pick up the highball glass and take a sip of the concoction.

He chuckles, "Paddy is the drink. Kole made a Gingered Paddy for you. It's Paddy Whiskey with simple syrup and muddled ginger. He thinks he can look at people and know what they want to drink."

The strong flavorful drink is refreshing and warming at the same time. "He may be right." I take another drink and feel it.

"Wonderful, lass. Let's not tell him and have it go to his head now." He grins, "May I get you anything else?"

"Your name? Maybe another of these drinks."

His voice low, "Ciaran."

"That's unique," I gaze at him intrigued.

"Not really. It's quite common. I share the name with Ireland's first born saint and many more after him."

"A saint? Your parents must be religious."

"No, mother has always been simple and obvious. It means "little dark one" and I was born with a head full of thick dark hair." He grins again, more mischievously, "I don't think she knew how dark I'd become."

"Did you follow your name or did your name follow you?"

"I think of myself as the darkest one." He leans into my ear and whispers, "There's nothing small about me."

"Oh."

"Don't mean to offend. Simply stating facts." He stops, "Let me get you another drink. Paddy can tell your story." He nods and walks away.

I sip on the delightful drink and slip off my coat, letting it fall on the bench around me. Paddy wants nothing more than to warm and comfort me. I glance up to find Kole watching me intently, more studying me really. Is he searching for something? What does he see? I think of myself standing in front of a mirror. Nothing special. Average build with a bit more hips than necessary and breasts to match. I've always thought of my chest as the extra weight I carry with my back and tie them down to maintain control of them. For some reason, they always want to escape. My mousy brown hair has a tousle to its wavy shoulder length, always a mind of its own which caused me to give up on it years ago. I can only imagine that I appear to be a wet shaggy dog after wandering in from the storm. I find Paddy in my hand and pound the rest of my drink at the thought. I remember that I set out on this walk aimlessly and didn't so much as paint on some lip gloss or stroke on mascara. I've been cold and colorless, probably look like I'm dead or maybe I'm wishing I were. The world hasn't been treating me well as of late. I've worked hard for everything, but it's always only been me even during the times when I'd been attached. Independent. Self-sufficient. My life, my money, control of my own orgasm.

A drink appears in front of me and I recognize the tentacled wrist that places it there. "The color in your cheeks tells me Paddy's taking care of you," Ciaran purrs at me, or maybe it was simply the combination of Paddy and his accent. "How about a bite to eat?"

"Another drink will be fine," I gaze up at the sexy man with hope. I may not look as dead as I'd thought.

"Anything for you, lass." I thought of telling him my name, but he'd already turned and walked away giving me a chance to think better of it. I like the way he calls me lass. Anything is good in his sexy accent. The anonymity of it is freeing, almost fantasy inducing.

Paddy seemed to be going down more smoothly with each glass. Waitresses were tending to their customers, flirting and providing a revealing view of their cleavage. They all had a shimmy to their step that had an extra bounce to it when they turned and walked away from the table. Kole was behind the bar still telling his continuous story. I wonder when his story started and if it's possibly endless, everyone sitting at his bar hearing an enticing piece and no one learning how it ends. He glances over at me and smiles. I return the greeting, adding a nod of my head. I should've kept to myself, I wasn't aware my actions could be taken as an invitation.

Suddenly, Kole is standing in front of me, "Are you enjoying your story? Paddy is quite the storyteller."

I smile, "The drink is delightful, but there's no story."

He furrows his brow, "Open your heart and your mind. Let Paddy in. Live your life. He won't disappoint." He winks and disappears as if he'd never been there.

I look down at the table and find another full glass. Kole must have left it. I'm not sure if it's number three or number four, I've already lost track. I giggle happily to myself, content to be in this place. I lean back and stretch my arms and legs, warmth meandering to the extremes of my limbs. Loose and relaxed, almost numb in some places.

"Lass, are you sure you don't want to order something to eat? The rain doesn't seem to be letting up, it's like a monsoon out there. It could be awhile before you wish to leave." He smiles at me and places his hand on my shoulder, "You are a refreshing sight in my section. Stay longer and have supper."

His long fingers lightly grasp my shoulder, sending an awareness shooting through my body. I reach out and pat his firm abs without thinking, "I'm enjoying the state I'm in and can't wait to find where this plot takes me. Maybe another drink?"

He angles toward me, "Maybe I should join you for one."

"That would be a lovely addition to my story," I croon and gaze directly into his eyes.

"You want me to be part of your story?" His eyes darken wickedly.

"I'd make it a special request with Paddy if I could."

Ciaran chuckles under his breath and walks away leaving me to my own thoughts. What's come over me? Paddy must be controlling my tongue or erasing my inhibitions. It's not like me to be forward or talk to any man like that.

Minutes later, the darkest one returns with drinks and smoothly slides into my booth with me. His arm winds around my middle like it belongs there. "Decided to join you for my break." I'm enveloped by his scent, a mix of the woods and cardamom with other dark spices. A young man from the kitchen sets a bowl of warm spiced nuts on the table as well as a platter of appetizers. "You are welcome to share with me." I watch as he sips a tall thick dark beer and picks at the platter with one hand until it's bare, and savor the way his other hand appreciates my curves. His hand and fingers actively explore me, moving from my hip to my thigh. He moves seamlessly in everything he does, without hitch or hesitation. Ciaran exudes confidence with every movement he makes, unconcerned with others around us. He leaves as quickly as he arrived, "I'll be back, lass."

A GLIMPSE OF LIGHT

Drawn to the music, I wander toward the back of the pub. The loud live music and energy flows from the band through the patrons that fill the dance floor. I'm struck by the brightness of the room and the light shining on the stage that somehow is reflecting and bouncing about. I survey the room and find at least half of it was at one time a walk in cooler, still covered in the cooler's interior. The rest is paneled in ornate metal tiles of different colors, all light colored or raw metal. There's no lighting on the stage, the shining light is the singer alone without any help from an electric socket. His dirty blonde hair, long on top and brushed to the side, yet still falling in his face. His full lips frame his pearl-white teeth when he smiles and the room brightens. I look closer and find myself standing in front of the stage, unsure how I got there. He's muscled everywhere, thick and solid. The plain white T-shirt he's wearing pulls at the seams as it's stretched across his broad chest, yet perfectly fitting at his waist and leaving a line of his tanned skin visible above his button-fly blue jeans. His snug-fitting jeans cup him in the front and accentuate his ass at the same time. He turns around slightly, shocked at how close I am and gleams at me with his familiar blue eyes, smiling at me flirtatiously with all of his facial features.

FOR ONE LASS

Melting like a teenage girl, I retreat to the safety of my alcove and finish my drink.

PADDY

Time was passing and my glass was always full. It had been some time since I'd seen Ciaran and the band was in full swing. Intrigued by the dark Irishman, I wanted more of him. I watched for him to walk out of the kitchen or stand at the end of the bar chatting with Kole. I found myself wondering how many tables he was serving and how many of those tables were women similar to me. Most likely, I'm not the only one. No sight of him. Maybe he left for the night or went off into a corner with another woman. It made sense. I was merely a patron in a bar, a single woman who'd come in from the rain and warmed herself with libation and heady thoughts about a certain dark waiter.

Or, maybe, could it be? This was all Paddy telling my story. The story of a woman who needed to live and experience an intoxicating world. Stepping into the pub for shelter from the rain, quite possibly could've been stepping out of reality and into the unknown.

This makes no sense. This is just a bar and I must be drunk to be thinking like this. Waiters aren't interested in their customers, especially not older women who have dragged themselves in out of the rain, wet as a dog. I'm sure they're not allowed to cavort with paying customers during work hours. It's an unending stream of constantly changing people to flirt with for better tips. Yes, that's exactly it. He's working for his tip. I'm older and appear established, perfect target.

Regardless, he's got my interest and I'm enjoying the entertainment of it all. I'd love for him to stop back by my table, maybe check in with me for a minute or two.

CIARAN'S RETURN

"How are you doin', lass? Paddy treating you well?" He grins and slides his arm around my shoulders. It had gotten louder with the band in full swing and people had been flooding in. It was almost impossible to hear myself think, let alone someone else speak. "I'd love to get you some food. What may I get for you?"

I'm drunk. No denying it. "Another Paddy please." I hesitate, "Directions to the ladies room?" Not the sexiest thing to ask for.

"I'm happy to get you another drink, but I think some food is in order." He smirks, "Nothing about all your inhibitions being lifted by drink that I don't like."

"I'll stick with the drink," I stare at him awaiting his response.

"Customer is always right. I'll get you another right away. Ladies is down the corridor to the left of the bar, keep going until you get to the end."

"Thank you, Ciaran."

I watch him walk away. He's a bit frustrated with me, though I'm not sure if he's trying to take care of me or attempting to increase his tip by adding food to the bill. I should eat some food, but I'm not going to. I haven't enjoyed a hazy state like this in too long and never with this atmosphere and company. It's silly to even think, but I'd love to keep Ciaran for myself. I'm dreaming, of course that's not a real possibility. I'm drawn to him. Different than I'd been drawn to other men. If I'm in a dream world, can I keep him just for one night? My whole body gets warm at the thought. My heart beats faster. My private parts awaken anxiously.

I get up quickly to find my way to the ladies room and be back before he returns with my refill. Walking toward the bar, Kole glances up and gives me a happy nod. I follow the bar to the left and step through the doorway. The hall is dim and lined with old photos on the walls, each individually lit and labeled with a description. They appear to be family from many years that are hung chronologically, some are black and whites. Nothing new since the wedding photo that resembles a younger version of the barkeep, labeled with the description "Introducing Mr. and Mrs. Kole O'Shea." The corridor turns and starts to descend. I continue to follow it to the end as directed. No more photos, all bare dark wood walls with the only light provided by a sliver of moon shining through a small window in a door near the end. I approach the end of the corridor and either I've missed the ladies room or there wasn't one. I turn to go back and run into a figure in the darkness.

His fingers grasp at my upper arms and pull me against him, "Ssshhhhh... Don't worry, lass." All of the air is forced from my lungs as our bodies are pressed together. He pushes me against the wall and traces the tip of his nose across my collarbone. His warm breath sends tingles down my neck. Exploring my body, his hands move down my sides to grasp my hips. He spreads my legs with his and pushed his thigh against my sex, encouraging me to rub against his leg. Hidden here in the darkness, I can't see his tentacled ink to take advantage of this closer look. I can only imagine what I would find. Do the tentacles cover the length of all his extremities? Do they continue onto his torso? Do they connect? The thoughts make me hot and curious to find out for myself. His lips are now on my neck, kissing every available surface as he finds his way to my ear. The heat of his breath is an intoxicating mix with his lips, sending shivers down my spine as he begins to nibble at my ear. Pulling at my earlobe with his lips and kissing, sucking below it. He tends to my jawline with open-mouthed kisses, stopping short of my lips. Both of his hands are on my head and his fingers tangled in my hair. He rubs his hard cock against me and I want more, but all I want to do is allow him to take me in my inebriated state. I'm his for that moment, for whatever he wishes. He places his forehead to mine and I feel his warm breath on my lips, sharing the same air with me. Insane electricity sparks between us. I want more. I want his lips to touch mine. I reach for his lips, but he steps back and is gone. I'm alone in the dark at the end of the corridor and my body is on fire. Remembering flashes of his body against mine. His exquisite lips and hard thick cock he'd teased me with. I want more. I need more.

I gaze out the window at the dark sky and moonlight. It's an ominous night that has taken over the weather and my life, but both are beautiful. The storm clouds with reflections of the moon bouncing off them as if it were their silver lining. Forceful drops of water penetrating from the sky, as if someone were playing with a hose to clean the earth and leave it refreshed. The dark one offering an escape from my everyday world, an invitation for an unexpected vacation into his.

I walk back through the corridor, the sounds of the bar getting louder and louder as I approach. The band is playing vibrant dance tunes, Kole is rambling on as he mixes drinks, large groups of men rollicking with laughter, tables of women chatting and giggling, the kitchen staff yelling back and forth across the kitchen, a couple arguing, and wait staff discussing who's drunk and needs to be bounced, all turns to an overdone fugue in my head that continues to intensify.

Needing an escape, I walk through the madness quickly toward the front of the pub and watch the rain fall. Listening carefully for the clickety sound of the raindrops hitting the ground and being blown against the glass of the window. Wanting it to overtake me from the frenzy of the pub. The storm succeeds in drowning out everything around me and I'm peaceful for only a moment before the storm echos with a raging thunder that shakes me to my core.

I'm no longer alone. His hands are on me. I don't need to look, I know who it is. I remember his hands and realize at that moment I will never forget them.

He leans into my ear and speaks softly, "Are you okay? You look in a rush, like you were heading for the door and you're all flushed." He turned to see who is watching and wraps his arms around me from behind. "You can't leave, we aren't finished yet." He smooths his fingers through my hair and down my back, gently caressing my hip. "Are you better? Come back and have another drink." He turns and walks me back to my table, making sure I'm seated and not a flight risk. Amazingly, the anxiety I'd felt releases and I'm comfortable once again in my alcove. He places his cool hand on my cheek, "I'll be back, lass."

I merely gaze up at him and nod.

He stares at me, unsure, searching the depth of my eyes. I have no idea what he's looking for or if he's found it. Probably confirmation that I'm not going to run. The coolness of his touch and his ice-blues ensure that I'm going nowhere.

He returns quickly this time with a large glass of water, another Gingered Paddy, and a plate of toast with some spread. "Try some toast for me, please. Drink some water. I don't want Kole to cut you off." His tone darkens, "You can't leave yet. I'm not done with you."

His words race through my body. He's not done with me. I grab onto his arm and pull him down to me. I kiss him below his ear and whisper, "I want more of you."

"Be careful what you ask for, lass," his voice is low and intense.

I gaze at him wide-eyed, "I'm in your world tonight and I want the full experience."

His eyes harden and his muscles clench visibly through his sleeves. "You already don't have a choice. Eat." He walks away without another word.

WAITING FOR DARKNESS

I need more. I'm growing impatient and the drink is driving my need. If I could simply have a glimpse of him. Something to settle my uninhibited, overactive mind. Did any of this happen? Am I passed out somewhere lying on a wet sidewalk?

The band is getting louder and invading my thoughts. I find myself clapping and moving to the beat. It's getting warmer and I enjoy the distraction in the comfort of my secluded booth.

Kole appears out of nowhere, "Beautiful woman! Why are you sitting here when you can't help but move to the music? Obviously you need to move to the back of the pub and enjoy the band. Dance, live a little." He reaches for my hand and pulls me up out of my comfortably secluded alcove without giving me a choice. He links his elbow with mine and leads me to the dance floor. He gives me a spin and grins impishly as he counts each time he twirls me around, disappearing somewhere around the count of ten and leaving me to dance alone in the sea of patrons reveling in the music.

THE LIGHT

I won't lie, it was thrilling to be on the dance floor in my intoxicated state. I was loose enough to dance and not care. My eyes are closed and I allow the music to move me. Not something that I'd normally do. Shaking and rubbing against other dancers, all of us enchanted by the beat the band has chosen for us. The band is playing a variety of different things from Irish ditties to pop and rockabilly, all with an Irish flair. I'd been dancing for some time when a man grabs me, appreciatively placing his hands on my hips and pulling me into him.

"How is it that a beauty like you is dancing alone?" Rolls off his tongue with a warm Irish accent.

I smiled uncontrollably, flattered and unable to connect words when I find it is the band's singer standing in front of me. I gaze at the floor bashfully.

"Well, I refuse to let that continue. I'll dance with you for the rest of the night unless you object," he states more than asks.

I don't object. Who wouldn't want this gorgeous mans hands on them? I'd been reduced to a giggle.

"My name is Angus."

"That sounds old school. Is it a family name?" I ask trying to continue the conversation like a human being instead of being reduced to a teenager. I wonder if there's a story behind his name and if his blue eyes truly are the same as Ciaran's.

"My mother named me after a chieftain lord who used his magical powers for pleasure," His eyes gleam when the word pleasure slips from his lips. "In Irish mythology, Angus is the god of love and youth. I'm not sure she considered where my name came from and if she did I don't believe she'd admit it. However, she's always felt my older brother and I balance each other out."

"Your brother?"

"Yeah, he's a waiter here."

"I've seen no waiters who resemble you. There's not another man in this building with a happy glow to them like you."

He blushes, "We share the same eyes and the same parents, but that's about it. Though often it seems we are connected deeper. I've wondered if I dream of the things he sees and does, my actions in my sleep are always darker like him and never bright. As long as I get to play with my Lovelights, their music washes away the parts that are more of a nightmare."

"Have you asked him if his dreams aren't his own?" I inquire curiously.

"In the past, but he's always been a man of thought and choice words. He'd never admit anything about himself wasn't dark."

"I'd love to be part of your light this evening," I stretch my arms up around his neck and gave him a peck on his jawline, the only place I can reach my lips to.

The muscled man immediately picks me up like I'm nothing and I find myself wrapping my legs around his waist as we sway on the dance floor. His eyes shine as he gazes into mine and his smile brightens. He presses his lips to mine and his fingers splay across my back, holding me tightly to him. It is an instant connection and I willingly push the kiss forward. His soft, full lips want more as his hair falls to tickle my nose. He sets me on my feet carefully and gives me a peck on the cheek before stepping back up on the stage. He takes the mic in his hand in time for the lyrics to begin and sings the song as he gazes into my eyes. It was romantic and familiar. I've heard the song before. "You're All I Have" by Snow Patrol. It's odd to have those eyes search my depths with the light Angus is filled with, when those eyes have been hard and dark with me all evening.

Brothers. What am I doing? This place makes me leave myself and act irresponsibly. Or maybe it's the Paddy. Regardless, how can I want Ciaran and have this moment with Angus? They're so different, yet both strong in different ways. Truly dark and light. Angus hasn't seen Ciaran with me and has no idea what's happened. Ciaran isn't done with me, his words. Though his brother might be a deal breaker for him. I'm just another woman in the bar, he probably doesn't care. What about me? Can I have both? Who do I want? I want Angus like no other, so the night can end on a positive high. But, I need Ciaran. I need his dark depths to take me with him and show me his world. I need to trace the tentacles that are painted on him to discover where they go. He's a map to darkness that I must experience.

Angus steps down off the stage with mic in hand and wraps his available arm around me. The band plays the intro to the next song, he sings from the dance floor refusing to leave me alone there. His smile brightens and he plays it up like he's singing to me. Dramatically overdoing "With or Without You" by U2. I laugh uncontrollably at his over-the-top entertaining ways. I should expect no less from a lead singer. The epitome of pleasure, love, and youth—he glows with all of it and more. He pulls me closer during the instrumental part, lifting me off my feet one-handed and kissing me sweetly. His soft, full lips taste of whisky and I wonder if Paddy is telling him a story this evening too. He's the center of attention and everyone is watching us as he nibbles and sucks tenderly at my lips right there on the dance floor. I don't know what's come over me. I pull away and he sets me back on my feet. Still dancing together with his arm snug around me. I gaze around the room and someone grabs me roughly from behind.

TAKEN BY DARKNESS

I'm snatched from Angus' arms without a word. He has a tight grasp on my hand and drags me through the crowd back to the dark corridor. His hand is holding mine high above my head against the hard wood wall and he glares at me, "Another man? And, he's my brother! Did I not make my intentions clear?" His eyes turn to ice and his tone gets colder, harder. "When I have touched you, you are mine until I am done." He shoves his body against mine, "You felt the pleasure I can give you. There's nothing like my darkness."

Something about the way he takes control and ownership of me trips a switch in my body. Any other day in my life I would've walked off on principle alone. Nobody controls me. Nobody talks to me the way he does. I decide who and when. But, this crazy night has released me from what I believed to be right and allowed me to be free. I've been given the freedom of having this fantasy at my own risk. It's now or never, and I'd be taking a chance on him getting darker, possibly too dark for me. I may not be able to escape him now and I simply don't care. I'm in completely, if only to find out what it's like to have his lips on mine, and what happens with his tattoos beneath his clothes. Who am I kidding? I want him and I'd do anything to have him, even give myself to him for his every whim. I don't speak, in response I lunge at his neck biting at the tentacle tattoo there and tracing it with my tongue, kissing it from the base of his neck up to his chin.

Ciaran pulls away before I can get to his lips and stares into my eyes, holding me at arms length. "My terms, I'll kiss you when and where I wish," he growls.

There's something hidden in the depths of his eyes that's trying to show itself to me. It's unclear yet intriguing and one more reason I would give anything to learn what makes this dark sexy man tick.

He steps away from me without releasing my hand, pulling me down the hall and into a dark room. He closes the door behind us. His hand grasps tightly around my wrist, he clicks the keys on a computer and the room lights up with monitors showing every nook and cranny of the pub. "Do you see this?" he says angrily as he points to the monitor showing the band. "I'd never do that to you," His gorgeous Irish accent even more prominent with his anger. "I'd never use you or tease you like that, especially when my woman was in the room. Angus does it every night. It's part of his show." I watch as Angus twirls another patron around the dance floor, picks her up, and kisses her. The whole time grinning at her wantonly with his perfect teeth. "You don't deserve that. You deserve better than his antics. You deserve better than me, but at least I'll give you pleasure, knowing it doesn't belong to another woman."

Pleasure. I suppose Angus was more about the pleasure than the love, and apparently gave some woman false pleasure every night. "His woman is watching?"

"She's the guitar player. They've been engaged for years and live together. She understands that his actions bring women out to see them play and accepts it." He turns to me with a dark deep tone, "I've never understood it and would never consider such actions. If I'm with you, I'm only with you. It's always been my way. Doesn't matter if it's one night, a week, longer… you deserve to be the only one if only for the moment." He turns to me and his gaze burns into my soul as he searches for something there. My inner darkness? My limits? My true desire?

"I didn't know…"

He cuts me off, "Would it have made a difference? Being aware that his woman was right there watching?"

"That's not…" I find myself stumbling over my words. Caught off guard and tongue-tied that he'd cut me off mid-sentence. "Stop! I never want to be the other woman, but that's not what I was going to say." Emotion gathers in my eyes and I take a deep breath. "I thought I was just another customer you were flirting with," I blurt out. "You vanished for quite awhile. Maybe you had left for the night or were off in a corner with another woman," realizing Paddy may have gotten the best of me. "Just forget it. Kole stole me from my alcove and said I should be dancing."

Ciaran's face hardens, "Kole? What else did he do?"

I glare up at him, "He stopped at my table to chat and left me a refill a couple times, and escorted me back to the dance floor where he twirled me around a bit until he disappeared."

"Damn it! He did it again!" Ciaran storms out of the room, leaving me behind. "Kole!" He yells.

I can't help myself, so I follow and watch from a distance. He approaches the bar, pounding his fists violently, "Kole! You did it again, didn't you? I told you to leave me out of your shenanigans!"

Kole turns and speaks calmly from the other end of the bar, "What are you talking about?" His green eyes shine, "I'm simply a pub owner covering a bartenders shift for the night." He smiles and continues to tend his bar, still telling his story to anyone who will listen.

But Ciaran isn't done, "Don't walk away from me. This shit always happens when you're here. Tell me, Kole, how many drinks did you give her? Did you add anything special? Did you give her to my brother on purpose?"

"I will say this, the lovely lady had been left alone for too long and I could see the music calling her. I helped her find her way." Kole walks directly to Ciaran and continues quietly, "Are you not satisfied with what you have? It seemed you needed something, too." I swear his pointed ears twitch and he floats when he's behind his bar, more when he's on defense. There's no denying the way his eyes shine and flash as he surveys the patrons in the pub, as if he can see things I couldn't, or maybe nobody else could. "Ciaran, you didn't need my

FOR ONE LASS

help. She needed to live a little. She's wanted you since you walked up to her table. You don't always need to be so dark, be you."

"I don't need you to tell me how to live. Keep your hands out of my life," he says angrily and is ready to jump over the bar. Then Kole nods my direction and his eyes flash. Ciaran sees me standing there observing, and his anger vanishes as he focuses on me and we are drawn together.

Our eyes lock together and his dark smile somehow brightens as he approaches me. I don't know what to expect. He'd made it clear that he was in control. I doubted that he'd kiss me. There is something coming to me from his darkness and I'd happily accept it. He wraps his arm around my neck and pulls me into him, kissing my temple. His lips are soft and silky against my skin. The warmth of his breath a caress all it's own. I'd already been awakened, and now my body was on high alert. I bite at the collar of his shirt and run my nose along his collarbone.

Kole pops his head around the corner into the corridor, "Ciaran, I've got your tables for the rest of the night. Enjoy your evening."

I was sure he'd be pissed at Kole for continuing to meddle, but he surprises me by nodding his acceptance and focusing on me. He kisses my temple repeatedly and his hands begin to wander, exploring my hips and ass.

"I think my brother is still in the house tonight. He's been after me to add something darker to our set. Ciaran! Find your way to the dance floor and we've got something to play for you coming up after this next song," Angus calls out from the back of the pub.

Ciaran takes my hand, lacing his fingers with mine and leads me to the dance floor. The Lovelights are playing a sexy song with horns and strings, "Heal Me," by Snow Patrol. Once we're in the middle of the crowd, he holds me against him and sways. One hand is on the small of my back, finding it's way to skin, and the other threads through my hair on the back of my head holding me as if I'm breakable. He brushes his lips across my forehead. My hands have a mind of their own, unbuttoning the top buttons on his shirt. I imagine what I would find hiding there waiting for me to discover it. I get a sneak peek of the black inked tentacle that's wrapped low around his neck and reaching up under his chin, I kiss it gently this time and commit it to memory. He leans down brushing his lips to mine, not a full kiss, yet enough for me to feel it in my toes. I want more. Swaying with me, his cock hardens and he rubs on me. His hold on me tightening, he kisses me open-mouthed on each cheek before moving to my mouth—it is electrifying.

STEPS INTO THE DARKNESS

The band starts to play the next song, "This one is for my brother. Never say I don't listen." "Take Me to Church," by Hozier begins, it's dark and the lyrics are a sexual metaphor. The lights have been dimmed and Angus is no longer glowing, there's a darkness that has overcome him as the vocals roar from within him. The sound of it all together is a haunting and controlling force with a sex drive. The music gets louder, engulfing us with its intensity. Everything around us ceases to exist. It's only us in this non-existent crowd and we're closer than before. The music has magnetized us and we're inseparable. Ciaran pulls back and gazes into my eyes, his own ice blue eyes have turned darker and glazed over. The corners of his lips become an almost undetectable smile as he leans in and presses his lips to mine. At that moment, my life changes. I both had to have him only for myself and knew I wouldn't be able to keep him. Yes, he'd intrigued me with his accent and tattoos, but this was more. My lustful crush had become what I needed to survive and I'd be whatever he wanted so I could have him. This world I'd been sucked into wasn't mine and I found myself never wanting to leave. I wrap my arms around him and dig my fingers into his muscled back, holding him tight and fantasizing about the ink drawn on his body as if its wrapped around him.

His lips are still on mine, I stretch up on my tiptoes not wanting to lose the contact. I'm intoxicated by his warm scent and push our kiss for more. He immediately stops kissing me and pulls away. His eyes gleam at me, dark and heavy like a wild animal. Fuck, I need to remember this is on his terms. It's what I want, too. I want him to have me the way he wants me, anyway he wants me—as long as he has me. Suddenly his hands are on my face and we're nose to nose. His gaze connects us and he devours me. His lips kiss mine with a need I've never experienced before. He traces my lips with his tongue. I open my mouth releasing a sigh and his tongue finds mine. His mouth closes over mine and he takes control with every step of our connection taking us deeper, making us hotter and needier. He releases me and grabs my hand, dragging me away from the dance floor with uneven breaths. Once in the dark corridor he holds me up against the wall and rubs against me while he holds my hands up over my head and kisses my neck. I roll against him appreciating his hard cock, I moan uncontrollably with sexual need and desire. He bites at my neck and earlobes, yet he doesn't allow me to touch him with my hands. All I have is my body to respond with and my lips at moments when I can reach him. I vine my leg around his, holding him to me as we stand there grinding against each other.

He lets out a low groan, "Are you sure? Do you know what you're asking for?"

I gaze up into his eyes, "I'm not asking for anything. I'm offering you everything."

He wraps his arm around my waist and kisses my temple as he walks me the opposite way down the dark corridor and to a flight of stairs. "You first. I'm right behind you," he instructs.

There was no light, only old wooden stairs that creak as I step on each of them not knowing where I'm going.

"Just keep going. I'm here with you," he must've detected my hesitance. "Not much further."

I hear the rain falling on something metal, it reminds me of the old patio cover outside my bedroom window when I was a child and it soothes my nerves. I have no clue where he's taking me, but it must not be far.

He's close, his warmth at my back and his breathing regulated. Sadly, I was slightly out of breath with all the stairs. But, that was quickly forgotten when he run his hand down the length of my leg and back up, ending at the top of my inner thigh with a needy manly sound. We'd reached a landing at the top of the stairs and his hands are on my hips. I reach out into the darkness for him and find him on his knees. His hands, one on each of my legs traveling from my hips to my ankles slowly, then back up on the inside and guiding me to spread my legs. His mouth is on my leggings at my willing sex and his hot breath penetrates me to my core. His hands slowly reach for the band of my leggings and slides them down over my hips, leaving them at my knees. "What have we here? I love the black lace, lass." He reaches around, squeezing my ass, "A thong as well." He places his hand on the band of my panties and hooks the front with his finger pulling them aside. He pushes his nose into my wet heat, smelling and tasting me, "You are lovely and sweet, lass. My favorite things." He pushes me back against the wall and licks me from end to end, sucking and nibbling at my folds with unforeseen skill. I whimper and move against him uncontrollably. The way he nibbles at me without biting, and licking like he could never get enough—I could never get enough. The unknown in the blind darkness adds to the heat. His repeated motions and long tongue push me to want more. I need more. He licks my seam and slides his tongue in between to taste me from the inside, slowly stroking me over and over as he delves deeper. He squeezes my ass cheeks and holds me to his mouth as he consumes me. He gets rougher with his tongue, moving to my clit and sucking hard. Still holding me to him with his strong hands and not allowing me to move. He continues to lick repeatedly and when I'm near my end he latches on and sucks harder than before. He's the only reason I remain standing, holding me to the wall with his hand splayed across my belly and his mouth slowly moving down to lap up my wetness. He groans in pleasure. His luxurious tongue tending to me more after I reach my climax.

When he pulls away and stands up, I reach down to pull my leggings up. "No, we're not done yet. Take those off," the command comes from his lips, not a request. I obey without hesitation.

THE ROOFTOP

He reaches around me and takes a key off a hook on the wall, then uses it to unlock a door I hadn't noticed was there. "It won't be cold for long. Don't worry, you won't melt or we will melt together," he pushes the door open and steps out into the rain taking me with him. We're on the roof and the only light is from the night sky. There are a couple of beach loungers with an umbrella and an ice chest off to one side, but they'd be no help having been soaked by hours of the storm. No other covering is in sight, the only shelter from the rain is inside and that isn't Ciaran's plan. "Come back here, lass." I'd walked away to inspect the roof. "Take your clothes off," he says as he strips and tosses his inside to stay dry. I stop in my tracks at the sight of him and watch as he bares himself to me and everything I'd wondered about was right there for me to see.

The tentacle I'd seen wrapped low around his neck winds around his torso multiple times. Those on his arms curl around his forearms and biceps before continuing across his shoulders and coming around to meet at his chest. There's one down his left leg that wraps similar to his arms and curls on his ass cheek. The two down his right leg crisscross a few times as they coil around his leg and when they reach the top of his thigh, one goes up the front of him to his chest and the other hugs his waist on its journey. The stark black ink in such dramatic thickness and design is striking on his pale skin. The monotone detail of the suckers and skin texture accentuate the ominous creature covering his body. I walk toward him and place my hand on his chest. Studying his ink in more detail, I find the tentacles are concealing, no, protecting his dark red heart in the formation of a Celtic love knot. I examine closer to find the words "For One Lass" tattooed there on the edge of his heart. Rather than fighting the darkness his whole life, he'd embraced it on the outside and didn't let it inside. I trace each of his tattoos lightly with my finger as he simply stands there bared to me. His brother may have been the bright light everyone was drawn to, but Ciaran was the purest heart.

His eyes turn angry, "Don't look at me like that. What's that? A look of sympathy? I don't need any of it from you. This is the true me. The inherent darkness in my soul."

"You appear dark, but your heart isn't," I speak without thinking.

"You know nothing about me. Remember I'm the dark waiter with the accent. All the women love the accent." He grabs me and claims my mouth hard, slamming me back against the wet metal door. I'm suddenly aware of how wet I am, dripping from the rain we'd been standing in. His dark hair is saturated, hanging longer and dripping as well. The storm clouds open up, pouring on us. Thunder shakes us and lightning reflects off our wet bodies.

I slick his hair back out of his face and search his eyes, "You don't have to put on an act for me. I'm yours for whatever you wish."

With no words, he lifts me and shoves his hard cock into me with my back up against the cold wet door. Repeatedly pounding into me with his thick length, he hits my wall on every pass and is still reaching deeper. "Ciaran!" I scream out and he kisses me roughly to silence me.

When he's finally sated himself all the way inside me, he pulls me from the door, "Arms around my neck. Legs around my waist." I don't respond. "Now, lass!"

I do as I'm told and he places his hands on my hips, gripping me and moving me on his cock for his pleasure. Shoving me down hard onto him. Needing to be completely wrapped in my wet heat. I bite his neck and he shoves into me even harder. I don't know what he needs, but I want him to have it. "Harder, Ciaran. Please, more. Anything you want," spills from my lips giving him permission. I'm suddenly back up against the door. He's bound my hands up above my head, tied together with my own blouse and is sucking at my breasts as he fucks me with long strokes of his huge cock. His breath turns ragged and I've already lost mine.

I'm hanging on by a thread enjoying the pleasure and pain when he starts moving faster and digs his fingers into my back, pulling me away from the door he cries out on his last few strokes, "Oh, lass!" He wraps his arms around me tight as I go with him.

REALITY

I wake up by the sunlight beating through my window in the middle of the afternoon. I'm alone and don't remember coming home. I lay there in my bed with the cat curled up to my foot, no clue what day it is and feeling as though many have passed. Everything around me is exactly the way I'd left it. Ceiling fan on low, nightlight glowing in my bathroom, grandmother's porcelain cats are all still lined up on their shelf, clean laundry stacked neatly on the dresser, my small jewelry box sitting on my nightstand with my phone charging next to it. I'm naked and sore everywhere. My dirty clothes are tossed over my desk chair. I'm warm and feel like I've been ill for days, not like I spent an evening at a pub. It was too real. It couldn't have been a dream. I look at my room through new eyes and I'm disturbed by the pale, non-descript decor. Life should be lived boldly. Color and things with thought behind them. Meek and mild may be safe, but it's not living. I stretch and attempt to sit up in bed, pulling myself up and leaning back against the pillows. I get my phone to check the date, and I haven't lost any days, but my phone has been changed to dark mode. I look at the pillows all stacked up neatly next to me except for one, a bit odd, and the blankets appear as if they've been slightly used. Then again, it wouldn't be the first time I'd tugged on my quilt and knocked over a pillow.

I walk into my bathroom and look in the mirror, surprised by the handprint shaped bruises on my hips. I shower, dress, and go for a walk in the warm sunshine to clear my head. I can't help but walk toward the pub, ready to walk in and take a look with sober eyes. As I approach the pub I find the doors chained closed. There's a new ownership sign in the window with a request for alcohol license for The Storybook Pub.

I return home quickly, confused to find the darkest red rose I'd ever seen waiting for me with a note.

You're a beautiful lass. Never forget it. I won't forget you. Make sure you live your life.

Tears stream down my face. I don't understand. It couldn't have been a dream. Startled by a noise in the hallway, I turn to find him standing there, "Ciaran?"

"Yes, lass. You're different than all the others. Am I different?"

"Yes. But, I'm completely lost."

"We'll get to it. First, I've never made sure anyone got home safe and I always walk away. I can't seem to walk away from you."

My heart pounds. I need to live my life filled with excitement and pleasure. "I don't understand. The pub isn't there."

"It was last night. Kole flew into town and wanted to try a trial night before he filed for the alcohol license. Stupid risk, but that's Kole."

"Last night was real?"

"Yes, and I'll be in charge of the pub when it opens. I need someone to keep me happy. I've been searching my whole life for one lass and it was only one night, but I've found her." He stops and wraps his arms around me, "Will you keep me, lass?"

I pressed my hand to his heart, "I offered you everything and I'll never take it back."

Learn more about Naomi Springthorp:
https://linktr.ee/naomispringthorp

FOR ONE LASS

ALSO BY NAOMI SPRINGTHORP:
    THE SWEET SPOT
    JUST A CALIFORNIA GIRL
    MUFFIN MAN

WISHES AND WHISKEY

TESSA MCFIONN

**"Wait.
You wished... for me?"**

Sub-genre: Contemporary Romance with a Twist
Relationship: Male/Female

Keep believing in magic!
♡ *Tessa McFionn*

1

A HARMLESS NIGHT OUT

"How the hell is a drink going to help me?"

Chloe hated the whine in her voice, but she had to resort to four-year-old behaviors in the hope that her cousin and life-avowed matchmaker, Melissa, would finally get the hint and let her go back to her self-imposed seclusion. Already she'd dragged her feet; she'd taken an hour to choose a coat, and had changed her shoes three times before even venturing out her front door. Not to mention, the bipolar April weather in Pittsburgh could mean anything from freezing rain, to surprise snows, to the rare balmy day. Inwardly, she'd prayed for a driving snow so she could have a legitimate excuse for her desire to remain indoors.

But it seemed the Fates were determined to screw up her night, and so, covertly flipping off the Universe, Chloe continued to stare out the window of their cozy Uber while Hurricane Melissa gave roundabout directions to a mysterious destination. Traffic was unusually light on Veterans Bridge. Perhaps the cool midweek evening had kept the smart people off the road. After crossing the Allegheny, the driver made a hasty exit and headed back toward the river on Penn Avenue.

"So where are we going, anyway?" Chloe asked. They had passed several suitable bars with no sign of slowing—the Ten Penny had zipped by, followed by the Backstage Bar and Olive or Twist. Her mouth watered as she remembered the delicious braised pork shanks she'd devoured the last time she'd splurged for a nice meal.

"Chloe Elizabeth Banning, would you just trust me?"

Chloe scoffed. "Yeah," she muttered. "Like that worked out so well the last time." Flashbacks flooded her mind: drunken businessmen braying like asses and behaving like frat boys, while unwelcome hands groped and pinched. Melissa had promised her a quiet night with some friends from work, and Chloe had stupidly believed that attorneys would make for polite company.

That was seven months ago and Chloe had remained happily confined ever since.

The buildings whizzing past the windows shifted, and the car veered away from the bridge across the Monongahela River. Relief and confusion intermingled and Chloe found her voice once again.

"While I'm glad we're staying away from the college bar scene, could you at least give me a hint as to our location?"

Am I underdressed? She glanced down at her demure, deep-plum sweater and black skinny jeans. Black suede ankle boots with a moderate heel gave her an additional two inches, leveling her out to an even five-foot-eleven, setting her out of reach for most men. Early in her dating life, Chloe had learned that tall, intelligent women spent many nights alone. Her family, insistent on seeing her married like the rest of her siblings, had fixed her up with every sports player in the area code. Yet her tastes were never for jocks, probably because all of her friends teased her about finding a man capable of handling her blue-collar temper.

Never once had she apologized for her humble origins, though, and she was not about to start, not even after rising through the ranks in the financial community.

"It's just a little farther down the road." Melissa finished the convoluted directions before she spun in her seat to face Chloe. "It's a new place that just opened. I heard about it on Instagram from Jessica. You remember Jess? She's always out and finding new places. So anyway…"

Chloe tuned out her friend's steam train of words as they filled the backseat. *Great,* she thought, *a spot recommended by the snobby social butterfly.* Melissa rambled on, gesturing broadly and tossing her perfect blonde spirals. Chloe scowled. Knowing that another beauty pageant queen was waiting for them at their ultimate destination didn't help matters. *Now I really feel underdressed.*

The sedan rolled to a halt in front of a rustic-looking building, its wooden facade out of place in the industrial setting. A plain-painted board announced the odd bar's name.

"Storybook Pub?" Chloe read, unable to hide her crestfallen tone. Melissa had already bounded out into the cold night and yanked open the door keeping Chloe safe inside.

"Oh, don't be such a grouch. Come on." Her friend grabbed her arm and dragged her out and up the two steps to the faded blue front door. She had just enough time to sling her purse over her shoulder and not slip on the slick steps before she stopped in front of the cashier's window. Melissa bounced beside her while Chloe rummaged through her small bag, assuming the place would have a cover charge.

"Make a wish."

Chloe frowned and looked up from her search. Behind the glass sat a young, fresh-faced boy. Freckles dotted his milk-and-honey skin while curious green eyes patiently peered at her. Black hair fell across his forehead, and she thought she detected a hint of an accent in his strange request.

"I'm sorry. How much?"

The boy shook his head, an impish grin tugging his lips upward. "Just need ya to make a wish."

Chloe floundered, trying to think of something witty that wouldn't make her sound pathetic or hopelessly romantic. Tall, dark, and handsome flashed into her mind, but she quickly derailed the thought.

"Uhh, I—"

"She wishes to have a strong, sexy man sweep her off her feet and—"

Chloe slapped her hands over Melissa's mouth before Melissa could continue with her loud over-sharing of Chloe's lackluster love life. "Omigod," she said. "Boundaries?" Then she turned her focus back to the smiling boy and blurted out the first thing that came to mind. No, make that the second thing. "A better job. I would like a new—"

A strange alarm buzzed, and the club's door popped open. He gestured inside. "Enjoy your night, ladies."

Chloe stared and sputtered, ping-ponging her gaze between the odd ticket taker and her friend's disappearing back. The boy waved her forward, and she quickly followed Melissa before the door clicked shut.

Darkness dominated the short entryway and Chloe blinked repeatedly until enough ambient light gave the interior some dimensions and edges. Melissa danced her way through the sparse crowd, then threw her arms around a small group gathered beneath one focused, overhead spotlight. Strings of tiny green bulbs outlined the mirrored display of bottles behind the thick, mahogany barrier. Tall, narrow tables sat amidst squatty ones, and all were scattered across the deep brown carpet. A small, rectangular stage was tucked into the farthest corner, and on it sat an empty stool beside an acoustic guitar. Cozy booths lined the walls, and a ramp led up to the only neon signs in the whole place, ones that marked both the restrooms and the emergency exit.

It truly was a pub, as if the door had transported her to the Emerald Isle. Chloe turned back toward the entrance to test her fearful notion, before scoffing at herself.

"Are you going to join us or not, silly?"

Jessica's shrill voice had cut through the comfortable murmurs with surgical precision, and Chloe used the relative peace of the dark entryway to paint on a believable smile. She could have said no when Melissa had called hours earlier. In fact, she'd made her desire to stay home very clear.

"Please let this night not be a complete disaster," she mumbled, a half-hearted prayer to any listening deity. Then, taking a deep breath, she spun around to join her cousin and the rest of the giggling girls.

2

THE PSYCHIATRIST IS OPEN

"What's your poison, beautiful?" Chloe looked to her right and left before realizing the handsome bartender was actually talking to her. Her eyebrows shot up, and as she rested her fingertips on her sternum, his responding laugh encouraged her to join in with the joyful sound.

"Yes, you," he said, adding a wink and a smile. Soft brown hair fell in careful disarray, framing his strong jaw and kind smile. He was dressed in the standard bartender uniform of a long-sleeve, black button-down with the cuffs rolled up to the elbow. She spied a hint of ink climbing up his arm, hiding beneath the slick ebony fabric, as well as a solid gold band around the ring finger on his left hand. Figured he would be married. In the five seconds she had spent with him, he seemed like a genuinely decent guy. "Don't tell me you're not used to the compliment?" he said.

After tipping her chin toward the runway crowd at the nearby table, she shrugged and met his eye. "You're kidding, right? Not with them around."

"Every flower in a bouquet is just as unique and beautiful as the others." He set a glass before her, its rich amber liquid two fingers high and exactly what she was craving. "Roses aren't the only pretty ones in the bunch."

A warm blush touched her cheeks before she even took a sip. And a romantic poet to boot? She envied the lucky lady who'd snagged him. "Thanks, uhh…"

"Kole," he said, reaching a hand across the bar. "Kole O'Shea." Mischievous green eyes twinkled as he smiled. "And this is my bar."

She returned the grin and shook his extended hand. "Hi, Kole. I'm Chloe Banning. Nice place you've got here."

"Do you really mean that?" He arched a brow as he returned his hand to his side of the barrier. "Seems like you had a different impression when you came in."

The upturned corners of her lips drooped in shy admonition. "Actually, I didn't know what to expect, especially with Melissa and her billboard bimbos leading the way."

He poured a glass of beer and set it onto the waiting tray at the server's station. "Seems like she has your best interest at heart."

Chloe's blasé stare must have telegraphed her opinion clearer than she'd expected and Kole smirked. She glanced down the length of the bar to her cousin and the rest of their party. Blonde, petite, cover-model looks. Yeah, she fit in with that cookie-cutter group. On cue, Melissa twirled about, showing off her newest outfit.

"She's got something at heart and it sure isn't me," Chloe mumbled around the rim of the glass. The heady aroma of aged whiskey hit her nose just as the strong liquor touched her tongue. Warm and soothing, it slid down her throat and eased a hidden tension in her shoulders.

Her new friend chuckled. "Don't you think wanting to see people happy is a noble endeavor?"

Chloe shrugged weakly. "It would just be nice every once in a while to be asked what I really wanted." She took another swig of liquid courage and continued. "Is it so wrong to be happy all by myself?"

Kole flipped the towel off his shoulder and wiped down the immaculate, deep brown wood. "Are you?"

Chloe swallowed hard, the burning alcohol twisting sideways in her throat, and she coughed down the final drops. "Am I what?"

"Happy by yourself?"

She pondered her response as he refilled her glass. *Was she?*

The soft background music shut off as the sounds of guitar tuning filled the quiet space. A few of the gathered patrons applauded, and the singer launched into a raucous version of "Whiskey in a Jar." Several voices joined in, further stealing away the quiet.

"I guess I'm as happy as the next person," Chloe said, and an explosion of bubbling giggles off to her left landed like ill-timed verbal shrapnel. "Unless the next person is them."

"Ah." Kole added a sage nod to his knowing interjection. "Perpetual matchmaker?"

"Yes," she exclaimed. "That's exactly it. None of my friends think I can be happy without a man in my life. It's like … I don't know." She gestured to the heavens for some answer before finishing her thought. "It's like I'm breaking some female taboo, or some spinster rule that says, 'Ug—me woman. Must have man to give life meaning. Must pop out puppies, or not real woman.'"

Her eyebrows shot up to her hairline as her cheeks warmed. She wished she could blame the alcohol for her lack of filter, and the laughter of her companion did not help in her embarrassment. She had always heard that bartenders were underpaid psychiatrists, but she had never put much stock into the idea. Until now.

"Why am I telling you these things?" Her eyes slid guiltily toward the group at the end of the bar. "I'm sorry. I'm usually not so bitchy. I—"

He waved off the rest of her apology. "No need. *In vino veritas.* Trust me, I have heard much worse from other patrons."

Chloe relaxed a fraction, though she was determined to be on better behavior. "Still," she said, "I mean, I should be grateful she does care enough to check in on me from time to time." Taking a final sip, she set down the empty glass and ran her finger along the smooth, crystalline lip. "It's not like I don't want to find someone. I just think dating is overrated, and I refuse to troll the internet like some … loser."

"So Mr. Right is just supposed to walk into your living room with an order of Lobster Thermidor and a bottle of Dom from The Carlton?" His playful tone coaxed her into a teasing mood.

"Personally, a good pizza from Pizzaiolo and a six-pack of Dr. Pepper would do the trick better."

Kole motioned to her empty glass, and Chloe shook her head. Any more and she might be tempted to do, or say, something she would seriously regret in the light of day. For now, she would enjoy the pleasant company of the non-estrogen driven variety.

"Besides," she added, "Eddie V's has the better seafood." With a heavy sigh, she turned about, leaning her elbows on the cracked, padded leather bumper. "Aw, who am I kidding anyway? I'm destined to live a single life and that's all there is to it. If only—"

"CH-LO-E!"

The combined screech of the gaggle of girls yanked every stare in the place over to her like a magnet. Even the singer stuttered in his lyrics, covering up his error with a laugh, and added his voice to the call. Chloe cringed as her friends continued to beckon wildly toward her. She inhaled deeply, hoping the circulated air would steel her spine.

"Prince Charming, where are you when I need you?" she muttered—an innocent question—under her breath and, painting on a pathetic smile, dug into her purse and slipped a twenty out of her wallet.

"Hey, Kole. Thanks for the—"

When she turned around, though, she discovered she was alone.

She glanced up and down the bar, but her bartender friend had simply vanished.

With a shrug, Chloe set down the payment and once again rejoined her cousin's group.

3

WHO'S SLEEPING IN MY BED?

The annoying racket of the alarm clock was like a spike through Chloe's brain. She'd only had a couple of drinks at the bar last night, not enough for even a light buzz, and she had gotten to bed before midnight. Throughout the night, she had searched for Kole, but he'd been absolutely nowhere to be found. Maybe he had simply locked himself in an office somewhere upstairs to do paperwork. After all, he was the owner of the place.

Dragging her heavy head up from the downy warmth, Chloe glared at the glowing red numbers. She peeled her arm from beneath her body and flung it across the space separating the nightstand from the bed. After a couple of sloppy swipes, she eventually found the snooze button, and silence again enveloped the room.

"Maybe I could call in dead?" she grumbled into her pillow and let her eyes slip shut.

"Sounds good to me."

"What?" Her eyes snapped open as the question flew out in perfect sync from a second voice.

She yelped at the unfamiliar tone, launching herself up off the mattress. Her right foot caught on the comforter and she hopped to escape the clinging snare.

Air burned through her lungs as she searched her room. *This is my room, isn't it?* Panic-stricken, Chloe dropped her gaze, praying she was wearing some form of clothing. Sure enough, she stood in her own once-white tank and pale green flannel lounge pants that served as her pajamas.

Even though she was fully clothed, her hands became impromptu fig leaves and she cowered behind her wrapped arms.

"Who are you?"

"Who am I? Who are—"

"And how did you get into my bedroom?"

"Your what?"

Chloe had fired off the questions at the mysterious bundle attempting to kick off the discarded bedding.

"What the bloody hell…?"

Her eyes widened. No way had she gotten that drunk that she didn't remember taking a man home. And she sure as hell didn't remember any delicious accent like the one bleeding its way through her heavy comforter. She recalled hearing the expected Irish lilts from a couple of the pub employees, but this definitely wasn't the same. Not quite Australian, but it was from that neighborhood for sure.

Long fingers appeared, connected to a broad palm, and before long, an arm emerged, deep bronze with inky triangular patterns trailing up to a defined bicep, continuing on to a strong shoulder.

"Bedroom? What do you mean bedroom? *Your* bedroom?"

With each new inch of him unveiled, Chloe's curiosity and heart rate increased. *Moment of truth.* When he pulled the rest of the blankets from his head, she gasped. Hazel green eyes peeked out from beneath thick black lashes, bright gemstones set in a dark olive complexion. Ebony locks, short-cropped and spiky, framed the strong, square jaw of her unexpected visitor. His regal nose sported wide nostrils and the receding evidence of a long-ago break. Tribal swirls and stylized sea creatures spilled across his left shoulder onto his pec, but the bulk of his bare and chiseled chest was a blank canvas.

Perfection. Absolute and utter perfection.

How the hell had the most perfect man in her mind just appear in her bed?

He scratched his head, confusion tugging his thick brows together. "How the hell did I get here?" he asked.

His accent was more pronounced now that he was unveiled. And nearly completely unveiled, at that. If her eyes did not deceive her, he was buck naked beneath her thin sheets. "That is exactly what I want to know, mister."

"Right now, your guess is as good as mine, sweetheart." His gravelly voice was encouraging the long-dormant butterflies in her blood to take wing.

Wanting to keep the higher ground, Chloe folded her arms across her chest and leaned back into her hip. "Is that all you have to say?" she asked, though inwardly, she prayed he had much more to say on any matter.

"For now. I'm shit without a cuppa coffee," he quipped.

"Can you at least tell me your name?"

Her guest smiled, his kissable lips curving upward, and all the blood in her body fled from her brain. He levered himself up, her deep green sheets pooling in his lap as he extended his hand. "Devlin Matene. But friends call me Dev."

More like the devil to me. She studied his offering, hesitating for a heartbeat ... then her arm trembled as she reached out for his fingers. "But who *are* you?" Only a hair's breadth separated their hands and apprehension held her back from closing the final distance. "I'm sorry if I sound like a broken record," she said, "but I don't remember seeing you last night in the bar."

"Bar?" He swung his legs off the bed and took to his feet. "What bar? What was it called?"

Chloe panicked as he strode closer. Damn, he was huge, his spiky hair adding to his towering height. She backpedaled until her ass bumped against the dresser, giving her no more escape space. He gripped the sheet around his tapered waist, and her eyes flared wide as her brain spun with images of what may lie beneath that makeshift toga.

She grabbed the tottering lamp behind her and brandished it like a bat. Yet before she could issue a challenge, Devlin backed away, one hand out as a shield while the other held fast the gathered material.

"Whoa, hang on. I promise I'm not going to hurt you." He hunched forward, apparently hoping to diminish his size. Instead, he merely flexed every muscle in his washboard abs, which was not helping to cool her head. Chloe swallowed hard, determined to focus on anything but the sensual stranger.

"You said you were at a bar," he said. "Was it a bar, or more like a pub?"

Chloe lowered her weapon and hazarded a step closer. "With a blue door and ... and some crazy, silly name?"

He relaxed his crouch a fraction. "Kinda quiet and new, but a friend of a friend of a friend said it's really cool?"

Chloe had bobbed her head each time he'd said *friend,* and soon, she stood toe to toe with him.

"And a weird ticket taker asked you to ... to—"

"Make a wish."

"Yeah," she whispered in reply, and his jaw hung agape, hazel eyes flared wide. Like lightning, her train of thought sped off its current course. "Wait a minute. You wished for ... for me?"

4

WELCOME TO PITTSBURGH

Devlin blinked rapidly as the prickly princess stared incredulously at him.

Last night, his coworkers had suggested a drink after the long negotiations. Usually, contract disputes were settled in a couple of hours, not a couple of weeks. But after the final, overly drawn out debates over minute details and inched concessions had wrapped up, he'd been ready for a good, stiff drink.

What he hadn't expected was to be waking up in a strange room. He knew he'd made it home last night; his roommate had driven, so he couldn't have ended up anywhere but their flat.

But the forest green sheets and dusty rose comforter was not his speed at all.

Maybe it was all a dream. A really vivid, realistic dream brought on by a lack of sleep over the past few nights. Hallucinations didn't talk back, though. At least the voices in his head had never provided feedback—until now. *Nor do any of my imaginary friends look that good in a pair of loungers.*

Statuesque, with some meat on her bones, the woman stood tall before him, flashing eyes of bright blue that blinked up at him as waves of shimmering ebony fell about her honey beige skin. High cheekbones and a slender nose directed his gaze to her lush and kissable pink lips. Full curves, and proud of them, she was beyond gorgeous.

In fact, she was exactly what the doctor ordered—his type, all the way down to her neatly trimmed nails and small, diamond stud nose piercing. One detail was still curiously missing, though, and his mind rewound to repeat her puzzled question: *You wished for me?*

"Well, yeah." He grinned, running his hand through his sleep-disheveled hair. "I mean, not that I had you—well, *you,* specifically—in my head, but yeah." But the longer he talked, the more he began to confuse himself. "Uh, hate to play the 'I'll show you mine, if you show me yours' game…" He paused and gave a sly wink, to which she responded with a deliberate blink. Damn, she was all kinds of sexy—in ways he was certain she didn't even know. He gripped his hasty toga tighter, gathered handfuls of the loose material to hide his growing interest. "But I gave you my name…"

He waited patiently for a reply. Her eyes narrowed, wariness oozing from her entire body.

Devlin heaved a deep sigh and tucked the sheet ends into the makeshift waistband. "Look, girlie, I'm just as baffled as you are. Hell, at least you're in your own place. And where is that, anyway?"

She eased out of his personal space, and the loss stole away some heat. "Nine-seventeen James Street."

With a defeated harrumph, he plopped down onto the mattress. "Wow, great. That might mean something to you, but it doesn't help me one bit. What city am I in?"

"What city do you think you're in?" she countered.

Fabulous, he mused. *Another negotiator.*

He clamped down on his back molars. Wherever in the world he was at the moment, it was morning, and he had no coffee mug in his hand to temper his patience.

"Well," he snapped, "it sure as bloody hell not Auckland."

"Auckland!" she squeaked and dropped her guarded stance. His eyes dipped down to admire the bounce of her breasts as her arms hit her sides. "Isn't that in Australia?"

Her voice had broken into his drooling, and he peeled his gaze away from her body, up to the deep blue eyes that regarded him coolly. He responded with a sheepish grin. He wouldn't apologize for finding her attractive, but he could show a little more tact.

"Not quite." Dev shook his head. "New Zealand, but in the same part of the world."

"So how did you end up in Pittsburgh?"

"Pittsburgh?" He sprung up from the bed once more, his own tone now incredulous. He paced away from the tempting bed and the even more tempting company, over to the curtained window. Taking a deep breath, he pulled aside the heavy fabric.

Outside were unfamiliar buildings—narrow red-and-gray brick dwellings and gaps where skyscrapers should be. Cars crowded along every available inch of curb along the two-lane street, and the sidewalks were devoid of pedestrians. Even the skies mimicked the colorless, bleak view, with thick, dark clouds keeping the sun's rays at bay.

"Crap."

How was he going to get home? He had no ID, no plane ticket. Hell, he wasn't even wearing underwear.

No clothes, no phone, no money.

He inhaled, hoping the cold air would encourage his mind to work, but his plan backfired as her mouthwatering fragrance permeated his senses. Dark and spicy, with notes of crisp autumn leaves, it filled the room, and the warmth of her nearby presence danced along his skin. Blood skipped through his veins, continuing on a southerly course.

Releasing the thick burgundy drapes, Dev spun back to face his gorgeous hostess, whose arms had returned to their shielding positions, squishing her lush breasts back into her. A frown had pursed her full lips into a kissable Cupid's bow. God, what he wouldn't give to taste those cherry red blossoms.

"Look, chicky," he began, and her eyes flared wide as an angry blush colored her pale cheeks. He hated using such slang with her, but until she told him elsewise, a safe nomenclature was gonna have to be enough. "Hey, not in my element, here, and I'm really trying not to be a right jerk, eh? Could you at least tell me your name for starters?"

5

INTRODUCTIONS COMPLETE

Embarrassment colored Chloe's cheeks, and she let her tough veneer slide. He was right. He had given her all the information he could and she hadn't even bothered to tell him her name.

"Oh, sorry. I'm, uh … I'm Chloe. Chloe Banning."

He was real, flesh and blood. She hadn't conjured him up from out of thin air and horny fantasies, though he did dominate the room adorned in nothing more than a bed sheet skirt. Maybe that was it. Had he been wearing clothes, he might not have been so delectable.

He flashed her an honest smile and extended his hand.

"Nice to meet you, Chloe."

Her name, as it tripped off his tongue, sounded like pure sin, and butterflies swarmed deep in her gut as she imagined other things that tongue of his could do. She forced down her awakening libido and accepted his courteous offer.

His broad palm nearly swallowed her entire hand, his fingers both strong and gentle. Her intention was to give a firm handshake, defining their roles, then back away. But her body had much different motives.

Standing so close, Chloe studied his intricate tattoos—they started just above his wrist with interlocking triangles and swirls that morphed into sharks and turtles as they climbed up his bicep and shoulder to trail across his chiseled pec. She itched to touch them, to lose herself in the strength that hid beneath.

"How has any of this happened?" She had breathed the words out to the universe as she dragged her gaze back up to his face. Mischief sat in his hazel eyes, and the soft tawny brown orbs streaked with accents of sea green roamed over her whole body. Simultaneously empowered and stripped bare by his hungered looks, Chloe stood frozen, waiting for either her heart or her head to give the final instruction.

Devlin's smile lost a bit of its light, and he gave one weak shake of his head.

"Right now, your guess is as good as mine, eh?"

Her alarm clock screeched out again, shattering the tender moment and yanking her back to reality. Chloe released his hand, dashed over to silence the shrieking from the nightstand. What now? Did she go on with her daily routine?

With her back to the towering mountain of handsome man flesh, she pondered the situation. She had a sexy, naked man in her bedroom and a budget meeting in two hours. Her colleagues could run the debriefing without her. Hell, the entire company would probably be fine if she just vanished. Only her deep sense of duty kept her firmly returning to her desk every weekday at eight am sharp.

"Holy shit! Is that really the time?"

Stunned by his sudden outburst, Chloe glanced over her shoulder. The bronze on his cheeks had paled as he stared at the illuminated numerals. Frowning, she turned back to the clock. Six thirty am. Why would that be so strange?

"Yeah. Why is—"

"Crap." He began to pace, his swearing setting the rhythm for his shuffled steps. An instant later, Chloe put together the pieces and joined him in his scramble. He was from the other side of the world and probably had a job of his own to worry about.

He slapped at nonexistent pockets, likely searching for an equally missing phone. Without skipping a beat, Chloe pulled her phone from the charger and handed it to Devlin.

"Hey, can I—?" He blinked, then took the phone. "Thanks."

His fingers flew across the keypad as he returned to his frantic path.

A stray thought pinged in Chloe's mind: Who was he calling? His boss, a roommate, his girlfriend? Maybe even his wife?

Of course someone that gorgeous would be spoken for. Chloe's shoulders drooped, and she made her way to the bathroom to give him some privacy.

"Hey, Erick, I ... Wait, what time is it?"

Erick? Promising. She leaned an ear toward the open doorway as she uncapped the toothpaste.

"After midnight! Ah, sorry, mate. Yeah, nah. I did go home ... Yeah, I know I'm not bloody there now, ya muppet."

Chloe shifted her gaze to the mirror, angled in just enough to show his back. His head dropped forward, bowing his spine, and the skirted sheet slipped down a fraction. Damn, even his muscles had muscles. She imagined those defined planes in serious sexual motion and nearly choked on her mouthwash.

The rapid fire, one-sided conversation continued, with many of the phrases not holding one ounce of meaning to her. "Chur" came up a few times, as did that weird combination of yes and no, nearly on top of each other. She caught snippets of work-related talk. *That* she understood fluently. Yet his enticing accent made even boring topics of "terms and acceptable conditions" swoon-worthy.

"I need ya to send me my fucking passport, yeah?"

She shut off the tap and, with water dripping off of her damp face, let that knowledge fully sink in. Here, she'd only been concerned about how he'd appeared in her bedroom wearing nothing more than a smile. He had no means to prove his identity and she only had his word about his name.

For all she knew, he could be a crazed serial killer loose on the streets of New Zealand. *You thought him up, dimwit. You've never been that inventive in your whole life.*

A timid knock at the half-open door pulled her back into the present. Devlin stood sheepishly beside the jamb, eyes downcast.

"Uh, sorry to bother you, but where's the nearest post? I need to get my mate to send me my passport and, well, some other stuff."

"Post?" she mumbled into the thick terry cloth, contemplating her answer. "You can just have it overnighted here."

Did I just say that? Chloe snapped her gaze up, locking stares with the solid hunk of stunned sexiness. The shadows in his eyes melted away as his full lips curled into a crooked, heated grin.

"I mean, it would make better sense," she said, her voice quavering from the possible scenarios within the single word "overnight."

"So, you're not kicking me to the curb just yet?"

His hopeful tone and puppy dog expression fanned the embers smoldering beneath her skin.

She chuckled lightly. "No," she said and returned the towel to the rack. "Even I'm not that cruel."

All at once, the bathroom door was flung open, and a massive pair of arms engulfed her.

"Thanks, gorgeous." The bear hug ended quickly, and Devlin slipped back out of the narrow room. Before completely vanishing, though, he poked his head inside, adding, "You are a total lifesaver."

His warmth lingered long after the door had clicked shut.

6

A MINOR LANGUAGE BARRIER

What did I just do?

Dev stood rooted to the carpet, his back inches away from the bathroom and the beautiful hostess within. He didn't think she would really toss him out on his naked ass, but he'd only truly met her just minutes before.

Chloe. Such a beautiful name. It fit her.

Considering proper introductions had just occurred, though, maybe his overly enthusiastic embrace hadn't been the best idea. Hugs had been the standard greeting at every family gathering while he was growing up. Not until he'd entered primary school did he learn not everyone like to be touched as much.

He'd merely acted on instinct. Yet in the heartbeats he'd held her close, he was in heaven. She hadn't flinched or tried to pull away, and her skin had been warm and soft against him, the top of her head resting just beneath his chin.

God, he loved the tall ones. His buddy, Erick, was drawn to petite girls, said they made him feel more like a hero with a tiny damsel in distress. But Dev liked a girl with more substance, one who could handle herself, and Chloe seemed just the woman to do whatever she set her mind to.

"Hey, Dev. You still there?"

His roommate's voice, distant and hollow, had whispered out from the forgotten phone and, jerked out of his reverie, Dev turned his attention back to the call, wandering around the room in search of something with an address. "Yeah, nah. She'll be right." She'd earlier rattled off the house number and street name so fast, he'd missed most of it. But, then again, he didn't realize there was going to be a test on it, either. Spying an unopened piece of junk mail, he slid the envelope off of the dresser. "You ready?"

"So what's she like?"

Dev paused mid-word. "Huh?"

"The girl. I heard her voice. Sounded choice as, yeah?"

As if on cue, the bathroom door swung open and the subject of their conversation stepped out. The sheet was a weak barrier to hide his growing hard-on. She still sported the loose pants and sexy tank top, her lush breasts filling out the stretchy fabric. His mouth watered in hungry anticipation. Maybe only a pipe dream, but every fiber of his being prayed for the chance to savor every inch of her.

"You have no idea," he replied into the phone, and a delicate frown tugged her brows together. He couldn't help grinning as he held her gaze, her pools of oceanic blue beckoning. Not a drop of makeup augmented her fresh, natural beauty; only the warm pink from a brisk wash had colored her creamy cheeks. He stared for a moment, and soon, her lips tilted up into a coy smile. He was lost. Dev had never been one to believe in love at first sight, though he was starting to change his tune.

Vaguely aware of the voice in his ear, he dragged his stare away to give Erick the necessary information.

"Got it. Hey, don't do anything I wouldn't do."

"Yeah, nah. She'll be right. I'll call you later, yeah?"

He thumbed off the call, ignoring his friend's braying laugh bleeding through the tiny speaker. While he knew his roomie had been speaking directly about sexual matters, Dev feared he might have gone and done just that. Had he fallen for her that fast?

"Right about what?"

"Huh?" Dev tightened the sheet, shifting the pleats into more strategic positions, and crossed to her. She lifted her chin to keep eye contact and did not shy away.

"You told your friend that I'd be right," she said. "Right about what?"

It was his turn to furrow his brow and he quickly filed back through the conversation, searching for the cause of her concern. Realization struck, and he chuckled. "Oh. Yeah, nah. Where I'm from, 'she'll be right' basically just means everything is okay, yeah? Guess you guys in the States might not be too familiar with all that stuff. I'll try to speak proper English."

His added wink only helped to dial up the intensity of her smile.

"Thanks for the phone," he said, extending the device to her. "And uh ... yeah. Sorry if I, um, kinda took you by surprise, there."

Her fingers brushed against his, lingering as she hesitantly retrieved the phone. "Sorry? For what? Magically appearing in my bedroom?"

Her playful, husky voice drove his last remaining brain cells below his belt line and he smirked, capturing her fingers. "That, I'm definitely not sorry about." Stroking his thumb in lazy circles on the back of her hand, he forced his feet to keep the gentlemanly distance between them. Her gaze slipped away to focus on her bare toes. "I mean, sorry about the hug earlier."

"Are you sorry you did it?" she asked in an odd, melancholy rhythm, and an uncomfortable tension oozed off of her. Did he regret his action?

"Not for a minute," he replied, and the stiffness in her shoulders vanished in a heavy exhale. "I'm a hugger, and sometimes I forget not everyone is. I just couldn't help myself."

"Oh."

The weirdness crept back into the scant space between them.

Damn. He was saying everything wrong. Certain his toga was secured, Dev brushed his knuckles along her jaw, then guided her chin upward. She followed his gentle lead, lifting her face to him. Doubt and confusion had painted shadows in her bright eyes, and the urge to kiss away those dark emotions thundered through his blood.

"Chloe," he breathed, the word a prayer to the heavens, "I don't think you get what I'm saying. I really couldn't help myself. Just like

I'm trying hard not to peel those clothes off you and taste every inch of you."

Her eyes flared, and a delicious blush crept up her cheeks. She coiled her arms together and stepped in. The cold metal rectangle still in her grasp pressed into his chest, but the slight discomfort paled in comparison to the heat of her body so close to his.

"Yes," she said, "I can tell how … hard … you're trying."

A hungry growl rumbled through his chest, and he snaked his other arm down her back. "Maybe I could start working on the doing part, yeah?" He splayed his fingers low across her ripe ass and ground his engorged cock against her.

Chloe dug her short nails into his pecs and, with a needy sigh, dropped her head back. Dev cradled it, her thick, sable hair like silk against his palm as he nipped along her jaw line. The aroma of fresh spring flowers melded with dark spices, and he buried his nose into the hollow behind her ear.

Dev marveled at the way her soft curves molded so perfectly against his body. Had she been made for him, and him alone? He trailed his tongue along the column of her throat, savoring her pulse against his lips.

A jarring buzz shattered the moment, and Chloe yelped, jumped away, the phone falling to the floor as it continued to blare. The distance gave Dev a chance to readjust the sheet.

Chloe snatched up the device and groaned when she saw the caller's name. "Oh, shit." She thumbed the green button and began to pace. "Yes, yes. I know, I know. I, um, don't think I'll be coming in to work today."

Dev tilted his head, caught her out of the corner of his eye. As he fumbled with his wrap, he crossed his fingers in silent prayer and sat on the edge of the bed.

"No, I don't have a hangover," she said, and her singsong tone brought a silly grin to her lush lips. His gaze followed each of her steps. God, she was all kinds of sexy without even thinking about it. As he returned to his active eavesdropping, her eyes landed directly on him. "Yeah, I guess you could say I've come down with something."

He flashed her a broad grin. *Nothing like being called a social disease.*

Chloe smirked, rolling her eyes as she shook her head. "No, you don't need to come and check on me. I'm not twelve." She tucked her free hand under her armpit, and Dev smiled at her petulant stance. He leaned back, locking his elbows as he planted his hands onto the welcoming mattress behind him. What had she been like at twelve? Judging by the strong woman before him, she'd probably been an independent and determined kid.

"Could you? Thanks so much. I'll talk to you later. Oh, and um … thanks for last night."

A curious smile curled her lips as she hung up. Dev arched a brow. Was he being toyed with?

7

FOOD FOR THOUGHT

Tingles still cascaded down Chloe's skin from his lips. His hint of stubble, rough and purely male, had driven her dormant libido to dizzying heights. Yet as she set her phone back onto her dresser and turned her wistful gaze toward Dev, his smile had already faded. Maybe he regretted his actions but didn't want to say it to her face?

Shyly, she gestured to the silent device. "That was Melissa," she said. "My cousin, and usually my ride in to work."

Once she had mentioned her cousin's name, his devilish grin returned in full force. "You had me worried there when you thanked them for last night. I hoped I wasn't butting my nose into something serious."

Chloe scoffed, running a hand through her tangled hair. "Hon, I haven't been in anything serious my whole life."

With Dev reclined on the edge of her bed, still wearing her bedsheet, it would be so easy for her to crawl into his lap and fill her body's aching need. And from the mini pup tent he was sporting, his thoughts were moving in the same direction. Would the day end up being nothing more than hours of meaningless sex? Although … was that such a bad thing?

Her stomach made its emptiness known in grand fashion and,

embarrassed, Chloe wrapped her arms tightly around her grumbling middle.

Dev smirked and leaned forward. "That was pretty impressive." He rose, and her knees fairly buckled. She had almost forgotten how huge he was.

Almost.

Perhaps she'd been single for so long because no man had ever made her feel delicate. Not like Dev did. And all he'd done so far was sneak in a hug. Fantasies upon fantasies spun in her mind, fired her blood. Caught in his sights and happily ensnared, Chloe held her ground as he approached.

"I'm a decent cook, yeah? How 'bout some breakfast? That is"—he laced his fingers with hers before going on—"if you happen to have something more than a sheet for me to wear."

His reasonable request brought on a smile, and she giggled. "I think I can find you a pair of sweats." Reluctantly, she released his hand to rummage through the dresser. After a quick search, she found a pair of hand-me-down joggers. "Can't vouch for the exact size, though."

She tossed the black fleece toward Dev and chuckled again as he scrambled to catch the flailing legs.

"Do I want know why you have a pair of men's sweatpants in your nightstand?" he asked.

Decency won over curiosity and she faced the door as he got dressed. "They belonged to my older brother. I borrowed them a couple years ago and he's never asked for them back." The hallway mirror over her shoulder only reflected his hunched back. Drat. She'd been hoping for a glance at his ass. Instead, she formed her own opinions about his still-hidden parts, each image more swoon-worthy than the previous.

A gentle hand on her arm drew her out of her statue impression and she blinked. Her sexy angel stood at her side, having paused at the threshold, smiling at her. "Lead the way."

Oh. Right. This was her place. Shaking her head to clear the daydreamy fog, Chloe entered the hallway, followed by her hunky shadow. Her brain fumbled for trivial topics of conversation, but her tongue refused to budge, and a heavy silence crept along her skin. She dared a glance over her shoulder.

To her surprise, Dev was studying every picture he passed along her hall, pausing to lean in and scrutinize the collection of memories.

"You got a big family?" He shifted his gaze to hers, and she nodded. His broad smile stole her remaining thoughts. "Yeah. Me, too. But all I got were sisters. Seven of them."

She whistled low. "Older or younger?" she asked as they arrived at her small kitchen. He passed her by, making a beeline for the fridge, and her eyebrows shot up as he opened drawers and cabinets, fired up the coffee maker, and gathered a variety of ingredients. He apparently had things well in hand, so Chloe sat down at the inset breakfast nook that doubled as her dining room.

He appeared to be completely in his element, easily ferreting out her supply of pots, pans, and … everything else. "A bit of both," he finally replied to her prior question. "I ended up plopped down closer to the end, though: five older and two younger." He cracked a handful of eggs into a bowl, then added several shakes of some aromatic spices. He continued explaining about his siblings, but Chloe was more fascinated by his powerful grace—he floated through her cramped cooking space, hip bumping shut opened doors, hand circling the pan over the hot burner. Her spatula had become an extension of his arm as he related an anecdote involving three of his sisters and a date gone wrong.

The eye-opening aroma of coffee filled the air, and Chloe poured two mugs full, grabbing the needed silverware, then returned to the table. She laughed as he reached the punchline, and he placed the gourmet breakfast in front of her. "Since then, no one in my whanau … um, family, can get a table there for love or money."

She breathed in the mouthwatering steam. "God, Dev, this smells amazing," she said. "Did I really have all this in my fridge?"

He nodded, setting down his own dish. "Sure did. And good thing I showed up here, too. Some of the veg was about to go tits up."

At his comment, she nearly choked on the delicious mouthful and struggled to get the food down the right tube. Dev chuckled and patted her back. "Don't waste all my efforts now," he said.

Still giggling, Chloe wiped away her tears and gratefully accepted his offered glass of juice.

"Tits up?" she croaked out and shook her head. Dev shrugged impishly and spun the chair around, pressing the low back against the edge of the table.

"Well, it's true, yeah? You can't just leave the peppers in the bin and hope they don't die there," he teased, a sinfully adorable twinkle in his green-flecked eyes.

"In the future, I will try not to neglect my produce," she quipped, then joined him in the thoughtful meal.

It was all perfect: the coffee, the juice, the eggs, and especially the company. Dev was ridiculously easy to talk to, even though the topics were a touch superficial. They discussed music and books, movies and fashion; they bonded over a love of police procedural shows, although Dev had surprised her with his guilty pleasure confession.

"Reality shows?" Chloe smirked as she sipped her cooling coffee. "Like *Survivor?*"

Dev chuckled, adding another shrug as he poured the remains of the coffee into her mug. "Hey, don't knock it, eh? Some of those guys are choice as, yeah? Mean, out there, tramping in the wopwops and all, yeah?"

The more he described the show, the harder she laughed. "I swear you're speaking English," she told him, "but I honestly didn't understand a word of what you just said."

His feigned shock dissolved quickly and mirth danced in his hazel eyes. "Gonna need to get you up to speed in your Kiwi speak, *e ipo*."

Heat blossomed on her cheeks at the odd new phrase. She turned her attention back to the home-cooked feast ... and to a plate practically licked clean. "Wow," she said, dabbing her napkin along the corners of her lips. "I think you sold yourself short. You are more than just a decent cook, Dev."

"Where I'm from, food is more than just what you eat," he said, and she shifted her curious gaze to him as he cleared the dishes. "Meals are where family gathers to talk about what happened during everyone's day. You take time, reconnect, share some laughs."

Chloe climbed out of the booth seat, following his path to the sink and, tapping him on the shoulder farthest from her, snuck around in front of him with a light laugh as he turned away.

"Sounds like you and I had a similar upbringing." She stole the towel and took over cleaning up. "But in my household, the person who cooked didn't clean up."

The warm water trickling over her fingers couldn't hold a candle to the heat pouring off his body as he stood at her back. She attempted to focus on scrubbing the plates. *You just met him. All you know is that he has a big family.*

Yet each logical reason her inner schoolmarm drummed up, her awakening libido dismissed. Dev trailed his fingertips down her bare arms, and a hungry groan slipped out. His hands engulfed hers as he stepped in, pressing her between the wooden countertop and his solid chest, and the temperature in the room climbed up in time with her shallow breathing.

Dev guided her hands in completing the mundane task, water flowing between their entwined fingers, and Chloe dropped her head back, sighing heavily, leaning into his powerful embrace. He dragged his tongue the length of her exposed throat, and she gasped, breathy and desperate. He spun her about, and clinging to his broad shoulders, she peered into his darkening eyes. The sound of running water vanished.

"Say the word, Chloe."

She blinked slowly, lids fluttering in the effort, while blood thundered through her veins and the pounding of her heart drowned out the world outside. His arms like banded steel had wrapped around her loosely, poised for her response.

Should she take the chance?

8

A LITTLE LOVE COULDN'T HURT

Dev fell into her turbulent, oceanic blue eyes, lost and praying for her to save him. He traced her pouty bottom lip with the pad of his thumb and counted the passing heartbeats, fighting to keep a proper distance.

A delicate blush painted her milk-and-honey cheeks, and she dipped her chin.

Releasing his held breath, Dev cupped her face and drew her near. "God, I've been waiting to do this."

Her lips parted in invitation, and he gratefully accepted the offer, slanting his mouth over hers and swallowing her escaping sigh, pulling her in tight. She tasted like heaven—a delightful blend of sweet and strong.

More. He needed more.

He maneuvered a hand beneath her thin tank top and caressed her smooth, hidden skin. She squeaked, jumping in surprise, but did not move away. Devilishly, he tickled her bare stomach and was rewarded with a deep, throaty laugh and sensual, squirming gyrations. He broke the seal of their mouths and, growling, nipped his way down her neck while he slid his hand higher. Soon, her ample breast filled his eager palm.

Chloe dug her short nails into the meat of his shoulders, and her fragrance took on a dark and heady flavor. The ill-fitting sweatpants strangled his swollen cock, and he fought the urge to tear them off; he might be stuck with them until his wallet arrived tomorrow. Instead, he concentrated on the passionate whimpers pouring down his bare back.

"Too many clothes," he grumbled against her skin and, using the scant space between them, peeled off her shirt and admired the plump mounds before him. "Much better."

Diamond-hard buds poked out from the centers of her rosy pink nipples. He cupped her breasts together, enjoying their weight in his hands, as well as their deep, tempting valley. Tiny bumps covered her bare flesh, and he exhaled softly against her skin.

Chloe gasped, and Dev buried his face in the pillowy softness of her cleavage, where he drew in a long breath, pulling her scent into his soul. The once-loose fabric still strangled his raging hard-on, and he thought he would pass out from the loss of blood to his brain.

Damn. Protection. No pants; no handy condom in the wallet. And asking her might cool the mood, so he'd endure the ache. But that didn't mean she had to go without some release. Dev gripped her hips and lifted her ass up onto the counter.

"Dev…" Panic laced her airy voice, and he turned his gaze up to her face where, although a heavy curtain of hair hid most of her features, he could see her eyes were squeezed shut. Her arms trembled, elbows locked stiff.

He reached up, brushed her silken tresses aside, and gently cradled her cheek.

"I am yours, Chloe," he said, and her eyelids fluttered open, a sad gaze pleading for something he did not understand. "And your wish is my command."

She groaned at his playful pun and relaxed a fraction, her fingers losing their death grip on his arms. Dev stepped in. The height of her kitchen counter was absolutely perfect, allowing him to look directly into her eyes while her core nestled comfortably against his solid shaft. Trailing his hand along the curve of her jaw, he pulled her close and brushed his lips against hers.

"Seems the Fates believe we should be together," he whispered, then traced his tongue across the seam of her full lips, drinking in her throaty response. "Aren't you even curious to find out if they're right?" He snaked an arm around her curvaceous waist, savoring the press of her breasts against him.

"But—"

The single word slammed the brakes on his rampaging libido and he eased out of her immediate personal space, though continued to share his body heat with her. This was more than chance or the promise of a hot night of action, and he had to prove it to her.

"But ... you're not sure," he said.

Chloe lifted her chin, leveled her troubled gaze at him. "You can't seriously think this is real," she replied.

He rested his hands on her knees, massaging her strong thighs with his fingertips. "You do realize I went to bed in Auckland and woke up here, without ever getting on a plane, yeah?"

Chloe shook her head, her thick tresses tickling at his nose. "How is *that* even possible?"

"Don't you believe in magic?" Dev looped a stray lock around his finger, its silky texture bringing him an unfamiliar sense of calm. Everything about her both soothed his heart and fired his spirit, all at the same time. He'd found his match; he knew it in his blood.

"Dev," said Chloe, "I'm an analyst. I look at facts and data and, and real shit like that." She tossed her hands up. "Wishes? Magic? That's..." Confusion radiated off of her skin as she broke eye contact.

"That's what?" Dev skimmed his hands up her flannel-covered legs, inching closer to the elastic waistband that separated him from paradise. His gaze slid up from her bared breasts to her flushed cheeks. "Impossible?" he asked, praying his rational tone would sway her indecision. "Why couldn't this be real?"

9
A MISSED OPPORTUNITY

Thoughts refused to connect. Always one in control, Chloe now trembled in debilitating indecision—her mind, her body, her very soul screamed out different messages at alarming levels of intensity. At the moment, her body and soul were nearly on the same page; they clamored for more of everything that was Devlin Matene.

Her mind, however, was unwilling to join in. None of this was logical. Everything in her well-ordered life had to have a basis in facts and data.

Yet the intoxicating hazel eyes of the fierce, tattooed warrior before her did not fit into the equation. His presence called to something buried deep within her spirit, something she dared not give voice.

Love.

Panic grabbed the reins, and Chloe scrambled off of the counter and away from him. Immediately, chills raced down her skin, bereft of his warmth. She covered her nakedness with her hands, keeping her back to him, and finally found her voice.

"It's not real, Dev. Wishes don't just come true. I should have never gone out last night."

No. That wasn't right. Even so, her harsh statement must have caught him by surprise, as evidenced by the thick silence behind her.

"I'm sorry. I—" She turned to face him, words caught in her throat.

But Dev was gone.

In mounting terror, Chloe jerked her gaze into every available corner and crevice of her kitchen. "Dev?" she called out. He couldn't have gotten past without her seeing him. "DEV!" Her heart pounded as she ran through her apartment, combing each room for any signs of him. But soon, tears blurred her vision and her legs gave out, dumping her on her ass in the middle of the hall.

Oh, God. What had she done?

She might have convinced herself it'd been all a dream … had it not been for the lingering scent of his cologne on her skin.

Curling into a ball, Chloe sobbed, awash in a torrent of emotions. Anger and grief bubbled up to the surface, and her body shook. Why couldn't she trust her heart? Why did logic always have to be right?

But this time it hadn't been. The magic had been real. Now, she was alone. She dragged herself up off the floor and numbly shuffled through her quiet apartment, adrift on a sea of tangled emotions. The world continued to turn, darkening the sky outside as day passed into night. Despondent, she flopped onto her bed as the latest bout of tears pressed against her closing lids.

The pub.

Her head snapped up, mid-snivel. Right. She could just go back to that bar.

Chloe jumped to her feet and dashed into the bathroom. *I'll just make the wish again. It'll be fine.* It had to work.

This mantra played on a continuous loop, driving her legs as she quickly dressed in a pair of jeans and a sweater she'd grabbed off the laundry pile. She muttered the last phrase over and over —*it'll be fine, it'll be fine*—after jamming her feet into the sneakers by the door.

What was the address of that place?

With keys, purse, and phone gathered, Chloe ran out into the cold toward her car, then asked Siri to dial her cousin as she warmed up the engine, unwilling to let anything slow her down.

"Hey, you. Hope—"

"What was the address of the pub?" Rude, but Chloe was on a mission and she didn't have time for pleasantries.

"Well, hello to you, too," her cousin's snark bled through the speaker as Chloe cranked up the heater and pulled out into the light traffic.

"I'm sorry, I just—" She fumbled for an appropriate response. Luckily for her, Melissa was known for her materialistic insight.

"Did you lose something there?"

Chloe stifled a sob. *More than you know.* She nodded, giving herself time to compose her thoughts.

"Yes," she replied. "I didn't notice it until just now and—"

Her phone pinged, alerting her of a new text message from Melissa and, grateful beyond words, Chloe tapped the address on the screen. Her course was charted, the final destination only twenty minutes away.

"Just let me know if they find it, okay? And don't worry. I'm sure whatever it is will turn up. You'll see."

Chloe crossed her fingers as she hung up. All her life, all of the hours spent staring at facts and figures, and she was betting her heart and her future happiness on magic and wishes?

"Please be open, please be open..." The faster the words poured from her lips, the more they lost cohesion. She didn't care if there was a line; she only wanted the place to serve an early dinner.

But as she rounded the last corner, her worst fears became real.

Gone. No sign, no line. No youthful smiling boy asking for wishes for entry. Nothing.

Chloe circled the block a second time, thinking perhaps she had the wrong side of the building. But no matter how many right turns she made, Storybook Pub never appeared. Her hands shook as she parked in front of the empty facade and exited her car.

Too much. This was just too much. She touched the boarded-up window, and the waterworks threatened to begin anew.

"Excuse me, miss?"

A polite voice at her back drew her out of her sadness. Sniffling, she wiped at her eyes and turned around. "Yes?"

An older gentleman stood before her, gray hair poking out from underneath a red-and-blue striped ball cap. His crisp uniform shirt that announced "International Courier" and his out-of-place shorts piqued her curiosity. He adjusted his glasses and shuffled closer.

"I think I got a little lost here. Could you help me find this address?" He presented the thick, padded envelope he had tucked under his arm. "It's been marked 'Urgent,' so I'm sure someone is waiting for it."

Chloe plastered on a simple smile. "Sure. Let me—"

She gaped at the name and address on the label, then her gaze bounced up to the kindly delivery man. "Wha... How? I mean... This is ... me."

"It is?" His bushy brows pulled together and he leaned in, scratching his head through the mesh hat. "That's quite a coincidence, wouldn't you say?"

Chloe clutched the bubble-wrapped package to her chest, laughing as tears of joy slipped down her cheeks. "I'm beginning to believe in luck." She threw her arms around the surprised courier. "Thank you. Thank you so much."

A renewed lightness propelled her steps and she climbed back into her car. Part of her knew the delivery man would be gone if she were to look back, so she waved to the empty street, her smile cramping her cheeks.

"Hey, Siri," she said, pulling out into traffic. "When's the next flight from Pittsburgh to Auckland?"

10

BACK TO LOVE

"Oy, Dev? You right?"

Dev blinked rapidly, dragging his mind back to the dreary meeting. "Yeah, nah. Sorry 'bout that, Erick. I'm here."

A bold-faced lie. Two days had passed since he'd been cast out of heaven. One minute, he was kissing the most beautiful woman, and the next ... he was sitting on his bed, staring at the old rolltop desk in his room, his return trip just as jarring as his original journey. His immediate reaction was to fire up his computer and search for her.

Google gave him 2,695,041 hits on "Chloe Banning," in 0.85 seconds. Even narrowing the confines to Pittsburgh proved useless; ninety-five people had some variation of her name, but none were his Chloe. Apparently, she didn't believe in social media, either. Or love.

He'd managed to convince his roommate it had all been an elaborate joke, and he spent the better part of his first day back getting a replacement phone and driver's license. His family had called on him, confused by Erick's odd message about his whereabouts. He didn't want to lie to his parents, but the truth was much harder to explain. His perceptive mother's stare had followed him around the house, though she hadn't pushed for answers. He'd even tried going back to the pub, with no success; in its place stood a fast food restaurant, its weatherbeaten sign and faded yellow leather booths showing years of wear.

Despondent and lost, Dev had driven home and crawled back under the covers. Every fiber of his being had known something miraculous had transpired. He'd arrived in the same sweatpants she'd loaned to him. No way had he imagined those things. And neither had he conjured up the taste of her skin or the silken softness of her sable tresses.

A hand on his shoulder jostled him out of his dark thoughts, and narrowing his eyes, Dev glared up at his well-meaning friend. "Don't say it."

Ever since he'd returned to work, Erick had been riding his ass about Chloe. The interrogation was seriously getting on his nerves.

"Chur, you gotta stop moping about over some made up girl."

"I didn't make her up," Dev said, slamming his palms against the table and lunging to his feet. Papers scattered in the wake of his sudden tantrum. He paced away from his friend, needing the space. "Erick, I can't … I can't explain it. But I know it was real. And now—"

"Now what?" asked a familiar voice.

Dev froze, then shifted his cautious gaze toward the office door. Was his mind playing cruel tricks on him?

"Chloe?"

Standing just inside the threshold was his statuesque beauty. His Chloe. The royal purple T-shirt dress accentuated more than her dazzling blue eyes, just as her high-heeled strappy sandals accentuated more than her long legs.

"Hi, Dev."

Her smile illuminated the room, and he remembered how to speak. "How … how did you find me?"

His hushed tone must have offered the wrong impression; the upturned corners of her sensual mouth twitched, then began to droop. She retrieved a large, opened envelope.

"Hey, mate," Erick chimed in. "She's got the package I sent you, yeah."

Chloe fidgeted, her gaze darting around the room. "I, um, caught the first available flight and—"

Dev rushed over and pulled her into his arms. Overjoyed, he claimed her lips, both losing himself and finding his sanity in the heat of her embrace. He broke the seal of their mouths and hugged her close.

"Dev, I'm so sorry." She clung to his shirt, sobbing, her voice quivering as her shoulders shook. He stroked her spine while he cradled her head against his chest. "I just got so scared, you know? But when you ... you just disappeared, I—"

"Shh," he whispered, the soothing sound trailing across the crown of her head. "No more tears." He pressed soft kisses against her hair, inhaling her intoxicating fragrance and centering his soul.

"I love you."

Their simultaneous pledge filled the quiet, and Dev laughed. He stepped back and brushed away the silver tear trails on her cheeks, smiling as he lost himself in her ocean blue eyes. He cupped her face and reverently touched his forehead to hers.

"Aw, you're stuck with him now, girlie."

Dev pried open his eyes to glare at his temporarily forgotten roommate, who ignored the dangerous glower and blathered on.

"That there's reserved for loved ones," he said.

Chloe smiled, her long lashes painting dark crescents on her pinked cheeks. "I think I'm okay with that."

"Good, *e ipo*." Dev said. "That is my only wish."

LEARN MORE ABOUT TESSA MCFIONN:
HTTP://AMAZON.COM/AUTHOR/TESSAMCFIONN

ALSO BY TESSA MCFIONN:
SPIRIT FALL
SPIRIT BOUND
TO DISCOVER A DIVINE

HIDDEN FATE

EMBER-RAINE WINTERS

They weren't supposed to be together,
they weren't even friends.
They could only be enemies.

Sub-genre: Fantasy
Relationship: Male/Female

1

KERRIGAN

I was still searching for the missing clan members. My father was worried about the missing people and sent me out to find them. It was taking too long, almost as if they had vanished off the face of the earth. No one knew anything about where they had disappeared to. I was hoping they just didn't want to be found and it wasn't something more nefarious than that.

I walked along the sleepy town on the ocean and smelled the salty water in the air. I loved the sea, but I wasn't there to sightsee. The entire town was deserted, and I was looking for any kind of clue as to what happened to them. I walked up to what had once been the bakery and tried the door. It opened easily. That was strange. I crept inside and the smell of rotting food caused me to gag. That was disgusting. I couldn't believe no one had sent a clean-up crew. I held my breath as I investigated further. The stench was completely unbearable the farther I went into the building. It looked like there had either been a fight or someone had left very quickly. There were papers and trays strewn across the floor. I bent to inspect a red stain on the floor. It resembled dried blood, but it could have easily been jelly from one of the baker's famous donuts. I couldn't be sure. I opened the mind link I had with my father and relayed the information I'd gathered so far as I left the bakery.

Each place I went held more of the same. The houses were ransacked and I was no closer to finding out what had happened to the clan. I rubbed a hand over my face and huffed out an aggravated breath. I kicked at a rock and heard an oof. Turning quickly, I drew my blade as I came face to face with Darius. "What the fuck?" I yelled at him but the infuriating being just grinned at me.

"What's the matter, Kerrigan? Did I startle you?" he chuckled.

"What are you doing here, Darius?" I growled, still brandishing my blade.

"You won't find anything here." He completely ignored my question.

"Then where do you suggest I look?" I asked with a raised brow. He shook his head, still grinning.

"You know I can't interfere."

"Then what the fuck are you doing?" I was exacerbated.

"I can point you in a general direction," he huffed out a breath. I glared at the idiot. I hated his cryptic attitude. He could never just spell things out because supposedly he wasn't allowed. Dealing with him was infuriating.

"Then point me, please," I yelled in frustration.

"Go to Blarney. There's a man named Kole there. He owns the Storybook Pub. He will point you in the right direction." He raised an eyebrow before disappearing as quickly as he appeared. I shook my head again and teleported away. It looked as though I was heading to Blarney.

I landed in the forest outside the city of Blarney. I wasn't a fan of the mortal realm but that couldn't be helped. I walked the streets looking for this pub Darius had told me about. I walked along the street until I came to a sign with scrolling cursive words written on it saying Storybook Pub, it even had shamrocks on each side of the name. I walked in and looked around; the dark wood reminded me of every other pub I'd been in. I sat at the bar and waited for a minute. There wasn't anyone else in the place and I thanked the gods for that. I wasn't sure who this man Kole was or more importantly *what* he was, but apparently he knew things about our kind, and I needed to have a chat with him.

A blonde man walked out of the back room with an easy grin on his face and I assessed him. I did a double take when I saw the points of his ears. "Are you Kole?" I asked bluntly. I didn't have time for subtlety.

"Yes, Kerrigan. I'm Kole, what is it that you desire?" He grinned.

"How did you know who I was?" I was on edge now. I hadn't told him my name, but I had a feeling Darius might have.

"I got a visit from an old friend who said you might be stopping by." He shrugged. "You going to answer my question? I don't have long. I need to get back to the US soon. I dropped in specifically for this meeting."

"I'm looking for someone." I was purposefully vague because I wasn't sure how much he knew about our world. Despite the ears he could have been human but if he referred to Darius as an old friend he might have known more than I thought. I couldn't be sure. His grin widened and his eyes sparkled.

"That, I can help you with." I had no idea what he was hinting at but if it helped me find the clan, I would go wherever he told me to.

2

TARRYN

I was shadowing the Leprechaun as he went through the small seaside town. I wasn't supposed to engage. I was waiting for him to leave so I could search for the item my boss required. I knew Kerrigan was looking for the clan and I needed to keep an eye on him. If the item wasn't in the town, I needed to find the clan and the item they were hiding from me.

I'd listened in while that fool Darius told Kerrigan where to go to look for the clan and waited until he disappeared. Finally, I walked to the clan chief's home and started going through his things. It looked like they'd left in a hurry. I knew they hadn't been attacked because my boss wouldn't have sent me to find them if he'd gotten there in time to attack. I wasn't even sure how they'd known what we'd planned. There were so many questions when it came to this particular clan but the longer I looked the more I realized they wouldn't have left something that precious behind.

I knew what I needed to do, and I was not looking forward to it. I teleported to Blarney and waited for Kerrigan to come out of the pub, shielding myself as best I could so he wouldn't see me. I felt a tap on my shoulder and cursed myself for letting some random person sneak up on me. I spun around readying my blade, but the man simply grinned at me. "He's already gone, love."

"What are you talking about?" I glared at the man. I noticed his slightly pointed ears and shook my head. *Stupid. This must be Kole.*

"Kerrigan. That's why you're lurking outside my pub like a creeper, right?" He grinned. I rolled my eyes. It was probably immature for a centuries old Light Fae warrior, but I didn't care.

"Yes. Where did he go?" I asked impatiently.

"What is it you most desire, Tarryn?" He was looking at me funny and it was making me uncomfortable. *Wait, how did he know my name?* I decided to ignore that detail and looked at him deadpan.

"Right now, what I desire most is to end this conversation and be on my way." I raised an eyebrow at him. Kole chuckled.

"You're feisty. Yes, you make an excellent choice," he said almost to himself. I tapped my foot in irritation. This guy was talking in circles and I needed to get moving. Kerrigan already had the jump on me. I needed to find the missing clan and get the item back soon, or the boss would be extremely displeased. You *never* wanted to fail him. You fail the boss and your life is forfeit.

"Are you going to tell me or not?" I grumbled.

"Where do people go when they want to stay hidden?" He was so cryptic and smiled so easily I wanted to punch him in the face, but with that question he disappeared. I growled in frustration. I hated it when people answered a question with a question. For the first time in my life I wished I was a wolf shifter so I could rip him out of that teleport and beat him until he made sense.

I decided to go back to the Fae realm. It really was the best place to look. I doubted the entire clan moved to the human realm. It had been done before. The lost had split off from the magical world for reasons I'd never known. I didn't really care. They were vicious blood suckers if the stories were true. I doubted the clan would risk it.

I teleported back to the seaside town and grumbled to myself. Kole hadn't made it easy. I had no idea why he was being so cryptic. Why couldn't he just tell me where he was? I searched the town for any clues as to where they might have gone, but there was nothing. I was wasting time. I needed to think. I sat down on a stump and racked my brain trying to figure out the damn riddle that infuriating being had left me with. Where does one go when they want to stay hidden? That could be anywhere. Obviously he knew about the magical world. He fucking teleported before I could get a hand on him.

Think Tarryn, think! Ugh. I was so irritated with myself. I knew the answer was right in front of me. I kicked a rock into the nearby forest and grinned. The answer practically jumped right out at me.

3

KERRIGAN

I stood outside the Black Forest looking at it with trepidation. I hated the damn place. It was meant to deceive. I doubted the clan was hiding there. It didn't make sense. Maybe Kole misunderstood when I said I was looking for someone? I was starting to have major doubts about that guy. I wondered if I had misinterpreted the riddle, but the Black Forest hides everything. You could get lost in there for weeks because the trees would move to block the way you'd just come. I'd only been there once before. My brother, the captain of the guard, had made it a requirement for joining the guard. There was a list of tests you had to complete to prove your worth, and the final test was surviving the forest without aid. I used to think he added the test to torture the trainees, but maybe he was smarter than I gave him credit for.

No time like the present. I huffed out a breath and took two huge steps into the forest. The tingling of magic beat against my skin. It was an oily dark magic. It crawled over my skin and made me shudder. Taking a deep breath, I squared my shoulders and continued my pace. Maybe I should have brought someone with me. I was psyching myself out in a major way, my brain remembering the last time I was there.

I walked for hours with no rhyme or reason. It was inescapable when everything changed constantly. I heard a twig snap and looked behind me, but the direction I'd just gone was a wall of trees. I shook my head and turned to continue forward but the trees had moved in front of me when I'd turned my back and the only path I had now was to my right. I shrugged and went right. I had to remember not to turn around or I would lose my way again. It was hard to be on full alert and not be able to turn around. I felt like I was being stalked but shrugged the feeling off. It was probably the trees. They were alive in a surreal way that was unlike anywhere else in the realm.

I heard a growl behind me and had to break my own rule. I spun around pulling my blade and looked for the source. A second later I fell to the ground with an oof. A weight was on top of me and it took a second to realize it was a girl and not some ugly beast that was known to roam the Black Forest.

I looked up into blue green eyes and grinned before it registered. Her strawberry blonde hair was in a long braid down her back and her eyes were still staring into mine in confusion. Her breath caught in her throat as my hand moved to her hip. Realization stung me as I thought about who she was and who she could be at the same time. Tarryn was the enemy, she was the top lieutenant in Jaren's guard, but as I laid there with her on top of me just staring at me, I saw the realization dawn on her as well. We could be mates.

She scrambled off me quickly, pulling her blade and getting into a fighting stance. I shook my head as I got up dusting myself off. "You landed on me, love." I grinned not taking my eyes off her in case she attacked. I picked up my fallen blade, twirling it once, completely nonchalant as I waited for her to decide what she was going to do. I wouldn't attack her first, but I would defend myself if I needed to.

"My mistake, Kerrigan." She raised an eyebrow at me but never dropped her guard.

"Well, this has been fun, but can you decide whether or not you're going to attack me so I can be on my way? I have important business to attend to." I raised an eyebrow back at her. I heard another growl and Tarryn spun around.

"You didn't wonder how I ran into you in the first place? Idiot," she grumbled the last part under her breath.

"What is it?" I asked suddenly on alert for a whole different reason.

"I never saw it. It blends with the trees. It's been stalking me for an hour." She shook her head.

"Then why were you running?" I was a bit confused. I knew Light Fae got their energy from nature and the world around them, but I had no idea what could possibly make a warrior run the way she was.

"I can feel animals. It's one of my talents. It's only really useful when hunting," she grumbled. "I felt something huge coming toward me. Something I was pretty sure I couldn't fight on my own." I could tell by the face she made those words tasted sour on her tongue. It took a confident warrior to recognize battles they couldn't win. Even though we were enemies, I had major respect for her.

Something huge and black like the forest came crashing through the trees behind her and I tackled her to the ground just before the thing would have rammed into her. It continued running and disappeared again into the forest and I breathed a sigh. "How do we keep ending up this way?" I chuckled.

"You tackled me. Saved me, why?" Her eyes were narrowed in suspicion.

"Who says I saved you? Maybe I just wanted you underneath me." I grinned salaciously. The suspicion turned to anger, then to fear as her eyes widened.

"Kerrigan watch out!" she screamed, and I rolled away grabbing my sword and staring into the mouth of whatever beast this was. I hadn't encountered one the last time I'd been in the forest and it was unlike anything I'd ever seen before. I thrust up, my blade cutting into the creature's neck, black ooze spraying everywhere as the creature screamed in pain and gurgled sounds. It took off into the trees leaving a trail of toxic smelling blood behind. The whole thing was over in about ten seconds, and I leaned back on the ground to catch my breath. I'd only been in that horrible place for a few hours and it was already trying to kill me.

4

TARRYN

Why did I feel the need to warn him? It's not like I needed him now. I could find the clan in the forest myself. It was just figuring out where in the realms they were. I would be lying if I said I didn't feel a pull toward the cocky leprechaun. I was about to tear his head off his shoulders myself before I saw big ugly coming back for round two. I wasn't about to let some big, ugly beast take my kill from me. "You okay?" he asked, even though he was the one nearly mauled.

"Fine," I grumbled back. Getting up I dusted myself off and glared at the stupid gorgeous leprechaun. *Gorgeous? No, no way.* My brain was running away from me. His light brown hair had golden highlights in it and his fractured irises were the color of moss and fresh soil. The combination probably wouldn't be so attractive to most but being a Light Fae the earth was where I got my strength from. He was thin but his muscles were toned, and his black T-shirt was pulled tight over broad shoulders. I had to keep reminding myself we were on opposite sides of the upcoming war. We couldn't be friends. We couldn't be anything other than what we were. Enemies.

Kerrigan chuckled and I wanted to throw something at him. I needed to get away from the infuriating male. I didn't need him to find the clan anymore. *So why haven't you left then?* I slapped the mental voice inside my head and continued to glare at him.

"Why are you so angry with me?" He looked confused. He scrunched up his brow and it was fucking adorable. *Gah! There I go again! Stop it, Tarryn. You are a warrior, things aren't adorable. He's not adorable.* I was seriously close to kicking my own ass.

"Cocky, Leprechaun," I growled, and started to stomp away.

"Wait, Tarryn. You're going to get lost," he called after me. I felt a strong hand gently wrap itself around my arm and spin me around. My whole body shuddered at the soft touch. No, this couldn't be happening.

"Why do you think I'm leaving? We aren't anything but enemies." I shook my head at him.

"That doesn't mean we can't help each other get through this maze of a forest." He shrugged. "How about a ceasefire until we get out of here?"

I was shaking my head before he finished speaking, not meeting his eyes because I knew I would cave. Then, I would have to betray him as soon as we found the clan. It was better for everyone if we just parted ways then and there. He squeezed my arm trying to get my attention and I stupidly looked up into his eyes. Fuck, I was in trouble. "Fine, but the second we are out of here the ceasefire is done." I glared at him and pulled my arm from his grasp. He looked at me with that cocky smirk again and I rolled my eyes.

"Who knows, you might change your mind." I was seriously going to be in some major ass trouble. I should have trusted my instincts and left when I had the chance.

～

WE HAD BEEN WALKING around that damn forest for days and hadn't seen any signs of the clan. Kerrigan never told me why he was in the forest and I didn't ask because I really didn't want to tell him why I was there. What was I supposed to say? *Oh, I'm here to steal the item my boss needs to change the tide of this upcoming magical war from the clan you're searching for.* If we left it in the hands of the Leprechaun clan, they could use it against us. I needed to tread carefully so I could grab it once we found them.

Kerrigan was starting to pale and was having to take more frequent breaks. He didn't say anything, but it was obvious his energy was waning. It had been a while since he'd fed I was sure. I could just leave him and let nature take its course, but we were in a ceasefire and after chatting amicably the last few days if I was honest, I didn't want him to die.

"You're slowing us down," I grumbled, stopping in the middle of a clearing.

"How am I slowing us down? We don't even know if we are going in the right direction." He sneered.

"Admit that your energy is tapped out," I said with a raised brow. His eyes widened as he shook his head.

"I'm fine." His eyes didn't reach mine and his cheeks tinted pink.

"Riiiight," I said sarcastically. You could practically blow him over he was so weak.

"It doesn't matter. It's not like there's a way for me to feed." I looked at him deadpan. "What?"

"Only doing this to save your stupid life. I can't let you die when we have a truce." Leprechaun's feed off sexual energy and as uncomfortable as it might be I would do this so he could live. I really hoped I didn't regret that decision.

"You're not serious. You know I have to touch you for this right?"

"If you'd rather die in this forest, then that's fine by me. You saved my life, so I do this and we're even." I shrugged. *Yup, that's a good reason to give. It has nothing to do with wanting his hands on my body. None at all.*

He stalked closer to me and ran a hand down my cheek. "I don't think that's the only reason." He smirked at me and crowded into my space. My breath hitched.

"No kissing," it came out a breathy moan and I mentally slapped myself. Kerrigan chuckled and the vibration went right through me to my toes. This was a very bad idea.

5

KERRIGAN

To say I was shocked was an understatement, but Tarryn was right. I needed to feed desperately. I chuckled when she said no kissing. When you kiss a leprechaun it almost always means a mating. We have a saliva in our mouths that absorbs into the glands of the other person and links us permanently. I make it a point to never kiss someone on the mouth, so I don't accidentally mate with them. It's one of our laws. You are never to mate someone without permission.

I put a hand on Tarryn's hip and pulled her in close to me. I'd be lying if I said I hadn't been thinking about this over the last few days. I was perpetually hard and walking around in the confusing forest hard as steel was uncomfortable. "I won't be kissing your mouth without your permission."

"G-good," she stuttered. My hand slid up her side under her tight tank top. She was absolutely fucking gorgeous.

"That doesn't mean I can't kiss you *other* places." She squirmed at the words. My finger grazed the underside of her breast and she gasped. "Are you sure you want to do this, love? It could change everything." I had no idea why I was giving her an out when there was nothing in the world I wanted more in that moment than to sink into her and damn the consequences. She looked unsure for a second and I cursed myself for being a gentleman and not just taking her against a tree. I needed it to live but something inside me knew it wasn't that simple.

"Y-you'll d-die." God I loved the fact I had this sexy warrior goddess a quivering mess for me. It was a heady feeling.

"That's not the only reason." I cupped her breast and skimmed my thumb across her nipple. I knew I wasn't being fair, but she was like a puddle and I wanted nothing more than to feel for myself how wet she was.

"Yes, no, maybe?" she groaned as I pinched it.

"I'm not hearing an answer, love. Are you sure?" I tweaked her nipple again and she groaned closing her eyes and nodding. It wasn't a verbal yes, but it was close enough. My free hand went to the button on her pants and popped it free and I shoved my hand inside. She bucked against the assault as I grazed my teeth over the pulse point on her neck. "Fuck, love. You're soaking wet for me," I groaned as my finger slid over her clit. A high-pitched sound left her throat that nearly did me in.

Ripping her shirt over her head, I didn't hesitate before taking her pert nipple into my mouth and nipping it with my teeth. "Fuck, Kerrigan. I need you," she growled and for the first time since this started, she touched me. Her hands slid through my hair tugging me closer.

I thrust two fingers inside her, but she was wearing too many clothes for me to do what I wanted. "Take them off." I released her nipple as I watched her slip out of her pants. We were in the middle of the Black Forest where anyone could have stumbled upon us, but I didn't care. I swooped her up and laid her down on top of her clothes. We were in a frenzy. I lifted both of her legs over my shoulders and grinned at the lust in her eyes. "I never said I wouldn't kiss you here." I ran my index finger along her slit and brought the digit to my mouth sucking her sweet juices off it. The taste burst on my tongue and if I would have been standing, I would have staggered at the exquisite taste and the overall feeling that this beautiful Fae, my enemy, was my true mate.

After a taste I couldn't stop. I was already feeling a little more charged, but I still needed more. I plunged my tongue inside her soft folds and thrust it in and out until her walls were clamping down on it. I pulled back smiling knowing my face was covered in her essence. Her sexual energy. It was mind blowing.

She twisted us around easily, so I was on my back. She grinned as she pulled my shirt over my head and scratched her nails down my chest. I growled, not in pain exactly, but that fine line between pleasure and pain. As soon as she was done raking her nails down my abs she started on my pants. I watched her with anticipation. "Your eyes are glowing, are you feeding?" She smirked as she pulled my cock out and pumped it lightly.

God, she was perfect. I already knew she was mine. I'd known from the first taste. Did I tell her she was my true mate before she sank down on my cock? No. But I should have.

She bent over and swirled her tongue around my tip causing my hips to buck. She giggled, the sound shooting straight to my balls.

I pulled her up until she was straddling my hips and she didn't need any more encouragement than that to sink down on me. I was going to be damned for eternity for this, but as the white-hot euphoria of having sex with my one true mate blasted through me all I could feel was absolute bliss.

6

TARRYN

I am so dead...

As soon as I sank down on him, I knew I was in trouble. I saw flashes in the blinding hot euphoria that came with being with my one true mate. I'd heard stories about the mate bond and how unbreakable it was. I never thought it would happen to me while I was with another magical being and one that was on the other side, nonetheless. Did I mention I was dead?

I must have passed out because next thing I knew I was opening my eyes to Kerrigan and he didn't look happy. "What happened?" I asked but all I got in return was a grunt.

"I should have left you there unconscious but seeing as we're mates the pain would have been unbearable," he roared.

"What are you talking about?" I groaned. He'd taken the time to dress me. How long was I out?

"We're true mates, Tarryn. You honestly can't be that stupid, right? I saw your memories just as you saw mine. Is that what all this was about? An edge to get to the enemy? A way to win the war? You realize what he is, right? He's the darkness that wants to destroy the universe. You're here to steal from the clan to get something that will destroy everything." He shook his head as he stood. I didn't know what to say because he was right. That had been what I was planning the whole time, up until I actually started to like Kerrigan. I wasn't sure what I was planning or not planning at that point, I just wanted to get the hell out of the damn forest. I had no idea what changed but nothing in my life was ever going to be the same.

"Hey! There's no reason to yell at me and call me names. I couldn't have possibly known we were true mates. I was saving your stupid life. Asshole." I jumped to my feet angry for no good reason. I could feel him now and I thought maybe his anger had affected me somehow. The plan *had* been to betray him though. His stupid self going on a mission without properly feeding first was just insane. It completely ruined everything. Jaren was going to kill me, then Kerrigan. "We need to get out of this forest," I said looking around. I found my pack and my sword laying not too far away.

"We aren't doing anything until *you* explain what I saw." He roared getting in my face.

"I didn't know you. I had a job to do, just like you did. I made my allegiance a long time ago and now I'm going to be punished for what happened. So will you. You know all my secrets now. Jaren won't let either of us live." I was freaking the fuck out. I knew the cost of failure, but as I looked at Kerrigan, I knew I couldn't betray him. *Fuck! I'm in so much trouble.*

"Jaren won't touch you," he growled, pulling me to him. His lips met my cheek because he wouldn't kiss my lips without permission. Even though we were partially mated, and he was angry, he was still giving me a choice. I melted a little at that. Fuck! How could I have thought I could actually betray him. I think I'd realized days ago what I was allowing myself to acknowledge then. This mission had failed before it ever began. That bitch fate had fucked everything up for me and it could end up costing me not only my life, but Kerrigan's too.

"There's no way around it. We are true mates and in case you've forgotten it is against the law in the magical realm." I rolled my eyes at him. "We aren't safe anywhere. Your people will never accept me, and Jaren would sooner kill us both than bring Kingston's little brother into the fold. We are dead." Kerrigan chuckled. I wanted to slap the stupid grin right off his stupid face. "What the fuck do you think is so funny?" I shoved at his chest, but he pinned my arms to my side and bent down to look me in the eyes.

"Kingston's mate is Fae. Actually, she is the daughter of Fae royalty. They will be ruling one day, and they will not be keeping the ban on magical mates. Jaren has been lying to you. Telling you this is the only way, when he's not Jaren anymore. He's Damian an evil creator who wants to destroy the universe because he's been locked up in a prison realm for Millenia." I scrunched up my brow at the words. There was no way I missed something like that. I'd been with Jaren for centuries and while he'd become a little more extreme over the last twenty-five years I was sure he was still Jaren.

Kerrigan's eyes widened as he looked at me. "What did you say?"

"I didn't say anything." I shot him a puzzled frown.

No, really, what did you say? I heard his voice in my head and his mouth didn't move.

"Oh fuck, it's happening already." Because true mates were tied to each other's life forces, the mind link was a fail-safe so they could protect the other even at long distances. Even with just a partial mating, I could feel him, and it would be excruciating for both of us if we were separated for long periods of time.

"Well, well, well, what do we have here?" My whole body froze up at that voice. I knew it well. I'd been in Jaren's service for centuries, but now it had a snakelike oily quality to it. Had it always been like that? When we were young he was full of ideas and life. He was charismatic, but now he's the shell of what he once was, and I briefly wondered why I stuck by him for so long.

He was your friend. Kerrigan's voice sounded in my head trying to soothe those turbulent emotions I knew he could feel.

He's not the same Jaren anymore, is he? I responded back.

No, love. Afraid not. Even in my head he sounded sympathetic.

"Oh, look at them, already using the mind link." Jaren clapped his hands together like a giddy child. The look on my face betrayed my disgust with the whole situation, and with him. "Did you really think I wouldn't know what was happening, Tarryn?" He tsked.

I shook my head, this was ridiculous. What was even more ridiculous was how he had us completely surrounded by wolves. We couldn't teleport our way out of the forest, but even escaping once we left would be impossible with the wolves' ability to rip someone from a teleport. I shook my head. We were well and truly screwed.

We will figure something out, love. His voice in my head was as reassuring as his smile. I wanted to believe him, but six wolves and Jaren standing in front of us didn't give me a whole lot of hope. "I knew the entire time you were on this goose chase. There was no item. It was a person. *Him.* I need the brother of the future king to do my bidding and it worked out even more beautifully than I had bargained for. True mates? I never saw that one coming," he chuckled, and the sound was like nails on a chalkboard. How had I followed this guy for so long and not noticed the difference? I was ashamed of myself for not opening my eyes sooner.

"You're really not him?" My mind was blown, and I was hurting for my friend who'd been taken by some dark evil force. It had to have been gradual because I never noticed the difference. Jaren, or whoever he was, chuckled darkly.

"This is what it took for you to see?" He was practically bent in half laughing. "You should see the look on your face right now. It's priceless."

"You are not my king," I yelled. It seemed to get his attention because his eyes narrowed.

"You will regret your disloyalty to me, Tarryn. One way or another," he warned. He turned to the six wolves surrounding us and commanded, "bring them to the palace dungeon. They will do as I ask." Then he teleported away.

The circle of wolves closed in on us and Kerrigan and I looked at each other with a grim determination. The wolves might have been powerful, but we were powerful too. There was no way we were letting them take us to the palace to be tortured. I would die first.

7

KERRIGAN

I backed up to Tarryn's back as we faced off against the wolves. They were in a circle around us and we were vastly outnumbered six to two. I felt a new energy pass through me, and I was supremely grateful to Tarryn for helping me feed. I needed my strength. I raised my sword, ready to take on as many as it took. They circled us probably looking for an opening to attack.

"You heard the boss, Tarryn. You need to come with us," one wolf snarled, stepping forward.

"You really think I'm that stupid Mik?" She smirked. "I know what will happen if I go with you."

"You really think the boss would hurt you?" His brows scrunched down.

"I'm not going to give him the opportunity," I growled at the wolf, widening my stance.

"Ryn, I really don't want to fight you. Please come quietly," the wolf said almost sadly. I shook my head growling at the familiarity this wolf had with my mate.

"You know I can't do that. He'll kill me after he tortures me slowly." She shrugged. The wolf shook his head in exasperation.

"Well, I guess you know what I have to do." He nodded and three of the wolves began to shift. *Shit, this is going to be difficult.*

I know. I heard Tarryn's voice in my head. Six shifters against the two of us would have been bad, but with half of them shifted into their animal forms--it's completely unpredictable. The wolves snarled.

I noticed vines moving by my feet as the wolf Mik took a step toward me. I narrowed my eyes at him as his hands turned to claws and he swiped at my head. The vines were still moving. He didn't notice as they wrapped themselves around his legs, not until he tried to take a step. He stumbled and they banded around his chest and arms trapping him to the forest floor. I looked to Tarryn, but she shook her head. Wind whipped at her hair as a swirling vortex blew through the place. I swiped at a wolf who was coming too close and the vortex changed direction and barreled into the wolf in question. Again, I looked at Tarryn.

"I'm not doing that, you are," she yelled trying to be heard over the howling wind.

"What?" I yelled back. There was no way I was doing that. I didn't have power over earth.

"Ease back on the tornado," she yelled.

"I don't even know how I'm doing it." The tornado blew through two more wolves throwing them into the trees which subsequently moved blocking them out. Watching it was crazy. The trees cut the wolves off so they couldn't get back the way they had come. I heard the clash of steel and turned my head to see Tarryn fighting with the last wolf. He snarled at her as he lunged. I growled low in my throat and lunged for the wolf, but I was too late. Tarryn slashed him across his chest and vines began wrapping around him leaving him immobile and gushing blood from the wound in his chest. Tarryn was breathing hard. I turned around and realized we were alone. I blew out a breath and the winds died down. I turned Tarryn around looking for any kind of wounds but found nothing. Her eyes glowed with a kind of bloodlust.

Tarryn jumped in my arms and her lips came down toward mine but I held my head back. "Are you sure, love? It's forever." I raised an eyebrow at her. Something in her gaze softened as she threaded her fingers through my hair pulling me to her.

"Kiss me, Kerrigan." It was a command. A command I wasn't about to ignore. My lips crashed down on hers and I plunged my tongue into her mouth, battling with hers for dominance. I felt the bond solidify and despite where we were and what had just happened, I was mindless in my need for her. I blinked and our clothes were gone. I shoved her up against a nearby tree as I pushed into her savagely, never removing my lips from hers. Tarryn's head fell back as she screamed. I could feel her need as much as my own and her climax had already begun to build. She pulled at strands of my hair, completely wild in her need.

My hands roamed her skin before making their way down to where our bodies were joined. I stroked a finger over her clit and felt her shudder as if it was my own. Her walls squeezed my aching cock as I thrust in and out, hard and fast. "Look at me, Tarryn," I commanded. Her eyes widened and locked with mine as I continued to circle her clit. Her orgasm was building as she continued to milk me. One final thrust and I grabbed her head molding her lips to mine as we both shattered.

8

TARRYN

I could feel everything. The most intense orgasm of my very long life crashed through me and wave after wave of white-hot heat seared my skin. I felt Kerrigan's orgasm as powerful as my own and reveled in it. He broke the kiss and we were both breathing heavily as he rested his forehead against mine. "That was incredible," he breathed, chuckling to himself. He blinked and my clothes were back on. I looked up at him in confusion. "It's an old Leprechaun trick." He shrugged. I giggled.

"Neat trick. We should probably get out of here." He nodded in agreement. I unwrapped my legs from around him and we gathered our things never breaking contact with each other. It was nice to have a connection like that.

"I'm starting to think the clan was never here." Kerrigan said as we walked through the forest.

"What do you mean?" I furrowed my brow in confusion.

"Darius sent me to this man named Kole for help finding the clan. He gave me some odd riddle that sent me here, but I think he was meddling in this by not telling me where to find them," he chuckled softly.

"He said the same to me," I admitted. Had this whole thing been a set up from the start? Why was Darius so interested in mates? I didn't know. He'd sent Kerrigan to Kole to help find the clan, but I was sure he'd already known what was going to happen before he did it.

"What kind of game is he playing? Why manipulate us into mating? Is he trying to make immortals stronger?" Kerrigan furrowed his brow in confusion.

"It would make sense. He doesn't want Jaren destroying the entire universe. He's giving us every advantage to fight him. But why send us on a wild goose chase?" I was slightly confused, but with my mind on other things we seemed to be making headway out of the forest.

"Would we have met and done what we did if we hadn't been lost in the Black Forest?" He arched a brow at me. "You probably would have just stalked me until you found what you needed, then you would have headed back to Jaren." He wrapped his arm around my waist kissing my temple.

"Yes, I probably would have," I sighed. He was right. We would still be enemies if Kole hadn't intervened. I couldn't even imagine it now that we were mates. The bond was so strong I couldn't fathom the idea that we were once on different sides and up until a few hours ago I'd had every intention of betraying him. He raised a brow at me. "Shit, I really need to work on shielding my thoughts," I grumbled. He yanked me to him glowering at me.

"You don't ever need to shield your thoughts from me," he growled. I heard a rustling in the bushes and tensed grabbing for my blade. Kerrigan spun around putting me behind him and wrapping his arm around my waist to secure me there like I was some kind of helpless female. I rolled my eyes and stepped aside to stand next to him. He glared at me, but I shrugged.

"Well, it looks like everything went according to plan." Darius stepped from the bushes grinning at us.

"You set us up," Kerrigan growled.

"Of course I did. I can't directly intervene, but I can push you in the right direction." Darius shrugged.

"Why?" I raised an eyebrow at him.

"We needed Jaren's most trusted lieutenant to see him for what he really was and defect. I knew you two would be formidable once you saw you were true mates and enlisted the help of a very persuasive bar owner to give you both the push you needed." This being was infuriating.

"So, the clan?" Kerrigan's hackles rose and I squeezed his hand.

"They are safe," Darius said pointedly.

"But not here?" I asked because he was so cryptic.

"It's best if the clan stays hidden for now so no, I can't tell you." He grinned like this was all some kind of game.

"This is some kind of crazy creator thing isn't it?" Kerrigan lifted a brow and Darius nodded. "Did you send us here because you knew this would be the only way to bring Tarryn to our side?" Darius nodded again, grinning. I wanted to punch the stupid creator in his stupid face but at the same time I was kind of happy he had done what he did. It brought me my mate and our lives may not be easy but at least we had each other.

"C'mon, I may not be able to do much, but I can get you out of this forest." Darius shuddered as he moved toward us.

"Sounds great," Kerrigan said as he put an arm around me and a hand on Darius shoulder just before he teleported us out. Thank fuck for that.

9

KERRIGAN

"What are we doing here?" I asked as Darius teleported us to Stonehenge. I looked around and blanched at all the faces I saw. It seemed like all the immortals who were on our side were there setting up tents and trying to find loved ones. "What happened?" I growled at Darius.

"From what I understand there has been a coordinated attack on all magicals not aligned with Jaren." Darius scrubbed a hand over his face. I heard a shout in the distance and in a second we were surrounded. Weapons were pointed at Tarryn and it caused a growl to burst from my throat.

"What the bloody hell?" I wrapped my arm around her and pulled her behind me. I didn't miss the exasperated breath that came from her as I did, but my people were treating her as if she were... oh shit, I'd forgot. I waved a hand at them and made them lower their weapons. My mother walked up with a smile on her face as she hugged me.

"We were so worried Kerrigan, when your father told me he sent you to find the missing clan, then immortals started being attacked in their homes, I thought something had happened." She looked around me trying to get a look at Tarryn. I knew mother knew her. Tarryn has been working with Jaren for centuries and in the immortal scheme of things I was a baby compared to most.

"Beatrix," Tarryn bowed her head in deference.

"Hello, Tarryn, why does my son protect you as though you need to be protected?" She raised a brow at her.

"I have no idea." She smirked. "I'm a warrior. Just because I'm also his mate doesn't make me weak, does it?" She challenged my mother, who gasped at the words. Her eyes widened comically as she looked between the two of us.

"She's your mate?" She looked at me with wide eyes and I nodded. I didn't know how my mother would react but a movement behind her caught my eye as I saw queen Arabella stalking toward us. Aisling's mother looked furious as she stomped toward us. I squared my shoulders and continued to stand steady in front of my mate.

"What is she doing here?" she bellowed, pointing an accusing finger at Tarryn. My shoulders tensed as I watched her. What the hell was she on about? This was my mate. My mother did the same thing she always did when easing Arabella. She went to her and hushed her before speaking quietly in her ear. Arabella nodded.

"Fine, I'll see it your way but only because she could be useful," Arabella huffed. She raised a finger to the guards who rushed around us in a circle. "But, that doesn't mean she gets to roam free until we've had a proper interrogation." She smirked as she walked away. *Shit! What the hell am I going to do?* I snarled at the oncoming guards, but they didn't seem to care.

"Mother," I called but she shook her head.

"She is the Queen. Right now, there is nothing we can do but cooperate." She kissed my cheek and followed after the queen. I stomped my boot and pulled my sword daring any of the men to come near her.

"You heard the queen, Kerrigan, she needs to be questioned." One of the guards had his hand up in surrender.

"Kerrigan," she whispered softly. "I'll be okay with them."

"No," I could hear the guttural tone of my voice in my own ears. She smiled reassuringly and kissed my lips. My arm wrapped around her back and we both moaned at the intensity of the kiss.

I'm right here baby. I promise I won't be going anywhere." My mind reeled at the sound of her voice in it.

"Fine, but if she calls out to me in anyway because you hurt her I will have no mercy." I warned the Fae before me. He gulped nodding his agreement before he grabbed her arm and dragged her away.

I stood a long time outside the queen's hut waiting for any sign that my mate was hurt. My mother came out hours later smiling at me. "Your mate is really something, darling one." She grinned. "She has quite the fiery personality."

"That she does, mother. What is going on in there? Can I see her?" I raised an eyebrow.

"The immortal race has been attacked while you were on your errand for your father. We must be sure she isn't on his side any longer." She couldn't meet my eyes.

"What do you mean attacked?" I growled.

"More clans have disappeared, and every town thought to be loyal to us has been snuffed out. We are all that's left, Kerrigan. We don't have the numbers to take Jaren on, and your brother and his team have not returned from their mission to find the shifters. We can't afford to have a mole in our midst telling Jaren where we are and every move we make. That's why your mate is being questioned." She didn't like it. I could tell by the look on her face. I walked over to the nearest hut and punched it. I hated not knowing. I felt a bit of reassurance over the mating bond and calmed considerably. We would be okay. Tarryn would be okay, and we would find a way to destroy Jaren, together.

∼

Hours later the queen came out of the hut and I glared at her. "Where is Tarryn?"

"She is perfectly fine and cleared to go. You are very fortunate to have a strong mate." I glowered at her words. What had they done to her that would make the queen respect her strength so much? I pushed through the curtains and came to a stop. Tarryn had one of the guards in a headlock as he tried to escape her hold. She kept shouting instructions at him on how to break it, but the guy just continued to flail.

"Ease up, love, we need every soldier we can get." I smirked as I sauntered toward her.

"I won't damage him. I was teaching him." She grinned maliciously. I chuckled as she released the guard, who glared up at her retreating form as he attempted to catch his breath.

"C'mon, love. We need some rest. There is still a lot of work to do." I wrapped my arm around her shoulder and led her outside to a nearby hut. For the first time I felt free and powerful, nothing could come between us and we could overcome all odds. As long as we had each other.

"I love you, Ryn." I kissed her temple. Her eyes shown up at me as her lips curved up in a smile.

"I love you, Kerrigan."

The End

EMBER-RAINE WINTERS
HTTPS://LINKTR.EE/EMBERRAINEWINTERS

ALSO BY EMBER-RAINE WINTERS:
LEPRECHAUN'S KISS
BEYOND THE WRECKAGE
CONQUEST

BEWITCHED BY THE BARTENDER

RAYNE ELIZABETH

Whatever you call it—voodoo, magic, serendipity—just say yes!

Sub-genre: Contemporary Romance
Relationship: Male/Female

1

THE READING

I should've known when Elle suggested I have my fortune read, it would be a bunch of bogus shit. And now, I can't get out the door of Madame Leget's damp, dusty backroom fast enough. *Jesus!* Just drop me in a maze and call me Mickey because twisting and turning through these rooms and dark, dingy halls, I'm nothing more than a mouse looking for the cheese at the end. *Oh my god, where's the fucking door?* Seriously, this place is creepy as shit. Between the voodoo dolls, candles, and skulls, I'm freaking out. I don't think it's been dusted since Voodoo Queen Marie Laveau herself was alive in the late 1800s. I refuse to touch anything, and I mean anything, including the door. I may not believe in all the hoopla, but I definitely don't want to take the chance of carrying out some crazy-ass mojo with me.

"Elle, open the goddamn door!" Stomping my foot, I glare at her.

Laughing hysterically, she finally pushes the door open.

I gasp for fresh air as I stumble onto the sidewalk. Okay, as fresh as you can get in the French Quarter on Friday night. Hell, maybe if I inhale enough, I can get a secondhand high.

"I'm telling you, Chayna, she's never been wrong. Madame Leget has always, and I mean always, been spot-on with everything she has ever read for me. Remember the time I told you I won at the casino?"

"Yeah, so?"

"She told me to go and what machine to play. I won $2,500! And that's just one of many things."

"Well, it isn't going to work for me. I'm not going to meet a man and fall in love, let alone a younger man. Come on, really. Look at my track record."

"So? What does that have to do with anything?"

Stopping abruptly, I whirl around to look her in the eye. "Seriously, I am giving up on finding a man, especially one I can love and trust. I spent eight years believing Adam was the one, and look what it got me!"

Elle stills, taking my hand and looking me dead in the eye. "Adam was an ass, Chayna, and you know it. He never did anything for you. Your world was him. His world was him. I'm sorry, but it's true."

Turning around, I look at the street signs. "Where's the fucking car? I thought we parked it right here. I hope we didn't get towed."

"It's probably just up the street a bit. Come on, Chayna, don't try to change the subject; you know I'm right."

I do know she's right, even if I don't want to admit it. Unfortunately, it took walking into Adam's office to find his secretary on her knees in front of him for me to finally walk away. Not waiting for him to respond to my shocked expletive, I just turned around and walked out. Well, I bolted. I didn't even know I could move that fast anymore.

"Hey, Chayna, you okay?" Shaking my arm, Elle jars me back into reality.

"Yeah, I'm okay. Just thinking."

A huge smile spreads across her face.

"Well, girl, stop thinking, cause we should be drinking. Let's check out the little bar we just passed, back up the street on the corner. I don't think I've ever been there."

"Yeah, I could use a drink. Maybe even two or three. But I know our car was parked right here. Weird."

Jerking me by the hand, Elle turns me around and we walk back down the crowded street, passing one drunken tourist after another, hurricane glasses in hand.

As we draw closer to the corner bar, I realize Elle is right; I've never seen this place before. I thought I knew every nook and cranny on Bourbon Street. Where the hell did this bar come from? It's like it appeared from out of nowhere. The exterior fits perfectly with the eccentricity of Bourbon Street, with its cream-colored brick, dark green accents, and gold-trimmed signage.

The Storybook Pub. I'm intrigued.

Tightening my grip on Elle's hand, I pull her toward the door.

"Hey, Chayna, slow down!"

"Sorry, hon."

Letting go of her hand, I push through the heavy wooden and stained-glass door. The scent of leather invades my senses as I scan the room, mesmerized by the quaint booths, mahogany-stained wooden floors, and brick walls. Most establishments in New Orleans are so traffic-laden they lose their gloss quickly, but this place is like a fairy tale. Tracing my hands over the bar, I lose myself in the intricate woodwork until a voice pierces my heart.

"Good evening, ladies. What can I get for ya?"

Lifting my head, my gaze locks with the bartender's piercing sky-blue eyes and my breath stutters in my chest. His loose, wavy, chestnut hair falls just below his brow, amplifying the brightness of his eyes. I drop my gaze to a wonderfully muscular chest and arms straining against the t-shirt he wears, exposing a hint of tattoos beneath its sleeves. I swallow the thickness in my throat, speechless.

I think Elle is, too, because I haven't heard a peep from her—which is highly unusual.

He steps closer to us. "Better yet, how about y'all let me fix you something special?" His thick, Southern with a hint of French Cajun accent is captivating, causing my knees to become weak. "Maybe something to help you forget the worries of the world?"

Like he's reading our minds, we just smile and nod in agreement, then watch him turn away from the bar.

"Holy shit, he is fucking gorgeous," I whisper under my breath, turning to Elle.

She just looks at me and smiles as we slide onto our barstools. "I told you, she's never wrong."

I slap her leg under the bar. "Come on, seriously! He has to be at least ten years younger..."

Elle smirks, and I flush as I recall what Madam Leget foretold about me meeting a younger man...

Nah, this is just a coincidence, right? Regaining my composure, I watch him as he makes our drinks. Unable to help myself, I take another peek at his lusciousness, scanning him from top to good Lord, bottom. His jeans have to be painted on, the way they hug every glorious inch of him. He obviously takes very good care of himself.

Dragging my eyes back up to his face—I freeze.

He's watching me in the mirror, a smirk dancing on his full lips.

I meet his gaze and quickly look away as embarrassment flushes my cheeks. Clearing my throat, I look down and straighten my top.

"Here ya go, cher. Tell me what ya think." Grabbing two napkins, he places them on the bar, then sets our drinks on top, sliding them toward us.

The hazy blue concoction has me curious. "What's in it?"

"Ah, a little of this and a little of that. Just take a sip and tell me how you like it."

I look at Elle and we both shrug our shoulders as we bring the straws to our lips.

Elle moans a bit as she takes her sip. "Oooo, yum."

"I know, right! Seriously, what's in it? Maybe a little pineapple? I love pineapple. And something I can't quite put my finger on. I don't think I've ever tasted anything quite like this before."

Folding his arms, he leans toward me. My pulse races as his scent envelops my space. His woodsy, citrus fragrance only pulls me in closer.

"No, cher, I assure you that you haven't." His eyes drink me in as he reaches across the bar, feathering his fingers across my arm, his touch leaving a trail of goosebumps in its wake. "It's one of those things, ya know, once you have a taste, nothing else will satisfy your thirst."

Holy fuck. I have officially melted.

2
INHIBITIONS

I'm entranced by his scent and his words. His touch elicits a shudder straight to my core, causing me to clench my knees together. The bell above the door rings and snaps me back to my senses. He quickly looks up and greets the group walking in. Skimming his fingers down my arm, he pushes back from the bar. He winks and moves down to the other end where the new patrons get settled.

"Chayna, oh my God. What the hell? Do I need to call myself a cab?"

"Elle, shush! Jeez, he's probably just surfing for good tips."

"Yeah, okay. Whatever you say. But, I would, so…"

"You would…?" the bartender drawls.

Shit, where did he come from?

"I would…like another one of these, please." Elle slides her empty glass back across the bar making a quick save.

"Not a problem. What about you, darlin? Would you like another, or are you still savoring the first one?"

Squirming in my chair, I clench my knees together once again. His gaze is intoxicating by itself, and whatever is in this concoction he mixed for us isn't helping my resolve.

"Maybe in a bit. I guess I'm still savoring this one." Looking into his eyes over the top of my glass, I take another sip.

Honestly, I'm not usually someone who flirts. In fact, I thought I'd forgotten how. I guess after being in a relationship for eight years, I didn't need to as much anymore. It's probably the reason Adam and I had become a bit mundane. Maybe he wouldn't have been banging his secretary had I realized. But tonight is a new beginning, so why not? What's a little flirting gonna hurt, right?

"Well, a woman who likes to take things slowly and enjoy the moment. I'll remember that."

I smile, trying to quell the heat rising to my face. Luckily, he's already halfway down to the end of the bar and doesn't notice my pink cheeks.

"Girl, he is *so* hitting on you! He isn't talking to me like that. And we both know if he were, you'd be tending bar for a bit because I'd be finding a storeroom in a hot minute!"

"Elle, you're so fucking crazy. You would not!"

"Chayna, babe, do I need to refresh your memory...?"

I nearly choke on my drink. "Nope, I got it. I know how many times I had to tag along with your ass to make sure you got home...*alone*."

"Do you remember the New Year's Eve when we were home from college and forgot we had a curfew?"

"Hell yeah. I had to follow your ass to the guy's house and drag you out at three a.m. And your mom—oh my god—she was standing in your driveway when I drove up!"

By the time our gorgeous bartender returns we are both laughing hysterically.

"What's so funny?"

"Just talking about one of our nights out when we were in college."

"Well, let's hear it."

"I don't think so, girl code and all. You understand, right?" Playfully, I touch his forearm, leaving my hand there as Elle and I continue to laugh about our antics when we were younger. He looks down at my hand, then back up at me. Our eyes meet and sparks fly, fueling the fire burning between us. Pulling my hand back, I quickly place it in my lap. Reaching out, he removes a strand of hair from my face and pushes it behind my ear. His touch scorches me causing every nerve to stand on end.

"Aw, come on, cher, you can tell me your secrets. I won't tell a soul. Scout's honor."

"So, you were a boy scout, huh?"

"Darlin, I've never been a boy scout, trust me." He flashes a devilish smile and walks down to the end of the bar to help another customer.

A man walks out from what appears to be an office in the back of the bar and makes his way toward us. "Good evening, ladies. How's your night progressing?"

"Very nicely, thank you." Elle flashes a flirtatious smile.

"And you, how's your night going?"

"Excellent."

"Wonderful to hear. I'm Kole, the owner of this establishment. Whatever you might need or *want* tonight, please don't hesitate to ask."

Elle kicks me under the bar.

I want to grab my shin, but it would be too obvious, so I grit my teeth and smile at Kole. "It's nice to meet you, Kole. You have a lovely place. Oddly, I've never seen this bar before. It's like it appeared from out of nowhere. How long have you been here?"

"Not long. We just set up shop recently, very recently. And may I ask your names?"

"Certainly, Kole." Elle extends her hand across the bar. "I'm Elle, and this is my very best friend in the whole wide world, Chayna."

Kole holds out a hand to each of us. I extend my hand and he turns it over, placing a kiss on my knuckles. Flirtatious bartenders must be common here. A smile crosses my face. It's nice to feel appreciated, even if from a stranger.

As I finish my drink, our gorgeous bartender returns.

"Cher, can I get you that drink now?"

"Yes, please." I slide my glass to him as Kole watches us intently.

"Tell me, is my new protégé providing you with everything you might need?"

Kole's stare into my eyes as he awaits my response is unnerving—stripping me of all of my layers, delving into my deepest, darkest thoughts—the way Madam Leget looked at me when she pretended to read my mind, or my future, or whatever else she pretended to do back there.

"Yes, thank you." I glance back at Elle, who takes her cue.

"Absolutely, thank you."

"Wonderful to hear."

"Here ya go, love. I hope it's as good as the first."

Kole motions toward us. "Finn, I trust you will provide Elle and Chayna with whatever a heart may desire?"

Finn reaches out and takes Elle's hand, kissing it, then he turns to me. Taking mine, he gently kisses the inside of my wrist, then responds to Kole while looking into my eyes. "*Everything* the heart desires."

My pulse accelerates when he places his thumb firmly on my wrist after kissing it. I swear I'm either losing my fucking mind or Madam Leget is legit. Either way, I'm enjoying every minute.

"Wonderful. Ladies, why don't you order from the menu? Everything is on the house this evening. I'm sure Finn would agree when I say we would love to have you pass some time here tonight."

Kole slides the menus down to us, still searching my eyes.

"Thank you."

Elle grabs my leg under the bar with a 'what the fuck is going on' kind of squeeze.

"Our pleasure. Enjoy. Finn, please ensure tonight is one to remember."

"Won't be a problem, sir."

With Finn's response, Kole turns and disappears behind the same door from which he appeared.

3

WHAT ARE FRIENDS FOR

Elle picks up her menu and opens it quickly. "You know, I am a bit hungry. Chayna, are you going to get something?"

Grabbing my menu, I replay the night's events in my mind as I stare blindly at the descriptions, unfocused.

Finn clears his throat. "Might I make a suggestion?" He places his finger in the seam of the menu and pushes it down to meet my gaze.

"By all means."

He takes the menu from my hands, turns it right side up, and hands it back to me. "It's quite easier to read this way, love."

I laugh at myself. "I guess it would be, huh?"

"Now, if you want a serious recommendation, I would suggest the fish and chips."

"Okay." I close my menu. "Fish and chips, it is."

"Yep, I'm leaning towards that myself." Elle closes her menu and slides it toward Finn.

"Perfect. I'll have your order right out. Be right back."

As soon as Finn disappears into the kitchen, I let out a sigh. "Elle, what the hell is going on here? I'm freaking out. This shit doesn't happen to me!" Burying my head in my hands on the bar, I take deep breaths, trying to avoid hyperventilating.

"Babe, yes, this is your life. This was your life before Adam, remember? Don't overthink it, just enjoy. I'll gladly take my exit at some point, but you know I'll want full details tomorrow."

"I don't do one-night stands; you know this about me! Especially with someone as young as Finn."

"You don't know how young he is, and besides, you are only thirty-four years old, sweetie. Shit, you're acting like you're old enough to be his mother or something. Enjoy the moment for whatever it is, for however long it may last."

Finn walks out of the back room, tray in hand. I push back from the bar.

"Okay, give this a try. If you need anything else, just let me know. I am here to serve." Winking, he turns and begins wiping down the bar.

The whole while I'm eating, I battle between what my heart wants, my body wants, and what my brain keeps telling me. My heart wants Finn. My body *wants* Finn. My brain, the level-headed part of me, says don't risk it. But, I am drawn to him. I am a moth to his flame. And each time I meet his stare, I ache for the chance to have him. I am totally under his spell.

While I stare into space, contemplating, Elle catches my eye in the mirror behind the bar. We have been friends long enough for her to know I am struggling. The fact that I haven't said a word since Finn brought our food out is a key indicator. She mouths 'you got this'. I turn to her and smile. Yep, she knows me.

As we finish, Finn returns and gathers our empty plates and utensils.

"I'll be right back to fix you ladies another drink."

"I think I'm going to make my exit now. There's obviously something going on with the two of you and *you* need to throw caution in the wind and explore it."

Elle starts fiddling with her purse, but I grab her arm, stopping her.

"No, you can't leave me, at least not yet. I'm not ready to be alone with him."

"Yes, you are. You've practically been alone with him all night."

"I'm sorry. I didn't mean to make you feel that way."

"Sweetie, I've enjoyed every moment of this evening. Seeing you, the old Chayna, has been wonderful. I'm so happy to have you back."

"Love you for saying all that, but you are not leaving yet. Please!"

"Fine. I'll stay a little longer, but I'll call for an Uber when I do leave. You can have the car in case you need an escape plan. Which I doubt."

"Thanks."

Elle drops her keys in my purse as Finn reappears. I swear he needs a fucking bell attached to him or something.

"Another drink?"

Elle and I look at one another and nod. As Finn makes our drinks, I look around the bar; we're the only two patrons still here. "You guys aren't very busy tonight."

"No, we tend to have a very selective crowd. Not everyone feels the same draw to this place as others do."

"Can't be good for business, though. I mean, keeping a place like this up and running costs money."

"We do just fine, cher. There are more important things than money. Kole has a very good handle on everything, I assure you. No need to worry."

"Sorry, habit. I'm in finance, so when I start doing the math and it doesn't add up, I can't help myself."

Finn chuckles. He has an amazing laugh—one you could live in. "Well, there's one good thing about not being busy. We can do pretty much anything we want. Care to dance?"

He turns and taps a few buttons on the back wall and music starts playing.

I narrow my eyes. "You can't be serious…"

"Oh, dead serious. Come on!" He jogs out from behind the bar and grabs both of our hands, pulling us off our stools to the middle of the floor. "Walking on Sunshine" plays over the speakers.

We definitely are.

4

THE HOOK

"Oh my goodness, how awesome was that? This has absolutely been a night I'll never forget!" I giggle and twirl around as the music slowly fades.

"Aw, darlin, the night is young, very young."

Elle glances back over her shoulder at us just as Finn reaches for my hand and raises her eyebrows. "Finn, speaking of young... if I may ask, just how young are you? Inquiring minds want to know." She plops herself on her barstool and swivels around facing us.

"What does a number really mean? Shouldn't life experiences account for years as well?"

Shit, is he younger than we thought? Finn grazes his fingers down my back and I stiffen just a bit. The way he dodged the question sends a huge red flag up in my mind.

"Well, I guess they could," Elle says, "depending upon the experiences. Care to share?" She is obviously determined to make this awkward, and I'm more curious than ever to find out more about our mysterious Finn and all of his *life experiences*.

Finn smiles widely as he makes his way back behind the bar and begins mixing another round of drinks for us. Sliding another hazy blue cocktail across to us, he leans on the bar, closing the distance between us once again.

"Well, you know, guy code and everything." His eyes sparkle with amusement. "I don't think I should. But, to answer your earlier question about my age, I will be—"

"Hold your thought!" I grimace. "I think all those drinks have just acquainted themselves with my bladder. Restroom?"

Elle laughs hysterically. She knows I must have to go very badly for me to interrupt him when he is finally answering the question I have pondered all night.

"Shut up, Elle. Not funny."

"Yes, it is. And you know it!"

Glaring at her, I hop off my stool.

"Follow me." Laughing and sensing my urgency, Finn walks hurriedly pass the door in which Kole disappeared earlier and turns the corner, with me close behind. "Right through there."

I push pass him like a woman on a mission.

When I've finished, I wash my hands, then stop to primp in the mirror and have a chat with myself before opening the door. Do I really care how old he is? I mean, really? He works in a bar, so he has to be of legal age. And, so what? It isn't like I'm going to marry him. Elle's right: he's amazingly enticing. Why not see what happens?

With that thought, I open the door and run right into Finn's arms. Shit!

"You startled me." I try to take a step back, but he curls his arms around me, pulling me even closer.

"Not my intent." Dipping a finger under my chin, he raises my face until our eyes meet.

"Well, then, what was your intent?" I don't know what possessed me to say those words. Maybe Elle has finally rubbed off on me after all these years?

"Cher, my intentions are definitely not honorable."

And before I can blink, Finn backs me against the wall. The contrast between the cold hardness of the brick wall behind me and the warmth of his body pinned against me sends a shiver up my spine.

"I want to taste you, *every* inch of you." His voice is a near-growl when he runs his tongue up the side of my neck and takes my earlobe into his mouth with a gentle pull.

Holy fucking shit. I swallow really hard.

"There's so much I want to do to you. Should we tell your friend it's time for her leave? I promise to take exceptional care of you, love." His voice is nothing more than a whisper, his breath hot against my skin. "Just say yes, Chayna. I need you to say yes."

His rock-hard body is pressed firmly against mine, every inch of him. *Every* inch of him.

My mind whirls with images of his tongue on my body—tasting, exploring every inch of me. I close my eyes and take a breath before opening them and answering, wanting, waiting to see his reaction to my words. "Yes."

His pupils dilate as he leans in, licking his lips. I close my eyes and he brushes his lips against mine gently, then pulls back.

I frown. I mean, seriously, what was up with that kiss after all the buildup?

"Ah, darlin', I see disappointment in your eyes." Raking his finger across my lips, he leans down until our lips almost touch. "I remember you like to take things slow and savor them. Trust me, every inch of you will be savored tonight. Now, let's go back up front before someone sends a search party. You can say goodbye to Elle in your own time, because once you do, Chayna, you are all mine. Every. Inch. Of. You." He grazes his hands down my sides, heightening the already alert nerve endings all over my body.

Dazed, I walk back up front to the bar and take my seat.

"Did you get lost?"

Swiveling my stool until our eyes meet, I look at Elle.

Her lips curl into the most impish of smiles as she glances over at Finn, who has his back to us. "Ohhh. Okay. Are you ready for me to leave?"

"One more drink, please?"

"Nope. I am not letting you talk yourself out of this, Chayna. Finn, can you call me an Uber please? I'm going to head home."

"Better yet, we have a car service for our patrons. Let me give

Vonn a quick call. Give me a sec." Finn disappears into the back once again.

"Spill, Chayna. What happened?"

Elle is sitting on the edge of her seat, anxious as a kid waiting to open presents on Christmas morning.

"Nothing, really."

"Seriously?"

"I mean, he kissed me."

"Get the fuck out! That is so not nothing!"

"It wasn't so much the kiss, as what he said."

"And what did he say, pray tell?"

The heat rises in my body and begins to fill my cheeks.

"This must be good if you're blushing. Spill. You know you're gonna spill the deets in the morning anyway!"

"Something about tasting every inch of me…"

"Yes, girl!" Elle slaps her legs with excitement. "All the deets tomorrow. *All* of them. Remember everything! This is so good."

The bell above the front door rings, causing Finn to reappear from the back.

"Vonn, thanks, man. Elle requires your assistance getting home tonight. Can you accommodate her?"

I look at Vonn, then at Finn, and then Vonn again. They could be twins. *Holy crap.* Are they twins?

"I would be more than happy to accommodate you, Elle."

Elle hops off of stool, eyes wide. "Wait, are y'all…?"

"Twins? We get that all the time." Finn chuckles. "No, not technically. We are Irish twins, actually. I was born ten months before Vonn."

"Holy, hell." Elle looks back and forth between the two men. "Vonn, how old are you?"

"I'll be twenty-nine next month. Shall we go?"

"Yes, please." Elle reaches over and hugs my neck, whispering in my ear. "Maybe we'll both have something to share in the morning."

"Knowing you, probably. Be safe."

"You, too. Come on, handsome!" Elle grabs Vonn by the hand and they exit the bar.

I am finally alone with Finn. My brain shifts into hyper drive, my insecurities plaguing my every thought. *What if I am not what he expects? What if...I am not good enough?* I shake my head to clear my mind.

5

ALL IN

"Cher, it seems like you may want another drink?"

"Maybe a water, if that's okay?"

"Perfectly."

Sitting here, I am lost in thought, my insecurities breaking through once again.

"Chayna?"

Startled, I shake my head back to reality. "Sorry, I was just thinking."

Finn leans across the bar and takes my hand, playing lazily with my fingers. "May I ask about what?"

Looking into his eyes is intoxicating. I have to look away to finally find the words to speak. "Honestly, Finn, I don't do this sort of thing. Actually, this is new to me. Well, wait, I didn't say that right."

Finn just chuckles and walks from behind the bar, sitting on the stool beside mine. "Love, take a breath. Relax." Pushing my hair back away from my eyes, he curls it behind my ear once again and leans in closer. His breath causes me to shudder in the most delicious way.

"I promise to take good care of you. Now, sit here and enjoy your water. I'm gonna close up and then our night can begin. And, I promise, it will be one you never forget."

He presses his lips to my skin; I turn to meet them before I realize what I'm doing. I have been dying to kiss him, to taste him.

What was meant to be a soft, parting kiss grows with intensity I haven't felt, if I'm being honest with myself, ever. His lips sear mine as his tongue lashes between them—venturing deeper, exploring, and taking my breath away. Bending me back against the bar, he encases my face with his hands, pushing my hair back as his lips mark their way down my neck.

I cross my arms behind his neck, guiding my hands over his shoulders and down his back. Sliding them up under his shirt, I explore the lines and ridges of his torso. Wanting to see and not just feel his exquisite frame, I tug his shirt over his head and pull it off. Finn slowly steps back from me, exposing the tattoos adorning his beautifully sculpted body.

"Cher, I need to lock up. Otherwise, we may very well be the entertainment on Bourbon Street tonight."

"Yeah." I sigh, but he's right. "Okay, lock up. I'll be right here."

Taking a sip of my water, I sit on my stool as Finn flips the sign to closed, pulls the blinds down, and turns off the lights. The only remaining light glows softly from the backlit liquor shelf behind the bar.

As he draws closer, I exhale. He's right; I will never forget this night.

"Just a few more things, then I'm all yours."

As he walks by shirtless, I take inventory of what exactly is all mine tonight. Mentally tracing every line of the detailed artwork on his chest and back, my eyes go wide when the lines dip below the waist line of his jeans, outlining the beginning of a perfect "v". The gods are smiling on me for sure.

Seriously, Adam could never look this good if he tried, and while I know I shouldn't be thinking, let alone comparing the two, I can't help myself.

Finn comes from the back room where Kole disappeared. Oh shit, Kole. Where the hell is he?

"Finn, where's Kole?"

"Kole has already left. He only pops in from time to time to check on things. It's just the two of us now."

He takes my hand, pulling me from my barstool. For a fleeting moment, I want to run, but I don't. Maybe it's the look in his eyes or how his hand feels in mine.

"Come with me."

I grab my clutch and follow him, hand in hand, toward the back of the establishment. Instead of turning the corner as we had previously, we continue until we reach a curved staircase leading to the second floor. I hadn't realized this place was a two-story when we came in earlier.

Finn stops at the bottom of the stairs, turning to search my gaze. "I live upstairs. Do you want to…?"

I glance up the staircase then meet his gaze and nod. "Yes."

Ascending the stairs behind Finn, I trail my other hand up the glossed, mahogany railing, taking in every moment. Once we reach the landing, Finn unlocks the door at the top. I step into his room, surrounded by shelf after shelf of books on every wall, leading to a window seat with an arched opening. The center of the room has a large oriental rug with a huge leather couch, a reading lamp on one side and a four-poster bed on the other. I make a complete three-sixty before looking back at him standing in the doorway.

"You really live here?"

"Yeah, Kole likes to have someone on premises in case there is a problem."

"It's beautiful. And so many books."

"I read a bit."

"A bit?" I laugh. "You've read all of these?" Dropping my clutch on the table by the door, I walk over to the shelves and run my fingers across the spines of the books, taking it all in.

"Most of them."

"Wow."

Finn closes the door behind him and turns back to me, the lust in his eyes making the books and bookshelves and all of New Orleans disappear.

Breathe, Chayna. Deep breaths.

6

ANTICIPATION

Unbuttoning his jeans, Finn closes the distance between us and pulls me in, encircling his arms around my waist. As he leans down, he brushes a kiss across my lips.

I'm totally under his spell. I know it, he knows it.

"Cher, I'm gonna take a quick shower. Wash off the day's work. You can get comfortable. I won't be long."

"Sure. I'm certain I can find something to get into while you take your shower."

"I'll be right in there if you need me." Finn points to the open doorway near the front of the room. "And besides, I'm an open book, so to speak."

I look up at him and smile.

"Cheesy, huh?"

"Maybe a little bit. Now, go. Shower. Now." Tearing myself away from his heat, I immediately get a chill.

"Yes, ma'am."

He disappears through the doorway. What a trusting guy. I mean, he doesn't really know me, yet he's leaving me in his room to roam.

So, roam I will.

I begin to scan the spines of the books nearest me, forcing myself to focus on *books* when there's a deliciously naked *man* just a few yards away, but the steam from the shower slowly wafts out into the room, and roaming becomes the last thing on my mind.

Good God, is he *trying* to test my self-control?

I close my eyes and breathe deeply, greedily inhaling Finn's intoxicating, woodsy scent.

Inching closer to the open door of the bathroom, I feel a bit voyeuristic peeking around the corner, hoping to actually steal a glance of him showering, but I can't stop myself, don't *want* to stop myself.

To my surprise, he's standing there, in all his scrumptious glory, looking straight at me as he washes off the lather. What a glorious, unabashed vision. It's as if he was waiting for me, knowing I would come.

I explore every inch of him with my eyes—his broad shoulders, sculpted chest, six-pack abs and perfect 'v'. My mouth waters at the sight of his cock. It twitches when I lock my eyes on it. I have never been so hungry. I drag my gaze back up to his face and a smile dances on his lips. Watching the water cascade down his body, glistening over every inch of him, highlighting his muscular frame, I am growing just as wet as he is.

"I was hoping you would join me."

Before I can respond, he steps out and extends his hand. I take it. I want to join him more than he knows.

"Let me help you get out of these clothes." Picking me up, he sits me on the vanity, running his hands down my legs as he kneels to take off my pumps, then gently massages the bottom of my feet. I can't take my eyes off of him. I am so caught in his web at this point, I don't care if he rips my clothes off—no matter how much I paid for them.

As droplets of water fall from his hair onto my chest, he licks them from my skin with the undoing of each button of my shirt. Slipping off my blouse, he hangs it on the hook by the door. I have never been so glad I wore a matching bra and panties set. Sliding the straps over my shoulders, he reaches around and unclasps the hooks in back, marking me with the heat from his touch. Gliding my bra around my torso, he removes it and steps back.

I am exposed and unsure and start to pull my hands up to cover myself.

"My god, you are beautiful."

And now, with his words, I can leap mountains. I lower my arms, then stand as he unzips my pants and gradually glides them down my legs. His touch is electrifying as he inches farther down until I can step out. After hanging my pants on the hook with my blouse, he turns back to me with his eyes firmly planted on the last article of clothing I have on.

I can't wait any longer. I need his touch, his mouth, his taste. I loop my thumbs on each side of my panties, pushing them to the floor, stepping out. Watching him totally take in my body is the most empowering thing I think I have ever done in my life. I hold my hand out for him; I want him to know I am all in.

And *that* was all he needed, apparently.

With one step he reaches me, pulling me to him. "Come on, before all the hot water is gone."

Stepping into the shower with him, I giggle a bit as I check out his fine, tight ass in front of me.

"What's so funny?"

"Oh, nothing…"

"Really? We'll see." Finn laughs and pulls me under the rain showerhead with him. Before I can react, he pushes me against the shower wall, pinning my arms above my head with one of his hands. The man has very large hands.

"I have wanted this since the moment you walked in tonight."

"Me, too. If I'm being honest."

His free hand trails down my neck, tracing the outline of my breasts and making an infinity circle around them before cupping one. Lowering his head, he takes my nipple in his mouth, biting it. Not painfully, but hard enough to send shockwaves through my body and straight between my legs. I lean against the shower wall and arch my back to meet his mouth as he moves to the other nipple, giving it the same attention. I moan from the exquisite pain and pleasure he inflicts.

Trailing kisses down my stomach, he releases my hands. I know what's coming next, but I don't know how much more anticipation I can take. God knows how long it has been since a man has touched me in this way. Adam was always very one-sided when it came to oral sex. He had no problem receiving, but he definitely took more than he gave.

Actually, in the last couple of years, he only ever took. I'm such an idiot.

Finn teases my clit with his tongue, and Adam is a distant memory.

My moans echo against the high ceilings, filling the room. Placing one of my legs over his left shoulder and the other over his right, Finn braces me against the wall and devours my pussy like no man has ever done. Pushing me up the wall until he is standing, I lose it. I have been on a guy's shoulders during Mardi Gras to catch beads. But this, this...

"Oh god, oh my god! Please don't stop." Bracing my hands against the ceiling, I writhe against him like there's no tomorrow, riding out sumptuous wave after shocking wave spasm through my body.

As the last wave subsides, I begin to laugh, looking down at Finn.

"What's so funny?" His eyes twinkle with wonder as his lips curl into a most deliciously wicked smile.

"I don't know, really. I guess I can't believe what just happened. I mean, I'm touching the fucking ceiling here, and I don't think I have ever—no, I *know*—I have never come that hard before, period."

Lowering me to the ground, he stands back up. I forgot just how much he towers over me looking up at him. I'm still weak, panting and laughing.

"Well, sounds like someone didn't know what they were doing, then."

"Obviously."

Looking down at me, he pushes back my hair. Cupping my face, he stares into my eyes. Call me a needy bitch, but I want more. I need more. I loop my arms around his neck and pull my legs around his waist and kiss him as if my life depends on it. With his hardness beneath me, I begin to tease his cock with my pussy.

At least until the water runs cold in the shower. I squeal as it hits my back. "Holy shit, cold!"

"Fuck! Yes, it is!" Carrying me from the shower, my body still encircling his, he doesn't miss a beat, making his way to the bed. He sits with me straddling him, his hardness against my slit; I grind against it. Thankfully, the cold water had no effect on his cock.

Taking my mouth with his, I relish the taste of me still on his lips. He possesses my breasts with his hands, owning them as I continue my pursuit of bliss. We are connected, but not yet in the way I desire. I want all of him. I am dripping wet, but not from the shower.

But, before I can go any farther, he stops me. He leans back, his erection standing to attention between us. "Cher, condom?" His words are strained.

I hadn't really thought about condoms. I've been out of the dating scene for so long, it never crossed my mind.

"I'm clean, Finn. It's up to you."

"I am, too."

Throwing caution into the wind, I lift myself and slowly lower onto his awaiting shaft. He fills me, stretching me in the most delectable way.

"Mmm, so good…" I moan, licking my lips once I am fully seated. He feels so fucking good. Looking into his mesmerizing azure eyes, I smile. Something inside me has awakened. Something I never knew existed, and this man has brought it to the surface. I should go slowly, but I can't.

I want rough.

I want reckless abandon.

"Oh god, darlin'. You feel incredible. Let's take this up a notch." Forgetting the strength he possesses, he thrusts his hips upward, holding my shoulders down, over and over again until the dam is pleading to burst.

Throwing my head back, I take in a sharp breath.

"No, no, no, not yet." Pounding into me again and again, Finn grips me harder.

A warmth passes through my entire body, starting at my toes and working its way up. I scream and beg for release, but he refuses, making me wait each time I get close. The stamina this man has is indescribable. Shaking, I fight to hold off the waves of orgasm teetering just beyond my reach. Until finally.

"Cher, you—"

"Yes, yes, please, yes!" And I let go as the warmth of his hot seed fills me. I'm sure they can hear my screams on Bourbon Street over the noise. We fall back onto the bed, my head resting on his chest while he's still inside me. His heart is pounding, and we are both breathless.

He strokes my hair. "Babe, you're amazing. If I were to die at this moment, I would die a happy man."

Pushing up from him, I look into his eyes. "Don't say that. I would be devastated."

"I truly am, though. Happy."

As he pulls me up to him and leaves my body, I immediately feel empty. He kisses me gently on the lips before moving me to his side. I snuggle up to him with my head on his outstretched arm and trace the beautiful, Celtic lines adorning his chest. His breathing shallows as I close my eyes and drift.

7

NO REGRETS

I wake to light shining through the window. Looking around the room, I try to get my bearings. Holy shit. I didn't just have the most fabulous wet dream of all time. It really happened, all of it!

The turn of the knob on the door startles me as it slowly opens. I grab the sheets around me in a panic until Finn peers around the opening with paper bags and coffees in hand. Relief rushes through me.

"Good morning, love. I didn't want to wake you. You looked so peaceful sleeping."

Leaning down, he kisses me. Mmm, he tastes so good. I lick my lips once he pulls away to sit down next to me on the bed.

I know I have no right to be jealous, but had I known he was going out, I would have had him wear something different. This man cannot wear a t-shirt and gray sweatpants out in public again, ever. If I weren't so hungry at the moment, I would tackle him for another round.

In good time.

"I thought you may be hungry, so I ran over to Cafe Du Monde and grabbed us some beignets and cafe au lait for breakfast." He shakes the bags in front of me.

I grab one without hesitation. I need the sugary goodness of beignets right now. "Yes, please! I'm starving."

I open the bag and a cloud of powdered sugar poofs into my face, covering me.

"I got this." He leans over and licks the powdered sugar from the side of my face. I nearly choke on my bite of beignet.

"Mmm, I told you I was going to taste every inch of you, cher. I still have a few more to go. How about we remedy the problem now?"

Finn jerks the sheet from me and pushes me flat to the bed, popping a small bag of powdered sugar. A cloud of sweet confection fills the air, quickly descending and coating me from head to toe.

"What are you doing, crazy man?" I laugh and hope I'm getting the treat I expect.

"Tasting every sweet inch of you."

Finn shuffles to the end of the bed, yanks off his t-shirt and pushes his sweatpants to the floor, then pulls my feet toward him. Gazing up at me, he sucks one of my toes into his mouth, caressing it with his tongue. Then another, and another. And, oh my god, while I have never thought this was something I would like, I'm delighted to discover I was so *very* wrong.

The moisture between my legs grows as he moves up my body, pushing my legs apart, stretching them with his knees once he reaches my mound. He's devouring my body as if it were his last meal. I buck as he laps my still tender clit before tonguing me.

"Sweet baby Jesus! What are you doing to me? God, please don't stop!"

He hums back to me, causing shivers to overtake every fiber of my being. He sucks two fingers in his mouth. Pulling them out, he inserts one into me, then the other, curving them, finding my most elusive spot inside. Placing his thumb firmly on my clit, he teases and tantalizes me as I move closer and closer to release.

His eyes are laser-focused on mine, daring me to close them, daring me to come, as he licks the powdered confection from my stomach, making his way to my heaving breasts. I hold my breath, wanting to wait, but knowing I can't take much more.

Removing his fingers, he quickly tugs me to him, cupping my

bottom and looping my legs around his waist. Drawing me onto his awaiting cock, he leans back, bracing himself with his hands, and begins pummeling me.

I entwine my arms around his neck and hold on for dear life, trying to stay my orgasm.

White light streaks my vision with pops of garnet, emerald, and sapphire. He smiles, knowing I am his to take. And he does. He rocks me into oblivion once again. I scream so many expletives a sailor would blush. Dogs are probably barking from the shrill of my screams.

I, more than likely, woke up the neighborhood.

Pushing me back onto the bed, he continues to hammer into me. Another wave is quickly approaching. God, stamina is such a good thing. His breathing hitches, and I know we are both there. I move in rhythm with him.

"Oh god, Chayna! You were made for me."

With the next thrust, he moans the most delectable sound, and we still as euphoria rakes over both of us. He rests on his elbows above me, and I reach up to push his wavy locks from his eyes.

A tear rolls from my eye.

Alarm moves across his face. "Did I hurt you?"

"No, not in the least."

"Why are you crying, then? Please don't cry." He wipes the tears from my face.

"I dunno." Then, like a ton of bricks, it hits me. I'm happy. I am, beyond words, happy.

Madame Leget may actually be a psychic, but I will never acknowledge the voodoo queen aspect. "Finn, I need to tell you something."

He sits up quickly with concern.

"It's nothing bad," I reassure him as I sit up. "Promise."

8
HONESTY IS THE BEST POLICY

I cross my legs beneath me and face him, then take his hand in mine and thread my fingers through his before I begin. Not really sure where to start, but I have to tell him how ridiculously happy he's made me. If he feels the same, he won't care about the how or the why, or the strangeness of feeling so strongly for someone I've only just met.

"First, this... the time I've had with you has been amazing, and words cannot adequately explain what I'm feeling for you."

He stiffens as I speak, but I have to tell him everything about the reading yesterday. If I don't, I'll feel as though I am lying to him in a way, even though I really don't believe in fortune tellers and voodoo magic.

"Cher, you're making me nervous. Just spill it."

"Okay, I am going to start at the beginning. I don't want anything hanging between us." Taking a deep breath, I begin. "So, about three months ago, I broke up with my longtime boyfriend of eight years. You know, being with him for as long as I was, I thought he was the one. But he wasn't. I found him with his secretary and that was it for me. Cheating is not something I can handle nor tolerate, so I ended it."

"As well you should have. Who is he? Do I need to have a little *chat* with him? I can't imagine a man doing that to you."

My eyes dart from side to side, I can't look at him. My hands begin to shake and my eyes tear up. I hate that this part of my life still rips me to pieces, but it does. He clenches his fists, so I look up and smile.

"Anyway, I spent the first month curled up on my couch, with a remote and a ton of junk food. It really did a number on my psyche. I couldn't for the life of me figure out what I had done wrong."

"Stop right there. You didn't do anything wrong. He did. He should have talked to you, not cheated on you."

"I know, but still, it did something to me, and I was spiraling. Elle finally had enough of my pity party, so she started dragging me out of the house—sometimes unwillingly—until the pain dulled. We've been friends since junior high school, so she can read me like a book…"

Finn smiles back at me, and I realize what I said.

"Oh, that was cheesy." I laugh and motion toward the shelves of books.

"It fits, not cheesy. Continue, please."

"I've been doing much better lately. Then Elle got the bright idea I needed to have my fortune read. So, last night, we visited Madame Leget."

Finn's eyes widen. "Wait. Madame Leget? From down the street?"

"Yeah, a few blocks. Why?"

"I know her. Well, technically Kole knows her. The two of them have lunch here a few times a week. I just serve their food." Finn waves his hand. "Sorry, didn't mean to interrupt. It's just a small world. Please continue."

While the idea of Kole knowing Madame Leget is interesting to say the least, I file it for a later conversation.

"So, she proceeded to tell me I had wonderful things coming my way, things that would eliminate my past heartbreak from existence. She said I would meet a man, a younger man, who would take me to places I had never been or experienced. Of course, I don't believe in all of that, so I ran out of there like a cat whose tail was on fire."

Finn chuckles.

"I know, but it's true. After leaving, though, we couldn't find the car. I still don't know if it's been towed, or we just had the wrong street. Elle suggested we come in here, to the Storybook Pub. Neither of us had seen it before and were curious. As I got closer, I felt this pull, drawing me inside. And…"

"And what, Chayna?" He brushes back the hair and cups my face between his hands. "Tell me, and what?" His eyes dart back and forth between mine, as he waits for my answer.

"I found you, Finn. I found you." Saying it all out loud makes it so surreal, so undeniable.

Finn smiles. "And I found you. It doesn't matter to me what brought us together. I'm just thankful you're here."

"You don't think I'm crazy?"

"Not in the slightest. Now, kiss me."

"Wait, shit, what time is it?"

"Umm, I don't know. Noon maybe?"

"Shit, shit, shit! Where's my phone? I have to text Elle. She's probably worried sick."

Finn starts laughing hysterically. "My brother texted me last night, saying he would check in before we open today at three." He scrunches his nose playfully. "I don't think you have crossed her mind."

"That bitch!" I shake my head and laugh. "I should've known."

"Yeah, I think he's got his hands full, for sure."

"You have no idea. Trust me."

We begin to laugh, falling back onto the bed. Turning to face him, I pick up where I left off, tracing the artwork on his chest.

"What time do you have to start setting up for tonight?"

"I usually go down around two-thirty, why?"

"I have some ideas."

"You do, do you?"

"A few…"

Finn rolls on top of me, pinning me beneath him. The weight of his body on mine is heaven.

9

IT'S NOT OVER YET

Finn's hand firmly grips mine as we wander through the quarter toward the car—or where it should be. What we shared was amazing, and I don't want it to end. Thoughts whirl through my mind. Does he feel the same?

The car sits exactly where we left it. "It's here." How the fuck did we miss it last night? I push the button and the door unlocks. Opening the door, I throw my clutch inside, scared to turn around and look him in the eyes.

Finn whirls me around, pushing me against the side of the car, pinning my body with his. He sweeps the hair from my face and runs his fingers down my cheek. My body ignites. I don't even care there are people all around us. He searches my gaze, the bright sapphire of his eyes even more striking in the light of day, like beams of light… stealing my thoughts. The rest of the world fades into the background.

"Chayna, I had an amazing time with you. But there is something I need to tell you…"

Fuck, here we go. I look down and do my best to try not to cry in front of him. I told him everything this morning—about Madame Leget, and how I feel about him—and now he's going to tell me it's been swell. *It's not you, it's me—*

"Hey, where are you going right now? Look at me."

I pull my gaze back to him with watery eyes.

"I know it's only been a day since we met, but I'm falling for you. I can't let you leave and never see you again."

The tears begin to trickle from my eyes. The realization of him feeling the same things I'm feeling is overwhelming. I never believed in love at first sight until now.

"You're cryin', why?" He wipes the tears from my cheeks.

"Because I feel the same way. I don't want to leave either."

"Cher, you make me feel things I've never felt before. I'm not willing to give it up. Come back tonight. I know we don't close until two, but I want you here. I'm off tomorrow. We can sleep in or do whatever you want."

A devilish smile curves on my lips. "Whatever I want?" Looping my arms around his neck, I pull his lips closer to mine. "I have a few ideas."

"More ideas?"

"Oh, tons more."

Finn leans in, taking my mouth with his, pressing his body to mine. I lose myself in his kiss. His cock hardens against my belly, and I pull back reluctantly, glancing down between us. His jeans are now tighter than ever.

"You know, you really need looser jeans, right?"

"No, I just need you."

"You can have me. Tonight. Be prepared."

"I will. Scout's honor."

Smiling devilishly, I give him a chaste kiss and hop into the car, rolling the window down as I start the engine. "Well, maybe you can earn some badges tonight."

"I look forward to earning each and every one, cher."

After another kiss, I put the car in drive and pull off down the street, watching him disappear in my rearview mirror.

Immediately, I call Elle on Bluetooth. "Hey, biatch! How was your night?"

She laughs on the other end. "Umm, maybe I should ask about yours since you're apparently just leaving... *well* after lunchtime."

I laugh and my cheeks heat. "I'll be over shortly to drop your car off. I'll fill you in then."

"Hey, can you pick up some beignets on your way? I'm in the mood for something sweet."

I beam from ear to ear. "Sure, love. See you soon."

The End...for now.

Learn more about Rayne Elizabeth:
https://linktr.ee/RayneElizabethAuthor

Also by Rayne Elizabeth:
  If the Boot Fits
  Booking Her Beau

COMING HOME

TERI KAY

Tonight, I'm not going to let the one who got away, get away.

Sub-genre: Contemporary Romance
Relationship: Male/Female

1

NATALIE

A high-pitched squeal pierces my eardrums. Two seconds later, I'm engulfed in a bear hug by my best friend from high school.

"Hey, Veronica," I say, attempting to wriggle myself from her clutches.

"Has it really been twenty years since we graduated?"

"It has." My tone is dry and flat.

Tonight is our high school reunion. I'd rather be anywhere else than here, but I promised Veronica I'd come with her. I hated high school. I was a nerd. I spent more time in the library reading than I did socializing with other people—which I was more than happy with. People have never really been my thing.

"I came. Can we go now?" I tease.

"Stop. It's not that bad and you know it. C'mon, let's go get a drink." She grabs my arm and yanks me toward the bar.

"French 75, please," I order.

"What?" the young, scrawny bartender snaps back. "We only have beer and wine."

"Two merlots, please," my friend tells the bartender. "Look at you and your fancy New York drink," Veronica teases. "Us hillbilly folk, down here in Tennessee, still keep it simple."

"I didn't know what a French 75 was until I got to go to Paris a few summers ago to study under a French pastry chef."

We grab our drinks and find a table with two empty seats. Veronica and I have only recently reconnected through social media, after ten years of not talking. There was no falling out or fight between us, just families and careers.

∽

"Paris, huh?" she asks. "Damn. I have to admit I'm a little jealous. Where else have you been?"

"I've been lucky enough to study with some of the best chefs around the world."

"It's not luck. You're one of the best chefs in the country. I saw the piece the Food Network did about your restaurant in New York."

"That special wasn't about me, just about the restaurant I work for." I sink down into my chair, uncomfortable discussing my success.

"Stop being so modest; it's your food bringing them in," she says. "Look at what you've accomplished, despite your parents saying you couldn't."

"Oh, my mom still constantly reminds me about how she doesn't have any grandchildren."

"Natalie Shaffer? Is that you?" A woman I vaguely recognize approaches us, eyes wide.

"It is," I quietly reply.

"Oh my god, everyone! We have a real-life celebrity here tonight." Her loud, southern accent echoes through the room.

I cringe, sinking down into my chair. "Please don't. I'm nobody special."

"Stop. I saw you on the Travel Channel on a piece about the cute little French bakery you worked in. You're the most famous person in the Spring Hill High graduating class of 2000." She turns waving toward a friend. "Lacey, come see who it is!"

Another woman I don't recognize steps up beside her. "Do you remember me? We had geometry together. What's it like to be on TV?"

A few more people sidle up beside the two women, quickly forming a suffocating half-moon of strangers looking down at me with stars in their eyes. "You look great. I guess it's true what they say, the camera really does add ten pounds."

I bite back a groan and try to force a smile—

"Is Chef Lockhart as gorgeous in person as he is on TV? Have you two ever hooked up?"

I scoff. Was that a serious question?

Veronica laughs, then motions for them to leave. "Shoo, shoo. We'll have a question and answer session after dinner."

Reluctantly, they all turn and leave us alone. As is always the case, nobody really wants to know how I'm doing, just what it's like to work with celebrity Chef Jordan Lockhart, or what famous people I've met in New York. It's always the same line of questioning, the same faux interest…

"See, I told you people would remember you." Veronica laughs. I glare at her and she anticipates my reply before I can say anything. "Well, at least they know how wildly successful you are."

I honestly couldn't give a flying rat's ass what these people think about me. I knew twenty years ago small-town Tennessee life wasn't for me, and I ran as quickly as I could. After a few more drinks and a handful of similar uncomfortable encounters, my head's in a vice and my cheeks hurt from forced smiles.

I turn to Veronica, pleading with my eyes. "I've spent the last two hours answering everyone's dumb ass questions. Can we go now?"

"I guess I'm done torturing you for one night." Veronica laughs.

We grab our coats and leave without saying goodbye to a single person.

"Are you ready to call it a night?" I ask as we walk to her car.

"Whatcha got in mind?"

"Let's go to the Young Buck Saloon in Franklin. Remember the hell we raised there the summer of my twenty-first birthday?"

"Oh, sweetie." Veronica smiles sadly. "Buck's burned down about five years ago. Big electrical fire."

"Damn. I had no idea."

She unlocks the car and we climb inside. "But there's a new little pub downtown I think we could salvage this night with."

"Think they'll know what a French 75 is?"

"I think Kole can make you anything your little heart desires." She starts the car and pulls out of the parking lot, easing onto the main road that runs through town, smiling mischievously.

That smile makes me slightly suspicious, but definitely curious. "Kole?"

"Kole O'Shea. He's the owner."

As she pulls up to the pub, the sign above the door catches my eye. I cock one eyebrow. "The Storybook Pub? As in, like, children's storybooks?" What have I gotten myself into?

"No, silly. It's like the perfect storybook romance."

"There's no such thing," I mumble under my breath.

"Damn, girl." Veronica raises her eyebrows. "Someone hurt you badly, didn't they?"

"Can we just go get drunk, please?" I beg.

"Hell yeah. Come on. My sister, Tara, and her wife, Mila, have already gotten us a table."

I link my arm through hers and let her lead the way.

"Natalie!" Tara barrels through the crowd to wrap me in the same hug her sister did just a few hours earlier. Even though Tara is two years younger, the three of us were once inseparable. "Come! We have so much catching up to do!"

"Go sit with them and I'll get us some drinks. I want to say hi to Kole anyway."

Tara leads me to the table and I settle onto a barstool. "What's your sister's thing for this Kole guy?" I ask. "She talks like she's got the hots for him." If there's something going on, Tara will tell me; it's always been in her nature to gossip.

"With Kole? Never. Kole is just the kind of guy who's friends with everybody. Good things seem to happen when he's around. I know my sister ran off, got married and had a shitload of kids after college. How did you end up being a television chef? I thought you wanted to be a teacher.

"I did and I was a teacher for a few years, but I quickly realized spending my days with thirty six-year-olds wasn't my passion. For once I did what I wanted and put myself through culinary school."

"Badass." Mila's smile is intoxicating.

Veronica returns to the table empty-handed and I frown. "I thought you were getting drinks?"

She flashes a smile. "Kole said anyone who is sophisticated enough for a French 75 deserves something from his special cellar reserve."

I raise my eyebrows, then turn to Tara. "So, Tara, how did you and Mila meet? When did you get married?"

"Last year. Kole introduced us at a party he hosted here. It was love at first sight and we married six months later."

"Dom Perignon French 75s for the ladies." Kole's smoldering green eyes and lady-killer smile make my panties a little wet.

"Thank you," I say, "but I can't afford that."

"It's on the house, beautiful."

"See! I told you Kole always makes good things happen." Tara giggles.

"Cheers, ladies." Veronica raises her glass and we all raise ours. "To old friends and new reunions."

"Cheers!" we say in unison.

The expensive champagne seems to be on an endless tap and we are taking full advantage of it. The only downfall is champagne turns me into a chatterbox. Poor Tara and Mila have been asked every question under the sun about being a lesbian couple living in the bible belt.

Mila sets her glass down and looks over at me. "So, why is a gorgeous woman like you still single?"

I grimace. "I was in a serious relationship when I was teaching, but when I chose to change careers, he wasn't supportive. He actually gave me an ultimatum: him or my dream. So, I kicked his ass to the curb. Since then, I just haven't had time."

"When the person is right, you'll find the time." Mila smiles at Tara.

"Come on," Veronica says, "let's go shoot some pool."

Five minutes in and not one of us has made a single shot.

"So, really? No one since Nicholas?" Veronica continues to pry.

"Nothing serious, but damn, you make it sound like I'm already a spinster," I say louder than intended as the music suddenly stops. The entire pub turns and stares, including the hot-as-hell bartender.

"What's the deal with Hottie McBartender?" I ask.

"He and his wife owned several pubs across the world. After she died he decided to honor her memory and their storybook romance by keeping each of their pubs up and running."

"What a tragically beautiful story. Do you think Wes is your Prince Charming?" I ask.

"I do. He swept me off my feet in college and our life has been pretty amazing since, even with the accidental fifth kid," she jokes.

I bet her mom doesn't complain about grandchildren. "You know who I bet could sweep me off my feet?" I hiccup, then quickly cover my mouth. How many glasses of champagne have I had?

"Who?"

"Xavier Roman," I yell over the music, which has, apparently, paused between songs again. Looking up, my eyes lock with Kole's for the second time tonight. If he could see the burning of my cheeks, he'd be calling the damn fire department.

"Like, the senior when we were freshman, Xavier Roman?" Veronica raises her eyebrows. "He was hot. You should have asked him out."

"Oh yeah, the fourteen-year-old nerdy girl asking out the eighteen-year-old star wrestler. Plus, he was friends with my brother. Talk about feeling stupid." I hiccup loudly to really drive my point home.

"I heard he married some chick he knocked up in college."

"Awesome." I quip, throwing back another glass of champagne. "Hope they're happy living in the suburbs, with their perfect kids and perfect pets. And have great, perfect sex all the damn time." I grab my pool stick and set up for my shot, closing one eye to focus. I hit the ball with such force it flies off our table and straight onto the table next to us.

"Oops." I giggle, grimacing. "Sorry."

"All right, Happy Gilmore. Time to get you home."

"I'm fine," I slur, wobbling over to our table. "Okay, maybe not."

"I'll have Kole call us a ride."

"Thanks, friend." I smile as I curl up in our booth and try my best not to fall asleep.

2

XAVIER

"Lay off, Dad. I'll make weight this week." My son and his girlfriend are sitting on the couch eating ice cream for the third time this week.

I take a deep breath. "Anthony, you have college recruiters coming to watch you this week. These matches could make or break your future."

"Thanks for the added pressure. Are you done? Jemma and I are watching a movie."

Before I can answer, I'm interrupted with a phone call. I glance at the familiar face on the screen and press the talk button. "Hello?"

"Hey, X. It's Kole. You rideshare driving tonight? There's a couple ladies here I think could use your assistance."

"You're not trying to set me up again, are you?" I joke.

"I've never tried to set you up. It's not my fault all these women hit on you. Try turning off the Xavier Roman charm."

I roll my eyes. "I can be there in fifteen minutes." I hang up my phone and slip it into my back pocket, then turn to resume my conversation with Anthony as he heads out the door. "Hey, wait a minute. We're not done—"

"I gotta take Jemma home. I'll see you later, pops." Anthony lets the door slam behind him.

"I only work this second job to make sure you can go to college!" I shout, but he's already out of earshot.

~

TRAFFIC IS UNUSUALLY HEAVY, taking twice as long as usual to get to the Storybook Pub. I've gotten to know Kole over the past couple years since the pub opened. Every once in a while, when he's in town, he'll call me when he has a group he wants to make sure gets home safely.

When I arrive, just before midnight, the pub is still packed full of people.

I walk up to the bar where Kole's making a fresh round of drinks. "You guys are packing 'em in tonight, aren't ya?"

"We are. There's a high school reunion in town, Oktoberfest starts this weekend, and three twenty-first birthday parties."

"Sounds like you've got your hands full. Who do you need me to take home?"

"The ladies back in the corner booth. I think you may know one of them."

I turn around and stop dead in my tracks, immediately recognizing a woman I haven't seen in almost twenty-five years.

Natalie Shaffer is just as beautiful now as she was back then. Long blonde hair, chocolate brown eyes, and a natural glow completely drawing me in.

A smile creeps across my face; she's not my buddy's fourteen-year-old little sister anymore.

Will she even remember who I am? Nah. Why would she remember us small town folk down here in Tennessee? Natalie's a bigtime New York chef now.

I smile as I reach them. "Kole said you ladies need a lift home."

"Oh, shit," Natalie's friend says. Her face is familiar, and I've seen her around town over the years, but I can't for the life of me recall her name.

"Something wrong?" I ask.

"Nope. She's the only one who needs a ride." The friend pushes Natalie right out of the booth. "We're, um, going to walk home. Come on, girls." She widens her eyes at the other two and they quickly slide out from the booth.

"Are you sure that's safe? It's late. And I don't mind taking all of you home."

"Veronica." Natalie attempts a drunk whisper. "Don't leave me alone with the super-hot driver. I don't trust myself." She giggles. Still just as cute as I remember.

"I'll get her home safely. Where's she staying?"

"Whiskey Hill Inn, up off the 96. Thanks. We're trusting you to deliver our friend safely."

Natalie stumbles down the steps as we exit the pub. I offer my arm for assistance.

She squeezes my bicep. "You have some nice muscles for an Uber driver."

"All the better to protect you with."

Opening the door for her, watching her sit down, my eyes lock on her long, tan legs.

"What big eyes you have there, sir."

Between her sexy smile and sultry voice, I'm having a hard time controlling myself. I close her door and breathe in the cool night air as I walk to my side of the car, hoping the brisk air will clear my head and help me focus on my drive, not my gorgeous passenger.

Each time I look over to steal a glance, Natalie is frantically typing away on her phone. Her arm is resting on the center console. I purposefully brush my arm against hers just to feel her soft skin.

"How long are you in town for?" I roll to a stop in front of the inn.

"Couple more days. I was dragged down here for this stupid reunion."

"You didn't enjoy the reunion?"

"People only talked to me tonight because they've seen me on television." Her words are slurred. "No one even acknowledged me in high school."

"I'm sure a gorgeous girl like you turned down dates left and right."

"No! I was awkward in high school. Plus, the one guy I had a crush on graduated when I was a freshman."

"Yeah? Did you ever see him again?"

"A few times before he left for college. He was friends with my brother. I still remember his jet-black hair, ocean blue eyes and those perfect muscles he got from wrestling. But I heard he ran off and got married. So la-di-da for him."

My hair's now mostly grey and always hidden under a hat; my eyes are still blue; those muscles are still there but covered in tattoos; and the wife, well, she's living in Mexico with her margarita dealer.

"Did you ever tell him you liked him?" I ask.

"Ew. No." She scrunches her nose. "I was fourteen. I wasn't trying to send him to jail."

Smart girl.

"But now, I'm thirty-nine and he'd be forty-three, so yeah, I'd do him."

I choke on the sip of coffee I just took.

My mishap brings out an explosive belly laugh from her. "This is me on the left."

"I've never been up here before. These are beautiful cabins."

"I like my privacy. Would you like to come in?" she slowly asks from lips I'm already aching to kiss.

"Thank you, but I can't. I'm on duty in the morning."

"Don't rideshare drivers make their own hours?"

"We do, but this is just my night job to help put my son through college. I'm also a cop."

"Oh shit. Well then, have a nice night, Mr. Rideshare Cop Man."

"You, too, Natalie."

3

NATALIE

The phone interrupts the pounding in my head, forcing me to roll over and open my eyes. Ugh. "Hello?"

"Oh. My. God," Veronica squeals. "Tell me everything."

I frown. Everything? Wasn't she with me last night? "Um… I have a hangover from drinking too much champagne."

"No, dummy, what happened between you and Xavier last night?"

"Who?" What is she talking about?

"Shit! You didn't recognize him, did you? Sweetie, your driver last night was Xavier Roman."

"What?" I scream loud enough for every cabin in this place to hear me. "How could you? Why would you? Ugh—"

Someone knocks on the door, stopping my rant. "I gotta go."

The person at my door knocks again. Fuck. They're probably checking to see why I was yelling.

"I'm coming. I'm coming." I open the door and my breath hitches.

"Everything okay here, ma'am? I heard screaming as I approached."

There he stands in front of me, all six feet of perfectly sculpted muscle. His once smooth, tan skin is now covered in impressive ink. His hair, which was once jet black, has become peppered with grey, making him look older but distinguished.

But those eyes.

Xavier Roman's ocean blue eyes are exactly as I remember.

How in the hell did I not recognize him last night? Too much good champagne from that Kole guy, that's how.

"Natalie?"

Shit. How long have I been staring at him? How could I not? Seeing Roman in uniform is making me want to break all kinds of laws to get frisked and hand-cuffed.

I giggle at the thought.

"Are you okay?"

"What? Yeah. I'm fine. Just woke up."

Shuffling my feet like an awkward teenager, I have no idea what to say next. What did I say to him on that ride home? Did I embarrass myself? Oh god. I search my brain for any glimpses of what happened, or what was said, but—

"After last night, I thought you might need some coffee. Grind Hut. Best in three counties."

"Thanks."

"Anything for a former teammate's little sister."

Ouch! I grimace from the imaginary punch I take directly to the gut.

"Shit… I mean…"

"It's okay. Would you like to come in?" I step aside.

He follows me, closing the door behind him.

"Natalie, do you… do you remember me?" Xavier asks.

"I do. I just didn't recognize you last night. Sorry. Twenty-five years and champagne goggles blurred my head a bit."

"Did you really have a crush on me?" he asks with a sexy-as-fuck smile.

My eyes widen. Just what the hell did I tell him during that ride home last night? I blink a few times, then just go with honesty. Fuck it. "I did in high school. I mean, it was kid stuff."

"I don't know." He tilts his head, smirking. "Last night you said you'd still do me." His laugh is just as hot as his smile.

"Alcohol will make you say all kinds of crazy things," I retort.

"So, you don't want to do me?"

"Yeah. I mean, no. Ugh! Is there something I can do for you, Xavier?" Why does this man get me so flustered?

"Go out with me tonight."

"Are you asking me or telling me?" I narrow my eyes. "And aren't you married?"

"Asking. And no. She walked out on us eleven years ago. Natalie Shaffer, may I please take you to dinner tonight?"

"No, I don't think that's such a good idea. You're friends with my brother," I respond with a slight chuckle.

"I haven't seen Johnny in twenty years and, even so, I'm sure he'd be okay with me feeding his little sister.

"I guess I do have to eat."

"Sounds like a date, then. I'll pick you up at seven."

Before I can protest that it's not a date, he kisses my cheek and leaves to finish his shift.

4

NATALIE

My nerves are all over the place. I haven't been able to sit still or get anything done since Xavier left me here earlier, and now it's damn near time to start getting ready. I draw a hot bath in a feeble attempt to calm myself. I haven't had a real date in over two years; it's been even longer since I've had sex. And now I have a date with the man I had my first sex dreams about. Fuck me. It's going to take much more than a bath to calm my nerves.

Finishing my make-up and my second glass of chardonnay, I'm slowly regaining my confidence. I slide into the only other dress I brought with me, then second guess myself. Maybe I should wear jeans? I glance at my suitcase, gnawing on my bottom lip.

Someone knocks on the door and I freeze, then turn slowly toward the sound.

"Here goes nothing," I whisper. Swallowing hard, I straighten my shoulders and walk calmly to the door, mustering all of my courage to pull it open.

"Holy shit," Xavier says under his breath. His gaze travels slowly down my body, then back up again, leaving a trail of heat as though he'd physically run his hands over me.

"It's too much. I need to change."

"Please don't. You look fucking fantastic."

With those simple words, the butterflies in my stomach launch their attack. As cool, calm and collected as I can be in the kitchen, I have no idea how to act on a date.

"Let's try this again," he says with a smile that makes me want to say fuck dinner. "Good evening, Miss Shaffer. You look stunning. It would be my honor to accompany you to dinner tonight."

His old-fashioned, southern charm causes me to burst out laughing.

"Too much?" he asks.

"Absolutely perfect," I say, unable to wipe the smile from my face.

"I was thinking the same thing. Are you ready? We have reservations in an hour."

Throughout the drive, I try not to stare at the gorgeous man in the driver's seat. How in the hell I didn't recognize Xavier last night? How is it possible that instead of aging, this man has just gotten more gorgeous?

"I had a hard time deciding on where to take you tonight."

"Why?" I ask.

"Where do you take one of the best chefs in the country on the first date? I'm sure nothing here compares to the food you've eaten around the world."

"And yet my favorite food is still chicken nuggets." I laugh.

"Good to know." He chuckles. "But for our first date, I'm trying to impress you a bit more than chicken nuggets. My partner's wife thinks she's a Nashville socialite and says this is the new hot spot." He pulls into the valet.

The sign above the restaurant says nick's in a simple font, backlit by an orange glow.

Xavier walks to my side of the car and opens the door, then extends his hand to help me stand.

"Thank you."

"For opening your door?" he asks. "They don't do that in New York?"

I laugh, shake my head. "No, just… thank you for tonight."

"Our night hasn't even started yet."

"Well, I'm looking forward to the evening."

Xavier slides his arm around my waist as we follow the hostess through the bustling restaurant. The flickering lights from the candles on each table create a romantic glow throughout the room.

As we take our seats, the young woman hands us our menus, explaining the night's specials.

She starts explaining the dessert and my ears perk up. "Wait. Did you just say chocolate whiskey pecan pie?"

"Yes ma'am. Chef's specialty. Nothing in the south like it."

Chef's specialty, huh? I close my eyes and the signage out front dances behind my eyelids.

nick's.

I bite back a bitter laugh, then quickly scan the menu for any other familiar recipes. Wouldn't you know it? There's a signature maple bourbon barbeque sauce. This has to be a fucking joke.

"I would like a piece of that pie, please."

"Now? Before your dinner?"

"Yes, before my dinner." I snap back. My hands are shaking worse than a California earthquake.

"Natalie, what's wrong?"

"Nothing."

"Don't lie to me. Your lips are pursed and your gorgeous eyes look like they are about to shoot daggers. Just like they did when you used to watch your brother get pinned to the mat in high school."

"Excuse me?" I question.

"You weren't the only one with a crush, beautiful."

His words should send my heart aflutter, but I'm too tense.

"Here's your pie, ma'am. Is there anything else?"

I hold my finger up as I take a bite, signaling her to wait before she walks away. The flavors assault my tongue, mouth-wateringly delicious and... too damn familiar to be a coincidence.

"I would like to see the chef, please." From the tips of my toes to my burning cheeks, my blood begins to boil.

"Ma'am, Chef Nicholas is busy at the moment. As you can see, we have a full house tonight."

"No problem." I remain calm despite wanting to rip someone's head off. I'll go find him myself. I stand, tossing my chair back harder than I intend. "Which way to the kitchen?"

"Please, sit down, ma'am. Let me see what I can do."

"That's better. Thank you."

"Natalie, what's wrong? Do we need to leave?"

"Oh, we're gonna leave, but not until I give this asshole a piece of my mind."

Heads turn toward me, but these people are not my concern. Let them stare.

"Natalie!" Nicholas hisses as he rushes toward our table. "Stop making a scene." He glances at Xavier, his eyes widening for the slightest of seconds, then he turns back to me and offers a saccharine smile. "It's been a long time. I can't believe you're still mad."

"Are you kidding me? You fucking ghosted me. Gone. After two years of dating, just gone. And coincidentally, my recipe journal went missing at the same time. You stole everything from me. My heart, my happiness, and my recipes. You fucking broke me."

"Well, I think you put yourself back together nicely. But I'm sure sleeping with Jordan Lockhart helped skyrocket your career," he sneers. "Even without your precious recipes."

Without a second thought, I clench my fist, pull back, then strike him square in his jaw. Nicholas flies backward, landing on his ass between tables. The customers shriek and murmur, eyes flicking nervously back and forth between the chef and the crazy lady that just knocked his ass down.

I turn back to Xavier, shaking my aching hand. "Can we go now?"

"With pleasure." Xavier grabs my other hand as I step over Nicholas, then we quickly exit the restaurant.

"I'm sorry for ruining our date," I say as we wait for the car.

He spins me around to face him. "Are you kidding me? That was so fucking sexy." Xavier places a small kiss on my left cheek and then one on my right. Resting his forehead on mine, he whispers, "I hope this isn't the end of our date." He brushes his lips against mine.

"Chicken nuggets it is." I laugh.

5

XAVIER

Remind me never to piss this girl off. Natalie's right hook could knock any man on his ass. Of all the places I could have chosen to go to dinner, I pick the one her ex-boyfriend runs. What are the fucking odds?

Natalie's fists are clenched, and her swollen eyes are fighting back the tears. Reaching over, I grab her hand, gently rubbing it with the pad of my thumb until I feel the tension leave her body, allowing her tears to fall.

"Wanna talk about it?" I ask.

"You don't want to hear my sob story."

"Of course I do. I wouldn't have asked if I didn't want to know. I want to know everything about you, Natalie." Even in the dark car, I can see her cheeks blush.

"I dated Nicholas in culinary school. He was a year ahead of me, and I looked up to him. But when the instructors started praising my work, he became jealous. He used to tell me I'd make it further in this industry than him because I have a vagina. One morning, I woke up and Nicholas was gone. So were all of his things. He also helped himself to my recipe journal." She sighs, shaking her head. "Thomas, my ex-fiancé, started the crack, but Nicholas broke me. Cooking has helped put me back together. I graduated top of my class and have spent the last seven years perfecting my craft. But, apparently, Nicholas would rather think I slept my way to the top rather than having any skills. I mean, fuck, he'd have a better chance of sleeping with Jordan Lockhart than I would."

"Seriously? I knew it! Gemma has a huge crush on him, and we always argue about it."

"Gemma?" she questions.

"My son's girlfriend. Gemma wants to be a pastry chef. She'd love to meet you. We'll have to plan something."

"Xavier, you do realize I'm going back to New York in two days, right?"

I did, but I was trying not to think about it. "Then I guess we're just going to have to make the best of the next couple days, aren't we?"

After grabbing a couple bottles of wine and making sure to stop for chicken nuggets, we make our way back to the hotel. Before going in, I pop the trunk and grab my bag.

"Little presumptuous, aren't we?" She cocks one eyebrow. "You seriously keep an overnight bag in your car?"

Fighting back laughter, I run my tongue over my teeth. "It's a gym bag. I was hoping that, since we're going to hang out for a while, I could slip into something a little more comfortable."

"Oh. Well, I guess I'll allow it. This time."

Damn, her sass is sexy.

We both change into something more comfortable and settle in on the couch with our chicken nuggets and wine.

I pour her a glass. "I'm sorry dinner didn't work out."

"Who says? I live my life around fancy food. Sometimes it's all about the simple things." She pops a nugget into her mouth.

"And good company."

"Cheers to that." She raises her glass to mine. "So, I gave you my sob story, now tell me yours. Why is a handsome man like you still single?"

"My ex-wife walked out on me and Anthony almost eleven years ago. I came home from work to find her sitting on the couch with her bags packed. She explained to me that being a wife and a mother wasn't for her." I shrug. "And then she left. My only concern became raising my son. Being a cop and a single dad was enough to worry about, so dating wasn't a priority."

"Wasn't?"

"You never know what the future holds." I reach out and pull her closer to me. Natalie nestles herself into the crook of my arm.

"And why drive Uber at night?" she asks.

"Because college is fucking expensive." I laugh. "We're hoping for a wrestling scholarship, but nothing's guaranteed. I work hard so I can watch him live his dreams."

"It's great you're so supportive. I wish I had that with my family. When I left teaching and went to culinary school, both my parents predicted I would fail and come crawling back to them."

"But surely your parents see your successes now? I'm sure they're proud of you."

"When my brother came out, my mom got it into her head that I was her only hope for grandkids… It doesn't matter how successful I become as a chef; I will never be a success to my mom because I'm not a parent." She shakes her head.

"And your father?"

"My dad has come around and is finally supportive."

"Well, I think you're smart." I tuck her hair behind her ear. "I think you're funny." I kiss the side of her head. "And I think you are drop dead fucking gorgeous," I whisper in her ear as I take her wine glass and set it on the table.

Natalie flips her body around and straddles me. My dick quickly grows hard, pressing against the inside of her thigh. I can't help it; I've desired this beauty in front of me for most of my life.

"Did you really have a crush on me back then or are you just saying that to be nice?" she asks.

"I did. There was an innocent beauty about you."

"I was innocent. I was only fourteen. It's funny how age is a number preventing us from going after something we want. We're too young to do this or too old to do that."

"Nothing is going to prevent me from going after what I want tonight," I say, wrapping my arms around her tiny waist.

"And what is it you want?" Her eyes blaze with the same lust I feel throughout my entire body.

"You, Natalie. I've dreamt about you so many nights. And tonight, I'm not going to let the one who got away, get away."

I slide my hand behind Natalie's neck and bring her face to mine. I start my kisses just below her ear and continue along her jawline until I reach her soft, pink lips. Our kiss starts soft and gentle, but the intensity increases with each passing second.

The first time her tongue brushes against mine, it takes everything in me not to lose my shit. The sweet taste of her mouth is something I could easily become addicted to.

And will, if she'll let me.

"If we start, I don't think I'm going to be able to control myself."

"Good." She pulls her top off over her head, granting me full access to her perfectly round, perky tits.

"Goddamn. Even more perfect than I imagined." Her plump, pink nipples beg for my mouth. I plan on giving them exactly what they need.

I suck hard on one breast, while gently playing with the other. The soft moans escaping her lips make me want to do this all night.

Natalie grabs the hem of my shirt, yanking it off in one swift move. Leaning back, she runs her finger down my chest.

"Damn." Her voice is deep with desire. "You were a good-looking guy back in high school, but now…" Her eyes widen. "Now, you are one fine ass man."

Speaking of ass… sliding my hands into Natalie's shorts, taking handfuls of her beautiful ass, I stand.

"Bedroom?" she asks.

Nodding, I hold her gaze. "Are you sure?"

Rather than answering, her mouth crashes on mine, giving me every answer I need. Without ever breaking our kiss, we make our way to the bedroom. I lay her on the bed and just stare at her, unable to even blink.

"What? Is something wrong?"

"Nothing. Just trying to convince myself this isn't a dream."

Natalie crooks her finger, calling me forward. I cage my large frame over her. "It's definitely not a dream." She reaches down, pushing my sweats off my hips. My hard cock springs free, hitting her in the stomach.

A playful giggle escapes her perfect pink lips.

"Oh, is that funny?"

"No. Sorry." She bites her lip in an attempt to stop her giggles.

"Two can play this game." Standing up, I awkwardly shimmy my legs out of my sweats. "If I'm naked, so are you." Taking the hem of her shorts, I pull them down her long, beautiful legs.

Standing over Natalie, I admire every part of her body. I run my fingers over her soft breasts, tickling down her taut stomach and finding my way to her exquisitely manicured pussy. Sliding my fingers down, she's already glistening wet.

"Fuck," I growl with disappointment.

"Well, that's not something a woman wants to hear when a man is between her legs."

"I'm sorry, beautiful. I don't have a condom."

"Oh, well, um… I haven't had sex in over two years, and I have an IUD." Natalie rolls on her side, looking away from me. Is she embarrassed? "You must think I'm a total loser."

I lay down next to her, pulling her body close to mine. "I have you beat."

"Huh?" She rolls over so we're now face to face.

"Three and half years for me. So, if you're a loser, I must be an even bigger loser. I think we're perfect for each other."

First our mouths, then our bodies seamlessly become one. I roll onto my back and Natalie straddles me.

"You're so fucking beautiful," I growl with the growing anticipation. "Fuck me, Natalie. I need to know every inch of your body, inside and out."

She reaches back, taking a firm grip on my aching cock, positioning just the tip in the entrance of her pussy. I grasp her hips firmly and want so badly to push her down, sink myself deep inside her. But I also want to make sure we move at her pace.

Natalie leans forward, kissing me. Hard. As she brings her body back up, she allows my cock to slide all the way into her wet and waiting pussy.

"Fuck," we moan in unison.

She begins a fast bounce, sinking herself deeper each time.

"Baby. Baby. Baby. Slow down. It's been a long time."

Her coy smile may prove to be the death of me. "I know. For me, too, remember? That's why we're gonna get this first one out of the way, go finish our dinner and wine and come back and do this over and over again."

I think I may love this girl.

Natalie pushes herself back up, using my chest to balance. She rocks her hips back and forth, sliding deeper each time.

"Come with me, beautiful."

Our eyes lock as her nails dig into my chest. Natalie's legs start to shake, and her pussy tightens around my dick and, together, we explode into sweet ecstasy.

6

NATALIE

"Tell me about your son." I'm laying across Xavier's chest after our third go 'round.

His deep, sensual voice is one I could listen to for hours.

"Anthony is an amazing kid. I would definitely say he's my best friend. After Ashley left, it was he and I against the world. I got him into wrestling to keep him out of trouble."

"Like it did for you and my brother?" I tease.

"Hey! We're not talking about me." He laughs. "I wish I would have taken it as seriously as Anthony does. He's been state champion twice; he knows this is his ticket out of Tennessee. I want my kid to be a thousand times more successful than I ever was."

"I think if he turns out anything like you, you did a good job."

Xavier leans down and kisses the top of my head. "My turn. Who's this Thomas guy? And where can I find him so I can kick his ass for hurting you?"

I sigh. "I met Thomas in college. We were together almost seven years. After five years of teaching middle school kids, I hated it. I told him I wanted to change careers; he told me he wanted to start a family. He made me choose."

"Are you happy with your choice?"

"Most days I wouldn't change my life for the world. Other days, I wonder what I missed out on when choosing a career over family. I was never opposed to having children, but if I wasn't happy for me, I couldn't be happy for a family."

"Sounds like you knew exactly what you wanted."

"I had no clue. But I sure as hell didn't want to be with someone who wasn't supportive. Hey, are you busy tomorrow?"

"Not at all."

"Will you go somewhere with me?"

"I'd go anywhere with you, beautiful."

Feeling more comfortable than I have in years, I close my eyes, drifting off to sleep.

THE SUN PEEKS through the cracks in the blinds, burning my eyelids, waking me from the best sleep I've had in months. Rolling over, I reach out for Xavier, only to find an empty bed. Burying myself in his pillow, I breathe in the lingering woodsy cologne, still reeling in the amazingness of last night. When I finally force myself to sit up, I find a note on the nightstand.

Good Morning, Beautiful-
I hated leaving you. You looked so peaceful. I enjoyed holding you in my arms.
I'm excited to spend more time with you.
I'll be back at ten to pick you up. And tonight, I don't plan on letting you go.
X

I doubt he'd be excited if he knew where we were going today. Fuck, I'm not even excited about going, but if I don't, I'll never hear the end of it.

Dragging myself out of bed and into the shower, I think about Xavier's note.

He doesn't plan on letting me go, but I fly back to New York tomorrow night.

Maybe seeing him again today or spending another night with him is a bad idea. What if one of us gets attached? Maybe I need to keep this what it is: a fun one-night stand. I don't do long distance relationships.

As soon as I'm dried off and dressed, I retrieve the note, his number scribbled at the bottom, and grab my phone to send Xavier a text before he heads back over this way. Best to stop this now.

Heart in my throat, I send the text.

We had a great night, and ending things before anything else happens between us is better for everyone. I'm heading back to the city soon—no need to pretend this is anything more than an incredible one-night stand.

Tapping my foot, I wait for my phone to chime with a response. Will he be pissed? Will he ignore my text and just leave me on read? Maybe he's feeling the same way I am and I just saved us both from an awkward conversation. I set the phone down and start pulling a brush through my hair.

Someone knocks on the door.

My pulse speeds as I look at the clock on the bedside table. Shit. I must not have caught him in time.

I hurry to the door, then pull it open, bracing myself for whatever he's going to say.

"So, you ask me out for the day and now you're trying to blow me off? You're not gonna get rid of me that easy, darlin'." Xavier steps past me into the cabin with the same glorious coffee from yesterday.

And damn if I'm not a sucker for good coffee.

And sexy men.

"I just think it would be better if we don't complicate things. I live nine hundred miles away. So, let's just call it what it was—a one-night stand—and go our separate ways."

"What if that's not what I want?" he asks. "What if I want things to get complicated?"

"Xavier—"

He closes the gap between us before I can finish. "Stop." He cups my cheek and trails his thumb across my lips. "Last night was not a one-night stand. Even if it never happens again, I will never think of you like that. Last night was a fantasy come true for me. The crush I had on you back then was very real. The crush I have now is even more real."

"A crush from twenty-five years ago. Come on, Xavier, let's get real, you don't even know me now."

"Are you telling me you felt nothing last night? You don't feel it every time we touch?"

"So what if I do? It doesn't negate the fact your life's here and mine's in New York."

"Give me the next two days. After that, you can go home to New York and never look back."

"I leave in thirty-six hours."

"Then we better use the most of our time." Xavier lifts me up, forcing me to wrap my legs around his waist. He walks us both to the bedroom, carefully lowering me onto the bed. "Do I have time to devour your insanely gorgeous body before we go?"

"I think we can make time." I giggle.

7

NATALIE

"Where are we headed?" Xavier asks, bringing up the navigation in his car.

"Um… 34 South Benton Street."

He side-eyes me as he exits the navigation system. "We're going to see your parents?"

"I'm sorry. I should have said something. I just thought that if I had someone with me, maybe my mom wouldn't be such a bitch."

"It can't be as bad as you're making it out to be."

"Just wait."

I nervously fidget. Xavier takes my hand and begins a gentle stroke with his thumb until I'm finally able to sit still. He has this calming quality about him.

"Let's make a signal."

"Huh?" A signal?

"Like a code word or something. For when you're ready to leave."

"How about, 'can we leave now so I can fuck you in the back of your car'?" I tease.

"That would definitely work. But let's try… 'sausage' to not make it too obvious."

Twenty minutes later, I'm walking into my childhood home with Xavier Roman on my arm. Is it too soon to use the code word?

My mother meets us in the kitchen. "Natalie, so nice of you to grace us with your presence. I heard you were in town."

She knew damn well I was in town because I told her myself.

I pull in a deep breath, trying to calm myself. "I told you I was here for the reunion and would only be able to visit a short while. Mom, you remember—"

"Xavier. So nice to see you again. What are you doing here?" She hugs him like he's her favorite person in the world.

"I ran into Natalie at the Storybook Pub, and we've been catching up. I hope it's okay I came."

"Of course it is, dear. I just wish Natalie would have been more considerate and told us she was bringing a friend. I'll put an extra plate out for lunch."

"Is it too soon?" I whisper to Xavier.

He leans in, kissing my forehead, giving me the reassurance I need to make it through the next couple hours.

"Is Joe home?" Xavier asks.

"He sure is. He's out back in the barn. You should go say hello." She smiles sweetly at Xavier, then turns to me. "Natalie, you stay here and help me with the food."

As soon as the backdoor shuts my mother rounds on me. "Why are you with Xavier? Are you two dating? Is there any hope for grandkids?"

I back away from her. "Seriously? I ran into Xavier at the pub after the reunion. He happened to be my Uber driver. We're just hanging out. I go back to New York tomorrow night. Please stop with the grandkids. Why can't you just be proud of me and what I'm doing?"

"When I go to bingo night at the church, all the other ladies are showing off pictures of their beautiful grandbabies. And there I sit."

"Are you kidding me right now? You're saying you'd rather me sit at home, popping out babies, than follow my dreams of becoming a successful chef?"

"Would that be so bad?" she asks.

"Unbelievable!" I storm out the back door to join Xavier and my dad.

My eyes burn as I fight back the tears. I can't let her win. I won't let her win. She acts like this is something I've done just to hurt her. Of course, I would have loved to have kids, but my life just didn't work out that way.

When I enter the barn, Xavier rushes to my side.

"Sausage! Sausage! Sausage!" I scream.

My dad's eyebrows creep up his forehead. "Is that the code word to signal it's time to get away from your mother?"

"Hi, Daddy. And yes, it is. Why can't she just accept that kids aren't in my future? I mean, damn, I'm almost forty years old. And I'm happy with the way my life turned out."

"Well, I'm proud of you, pumpkin." He kisses the top of my head like he used to when I was a kid. "I'm going to talk to your mother. X, why don't you show Nat some of the improvements we've been doing around the farm."

"Wait. What?"

"Come on, I'll show you." Grabbing my hand, Xavier pulls me to the back of the property.

Just at the bottom of the hill is a brand-new horse stable. All I ever wanted growing up was a horse, but my mother always said they were too expensive. Being an adult now, I get it, but seriously? Now they have a stable?

"What is all this and why are you helping my dad? And how come you never told me?"

"So many questions, beautiful. One night at the station, your dad was telling us about these race horses being put down when they are no longer needed."

"My dad was at the station?" I question.

"You didn't know he's a community volunteer?"

I shake my head in confusion.

"Yup. So, we were talking about how a horse rescue in this area would be beneficial. Your dad offered up his land, me and a couple of the other guys offered up our carpentry skills, and the community offered up their wallets."

"Who's going to take care of the horses?"

"That's the best part. Let me show you." He leads me behind the stable to a half-circle of tiny houses. "These are the caretakers' quarters. Fully furnished."

"Fully furnished, huh?" Throwing my arms around his neck, I jump into his arms, forcing him to carry me.

"What about lunch?" he asks.

"They can't start without us." My lips crash onto his, letting him know I want him for the second time today.

Entering the tiny place, Xavier kicks the door closed behind us. Knowing he's got a tight hold on me, I let go and pull my shirt off over my head.

"Your body is so beautiful." Xavier lays me on the bed, staring at every inch of my body. The lust in his eyes sets me afire. I need this man in every way possible. I shimmy out of my leggings and panties, offering myself up for Xavier to take control of my body.

He strips off his jeans and shirt, then I wait for the boxers to come off, but he just stands there.

"Are you okay?" I frown. "You look a little nervous."

"Not nervous. Just taking you all in."

"Well, hurry up and take it because we have about ten more minutes before my parents come looking for us."

Xavier strips off his underwear and plops down next to me, causing us both to crack up laughing. He slides his hand behind my neck, pulling my lips to his. His kisses are so soft and gentle, yet toe-curling at the same time.

Caging his body over mine, Xavier never breaks our kiss. I wrap my legs around his hips, pulling him closer to me. Quickly finding my aching pussy, Xavier slides in and out with the perfect strokes.

"Fuck, baby." My voice comes out in a growl I've never heard before.

He just smiles before leaning down and kissing me until we both come.

8

NATALIE

Forty-five minutes of silence on our way to the airport, and I've chewed my fingernails down to the nub. My chest is tight with anxiety. He hasn't said more than two words to me for the entire drive. Every time I try to strike up a conversation, he answers me with single words or grunts.

What's he thinking about? Is he mad? He knew I was heading back to New York. He knew it.

Maybe I should have ended things before we got too close.

"When will I see you again?" he finally asks. So that's what he's been thinking about.

"I'm not sure. The holiday season is our busiest time at the restaurant, so I usually can't get away."

"Can I come visit you?"

"Xavier, is that really what you want? A relationship of just phone calls and the occasional weekend visit?"

"If that's all I can have you, then yes. I'll take it. Natalie, the last two days have been some of the best of my life. You've made me feel something I thought no longer existed. I know you feel our connection. It's there every time we touch."

"I do, but our lives are just too far apart. I'm sorry."

"So that's it? We just say goodbye and go on with our lives like nothing happened?"

"We can still be friends," I suggest.

"I have enough friends." He pulls up to my terminal and parks between two taxis, then stares straight ahead. "Safe travels, Natalie."

I grab my weekender and climb out of the car. "Bye, Xavier."

The second my door shuts, he pulls away from the curb.

My heart pinches as he drives away, and disappointment twists in my gut, leaving me to question whether or not I've chosen my career over something great.

Again.

9

XAVIER

Six Months Later

I run my hands through my hair for the thirtieth time in the last five minutes, my brain still unable to comprehend what my son and his girlfriend have told me. In the blink of an eye, everything we've worked so hard for is gone.

"Please tell me you two are pulling some kind of video prank because this shit isn't funny."

"I wish we were, Mr. Roman. We're so sorry. We were careful. It was an accident," Gemma says, bursting into tears.

"Most teenage pregnancies are." I run my hand over my face. "What about college? What are your plans now?"

"Gemma and I have talked a lot about this, and we want to give the baby up for adoption."

My heart pinches. Adoption? This can't be happening. "Anthony, you can't—"

"Neither of us are prepared to take care of a baby, Dad. So, we think this is the best option."

"To give my grandbaby to a stranger. Are you kidding me?"

"We thought you'd be happy that we decided not to drop out of school and do the right thing," Anthony says.

"I am. I don't know. I need some air." I grab my keys and jacket, rushing to my car. I take off down the road, away from town, just driving with no destination.

Seven hours later, I'm sitting in a McDonald's parking lot in Roanoke, Virginia, crying like a baby. I've worked so hard to give Anthony the world and he goes and does this? To us? To his future? My son is giving up his child. My heart shattered the moment he uttered those words.

Where the fuck did I go wrong?

I wish I could just lay my head on Natalie's lap and have her soothing voice tell me everything's going to be fine, the woman I have fallen for is nine hundred miles away.

I miss Natalie. I miss her more than words can explain. Even though we only spent two days together almost six months ago, she invaded my heart. We've talked a few times since she left, but she always cuts the conversations short. It's been two months since we've last talked. I'm trying my damndest to respect her wishes, but I wish she were here to calm my soul.

Then it hits me. I can fix all this. Maybe, just maybe, I can make everyone's dreams come true. Without giving it another thought, I throw the car into drive, speeding north up the interstate.

It's close to ten when I arrive in New York City. I just drove the last fourteen hours to see Natalie. Pulling in front of Mangiamo, I wait for her to leave for the evening. She doesn't know I'm here, so I don't want to just show up at her work.

She exits the restaurant on the arm of a tall, blond man. The umbrella they are using to shield themselves from the spring rain, is also hiding their faces. Has she found someone new? Did I really mean so little to her? Should I just turn around and leave?

No. Fuck that. I came here for my girl and my grandbaby; I can't leave without even trying.

"Natalie!" I call, running across the busy street.

Both of them stop and stare at me.

"Xavier?" Natalie's eyes widen. "What are you doing here?"

"I need you. I mean, I need to talk to you."

"Thanks for the evening, Natalie. We'll talk soon." Her new man kisses her on the cheek and walks off.

"Are you dating him?" I ask.

"That was Jordan Lockhart. We were discussing a job offer."

"Oh. Sorry."

"Why are you here? Did you drive all the way from Nashville?"

"I did. I got some news and I needed you. You calm my soul. So, I've been driving since eight this morning."

"What news?" She searches my gaze. "Is everything okay?"

"No, not really. Can we go somewhere and talk?"

"Come on, Follow me back to my place."

"Wow. You weren't kidding when you said your apartment was small."

Natalie turns toward me, frowning. "It's just me, so I don't need much. Xavier, why are you here?"

"Are you not happy to see me?"

"Of course I am. I'm just a bit confused. You said you got some news. What does this have to do with me?"

Sitting down on her couch, my face sinks into my hands and I'm not sure where to even begin. Natalie sits down, putting her arms around me. Before I can stop them, tears begin streaming down my cheeks.

She grabs my chin, turning my face toward hers. "I'm here for you. No matter what. But please tell me what's going on, because you're starting to scare me."

Leaning in, I kiss the lips I've missed so much for the last six months. "I've missed you. I fell in love with you during the short time we were together. And now... now I need you. I need you by my side."

"Xavier—"

"Please let me finish. Gemma is pregnant. Six months already."

"What the hell? What about college, and your son's possible scholarships?"

"They've made the decision to give the baby up for adoption," I explain.

"Oh." She pauses, searching my gaze. "How do you feel about this?"

"I hate it. The thought of complete strangers raising my flesh and blood kills me." The tears start again.

"How can I help?"

"Move back to Tennessee with me."

"Excuse me?"

"Hear me out. I want to adopt this baby. I want to give him or her the best life they can possibly have. I did it alone once, and I know I could do it alone again if I had to, but I want to share it with someone this time. I want to share this with you, Natalie."

Her eyes widen and she rocks back a bit like my words are a physical blow. "Wait. You want me to move back to Tennessee and adopt a baby with you?"

Okay, when she says it out loud it does sound kind of crazy.

"Yeah, I do. If Anthony and Gemma are going to give this child to strangers, why not give it to us? I love you, Natalie Shaffer. I don't care how crazy that makes me. Or how crazy any of this is. I want to spend the rest of my life kissing you goodnight and waking up next to you each morning. I want to sit on a porch swing and watch our baby play in the yard. I want to grow old with you."

Her tears now match mine and we're both crying like babies.

Finally, she wipes her eyes and shakes her head in disbelief. "Maybe."

"Maybe?"

"Yeah, maybe." She smiles. "Aren't you going to ask me about the job offer from Lockhart?"

So consumed in my own needs, I forgot about hers. She's worked so hard for her career and now, in the blink of an eye, I'm asking her to give it all up. I'm afraid to ask, knowing my heart would break if she doesn't feel the same way I do. My silence causes her to continue.

"Jordan came to see me about a month ago after he got back from Europe with his husband, Nicoli. Unbeknownst to me, they are the owners of nick's in Nashville and heard about my incident with

Nicholas. Apparently, I'm not the only chef he's stolen from. Needless to say, he's no longer working for them."

"What does that have to do with you?"

"I accepted a job as head chef at nick's."

"Holy shit, Natalie! That's amazing! Congratulations, beautiful." I reach for her but she pulls back.

Eyes narrowed, she watches me warily. "Aren't you going to make me choose? Everyone always makes me choose."

I close the space between us, wrapping my arms around her waist. "Of course not. I want you to have everything you've ever dreamed of and I want to be the man proudly standing by your side, lifting you higher than the moon, supporting you, loving you."

Her eyes glisten with fresh tears.

"So, what do you say?"

"Yes, Xavier. I will take this crazy adventure with you."

Before she has the chance to change her mind, I kiss the lips I've been craving. As her sweet tongue enters my mouth, I know I'll never be able to let her go again.

And now I'll never have to.

THE END

LEARN MORE ABOUT TERI KAY:
HTTPS://LINKTR.EE/TERIKAY_AUTHOR

ALSO BY TERI KAY:
RECKLESS ABANDON
SINICAL HEARTS
ONE-EIGHTY

TRADING LIVES

MARY DEAN

Sometimes the chaser helps with the burn.

Sub-genre: Romantic Suspense
Relationship: Male/Female

1

DYLAN

I sighed as I crossed the street from my office and headed towards Storybook Pub, my favorite place to get a drink and unwind after a long day. And that was definitely this day. It was tax season, the busiest time of the year for me. I was an accountant so this was my season. Don't get me wrong, I loved what I did. Numbers and me always had a lovely relationship. While others saw math as torture, I saw it as a fun puzzle to solve. That's why I started my own company. It was just me and two other accountants who worked part time. In the two years that we had been open, we had become very well known in my home town of Huntington Beach, California. We were an honest company and usually went out of our way for our clients. We were about making money, of course, but also about helping people and I took pride in being honest.

I opened the door to the pub and was greeted by the smell of chicken wings and beer, two of my favorite things. I took my usual seat at the counter. It was Friday night so it was busy. I didn't mind the crowd. The noise took me out of my head a bit. I would grab a quick drink and then head home. There wasn't much there for me except my DVR, so I wasn't in a rush.

"Good evening Dylan," Kole, the bartender said to me. He was a slender man who always had an ear to listen and advice to give. His eyes told me that he had a story but it wasn't my place to ask. I spilled my woes to him and he always listened with kindness. "What can I get for you?"

"Just a glass of the signature brew tonight. Thanks." Kole nodded, then turned away to get my drink. This was always my order. I liked the surprise. Some days it was a good choice, some days not so much. The fun was in the mystery. The phone rang and Kole answered it. I figured my drink would be a little delayed and I took the time to look around. There was the usual Friday night group of businessmen letting loose, college students partying, groups of friends making memories, and even some couples on dates.

"Here you go," a female's voice said next to me. I turned my attention from the crowded room and was met by a pair of beautiful green eyes. I was frozen. This woman was gorgeous. Her face had a delicate shape and her skin looked so soft I

longed to feel it beneath my fingertips. Her brown hair looked silky and smooth. It was in a high ponytail. I looked down and saw she had a curvy build. She definitely was a knockout. I then noticed that she had on a shirt that said *Storybook Pub* over the left breast and an apron around her waist. She was a waitress. She must be new because I had never seen her before.

"Uh, thank you," I said like a nervous school boy. I couldn't sound more lame. She smiled and went off to help the next customer.

"Sorry about that," Kole stated as he came back over to me. "Ever since I put out the ad for a waitress the phone has been ringing off the hook. I need to take it down. Kelsey is perfect."

"Is that her?" I nodded my head towards the waitress that had helped me, who was now smiling with a group of frat guys. I felt a little jealous. I wanted to be the one to make her smile.

"Yeah. She started yesterday. She seems to be a good fit. The weekend rush will be the test." Kole started drying some newly washed glasses with a towel as he spoke.

"Do you know, um, her situation?" I asked. As soon as the words left my mouth I rolled my eyes at myself. Real smooth Dylan. Kole must have caught on as he let out a chuckle.

"She didn't have a significant other listed as an emergency contact. She actually didn't list anyone. But that's all I know."

"Hm." I took a sip of my beer. It was a dark lager. I liked it. I watched Kelsey move around the room as I drank my beer. Before I knew it, I had finished it.

"Would you like another?" Kelsey asked approaching me with a sweet smile.

"That's it for me tonight, Darlin'. I'll pay my bill and take your number please." I winked at her putting on the charm. I expected her to giggle or give me a smile. I wasn't too full of myself but I had an effect on women. I didn't usually get turned down.

But she didn't smile. She didn't giggle. Her sweet demeanor seemed to fade a bit. She looked at me like I was an annoyance. That was new. "My name isn't Darlin'," she responded and then walked off to charge my card that I kept on file. I heard a chuckle behind me and turned around to see Kole shaking his head. I shrugged. Other men might have moved on, not wanting to deal with a difficult woman. I wasn't like most men. I saw the challenge and it just made me want her more.

"Excuse me. You forgot your number," I said to her with a smirk after she brought me the receipt to sign.

"Trust me, I didn't," she said and walked off. I sat there with a surprised look on my face, then I grinned.

This would be fun.

KELSEY

I saw him the minute he walked in. I hated to admit it but he made me pause. I had to catch my breath. He was stunningly handsome. He was tall, dressed in a dark business suit. His hair looked like he had been running his hands through it all day. I was jealous of those fingers. He had a brooding look on his face as if he was always in deep thought. As he approached the bar, I saw him smile at my boss Kole and that smile took my breath away. He had a dimple. Oh man. That was a weakness of mine.

"Kelsey," Kole called to me while he was on the phone. "End of the bar. Signature brew," he told me and then went back to his phone call. I nodded and grabbed a glass from under the bar. I went to the barrel with a star sticker on it to show it was the night's signature brew and poured it into the glass. I put on a smile as I served it to him. Then I quickly went to help other customers to distract myself. I felt myself blushing, stupidly. It wasn't the first time I was around a hot guy. I served many of them each night. There was just something about this man. When I came back around I told myself to suck it up and I checked to see if he wanted anything else. Then he did the one thing that was like a bucket of ice water. He called me Darlin'. I stopped myself from telling him to go to hell. I hated when men called women they barely knew pet names, sweet names. It's like they thought we should just swoon on the spot because they showed us attention. Dream on. He then ordered my phone number. I almost laughed. I wondered if that move worked on other women. It definitely didn't work on me. I went to the cash register to charge his account. The annoyance was taking over. I returned with the receipt for him to sign without my number. He paid with a smirk and left the pub. I let out a breath of relief when the door closed behind him.

"He's a good guy," Kole remarked from behind the bar, watching me.

"Good for him," I spat back and instantly regretted it. That was no way to talk to my boss. I couldn't blow this job, especially so soon. I had only been here a few days. I liked it here, in this town. I didn't want to have to leave again. "I'm sorry Kole. That was rude."

He waved his hand at me. "No offense taken. I told you it's kick back here." He smiled at me. I was so lucky to have answered Kole's ad for a waitress at the right time. After he hired me, right after my interview was over, the phone was ringing off the hook. I could see why. The pay was good, hours flexible, and Kole seemed like a decent man to work for. I needed to regain my trust in men again.

"Well if your friend thinks he's going to woo me like he probably does other women, he is mistaken," I stated and was happy to see a table waving me over. I didn't want to discuss this with Kole. Especially since he seemed friendly with the charmer.

The rest of the night went by quickly. I was relieved when Kole announced it was last call and customers slowly started to take their leave until finally the pub was closed. I cleaned up the seating area while Kole wiped down the bar and the cook Rickard cleaned up the kitchen. I was happy for the silence. I think Kole knew I didn't want to talk about his friend anymore. That's another thing I liked about Kole. He didn't ask too many questions. I was relieved. I didn't want to talk about my life before a few days ago.

"Why don't you head on home? I can handle the rest of it," Kole told me.

"Thanks." I took off my apron. I went through the bills in my pocket. As I counted the tips I had gotten my eyes widened. I had made $300 in tips in one night! The night before it hadn't been much but I hadn't expected a Thursday night to be busy. But that night, it was packed.

"Those are for you." Kole told me as he watched me stare at the bills in my hand.

"What about Rickard?" I nodded towards the kitchen. I had a few waitressing jobs before and we split the tips with the cook usually.

"Don't worry, he isn't forgotten." That's all Kole told me and I didn't question him on it.

"Well thanks." I grabbed my purse from the safe, putting the wad of cash into the inside pocket. This many bills wouldn't fit into my wallet. I waved goodnight and headed out the door towards the motel I was staying at down the street. The tips from the night would buy me a few more days. And when I got my first paycheck I could start looking for a cheap car just to get around in. This was how it was starting over. I had done it before so I had what I needed to do down.

I looked across the street at a small building with a sign that read CARTER ACCOUNTING SERVICES. But it wasn't the sign that caught my attention. It was the sight above the sign, in what looked like an apartment. In the window a bare chested man could be seen with his pecks on display, running on a treadmill in basketball shorts. I was captivated watching his body move. It was when he turned his head and made eye contact with me that I gasped. It was the charmer who was in the bar earlier. He smiled at me and I turned my head and walked quickly down the street. Crap. He totally caught me staring at him. This would be an issue.

2

DYLAN

As she faded from view, I shut off the treadmill and went over to the far window to see where she was going. No I wasn't a stalker. This wasn't some episode of *You*. But I was curious where she was going. It was late and she was walking. I was concerned about her safety. Yeah, that was it. I saw her walk into the parking lot of Rudy's Motel. She was staying in a motel? Did that mean she wasn't planning to stay long? I had to up my game. I needed to know more about this woman before she was gone.

The next day I occupied my time with an early morning surf session with my best friend Chandler. He was married with three daughters, triplets. His life was hectic but we always met up Saturday morning early, before the beach was swarmed with people, to surf together and catch up. This morning it was the same old for him, busy with the family and his law practice. I didn't tell him about Kelsey. She was a fun little secret I suppose. Plus he would just lecture me on how I needed to settle down. The right woman was out there. Blah. Blah. Blah.

Once I was back home and showered I headed into my business

office to get some work done. I didn't usually work on the weekends but I needed a distraction until the evening. As I was typing away entering in a client's information on the computer, I heard the bell on the door chime. Shoot. I had meant to lock it. "Sorry we aren't open today," I called out. Then I looked up and a smile spread across my face. Kelsey was walking towards my desk with a look of determination.

"This won't take long," she said to me as she stopped in front of my desk. "I just want you to know I wasn't checking you out last night, ok?" She put her hands on her hips in a sassy way that had me chuckling. She frowned. "What's so funny?"

"You," I admitted and stood up. I leaned over my desk towards her. "I saw you watching me. I bet you were thinking about me all night. That's why you had to come in here and talk to me." I smiled at her and that seemed to enrage her more.

"You are wrong," she huffed. "I don't care about you. I just didn't want you to come into the pub tonight with the wrong idea."

"So you were hoping to see me tonight?" My smile widened.

"No," she defended. "I just, uh, ugh!" She turned around and stormed out of my office letting the door slam behind her. I still had a smile on my face. I was getting under her skin.

KELSEY

Stupid. Stupid. Stupid. Why did I go into his office? I wasn't even sure it was his office. I just figured if he lived above it, he owned it. Looks like I was right. I had paused for a good few minutes outside the door getting the nerve to go inside. He didn't notice me. He was busy looking at some folder and typing at a high speed. Finally I took a breath and entered. I had rehearsed what I was going to say all morning. All night I kept thinking about him and it bothered me. So to my sleep deprived brain the logical thing to do was confront him before he got the wrong idea. Well that backfired in my face. He had instead thought I was more interested.

I busied myself the rest of the day sorting my finances. I paid for another two nights at the motel and then looked at the local ads for anyone selling a car I could afford. I found some I would call at the end of the following week, after I got my first paycheck. I also found a few rooms for rent to call on. I was feeling good about my future. I had hoped I could stay in this town. I just had to be smarter than I had been. No friends. No one could know anything about me. That was the only way. I put the remainder of my cash in my purse. I never trusted that someone wouldn't break into my motel room.

The night at the pub was busy and I liked it. It kept me out of my head. I didn't think about all I had to still do for myself and all I needed to be afraid of. As it got later I was relieved the charmer hadn't come in. Kole called out "last call" and I smiled, excited to be closer to getting off my feet. They were aching.

"Can you stay and clean up tonight? I have a friend coming in for a small meeting." Kole said to me as most of the patrons filed out. That made me curious. What kind of meeting was that late? I didn't question him out loud, though. I nodded and got back to work, not complaining that I just wanted to get off my feet.

"Did you miss me?" A voice said behind me and I spun around quickly. I was relieved it was just the charmer. Then I was annoyed that he had shown up after all.

"We're closed," I told him and went back to cleaning the table.

"Dylan, over here!" Kole called from one of the back booths. We both looked over at him as he waved. I now knew his name. I had thought it would have been Carter from his business name. Now it made sense that it was his last name.

"I don't mean to disappoint but I have other plans." Dylan smiled at me with a wink and then walked over to Kole. He set a blue folder on the table and they started to chat. I couldn't hear what it was about and pretended not to care. The nerve of him thinking I was waiting for him to show up. I couldn't help but watch them out of the corner of my eye, curiosity getting the best of me. It was a habit. I didn't trust anyone. I couldn't afford to. I watched Dylan hand Kole some sort of spreadsheet and they went over it line by line. Was Kole some sort of underground crime boss? Maybe Dylan ran the books for him. My mind came up with all sorts of crazy scenarios. Before I knew it I had finished wiping down the tables and was working on the booths, closer to their meeting. But as soon as I got close enough to hear, they were finished. They shook hands and Kole took the folder.

"Everything looks great. Thanks Kelsey." Kole smiled at me.

"Kelsey," Dylan nodded at me. Alarms went off in my head. He now knew my name. I never told him my name for a reason. It wasn't my real name but still. I told myself to relax. I was being too paranoid.

"Need anything else from me?" I asked as I wiped down the last booth, the booth they had been in.

Kole shook his head. "See you Monday." Kole disappeared into his office. The pub was closed on Sunday. I was looking forward to a day off. I liked this job but it was tiring on my feet. I was so grateful to have it, though.

"Can I walk you out?" Dylan asked me. I made the mistake of looking up into his dark brown eyes. My knees felt weak. I told myself to pull it together. I wanted to decline. I wanted to tell him I didn't need anyone to walk me out.

"Sure," I responded instead. As soon as the word left my mouth I was shocked. I grabbed my purse and walked ahead of Dylan, who held the door open for me like a true gentleman. It made me uncomfortable. I had a hard time with nice gestures. Especially from men who I knew were interested in me. I had fallen for those tricks before. They are the reason I was in the position I was in. I heard the door shut behind Dylan. I expected him to say good night and cross the street. But instead he kept walking with me. "Aren't you going the wrong way," I finally asked after a few feet.

"Nope." That's all he said. No explanation. No volunteered reasoning.

I stopped, blocking him from walking any further. I gave him a stern look. "I can walk by myself. I don't need you to walk me like I am some helpless female." I promised myself that no man would ever make me feel weak again, forcing me to depend on them.

"I know you don't need me to." He looked me in my eyes and I told myself to ignore the heat running throughout my body. "I want to. Not for you. But for me. I would feel better knowing that you got home safe. Can you please let me do this for me?"

I eyed him suspiciously. Was this just a line? Or was he serious? I decided I was tired and I didn't want to argue any further. I sighed and turned around heading towards the motel. I figured he could follow me if he wanted to.

"So where are you from?" He asked me as he caught up to me. We walked side by side. I made sure my fingers didn't hit his. I had to really focus since it seemed like he was trying to make his fingers touch mine. His touch would be my downfall, I just knew it.

"I am from somewhere else," I answered. No personal information shared. I couldn't do it. Even the smallest details. It wasn't just for my safety, but for Dylan's too.

"Wow. That sounds like a fascinating place," Dylan teased. But he seemed to take the hint and didn't push me for anymore information. "I grew up here." He was offering up personal information about himself to me. I just nodded. I wanted to ask him more but I knew I had no right. We walked the rest of the way in silence. I swear it was the longest walk back to the motel I'd had yet.

As we neared the motel I suddenly smelt something smoky. I looked up and the sight in front of me made me freeze just steps away from the entrance to the motel. It was ablaze. The motel was on fire!

"Oh no," I whispered. "He found me."

3

DYLAN

I pulled Kelsey back as soon as we were at the entrance to the motel. It was on fire and the fire department hadn't arrived yet. People were running from their rooms. Pretty soon the entrance was crowded with people spilling into the street.

"No! This can't be happening!" Kelsey crumbled and I caught her before she hit the ground. I expected her to push me away, but she seemed to be clinging to me for dear life. "I was careful. I didn't screw up this time."

"What do you mean?" She wasn't making any sense.

"This is my fault." She looked around. She was addressing all the other patrons of the motel. "I'm so sorry."

"Why are you apologizing?" A large grey haired woman looked at Kelsey as if she was crazy. She had a name tag that listed her as the motel manager. "This fire isn't your fault. You weren't even here."

"Trust me. It is," she said in a soft voice and I am sure only I heard her.

"She's just in shock," I quickly said. I had to cover for Kelsey before she incriminated herself. Of course this wasn't her fault. But I didn't want her putting it in anyone's head that she was to blame. I didn't want anyone to claim she confessed.

"I understand." The grey haired women nodded with a sympathetic look and walked away to talk to other people who were just as freaked out. The fire engines had arrived, and I pulled Kelsey a few feet down the street to get out of the way. The firemen rushed in putting out the fire. The fire had taken over the building quickly and fiercely.

"I am sorry to announce," the fire chief addressed the crowd, "you will all have to find somewhere else to stay for the time being. The building is not safe to be in at the moment."

A few people started to complain and pretty soon everyone was talking over each other. I looked at the grey haired woman. She was trying to keep everyone under control but she looked like she was going to lose it herself.

"I have nowhere to go. I have nothing." Kelsey's voice was quiet, hopeless. She looked up at me with tears in her eyes. "My whole life was in that room. I didn't have much but now it's all gone." Tears fell from her eyes leaving a trail down her face. I had a sudden urge to comfort her. To protect her.

"You don't know that. Maybe some of it survived. We can find out tomorrow. But right now you need to rest. Come on." I started to lead her down the street back the way we came.

"Where?" She wiped the tears from her eyes.

"You can stay with me." I quickly snapped my mouth shut. Where had that suggestion come from? But I meant it.

"No." She pulled back taking her hand from mine. "I can't stay with you."

"Yes you can," I told her. "I have a guest room."

"But I don't know you."

"What's going on?" A voice said to us from a red sports car that pulled up. I stepped in front of Kelsey protectively. It was then I saw his friendly smile. It was Kole.

"There was a fire at the motel," I explained.

"Oh no." He looked past me to Kelsey who looked in shock still. "Weren't you staying there?" Kelsey nodded. "I'm so sorry Kelsey."

"I'm trying to convince her to stay with me. But I'm a stranger to her," I explained, widening my eyes meaningfully, hoping he could help me out. He nodded, pulled the car to the curb and parked. He got out of the car and walked over to us.

"Kelsey, let me talk to you." He motioned for her to follow him a few feet away. She didn't respond but followed him. I wanted to hear what he said to her. But I knew it would be better if I stayed where I was and let them talk. After a few minutes of Kole talking and Kelsey nodding she hugged him and they walked back over to me. "She will go with you tonight and we will figure things out tomorrow. I'll come to your apartment around noon. Does that work?"

"You don't have to Kole. We can work it out." I appreciated him offering to help but I sort of wanted to be her hero at the moment. I know it was selfish. But it was the truth.

Kole now pulled me to the side. "She needs me there tomorrow. She needs me to see that she is okay with you. She's scared. The only reason she's agreeing to go with you at all is because she's in shock. She might flee in the morning. I don't know what happened to her but she has trust issues. She seems to trust me. So me promising to check on her tomorrow is her only sense of safety at the moment."

I nodded. I understood. I had to take this slow. For some reason I cared about this woman. This woman that I had just met. She wasn't just an infatuation anymore. She was damaged, but strong. She was also running from something or someone. I wanted to protect her. I would. My new goal wasn't just to win her over any longer. My goal was to get her to trust me fully and then maybe she would give herself to me, in more ways than one.

KELSEY

The rest of the night or shall I say early morning was a blur. The motel on fire. Kole promising me that I would be safe staying with Dylan. The walk towards his apartment. I don't remember going into his apartment or going to bed in this room. But I woke up to the sun shining through the blinds. I shot up out of bed. All my fears and worries came forth. I ignored the headache I felt and grabbed my phone connected to a charger on the nightstand next to the bed. It read 11:30 a.m. I relaxed a little bit. I looked around the room. It was a pretty bare room. There was just a black dresser and the twin sized bed that I was in. The walls were a beige color. There was a walk in closet across the room. I saw the bedroom door was shut. I was alone in there. I searched for my purse, it had all I owned in it since I was sure the fire took everything. I spotted it on the floor next to the bed. I grabbed it and inspected it inside. Nothing was missing. A sense of relief came over me.

I got out of the bed in the clothes from the day before. I needed to get out of there and go to the motel. I needed to see how screwed I was and come up with a plan on what I was going to do. I flung the purse over my shoulder and cracked the door. The television echoed down the hall. I had hoped that Dylan wouldn't be home. But then I wondered why he would leave me alone in his apartment? I was a stranger. I walked slowly down the hall and entered the living room. Dylan was sitting on the couch in a pair of blue jeans and a plain white shirt that hugged his arms tightly, his muscles bulged out. Damn.

"Good afternoon." He smiled at me and stood up. "Are you hungry?" He turned around and started walking towards the kitchen behind the couch.

"You don't have to," I offered but I was hungry. Actually I was starving. I hadn't eaten much the day before.

"You have to eat." He reached into the refrigerator and pulled out a bowl. "I made chicken and rice. I hope that sounds good."

"That's great. Thanks." I wanted to fight him but I couldn't. I needed to eat. I'd accept his meal and then be on my way.

"So, I went over to the motel this morning," he told me as he put the bowl in the microwave. I stare at him waiting for the news. "They are going to have to rebuild." He paused, his eyes scanned my face. "Nothing could be saved in any of the rooms."

The words hit me like a ton of bricks. I don't know why. I figured that nothing was salvageable. But there had been that sliver of hope. I held back the tears of hopelessness. I really didn't have anything to mourn. Everything was replaceable. I had nothing truly valuable and personal. I had lost that already. I told myself to get over it. I had been through worse. No sense being sad. I needed to figure out what to do next.

"Also they know the cause of the fire," he stated. I felt my stomach tighten. I was afraid of the truth. The truth I thought I knew. "It was caused by a group of teenagers playing with fire in one of the rooms."

I sagged in my seat, my stomach unclenched. Relief set in. It wasn't my fault. He hadn't found me. The fire was just an accident. Sure I was upset I had nothing left. But the feeling that I didn't have to shoulder the blame almost made me want to sing. I was okay. I was still safe.

"Well thank you for looking into that for me and also for letting me stay here this morning." I did have manners. I was raised right. I just didn't always make the best choices.

"You are welcome. That's what I wanted to talk to you about." My stomach flipped. Whatever it was he was going to propose I knew I was going to refuse it. We were interrupted by a knock on the door. I felt my body tense. Dylan eyed me suspiciously. Then he was at my side patting my hand. I quickly pulled my hand away. He didn't seem to take offense.

"It's just Kole. Remember, he promised to stop by?" He walked over to the door and opened it. Kole walked in with a smile, I took my first deep breath since last night. There was something about him that made me feel safe. I wasn't attracted to him, even though he was a good looking man. Something told me I could trust him. Usually, I ignored that voice because it had been so wrong before. But Kole had shown me that he was a good man. I saw him with his customers and how he helped people too. I eyed him giving a hug to Dylan. I wondered, was Dylan just as good of a man?

"How are you doing?" Kole asked me, sitting down next to me. The microwave beeped and Dylan walked over to it removing my lunch. He set it down in front of me. He offered one to Kole who declined it respectively.

I shrugged and started to eat. I could avoid talking by eating. Kole didn't press me for more. He and Dylan started talking. I realized they were talking about their meeting last night. It was about taxes. Kole wasn't some crime boss. My imagination and paranoia made me almost laugh. But then I remembered my imagination also had gotten me in trouble before. I shook the memories from my mind. The past was not a place my mind needed to go right now.

"Well everything seems to be ok here. I have some errands to run today. I also need to prep for the week." Kole stood up.

"I can help," I immediately offered. It was my day off but I could use the distraction.

"I'm good." He patted my arm and I didn't brush off his touch. Dylan definitely noticed by the way he eyed us both but he didn't remark on it.

"While you're here Kole," Dylan started, "I wanted to offer something to Kelsey. I figure you could back me up." He looked at Kole then at me. "I want to offer my guest room to Kelsey until she can get on her feet."

"I appreciate that," I quickly stated. "But I don't need help. I'll be fine." I took a bite of chicken before I said anymore. I started to get defensive but I couldn't offend this man in his home, especially when he had been there for me last night.

"I didn't say that," he defended, calmly. "But I would like to help."

"I would take the offer," Kole stated looking me in my eyes. "If you need me to vouch for Dylan I will. I've known him for a few years and I trust him. You can too."

I sighed. I know I needed to refuse further. I needed to tell them to mind their business. But the image of the fire came into my mind. The realization that I had lost pretty much everything took over. I had some cash but that wasn't enough for a room in this town. I was lucky to find that cheap motel. But that was now gone. I eyed Kole. I didn't see anything but truth in his face. I told myself maybe I could really trust him. Really I had no choice unless I wanted to sleep in a park and that really seemed more dangerous.

"Okay," I agreed quietly. Dylan jaw dropped in shock and I almost laughed. "But I have some rules."

"I'll leave you two to sort it out. See you tomorrow." Kole nodded at us both and then left the apartment.

"Hit me with your rules," Dylan said with a smile. The fact that this man was happy to have me in his apartment would have usually made me suspicious, causing alarms to go off in my head. But at this moment, it didn't. Weird.

"We aren't anything but roommates," I started to tell him. "I am not some hook up for you to go to. And I need my space. I appreciate you letting me stay here. I can't pay you until next week but I will clean and cook as part of my keep."

"Not necessary." He waved his hand at me. "I have a maid that comes in once a week and I'm a big boy. I can cook for myself. Don't worry about paying me. I am offering this to be kind. Not to get something out of you. I'll give you your space." He walked up to me. I tensed, fearing he was going to touch me again. I couldn't handle his touch. It made my body feel things I had no business feeling. But he just looked into my eyes. "You can trust me." He gave me that panty melting smile and I was almost a puddle on the ground.

"Thanks," I said to him and looked away. I focused on my food once more as Dylan walked out of the room and down the hall. Seconds later, I heard his bedroom door shut. I let out a breath of relief. I could do this. I could resist him. I had to.

4

KELSEY

The next week flew by quickly. I had actually gotten myself into a routine. Dylan had stuck to his word. He has given me my space. He hadn't tried to make a move on me at all. During the day, I was alone in the apartment while he was working in his office downstairs. At night as I was working, he would come into the pub for a drink but left after he was done. He was friendly with me but didn't try to take up my time. Which I am grateful for because he would be a distraction. I may not have been in the business for anything romantic but I wasn't dead. I knew he was sexy as hell and his kind heart just made him that much more appealing. And did I mention what a gentleman he was? Every night after closing I found him waiting for me at the entrance to the pub to walk me across the street. I told him it was silly but there he was every single night to make sure I got home to the apartment safely. This man was quickly chipping at the ice on my heart.

We also had been getting along like friends. When he was in the pub we joked a bit. And when we ran into each other in the apartment it wasn't awkward. I could get used to this. I did get my first paycheck and after I cashed it at a check cashing place I left him some money for rent. But it just ended up back in my wallet somehow. After a few attempts of giving it back I kept it and decided that I would pay him in another way.

It was Sunday late afternoon and I had just gotten back from my walk to the grocery store. Thankfully it was just a block away. I was still looking for a car but no luck yet. I was relieved to find that Dylan wasn't home. He left me a note on the fridge that he was down stairs getting some work done if I needed him. He would be done at about 6 p.m. That worked out perfect for me. I was going to make him my homemade mac 'n cheese with ham and bacon. I had hoped he would love it. I noticed he mostly ate healthy. That made sense because he was in amazing shape. And boy did I notice.

At 6 p.m. I had just taken the casserole dish out of the oven and I was pulling out the garlic bread as the apartment door opened. Dylan walked in looking tired. He stopped as soon as the smell of my meal hit him and he smiled the biggest smile at me.

"What's this?" He asked.

"Since you won't let me pay you in cash for letting me stay here, I thought I could pay you with a nice meal. I know it's not healthy..." I started to explain but he put up his hand to stop me.

"It's wonderful. Thank you." His words were sincere. He puts his phone and keys on the counter. "Let me plate us up." He started walking towards me.

"Nope." I shook my head and he stopped. "I am treating you. Take a seat." I nodded towards the small dinning table in the corner of the living room. His apartment wasn't too small but it also wasn't very big. It was perfect for us both. But I reminded myself it wasn't mine. It was his home and me being in it was temporary.

We ate together in a comfortable silence. Dylan did remark how good the dinner was. My smile expressed my pride. I did something right. I was not used to that feeling. In my past I tried to please and was left to feel like I never could. I pushed those memories away. They wouldn't taint this moment.

After dinner I had planned to go to my room and just read. But Dylan asked me to watch a movie with him. I froze. I told myself to calm down, it was just a movie. Friends do that right? I could hang out with him. We joked that it was a pajama party and we both went to our rooms to change. I did manage to do some clothes shopping at the discount clothing store down the street that past week to replace the clothes I lost in the fire. I returned to the living room in a pair of black sleeping shorts and a red tank top. Dylan was already on the couch with a remote in his hand. I took a deep breath. He looked so hot in just a pair of black sweatpants and a plain black t-shirt, that hugged his abs just right. How could an outfit so simple make him look so appealing? I told myself to ignore it and I sat on the opposite end of the couch.

Dylan put on a movie, a romantic comedy, for my benefit I'm sure. He doesn't strike me as a Katherine Hiegl fan. We laughed throughout most of it. Then the epic romantic scene happened. I found myself having mixed feelings. It wasn't that I didn't want romance, it was that I couldn't bear to give my heart away again. As these thoughts were in my mind I felt Dylan's gaze on me. I turned my head and we locked eyes. I looked at the man that had invaded my fantasies each night since we met. I can't tell you how it happens or why I let it happen but suddenly I lunged across the couch at him. He caught me in his arms and our lips met. The kiss was urgent. We were both desperate for each other. My alarms were going off in my mind. But my body was shutting them down telling me I needed this. I deserved this.

I started to lift Dylan's shirt off and he stopped me by pulling back from our embrace. "Are you sure this is what you want? I don't want you to do anything you'll regret."

I stared at him. I know he wanted me. He had made that obvious since I met him, but he was being a gentleman and giving me the option to stop us. My mind said to take him up on it. But at that moment, I wanted him more than I had wanted anything in my life. "Shut up and kiss me," was my response and quickly our lips were meeting again and our clothes were being stripped off. Dylan picked me up exposing my bare ass to the window that faced the street. I didn't even care if anyone could see. He carried me to his bedroom and set me on his bed. We were kissing again. Our hands were roaming each other's bodies. I pulled away and gave him a look that showed him what I wanted, what I needed. He went to his night stand and pulled out a condom. I waited patiently as he slipped it on and then positioned himself between my legs. He looked down at me as if waiting for permission and I pulled him into me. As soon as our bodies connected I let out a moan. He moved in and out of me with sweet and gentle strokes, and I couldn't handle it. I pulled him further in me and demanded more. As we moved together, both of us panting and moaning, I knew that I was falling. Falling for this man who was genuinely good. This man who treated me with such care that I hadn't ever really experienced before. I was in danger of doing the one thing I promised I wouldn't do. And as we both reached our climax together, I realized I was doomed. I could see myself falling in love with Dylan Carter.

DYLAN

I looked down at the beautiful goddess beneath me who was trying to catch her breath. She wasn't the only one. I didn't want the moment to end. Us connected. Her baring herself to me. I knew I wanted her when I first saw her. She was gorgeous. In the beginning it was just a physical thing but getting to know her that past week, really learning who she was inside her heart, it had me falling for more than just her body. And that wasn't what I normally did. I wasn't a sleeze ball who slept with tons of women and then never called them again. But I didn't fall in love. It was too messy. I had seen my friends burned too many times and that wouldn't be me. But this woman, I feared, could break me. She let out a breath and looked up at me with that smile that made me forget my fears. I leaned down and gave her a sweet kiss. Then I disconnected our bodies, disposing of the condom in the bathroom connected to my room. I ran the water and splashed my face to make sure it was all real. I looked into the mirror. Yup, it all had happened. I felt like a lucky man. Kelsey gave me her body, her soul and I had hoped to win her heart. I came back into the room expecting her to be leaving but she was under my sheets, asleep. I slid into bed next to her and wrapped my arms around her falling asleep with a smile on my face.

I woke up the next morning when my alarm went off. I shut it off and groaned. I usually didn't mind going to work. I liked my routine and staying busy. But that morning I wanted to ignore my appointments and just stay in bed. Kelsey was still in my arms. She hadn't ran.

I tried to sleep for a few more minutes but my back up alarm went off telling me that I needed to get up and face the reality of the day. As much as it pained me, I removed my arms from around Kelsey's sexy body and forced myself out of bed and toward the shower. As the water hit my face I noticed the shower curtain moved to the side and my mouth dropped open at the sight before me. Kelsey, naked, with hungry eyes. Yes we were naked the night before but in the heat of the moment I didn't get a chance to look at her body like I was now and I swore she was perfect. Her body was perfectly sculpted. She bit her bottom lip as she took the sight of me in. I pulled her into the shower and our lips met under the stream of water. In movies they made it look sexy but in reality it was so not. We laughed as Kelsey backed up spitting out some water. We exchanged a look of amusement but that passed and passion took over. I pushed her against the wall and she smiled at my need for her. The night before I made love to her sweetly. At this moment I just needed to be inside of her. She opened her legs giving me permission. I went to leave the shower to grab a condom but she stopped me.

"I'm on the pill. And I trust you." She looked into my eyes.

Those words, *I trust you*, hit me hard. They weren't something to take lightly. I know they meant the world to her. And I was not going to make her regret them. I slid into her and I showed her how much those words meant to me with each thrust.

"Harder," she demanded and I obeyed. Soon we were both finding our release, her moaning loudly. That's when I realized I was screwed. I was quickly falling in love with this woman. I had just hoped she wouldn't break my heart.

5

KELSEY

I felt like I was in a dream. I expected things to be weird between Dylan and I after we had sex. But they weren't. He was still so sweet. He hadn't changed at all. He wasn't being possessive and his sweet demeanor didn't fade. But things did change between us. We weren't acting like just roommates anymore. And I hadn't spent a night in the guest room in a week. Dylan wanted me in his bed every night and I didn't fight him on it. Every night he brought my body to such heights that I never wanted to let him go.

It was Saturday and I was alone in the apartment getting ready for work. Kole had called early in the day to ask Dylan to help him fix something in the pub. I hadn't pegged Dylan for a fix it himself kind of guy but I guess Kole asking him to come help meant he was. As I left ten minutes before my shift started I noticed that Dylan hadn't gotten back yet. I didn't think much of it as I locked up and headed across the street. I also didn't think anything about the closed sign that was still lit up in the window. But I did find it odd that the door was locked. Kole usually had the door unlocked by the time I arrived. I knocked and then heard a voice on the other side that I thought was

Dylan's yell, "Kelsey leave!" I didn't listen. I knocked again and the door opened up. I pushed it to see what was going on. That's when I saw Dylan across the pub tied to a chair. He looked at me with fear. Before I could question what was going on I heard the voice of my nightmares.

"How nice of you to join us Raelynn." His voice was sinister and it sent chills down my body. I froze. This wasn't happening. This was a nightmare. I shut my eyes and then opened them quickly. I was still in the pub. Stephon was here. "You can't blink me away, Sweetheart."

I quickly turned and was faced with those eyes that held so much anger. Those eyes that used to fill with enjoyment at my pain. Those eyes that I wanted to never see again. He had Dylan tied up. He was here for me. He found me. Again. But this time I wasn't able to run before he reached me. This time he was smarter than me. I tried to take the look of fear off my face and put on a fake smile. "Hi Stephon," I said sweetly as if he wasn't a man I had been running from.

"Cut the crap." He glared at me. Then I felt a slap and I was on the floor with my face stinging. This was bad, very bad. I looked over at Dylan and mouthed that I was sorry. I knew Stephon. I put up with his abuse for months. Things weren't going to get better. And it was all my fault Dylan was in this now.

"Don't touch her!" Dylan yelled. I quickly looked up at Stephon who had a grin on his face. Dread pooled in my stomach, I knew that grin.

"I see you've been busy." He then walked over to Dylan addressing him. "Trust me. She isn't worth it. She may seem sweet. But one day she'll leave with your cash never to be heard from again." Stephon then sneered at me. What he was saying was true but it wasn't the whole truth. I only left after he had almost put me in the hospital. I had packed up my things that could fit in one bag in the middle of the night and took the money that was mostly mine saved up in the safe and I bolted. That was almost a year ago. "Well it's time for you to pay me back." He stalked over to me and bent down and lifted up my chin. His touch made me cringe. I couldn't believe I had loved this monster once upon a time.

"I don't have anything," I squeaked out.

"Oh I know." He smiled. "I burned it all and paid those teenagers to take the blame." My eyes widened. I knew it was him! "So you'll have to repay me in another way." His hand moved from my chin and I felt it slide down my neck to my collar bone and inch it's way down the inside of my shirt. I tried to hide the tears that were forming in my eyes. I had to find a way out of this. Then Stephon removes his hand from the inside of my shirt. He reached a hand inside his jacket and pulled out a black handgun, putting the barrel up to my temple. "You're tainted. I saw you in the window of his apartment. You were supposed to only bare yourself to me! I don't want you. But you still have to pay." Then the explosion echoed in my ears and I braced myself for death.

DYLAN

I grounded my teeth watching this waste of a man touch Kelsey, or I guess Raelynn as he called her. I wasn't even upset that she had lied to me about her name. As he talked I understood why. And those lies he said about her only fueled my anger. I was helpless. He had surprised me when he came in. He had approached me from behind and hit me in the back of the head. The next thing I knew I was waking up tied to a chair. I didn't have time to think of how to escape because he was opening the door to Kelsey's knock. I tried to warn her away but failed. Then he pulled a gun out of his jacket and my heart felt like it was about to burst out of my chest it was beating so fast. He put the barrel up to her temple and all I could do was cry out for him not to. Then the sound of the gun hit me and all hope left me.

But then I discovered it wasn't his gun that went off. That gun dropped out of his hand as his body fell to the floor. There was a bullet in his forehead. It took me a minute to understand what was happening. Then it clicked. Kole. He never came back from the storage room. In my panic of Kelsey arriving I hadn't even thought about where he was. I turned my head towards the back of the pub and saw Kole standing there, gun lowering to his side. He then walked over to me cutting the rope around my wrists with a switchblade. As soon as my hands were free I rushed over to Kelsey and took her in my arms pulling her away from Stephon's body. She looked like she was in shock. Truthfully, I was too.

"I'm here. You're safe," I said into her ear.

"Is he dead?" She stared at the body across from us.

"Yes. He can't ever hurt you again." I squeezed her and I felt her tears hit my arms. I wished I could erase them. I wish she didn't have to feel them. But I'd make sure she never had to cry them again. That's when I uttered something that I had never said to a woman before. Something that I am sure was too soon but I couldn't hold back while holding this woman in my arms. "I love you."

"I love you, too," she whispers back and then shut her eyes, the exhaustion taking over. I stood up with her in my arms. I turned to Kole who was texting someone on his phone.

"Take her home," he said to me. "I got this."

"Thank you. Words can't express..." I started to tell him but he interrupted me.

"Just take care of her."

"I will. I promise." I meant every word of it. I would never let her go.

KELSEY

I woke up to the morning light with a headache and my face throbbing. The events from the night before came back. I was sure I was going to die. But to be honest that's not what my heart cared about. I just wanted Dylan to be safe. I looked next to me and he was there, watching me. I smiled at him. I don't think I have ever been so happy to see someone looking back at me. He was alive. We were alive. The man who tormented me, broke me, made me constantly look over my shoulder was now dead. I didn't have to live in fear anymore.

"Are you okay?" Dylan asked me as his hands cradled my face planting a soft kiss on my lips. He pulled away and I looked into his eyes. I felt safe. I felt freedom for the first time in a long time. This was where I belonged.

"I'm good. Because of you," I tell him.

He shakes his head. "No. I couldn't save you." He looked down, hiding his eyes from me.

"Hey." I lifted his head up forcing him to look into my eyes. "You did save me. Kole may have pulled the trigger but you saved me before I set foot in that pub last night. You showed me kindness when all I did was push you away. You took me in when I had nowhere to go. And you showed me what it's like to be truly cared for. You showed me real love." I leaned down and kissed him. "And now you are stuck with me." I smiled.

"Lucky me." He smiled back and kissed me sweetly. "Raelynn."

I pulled back quickly. "No." I shook my head. "It's Kelsey. Raelynn died with that monster. Kelsey is the woman who took a chance and fell in love with a man who didn't give up on her. A woman who found her happiness."

"And now you're stuck with me." He pulled me into his arms.

"Lucky me."

THE END

Learn more about Mary Dean:
HTTPS://LINKTR.EE/MARYDEANWRITES

Also by Mary Dean:
The Secrets Within
The Fire Within
Witch House

THE SHOW'S NOT OVER

MARY ROGERS

What's harder than your first love
breaking your heart on national television?
Taking a chance on the one who did it.

Sub-genre: Second Chance Romance
Relationship: Male/Female

THE SHOW'S NOT OVER

Nothing ever smelled like an Italian neighborhood in Brooklyn on a Sunday, and nothing ever would. Catherine "Kicks" Malloy turned the corner from her apartment to the Storybook Pub on one of the windiest days in the history of Brooklyn, bringing that smell whirling all around her reminding her she was hungry. The wind pushed a rogue piece of unidentifiable garbage toward her. She dodged it, spilling her Dunkin' Donuts coffee. It wasn't a tragedy, but her suede glove would need triage. It was her new silk blouse, and what she wore under it she was worried about.

It had already been a long day worrying about this evening's meet of the cast of *Growing Up Brooklyn*, the show they all literally grew up in front of America on, so she didn't need any more aggravation. She trudged on, head down, thinking to herself, *How long is a block and a half?*

She looked up when a man answered with that accent she both loathed and loved. "Yo! It's a block and maybe… a half." He smiled and faux punched her arm. "You got this, Kicks," and he continued on.

Okay, so not to herself this time. "Thanks, Benny. Have a good night!" He didn't answer but he didn't have to, more than likely the wind blew her words away. She smiled to herself. She'd see him again. After all, they lived next door, as they had since he was born. She loved Benny, as she had since he was born. He was the first child she had babysat for in the neighborhood. This was what made Boerum Hill great. This was family. This was her place, her turf, and even if she was a little worried about seeing everyone again—okay, Hobie Daniels again—it was still home to all of them.

They truly were the lucky ones. Some left Brooklyn, most of them not by choice. Brooklyn people stayed. Most would have to be dragged out kicking and screaming. It was their opinion that you'd have to be crazy to be anywhere else. She had stayed on the block along with Vinny and Toni, happily married since about six seconds after their shared eighteenth birthday, against everyone's wishes, but proving everyone wrong daily. It lightened up for them when they gave their parents a grandchild in nine months and two days, and the public a spin-off show. Kicks sighed. Her having a child was her parents' long suffering *very* vocal dream, and one they shared with everyone, as passive-aggressively as possible. Ev. Ry. One. Oy! The Irish had a handle on a very special form of guilt which they practiced on generations of children. She fully expected to become a victim who in turn victimized another generation someday.

Sorry, oh poor unsuspecting unborn potential children. She held her stomach. *Sorry, eggs. Changing this is probably above my pay grade.*

She looked up as she hurried along. "Prakesh," she nodded.

"Hey, how's it goin', Kicks? Some wind, eh?" He turned around to face her jogging backwards at a good clip. "You still single, gorgeous? 'Cause I'm available. Call me."

"Hmmm... tempting, but I think Shareeza would be a tad upset. When are you going to marry her, Prak? She's a beauty, *and* it seems she loves you despite you offering your love to half this city. I'd step on the gas, buddy."

"Done. Date is September. You'll be there." He turned and moved on.

She stopped, ran back, and hugged Prak with all her might. "Try to stop me! Finally! With bells on, buddy. I'll be there with bells on."

When they broke the clinch and moved on, she saw Vinny and

Toni outside the Storybook Pub, neighborhood watering hole for the cast of *Growing up Brooklyn,* and pretty much everyone here. It was a madhouse during the run of the show, she didn't know how the bar survived. Rumors of the kids in the bar set off gawkers from as far away as New Jersey. They weren't allowed to drink yet, but since everyone knew everyone and the parents were there, it was never an issue. It was a family place. It was where she had her first communion party with Hobie, Toni, Vinny, and the rest of the Catechism class from Saint Agnes. The Christenings for Vinny and Toni's kids had been there. She remembered how honored she'd been to hold little Colleen as her Godmother, and how Father Kim spent a month practicing English words he had trouble with, and how he gave a long-winded sermon about love and children for the cameras. It was his fifteen minutes of fame, in the last show of season one, "Vinny and Toni D'Abruzzi's Happily Ever After." The show went on until they had three kids, zero marital strife, zero problems, zero affairs, and zero drama. At least that anyone knew about. When it was cancelled, Vinny had been an amazing investor, and the "happiest family in Brooklyn" was well taken care of.

It was also the cancellation of what she had thought of as love, but that could hardly be blamed on the show.

"Hey, Honey, we thought you'd never get here!"

She moved in for the hug. "Toni! Like I would miss it for the world?" She moved to hug Vinny next.

"Hey, kiddo. Come on in! The gang's all here."

She shook her head. "You know that's what I'm afraid of, Vinch."

"Kicks."

When she didn't look straight at him, he grabbed her chin and turned her to him. "Catherine. He's here. He seems the same, only more mature. It's been a bit, honey. I hope we're all more mature. You gotta let it go. Just let it go." He smiled and put an arm around her. "Come on. Let's go in."

Toni grabbed her arm as they led her in and leaned in whispering conspiratorially. "We're at the stage where the only words and phrases we can speak come from Disney movies, currently Anna and Elsa. We expect to recover by the late twenty thirties."

Catherine looked up at Toni, always so tall, curvy, and gorgeous. "Hold my hand?"

"Always, Kicks. Always. That's what friends are for.

Kicks continued. "And this is Brooklyn—"

"And Brooklyn is for friends!" all three said in unison, the tag line for *Growing Up Brooklyn* that chronicled their lives and loves from middle school to high school graduation. It seemed like forever ago, but occasionally, she'd be noticed, and someone would look at her and call, "Hey Kicks! Brooklyn is for friends!" They had to say it every week, all of them, in unison. They each had their own catch phrase, none of them were ever said by any of them before the writers wrote it for them, except for Vinny, but it became a part of their identities. She had to admit the writers got good at summoning up the essence of their personalities with a seemingly silly phrase. When confronted with this strange and privileged past, she would smile and wave. Those times were getting less and less, and that was good. It was a little hard to reconcile that her childhood, her first *maybe only?* love, the loss of her virginity (never shown but heavily hinted at) and the devastation left behind when she realized it was one-sided had been broadcast for the world to see along with every zit, every fashion faux-pas, every flub, and every bad haircut. There were soooo many bad haircuts, each kept for posterity somewhere on YouTube. Kicks could count on making the top ten in a few 'bad haircuts' countdowns at least once a year. Lucky her.

"Chin up, Cherub." That was Vinnie's line, and it was the only one they knew was actually his. His mother, the greatest woman you could know, would say something like it in Italian, and Vinny translated. The Italian audiences would adore the scenes shot in his house and Toni's— the Italians being, well, Italian. Cooking, cleaning, cooking, speaking Italian, and cooking. The producers tried to get to their houses every Sunday. It may have been a plot to get good meals, despite Vinny's mother forcing them all to church beforehand or to say Catholic prayers. No one complained. Not even the non-Catholics. People would do a lot for Italian cooking. She took one last good whiff of paradise. No, Sir. Nothing ever smells like Brooklyn on a Sunday in an Italian neighborhood, and nothing ever would. It shored up her courage. This was home.

"Here we go." Vinnie opened the door, and Toni and Kicks entered the bar like it was *Cheers*.

"Toni! Kicks!" Everyone got up to hug, including Hobart Daniels. "Hobie." Moderately wealthy, pre-revolution pedigree political family, Blue Book-er, exceptionally gorgeous, breaker of hearts. Specifically? Hers.

Kicks held out her hand to shake his, but everyone moved in. The group hug was so tight she wouldn't be surprised if they all went through each other. There was a small tense moment as they were smashed together, but finally the past gave way and they hugged.

"You guys, we're here!" Pedro Seymour "Peps" O'Brien was always the happiest, you could hear it in his voice. Peps was the Puerto Rican/Irish/Jewish/gay cast member. "They got a lot of diversity with me, because I got the best of everything," he'd say, and it seemed he did. Always upbeat, always kind, and always the most generous of all of them, he was everyone in the group's unofficial bestie. "I can't believe we're all here!"

That was echoed by all. They *were* all here. Kicks, Hobie, Vinnie, Toni, Peps, and Eliza "Liza" Salazar, Jeremiah "Jersi" Singh, Brenda "Star" Stanislawski, Anya "Anchovy" Barischova, and Danny "Dan-Van" Van der Hoff - the entire regular cast of *Growing up Brooklyn*. It was, after that awkward beginning, nice. Comfortable.

Okay. Maybe not. Thank God Vinny and Toni were here.

Danny Van der Hoff started off by having the first round sent over, something they weren't legally able to do in the beginning, and only occasionally in Vinny and Toni's spin-off. "What's everyone drinking?" When the owner of Storybook Pub, Kole O'Shea, sent over a complimentary bottle of champagne, it was decided that a toast was in order first, then on to whatever else.

Anchovy, a name that couldn't be further from the gorgeous woman speaking, asked the question. "What do we say, guys?"

Like it was yesterday, and like the camera was rolling, they all picked up the flutes of champagne, and said the opening and closing lines of every episode. "That's what friends are for, and this is Brooklyn. And Brooklyn is for friends!" Glasses clinked and toasts were drunk, and in minutes they seemed to be like they were a decade ago.

Brenda downed her glass, said no to another in favor of her vodka gimlet, and shook her head. "Did any of you grow up and think how that line is the ultimate in cheesy?"

"Yes, but college," Jersi Singh said. "I mean, cheesy and all, it paid for school." Everyone nodded in agreement. "I'll probably never make that kind of money ever again, and to think I had a blast doing it with the people I wanted to be with. Not exactly a normal first job, but as a doctor with a specialty, having zero student loans and a practice I own is a damned fine thing. Bring on the cheese if it pays that well. Hell, I'd do it again in a heartbeat."

There was a momentary quiet. Everyone there seemed startled he said that.

"Wait. You guys never thought about that? That 'what if?' What if the producers wanted us back, and this time instead of following us around school, they'd follow us around our jobs, and our lives, and loves, and—well, whatever we were doing or what we were up to. What if? There was a moment before Jersi added, "You mean to tell me not one of you has given the matter a bit of thought?"

Small mumblings turned into some agreement, and finally, a lot of agreement on that. Kicks taught at Brooklyn University, but she wrote romance on the side. Only Toni and Vinny knew that part. Having that buffer, allowed her to get degree after degree without a side job or loans, and God knew academia was no pot o'gold. Most everyone she knew had a future saddled with student loans. She was very lucky.

Dan spoke up. "I know you know this, but I used my money to help out small businesses. I made more from that than I expected, and I feel good about it." After a collective groan, he continued. "Okay, okay, trust funds are a good cushion, but it was still nice to have mad money outside of my grandmother, and to not have to wait for the checks every month." In a conspiratorial lean-in he whispered like he was imparting great personal heartache. "Guys, life isn't perfect for me, either." With a face that hinted of some deep revelation, he continued. "Sometimes? The checks are late." When the eye rolls were over, he

THE SHOW'S NOT OVER

began again. "I could do a lot *more* very good now, bring attention to *a lot* of very worthy causes."

Peps questioned that. "Is the world still interested in us and what we do now?"

Vinny added, "They certainly got bored of us in our spin-off."

"That's because the roughest conflict on the show was when you were down to two diapers for Connie!" Kicks added.

They all laughed, then everyone sat back, seemingly all wanting to mull over a return to a very special time for all of them. Finally, Hobie spoke.

"What if... they were?"

Glasses stopped midair as heads turned to Hobie. He motioned to the bar. Kole O'Shea came over with another bottle, this time Don Perignon, and Hobie nodded his head. "Thank you, Mr. O'Shea."

"Kole, please."

"Okay, Kole, thanks. You know I'm Hobie Daniels. Please, sit. This could very well concern you, too."

Now thoroughly confused, they all moved in tighter to let Kole in, pushing Kicks closer to Hobie. Great. He still smelled amazing, making her cross her legs tighter. Hormones were total asshats. No discretion whatsoever.

"Go on," Kole said, "I'm listening."

They were all listening.

"You all know what I do for a living." They all did. He drove them crazy as a kid. Instead of being part of filming, he ended up taking an interest in what happened on the other side of the camera, and being a kid and their current meal ticket, the people behind the show let him follow them around. He hung with the lighting crew, the cameramen, the producers, the directors, anyone he could. They practically had to shove him in front of the camera because all he did was try to be behind it. Mission accomplished. That desire and an NYU film school education landed him an internship with the biggest NY-based people in the film and television industry, and now he was the producer and associate producer of two of the hottest shows filmed in NY. He worked at the famed 30 Rockefeller Plaza, or "30 Rock." Not like she checked up or anything.

He went on. "So, here's an update. We have these, for lack of a better term "meetings." I guess they're called "brainstorming." Some weeks, you're sure everyone has a brain bigger than you'll ever have. Other weeks? You think they have a quarter of the brains in your left shoe. It's a bit of a merry-go-round with the insecurity, but we all have one goal. A show, one people will want to watch, love if possible, one that will be a success."

Kole nodded. "I understand how that would be rough. Tastes change. I'm missing how it would affect us here at Storybook Pub, unless you want to use us in a scene or two?"

Hobie's answer was brief, and to the point. "Many scenes."

Kicks waited a moment to listen to Kole's reply. She didn't want to cut him off. When Kole didn't say anything right away, she couldn't wait. She asked the question they probably all wanted to know. "Why are you telling us this? What has that got to do with all of us?"

"Well, at this last brainstorming session—" he hesitated, uncharacteristically playing with the cocktail napkin. He was obviously nervous. Kicks was well aware that Hobie wasn't usually nervous. He was almost always cool under any circumstances, like the time the block flooded, or when she almost drowned at Brighton Beach episode, or like cheating and breaking her heart. Very cool, like he had no cares. For her, she guessed. What was different here?

"—it was commented on that one of the new writers was a huge fan of *Growing Up Brooklyn*, and specifically tried to get in with my team. He said he was on a lot of Facebook and community groups for fans, and they all want to know what we were up to. There are 'sightings' groups for when a fan sees one of us out and about. Any of you on them? Even anonymously?"

"I've heard of them." Peps added. "And I stay off them. We probably all do."

Liz continued. "If that reason is you don't want to know that when you're shopping at Shop Rite's can can sale someone is surreptitiously filming you, and you don't need to hear the comments that you're down and out and need to shop the sales, yeah. I can tell you if I won lotto I'm still going to shop the can can sale. I get my chickarina soup supply for the year!"

Most agreed. "Not everyone is D'Agostino's or Zabar's material," Liz added.

Hobie went on. "All the writers were fans, so the idea got amped-up. Before I knew it on a late Friday night with some adult beverages, I said I'd speak to you all— get your opinions."

Kole opened the new bottle of champagne, poured and handed him one. In the following silence, he nodded his thanks and downed it like he needed it to live.

When everyone looked dazed and no one said anything he continued. "So, does anyone have, like, an opinion or something, because the silence is killing me, folks. We spent our entire lives together here. I've known you all since then, and none of you, not one, is the quiet type. At least not with each other. Someone?"

"Ah, well," Kole said, "I think it's something I would have to consider. We've done it before, at least my wife's family did, and I can't see how it could hurt, but it looks like you all need to choose what you're going to do before I need to worry." He stood up. "Shall I send the waitress over?"

Danny nodded and Kole left. "Will you all be having your favorites?" When no one said anything, he said, "Right. Favorites it is." He got up to give the waitress their order, as only he could remember it all. He sat down again. When still no one spoke, he continued. "I don't want to be an ass, but there're a lot of upsides to this for me. The money, the assistance I could give, it would be incredible. How personal do they want it? I'd focus on the charity angle, not me."

Brenda said, "Hey, I'm a professional comedienne. I'd love free publicity. *GUB* basically still allows me to work without crying, so for me it would be a win. What about you all?"

"I live in LA." Peps continued. "I'd love to move back to Brooklyn, but the business is a bit scarce here. Los Angeles is *not* Brooklyn. How would that work in my case?"

Everyone offered an opinion— most positive. Peps still wondered about how it would work, Vinny and Toni both nodded that they could use some college funds for little Collie, Carly and Connie. That —left her. Of course he noted the one abstention.

"Kicks?"

She looked at him. *God he's beautiful.*

She thought for a minute. "I—I don't know."

"Is there something I could do to make your decision easier? I mean, this is fast, sure, and despite you all being positive, you'd really all need time to think. In the interim if there's something you need from me to allow you to consider it, Kicks?"

How about you take back being the love of my life and then ruining it? Unbreak my heart. Unhurt my self-esteem, and maybe give Renee a case of raging halitosis?

Everyone was staring goggle-eyed at her. "What?"

Toni grabbed her and said, "Potty break." When everyone continued to stare, she said, "People, we have kids, and some are toilet training. Potty is the word. Stare at someone else."

She stood, not like she had a chance against Toni's insistent pull. They rounded the door, and Toni closed it. Kicks put her head in her hands. "Please tell me I didn't?"

"You did." Toni grabbed her and pulled her into a hug. "You did."

"That was out loud?"

"Yup."

"Oh, thank God in heaven it's been a while. You should have heard what I used to wish that woman."

"Oh, I did. Out loud, in my kitchen over tea, in your kitchen over whiskey, after we saw her in the diner, after you threw up your guts in my bathroom after seeing her in the diner, at the other diner, in your living room, on the phone, and basically everywhere for a year after the events as you know them. Just not, you know, in front of ground zero, himself."

"As I know them? We all know them, and thanks to G-U-B, a lot of America knows them."

"For one thing, it was on our spin-off. For another, we were not as popular. I'm sure no one remembers that. Not even you."

"Oh, really? There are entire fan pages devoted to my heartache, and how could you say I don't remember" she made air quotes, 'the events' as you call them."

Toni smiled, sitting back on the sink. "So—you are on the boards, and you do care."

Shit. "Yes, of course I care. I mean it's our life, Tone, and I'm surprised you don't."

"Meh. I do. I tried it a couple of times, but it's really silly stuff from people who long to see drama where there is none.

"Toni, that's you and Vinny, the perfect couple, the 'happiest family in Brooklyn.' You guys never have drama."

"We have *you* guys, who says we don't have drama?" She moved over to the sinks. "As for you and Hobie? No one knows what happened. You know that we all took care of that, protected you. No one, not anyone outside this magic circle and Renee knows what *really* happened. They just know you and Hobie went from a thing to a no-thing.

Kicks smiled. "True that, but your *own* drama. You guys could have married in Kindergarten, and you'd still be perfect together."

"I wasn't into sharing my crayons back then."

Kicks had to smile. "You know what I mean. What might have seemed harmless to you almost killed me back then. He cheated on me. He was my first and only love since I can remember. We gave each other our virginity. That thing with Renee? I was devastated."

"Sit." Toni took Kicks' hand in hers as she scootched over on the sink. "Hmmm... hope this thing holds us." She bounced up and down experimentally. "Sound enough." She turned back. "He didn't lie. He never lied. You never gave him the chance to tell you what *did* happen."

"Toni can't you see? I was over-the-moon in love and writing my name 'Mrs. Catherine Daniels' all over the place. I was dreaming we would be like you and Vinny. I thought it was forever for us."

"I know, but Renee and Hobie were never a thing. It wasn't real. Vinny and I have told you a million times why he didn't run for you, but it's up to him to tell you everything. It's up to you to finally listen. His reasoning holds true."

Kicks looked at her best friend since... she remembered life at all. "You're standing up for her?"

"No, but in this case, yes. It's more I'm standing up for *you*. And for Hobie. He told us tons of times she set it all up and he had no idea. She wanted in, Kicks. She wanted a role on the show, and she always did. She hung around us looking for camera time the whole time we were on. Remember when we'd film in public places? How she would always show up there? Did you ever wonder why or how? She made friends with us and got the information, and when she figured out you and Hobie were a couple she could exploit, she figured having drama would do it. She'd be in, even as the bad girl. She didn't care. She just wanted in."

Kicks wasn't having it. "You know, even if that was the truth, what about Hobie's part in this? Huh? He was there, you know. More, much more than there, if you get my drift."

"Have you ever considered that he was set up, and just as blindsided as you would have been if someone set you up?"

"No, because I wouldn't have had a hard on."

Toni made a face. "Um, maybe not, but no one can deny Renee is gorgeous, and she was practically naked. She waited until she knew you were about to come in the back, and she draped herself over Hobie. In the process she put her very large breasts all over him while going for ground zero. She actually wriggled one of them in his hand as he was pushing her away."

"Is that supposed to make me feel better, Toni?"

"No, honey. Of course not, but it's supposed to make you see it for what it was. You saw what she *planned* you would see, and you reacted like she hoped you would. The only problem was that she hoped she'd be a character for a few shows, maybe parlay that into something for herself. She didn't count on all of us protecting you instead of the show. She didn't get her wish, and I bet she wished she didn't do it after she did."

When Kicks made a face of disbelief, Toni added, "Okay, maybe she's happy. No one's saying she's normally a great gal."

"Tell me something I don't know," Kicks said. "And don't, I mean it, protect Renee."

"Not protecting her, just letting you know it's time you let it go."

"Really Elsa?"

"Oh come on, you'll see when you get here. You're lucky I didn't tell you to put your behind in the past. Still, it's true. Hobie was ambushed, and he reacted like any nineteen-year-old would, with a

'Holy shit, there's a tongue in my mouth, a big tittie in my hand and another going south on my zipper's freeway,' and all for anatomy, you might have, too."

"I think you know better."

"Sure, but I also think you could have listened better, noticed all the signs everyone pointed out to you. Taken Hobie's calls or met up with him, actually talked to him."

"For what? So that he could hurt me worse than he already had?"

Toni got up and pulled Kicks down. "Now wash your hands completely," and when Kicks made a face, she apologized. "Sorry. Mommy-speak. But do it."

She smiled as she rolled up her sleeve, noticing belatedly that her silk blouse did not die a Dunky D's death by coffee. "Now what am I going to do? I can't believe I said that out loud."

"Really? You can't? You always say what's on your mind out loud, and that's why you can't lie. Also? You don't seem to recognize you did it." Toni shook her head. "Kicks, we have to go back out there, and we have to give at least a thought to Hobie on this *GUB* reunion. I know you may not need this or even want it, and that's okay, but you're still going to have to hear about it and then decide, even if the decision is no. And another thing? You have to go out there now and face your inner monologue's repercussions. Remember one thing. You called him the love of your life just now, and he heard you. We all heard you. You still have feelings for him and you have to face that, too— no matter what you think. Have you ever thought that's why everyone you date is not for you, or has zero chemistry? Maybe because you still have the hots for Hobie? Just a thought."

"Jaysus, right when I think I have my ducks in a row."

Toni smiled. "Ducks never go in a row for long, not for you, not for me, not for anyone. Just be happy they're in the same pond. Ready?"

She shook her head no, but Toni grabbed her hand and pulled her out of the bathroom. "That's what friends are for," Toni said.

"And this is Brooklyn." she added, then together they said, "And Brooklyn is for friends!"

They hugged quickly and left. Kicks stood up straight, and fell in behind Toni. "Let's hope so."

Toni turned back to her and smiled. "Hope's for other people. Me? I *know*."

~

When Kicks and Toni returned to the table, it was empty except for Vinny and Hobie. She didn't consider this a good sign, and she hadn't since they were nineteen. Prior to that it was the configuration of her life. Vinny and Toni and Hobie and her, since forever. At the door everyone was "just leaving." Sure. Everyone just had, what? An emergency call from the Pentagon? Simultaneously? "Hey, I'll call you this week, you up for a night out?" or some variation was said by all, but they all left as fast as they saw her. Hmmm.

Like she was headed for the guillotine, she kept walking, head down. Okay Everyone and their brother wanted her and Hobie to talk, and this was the time everyone, *or their brother*, had set for that. Arriving at the table in seconds instead of the mile it felt like, Kole came over, motioned for the waitress to drop the food off for the four of them, and he moved off. Some of the food was already in to-go containers. Boy. They really had no faith in her.

"I'll be leaving you now, it's almost closing time. Feel free to stay as long as you'd like, because I'll be doing paperwork for ages. I'm just going to be in the office." He was halfway down the hall before he finished. "Enjoy!" If she didn't know better, she'd swear she was carrying bubonic plague, but that would be too easy for what came next.

Vinny gave Toni a hand getting up from the table, "Gotta move it home, guys. The sitter is getting anxious."

Kicks knew the smell of verbal fertilizer. "The sitter? Is your family all away or sick?" Vinny knew better than to try that one. Those three kids were adored by an extended family the size of Connecticut. They had never seen an outside babysitter, and there were regular fights about who got asked to sit, she had been in a few of them herself.

THE SHOW'S NOT OVER

He smiled. "No, my Mother is watching them, but her shows are on. She wants to get home for them."

"Nice try, Vinch. So… General Hospital is in Italian now? Or wait, Fordham University dropped the Irish program for the Italian one?"

Vinny shook his head. "Kicks, Kicks, Kicks. You know too much. Okay, we're leaving. It's up to you and Hobie here to talk and to see what you can do to clear the air. It's been a long time coming, Catherine."

"How is it, Vin-CHEN-zo, that when *you* use my given name, it's more effective than when my parents use it?"

Toni smiled and fielded this one. "Because, *Catherine*, all children know they're in trouble when you use their saint's name. You, my dear, are not only *in* trouble, you *are* trouble. They don't call you Kicks for nothing." She spun into Vinny, who held her coat. "Have fun, kids." They were out the door almost immediately, carrying the to-go boxes.

She turned and looked over at Hobie. He was staring at her so intimately, she wanted to get up and haul ass out of there. She'd be damned if she'd let him take any more of her dignity, so if this had to happen—and even she knew it had to— now was the time. Ugh. When he opened his mouth to say something, she cut in. *Not on your time, Hobie. On my time.* "Is that my order?" Of course, she knew it was. Same since P.S. 261.

He passed the plate to her, but not before stealing a French fry. "Okay, on your time, although I think you didn't mean to say that out loud. You want to talk about the show, or do you want to talk about what happened? Finally. I don't think there's a show or anything that includes you *and* I unless we get through this mess."

Shit. She had said it out loud. Again. "Okay."

He smiled at her and took another fry. Just like in the old days, she slapped his hand. "You don't get that privilege anymore, Hobie."

His smile dimmed. "Sorry." He asked for another though. "May I?" His brows went up, and that hair, that soft blond hair that she had always loved, fell into his eyes. She remembered when she first started reading romances, she discovered the word "rake" wasn't just a garden tool. Even way back then, she thought he would be an excellent rake.

She was so enthusiastic to know his hair, or the style of his hair was actually known as "the rake." More like rakehell. "Yeah, why not. You know I'll never—"

"…finish them all." He used to finish a lot of her sentences for her. It seemed either she hadn't changed much, or he knew her too well. Or both. "Ketchup on the side?"

"As long as it's catsup, why not?" They had argued about how her family called it catsup, C-A-T-S-U-P, instead of K-E-T-C-H-U-P, like his. It was weird, but it was one of their things like Vinny and Toni with the sauce or the gravy.

"I've missed this."

She looked up. "What? Correct spelling?"

He reached over and took her hand as she went for another fry. He smiled at her so his whole face became lit from inside. "No, Kicks. *I* have missed *you*." He squeezed her hand and let it go before it became "a thing."

She frowned at that. "You know there's a reason for that, right?"

He nodded. "Yes. I do. Is it time for the reckoning?"

"What? Are you Stephen King now?" She had to laugh. Here she sat, talking to the person who had been her forever love, and who had pretty much chewed her love up and spit it out, but yes… she missed him, too. "Okay. I guess."

"Okay. Shall I start?"

"Why not?" She pretended not to care, but it was hard. Her heart began to beat faster.

Hobie shook his head. "I tried to talk to you a million—"

"Please, Hobie. If you want this to work here tonight, for us to 'clear the air' as it were, let's not start with any accusations or recriminations. I know I could have listened, but I wasn't ready. I'm here now, slightly forced into it, but we both know I could have left, and we also know it's time—especially if my not getting past this would hurt my best friends since forever and I would be holding them back. If it helps - I know. I fully acknowledge that you tried, even that million times. I should have sat down with you and done this sooner. Okay?"

"That took a lot, thank you."

"On the other hand, *Ho*bart, you don't have to cajole me with praise if I state the obvious. I was wrong. I admit it. Move on."

He bowed his head. "Noted, *Cath*erine."

She rolled her eyes. "Oh, good Lord! Go on, Hobie."

"Back to Hobie, this is good. Progress." He took a healthy portion of fries. "I tried to talk to you, and I recognize that you were hurt, and you had what appears on the surface to be a good reason."

She was angry now, because it was on the surface, in the middle, and way down deep a damned good reason.

"I see you there, Kicks. I see you steaming, but how about you let me get this out and then you reply. Are you okay doing it that way?"

So. Hobie wanted to take the high road, eh? Make her the bad one for feeling justifiably angry. Okay, two could play at maturity. "Fine with me." *Cool. That's it. I am cool, and I don't care nor am I saying this out loud. Hah!*

Hobie screwed up his face in thought, leaning in over the table to get up in hers. "Man, I do not know what's going on in there, but I know it's something." He sat back in his seat. "Looks like the redhead is coming out to play."

She made a face and was about to lecture him about Irish stereotypes, but she decided not to. Whatever. But he shouldn't use the language they used to make love. Okay, screw. The redhead definitely screwed more than made love. The Irish temper was fast and furious, and apparently so was the Irish libido.

"Okay, I'm just going to do this fast as it feels that I'm getting it all right, then you can talk, or ask questions." He took a sip of his drink. "Renee. She was absolutely nothing, and no one. Not to me except for how some of you all noticed her constantly coming around during filming and noted it. I knew her, sure. We all did, but I honestly never gave her a thought before what happened." He stopped and looked her directly in the eyes, which she knew meant he was one hundred percent serious. He reached for her hands, and in a moment of, what? Longing? She let him, and he continued.

"I don't know. Even to this day, I have no idea what happened outside of that it *did* happen, and still I don't know how. I swear to you on whatever you want, a stack of bibles, my soul, I'll even pinky swear. I had no idea what she was up to, nor did I encourage her in any way. To me, she was a hanger-on, like a lot of the people around us when the show was on. I did *not* try to kiss her, and the second I realized what was going on, I tried to push her away. You walked in that exact moment." He looked down, then up to her eyes again. "This is the God's honest truth, Kicks. I never tried to do it, she actually just launched herself on me, and you? You were caught in the crossfire. I loved you, Kicks, and we had just made love an hour before taping. I would never do that. Maybe it—we—would never have worked out in the long run, but at that time, and in that place, I thought we were forever. That you and I were unstoppable."

He had shot the last bit out like he didn't even know it was coming. He broke one hand from hers, and she realized that they were still holding each other. It had been so long, but it was so natural she fell into it. He used that hand to brush that hair back and returned it to hers. She shouldn't let him keep holding her hand, but she did. Lord help her, she liked it. She had always loved his hands. What he could do with them. He used to build her things, first in his grandfather's basement as a child, later on in wood shop, and then he set up in his basement. She still had them all, from the first birdhouse to the hooks that he had painted for her on her wall when she moved downstairs. She had taken it with her everywhere. She couldn't let it go, although she had many times fantasized about burning all of them. Even if she hated him fiercely at times, she loved him, and she couldn't do it. Later on, she learned along with him that those talented hands could do more than carpentry. They had given her so much pleasure. Mere memories of that made her wet. She tried to stop this mood, or she would go home and cry. Or deplete the world's battery supply. "Are you done?"

He sat back fully and looked at her. "Maybe. Do you have questions?"

She wanted to say no. She wanted to say she couldn't care any less about him than she did right now. She knew as he probably did too that she cared. Too much. She sat back, adding that small bit of distance as if it would help to protect her or her heart. As if it was a kind of armor that would help keep her safe. She knew how silly it was. When had anything protected her from him? Never. "Will you be okay if I take some time thinking things through?"

Breda, the waitress, came over and brought a bottle of her favorite wine. "Compliments of Kole and Storybook. I'm off, so I'm going to lock up behind me. You two know he's in the office right in back. When you want to leave, just knock, and he'll let you out. The door is totally locked from inside, and only he can let you out so don't panic! This place has been around since prohibition; it's all good. Just knock for Kole. If you're good, I'm off!"

They both nodded their agreement, and with a wave and a door shutting with lock and key, Breda was gone for the night. Hobie poured two glasses of a 2013 Chapin Montepulciano.

He looked at the bottle. "Your taste has changed."

"Yes, I mean, I guess. I love wine now."

He nodded. "You didn't used to drink red."

She had to laugh. "None of the girls drank reds. We all drank whites because we thought it would keep us skinny. We all drank the famous 'white wine spritzer' because not only was the wine white and therefore had less calories, but the soda water cut the calories even more."

Hobie nodded his head, laughing. "That sounds right. You all were skinny, and you all kept saying you weren't."

"It's the being a woman thing. Like it or not, agree or not, we all feel fat as teenagers no matter what. All we saw, all we *still* see is women who are tiny. I mean, down to their birth weights tiny. No one feels adequate up against that."

"You were never adequate, Kicks. You were perfect. To me, you were perfect. Although you probably don't want to hear it, you still are. You were always perfect to me, Catherine."

Jaysus, she would die this evening. "Thank you."

"I hope I showed it. I was always grateful you were mine, proud you were mine, and more in love with you daily."

She looked down. When she looked up again, she saw her hand in his. How had that happened? "That was—"

"…before. I know."

It was. But he still knew her. He could always read her like a book.

They could always read each other, and here he finished her sentence again, after all this time. "Hobie, are you ready for my questions?"

"Go ahead."

So. Here it was, the chance she should have taken, and never did. At first, her pain was too intense, and then it became a point of pride. How much was her pride worth to her now? Not a lot at night. She picked up her glass and drank the wine straight down.

"Wow. Fortification?"

She nodded. "Why not?"

"Why not indeed." He drank his down as fast as she did and nodded. "Ready."

She was warm inside between the champagne, the wine, and Hobie holding her hands again. "I think it's going to be hard to do this with our hands together."

He looked up and leaned over. He brushed her hair back, his hand stopping behind her ear, on her neck. He closed his eyes and inhaled deeply. "Same shampoo." He opened his beautiful light blue eyes and said, "I think if I give you the chance to run, you might. Only the locked door would stop you. Maybe you don't have to hold my hands, but please, Kicks— allow me the pleasure of holding yours?"

He moved his hand from her neck and back to her hands, and she didn't know what to do. "Oh, okay." Or did she? She nodded to the wine, and he poured for her, then for himself. She took one small sip, already a little buzzy and not needing more. He moved his hand back to hers. Time to compose her thoughts was up. "How long did it take you to realize what Renee was doing?"

He nodded. "Almost immediately. She was hanging around the back bathrooms, looking around for something, or someone. That was all I remembered. Seriously. She was there, I must have noted that. She didn't even speak to me as I went by. Then she seemed to jump on me. I was confused. Then I felt it, the '*Oh, my God, this is bad*' thing. I tried to get away. She really leaned into it, and I was half disbelieving what happened and half hysterical because like always, I could tell you were there. Electricity pulsed through me when you were in the room. And I was right. When I looked up, you were standing there, looking at me, at Renee, your mouth open like you had been shot. Before I could get her off of me, you were gone."

"You could have come after me."

He shook his head and looked directly at her. "Don't you know what happened next?"

"I do. I was there, Hobie. I saw what happened, and it almost killed me. Did you know, and maybe I shouldn't even say this to you, but up until that very day I was running around writing Mrs. Catherine Daniels on everything? My God, what a fool. I was—"

"Don't call it foolish, Catherine. It wasn't. Did you think *I* didn't feel that way? Was that it? You assumed that *I* didn't love you? Because I was already *in* love forever. Did you assume we would do all those things like get married and have those kids who looked just like the best of both of us that we always talked about? I did. There's one more thing, if you felt all that like you say you did? You probably only loved me a tenth of how I love you."

She couldn't hold back the tears, but she didn't shy away from him seeing her cry. Maybe he should know what it did to her. "Then why didn't you come after me?"

"I tried but I was stopped. Vinny, Toni, and Peps saw what happened. That's when Toni got you out of there, Peps cornered Renee, and Vinny got a hold of me. Peps got Renee out of there before anyone would know. Before anyone like the producers or the cameramen would get wind of it and get it on film. Toni told the crew that you were sick, and Peps hustled Renee out the back, told her some story that he needed to get her input on something. Renee was pretty desperate for a connection to the show. You know him. He knows how to defuse a situation, and she went willingly. When you were out the front and Renee out the back, Vinny and Toni had me sit. They blocked the camera and made sure I sat for over an hour so that the crew wouldn't get wind of the drama, or that would have been front and center on the show for the next weeks until the last episode. You know what else would have happened? Renee would have gotten her way. I may be a lot of things, but uncaring isn't one of them. I didn't come to you immediately, because Vinny, Toni, and I were trying to protect you. I didn't need you to have to see that on national television. I didn't need that, either."

Kicks put her head in her hands and wept. He moved over to her and put his arms around her. It felt so good, and it had been so long. She leaned into him and cried. How many times had he held her this way? Too many to count, but not enough. Never enough. He smelled of that Hobie smell she had always loved. She remembered his scent intimately, like how he smelled like him but peppery when they made love. She had missed that so much.

"When I got out of there, I walked to the corner, and then ran full speed to your house. I didn't even stop for the light. My God, I almost got hit but I didn't care. The only thing I cared about was you. Getting to you. Telling you what happened wasn't anything I could help. That I only tried to pry Renee's hands off of me, and never had a thing for her at all. I never could. I have you."

She looked up into eyes she had always adored and pushed his hair away from his forehead. He smiled at the familiar gesture. "Have?" His look of confusion prompted her to go on. "You said 'have,' Hobie. You 'have' me."

He looked into her eyes and when his gaze lowered to her lips she licked them. She felt ridiculous, childlike, and embarrassed, but she couldn't resist. His pupils dilated, and he breathed heavier. She knew him like a book, and he was as aroused as she was. Could it be this easy? *It always was with Hobie.* He bent down and took her lips, gently at first, then with a building intensity. She had missed this as well—so much. His hands circled her slowly, and then came around and grazed her side. When he reached up, he stared at her. Breathless, she leaned into him. The silk brushed against her skin. He looked down, and moved his fingers flicking one. Two. Three buttons of her shirt, moving one side over her shoulder and baring her bra to him. Did she know this might happen? Had she secretly wanted it to? She was wearing lingerie she knew put her best assets on display. He moved his hand up and touched her, gently at first, then knowingly, grazing the nipple until it hardened. Her head floated back, baring her neck to him. Then she remembered where they were, what they were supposed to be doing. With effort, she sat up and opened her eyes. His eyes were still closed. She watched his Adam's apple go up and down as he swallowed then opened his eyes.

He moved his hands to cradle her face. "Do I have you? Do I still have you?"

She didn't answer, and he didn't miss a beat. Leaning into her neck, he bit softly and then licked the spot to soothe. He began kissing his way down her neck while his hands zeroed in on her swollen breasts. It felt so right she could have whimpered. When the soft moans became hers, she had to stop. If she didn't stop now, she would be tossed on the table like a feast in a minute. While that idea had its merits, they still needed to talk. Reluctantly she pulled back, grieving the loss of his fingers softly playing at her nipple. He knew her. He knew what she liked, what she wanted, what she feared but still wanted. He knew just what to do, how hard, when to get harder, and for how long. She could tell he hadn't lost his touch. With effort she opened her eyes and pulled his hand into hers. The intensity in his gaze held her riveted to the spot.

"I—I don't know. I'm not sure. Is that what you want?"

"Yes. It's what I wanted that night, when you had your parents tell me to go home, and then you refused to take my calls. You had everyone run interference so that no matter how many times we all got together, you and I hardly ever got near each other. It's what I wanted when I drove up to New Haven to see you at school. It's what I wanted always. It's you, Catherine. *You* are what I want. You are *who* I want. Do you believe me now? Do you understand what happened and how?"

"I do. I mean, I never realized how hard I made it for you. I thought if you wanted me, you'd get to me. You'd find me no matter how many roadblocks I set up. And I did. Set up roadblocks, I mean." She looked down, smiling sheepishly. "Maybe I'm better at setting up roadblocks than I thought."

He nodded, then kissed her again, a kiss filled with all the things she had always hoped for. He came up for air, eyes still closed. "No matter how much I wanted you, I don't go where I'm not wanted. *Won't* go where I'm not wanted, even if it killed me. I admit, there were times it almost did."

He kissed her again, harder this time. She was going under, and she liked it. He broke the kiss quickly, making her fight for balance. He leaned down, breathing heavily, and put his forehead against her own. "Do you want to go somewhere else? Like, maybe to my place?"

She did. She wanted to go there and never come back. "I'm off tomorrow. I could go somewhere but I'm only a block and a half away."

"I said *my* place, Kicks. That's my place, not 'somewhere,' and *not* in your parent's basement, even if it's all yours and private. This is post #metoo, Kicks. I don't go where there are no trespassing signs."

"Noted. And admirable."

"So yes?"

"Hell, yes."

Hobie grabbed her coat and his, brought them over to the table, and practically shoved her into it. He threw his own on one arm and moved her to the door.

"Hobie, no! The alarm will go off, remember what Breda said?"

"Oh, yeah. The alarm will go off, and we *still* can't get out. Okay, over to the office. Kole is doing paperwork, right? He'll let us out."

She nodded and they practically flew to the office. There was no need to knock because it was open with no Kole inside. There was a note on the desk, however, with their names on it. "Are you thinking what I'm thinking?"

She shook her head. "What? That we're locked in?"

"That, too, but I'm thinking we've been set up."

"There's an Air B&B upstairs over the office and the storeroom. Maybe he's there. Read the note."

"'Hobie and Kicks,

I guess you finished talking. Hopefully everything worked out well for you. I would like to confirm that if there is a show being done for you all , you may use the bar again with the same rules and understanding as last time. Storybook Pub was my wife's family's place as you know, and I'm sure she'd want to have us keep up with the show as she was a fan. So was I.

The upstairs has two short-term rental units, neither of which is rented tonight. I'll leave you to use one, or both, or call me and I'll come right down to let you out. Up to you.

Here's to *Growing Up Brooklyn*, and to you.

Kole O'Shea'"

"What do you want, Kicks?"

"I want you." Admitting it didn't even cost her pride.. This was Hobie, *her* Hobie, and she wanted to be his again. She had always wanted this, and silently she breathed her thanks that he wanted her, too.

"Upstairs. Got your stuff?"

"Huh?"

"Your coat is on. Your purse, anything else? The wine? There's still more. If we don't get up that early, I don't want people coming in here to see it all."

She nodded over to the table. "I'll get the purse, you get the wine, and maybe if we got too old for this, we'll have time to drink it."

He stopped, grabbed her, and kissed her fiercely. "Get up there. I'll be right back."

She ran up the stairs, hardly thinking of where she was going. She opened the first door, and found a room made up for guests. There was a note on the bed. Before she had put her things down, Hobie was back up.

He nodded toward the paper in her hand. "What's this?"

She handed the note to him. "It's addressed to us. How did they know which room we would choose, or even if we would stay? Go open the second door, would you, Hobie? See what's in there."

"First read the note. I'll hear you, read loud."

She held the note closer to her face.

'Dear Hobie and Kicks:

Congratulations on making a good choice. The bar opens at 10:00 for the staff, and your breakfast will be outside by then. Enjoy your evening, and remember – we all have a story. This must be yours. - Kole'"

She put the note down. "What does the other note from the second bedroom say?"

Hobie opened it.

"'I figured you'd check. Go back to the other room. -Vinny and Toni'"

He looked at her. "You'd think they know us or something."

"You would think. But Hobie? I'm a little tired of thinking right now. Can you help me to stop thinking at all for a time?"

"Is all night good, or is it too soon to say for the rest of our lives?"

She laughed. "Too soon. One day at a time, but let's forget time for now, okay?"

He tossed the note down on top of the other and moved toward her slowly. "Do you want time to go fast, or slow?"

"How's fast the first bit, then slow as hell for the rest, okay? I have some making up for lost time to do."

He registered her words and nodded. Standing there silently, looking at her, he made her nervous. Why wasn't he doing something? Anything. "Hobie? Is something wrong?"

He shook his head. "Slow it is."

"I said—"

"I heard you. I just don't want to go fast." He continued the short distance, then turned around, began moving away. He shut the door, locked it, and moved back to her. "Show me the underwear. The lingerie." He leaned in and used one finger to undo the other buttons. That was all. He didn't touch her, just her shirt. When they were all undone, he used his hands to pull the shirt down over her shoulders, slowly. The silk, oh she was happy she was wearing silk, moved down her shoulders, to her upper arms, and lower—then he pulled the sleeves behind her, effectively holding her arms down. He nodded appreciatively at her choice, a pale pink glimmering see-through bra, lined in black. He reached up the other hand and cupped one breast. Then he kissed her and pinched her just the way she liked it, rolling the nipple between his thumb and fingers. She wriggled around, effectively caught in her own shirt. She could have gotten free, but why? It would only get better. When Hobie commanded her, she could relax. He took her only where she wanted to go, and never further.

"I want to touch you, too."

He smiled. "Later."

"But—" Her words stopped when he pinched her harder, then he turned his attention to the other breast. She was already wetter than she had ever been, and if absence made the heart grow fonder, the heart was not alone. She could feel her sex clenching, desperate to have him inside her. He let her arms go and they fell to her sides.

"Turn around."

That was all he said, but she was done arguing. She did as he asked. No, she did as he said.

"Bend over. Put your hands on the bed and spread your legs."

Oh my God. She was sure she couldn't be more turned on, but she was willing to see. She did. She was rewarded with his grunt of satisfaction. He massaged her neck for a moment, then slowly ran his hand down her back, while his other hand came around her middle. She was so wet and so turned on her breathing was coming short, sure she couldn't wait another minute. When he reached her panties, he slowly ran his hand over her ass. Coming to the top of them, he hooked a finger inside the top and pulled them gently against her swollen clit. Her head hung low, and she heard herself cry out as he sawed the soft fabric back and forth, increasing the pleasure, and the pain of waiting.

"Is this good?"

"Yes." That was all she could say.

"Good. Would you like me to make it better?"

God, yes. "Yes."

"Good. I want to make it better for you. Stay like that."

When she nodded her head, she heard him undressing. The belt, the zipper of his jeans, the shoes being toed off, the socks, the pants coming down. He moved into her, letting her ass feel his hardness, up and down until she was almost mad. Then he stepped back again, and she heard the rest of his clothes hit the ground. He came back up to her and palmed her ass again. She quivered. "Hobie, I need—"

"I know what you need. I need it too, baby. Hold on. You'll get it."

"But I want—"

She gasped when his hand came down in a light spank across her bottom.

"I know what you want. I want it too, but you'll have to wait, baby. Good things come to those who wait. Who wait for it to come."

She gulped and nodded her head.

"Good girl." With that he pushed her legs in and she complied. He licked her back, down to the panties, and bit them, pulling them slowly down. His hands reached to finish the job, and then he spread her legs again. "Good, baby," he praised her.

He reached around her and took hold of her breast, rubbing his hand over the rigid tip until every touch had her so sensitized she thought she would come right there. His cock was hard and throbbing in the fold of her ass. While one hand moved back and forth over her breasts, he used his other hand to rub her swollen clit. Between her breasts, his hardness, and the pressure on her sex, he moved his pointer and middle fingers around her clit and slowly moved them back and forth in a pattern she knew well. It took only a minute more for her to come, and when her head snapped back with the force of it, he entered her from behind. Now her orgasm shattered her. He was finally inside her. She came again. She heard herself screaming his name. He thrust in and out of her until she felt another orgasm coming, but he pulled out. Turning her quickly he kissed her, pushing her back gently onto the bed. His words were short, but she didn't care.

"Move back. All the way back."

She did. He moved over her, cupping her as he kissed her, and then moved down to the center of her world, slowly kissing and licking her home. She wasn't squirming anymore. She'd been too satisfied for that, but she wasn't sure she could go on. That never stopped him before, and apparently not now. He used his hands to spread her legs so she was completely open to him. He pulled her ass so she met his mouth like she was a feast. When he murmured his satisfaction, she laid her head back. Oh yeah, this could get better. He licked her once, twice, then blew on her so she squirmed again. He looked up at her.

"Look at me." She lifted her head and did as he said. "I miss this. I miss you. You are what I want. You are what I need. You are everything, and I'm going to spend the night showing you how much you mean to me, how much you always have. And always will." Then he moved his head back to her sex and began in earnest to pleasure her. When her breathing picked up, he moved, played with her nipples, and pushed her over the edge.

"Oh my God. I can't—" but she couldn't come up with a sentence, not that she had time to because before the final shudder of her orgasm, he was up on his hands above her, kissing her. She tasted her love on his lips as he entered her. He went slowly, pushing all the way up to the hilt. She rose to meet him each and every time. When he started to move faster, she reached down between them and fondled his balls. He looked down at her.

"I want you to come for me one more time."

"I don't think I can."

"You can. Come on. Concentrate. Move with me, rub on me, tell me to go harder, slower, faster, softer, anything it takes, baby. I need you to come for me again. I need you to look at me, come for me. I want to see you come up close. I want to see the pleasure I give you. Can you do that? Can you do that for me?"

She really wasn't sure. "I—I can try."

He smiled. "Good, baby. Good."

He began to move slower, holding each thrust like being suspended at the top of the swing set before coming down again, that giddy feeling that you might fall, but you know it's going to be okay. The trembling began again. "Come on, baby. I feel you getting ready. Come for me. Look me in the eyes and come for me."

She did.

"I love you, Catherine."

That was all he said before he joined her. His eyes finally left hers, and he threw his head back, teeth bared, breathing hard. His thrusts slowed as he emptied into her and she held his back and his beautiful tight ass. Then he moved to the side, and came down, pulling her into an embrace.

She had been given the ultimate pleasure, and she was alive for the first time in so long. She had given him pleasure, too, so did he mean it when he said "I love you?" How could she be sure?

"I meant it, Kicks. I see you and your crazy questioning. Sometimes, a cigar is just a cigar. I love you, and I have since I knew love was possible. Since I formed the idea. Since we met. It's not the orgasm, Kicks. Don't be doing that crazy second-guessing and the Irish thing."

Irish thing? "What Irish—"

He rolled his eyes. "The whole thing. The side eye to all that's good. Seriously, I don't know how you guys survive all that 'if it feels too good it's bad' stuff."

"DNA. Thousands of years of programming. Shut up, heathen Protestant. I'm tired. I need sleep."

"No second act?"

She turned over in his arms, so he spooned her. "You took any and all motivation away right there, I have none left. I need sleep."

"Good to know. A satisfied wife is a compliant wife."

With that she shot up. "Oh, it's compliance you—" then she heard the full sentence. "Wife?"

"Have some wine, Catherine."

"Oh, it's Catherine now, Hobart?"

She leaned up as he left her and handed her a glass of the last of the wine. And a ring. A gorgeous emerald ring with tiny diamonds all around it.

"I got it ages ago, but... things happened. I thought it would go nicely with your hair and your skin, and your eyes."

"My skin? It's gorgeous, and perfect. Are you sure?"

He rolled his eyes again. "Stop with the Irish shit. Yes, I'm sure. No, I'm not crazy. And yeah, good things come to those who wait. By the way, I'm the one who had to wait, and you're the good thing here."

She took a sip of the wine and handed him back the glass. She took the ring from him to try it on, but he took it away, left the bed and got down on one knee. He put it on the top of her left ring finger and spoke. "I would be honored if you, Catherine, would be my wife. I want to live with you forever, and have children with you, and of course, I'll provide the sound-proof room so that we can continue to do what we did tonight without warping their little Irish brains."

"They won't be Irish only, they'll be half yours."

"What does that even mean? We've been here so long I have no idea what we are but American. I know we're semi-sorta Protestant, but Episcopalians are Catholic, just not Roman Catholic, and we don't really have many rules. I'm pretty sure you'll thoroughly ruin them

THE SHOW'S NOT OVER

with guilt, and it may not be the worst thing. After all, you managed to survive. They're staying in on Saint Paddy's day. No other rules."

She kissed him as the ring slid home. Slid true. "Then yes. I will.

∼

At nine am they woke, and made love again – slowly, and surely, and like they had the rest of their lives. They did. At ten they heard the sound of a person on the steps, and a tray rattle. Getting his pants on quickly, Hobie opened the door to a huge breakfast, one they had earned honestly. After two showers, one before, and one made necessary by another round of lovemaking, they finally emerged. Everyone was downstairs, the entire cast and Kole O'Shea.

"How'd it go?" he asked, but their smiles led them all to know, the show wasn't over.

Learn more about Mary Rogers:
www.AuthorMaryRogers.com

SPEAKEASY

TARRAH ANDERS

What's on your menu?

Sub-genre: Contemporary Romance
Relationship: Male/Female

1

BIANCA

I wasn't aware of what I was getting into when I first started working at Storybook Pub, and I also wasn't prepared for what my role, all my roles would entail until my interview.

I once heard that Storybook Pub was where all your wildest dreams come true. That you can come here for a drink and a little something more. And now, I know what really happens here.

I thought it was just rumors, I didn't know that what was said by the lips of many, were true.

And now, I'm working here, in one of the highest coveted positions at the bar.

I'm a bartender.

And I'm a wish maker, if I so choose.

And I am thinking that I will give it a try, what can it hurt?

You only live once.

I don't have a significant other and I do like to think outside the box.

I am though, first and foremost a bartender, because that's me.

While to some, it may not be a flashy job, for me, it's all I know.

Tending bar is what I'm good at.

Hell, I was born in a bar, so I should be good, right?

Today will be my first shift at the pub, and I'm supposed to meet with Dwayne, the bouncer, or enforcer—I'm not really sure what his role is. Either way, I am to get a hold on what my other *talents* are, whatever that means.

I'm parked in the alley with my nerves taking over my body. My palms are sweaty, there's a trail of sweat running down between my tits and I'm pretty sure that my make-up is already faded.

I look at myself in the rear-view mirror and reapply my lipstick, smack my lips together, and smile.

It's now or never.

I take a deep breath and exit my shoddy little Honda.

I pause at the door, take in a deep breath, then enter.

The interior is dim lit. I can see that the majority of the inside walls are made of stone bricks giving the space a slight chill, but it's welcoming. The inside looks like what I image a wine cellar with the stone walls lined with sconces throughout the vast space alternating in white and green. In the rear of the bar is an arch that holds a few recreational standard bar games and along the walls are booths and a few tables. I turn to my area, the bar is immaculate, reclaimed oak with a finish that is smooth to the touch. Behind the bar are glass shelves that showcase the liquors with a green glow from behind. It's a beautiful sight.

I feel right at home immediately.

"Are you the new bartender?" A large bald man with arm muscles the size of my thighs asks interrupting my perusal of the space.

I nod my head eagerly and adjust the purse strap on my shoulder.

"How old are you?" he tilts his head, looking me up and down with a confused look.

"I'm twenty-five, why? I wasn't aware that there's an age limit," I say, my voice shaking with worry.

Am I too old for this job?

Was my job offer a mistake?

Who the heck is this Vin Diesel lookalike?

He holds his meaty hand out to me, "I'm Dwayne, I am the connection between the two establishments here. My apologies that I didn't recognize you from your interview, I see a lot of people come and go. Since it's your first day, I will not overload you with too much, but during your next shift, we'll begin discussing your menu and what kinds of wishes you will be exploring, should you have the chance. You will train with Mike, one of our other bartenders and he will give you an in-depth guide to the bar."

I feel the lump in my throat of nervousness while I swallow and nod.

He gives me a general run-down of the bar, the drink menus and the types of tapas that they have, which is partnered with a restaurant less than a block away.

He also gives me instructions for those who are members of the other establishment within Storybook Pub and directs me on how to assist them.

Mike comes in soon after I get behind the bar and does as Dwayne said he would. Throughout the day, I see a lot of diversity while working my shift. I notice that as my day goes on, it's clear that not everyone knows about the other side to Storybook Pub. The entrance to the other side, what I like to call the speakeasy, is down the hallway, which is close to the restrooms and another exit. So, if someone disappears down that hallway, other patrons of the bar won't think that it's odd if they don't come back.

In a single day, I've seen couples and individuals walk in and access the back hallway. I've also seen folks leaving alone, with a smile on their faces.

I wonder; *will that be something that I can handle being a part of?*

2

WESLEY

I hate Mondays.

I know that I'm not alone in this, but I terribly hate Mondays for the sole reason that it's the day that my uncle, the owner of Brockmire Industries comes into the offices that I oversee and tries to pretend that he has a hand in direction when the fact is, he has no clue what each office does. Since he took my cousin, Ash away from my department to begin recruiting new cities throughout the United States. I'm stuck here with the development side of many of the products that work together to make a city SMART and our line of products better than others.

It used to be Ash and I against the big bad mean man, and I could handle that. But now… now, it's just my team leader and I who is pulled between too many tasks, and also someone whom I shouldn't complain to.

So, I'm stuck with my assistant, who cannot assist. I didn't hire her. Which annoys me to all hell, because frankly, I wouldn't have.

So today, when she didn't check the calendar for the department meeting and showed up thirty minutes late, I took note of that to add to my long list of issues I have with her performance and plan to bring up on her next evaluation.

"Sir? Sir? I have some correspondence from Mr. Brockmire," she holds out a manila envelope.

"Which Brockmire, Vanessa? There's at least four of us all together," I reply with an internal eye roll, but with an audible sigh of frustration.

"Um, I think it would be Ash, or it could be your uncle, I'm not sure. What's your uncle's first name?" she asks while shifting her weight from one foot to the other. Her large blue eyes looking at me, with a puppy dog stare. I don't feel any sort of pity for the girl. She's got large tits, big hips, and even bigger hair. But under all that, a pea sized brain.

It's bullocks.

I take the envelope from her and do my best to not display further frustration.

"Anything else?" I ask her, evening out my tone and looking at her.

She lingers for a moment, smacking her gum, looking down at her finger tracing the hard lines of my concrete desk.

I'm growing impatient with her.

"I was wondering if I could leave in the afternoon, I'm not feeling good. I think I need to go to the doctor," she says finally looking up.

I wave my hand, "that's fine. Please make sure that you have the purchase orders completed and approved by me before sending. Also, I will need for you to make some bound copies of the instruction manual for the compact grid."

"How many, sir?" she asks.

"Take a look at the volume orders and decipher the number based on the current amount listed." I say looking at the manila envelope, turning it in my hands.

"Okay," she says meekly clearly unsure of how to complete the task, despite going over it a few times with her already.

"That is all, you're excused."

She quickly leaves my space and I hesitantly begin to open the envelope.

Inside is a glossy gold envelope.

With a note attached and my cousin's scribbled writing on the paper.

You need to have a little adventure, brother.
A one year membership, on me.
You'll thank me for this.
-Ash

I open the envelope and pull out another glossy gold postcard, with what looks like a membership card attached to it.

The postcard is gold with black and green lettering.

Storybook Pub - Where you can have a drink and much, much more.

I've heard of this place, it's a bar with some sort of sex club in it. It's an exclusive membership that many people around Manhattan Heights whisper about and no one that I know will admit to being a member.

I've never paid much mind to any of the whispers, nor have I ventured towards the establishment regardless of curiosity.

I could use a release, a break from this job and place the membership card in my wallet, while I leave the invitation postcard out for me to look at for the remainder of the day.

IT'S NEARING dark and I'm casually sitting in my car across from the Storybook Pub. I'm not afraid to go in, I'm just probably not ready.

I notice movement from my peripheral vision, and I see a beautiful vision walking out of the Pub.

She's gorgeous. She has jet black short hair that falls just at her chin. From where I sit—trying to not be obvious by staring at her—she has a perfect profile. If only I was closer, I want to see more of her. She briskly walks down the street in a jean skirt and thigh high boots. I watch her long legs carry her to a beat-up Honda before she slides into the driver's seat and is gone.

I'm curious about her.
Is she a member?
Does she work there?
I must know more.

3

BIANCA

Dwayne hands me a piece of paper and a pencil.

"Take notes," he instructs, dimming the lights in the room while the lights in the adjoining room illuminate the space. The entire wall is glass, and I feel like a voyeur.

I kind of like it. I make a mental note to think about adding that to my menu, but don't jot it down out of embarrassment or over-eagerness at the first thing that I feel.

The scene before me is a man wearing tight boxer briefs strapped to a St. Andrew's Cross with a blindfold covering his eyes. The woman standing before him is wearing leather pants and a fishnet top. The choker on her neck has a ruby red jewel in the center which matches her lipstick and the electrical tape covering her nipples. She yields a cat o' nine tails and gently whips it along the bare legs of the man.

I hear the man take a deep breath as the tails lick his skin harder my skin erupts in goosebumps.

"Um, Dwayne? What exactly am I supposed to be taking notes about? I'm confused," I say, my eyes never drifting from the other room that the preview room is attached to.

"Watch her, watch him, if anything looks exciting to you, or like something that you would be comfortable doing, then write it down. This is an intro to what happens in the club."

"What do you mean?" I ask.

"You will create your own menu."

"Oh, like my favorite foods and drinks?" I say, hoping that's the avenue he's going down.

"Funny girl. As you know, we are not a brothel, but we do make fantasies come true. Your menu will entail what your limits are. If a customer requests a flogging, and that's on your menu—you may be requested for a scene."

"Do people, do people have sex here?" I stutter.

"Some do. This Storybook Pub isn't purely about intercourse, the majority of our clients are here to get something that they can't do elsewhere. They are here to release their inhibitions and to express their carnal desires."

"And that's where the role of a wish granter comes into play?" I say nodding, almost as if to myself.

"Exactly. The Storybook Pub franchise was created in mind for those who need a safe place to let who they are out."

"Let their freak flag fly!" I laugh.

"You're an odd one," he tilts his head.

I continue to watch the scene, and when that one ends, with the man ejaculating in his boxers from his scene, the lights dim in that room and the wall to my right illuminates.

The preview room is a glass box, with sight into each room that line the four walls.

I turn in the chair to the next scene that is a little more graphic than the previous.

It has a woman in the middle of a man and a woman. Her skin is being kissed and rubbed by both and she's the monkey in the middle.

That goes on for a few minutes, they never take it any further. The woman's clothes are still on, she's just getting the attention that she is likely craving.

She pays a membership for this?

The room dims and the next room illuminates. I watch that scene which has more play and more nudity with the act of the scene being oral sex.

The final room that I get to view is straight on fucking. Not just any fucking, it is a pure orgy. There are three women and two men. Overall, it looks like a complicated game of naked Twister, but there's are cocks in pussies and mouths on other parts. It's definitely sexy as hell, and I feel a little anxious to have some alone time where I can do something about the building frenzy that I'm feeling.

A part of me feels guilty for watching this moment between these strangers, the other is turned on.

What the hell is going to be on my menu?

I'm in touch with my sexuality, but holy hotness.

What am I willing to do with a complete stranger?

Can I bring myself to satisfy a complete strangers needs?

It's not prostitution, there is no money that is exchanged. The club participants pay for a membership, which allows them to do whatever in the space, while there is a menu from each wish maker, it's a consensual experience through and through.

Which is why I'm having a hard time trying to figure out what my menu will entail.

I have a month to get it together. If I choose to not partake in the other side of the club, I won't get fired, which is nice. But apparently, the owner likes my look and think others will too.

Whatever that means.

After my time with Dwayne, I walk back out into the front of the house and slide behind the bar and do what I do best. My shift goes quickly and I'm exiting the building just as a well-dressed man, is walking toward the front door. He is looking straight at me, with a smile.

He's attractive as hell. He's tall and slender with dark brown hair and a dusting of facial hair grazing his face, making him look smoldering hot. I hold the door open for him, he gives me thanks in what sounds like an accent, and I give him a smile before walking down the street to my car, as he disappears inside.

He's handsome, unattainable, and definitely there for the club.

4

WESLEY

She's even more beautiful up close.
I watched her open the door as I was already walking across the street. I knew I should have gotten here earlier. Whether or not she's an employee, a wish maker, or a member, she's leaving here every day around the same time. I've been sitting like a creep outside the pub for the past few days, luckily, no one has spotted my sketchy behavior, but either way I felt today was the day to enter and finally access my membership benefits, in hopes that she would be involved one way or another.

Up close, she has full pink lips, a slight upturn of her nose, and beautiful hazel eyes. She has light freckles on her cheeks and a sultry smile. I don't know what to do, as she holds the door open for me. I have to go in now. As she walks away, I watch her walk to her car and then get in.

I show the bartender my membership card and ask for clarification on how things worked. He mentions another space, that there is a cast of menus, and that some of the staff in the pub also participate. He calls someone, and a giant of a man comes out from the hallway and takes me through the hidden door to give me a tour of the facilities. I sign the waivers that are required to enter the space and become a full-fledged member right then.

Part of the tour was watching some of the scenes playing out. I saw things from touching to fucking, it was intense. While I can say I'm not sure that I would be able to fully fuck in this place, I could definitely watch.

The next day, I'm here again.

I left work an hour earlier than usual and walk into the pub, to find the woman that I've been obsessing with behind the bar mixing a drink.

So, she works here. I smile as I approach the bar and pull out a bar stool in front of her.

I unbutton my jacket and take a seat as I wait for her to finish what she's making. I lean my arms on the glossy bar top and wait for her eyes to reach mine.

She offers me a smile that I feel right to my dick and I remember why I'm here.

"What can I do you for?" she pours the drink into a tumbler and slides it to the gentleman that I didn't notice at first at the end of the bar with preciseness.

"I would like a menu, please?" I ask.

She gives me another small smile and pulls a drink menu from below the bar and hands it to me.

I shake my head and put my hands up refusing the menu politely.

"No, Love. I'm talking about *your* menu."

"My menu." She says quietly, not a question but a statement as she nods her head slowly.

"I would like to see your menu and to see you downstairs," I say cautiously, hoping that I don't startle her.

"I, uh, don't have a menu, I mean not yet, I just started, and I don't know—" She stutters nervously.

"Calm down, Love. I'm a patient man, but don't keep me waiting for long. I know what I want, and that's you. But I will wait until you're ready," I say licking my lips, trying to put her at ease.

I can tell that she's nervous as her eyes widened when I mentioned her own menu.

I knock gently on the bartop and walk back out of the establishment.

I linger at my car and turn to look back at the pub.

She's a bartender there.

She's new.

She's beautiful.

"Sir?" an Irish accented man calls from behind me.

I turn and smile at him, the man that was sitting at the other end of the bar. His dirty blonde hair and green eyes sparkle under the streetlights.

"Can I help you?" I ask.

"Name's Kole, I own Storybook. Don't let her nervousness deter you from your goal. I can tell that you two are meant to be connected," he says.

"Okay," I say slowly.

"I have this feeling about the two of you. Be persistent, it will pay off." He shoves his hands in his pocket and then walks back into the bar leaving me unsure of that interaction and wondering just where the man came from. I didn't see him leave the bar, nor did I hear the door open or close after I exited the establishment.

I will take what he's said into consideration, I will not give up on what I want.

5

BIANCA

My menu, my menu...
What would my personal menu say?

And truly, who would want to choose items from my menu?

Dwayne said that it would be rare that I would be requested for anything, but he said the bossman liked what he has seen of me and to not underestimate the power of a bartender.

Whatever the heck that means.

Besides, who is this bossman? I've heard whispers of the name Kole, but I don't think I've been introduced to him yet. And what has he seen of me?

What fantasies would I have the I would like to fulfill?

I click the pen and scribble on the notepad.

1. *Strangers.*
2. *The fantasy that could never be...*
3. *Voyeurism.*
4. *Voyeurism inspired play.*

I can feel my cheeks flame with the mere thoughts of participating in each.

Participating in the other side of the pub is not a requirement, but a bonus of working here, where I can explore myself - my sexually.

I haven't seen the Welsh man in a few weeks, and I'm a little terrified that when I next see him, I will have to show him my menu.

When asked, we have to disclose our menus. I haven't been asked by any others aside from him—and I'm nervous as hell.

His ears must have been ringing.

"Well, hello Love," he says standing in front of me.

I look up.

Butterflies swarm my stomach; my palms get clammy, and my heart beats out of my chest.

"You know, I don't even know your name, what do I call you?" I ask.

"I'm so daft, names Wesley, Wesley Brockmire. Shall I continue to call you 'Love', or would you prefer your name?"

"I'm fine with 'Love'."

He smiles and leans back, "Splendid."

"So, can I get you a drink?" I ask nervously, hoping that will stall him from asking for my menu.

He orders a whiskey and I quickly place his drink in front of him.

"What brings you to work here," his finger traces the rim of his glass.

"I love bartending, I'm good at it," I reply with a shrug of my shoulders.

"Can I ask you a personal question?" he asks.

I look him in the eyes and give a small nod.

"Have you participated on the other side yet?"

Should I lie and say that I have.

I don't answer him right away, but I know I should be honest with him.

"No," I reply.

"Marvelous, now I have another question. Have you got that menu of yours ready for me to peruse yet, Love?" he asks with a mischievous grin and his sexy welsh accent that makes him even hotter.

"Why are you so adamant on my menu, when you know as well as

I do that there are many women downstairs who will see to your needs whatever they are?" I lean forward asking with pure inquiry.

"Because, I'm a man who knows what he wants, and that is you."

I stand straight and laugh while shaking my head, "oh, you're good!" I smile. "How often does that line work for you?"

"Truthfully, that's the first time, I've said it," he says scratching his temple.

"So, let me use a line on you," I lean forward again, and my finger catches a runaway strand of hair and begins to twirl.

He leans forward as well, eager to hear what I have to say. He licks his lips as his eyes dance with excitement.

"Yes, Love, please feel free to ask me anything."

"Come here often?"

"I do not actually. I just received this membership here as a gift, I've gotten the tour, but the most I've done here, is drink."

"And you've asked for my menu now twice," I lean forward and say with a smirk.

"And I would ask a third, fourth, and fifth time."

I stand up straight and cross my arms over my chest, liking his answer.

"If you must know, I am working on what will be on my menu," I say feeling my face flame.

"I can definitely help you out with that," he grins.

I take a deep breath and steady myself. I reach under the bar for my menu. Before he even can ask for it, I slide it across the bar in front of him.

"Your menu?" he asks meeting my eyes as I give a small nod.

He gives me a panty-dropping smile and holds it up, and while there are only four items on the page. He's engrossed in it, and takes his time reading each letter carefully, as if he is tracing them as he reads it.

The pub atmosphere is on hold for what feels like an eternity, until he looks back to me with a smirk.

"So, when can we schedule? What's your availability?" he asks with a Cheshire's grin.

6

WESLEY

ednesday.
 Wednesday is the day.
And today is that day.

I had to wait two days to wait until her next day off. While that's not a rule of the club, it's one of her limits. It's also clever. That way, she doesn't feel like she's being paid for doing whatever we will be doing.

I spent the last two nights, jacking off to thoughts of what is to come and what I want to do in the future.

I took the afternoon off from work to get ready for my date with her.

It's not a date. This is a scene.

We will be participating in a scene of strangers. After sitting at the bar for an hour discussing what each menu item meant, we felt that we were in fact strangers, so that would be an excellent starting point. I'm not entirely sure what that would entail, but I was given the explicit direction to meet her at a high-end bar down the street, a place where the drinks are over-priced and they barely pour the liquor, let alone the good liquor. We will meet and leave the other bar together to venture off to Storybook Pub and complete our menu selections.

I park my car between the pub and the other place. I enter and immediately see her, although she's done something different with her hair. It is slicked back into a tight bun, her hair looks shiny and… wait a minute… she's wearing a wig; her hair is definitely not blonde. She's wearing a black backless dress and sitting with her legs crossed.

I straighten and take a deep breath as I begin in her direction. I take the empty barstool to her left and motion for the bartender. I order a drink and look over to her. She smiles shyly then looks down at her nearly empty tumbler. The bartender puts my drink in front of me.

"Please get this beautiful woman, another drink," I ask.

The bartender looks to Bianca for confirmation and then gets her drink.

I turn to face her, unbutton my jacket and put on my best smile.

"I noticed that your drink was low, I hope that you don't mind," I say quietly.

"Well, thank you for refilling it," she turns to me and smiles.

"Name is We—" I'm cut off by the palm of her hand.

"No real names," she says quietly.

"Right. My name is Marcus," I reply using the first name that I can think of.

"Hello Marcus, my name is Linda, it's very nice to meet you."

"Same." We shake hands, with her hand fitting perfectly in mine.

"I was going to have one more drink tonight, and then I was going to head out, would you like to join me?"

"Ah, that sounds like a brilliant plan. What do you have in mind?"

"Are you up for a little adventure?" she smirks.

～

WE STEP into the dark hallway with my hand at the small of her back. I'm curious how far this will go and if this obsession of her will fade after I touch her.

She smells like candy, and that makes my mouth water. I want to taste her rainbow; I want to touch her smooth skin and be as close to her as humanly possible. I want to be wrapped up in her in all the ways possible.

She leads us to the glass-walled preview room and we take a seat in the rolling chairs that sit inside. We have the space to ourselves, and I'm curious as to what's going to happen next when she turns to face me and says.

"We're going to watch some things tonight. Tell me, what's your fantasy?"

I believe that I already wrote it down in my paperwork when officially requesting the scene, but she may need me to say it out loud as this may be her process.

"My fantasy, well dear Linda, is watching an orgy. I want to watch two women being serviced by the two men." I reply strongly to her. "And if we're inclined, a little play as well."

Her eyes sparkle and the corners of her lips twitch into a smile.

"Mine too," she whispers and then turns away. She stands up and pulls a remote control off the door that we entered from, takes a seat, then looks at me. She spins around and I follow suit while she points the remote to the wall we're now facing.

Lights go on in the room. The scene unfolding in front of us is simple and the surroundings in the spacious room are plain, yet comfortable.

Clothing is slowly being removed, lips are touching bare skin, and hands roam the various bodies in front of us. Necks arch, throats moan, and eyes roll in pleasure.

My dick twitches at the start of the orgy unfolding in front of us. I look over to the beautiful woman by my side and she's biting her lower lip with her fingertips grazing along her collarbone.

7

BIANCA

I can feel my heart beating, not just in my chest but between my legs. I wasn't lying when I told him that this is my ultimate fantasy as well. The women in front of us look like they are ready to jump out of their skin with pure rawness as the men do what they can to bring them to the height of pleasure.

I look over at Wesley and I can see the lust in his eyes.

He's watching me. Not the room.

My fingers were running along my neck absentmindedly when I noticed his gaze on me.

I turn to him and he turns to me with a lopsided smile. He scoots closer to me which closes the distance between us.

Slowly, his hand grazes my knee while he looks to me. I nod and his hand travels up my thigh, around my hip and to my waist. I lean into him and we're moving in slow motion until our lips touch.

Upon contact, we press our bodies against one another. The speakers from the room echo into the space we're in.

His hands run along my back, our heads angle opposite as our tongues happily invade one another's mouths. I grab the back of his neck and lightly moan into the kiss.

We pull a breath apart and I smile. "We should watch our show," I say.

He nods, then we turn towards the wall. One man is sucking on a woman's breast, while his dick is getting sucked by the other woman, who is getting fucked by the other man. It's quite the scene and it's only making me hotter sitting beside this extremely attractive man who is amazing at kissing.

My breathing quickens as the sexual acts resume in front of us, and the soft sweeps of Wesley's hand stroking the inside of my thigh gives me the butterflies.

"Am I distracting you?" he leans in to whisper.

I turn my head slightly and catch his eye.

I lick my lips again lean in toward him. Another kiss, this time a sweet one. One full of passion and desire.

I pull him to stand up and with his confusion evident on his face, I lightly push him back until his back hits the glass with the people behind us continuing with their activities.

"Oh, bloody hell," he whispers pulling off my wig and releasing my hair underneath from the wig cap that I was wearing, so my hair brushes across my neck with my head leaning back, arching slightly at the movement. He then threads his hand through my hair and yanks me closer to him.

Our lips crash again and everything else disappears while Wesley and I get wrapped up in one another.

We do nothing but kiss and touch. And once the scene behind him ends, I have to force myself to pull back.

"What? Why did you stop?" he asks.

"I don't—I don't know how to do this, are we supposed to stop? Do we continue? Is your fantasy fulfilled?" I'm nervously word vomiting.

He grins and tilts his head, as if he's trying to figure me out.

"Love, I would love to continue, however, it appears that there are others who are waiting for this room," he looks around me and my eyes follow his to the doorway, where two women are standing.

"Oh, please don't mind us. You two can continue. This," she points between us and the empty room behind us, "has been fucking hot.

Watching you two going at it, while those people were going at it just the same. Wow, H-O-T, hot!"

"With due respect, ladies, I think we will be going. You two may have the room," Wesley grabs my hand and we walk out of the room, past Dwayne and through the hallway.

We sit down in a booth and I burst into laughter.

"That was not what I was expecting," I say catching my breath.

"What?" Wesley asks.

"We were voyeurs and then we were getting voyuered just the same. I mean, that's voyeurism squared."

He cracks a smile, looks at his hands folded in front of him and then looks back up to me.

"I would like to have another with you?" he asks.

"Another?" I ask.

"I would like another menu glance, please?" He asks.

"But we literally just finished," I start to say then pause, "but that doesn't mean that we can't get the next one planned." I give him a smile.

"Perfect, I would like to schedule for eight," he says.

"Eight? Eight when?"

"As in eight tonight," he leans back in the booth.

"You've got to be kidding me. That's in an hour!"

8

WESLEY

I look at her as her mouth drops open.
"I've had a fabulous time with you, I'm hoping that you did as well. I definitely do not think that I've gotten enough of my fill this evening, I still have some fantasies that I would like to explore with you and you alone. So, my question to you is; do you want to continue on in the privacy of the club, or would you like to take this out and explore it naturally?" I shock myself in asking.

I can see the cogs in her head turning as she contemplates my proposal.

Do I want to take this out of the club? The privacy of the club makes it less real and taking it out, means that we're looking into pursuing something more like a relationship.

Is that something that I'm wanting to do?

Is that something that I have time for or am I just kidding myself and that's more than I can manage at this current time.

I don't date. There's no time. And I can't for the life in me recall the last time that I've gotten laid.

I work a lot and I'm sure any woman would be hesitant to be with someone who doesn't have the time or energy to tend to someone else needs.

What could I offer to her?

Pure unadulterated sex.

I have the capability to please her, likely as she's never been pleased before.

I know that.

"Yes."

I look up at her words and a smile forms on my face.

"Yes?" I clarify.

"Yes, we can do another scene. I'm not completely sure whether or not, I could take this out of Storybook, at least not right now. We're strangers, remember."

"While that may be true, Love, I did have my hands all over you a short while ago. Care to expand your palate of your menu?"

"What do you mean?" she asks with a tilt of her head.

"Maybe together, we can come up with a few new items to add, but only if they pertain to certain people, for instance, my own personal menu," I say with a grin.

"Your own private menu, something that I wouldn't share with anyone else?" she clarifies.

"Why not?" I shrug with a smirk.

I know that she's interested. And I damn well know that even though she's playing hard to get, this will be something that happens.

"Then, what do you suggest?" she fingers a strand of her hair.

"Depends, what are your limits?"

She blushes, looks at her hands as she massages them, and looks up directly into my eyes.

She shakes her head and then looks down at her hands.

"Don't get all shy on me now, my tongue was just in your throat."

She laughs quietly and turns her attention beside her, rummages into her purse, and then pulls out a pen and paper.

She poises the pen, looks at me, then begins writing something. She folds the piece of paper and slides it across the table to me.

I read her note and then fold it. I do my best to school my features and play off my expression to something other than extremely excited about what she's proposing.

9

BIANCA

I cannot believe what I wrote on the paper to him.
I cannot believe that I am so bold to have written what I did.
And when he read it, I could tell that he was thrilled, but was trying his best to not look over eager.

My leg is bouncing underneath the table and I'm pretty sure that I'm about to jump out of my skin in anticipation, until he smiles and nods.

"Let me go and discuss with Dwayne on what we're supposed to do," I say moving from the booth.

Dwayne stands stoically just inside the door. I lean up and ask him for direction. He smiles, shakes his head and reaches into his pocket to hand me a key card.

"This will grant you entrance into a private room. There is a black button that you can hit for any reason you need security to come, are you sure about this?"

I nod my head, then turn on my heel and head back to the booth where Wesley is sitting.

I flash the key card and his eyes light up.

"Shall we? While I still have the nerve."

"You know that we don't need to continue if you don't want to."

"I know."

He stands and offers me his elbow. I loop my arm through his as he offers me a slow smile that's hot enough to make my panties melt.

I wave my key in front of the door's lock that matches the number embossed on it, and it opens to a dim-lighted room with a bed in the middle of the space. The walls are a dark gray and there is a wall full of different sized whips and a shelf with packaged sex toys. I look to Wesley and see laughter dancing in his eyes.

"There won't be any toys going close to any of my openings," he says with a straight face.

"Got it. Now, I want your clothes off," I say with a commanding tone and pointing to him.

He removes his jacket slowly and begins to finger the buttons on his dress shirt with his gaze never wavering from me.

"Am I the only one here getting naked?" he asks.

"No, but remember this is my game right now," I remind him.

Once he's down to his boxer briefs, he pauses with his fingers hooked into his waistband.

He is even more stunning than I thought that he would be. His chest is broad with a sprinkling of chest hair, there's a rippling of well-defined muscles from his pecs to his groin that highlights the promise zone.

My eyes move downward waiting and expecting the grand reveal. He smirks, then bends at the waist and when he comes to his full height, my eyes are locked on the most attractive penis that I've ever seen.

And penises are definitely not attractive.

"So, what now?" he asks.

What next? Oh, shit! What next?

"I want you to undress me," I order him.

He approaches me slowly, and then does what I ask him. With each layer being removed, my skin breaks out in goosebumps at the contact.

When I'm completely naked, I turn and offer him a smile.

My heart is beating out of my chest, my palms are sweaty and I'm suddenly not sure if I can do this.

I want to.

I want him.

But can I do this under the guise of being in Storybook?

This place lets all fantasies come to life, but what if I'm unable to go through with having sex with him here.

His hand grazes my arm and he moves to intertwine our fingers together as he guides me to the bed.

"What do you want?" He whispers, his lips a breath from mine.

"I want you," I whisper.

I see his eyes dilate and all my hesitations cease.

"You have me," he whispers, leaning in and brushing his lips against mine.

I lean into him and give into the kiss, getting dizzy in the taste of him and the sensations that my body is feeling at his touch. I've forgotten about my plan of action for this scene.

I was going to let him dominate me in a swapped role. But all I can think of doing is exploring what is happening in this moment. There's time for that at a later date.

I push him back and shake my head.

"I like this, I really do, but we need to stick to the plan," I tell him.

He slowly nods.

"I'm going to get on my hands and knees, you're going to fuck me from behind and spank my ass," I tell him.

"Yes, that. Let's get back to that." He nods eagerly.

I move to the bed and into the position that I had asked of him, he comes to stand behind me and kneels down with his hands on either side of my ass. Then I feel his hot breath against my sex, and soon a swipe of his tongue against my center pulls a light moan from me.

He laps up my wetness, and moves between using his tongue and fingers repeatedly until I can feel my orgasm coming and the clenching of my pussy.

In what feels like minutes, my orgasm pulls my thoughts from his mouth on me until I can no longer feel it.

I hear the tearing of a condom wrapper, and soon a different feeling against my center as Wesley presses his cock into me from behind. He slowly thrusts into me as my body gets used to him. A moment later, Wesley picks up speed and just as I moan loudly, he catches me by surprise and lands a loud slap across my right cheek, then while still thrusting, he rubs the sting away with his palm. I reach in front of me and clutch onto the sheet to get a hold on something as I push my ass into him.

He reaches his arm around my waist as his hands fumble across my pussy to my clit.

"Yes!" I hiss, arching my back.

Wesley pulls away and out, rolls me onto my back, and then my legs wrap around his middle as he quickly buries his cock into me.

A rushing current of desire pulses through my body while Wesley's carnal gaze never leaves mine.

"I'm going to come," he breathes out in-between thrusts.

"Me… me… too," I moan.

"Now." He commands.

My body reacts to his words, and all the sensations come to the surface as we come together. Wesley pulls me up, so our bodies are flush against one another, with his head in the crook of my neck, he turns so I sit astride him.

I cling to him, not wanting to let go, not wanting to break the contact. Our breaths become one as his hands rub my back lightly to fall onto my hips where he gently moves me, so I am still fucking him.

He lays kisses across my shoulder and up my neck to just below my ear.

"You are amazing," he whispers into my ear.

I smile and nuzzle into him.

"What are we supposed to do now?" I ask in a whisper against his neck.

"Whatever you wish to do, you're calling the shots," he declares.

"Technically, you're supposed to dominate me," I pull back and point out.

"Oh, Love. I did dominate you; do you not recall?" he smirks, his accent thick with innuendo.

And now, I just want more. But I don't want it to be only here at Storybook.

10

WESLEY

I'm sitting in a meeting full of executives and my thoughts continue to replay over and over again from the previous night with Bianca.

I wasn't expecting that we would have gone as far as fucking one another, but I'm sure as shit happy that she asked for the domination scene.

I know she's working today. I look at my watch and note that she's likely just starting her shift.

Are other patrons asking for her menu?

Is she fucking other men?

I know that I'm jumping to conclusions. I had just seen her last night, and hopefully will be the only partner that she will have at Storybook Pub.

I sit up straight in my chair with that thought.

Where did that thinking come from?

I'm not a man who can be in a relationship right now?

But I want her and do not want her with anyone else. Does that constitute a relationship?

I pull out my phone from the pocket inside my jacket and scroll through the contacts.

I don't have her number. The realization hits me. We didn't exchange numbers and I have no way of reaching her, other than to go to her. The meeting still has another hour left in it, and the remainder of my afternoon is also full of additional tasks that I cannot put off for another day.

With my thoughts torn between work and Bianca, I know that in order to see her, I need to do the latter, so I set my intentions forward and do just that.

∼

SHE'S NOT at the bar when I arrive.

Maybe she's on a break.

But what if she's downstairs?

I see another bartender and walk up to him.

"I'm looking for Bianca?" I ask him once he looks up.

"She's, um, not here at the moment, can I take a message? I didn't know she had a boyfriend."

"I'm not her boyfriend," I say.

"Oh, in that case, if you're looking to schedule something, she'll be back in about another ten minutes, care for a drink while you wait?" he asks.

My mind immediately goes to that she is with another man, and my head begins to spin.

This is entirely out of character for me.

What is happening?

"I'd like whiskey, two fingers on the rocks, please?" I say settling into the barstool at my side.

Within the amount of time that I'm waiting, my mind races to several different scenarios.

Ten minutes later, Bianca walks in through the hallway with a smile on her face. She says a quick hello to the other bartender and then turns to me. A brief look of shock is on her face, but she straightens and offers me a sexy smile, that I would like to think is just for me.

"Hey, you, what are you doing here?" she asks leaning on the bar.

"Were you just in a scene?" I blurt out, feeling insecure.

"No, I was on a break," she says, a smile still on her lips. I release a breath and she tilts her head. "Are you worried about something Wesley?"

"I don't know what is happening to me," I say meeting her inquisitive eyes. "No, no that's not it. I know exactly what's happening to me. It's you."

"Me?" She points at her chest.

"Yes, you've captivated me. You're all that I can think about, even from before we officially met."

"What do you mean?" she asks.

"I saw you, I came here and sat outside. I was debating whether or not to come in, and that's when I saw you. I didn't know if you were a customer or if you worked here. But I just had to know you, and now I cannot get you out of my mind. You're all that I think of, and I'm not sure how to handle it."

"Oh," she says quietly.

"I work too much. I don't have relationships. And I don't do feelings. But suddenly, I have time away from work, I don't want you to be with anyone else, and now, I feel an intense amount of feelings for you."

"Oh," she repeats.

"What time are you out of here?" I ask her.

"At about seven," she replies.

"Can I take you out to dinner? Like on a date?" I shock myself with the words that come out of my mouth.

"A date?" she asks.

11

BIANCA

My chair is pulled out for me and I slink into it with a smile as I look up to Wesley before he takes his own seat beside me.

"Thank you for agreeing to come out with me tonight," he says placing his napkin across his lap.

"Well, thank you for asking me out," I reply.

"I meant everything that I said. Before you and I had a scene together, I had to know you," he tells me.

I've thought about him constantly all day, I didn't want to let go of him and I definitely do not want him participating in scenes with anyone else. But is that too much to ask? We just met, we only had one night of scenes. Amazing scenes.

"I'm not sure how the whole fantasies thing at Storybook operates," I admit.

"Do you think that you have more fantasies?" he asks.

"I'm sure that I do, do you?" I ask.

"I do, but I would rather explore those privately, and with you."

His words warm me.

"Is there an option to pull out of the fantasy side of the pub?" he asks.

"There is," I say cautiously.

"Bianca, I can't share you," he tells me.

"Does that mean you won't be attending either, for scenes with others?"

"I've only come there for you; I've told you that. I haven't and don't want to share scenes with anyone else, only you."

"I just want to make sure. But what you were saying about work and relationships?"

"I meant everything. Before you, I didn't have a reason to not work so much and I didn't have a desire to date anyone. I want to make time for you, I want to be with you." His hand slides on top of mine and squeezes.

"Well then, let's see if us meeting at Storybook Pub was fate just waiting to happen."

He leans in and I meet him halfway when he takes my mouth with his.

Dinner is relaxing and full of conversation. Once we leave the restaurant, I get anxious.

"What now?" I ask.

"Now, I want to take you back to my place and devour every inch of you," he tells me.

12

WESLEY

Her short hair is fanned out on my pillow and the sight in front of me is now my most favorite. She lays on my bed in a matching black lace bra and panties. She spreads her legs as I move up on the bed. My eyes drop to her breasts, and the quickening of her breath as my hand lightly trails across her skin.

I kiss the top of her hip, then move up her body, laying kisses along my path up to her lips. I grin when I look up at her from the valley between her heaving breasts with our eyes connecting, I lick a line from the center of her chest to under her chin, along her neck and up over her chin to her lips.

My tongue dips into her mouth as my hand fits to her breast. Bianca moans into my mouth while I hover over her. I want to take my time with her, but the other part of me wants to ravage her.

I'm wearing my boxer briefs and my cock is anxious to get closer to her. I press myself against her center, mimicking fucking her as she writhes underneath me. I continue kissing her, continuing to grind my hips against her center and keep exploring her mouth with mine.

I want her.
I want to be inside her.
I want to just be with her.

I pull away from her, look down and smile.

"You're driving me insane," I whisper.

A slow smile spreads on her face as she licks her lips.

"If you don't hurry up and fuck me, I might combust from all this pent up sexual tension," she coos while cupping my cock through the fabric.

I lean up on my knees and pull my boxer briefs down. My cock springs out from the waistband and drips in precome in anticipation of what's coming next.

I sheathe myself and enter her swiftly.

I bury myself to the hilt, then lean down and take her lips as I thrust into her repeatedly. I build up to the crescendo of pleasure and pull myself back as I piston my hips into the beauty below me.

I lean down, place my hands under her ass and we roll over, so I'm underneath her and she takes control. Her hands are on my chest as she uses her knees and pushes up and down.

She stops and turns with my cock still in her and clutches onto my upper thighs as I grab her hips to help her movement.

Fuck! This feels so damn fucking good.

I want to feel like this, forever.

BIANCA

"And how is everything between the two of you?" he asks in his thick accent leaning on the bar toward me.

"Well, I didn't think that this would come out of working at Storybook Pub," I reply holding up my hand showing the massive engagement ring on my finger.

A large smile erupts on Kole's face. "I had a feeling about you two. I knew it the moment that I had you hired."

"So, it was you who orchestrated it all?" I ask drying a pint glass.

"That's what I do. I come and I go. I see all and I know all of what happens here in the Pub. The moment that his brother got the membership for him, I saw your future together. So, cheers," Kole holds up his glass.

"What are you a fortune teller?" I ask him pouring myself a glass of soda.

"I had happiness and love once before, and when she passed, I made her a promise to carry on with Storybook Pub. So, that's what I do," he explains as the door of the pub opens.

One year after meeting Wesley, and every time he walks into the bar, it gives me chills. This is the place that we met, the place where we explored one another for the first time. And the man seated—I look over to where Kole was perched—but he's gone. Well, that guy apparently had intertwined in whatever way that he does, and here I am, happily engaged to the love of my life.

The man that I will forever explore my fantasies with.

The man who learned that he was missing something and found it with me.

"Hello, Love. May I see your menu?" he smirks.

Learn more about Tarrah Anders:
https://linktr.ee/tarrahanders

Also by Tarrah Anders:
- More than Friends
- Clutch Endgame
- Sinful Secrets

LOVE IS BLIND

FAITH RYAN

"I want to know what it feels like to possess you;
body, heart, and soul.
To own all of you the way you own me."

Sub-genre: Contemporary Romance
Relationship: Male/Male

JOSH

"You'll be fine. Aidan is going to stay with you. I have to go Josh. This is my job. I can't keep putting things off because you're scared. You need to face things sooner or later."

I adjust the shaded glasses that help hide my eyes, then huff out a breath and listen as my brother Jason packs for a month-long trip to Japan. He's not wrong, it's just that I don't want to. Facing things means accepting, and I don't much like my current reality, so why would I accept it.

The mattress bounces under the weight of what I'm assuming is Jason's suitcase. A moment later the zip sounds and Jason sits beside me, slinging an arm around my shoulders. "I wish I could make your life better, easier but I can't Josh. This is something only you can do. I have no experience with being blind."

"Neither did I until six months ago." I clench my hands into fists and press them into my thighs. "I don't know how to live like this Jason. How am I supposed to be me when I can't see?" Tears leak and slowly cascade down my cheeks. "Tell me. Who am I if I can't see?"

Jason pulls me closer to him, wrapping me in a brotherly embrace. "Oh, Josh. I wish I had the answers. Maybe you can let Aidan help while he's here."

"Aidan hates me. Why did you ask him to babysit anyway?"

"He's not babysitting you. He'll be here to help you when needed, you're an adult whether or not you can see, and I won't treat you like a child. When you come to your senses you'd hate me if I did."

"Fuck. It's like losing my sight made me an emotional mess. I need to drink a case of beer and get laid." Jason grunts out a laugh and with a final squeeze releases me from his hold.

"Come on, Aidan will be here any minute." He grabs my hand and leads me back to the living room, straight to the couch. I'm learning to maneuver around the apartment on my own, but I'm constantly bumping into shit.

"You need anything before he gets here?"

I shake my head no and settle into the cushions. The TV clicks on and I hear pots and pans being knocked around as Jason puts on the annoying cooking show he likes to watch. "Seriously, Jason. Just because I can't see it doesn't mean I want to hear the damn show."

Jason's laughter is interrupted by a knocking at the front door. I want to run and hide. Aidan has been Jason's best friend since sixth grade. I had a crush on his dark emo-esque looks back then, but I haven't seen him in the four years since I left for college. And now thanks to a fucking freak accident I'll never see him again.

Yeah, I know. I'm a barrel of fucking sunshine. Which is another thing I'll never see again.

"Hey Josh, how's it going?" Aidan's voice gets closer as he talks, and the cushion gives under his weight as he sits beside me. "It's been a long time. I'm sorry about, you know. Anything you need while Jason's away, let me know." He pulls me into a hug and I involuntarily inhale. A whiff of the sandalwood soap I remember him using years before assaults my senses and stirs improper memories of the time I jacked off while sniffing a shirt he'd left behind in Jason's room.

I feel myself getting hard, so I pull away and reach for one of the decorative pillows. Instead of cloth and fluff, my hands find rough and warm. *Fuck.* Aidan must have stood when I shifted, the normal disruptions in movement not registering with my senses because I was distracted by my dick.

"Do you need something, Josh?" Aidan asks, and I realize my hand is still on what I guess is his thigh. I quickly pull back and sink into the couch as far as the cushions will let me, mumbling "I'm fine."

"Hey Aidan, will you come help me for a minute?" Jason calls out from what sounds like the kitchen.

"Sure, Jase." Aidan pats my shoulder on his way out of the room. I feel like the pest he's always claimed me to be. Only now it's a million times worse because I really am the annoying little brother who won't go away.

AIDAN

Josh Klein isn't the scrawny teen I knew a few years ago. He's grown into a man. For a second there, I was glad he couldn't see me. My dick would have given away my attraction to him. I've only been out of the closet a short time, and while Jason is understanding, I doubt he'd want me anywhere near Josh if he knew I wanted to gag on his brother's cock.

"You sure you're up for this?" Jason asks as we make sandwiches for a quick lunch before he has to head out. "Josh has been difficult since the accident. I can hire a nurse if you don't feel you can handle him by yourself."

"No. I can handle Josh. Stop worrying. Everything will be fine."

"Thanks, man. I don't know what I'd do without you. He's taking this hard. It's been six months; I can't keep asking for time off. My sick leave ran out three months ago, my vacation time, last week. We'll be out on our asses if I don't start working again."

"Six months isn't long to adjust to losing your sight, Jase. Give him time. I'm here. And my offer to move in still stands. It'll help all of us."

"Aidan, why didn't you tell me?" The hurt in Jason's voice causes my throat to tighten.

"I didn't want to lose you." I whisper the words, choking on my emotions. Jason is the only person to stand with me no matter what. He's had my back and I've had his, and the guilt of this betrayal eats at me. I make a promise to myself to never let him down again.

My forced coming out a month ago was not the best, and things have been stressful and exhausting. I'm lucky to still have a job, but that's only because they haven't found the right loophole to get rid of me without discrimination playing a part. I kept things to myself because Jason was already dealing with so much when it came to Josh.

"You'll never lose me, dipshit. Now, stop being a pussy and help me carry this shit."

I laugh, grateful for Jason's ability to sense when things are too tense. I grab the few sodas and follow Jason as he moves toward the living room where Josh sits.

Jason sets a plate on Josh's lap. "Ham and cheese. Unopened soda on the coffee table directly in front of you."

What must that be like. I close my eyes, imagining I'm as blind as Josh. It's hard to see the world encased in total darkness when the brightness from the high watt lightbulb turns the back of my lids a pinkish red.

"Dude. Are you sleeping? Are we boring you?" Jason kicks at my feet and I immediately open my eyes. I glare at him for a moment, before my gaze is drawn to Josh.

He eats his sandwich slowly, tearing pieces with his fingers and putting them in his mouth, chewing longer than necessary before swallowing. Dejection pours off him in waves that roll over me, suffocating and choking any happiness I might have found in the thought of spending more time with him.

"So, Josh, wanna be my wingman tonight? I'm sure it's been awhile. Damaged guys get all the attention at the club ya know." He cracks a smile at my attempt to alleviate the depressive atmosphere of this apartment, but it's gone in a flash.

"Aidan, that's not funny." Jason smacks me in the chest.

"Who said I wasn't serious? You'll go with me, won't ya Josh?" I didn't intend on going to a club, but the more Jason insists Josh shouldn't go, the more I want to prove he should.

"Uh, yeah. Sure. If that's what you want, to babysit me while trying to get laid."

"What's the matter? Afraid you'll realize you can still have fun without your eyes?"

"More like I know I can't and don't want to ruin yours."

"Challenge accepted." I tell him.

The look of shock on both their faces is priceless.

JOSH

Aidan drove Jason to the airport. They wanted me to go with them, but I said I was tired and headed to my room. I don't know how long they've been gone; time moves differently for me now and I can't quite grasp it.

I roll from my side to my back. I can't get comfortable. From this position my blank stare once locked onto the popcorn bumps in the ceiling, but now—today—Aidan fills my unseeing vision. I remember the way his dark hair was just long enough to flop down to cover one dark eye from view. I loved his eyes. So dark, they were almost black, a deep tunnel of darkness that called to me. I wanted to sink into their depths and lose myself there forever.

The faint scent of sandalwood permeates the air and I groan. The aroma combined with my reminiscent thoughts has me growing hard again. I reach down and squeeze my length, wanting to avoid an awkward erection when Aidan returns. *He's not here. He'll never know.* My mind whispers, and I eagerly fist my cock, stroking slowly from base to tip.

I try to imagine what Aidan might look like now, how his body would feel under my hands, but I'm stuck with my teenage memories.

Even with the outdated version of him in my mind, the thought of Aidan has me coming quickly.

I let my body relax into the mattress, the tension easing somewhat from my body. My release is cooling on my stomach and I'm drifting into sleep when I hear the front door close.

"Josh?" Aidan calls out and I frantically reach toward my nightstand for a tissue to clean myself. I manage to grab a few but in my haste I knock something over and it rolls off and onto the floor, making a loud thump when it lands.

"Shit." I swipe at my stomach, then toss the tissues in the direction of the trash can.

Hurried footsteps sound down the hall getting louder and closer with every step. "Josh? You okay, man?"

"I'm fine. Just knocked something over. Don't worry about it."

"Okay. You want some help getting things back in place?" Aidan sounds like he's in my room.

"No. Thanks anyway, but I got it."

"It's no problem," he says and places his hand on the bed near my leg. I can feel the tips of his fingers brush my thigh. My breath begins to come out in rapid bursts, so I hold it on the next inhale, praying Aidan won't notice my reaction to him.

"Oh, uh," a soft thud sounds from the nightstand, before Aidan manages to speak actual words. "There you go. Everything back where it, uh, belongs. I'll just leave you to, um, to whatever it was you were doing."

Aidan brushes past the bed and out of my bedroom as if his ass is on fire and I am the fuel to the flames.

What the fuck was that about?

I tentatively reach my hand out to see what I had knocked off earlier, not wanting a repeat of knocking it down again. When my fingers collide with a rubbery texture, an embarrassed blush covers my face and the realization of what I accidentally left out dawns on me. I can feel the heat of my shame pouring from my cheeks. *Fuck being blind.* Aidan Montgomery, my lifelong crush and my brother's best friend, just had his hand wrapped around my dildo. Someone kill me now. Please.

AIDAN

Josh has a dildo. A realistic looking piece of silicone that I want to use on him. *Fucking holy hell.* The thought of fucking his ass with the dildo, watching his face as his orgasm consumes him has me running from his room.

Jason let me know years ago of Josh's sexuality. He even suggested Josh had a crush on me. At the time I was in denial of my own attraction to men, and Josh was just Jason's pesky little brother. But now, now I don't know how I'm going to keep from coming on to my best friend's kid brother. At least he can't see the hunger I have for him that's surely written all over my face.

I close the door to the guest room, my room for the next few weeks, and lean back against the cool wood. I thump my head onto the hard surface a few times to knock some sense back into my brain. As much as I am attracted to Josh and would love to spend a night or two learning his body intimately, I won't ruin the friendship I have with Jason.

Fuck. This is going to end badly if I don't get my dick under control. Maybe heading out to the bar or a club will be beneficial to both of us. I'll get Josh out of this apartment, show him he can still have a life, and find someone to relieve this lust pulsing through me.

Decision made I call out to Josh, still too excited to be face to face with him. "Hey Josh! Get dressed man, we're heading out." I hear some mumbled words but can't make out what he's saying. Before I can ask him to repeat himself, the shower down the hall turns on.

I use the shower attached to the guest room and get myself ready. I dress in dark jeans, a forest green button up, and a pair of work boots. Then I style my hair to fall into my eyes and give me that just fucked bedhead look that drives the men crazy. I'm feeling sexy and confident, but it's tempered when I realize my attempt to impress is wasted on someone who can't see the finished product.

No. This is not for Josh. This is for some random hookup.

It doesn't matter if I can impress Josh. I can't have him.

I head out to the living room to wait on Josh to finish getting ready. I flop onto the couch and aimlessly flip through the channels on the TV to distract myself from more thoughts of having Josh naked and beneath me.

Josh clears his throat and when I look his way, I let out an audible breath at the sight that greets me. His blond hair has been carelessly brushed away from his face and his outfit of holey jeans and a plain black t-shirt screams "I don't give a fuck." He's put minimal effort into his looks and somehow it's the hottest he's ever been. I don't know if my reaction is because I finally see him as a man, or if my mind is sexualizing him into my fantasy because of the dildo incident earlier, but Josh Klein has my body reacting in ways I've only dreamt about. He has my—and my dick's—full attention.

"Sorry if this isn't good enough for the club. I can stay here. You don't need me around while you're trying to find someone to fuck."

Josh's words are self-deprecating and defensive. I watch his honey colored eyes shift unseeing over the room, weighing my response carefully. He needs this, needs to feel more like himself, but he's going to deny what he needs for what he feels he deserves.

"Nah, man you look fine. You'll probably get some before I do tonight."

"Ha. I doubt that. I know Jason doesn't shout from the rooftops that I'm gay, but I am. So, no, I won't be getting laid at whatever club you take me to. More girls for you." He smiles in my direction. It doesn't reach his eyes and my heart aches for the sadness I can feel encompassing the room.

"There won't be any girls for me," I tell him.

"Fuck you. Just because I like dick doesn't mean you can't go out and find some chick to bring home."

I laugh. "You misunderstood, Josh. There won't be any girls for me because I like dick, too."

He opens his mouth to say something, then closes it, keeping whatever thought he had to himself.

"Okay, well, what are we waiting for? Let's go find you a cock for the night."

As we head out to my car, me guiding Josh, I wonder if this is such a good idea after all.

JOSH

The music pounding through the club is a throbbing pulse behind my eyes. I hear Aidan shift on the stool beside me and I've had enough of his babysitting.

"Go dance or something. I promise I'll be right here when you're ready to go. It's not like I can manage to make it out of here on my own anyway."

"Josh—"

"Aidan just go. Have fun. Please. It's killing me that you're just sitting here because of me. I'll be okay."

He sighs. "Okay, fine."

The stool beside me loudly scrapes across the floor and I feel Aidan brush by me.

"You look miserable."

The voice comes from the other side of the bar top.

"Listen, I'm not up for chit chat. I know it's your job, but if you could just get me another drink then leave me alone, I promise you'll get a nice tip at the end of the night."

"Noted. But if it's any consolation you should know, he looks just as miserable and not really into the girl he's dancing with."

"Girl? I thought this was a gay club?"

"We don't discriminate here at Storybook Pub. We're not a club either. I know it gets loud in here and the crowd likes to have a good time, but we're nowhere near the hookup, bump and grind scene of a nightclub."

"Sorry. I should have asked for more information. In case it's not obvious, I'm blind."

He laughs, a friendly sound that makes me smile in response. "No worries. The sunglasses kinda gave it away."

"Yeah, well it's a new development for me and not one you start a conversation with, if you know what I mean."

"I get it. I see all kinds being a bartender, nothing shocks or surprises me anymore. Except maybe how your friend is suffering unnecessarily. That woman is rubbing herself all over him and he looks like he wants to be somewhere rather than on that dance floor."

"He does? Shit." I knew I shouldn't have tagged along on Aidan's night out. "I guess I should have him take me home so he can head out to where he really wants to be."

"Does your friend know how you feel about him?"

I raise a brow in question.

"It's all over your face. You don't control your facial expressions very well."

"You mean, does he know I've been in love with him since I met him. Uh, no. Besides, he doesn't think of me that way, so why bother bringing it up. I am and will always be his best friend's little brother."

"Hmmm. If you say so. Let me get you that drink."

The man places a cold glass near my hand moments later.

"Name's Kole, by the way."

Making a connection to someone outside of Jason, and now Aidan, hasn't been something I wanted since my accident, but Kole's friendly manner seems to have a magical effect on me. He makes me want to open up and tell him all my insecurities along with the longing for Aidan I've already shared.

"Josh."

"Well Josh, I think that man out there is interested in you for more than the fact you're his friend's little brother. The way he keeps looking over here, it almost seems like he's jealous." Kole's voice was closer and

I felt his breaths against my cheek. "Wanna mess with him? Test out this jealousy I'm seeing?"

There was no way Aidan was jealous of me talking to Kole, more likely he was concerned because I am his responsibility.

"Come on, I have a feeling you'll thank me for it later."

Another glass brushes my fingers and I down the contents. The liquid burns a path down my throat.

"Aidan isn't jealous, but if this is your way of asking me out… a few more drinks and it just might work."

Kole laughs and I hear him pour more of the alcohol into my glass.

"You're not my type, but I'm positive you'll have a date before the night is over. Bottom's up."

"Cheers."

I down my drink and slam the empty tumbler on the bar top.

AIDAN

I watch the bartender flirt with Josh. I gave up pretending to dance and have a good time hours ago when I noticed the attention the handsome man was bestowing on my date.

But he's not your date, is he?

Fuck. My mind keeps reminding me that no matter how much I want Josh, this is just a night out between… what are we? Friends. Acquaintances. I don't fucking know. I just know that I want him.

Josh laughs loudly at whatever the man says and sways on his bar stool.

"Okay lush, I think it's time to go."

Josh pouts and the look is adorable, but I want out of here. "I'm having fun Aidan, isn't that what you wanted?"

Yes. But I wanted the fun to be with me, not the green-eyed Casanova mixing drinks.

"It is, but if you drink too much more I won't be able to get you home by myself, and I doubt your new friend can leave his post long enough to help me."

Josh snorts. "Oh my God! You're right Kole, he sounds jealous." Another snort and they're both laughing.

I frown. I can't deny I'm jealous, but I think I've hidden it pretty well.

"Don't look so sad about it, kid. I have an eye for these things. Plus, your boy here probably won't even remember in the morning. Take him home, take care of him, then when he's sober, show him how you feel about him." The bartender gives me a wink before walking away.

"How do you feel about me Aidan? What does Kole see that I can't?"

"That you're drunk as fuck. Come on."

I put an arm around his waist and place his limply across my shoulder, using my other hand to hold his and keep him in place. Josh turns his head and leans his face into the crook of my neck. He takes a deep breath, then releases it on a happy sigh that drifts over my skin. My cock immediately tries to harden, but it's been hard for hours. Watching Josh flirt might have pissed me off, but it also has me horny as hell.

I manage to get Josh out of the bar and down the street to where I parked the car. Once I have him buckled in, I take my spot behind the wheel and get us back to his place as fast as legally possible. Wouldn't do me to get a ticket with my dick tenting my pants.

Josh is quiet on the drive, so I assume he's fallen asleep and try to gently lift him from the car. He doesn't weigh near as much as he looks. I don't know if that is a side effect of his depression since the accident, or just his natural physique; either way it's a blessing as I carry him from the car to the apartment. When I get to the door I realize Josh has the key in his pocket.

"Hey, Josh. Man, I need you to wake for a minute and give me the key."

"Jus' take it." He mumbles the words into my neck.

"I can't. I need you to get it for me. It's in your pocket."

His response is a hum, followed by a snore.

"Fuck it. Just reach in a grab the key."

I don't know why I'm talking to myself, but the little pep talk works. I set Josh to lean against the wall, braced between the hard brick and my body, then I reach into one of his front pockets. I feel around for a moment, my fingers brushing his cock through the thin lining of the fabric. No keys. I reach into the other, my fingers skimming down the length of his now hard length, before finding the set of keys. I wrap my fingers around the key ring and begin to pull them from the pocket only to repeat the same skimming movement along his dick in the opposite direction.

Josh lets out a moan and I make a conscious effort not to do any of the hundreds of X-rated fantasies flowing through my mind. Not while he's drunk and passed out. I won't take advantage of him.

JOSH

I'm having the best dream. Aidan is manhandling me into my bed after he felt me up outside my apartment. Now he's undressing me, his hands touching me in feather light caresses.

"Mmm, feels so good."

Aidan stops moving for a minute then curses. I wish I could see him, but this dream stars Aidan as he is now and not from my memories, which means I can only imagine what his face looks like when he's drowning in lust.

"Fuck. Josh, you have to stop. I need to take these clothes off you."

"Yes. Clothes. Off." I reach for his shirt and begin to push it up his chest with one hand and feeling the grooves of his muscles with the other.

"Josh. No."

The words bring me back to reality for a moment before I decide to pretend I'm still half-dreaming. Aidan pushes his shirt back down, moving my hands away from his body, and continues undressing me. When I'm left only in my boxers, Aidan tries to get me to move under the comforter on my bed.

"No. You. Naked too." I can hear myself speaking in half sentences that barely make sense, but my mind is a glorious combination of alcohol induced fog mixed with waves of lust that make it hard to think. I'll blame the booze for my actions and to help cushion the finality of his rejection when I wake in the morning.

"No. Josh, stop." Aidan pushes me under the comforter then wraps it around my body, sealing me in a warm cocoon of fluffy down. "I must be an idiot," he says.

"You're not an idiot. But you are overdressed." I pull my hands free of the comforter and finger the hem of his shirt, trying to slip it up his chest again.

"Fuck me."

"No, silly. You're supposed to fuck me."

"Josh, you're drunk. Tell me it's what you want again in the morning when you're coherent and I'll fuck you until you can't walk, but until then, my answer is no."

I groan at the promise in his words before sticking out my bottom lip, exaggerating a pout. "Fine. But will you stay with me?" I ask. The fun of the buzz is starting to fade, and I don't want to feel alone anymore. I think I have just enough sway at the moment to get him to do just about anything. Well, anything but fuck me apparently.

"Josh, I don't think that's a good idea."

"Please, Aidan. I don't… I don't want to be alone again. I'm always alone even when I'm not. There could be a hundred people standing around me and I wouldn't even know. But I know you're here now, and if you stay I'll wake up knowing someone else is here. That I'm not alone."

A tear slips from the corner of my eye and makes its way down my temple. Before it can disappear into my hair, warm, wet flesh swipes it away. It takes a moment for my senses to register exactly what happened, by then Aidan's hands are in my hair and his lips are pressing a tender kiss to the flesh where he'd just licked away my tear.

"You're not alone Josh. Never." Aidan climbs onto the bed and beneath the comforter, pulling me to him until we are spooning, my back to his front. "I'll stay as long as you need me to."

"Promise?" My voice sounds small, childlike and my vulnerability wants me to take back the words, but it's too late.

"Always. I'll stay forever if you need me."

I close my unseeing eyes and relax into the hold Aidan has on me, letting sleep claim me fast and deep.

AIDAN

Sleep is impossible. Josh is a cuddler. Every time I move he follows and somehow ends up closer than before. At the moment I'm on my back and he is snuggled up to my side; one of his legs is thrown over mine and resting dangerously close to my throbbing erection. I need to extract myself from his hold and go to my own room so I can relieve the ache in my balls and maybe get some sleep before morning. But whenever I move to go, and Josh's grip tightens I remember how his words from earlier were drenched in loneliness. Even if he doesn't recall tonight when the sun rises, I just can't bring myself to disappoint him.

Josh shifts, his leg making contact with my groin and his hand moving from his side to my chest. I hold my breath, not daring to move in case he wakes.

"Mmm, you have more muscles than I imagined." Josh's hand moves over my pecs and down my abs, playing with my happy trail of hair before moving back up my chest to repeat the movement again. On each pass his fingers move closer to my cock, which is begging desperately for his touch, or even my own. Any skin on skin contact to bring me some relief.

I squeeze my eyes shut, trying to will my erection away. The wet heat of a mouth engulfing my nipple has me moaning and instinctually gripping the back of Josh's head. His tongue twirls around the stiffening peak before he takes it between his teeth and bites down with just enough pressure to send a zap of pain to mix with the pleasure he's inflicting on me. I need to stop this before it goes too far so I tighten my grip on his head, twisting the strands of his hair around my fist and begin to pull him away from my body, which protests by arching into him.

His fingers are once again trailing down the patch of hair to where I crave his touch. His mouth follows, sucking kisses into my skin and disrupting my train of thought.

"Josh, wake up. You need to stop."

"Who said I was sleeping?"

Fuck. "Josh, I don't want to take advantage of you, but my will is only so strong." I groan as he goes lower still and my hand falls from his hair.

"You said when I woke, if I still wanted you, wanted this, you'd fuck me until I couldn't walk. Did you lie to me Aidan?"

His hand finally—fucking finally—wraps around my cock. "Did you Aidan?"

What? Am I supposed to be having a conversation right now?

"Did I what?"

Josh licks the tip of my dick before answering. "Did you lie to me? Or are you going to fuck me?"

I'm certain he's still drunk, but his words make sense and he's not swaying and slurring anymore, so the buzz of the alcohol is wearing off. My mind is telling me I should wait until he's had more than a few hours to sober up, but my body says I should fuck waiting and take what I want.

"Aidan?" Josh releases his grip on my dick and pulls away from my body. "Oh, God. I'm sorry. I thought… you said… fuck, I should have known better." He rolls over to the opposite side of the bed, his back to me.

Shit. My hesitation has brought back that hurt and lonely boy from earlier, the one I promised myself I would not disappoint or make feel alone. Fuck me, I'm really screwing this up.

"Josh—"

"It's fine, Aidan. I should've realized you were just being nice. I made a fool of myself, nothing new. Just leave me alone, so I can wallow in my humiliation."

"No. You misunderstood my hesitation. It's not that I don't want you, I do. I want you too much to risk ruining it by letting you do something you might regret once you're sober."

"I'm not drunk Aidan. Not anymore."

"You're not sober either."

"Whatever. Just go, please."

"No." I reach over and turn him back toward me. I know he can't see the sincerity in my eyes, so I'll have to convince him of my intentions in another way, but first, "how about a compromise? A renegotiation of sorts."

He doesn't answer, but he tilts his head toward me as if to hear me better.

"I won't fuck you," I begin. He frowns at my declaration and his pout is adorable. "Let me rephrase. I won't fuck you tonight. I want you fully with me when I take you for the first time. But if you tell me in clear words that you want me, now, tonight, I'll give you what you want in other ways."

"Oh God yes, please."

"I need the words Josh."

"Please Aidan. I want you. Now. Please."

I smile to myself and run my hand through his hair. "Okay." I apply pressure to the back of his head, maneuvering him back to my cock. "Now, where were we?"

JOSH

The heavy weight of Aidan's hand at the base of my neck is as much a turn on as the smell of his arousal. His cock's musky aroma fills my nose as I inhale, the scent stronger the closer I get.

I owe Kole a thank you. I'm not typically this bold with what I want, but between the alcohol and his encouragement I convinced myself to take a chance. It hurt when I thought my risk had ended in rejection, but now, with my face an inch from taking Aidan's cock in my mouth, I can't imagine not taking the leap.

I tentatively lap at the tip, my tongue dipping into his slit to collect the precum seeping out. Eager for a better taste of him, I suck him into my mouth. I take him to the back of my throat and swallow.

"Fuck yeah. That feels incredible," he tells me, and I feel his fingers flexing in my hair, a clear sign he's holding back on what he wants because he thinks it's not what I want.

I pull off his cock, sucking until my cheeks hollow and he leaves my lips with a loud pop. Grabbing his other hand, I guide his palm over my head until he digs his fingers in the strands of my hair.

"Don't hold back Aidan. Take what you want from me."

"This is about you, not me."

I smile in the direction of his voice. "Exactly. And what I want is for you to take what you want. As hard as you want. As fast as you want. For as long as you want. Use me for your pleasure, Aidan. Please."

I don't wait for him to answer before sucking him back into my mouth. I tongue the length of him, following the vein on the underside of his cock up and down, over and over.

"Josh." Aidan groans out my name causing me to moan around him. I suck harder, my head bobbing faster. His cock hardens even more against my tongue and I'm ready to swallow his release, ready to taste him.

His fingers tighten in my hair and he pulls me off him, his dick smacking wetly against his pelvis, and a whine leaves my throat.

"I'm too close, and I refuse to come before you're taken care of. Come here."

Aidan guides me where he wants me with his hands on my hips. He places my legs on either side of him, my knees resting on the pillows near his head until I am straddling his face.

"My turn."

His hands glide up my sides then down my arms; he takes my hands in his and directs them to the headboard.

"Hold on." His words don't register fast enough, and I almost lose my balance when he takes my dick into his mouth. I tighten my grip on the headboard and let the sensations from his magical tongue wash over me. I haven't had sex since my accident, but I'm beginning to think that has been a mistake. The inability to see Aidan as he swallows me down is enhancing my other senses. The slurping noise of him licking and sucking my length combined with the feel of the wet, saliva drenched heat of his lips has my long overdue orgasm rushing through me.

"Aidan, I'm not gonna last. Fuck. I'm gonna come."

Aidan doesn't pull off me. He sucks harder, and when I shoot my release down his throat I swear I propel my heart and soul, all that I am, into him with it.

I'm too exhausted to move, hanging weakly off the headboard as Aidan releases me from his mouth with little licks and sucks that send painfully pleasurable aftershocks through my body. I drift in and out of consciousness, fully succumbing to sleep once Aidan has maneuvered me into his arms and slowly strokes my back as he holds me.

"Sleep. I'm not going anywhere. I'll still be here when you wake."

His reassurance, whispered against my forehead and followed by a soft kiss, wraps me in a cocoon of safety and love.

AIDAN

Despite not coming last night, I fell asleep shortly after Josh. I woke a few minutes ago and have been relishing the feeling of him against me, the way his breath puffs against my chest, and how he looks like he belongs in my arms, always. If I have any say in it, he's never leaving my side, but it might be a bit early to tell him that.

Josh stirs and his hand smooths over my ribs. "Aidan?"

"Were you expecting someone else in your bed, brat?"

"No." He shakes his head and buries his face in the crook of my neck. "I thought last night was a dream."

"Not a dream, brat."

"Quit calling me that. It reminds me of how much you hated me hanging with you guys when I was younger."

"I never hated you tagging along. I actually liked it. A lot. I was struggling with coming to terms with who I was, and there you were, making it harder for me. My reaction was to push you away and build walls to hide behind."

"Well, you did a great job of that."

"I know." I pull him closer to me, hugging him to my side. "I'm sorry, brat. I should've dealt with my feelings back then. Maybe things would be different if I had." Maybe if I had been with him, Josh would still have his sight.

As if he read my mind, Josh responds to my unspoken thought. "No. None of that. I think I liked the idea of wanting the unattainable back then. And even if we had somehow found each other then, I would still be blind now. I always wanted to be a photographer. I would have ended up in that dark room no matter what. I know the splash of chemicals was an accident, preventable maybe, but a freak anomaly of events that left me bereft of my dream regardless."

"But—"

"No buts. I know I haven't been dealing with my loss well. I wasn't ready, but I think I'm getting there. Maybe with you helping me, I can learn to accept this new reality and find myself again." A blush creeps across his cheeks and his voice gets quiet at the end.

"I told you last night, I'm not leaving you alone. You're stuck with me, brat."

"Good." His hands find my face and pull me in for a kiss. He tangles his tongue with mine and it feels like he's giving me everything of himself.

He pulls away and I try to follow with my lips, wanting more of him, wanting all of him.

"Are you going to fuck me now? Because if you're not, I need to go take a cold shower."

"You have a one-track mind, don't you brat?"

"Only when the man I've wanted for what feels like forever promises to fuck me until I can't walk, then makes every excuse not to."

That pout I love makes its appearance again and I contemplate holding out longer to keep the adorable expression on his face.

"That pout doesn't have the effect on me you're thinking it does. Don't get me wrong, it's cute and makes me want to give in to you, but it also makes me want to deny you, so you'll pout again."

"So, does that mean I'm getting fucked or not?"

"You're incorrigible."

"I'm in desperate need of a good fuck."

I lean up and take his lips in a hard kiss. The brat is going to be the death of me.

"Fine. But next time you fuck me. You're not the only one who needs to be ridden hard."

The shock on his face is priceless.

"You'd let me fuck you?"

"Yeah. Why is that so hard to believe?"

"Because no one else has wanted me to. You might not like it. I've never done it before."

"So, I'd be your first?"

He nods shyly and I decide a change of plans is needed. Our first time is going to be an experience to remember.

"Those douchebags don't know what they're missing." I roll us until he is beneath me, then I straddle his waist, his cock resting along the crack of my ass. I rock over him until his body takes the lead, rolling his hips up into me. Leaning forward, I give him another kiss. "Fuck me, brat. Take me the way you've fantasized. You have fantasized about fucking me, haven't you?"

Josh bites his lip; lost to the sensations, all he can do is nod.

"Tell me."

He releases his lip, his teeth leaving impressions in the pink skin I want to lick away. "I've dreamt about fucking you, Aidan. I want to know what it feels like to be the one to possess you; body, heart, and soul. To own all of you the way you own me."

"Fuck, brat. I want that, too." I give in and lean forward to lick at his lips. I lead his hand to his cock and press the tip to my puckered entrance. "Own me, brat. Give us both what we want."

JOSH

"Where's your lube?" Aidan asks me as he reaches over and begins rummaging through my nightstand. "Found it. We'll play with some of your toys another time."

The sound of a cap being opened followed by a liquidy squirt distracts me from embarrassment. Aidan's hand is cool and slippery as he rubs the lube over my cock in a few strokes before placing it at his hole again. I'm holding my dick upright, but Aidan is the one in control of this encounter. He lowers his body onto me slowly until he is full, and I no longer need to hold my dick in place. My hands find his hips and I take hold of him, my grip bruising.

Aidan begins to lift off me and the way he contracts around me as his inner walls rub along my length has me close to coming. When he tries to lower again, I use my hold on him to stop the movement.

"You okay Josh?"

"Yeah. Just trying not to come before we get started."

Aidan leans forward, placing kisses up my chest, along my neck, and across my jaw. I slip from his body the higher he moves up mine. I want to be back inside him, but I also want to last, to make this good for him.

"You want to last longer brat? I have something that could help with that. You want me to go get it?"

"Yes, please."

I regret my choice when Aidan lifts his body from mine and the rush of cool air marks the absence of his warmth.

"That pout will be the death of me."

"I changed my mind. I just want to be back inside you."

"Tsk, tsk, brat. I brought you a gift, don't you want it?"

It seems like a trick question, so I wait for him to make the next move.

I'm not disappointed. The bed dips beneath his weight and he kisses his way from my ankle to the crease where my groin meets thigh. He takes me in his mouth sucking me into what feels like an impossibly hard state before placing something around the base of my cock. Once it's secured in place Aidan pulls away just far enough that I can feel his breath along my length.

"Now that's a pretty sight. Your dick hard and ready for me to use to fuck myself until I come."

My dick twitches and I feel like I'm going to come from those words alone but whatever Aidan put on my cock prevents me from doing more than feel the pressure build.

"Oh, fuck." I reach down to finger the contraption.

"It's a cock ring, brat. You've never used one?"

"No. You sifted through my toys; I'm very vanilla." It's the truth. I've never been very adventurous. I use my dildos when I can't find a worthy fuck—which has been a lot since my accident—but it was always just a means to an end. With Aidan though, I find myself curious enough to try whatever he wants.

"We'll fix that brat, later. Now, I want to use you as my own toy."

Aidan climbs over me again and applies more lube to my cock. This time when he takes me inside the squeezing of his passage is amplified by the restriction of the cock ring. I'm covered in sweat and ready to beg Aidan to let me come by the time I'm fully inside him. When he wiggles around on top of me, changing the angle of my cock until I hit that place inside him, I almost come despite the ring preventing my semen from leaving my body.

A low groan leaves Aidan as he pulls himself up my length then slams back down, over and over. I can tell when he gets close, his channel tightens further, and his breathing becomes harsher. He reaches for one of my hands and wraps it around his dick. He uses my hand to jerk himself as he continues to fuck me as if I'm his own personal dildo.

"Fuck brat. You're fucking perfect." A few more strokes and thrusts and Aidan comes all over my chest. "I wish you could see how gorgeous you are right now, covered in my come." He swipes a finger through the mess and presses it to my lips. I open eagerly and suck his essence into my mouth. "So hot." He takes my lips in a rough kiss, his tongue dipping inside to take a taste of himself from my own.

He continues to kiss me as he reaches down and removes the cock ring. I'm still inside him so it takes a bit of work, but he manages somehow. Once the ring is gone, Aidan fucks me hard. His body sucking me inside as he lowers and tightening to keep me there when he lifts.

"Oh God, Aidan." I can feel the come leave my tip and the warm creaminess spurs me into a second orgasm. Thoughts cease and I'm left as a boneless lump unable to move.

"I take it you liked that."

"Fuck yeah. I mean I think I prefer to be on the receiving end, but I won't tell you no if you want to do that again."

"Good to know brat."

"Just not any time soon. I think you killed me, and I need to recover."

Aidan's laugh fills the room as he lifts off me then spoons against me. "Whatever you want brat."

AIDAN

It's been a month and Josh and I are inseparable. Jason is due home in a few days, and I'm worried about his reaction.

"Stop worrying, it'll give you wrinkles."

"Good thing you can't see them then." Joking with Josh about his blindness has become a way to help him accept his reality. He told me to never hold back, and I'll never tell him that I keep the worst of them to myself, but I do indulge his little display of bravery whenever I can.

"Jason will be fine with us. I promise. He already loves you like a brother."

I hope he's right. My phone chiming with Jason's ringtone pulls me from wallowing further into despair over my best friend's reaction to me fucking his baby brother. When I see he wants to facetime, I automatically answer.

"Hey! Can't wait a few more days to see my handsome face, huh?"

Jason laughs at my joke and we exchange stories of our time apart. I feel like he's leaving something out, but I don't call him on it since I'm avoiding telling him about me and Josh. I figure we can both keep our secrets for now.

A tug on my sweats distracts me for a moment. Josh is pulling my cock out and before I can tell him no, he takes me down his throat and I let out a groan.

"Aidan, what the fuck? Are you getting head while on the phone with me, again?" Yep, I've exposed Jason to my "O" face before.

I try to deny it. "No, I—" Josh sucks harder, daring me to lie. "Shit."

"Man, call me back or better yet, let me talk to Josh while you get your rocks off. I miss the little brat."

Josh audibly chokes at Jason using the nickname I've given an intimate association to.

"Damn Aidan, let the man breathe." Jason laughs at his own joke. "Give the phone to Josh, will ya? Then you can gag your new fuck toy all you want."

"Uh," I try to come up with a reason why I can't, but I am saved—fucked—when Josh takes the phone from me. I have to give him credit, he avoids showing my cock in the little screen, how he does that without being able to see I don't know. He is now jerking me while he talks to his brother. And he's not trying to hide what he's doing judging by the smirk on his lips.

"Josh?" Jason calls his brother's name.

"Yeah."

"What are you doing?"

"Nothing, why?"

"Because it looks like you're jacking off while talking to me."

Josh's hand squeezes around me as he laughs at Jason's words. The added pressure causes an unexpected jolt of pleasure and I can't stop the moan that leaves my lips any more than I can stop my come from landing on Josh's t-shirt and chin.

"Fuck." The word is both a curse and a compliment.

"Was that Aidan? Did he—is that his come dripping from your chin?"

Josh swipes at his chin and sucks my spunk from his fingers.

"Josh!"

Jason sounds shocked and worried. I grab the phone from Josh as he lapses into hysterical laughter. "You think you're funny don't ya brat? Just wait," I tell him. To Jason I say, "Don't freak out."

"Don't freak out! You just came on my brother!"

Okay, he has a point. "Well, yeah, but it was his fault." Maybe I shouldn't have said that. The silence that greets me tells me it was a mistake, but I can't take it back.

"Are you with Josh? Are you guys a thing? Or is this just a fling of convenience?" Jason goes on before I can answer. "Because if you aren't in it for the long-haul Aidan, if you break his heart, I'll kill you."

The threat is delivered in a deadly tone, one I've never heard from Jason before.

"I'm in this for forever, that is if he wants me for that long."

Josh climbs up my body from his spot on the floor and crawls into my lap. Grabbing my face, he kisses me. "I don't want you for forever, I want you for beyond forever Aidan. You own me, I'm yours."

"And I'm yours brat."

"I'm still here!!" Jason's exclamation brings my attention back to him as Josh lays his head on my shoulder, his face turned in the direction of Jason's voice. "I'm really happy for the two of you, really I am, it's long overdue. But I'm actually calling for another reason."

"What's wrong?" Josh asks, picking up in Jason's voice what I'm seeing on his face, worry and fear.

"I can't go into details. Not yet. I just wanted to let you know I'm going to be gone for a little while longer. I promise when I can I'll explain everything, but you don't need to worry about me right now. Enjoy each other, get the PDA out of your systems, 'cause when I get back, that shit has to stop. Eww. That's my brother Aidan."

Taking the hint to deflect Josh from worrying, I promise to be good before we say our goodbyes.

"Is Jason going to be okay?" Josh asks me after the call disconnects.

"He'll be fine. He's a consultant, what kind of trouble can he get into? Besides, he'll be home to bug us in no time at all."

"You're right."

"Of course I am. And now it's time for payback, brat."

I stand with Josh in my arms and carry him into our bedroom, so I can devour this man I can now call mine.

Learn more about Faith Ryan:
https://linktr.ee/FaithRyan

Also by Faith Ryan:
    Bad Deal
    Giving Up the Fight
    Fighting Chance

HEARTS COLLIDE

KENZIE ROSE

My heart is beating out of my chest when I think of her...

Sub-genre: Second Chance Romance
Relationship: Male/Female

1

NATHAN

"Come on, man, you need a night out," Jonathan said. "You can't keep working like this."

I looked at my boss and shook my head. "I'm not in the mood." I stacked another box of beer. I'm the operations manager for Giovanni Cellars, and I've been working late for the last few weeks.

He watched me, while I stacked more cases, waiting, one eyebrow crooked.

"Fine. Just one drink and then I'm going home. I'm not in the mood to go out."

He nodded and left the room.

I stared at the door as it closed behind Jonathan. Why did I agree to go out after work? I would have rather gone home to be alone. Sarah left six weeks ago and I still couldn't believe it. We were planning on getting married and then bam, she left me a Dear John letter with my ring, apparently she met and fell in love with a guy who was in a band and she was following him around the world.

I finished stacking the boxes, then went into the office to file the paperwork so the shipment could be wrapped and delivered. I made my way into the locker room, grabbed my jacket, clocked out, then headed to my truck. I waved to the night crew as I walked through the parking lot, then unlocked my truck and got in. After starting the truck, I sat there and closed my eyes.

Why am I going out? I just wanted to be left alone. But if I didn't go, Jon would be all over me tomorrow. Better to just get it over with. One drink and then home.

As I drove towards my house, my thoughts drifted to Sarah, who I met when I was running on the beach. No, I don't want to think about her, I need to forget about her. I decided to drive home and run to the pub, I needed to work off this feeling and a good run would do it.

After changing clothes, I ran down the road to the stairs that lead to the beach. About two miles down the beach, then I ran to the boardwalk to cool down. I stopped outside the pub and looked around. I saw Jonathan's truck and his girlfriend's car, so I knew they were already there.

One drink, that's all I will have. I walk into the bar, waiting for my eyes to adjust to the low lighting, you can hear people cheering for some team that was on the TV and the band playing in the back room. I waved to Kole O'Shea, the owner of the Storybook Pub, and headed towards the room where they always sit.

I walked over and pulled out one of the chairs at the tables they had pushed together in the whiskey room. After saying hi to everyone, I got up and ordered a beer before sitting back down and talking sports with Jonathan and Thomas Anderson, the general manager of the Mill House where I work. A few minutes later, Kole walked over with a tray full of drinks and placed them on the table. After shaking Jonathan's hand and kissing Emily's cheek, he looked around the table nodding at everyone. "This round of drinks is on the house."

"Thank you, Kole," Jonathan said.

The rest of us murmured our thanks.

"Your family's wine was one of Rebecca's favorites, Jon, so I don't mind doing something nice for your family." If you were looking at him closely, you could see the sadness in his eyes, but it was quickly masked when he looked up at the woman that walked through the door. "Excuse me," he said, then turned away from us to greet her, throwing his towel over his shoulder.

My eyes followed Kole as he spoke to her and then showed her to a table. She had long, strawberry- blonde hair pulled in a ponytail, with jeans and a tight t-shirt. Kole leaned down and said something to her. Her face brightened when she smiled, and I found myself smiling as well.

For the first time in months, I was curious about a woman. While I watched her, the conversation around me kept going. I never even noticed Thomas leave the table and walk towards hers. Her face lit up when she saw him. He leaned down to give her a hug and kiss on the cheek. I wonder how they know each other. I tried to pay attention to the conversations around me, but my attention was drawn to her and I cannot figure out why.

2

NIKKI

The drive down the coast was beautiful, the hills to the east were emerald green, and the sky was the same shade of blue as the Pacific Ocean, it was impossible to tell where one ended and the other began.

The GPS indicated just fifteen minutes left in my drive to the house that my boss, Genevieve Anderson -aka bestselling author Kimberline Evan-rented for me to stay in while I'm here in California working with her.

As I drove down the narrow roads that led to the rental, it was clear that I was no longer in New York; instead of high rises and people everywhere, I was surrounded by trees and wildlife. I pulled up to a cute little red bungalow right on the beach that looked like it should be on Block Island, Maine, not the beach in California. I grabbed my bag, closing the car door and walking up to the home. I unlocked the front door, then stepped inside. The first thing I saw was the beautiful blue and white hydrangeas sitting on the counter in a crystal vase beside a pie in a basket, just like my grandmother used to have.

I dropped everything and went right to the glass door, slipping quickly outside to the deck. I took a few deep breaths of the salty air and closed my eyes, enjoying the sound of the waves. Taking my shoes off, I stepped onto the sand and, wiggled my toes. The dry sand was warm under my feet, as I walked down to the water's edge, then right into the waves letting the water rush around me. I stood there and enjoyed the feel of the waves lapping at my ankles. As I turned around to return to the bungalow, I noticed that it was a secluded beach. I have so much to do but I want some time on the beach to since it is incredibly warm for November. It is normally cold and snowing in New York this late in the year, so I planned to enjoy this as much as possible.

I walked back into the house and sent Ginny a text to let her know I arrived safe.

Once I'm unpacked, I decide to walk down the beach to see if I'm close to some shops or restaurants. I grab my keys and some cash and set off to explore. I pick up some rocks and throw them into the water and notice a few silver dollars that I pick up along the way. There is a boardwalk not far from the bungalow, so I decide to take the stairs and give my legs a break from the sand. I look in the windows of the shops and stop to buy some saltwater taffy before continuing down the picturesque street. I could hear loud music coming from what looks like a bar. As I got closer, I noticed the sign in the window that said Storybook Pub. Well, I definitely need to check this out since I work for a publishing house. I walk through the door and I am immediately hit with a sense of Deja vu.

Pausing just inside the door to allow my eyes to adjust to the soft lighting, I scanned the small pub.

A sexy blonde approached me, smiling widely. "Hello. Welcome to the Storybook Pub. I'm Kole O'Shea, the owner of this fine establishment. Can I show you to a table or would you rather sit at the bar.

"A small table would be great," I said as I followed him to a quieter side of the room. "Thank you."

"Can I get you something to drink?" Kole asked.

"A glass of cabernet, please.

"Coming right up."

My eyes followed him as he walked away, throwing a rag over his shoulder, as my eyes moved across the room to a table of guys laughing. I noticed that Ginny's husband, Thomas, was sitting with them. All of them were good looking, but my eyes stopped on the guy with the curly red hair who was talking to Thomas. I am not sure what it is about him, I just can't take my eyes off him. He looks familiar, like I have seen him somewhere before.

Kole brought my wine and placed it on the table. "Enjoy, just let me know if you need anything else."

"Thank you." I picked up my wine and took a sip as I looked around the room. Shelves of whiskey were backlit above the bar, old wooden signs with Irish sayings hung in various locations throughout, and beautiful old photos of Ireland decorated the walls. Big screen TVs hung in various places behind the bar, most of them were airing soccer games, and to the back of the bar, an Irish band played loudly.

Thomas walked towards me with a big smile on his face. When I get up to hug him, I notice that the guy with the curly red hair is watching us.

3

NIKKI

Thomas leaned down and kissed my cheek, then sat across from me. "What are you doing at the pub? I thought you would want to sit on the deck and enjoy the warm weather."

"I wanted to walk and stretch my legs, and I saw the name, so I had to come in. After all, it is intriguing and fits in with my job. What are you doing here? I thought for sure you would be at home with Ginny." I took another sip of my wine.

"We had a meeting at work and then decided to go out for drinks to check out Kole's pub since he is a new customer of ours."

"How is Ginny doing?"

"Better than expected but still on bedrest and I can't thank you enough for agreeing to come out here and be her assistant."

"I would do anything for her and the publisher would be crazy to not agree to it. Plus this gives me time to get to know Tommy. I can't wait to meet him and see Ginny."

"She's looking forward to seeing you, too. In fact, we are planning a barbeque tomorrow and she wants you to be there."

"Sounds like fun, So, are any of the hot guys you promised to introduce me to going to be there?"

"Well, I don't think any of them are hot, but I will introduce you to some guys at the barbeque tomorrow."

I laughed. "Deal," back in New York, I'd helped Thomas set up the hotel balcony for his proposal to Ginny and told him he needed to introduce me to some hot guys.

My gaze darted to the table where Thomas's friends gathered, and the redhead's eyes met mine. Heat rushed my cheeks, so I lifted the wine glass to hide my smile. "Who's that?" I asked Thomas quietly.

He looked over his shoulder.

"Thomas, don't look!"

"Well, how else am I supposed to know who you're asking about."

I shook my head then drank the last of my wine. "The one with the curls."

Thomas crooked one eyebrow. "Nathan? The redhead?"

Nathan, I nodded, my cheeks heated farther, then got up to leave, dropping a tip on the table. "I should head back to the house so I'll see you tomorrow." I gave Thomas a hug, then left enough cash to cover my drink and a tip.

"Let me drive you."

"No, you stay here and enjoy your evening. I want to enjoy the walk back. Tell Ginny I'll see her in the morning."

"Will do, have a good night." I kissed Thomas's cheek, then stepped out into the cool evening air.

I felt the ocean air against my face and realized my face was hot. Why did I blush just now? I never blush.

I ended up jogging back because the tide was coming in. Once at the house, I made myself some coffee and took it to the deck with a blanket and my phone. I wanted to enjoy the sunset on my first day in California. Once I was settled on the lounge chair, I pulled out my phone to do a little research on the area, so I knew where the store and bank were. I also checked to see how far Ginny and Thomas's house was from here.

I looked up and watched a dog playing catch on the beach. I smiled, then I saw someone move out of the corner of my eye; it was a guy running on the beach.

I sat up straighter when I noticed that it was the red headed guy that was sitting at the table with Thomas tonight.

I couldn't take my eyes off of him. I love his red hair that is full of curls. What would it feel like to run my fingers through his hair?

Okay, where did that come from?

He ran down the beach and up the stairs to a house four doors down.

Holy crap on a cracker, he's practically my neighbor!

I have to get Thomas to introduce us, I mean, he did say he would introduce me to some hot guys, and the redhead was sitting with him.

I was going to ask Ginny to mention it to Thomas. I walked down to the beach to see if he would come back outside but there was no movement on the deck, so I returned to the bungalow and headed inside, made myself some dinner, and found a movie on the Hallmark channel to watch.

4

NATHAN

She walked towards the door, then stepped out into twilight. I pulled my attention back to the table and the conversation going on around me, unable to focus on the words. She was beautiful, with legs that went on for miles, and an unforgettable smile. There was something familiar about her, but I couldn't put my finger on it. Thomas returned to the table, settling back onto his barstool.

"Who was that?" I nodded towards the door.

Thomas tilted his head, assessing me. "That was Ginny's assistant. She's staying out here for the next few months to help with Ginny's book release."

The next few months, eh? Thomas smiled mischievously. "You comin' to the barbeque tomorrow?"

If there was a chance to see that gorgeous woman again? Hell yes. Nodding, I turned to Jon, raising my empty bottle in salute.

"I'm going to head home. See you guys tomorrow. Thanks for the beer." I got up and left before they could stop me.

Waving to Kole, I exited the pub, jogging down to the beach. I headed home, wondering if I would run into her. Probably not. She's probably already back over the hill, working with Thomas's wife. I sprinted down the beach, climbing over rocks to avoid the tide coming in and headed to my parents' beach house. They moved back home to New York, but I'd stuck around after I started working at Giovanni's Cellar. I ran up the stairs and then stopped to stretch the muscles that I pushed a little too hard dodging the waves. I went into the house and grabbed a water before heading to the shower.

―

THE NEXT MORNING, I did my five mile run, but instead of running down the beach, I headed down the road to the boardwalk. I couldn't stop thinking about the woman from last night and how much she looked like Nicole from back home. I stopped to tie my shoe and realized I was in front of the Storybook Pub. I saw Kole in the window, so I knocked on the door to see if I could buy a bottle of water. He smiled when he saw me and opened the door. Holding out his hand he welcomed me.

"Hey, man, good morning. What are you doing here so early?"

I looked at the clock and realized it was only seven o'clock in the morning. "I was out running and wondered if I could buy some water," I said as I looked around. "Place looks different in the morning when no one is here."

He handed me a bottle of water.

"How much?" I started to pull my wallet out...

"No charge."

"Thanks, I wasn't expecting it to be warm this morning. I mean, it is November" I said as I took a long drink.

"I can't get used to this weather. But Rebecca loved Cambria, so this is where I have been spending my time, at least until another pub needs me." Smiling, he raised his eyebrows. "So, I noticed you left right after Nikki did last night, did you happen to run into her?"

I stopped mid-drink and stared at him. "What? Why would I run into her?"

"Because she is staying in the rental four houses down from you on Windsor Drive."

Shocked, I put my water bottle down on the counter. How did I miss this? "I had no idea." I said, thinking back to yesterday. Is that why she was on my mind all evening and why I woke up thinking about her first thing this morning?

"Maybe you should offer to show her around the area. All work and no play makes for a boring work trip."

I nodded and shook his hand while trying to wrap my head around the idea of showing her around.

"Thanks again for the water. I need to finish my run before I head to the gym."

"No problem. I will see you Monday for the delivery."

I drank the last of the water, threw the bottle away, and shook his hand again. "See you then."

As I turned to leave, he stopped me. "Nathan, my wife Rebecca was a true romantic and believed in destiny. Maybe you need to see where destiny leads you with Nikki. There is a reason you can't get her off your mind."

I looked at him, shocked. How does he know that I have been thinking about her all night? I nodded and waved before leaving the pub. I ran back down the beach towards my house, slowing when I turned past the rocks in front of the only rental on the street, just in time to see her disappear into the house and close the door. Stopping, I stared at the house, willing her to come back out.

Just as I was about to head to my place, there she was, walking back outside with her coffee cup. She sat at the small bar on the railing and looked out at the water, slowly drinking her coffee. I walked over to the house, pausing at the bottom of the steps. I could feel my heart beating hard in my chest. When she didn't notice me, I cleared my throat.

She looked down at me and slowly smiled.

"Hi," I said. "I saw you at the bar last night…."

"Hi, you work with Thomas, right?"

I walked up a couple of steps then paused "Yes, I do. My name is Nathan."

She grinned. "Nice to meet you. I'm Nikki." She held her coffee close to her lips but I could see the grin forming. "I'm being rude, would you like a cup of coffee?" She motioned for me to continue up the stairs.

"I would love a cup of coffee."

She smiled sweetly, then went into the house. A few minutes later, she returned with a cup of coffee. "I hope you like it. It's coffee from back home."

I took a sip, smiling. "This tastes like Third Rail Coffee at NYU."

Her mouth dropped in shock.

"It is. You went to NYU?"

"I did. Studied business and finance, and minored in film history."

"My brother and I both were there. He majored in finance and minored in film history too."

"And you?" I asked, taking a sip of the coffee. This is literally the best coffee in the world. Giovanni's wine-infused coffee came close.

"English lit and marketing. I work for a publishing company in New York City as the personal assistant to a bestselling author."

"What's your brother's name?" I knew but I wanted to see if she remembered me.

"Frank."

I was right. It is her. "I had classes with him all four years. I think we did a film project together for graduation." I thought he had a sister named Nicole." Her cheeks turned pink while she sipped her coffee.

"That's me. My name is Nichole; I just go by Nikki because I like the name. So, have we met?" Then all the sudden, it was like the lightbulb went off. "Oh my God, Nat. How did I not recognize you?"

Finally, I smiled and nodded. "I didn't realize it until I saw you this morning. How are you doing?"

Her cheeks turned bright red and she bit her lip. "I'm doing good, as you can see. I love working for Thomas's wife, Ginny. I get to travel around the country, and I get to spend the holidays here in California."

"Not married?" She shook her head and laughed and it did something to me.

"No, not married and not dating, yet." She winked. "So, what are you doing out here?" She pulled her legs up and hugged her knees, giving me a glimpse of the backside of legs.

Forcing my eyes back up to her face I took a sip of coffee. "I took an internship with Giovanni Cellars two years ago and then Thomas asked me to be his Operations Manager and I have been here ever since." I finished my coffee and tilted my head. "How long do you think you will be out here?"

She shrugged. "I don't know. Ginny is supposed to take it easy until the baby is born, so I'm here to help her with anything that is book-related since she has a book due to her editor in a month and it has already been pushed back a few months because of her accident and hospital stay. So, I'll be here until she doesn't need me anymore. I mean, it's not like I am living in a shack. I get to live on the beach in California and miss winter in New York." She laughed "And I have an amazing job and the bonus is Genevieve and Thomas are amazing people."

I want to spend more time with her, just the few coffee dates that we had in college weren't enough. "Would you like me to show you around? You need to do more than work while you are here."

She worried her lip and that made her look adorable.

"Come on, what do you say? I know a few of the hot spots and this is the time to do it. With the mild weather, we can hike and maybe hit the hot springs. I can give you a tour of the Mill, what do you say?"

I could see that she wanted to do it.

"It's nice to find someone from home to spend time with."

And maybe pick up where we left off.

"I think that could be fun. I need to check in with Ginny and see what she needs me to do today. Why don't I text you and let you know when I'm finished?"

I pulled out my phone so we could exchange numbers since I was sure our numbers has changed over the years. I'd received a message for Thomas, reminding me about the barbeque; I hadn't even felt the phone vibrate. "Looks like Thomas is having a barbeque at his house tonight." I looked at her. Want to go together?" I flashed her a smiled and saw her cheeks flush, again.

"He mentioned that he was doing it so I can meet everyone, sure, why don't I meet you there?" She asked as she stretched her legs out in front of her.

Standing I placed my coffee cup on the railing. "That sounds like a good idea." Looking around I knew I should leave but I didn't really want to. I wanted to spend more time together. "Thomas and his wife picked a great house for you to stay in, I always admire it when I run the beach. It reminds me of Cape Cod, or a home on Block Island."

Her mouth opened in surprise. "Oh my God, that's what I said to Ginny yesterday. I helped Thomas not only set up his proposal, but I helped him with their trip to Block Island as well which is where my family always vacationed. It's one of my favorite places."

Is she for real? Where has she been this whole time?

"We vacationed on the island too. My grandparents ran a hotel and a restaurant for fifty years. When they retired, my aunt took over so they could move to California. Now they live in Palm Springs and love retirement."

"Maybe we were there at the same time? My parents always rented a house in town so we could walk everywhere."

I felt my chest squeeze, like someone was sitting on my chest. What the hell was that?

"Maybe we were." At that moment, my phone started ringing. I looked at it and sighed. it was my Thomas. "Excuse me, I need to take this." I went down a few steps and noticed she took the cups into the house to give me privacy.

"This is Nathan." I watched her walk around the house, wiping the table off.

"Hey, it's Thomas. I know today is your day off, but can you come in today and run a delivery? Gino's wife is in labor." Gino was one of our delivery guys.

"Yeah, no problem. Give me an hour? I'm out for a run."

"Didn't you run last night?"

I rolled my eyes. "Yes, I did, but I usually do a five mile run on Saturday."

"Trying to use up some pent-up energy? Man, you need to forget about her and go out with someone and release that energy another way." He laughed.

I looked up and saw her watching me. She licked her lips.

"Maybe I do. Let me go and I will be there in an hour." We said our goodbyes and I put the phone back in my pocket and zipped it up.

As I looked at her, I realized I hadn't thought about Sarah since yesterday afternoon and I was all right with that. Nikki walked back out and stood at the top of the stairs.

"Is everything all right?"

"Yes, one of our driver's wives went into labor, so I need to go into work and take care of some deliveries. How about I meet you at Thomas's house tonight?"

"I am looking forward to it."

I slowly walked backwards down the stairs until I was on the beach. "Have a good day with Ginny. See you tonight."

She waved and I turned to jog back to my house.

Now that I know she was Nicole, I was more than willing to get to know her better, because there was something about her that just drew me in.

5

NIKKI

Oh my God, he's just as gorgeous as he was in college. What were the odds that Nat would be here, in Cambria, when I am? I watched until he was out of sight before I went into the house to get ready for my day.

An hour later, I was on my way to my friend and boss's house. Following the GPS directions, I drove through the hills and vineyards to the ranch they were renting. I noticed the security guard at the end of the driveway. After letting him know who I was and confirming with Ginny that I was indeed supposed to be there, I made my way up to the house. I grabbed my bag and headed to the door.

Tommy, Ginny and Thomas's son let me in. "Mom, Nikki is here," he yelled.

I leaned down and gave him a quick hug. "How are you?" I asked as I followed him into the house.

"Fine, Mom said I could play outside with my dog when you got here."

"Well, take me to your mom."

He ran into the room at the back of the house, and I saw Ginny laying on the sofa, with a pillow on her lap and the computer propped on it.

She looked up and smiled at me. "There you are. I was afraid that you got lost."

I leaned down and hugged her. Careful not to lean on her. "No, it was rather easy to find your house. Especially with the security guard out front." I raised an eyebrow. "I did make a note to drive around and see the vineyards and hills. It's just beautiful here. And the horses next door are just stunning. You are so lucky to live here."

"The security guard is there to keep unwanted people away. Thomas will have to show you the ranch we just bought. We wanted to buy the one next door but with the news of my "double life" as they are calling it, we decided to move closer to his sister and his work. So we bought a twenty acre ranch in the hills. It has a security gate and everything, plus room for Tommy and the baby to move around, and we can finally have the horses we want."

I sighed. "That sounds amazing." My phone buzzed with a text. I looked down and saw it was from Nathan.

Nathan: how about a moonlit stroll on the beach after the barbeque?

I must have grinned because Ginny hit my arm.

"Well, well, well, who was that from? Must be someone that makes you hot, in all the right places by the look on your face." She wiggled her eyebrows.

"Stop, it's just a guy I had coffee with a couple of times in college, I actually saw him last night and then he stopped and talked to me this morning."

"When? Where? What guy? Give me all the details. I am cooped up in this house and I need to know what is going on in the outside world."

I laughed; I mean, how could I not?

"We both went to NYU and I had coffee with him a few times, I really liked him but, eventually, our schedules didn't work and we went our separate ways. Anyways, last night, I was at the pub in Cambria…"

"Oh yeah, Thom said he ran into you there," she interrupted.

"Yeah, so this guy with curly red hair caught my eye, but then I started talking to Thomas. Then, last night I saw him running on the beach, and this morning he came up to the deck and started talking to me. Turns out, it was Nat, but he knew me in college as Nicole. Anywhoo, we exchanged numbers and I agreed to let him show me around."

"Oh, I love Nathan. He comes over here and spends time with Tommy a lot."

"He does? And he's even better looking now then he was in college. I mean, he is built, and hot as hell, and the curly hair just makes me want to run my fingers through it."

She laughed. "He is kind of hot." She fanned her face dramatically.

"Ginny," I said shocked.

"Oh, please, I'm not dead, just married."

I laughed, hard. "He asked if I wanted to go on a moonlit walk on the beach after the barbeque tonight." I bit my lip while I looked to her for advice.

"Girl, you better say yes."

"I want to…"

She took my phone out of my hands and sent him a reply.

"Ginny!"

"What? You would have waited and driven him and yourself crazy. So, I answered for you."

I took my phone back and saw what she said.

Me: I would love too.

"Doesn't that make me sound too eager?"

"Hell no. He's hot, go for it. If I learned anything from my past with Thomas, it's that you can't let fear win." She looked like she wanted to say something else but stopped.

"What?" I asked.

She shook her head. "I shouldn't say anything."

"Too late now, spill it." I sat down next to her.

"Ahh, I am blaming my hormones. Don't tell Nathan I said anything."

Oh, great, what's wrong with him?

"I won't say anything." I hoped I could keep this promise.

Sighing, she looked at me, sadness filling her eyes. "He just went through a horrible breakup about six months ago. His ex ran off with a bass player for a band that was in the area for a concert. He's been having a hard time moving on. He thought that they would be together forever. Instead, she left and is traveling the world with this guy."

Poor Nathan. I placed my hand across my heart. "Wow, you hear about that in movies and books but not in real life."

"I know. I felt so bad when Thomas told me. The guys have been trying to get him to leave the house for months. All he does is work and go home."

"Well, you couldn't tell he was heartbroken this morning. He was the one that came right up to the stairs and started talking. He even remembered me from back home."

"Really? Well this is an interesting development." She said as I watched her eyes light up.

"Why are you looking at me that way?"

"No reason…"

"Ginny…"

"What?"

"What are you planning?"

"Oh, nothing……"

My phone rang, I saw that it was the publishing house that I work for. I walked into the kitchen to take the call from New York and got consumed with work, our conversation long forgotten.

I DIDN'T EVEN REALIZE what time it was until I walked into the living room five hours later when Thomas came into the house with Nathan and several other people that seemed to know their way around the house.

Nathan caught my eye and smiled.

I did a small wave, which I never do, and he waved back.

After helping unload bag's of food and drinks, he walked over to me and brushed the hair behind my ear.

"Hi," I said, suddenly shy. I am never shy.

"Hi. How was your day?" he asked as he leaned against the counter.

"Busy. I had a lot to catch up on for the New York office, calls to make, and emails to answer. I still need to reschedule some interviews for Ginny after the baby is born, but I can do that Monday." I'm rambling.

"Well, you don't let the grass grow under your feet for long, do you?"

"No, I don't. I hate wasting time." I looked into his eyes.

"So do I." He took my hand and linked our fingers, and I felt a zap of energy run through my body.

Did he feel it too?

Before I could ask, we were interrupted.

"Nikki, have you met my sister and brother-in-law?"

I turned to Thomas and had to take my hand from Nathan's to shake hands with Thomas's sister. The next twenty minutes were filled with meeting people that Thomas works with and family members. I could feel Nathan watching me across from the room while I helped get the food ready, and I thought back to something that he said to me. He hates wasting time. I wonder what he meant by that?

6

NATHAN

I watched as Nikki moved around the room and mingled with everyone I work with or for. I never saw an ounce of shyness while she talked to a room full of people. I am sure that her job had a lot to do with that. But, when she was with me, I saw just a hint of nervousness and it's endearing, I'm sure that she shows everyone a tough New York side but I bet she has a softer side that I would love to get to know.

Sometime this morning, on my run back from the pub and talking to Kole, I realized that it was time to move on from Sarah and live again. She took six months from me and that's enough. There is something about Nikki that appeals to me; I can't wait to spend time with her later tonight.

I started to walk over to her when Ginny touched my hand to stop me.

"Hello, Ginny, how are you and the baby doing today?" I sat down next to her, leaning closer so we could hear each other.

"We're doing great, but I'm tired of not being able to move around much." She placed her hand on her small baby bump. "As long as I stay down and don't move around too much until after the second trimester is over, everything will be just fine."

I smiled at her. Ginny and Thomas are some of the nicest people that I have ever met.

"So, Nikki said something about you two going to NYU together and you went out for coffee a few times . That's kind of interesting, or, as my brother-in-law would say, it's fate."

Fate….. never thought about it much.

"I have heard Jon and his brothers talk about it at work, 'bout how fate and destiny brought them together with their spouses or girl-friends." I looked over at Nikki talking to Abby, Ginny's sister-in-law.

"They are big believers in fate, destiny and love at first sight. I'm just wondering if that's happened to you before?"

"What?" I asked, looking at her with a puzzled expression on my face.

"Love at first sight?" She looked at me, intently, almost like she was trying to read my mind.

"I don't know. I thought I loved Sarah, then she left me, and I felt like I was never going to get over it. Then, last night, I saw Nikki and I couldn't get her off my mind."

Ginny smiled.

"What?"

"Oh, nothing, I just think that you've just had your first experience with fate. You can't get her off your mind and you want to spend more time with her, right? That's how fate works. Trust me, I know."

I stared at her like she has two heads.

"Trust me, don't fight it."

I shook my head.

"Don't fight what?" Nikki asked as she approached, Thomas right beside her.

"Oh, nothing, " Ginny said.

"What are you talking about?" Thomas asked.

"Fate and destiny." Nikki turn a bright shade of red and I felt the heat in my face rising, too.

"Um, excuse us." I took Nikki's hand and we made our way outside to the deck, then down the stairs to the grass, walking to the fence line to give us privacy. I turned to look at her. "Are you all right?"

"Yes, I just wasn't expecting that conversation to be happening when I walked up with Thomas."

I rubbed the back of my neck, hoping that I could ease the tension building there. "Let's try and forget about what Ginny said and have a good time tonight," I said as I brushed the hair off her face and pushed it behind her ear. It was a simple move that felt personal to me.

"I should be used to the way she talks about all that stuff, but to hear her talk about me that way, right now with you, well, it was a shock."

Placing my finger under her chin, compelling her to look at me, I said. "She didn't mean anything by it. She probably just wants you to be happy. That's all. And she writes romance novels, so she always looks for the happy ending."

Where did that come from?

Standing on her tiptoes, she kissed my cheek "Thank you, I shouldn't be so surprised."

I stood there and looked at her. Did she feel the zing of electricity when her lips touched my cheek? It wasn't the first time, I felt it when I moved her hair. Before I could say anything else, I could hear Thomas asking Nikki if she has met his parents. She touched my arm and excused herself while I stood there and watched, stunned by what I was feeling. Could Ginny be right and I am falling for her?

7

NIKKI

What just happened? Had he felt the zap of electricity when he touched me? Was I imagining it? Or was Ginny getting in my head and making me believe all that mumbo jumbo? I couldn't concentrate on what was happening around me.

Thomas was introducing me to his parents, and all I wanted to do was talk to Nathan and find out if he felt the same thing. My heart was pounding in my chest while I listened to the conversation around me, and all I could think of was how I felt when he touched me. I felt his presence when he came up behind me.

Placing his hand on my lower back, he shook hands with everyone, then asked me if I wanted a beer.

"Yes, please."

He smiled and walked to the cooler to grab a few beers, once back he handed them out, he also had a small bottle of wine for Thomas's mom. Once the drinks were handed out, Nathan placed his hand on my back again.

My stomach tightened and a rush of electricity pulsed through my veins.

What in God's name is happening here?

"If you all don't mind, Nikki and I have some catching up to do.

We knew each other in college." He led me through the gate and out to the front, where we could be alone. "I thought you might need some space from the insistent introductions."

Looking at him for the first time since we left the chaos of the yard, he was looking at me with an intense expression on his face.

"It was getting a little overwhelming. I know Thomas means well, but I didn't need to meet everyone all at once. I will be here for months, so there will be time to get to know everyone important to them. In fact, I think that I might end up moving here to be her full-time assistant."

The hopeful look in his eyes was enough to make me want to tell him about the strange feeling I have been having when he touches me.

"Really? When did you get the news about being transferred to California?"

"Today, when I spoke with the publishing house about the schedule for her next year. With the baby due in about six months, and the need for her to be on bedrest, we realized that I need to be here full-time."

Linking his fingers with mine, he kissed my hand. "Does this mean there is a possibility for us to pick up where we left off? I know it's been a couple of years, but I never stopped thinking about you. I just couldn't find the time to give a relationship my full attention. And it wouldn't have been fair to try. You would have resented me in the end." Pulling me a little closer and looking into my eyes, he smiled. "Finding you here was like fate brought us together at the right time. When I realized it was you, I felt like my heart was going to beat out of my chest."

"You did?" I asked, moving my hand up to his cheek and smiling.

"I really did. I regretted not keeping in touch with you. I always thought you would be married by now."

Laughing, I said, "Nope." I covered my mouth, embarrassment written all over my face. Wishing the ground would open up and swallow me, because I didn't mean to blurt that out!!

He leaned down, hesitating just a few inches away from my lips as if waiting for me to stop him. Instead, I leaned closer and pressed my lips to his. The spark was instantaneous, and I felt it all the way to my toes. His tongue sweeping against my lips, asking for entry. I opened my mouth and he deepened the kiss. Placing his hand behind my head, anchoring me to him, his tongue danced with mine. It was the most intense kiss of my life. Kissing anyone else had never felt like this.

Breaking the kiss when we needed air, I looked at him, not believing what just happened.

"Holy crap, that was intense," Nathan said as he ran his thumb over my kiss swollen lips.

"Yes, it was. I….. well……" I closed my eyes.

"Have never been kissed like that before?" he asked, leaning down and kissing me again.

How could he tell? I could hear someone calling my name in the distance, it permeated my addled brain. The voice got closer and I pulled back. Feeling my cheeks heating from the intensity of the kiss. I licked my swollen lips and looked down at the ground.

"Someone is calling your name. He said while he tipped my chin up to look at him.

I swallowed hard and nodded. Turning around, I saw Thomas standing on his porch. I turned and waved. "I will be there in a minute," I yelled.

He nodded and walked back into the house.

"I should really get back to the party."

Cupping my face, he kissed me softly. "I can't wait for our walk on the beach tonight." He smiled down at me.

I swear he is scrambling my brain. Licking my lips, I smiled. "I can't either." Taking his hand, I led him back into the house. All the while, my mind was spinning. I was so confused by what I was feeling.

If he had been thinking about me all this time, then why didn't he contact me? And what about the girlfriend that left him? Ginny said he's been upset for six months, but he doesn't seem upset. I need to talk to her before we leave. I didn't want to set myself up for heartache if the ex came waltzing back into his life.

Before we left, I asked Ginny if I could talk to her in private. I helped her into their room and closed the door. After getting her settled on the bed, I sat down next to her and took a deep breath.

"What's wrong, Nikki?" she asked as she took my hand.

"I am so confused about Nathan." I played with a tassel on the pillow next to me.

"Why? You both seemed to be getting along very well, if my eyes weren't playing tricks on me." She winked. "Please, tell me what's wrong."

Sighing, I closed my eyes, not wanting the feelings that were just below the surface to boil over. "I really like him. I always have. And he said that he never stopped thinking about me, but ... he never contacted me. Then, there's the ex who you said broke his heart, but he shows no sign of heartbreak at all, and I don't want to get involved with him if there is a chance that she will drop back into his life. And this is all happening so fast. I mean really fast."

She just stared at me, her mouth agape.

"Well, you asked," I said.

"First of all, the ex isn't coming back. This area doesn't have enough glitz and glamour for her. Second, he was heartbroken until he found you, again. Trust me when I say that she is the farthest thing from his mind. You consume his thoughts. I saw it in his eyes." Squeezing my hand, she compelled me to look at her. "Have you asked him why he never contacted you again?"

"He told me that he was busy with school, and because of the time we spent apart, he figured I was married by now." I shrugged.

"Don't you believe him?" she asked.

I bit my lip, trying to stop the tears. "I want to, I really do, but it happened so suddenly."

She tugs on my hand. "This wasn't suddenly, if I am reading things right, these feelings have been under the surface since the last night, right?" she asked, and I nodded "You tell me all the time that you wish you could find someone like Thomas that will sweep you off your feet, or like the guys in my books that will suck the air out of the room, or make it feel like your heart is colliding with his. That's Nathan. He's that guy. I have known him for a few years, and he treats his mom or any woman like they hung the moon. He isn't giving you a line. If anything, he is looking for the same thing you are. I will tell you the same thing that I told him, that fate and destiny all played a part in you and Nathan finding each other again. I am a big believer in destiny, but you already knew that."

I did; she has been talking about it since she brought Thomas to New York last year.

"Take the leap and give him a chance."

I leaned over and hugged her. "Thank you. I think I will."

The door opened and Tommy ran into the room, stopping short of jumping on the bed.

"Mom, Grandma said I can spend the night. Can I, please?" He jumped up and down next to the bed.

"I will leave you two to talk. I am going to thank Thomas for the party and find Nathan. Talk tomorrow." I turned to leave…

"Nikki, let go of the worries and see where it goes."

I nodded and left the room.

8

NATHAN

I followed Nikki back to the beach house and parked in my garage. I told her I would meet her on her deck in twenty minutes, so after grabbing a sweatshirt and blanket, I walked down the beach to her cottage. With every step, my heart pounded, drowning out the sound of the ocean. The anticipation of spending time alone with her was something I had never felt before . My hands were beginning to sweat, even though it's cold outside. I walked up the steps to her cottage, and there she was, standing in the doorway, with a NYU sweatshirt on and a big smile on her face. She opened the door farther and bit the side of her lip. I reached up and pulled her lip from between her teeth, then ran my finger over the mark.

"Don't bite your lips; they are too pretty to have bite marks and bruises." I leaned down and lightly kissed her. "Hi."

"Hi. Do you know that you said the same thing to me the first time we had coffee?"

Shaking my head, I brushed some hair behind her ear.

"We were meeting for coffee before a movie, and I have a nervous habit of biting my lip. You said the exact same thing then, too."

"And you remember that specific detail? Out of everything else that people have said to you over the years?" I cupped her face in my hands.

"No one ever made me feel like you did, even with just kisses and holding hands. You made me feel special."

I dropped the blanket and took her in my arms, not caring that people could see us if they were walking on the beach with us backlit by the house lights. She wrapped her arms around me and leaned into the kiss. Deepening the kiss, her moan vibrated through my body.

"What are you doing to me?" I asked, kissing her neck.

"The same thing you are doing to me." She ran her hands through my hair in a gentle caress that made me shudder.

Pulling back, I looked her in the eyes, cupping her face and running my thumb over her bottom lip.

"Come on, let's take that walk while the moon is out and the tide is low. I brought a blanket so we can sit and talk."

"I have one, too." She reached for the blanket that was on the barstool.

After closing the door, I followed her down the stairs, and we held hands as we walked down towards the water. The foam from the waves glowed in the moonlight. We found a spot on the sand, placed one blanket down and left the other for later. Then I took her hand and we walked towards the outcropping of rocks. Leaning against them, I took her in my arms again, nuzzling her neck.

I inhaled deeply, "Mm, you smell so good… like roses and peaches." I nibbled on her ear.

Leaning her head to the side she held on tight. "It's my favorite shampoo; it always smells like summer."

"Yes, it does." I pulled back and looked at her in the moonlight. "I want to apologize for not calling you again. I never should have let school take over my life. I have regretted it all these years. I just wanted you to know."

Placing her finger over my lips she leaned over and kissed me. "I was just as much to blame; I had your number and could have called." Leaning her head against mine, she took a deep breath. "You know, Ginny told me to take a chance and let destiny take its course."

"Funny, Ginny and Kole said the same thing."

"Kole? From the pub?" she asked, shock apparent in her voice.

"Yes, Kole from the pub. I stopped by there yesterday and he told me where you lived and that I should see what destiny had in store for us. His wife was a big believer in destiny."

"I don't understand, how did he know where I live? How did he know about us?" she asked, incredulous.

"I have no idea, but with two people saying that same thing, I think we need to listen to them and see where this goes."

"I……..um……. I do, too."

I took her face in my hands and kissed her, starting off soft and light, but feeling the spark of desire igniting between us. I felt her start to shake.

"Are you cold?" I asked, pulling her closer to me.

"A little."

"Let's go back to the blanket, wrap up, and get to know each other again."

Once we were wrapped up in the blanket and reclining on our sides, I pulled her to me again, kissing her with the same intensity as before. Next thing I knew, I was laying on top of her, pressing my erection into the warmth of her body. "Nikki, God I have never had these feelings before. I don't want to move too fast."

Placing her finger on my lips, she smiled. "I feel the same way, and if we were going too fast, I would stop you. I never do this with someone I just met, but I was reminded earlier tonight that we are picking up where we left off, not starting over again. So, it is not too fast. I promise." Kissing me, she said against my lips, "I want to be with you, and I think that we needed the time apart to realize that we were meant to be together. If not, then why does my heart practically beat out of my chest when I think of you or see you, or when you have your arms around me?"

Leaning down to nibble on her ear, I said, "Your house or mine?"

"Mine is closer."

I helped her up, grabbing the blankets, then we ran to the house. Taking the steps two at a time, she opened the door and stepped inside, then I closed it behind me. Turning to me, she ran her hands under my sweatshirt, pulling it up and over my head. Everywhere she touched, I felt the heat of her hands. I unzipped her sweatshirt and pushed it off her shoulders. She stood there in a sexy black bra that pushed her breasts up, making them spill over.

"You are so beautiful," I said, running my thumb over her nipples through the black lace, making them harden.

"Nathan…" she said, letting her head fall backwards.

I took the opportunity to kiss her neck, moving my hands down her body to the waistband of her shorts. Feeling her tremble , I unsnapped them and left them on her hips. Moving my hands around to her back, pulling her to me, feeling her skin against mine, I groaned and let my hand travel down to her ass, squeezing and pulling her against my erection, letting her feel what her nearness did to me.

"Nikki, I want you so bad," I panted.

"I want you, too, just as bad."

"Bedroom?" I asked, picking her up in my arms and walking through the house.

"The door at the end of the hallway," she said.

Once inside, I placed her on the bed and just looked at her. She was so beautiful, flawless skin and sexy kissable lips. I was a stupid fool to let school and life get in the way.

Never again.

This was a new beginning for us both. I slowly removed the rest of her clothes, leaving her in just a barely-there black thong. As I quickly removed my clothes, she shimmied out of the thong and scooted back on the bed, opening her arms to me.

I climbed on the bed and hovered over her. "You are so beautiful."

A faint blush spread from her cheeks down her neck.

So sexy. I ran my hand from her neck down to her breast, where I played with her nipple. Leaning down. I took her nipple in my mouth and sucked, swirling my tongue, then sucking again. She arched her back into me, calling out my name. My hand moved down between her legs and I found her wet and ready for me. Letting her nipple pop from my lips, I kissed my way down to her core. I pressed my finger to her sensitive spot, and she gasped. Moving so her legs were over my shoulders, I swirled my tongue around her clit, gently sucking until she cried out in pleasure. I slipped a finger inside her, then a second, testing how ready she was for me. Withdrawing my fingers, I moved swiftly to my jeans and I pulled a condom from my jeans.

Rolling it on, I moved back up her body until I was seated between her legs, nudging at her wet entrance with the tip of my cock. "Nikki, look at me." Her eyes fluttered open to stare into my eyes. "Are you sure?"

"Yes, I am very sure."

I slowly pushed into her, giving her a chance to get used to my size.

"Nat…"

I looked down at her and was instantly hit with the feeling of rightness. She is the one. Once I was seated to the hilt, I didn't move, just feeling our hearts beat as one.

"Nikki, God, you feel amazing."

I started to slowly move and, she met me with every stroke, the squeeze of her internal muscles making me grit my teeth. While I moved faster, she held me tighter.

"Nathan, oh God, almost there……"

I moved my hand between her legs and pressed on her clit, causing her to detonate. She squeezed my cock so hard I saw stars. She wrapped her arms around my back and held me tight.

"Nathan, I've never…"

"Felt anything like that before?"

She grinned. "Yes, it was amazing."

I leaned down and kissed her. "I guess everyone was right."

"About what?" she asked, rubbing lazy circles on my back.

"That we were meant to be together."

She smiled and brought me down for a kiss. "I guess they were."

THE END for now

Learn more about Kenzie Rose:
https://linktr.ee/authorkenzierose

Also by Kenzie Rose:
　Everlasting Love
　She's My Destiny
　Love in Texas

THE SCENT OF HER

PEPPER NORTH

**Sometimes fate matches two people.
Or is the magic of the Storybook Pub at work once again?**

Sub-genre: Shifters
Relationship: Male/Female

1

A movement at the door captured Kole O'Shea's attention. The pub was packed on the cold Saturday evening. She shouldn't have attracted his attention, but she did. He paid attention when someone stood out. Kole considered it was a sign from his late wife, Rebecca. He would always heed Rebecca's signals.

Catching the newcomer's gaze as she froze indecisively at the entrance, Kole waved her forward to a suddenly vacant seat at the bar. The stocking-cap-clad woman glanced behind her to double-check that he wasn't talking to someone standing behind her. When that space was empty, she touched her chest in a silent, *Me?*

Laughing, Kole nodded and waved a bit more enthusiastically. His movements drew the attention of the gentleman on the neighboring stool to the newcomer as well as he traced Kole's line of vision to the door. Out of the corner of his eye, the bar owner saw the man smile at the adorable picture she presented. When she approached, Kole noted her neighbor's shocked, deep inhale.

"Um, hi!" The hesitant words tumbled from the young woman's mouth as she scooted her bottom onto the tall stool. She pulled that bright pink stocking cap from her head, unleashing a static-cling-fueled array of light brown hair in all directions. Then, as if she'd forgotten that she wore mittens, the new arrival yanked off their mismatched lime green and blue polka-dotted warmth.

"Hi! Welcome to the Storybook Pub. I'm Kole, the owner. I don't think I've seen you in here before."

"I just started a new job down the street. It was a pretty rough day. I thought I deserved a drink," she explained. "I don't ever drink. I don't even know what to order," she admitted.

"How about a Shirley Temple for the newest devotee of the bar?" the quiet man to her left suggested.

Startled by the man's words, the brunette turned her head to meet her neighbor's gaze. Her mouth fell open slightly as she stared at him. After several seconds, she seemed to realize that they were waiting for her to say something. She repeated, "Um, hi?" This time her voice rose as if questioning why he would waste time talking to her.

"I think a Shirley Temple is a perfect drink choice for..." Kole allowed his voice to trail away as he waited for her to give them her name. When she didn't answer, he smiled. She couldn't tear her eyes from the distinguished man next to her. Nodding, Kole faded into the background as he mixed the nonalcoholic, sweet drink for his new patron.

2

"Tell me your name," Vincent commanded. His deep voice contained the force of his dominance and his interest in the adorable woman beside him.

"Um... I'm Brea. Brea Scott."

Vincent stared at the oval face of his newly discovered mate. He tried to memorize her appearance, knowing that he'd never forget the moment he'd met Brea Scott. When she looked away in discomfort at his studying gaze, Vincent spoke quickly to reassure her.

"Brea Scott, it is my pleasure to meet you. My name is Vincent Woods. You must forgive me for staring. You reminded me of someone I met years ago." He invented an excuse smoothly and was pleased to see her tense posture relax.

When Kole slid the pink drink in front of her, Vincent nodded his thanks. The owner's acknowledgment confirmed his suspicion that Brea's presence next to him had not been solely chance. The rumors of Kole's touch in pairing couples together were obviously correct. As Brea picked up the drink to sip it tentatively, Kole faded away, leaving the two of them enwrapped in an intimate bubble created by the noisy atmosphere around them.

"Mmmm! This is absolutely yummy!" Brea complimented as she took another larger drink. "I hope this isn't too dangerous."

His lips spread in a delighted grin. "A Shirley Temple does not have a drop of alcohol in it. It is the perfect drink for someone to enjoy as they relax from the day."

"It is delicious," the young brunette agreed. "Oh, I'm sorry. I didn't mean to monopolize your time. I bet you were holding this seat free for someone to join you." She started to scoot off the stool and lost her balance. As she began to tumble, Vincent's arm quickly wrapped around her and steadied her in place.

"There is no one else who I'd like to talk to, Brea. Take pity on an old man. Enjoy your drink and chat with me," he requested as he reluctantly released his arm from her body. The touch, even through layers of clothing, had reinforced that she was his mate. There was no doubt.

"Oh, you're not old. Just a few years older than me. I'm probably older than I look," Brea reassured him, leaning in to whisper confidentially. "I'm twenty-seven."

"You are correct. I am a few years older than you," Vincent agreed without disclosing his age. Those in his family lived longer than most. He would share this information later with her. Smoothly changing the topic, he asked, "Tell me about your first day at work, Brea."

"Oh, gracious. I'm a bit accident-prone," Brea admitted. "I didn't even make it into the building before someone bumped into me at the door. I fell and tore my hose." Scooting back on the stool, she slid her coat off to the side to display a large hole in the suntan pantyhose she wore.

Admiring the plump thigh that she also displayed for his view, Vincent narrowed his focus to her injury that still oozed slightly. "Ouch! That must have hurt!"

"It did. And the guy didn't even stop. I cried. Unfortunately, that made my mascara run. I had to run to the bathroom to clean my knee and wash off the makeup I'd applied so carefully to make a good impression. Thank goodness, I had arrived early. At least I wasn't late."

Vincent studied her bare face, enjoying the look of her, not the layers of makeup that many felt they needed to wear. Her eyes were dark brown and filled with life. She might be accident-prone, but Vincent could tell that Brea didn't focus on negative things. Her face shone with positivity.

"That is a tough start to the day. I'm sure it must have gotten better." Leaning in, he tried to focus on her response, but her scent tantalized.

"Oh, no. It kept getting worse," Brea laughed and lifted her glass to take another large drink.

Seeing Kole reappear in front of her, she complimented him, "This is so good. How much do I owe you?"

"It has already been taken care of," Kole answered with a slight nod of his head toward Vincent. Before she could react, he added, "Your table is ready, Mr. Woods. It's there in the corner." He pointed to an isolated spot in the bustling pub.

"Oh! Thank you for the drink. It's been nice talking to you," Brea rushed to say as Vincent stood.

He watched her eyes trace his form. Arrogantly, he stood still, allowing her to study the powerful muscles that he had built over the years. Vincent had grown used to women throwing themselves at him. Now, he realized that only his mate's opinion was important. He wanted his body to attract her.

"Oh!" Brea exclaimed again, and her face blushed a beautiful shade of pink. "I'm sorry for staring," she apologized.

"Come have dinner with me, Brea. I wish to hear about the rest of your day." His hand cupped under her elbow to help Brea gently to her feet. His other hand lifted her drink from the bar as he guided her toward the empty table that waited.

"Really? You want me to join you?" she stammered.

"Yes," he said simply before sliding his hand down the enveloping sleeve of her coat to link his fingers with hers. As her bare skin contacted his, an electric thrill spread from their joined hands.

"Oh!" she repeated for the third time.

Vincent decided that it was his new favorite word. He looked forward to hearing her scream those two letters in passion. With his goal set in stone, he tugged her gently to their table.

3

Brea hid behind the menu the waitress had given her. Her whirling thoughts tumbled in her head as she snuck peeks at the handsome man across the table. *He can't be interested in me. That's crazy. Look at him!* She peeked again.

Studying the dark brown hair that brushed his collar, Brea realized the brighter light in the dining area revealed that his hair contained streaks of red and blond highlights. She clenched her fingers around the menu when a sudden desire struck her to reach out and brush her fingers through the silken strands. He'd think she was a complete weirdo, she told herself.

"Never, Brea," Vincent promised.

Startled, she realized that she must have said that last line aloud. Rushing to apologize, her eyes linked with his. Those devastating brown eyes flashed red and then returned to their usual brown. "What...?" she began to question but stopped as the waitress came to take their order.

Desperately, she looked down at the menu she hadn't even read. A warm hand covered hers as it clenched the stiff paper. Looking up, she watched Vincent wink at her. It was so conspiratorial that she almost laughed.

"We'll both have the special, please," he smoothly ordered.

When the waitress smiled and darted away into the busy pub, Brea leaned forward to ask, "Do you know what the special is?"

"Not a clue," he admitted. "We'll find out together."

She felt her lips smile genuinely for the first time that day. Not the fake smile she'd shared throughout the awful day as she tried to look at things positively. This was real. It felt good to have someone to do silly things together. Brea lifted her Shirley Temple to salute him and took another drink.

"Thanks," she impulsively blurted.

"For what?" he asked with a puzzled frown.

"For inviting me to dinner," she explained.

"Take your coat off, Brea. Stay for a while," he invited. "I don't intend to let you go."

His words could have been threatening, but they weren't. A thrill ran down her back as Brea shrugged out of her coat. She waited to see his disappointment when she revealed her too-curvy body. At the sight of desire flaring red in his gaze again, she relaxed her desperate attempts to sit up straight with her tummy sucked in. Vincent seemed to like her just as she was. He held her gaze as he helped her settle her coat and purse on an empty chair.

When their meal came, she enjoyed the delicious flavor of the dishes. Forking another bite into her mouth, she almost hummed with delight. *This is so much better than salad.* Brea watched Vincent consume his entire plate with impeccable manners. To her delight, he caught the waitress's attention to order another plate.

"Brea, would you like another serving as well?" he checked with her before the waitress left for the kitchen.

She instantly regretted all the leafy greens she had eaten during the few first dates she'd had in the past. This was a man who invited her to eat more. "Oh, no. Thank you. I have plenty here," she reassured him as she took another bite. She relaxed a bit more in his company. She'd been on dates where the man had watched her eat so closely that she'd only eaten a few bites before going home to cook another dinner. Vincent seemed to want her to eat.

Impulsively, she set down her fork and reached her hand across to him. Brea needed to test that reaction she'd had to his touch. Surely, she'd imagined that zing of pleasure. When his fingers wrapped around hers, she shivered. She hadn't imagined it.

"Brea, I know you can feel it as well." Vincent's low voice demanded her response. When she nodded, he continued. "I have been searching for you for many years. For my people, there is only one fated match. The desire we both feel as we touch is one sign that you are mine. I don't intend to let you go."

A red flash filled his gaze as she stared at him. "I don't understand," she whispered after several seconds.

"Search your heart. Does it recognize me?" he asked, softly squeezing Brea's hand to remind her of that electric zing.

Immediately, her mind wanted to deny his question. Starting to shake her head, Brea found that she couldn't. She couldn't lie to him. Nodding, she repeated, "I don't understand."

Vincent's hand released hers, and instantly she missed his touch. When he reached forward to cup the back of her head, she moved forward as he drew her close. Brea fixed her gaze on his lips. Her eyelids fluttered closed at the last moment to concentrate on the feel of his mouth against hers.

The ambiance of the pub faded from her mind as his lips seduced hers. Holding her securely in place, he tasted her as if they had all the time in the world to explore the desire that drew them together. Brea melted against him. There was no resistance possible to his dominance. He would always be in charge.

4

Brea didn't know where the time had gone. Standing in front of her door, she studied the handsome man beside her. As she tried to come up with something glib to say, expecting that she'd never see him again, Vincent leaned in to kiss her again. Her body arched toward him, seeking contact with his body.

"I hope that tomorrow will be a better day. I will meet you at the doors to your building at 5:00 p.m. If you allow me, I'll take you home for dinner," Vincent proposed minutes later when he raised his head.

It sounded like an invitation, but it was more. Brea knew she couldn't refuse him. "Yes, Vincent. I'd like that," she answered with a smile.

Watching him walk away, Brea couldn't understand how anyone could move as he did. She traced his athletic form with her gaze and allowed her mind to picture him nude. The resulting wave of arousal made Brea clench her thighs tightly together.

When Vincent glanced back over his shoulder with desired chiseled into his expression, Brea felt a gush of arousal dampen her upper thighs. Her panties had been wet from his first touch. *He knows*, she thought.

At the sight of his matching desire, she didn't blush. She felt her lips curl into a knowing smile. She wanted him to know she was aroused. After lifting a polka-dotted glove to wave, Brea ducked into her apartment. She couldn't wait to dream of him.

5

Weird dreams filled Brea's sleep. The distinctive sound of a howl echoed in the images that drifted through her mind. She pictured a large wolf with brown fur gleaming with red and golden threads. It paced through the edges of her dreams as if marking his territory.

Brea wasn't afraid of the massive animal. Her heart beat faster each time he appeared or she heard his call. She knew the beast was speaking to her—not summoning her yet but letting her know he was there. Reassured, she relaxed into a deeper sleep.

The ring of the alarm jolted her from the best dream. Replaying it in her mind, Brea smiled as she remembered the shadowy figure that had wooed her. There was no doubt that he was Vincent.

Catching a glimpse of the time, Brea burst from the bed in a flurry of rushed activity. She dressed professionally in a pantsuit she hoped would redeem her from the bedraggled appearance that she'd shown everyone on her first day. Brea managed to drink a cup of coffee while putting on her makeup without spilling a drop on her cream-colored shirt.

She grabbed a totally non-nutritious packet of toaster pastries and ran for her purse. Brea needed to leave now. To her delight, the bus arrived minutes after she did, and there was even a seat left for her.

Sailing off the bus, she walked into her new office building with ten minutes to spare. Brea offered smiles and good-mornings to each person she passed. Their responses were not as enthusiastic, but she hoped maybe she'd helped turn their day around.

Brea checked her schedule on her computer and discovered once again that a financial spreadsheet had been emailed to her. The copy-and-paste directions were to approve the account logs and submit them to her superior. A terse message provided his name and email.

She looked around, disoriented. Yesterday, she'd assumed that being asked to dive into work was a test to check her work ethic. The receptionist had pointed out her desk and told her to look for a computer with her directions for the day. Now, on the second day, it just seemed wrong. This was it? There wasn't an orientation? No forms to fill out for payroll and benefits? Shouldn't she meet her boss?

Brea looked around to see if there were any friendly faces she could approach to ask some questions or at least to find some supplies. She worked best on paper. No one would meet her gaze. Finally, she resorted to stealing paper from the copy machine. Thank goodness, she'd brought some essentials from home.

Opening her purse to find the pen, pencil, and eraser, Brea dug through all the miscellaneous stuff in her purse to the bottom where everything collected. Her fingers closed on a cold metallic disk. Immediately a tingle went through her body, feeling just as it had when Vincent had touched her last night.

She pulled the coin from her purse to examine it. The profile of a wolf was etched into one side. Flipping the coin, she read Vincentius. Vincent! Brea somehow felt protected holding on to the coin. Without understanding why she was secretive, Brea slipped it into her pocket to have it close to her. Instantly, it seemed to warm in her pocket.

Oddly comforted, Brea began to crunch the numbers on the accounting sheet. Something bothered her. She went through the sheet three times before she found it—an odd discrepancy. The figures appeared to add up in each column. Brea noticed at irregular intervals an unexplained debit would occur.

In a mass of numbers and entries, she would expect it that the varying amount would be overlooked as a standard business charge. Now that she had detected it, the entries seemed to become neon signs capturing her attention. She began to star the questionable withdrawals.

Had she missed this yesterday? Opening the drawer where she'd stored her calculations and notes from yesterday, Brea looked astonished at the bare metal. She slid a hand inside, sweeping to the back. Nothing. Who would have taken her notes? No one other than herself would have been able to decipher the random numbers and codes she'd jotted on the sheet of paper with her name and login information.

Perhaps the cleaning crew had collected it as trash. Dismissing the concern, she hunched over the figures and began to complete a report. At lunch, Brea ate the peanut butter sandwich she had thrust into her purse just in case.

The other employees ate at their desks. Surrounded by the cubicle walls, Brea could only see the tops of their heads, angled over their computers. When she'd approached the people on each side of her cube, they'd just tapped their earphones and shook their heads. Checking with the receptionist, she'd gotten a chilly response, and another waved a hand toward a far hallway. No one in Human Resources yesterday or today had answered her knock on the door.

When people began to disappear from their desks, Brea looked at her watch. Unable to stop her smile, she felt the coin warm in her pocket. She emailed the supervisor listed on her work assignment, sharing her preliminary findings and asking to schedule a meeting. After taking a few minutes to hide her notes surreptitiously behind the back of the bottom drawer, Brea powered down her computer. She plugged it in to be ready for the next day.

Finally, it was time to go see Vincent. *What if he isn't there?* The negative thought popped in her head as Brea donned her coat and pulled on her mismatched mittens. The coin seemed to warm in her pocket to reassure her. He'd be there.

6

Vincent stood quietly positioned before the bank of doors to Brea's new company. A thick stream of frazzled employees hurried through as if seeking their freedom. He frowned at the thought that everyone disliked working there. That was not the right atmosphere for his mate. Thank goodness, she would not be there for long.

When he spotted Brea's bright pink hat, Vincent moved forward to meet her. The flow of employees automatically adjusted for his presence. Even those glued to their phones moved out of the trajectory to avoid crashing into him. He loved the genuine smile that replaced the one frozen on her lips as she noticed him and changed her path to meet him.

Without a word, he swept her into his arms and pressed an urgent kiss to her lips. "I missed you, Brea," he breathed as he lifted his mouth slightly from hers.

She blinked at him as if in a daze before admitting, "I missed you so much."

His mouth captured hers again in a heated kiss as he pulled her body against his. This longer exchange left them both breathless when he finally lifted his head. Her adorable reaction captured his heart as that polka-dotted glove covered her mouth.

"Come, Brea. I am eager to show you my home," Vincent urged. With one arm wrapped around her waist, he escorted her to the waiting car and driver. Not a limo. Vincent was too practical for that type of car in the city. Who really liked to crawl into those things, anyway?

The luxury sedan stood at the curb with the driver at the ready. As they approached, Vincent took the time to introduce the staff member to her. "Brea, this is Eric. He has negotiated these streets for me for over ten years now. He is at your disposal now."

"Miss, it is a pleasure to meet you," Eric greeted her with a smile as he opened the rear door.

"Thank you… Eric." She stumbled through her words and lost her balance. Vincent's arm steadied her smoothly as he helped her into the car. Brea turned to stare at the enigmatic man that slid in beside her. "You have a car? Who are you?"

"I am Vincent Woods, nothing more and nothing less. I am the man who was delighted to meet you last night and has looked forward to spending the evening with you. Is there anything more important than that?" he asked, distracting her from the plush interior of the vehicle.

"Um… no," she answered hesitantly.

When he held his hand out to hold hers, she paused for a few seconds before pulling off that famous mitten and linking her fingers with his. Almost instantly, her posture softened as she relaxed against the seat. "I missed you too," she confided.

"Then, it is good that we are together again," Vincent replied before leaning in to kiss her once again. When Brea's eyes darted to the back of Eric's head as he pulled into traffic, Vincent reassured her in a low voice that would not be overheard. "Eric is very well trained. He is not listening but paying total attention to the rush-hour traffic. I can put up the privacy screen if you wish?"

"Oh, no," Brea answered quickly before sitting up slightly to stare at the back of the front seat before her. He could tell she was searching for the hiding place of that barrier.

"How was your day, Brea?" he asked to distract her once again.

"I didn't cry in the bathroom," she answered with a laugh. "It was weird. No one talks. I hope I'm doing what I'm supposed to do. I haven't even talked to anyone in HR." Unsure what she should share, she added, "I'm intrigued by the work they have given me."

Vincent's staff had rapidly compiled a dossier of information on Brea Scott, age twenty-seven. He had not been concerned about her background but supremely curious. Immediately after reading the information, he had shredded it in his office.

"Tell me, Brea. What do you do?"

"Oh, I'm pretty boring for you, I'm sure," Brea shared before rushing ahead when his eyes darkened at her unflattering words about herself. "I'm a forensic accountant. You know the kind of number cruncher that searches through old records to find mistakes or investigate something."

"That does not seem boring at all. You must be very skilled in finding what others have missed or… hidden," Vincent shrewdly commented.

"You wouldn't believe the stuff I've found," she confided. "But usually it's super boring. Especially to non-number people."

Glimpsing the large iron gate ahead, Brea sat forward to peer through the windshield. "You don't live here, do you?"

"This is my house. Welcome," Vincent answered smoothly as the car proceeded down a long, tree-lined drive to park in front of a historic, stone mansion.

His lips quirked up at the corners when she inhaled loudly at the sight of the home which he intended to be hers—soon. Studying the vast stone façade glowing from the modern lighting, Vincent knew that the estate would appear striking to the young woman next to him. He squeezed her hand to quiet the nervousness that stiffened her body.

"It is simply a house, Brea—a beautiful one granted—that I have worked hard to establish for my mate. I am looking forward to showing it to you. Will you come in for dinner?" he murmured, close to her ear.

When she nodded, he pressed his lips to the warm skin just behind the enchanting curve of her ear. Her responsive shiver made him dare to nip lightly at her earlobe, drawing a stronger response.

"Oh, Vincent!"

Leaning slightly away, he met her heated gaze. "It will be so good between us, my heart. But only when you are ready."

She nodded at his reassurance and clung to his hand. Whispering, "I don't understand this," she searched his face for answers.

"Dinner first, and then I will explain," he promised her. When she nodded again, he pressed a small button to alert Eric that it was time to open the car door.

Vincent slid from the seat and leaned in to scoop his mate from the car. Her arms clutched his neck as if she expected he would drop her. "Relax, my heart. I would never hurt you. Your safety is my highest priority." Effortlessly striding up the stairs, Vincent held her to his body, cherishing the feel of her body pressed to his. Then, when she relaxed into his arms, the thrill of knowing that she trusted his strength to guard her against harm.

7

Dinner had been a whirlwind of one delicious plate after another. She'd loved the delightful, scant glass of wine that Vincent had poured her. Brea loved that he had not pressured her to drink more. She'd wanted to stay clearheaded, and even the small amount had been slightly intoxicating.

Now, sipping coffee with the delicious cheesecake served as the main course, Brea wondered at the number of calories she had just consumed. Surreptitiously scanning his athletic form, she wondered how he stayed so fit while eating like this regularly.

"My chef is very skilled in preparing dishes that I enjoy eating, Brea. Did you enjoy tonight's meal?"

Laughing at herself, she admitted, "You caught me. I was just calculating all the calories in my mind. You are a dangerous man to hang around. I won't fit in any of my clothes after another meal like that." Unable to resist, she took the last bite of the creamy dessert.

"You are beautifully formed, Brea. A few more pounds would only make you more delectable," Vincent complimented her. Then he continued. "At your wish, however, the chef will be delighted to prepare a lighter fare for our next meal. Tomorrow, I think you will find his dishes to be delicious at a lower calorie count as well."

"Will I be having dinner with you tomorrow?" she asked in surprise.

"Yes. I think it is time we talked." Signaling to the table attendant, Vincent directed, "We'll retire to my study."

He stood and held his hand out to Brea to assist her from her chair. "Let's stroll through the greenery. I enclose it to combat the cold at this time of the year. I think you will enjoy the moonlight."

When she nodded, Vincent placed a hand at the small of her back and escorted her through a set of outer doors. He paused to allow Brea to look around the beautiful area. She breathed deep, enjoying the fragrance of the flowers and foliage that filled the room.

"It's like being outside in the springtime," she enthused.

"This is one of my favorite places. Look up at the moon. It is almost full."

She followed his sweeping gesture up and gasped at the beauty almost within her touch. Unable to resist, she lifted her hand to reach upward. The moonlight enveloped her hand its pale radiance. "So beautiful," she sighed, dropping her hand to her side.

Impetuously, Brea turned to ask Vincent how he could ever bear to leave his beautiful home. She discovered that the handsome man had been distracted from the view and, instead, studied her. "Vincent?"

"Your beauty and allure easily hold my attention, Brea." Stepping forward, Vincent wrapped his arms around her waist. "You, I can't resist."

Feeling beautiful and desirable as never before, Brea threaded her fingers through the silken hair that lay against his collar. Rising on her toes, she pulled Vincent's face to hers. Her lips pressed soft kisses to his square jaw before daring to meet his lips.

Instantly, Vincent took control of the kiss. Holding her in place with a firm hand cupping her skull, his mouth explored hers. His other hand pulled her closer to press their bodies together.

With a gasp that Vincent muffled with his kisses, Brea arched her body against his hard form. His rigid staff pressed against her pelvis, its thickness revealing that his desire rivaled hers. She shifted her hands to clutch his shoulders as he swept that hand down her body, cupping her full bottom to pull her even closer.

Vincent groaned, low and deep in his throat. She smiled against his lips, pleased that he found her bewitching. Unaccustomed bravery fueled her request for more. "Vincent, please," she whispered.

Lifting his lips from hers, Vincent's eyes seemed to glow a deep red in the moonlit room. "You are sure, my heart? There will be no going back afterward."

"Please," she dared to repeat.

With a low growl, Vincent scooped her into his arms and carried her through a hidden set of doors into his bedroom. An impression of luxurious, dark wood entered Brea's mind before his mouth retook hers. Lowering her onto a soft, thick comforter, Vincent quickly took his place beside her.

His fingers explored and caressed her body through her clothing. Pushing her jacket from her shoulder, Vincent dropped it to the floor as he touched her, raising her desire to a level that required more. Sitting up, Brea began to unbutton her blouse. Her eyes scanned his reaction as she daringly revealed all her flaws to his eyes.

Only, Vincent didn't seem to detect any blemishes. His hands reached forward to caress her smooth skin. As she dropped the unwanted garment to join the other, his fingers skillfully unfastened the bra that contained her large breasts. Cupping the heavy globes, Vincent bent to kiss and taste her flesh.

He paused only to rip his dress shirt from his body in a flurry of scattered buttons and cufflinks. When Brea urged, "More!" Vincent stood to remove his remaining garments. His gaze never left her. Its passionate touch was almost as real as the feel of his hands.

With a few flicks of his fingers, the passionate man unfastened and pulled her trousers off. Her shoes and socks removed simultaneously. Vincent stood at the end of the enormous bed for a few seconds, scanning her body as if memorizing the look of her in his bed. His body was rock hard and eager for her. She could not doubt his desire for her.

The low growl strained from his throat as he crawled over her. The feeling of being stalked flooded through her brain, making Brea hold her breath. She'd never been so turned on in her life as he caged her in place. When he dipped his head to kiss her passionately, Brea wrapped her arms around his broad shoulders.

Treasuring the feel of his muscles bunching under her fingers, Brea pushed away any doubts of why this gorgeous man was attracted to her. He was, and she was going to enjoy this while it lasted. She'd never been a live-in-the-minute type. Following her head instead of her heart had been her normal.

"My heart," he whispered against her skin as he kissed a blazing path down the center of her body.

Yielding automatically to his urging touch, Brea spread her thighs to make room for him to settle between them. His hands slipped behind her knees to press Brea's legs up and apart. She held her breath as he looked at her intimately.

Her eyes closed as he leaned to press a kiss to the plump mound between her thighs. She heard Vincent inhale deeply and compliment her with an "mmm." Brea dug her fingers into his shoulders as he began to taste her plentiful juices.

Quickly, his fingers and tongue brought her to the edge of pleasure. When he paused, her eyelid flew open as she gasped, "Don't stop!"

"Your pleasure is mine from this moment, my heart. There will be no one else," Vincent warned her. Those eyes flashed red as he watched her, awaiting her response.

"No one else," she promised. She barely knew him. That didn't matter.

With the speed of a lightning bolt, Vincent bit the tender flesh of her inner thigh. As she gasped in agony at the savage grip of his teeth, Vincent's talented fingers pinched that sensitive bundle of nerves, topping her tight channel. Pain blended with pleasure as her body arched in a climax that overwhelmed her mind and senses.

When he shifted to hover over her body, she watched him lick her blood from his lips. "Mine. You are mine, my heart." Fitting himself at her entrance, Vincent drove into her body. The ecstasy his caresses lavished on her overwhelmed her. Weakening from the pleasure he lavished on her body, Vincent joined her in one final orgasm.

Pressing a kiss to his lips, Brea allowed her mind and body to escape into oblivion.

8

Nibbling at the sensitive hollow of her neck, Vincent purposely roused his mate. Their lovemaking had pushed his intended conversation with her away. Now, it would need to wait for a bit more. She would wish to put in her notice at work and would not be pleased to arrive late. "My heart, it is time for you to awaken. A new life is awaiting you."

"What? A new life? What happened to my old one?" she sleepily mumbled before turning to press her body against his. "Warm," she sighed happily. At the sound of his low laugh, her eyes flew open to meet his.

"Vincent? It wasn't a dream?" When he dismissed that idea with a denying shake of his head, she accused, "You bit me!"

"I did. I will probably do that again. Was it so bad?" he questioned, carefully observing her body's response.

When she dropped her forehead to his shoulder to avoid his gaze, Vincent stroked the length of her spine. He enjoyed the feel of her skin against his. Already he could feel some of the changes beginning to happen in her body. Her heart rate slowed at rest, and instinctively Brea sought contact with him.

His mate would never be a shifter, but the small amount of his saliva that had entered her bloodstream through the wound would build her strength and stamina to stand by his side and bear his children. He would not know the full extent of the changes for several months. She would be the most vulnerable now.

With a jerk, Brea realized that it was morning. "Oh, no! What time is it? I have to go home for clothes and get to the office."

"The shower is through there, my heart. You will find your makeup and a change of clothes waiting for you. We will have time for a snack and coffee in the car if you hurry," Vincent said. Feeling his lips curve in an affectionate smile, he memorized a new picture—his tousled mate was endearing.

In a burst of energy, she jumped from the bed and ran to the bathroom door. Vincent watched her slide to a stop in front of the large vanity when she noted her familiar makeup case and ran a hand over the comfortable but businesslike dress hanging on a hook nearby. Whirling, Brea blew a kiss to Vincent before dashing into the shower with a relieved look.

He would need to talk to her about her job. For now, Vincent would allow her to shower and dress. Brea would feel less vulnerable when she was dressed and wearing her makeup.

9

"I have to put in my notice? Why?" Brea looked at him in shock. He'd broached the subject as soon as the car glided from his estate.

"Do you like your job? Are the people friendly?" he asked pointedly.

She tried to dodge the question. "Well, I've only been there for two days. I haven't met everyone."

"Does your job hold the possibility of fulfilling you?"

Brea squirmed on the leather seat. She looked down to avoid his knowing eyes and took a bite of the delicious pastry the chef had boxed for them to eat. With her mouth full, she had an excuse not to answer.

"You do not know everything about me," Vincent shared. "We will talk tonight, and I will answer all your questions."

"Are you like a serial killer?" The words blurted from her mouth with a spray of crumbled pastry. Appalled, Brea immediately began brushing them from his immaculate trousers.

Vincent's hand wrapped around hers, stilling her frantic motion. "You know that answer, my heart."

She exhaled noisily, allowing a few more bits to escape from her lips. As her shoulders settled back into place, her tension ebbed. The touch of his skin immediately calmed her. Swallowing hard, Brea dismissed that idea. "You're not a serial killer. Sorry. I just don't know much about you," she admitted, allowing a bit of her fear to echo in her words.

"I promise. I will answer all your questions this evening."

"I have to quit my job?"

"You were fired as soon as they saw me pick you up."

"What did you do to them?" Brea asked.

"I've stripped away their funding and revenue streams. I'm assuming you have not seen their financials yet," Vincent asked with arched eyebrows. The once vital firm had declined rapidly following a change in leadership. Shifty business decisions had severed past business relationships, and the company now floundered. Those impacted by the negative interactions, including Vincent, acted swiftly to recuperate their losses.

"How are they going to pay me?" Brea's financial mind went directly to the bottom line.

"They most likely weren't. The business will close in a couple of weeks. I would guess that they planned to use your brilliance to salvage whatever they could before disappearing before your first paycheck cleared."

The car pulled up at the front of the building. Brea had to ask, "Did you talk to me at the pub because of who I am?"

"No. I knew immediately that you were my mate. Even though the stench of the tarnished air clinging to your coat from this building, your natural scent captivated me. Even if you had been the chief operations officer of this cursed place, you are my mate. Nothing else matters," Vincent rushed to reassure her. He wrapped an arm around her shoulders to pull her close to his body.

"If I quit my job, I'll lose my new apartment," she thought aloud.

"My staff moved your belongings to my home, following our bonding. Your place is with me. Your job will be at my firm. Who else would I trust my finances with, other than my heart?" Vincent informed her.

"You took all my stuff and moved it to your home? Who gave you permission to do that?" Brea protested.

What had she gotten herself into? Who did he think he was? Her mind raced in circles as she tried to decide what she should do.

"We are now bonded, my heart. Stop and breathe for a minute. Listen to what your body is telling you. Your mind is scared. Is your heart?" he asked. His hands plucked the coffee cup from her hands to set it aside. Cradling her hands in his, Vincent sat quietly, giving her time to take in everything.

At the touch of his skin, Brea felt her pulse and mind quiet. After several minutes, she squeezed his fingers. "What does it mean that we are bonded? That I'm your mate? I need to know now. Don't put off telling me until we're alone again."

10

Vincent met the driver's gaze in the rearview mirror. "Eric, I will need you to drive to a quiet spot, please. It will not matter if we are late."

Looking back at Brea, he apologized, "I am sorry, my heart. I should have kept control of myself yesterday, but I couldn't resist your allure. I have waited for you for too long."

"You've said that before. How long could you have been waiting for me?" Brea protested.

"My search for my mate began eighty-two years ago." When she shook her head in disbelief and started to speak, he placed a finger over her lips to silence the protest. "What I will tell you will not make sense to your mind. I ask you to listen to your heart."

When she nodded after a pause, he continued. "In this world, there are those of pure human lineage and those who appear human but have additional abilities. My family descends from the latter group. My genes are a mixture of human and wolf."

Taking Brea's hand, he pressed it to his chest. He could read the disbelief on her face and felt the indignation radiating from her body. "Feel my heart beating. Watch my hand," he instructed. Slowly, he allowed the one he extended between their bodies to change. The digits began to lengthen and thicken as a fine pelt covered them. Then he allowed his hand to shift as well.

Watching his mate, Vincent held his breath. Would she listen to her heart or think only with her mind?

"Oh!" she exclaimed and froze, staring at the change. Then to his delight, he watched her stiff posture relax. Brea reached her free hand to touch and then stroke the soft fur. "It's the same color as your hair," she marveled. Her fingers traced the red and gold strands of fur sprinkled into the dark brown pelt.

"Yes," he answered simply.

"Your whole body changes?" she asked, an expression of absolute wonder replacing her anger.

"Yes," he repeated. "I will show you. The wolf inside me is the other half of my mind, body, and heart. The wolf has searched for his mate. There can be only one. You are that one. He sensed you immediately as you approached the bar. You are the mate who has eluded us for eighty-two years."

"The coin! You are the wolf on the coin. It has your name printed on it," she gasped as she remembered. "It heated when I thought of you."

"It is a token of my protection. Call on it, and I will move heaven and earth to get to you," he promised.

Eric turned into a private wooded area. Pulling the car to the side of the unpaved road, he turned off the engine and slid from behind the wheel. Soon, the door next to Vincent opened.

"Come with me, my heart. I will show you all you wish to see. Then I will answer any questions you have." Exiting, Vincent held his shifted hand back inside to assist her from the vehicle. Without hesitating, she placed her hand in his. They both felt that familiar electrical zing as the wolf and woman connected palm to paw.

Vincent led her into a deeper section of the trees where privacy wrapped around them. "Do not be afraid, my heart. The wolf is as incapable of hurting you as the human side of me is. Will you trust me?" he asked.

"I'm trying, Vincent."

Scanning her features, he leaned forward to kiss her. When she lifted her mouth to meet his, his nerves settled. His touch did not repulse her, and she was willing to listen. He could ask for nothing more.

Holding her gaze to reassure her she was safe, Vincent stepped backward to give himself space. He stripped off his suit jacket and began to unbutton his shirt. She watched now human fingers as they revealed the tanned skin that she had caressed and tasted so uninhibitedly. Her face blushed slightly, and Vincent knew that she remembered their passion as well.

His low growl brought her gaze to his face when he proudly displayed his strong, nude body before her. His voice was deep and resonated as he spoke. "If you get scared, look at my eyes. I will always be the same, whether in human skin or wolf's pelt."

Vincent allowed the wolf to envelop him. As his body shifted, lengthening and morphing, Vincent ignored the pain involved in the shift. The pain would always be there. His attention focused solely on the curvy brunette before him. Several times, her body tensed and began to turn away. His pride in his mate grew as each time, he watched her battle the fear stiffening her body and remain with him.

When finally he stood in front of her on four legs instead of two, Vincent allowed her to make the first move. Fierce admiration for his brave mate grew within the wolf as she took small steps to approach him. He watched her search his lupine gaze, searching for the man she'd had known for such a short period.

"Vincent?" she whispered hoarsely, the tension in her voice betraying her anxiety.

His low growl could have frightened her, but to his delight, he watched her lips quirk up in an amused grin. She quickly took two more steps to cover the distance between them. Her outstretched hand reached forward and paused.

"May I touch you?" she asked.

Vincent paced forward to press his muzzle into her palm. His brown eyes flashed red as she dropped to her knees beside him. Her tentative strokes over his head and shoulders pleased the wolf. He lapped at her face, allowing his beast to taste Brea.

Her giggles filled the silent woods as her fingers tangled in his thick undercoat. Vincent felt his fears evaporate. His mate had accepted him. Nature had chosen well for him. She was his. He swore he would never let her go.

11

Triumphantly, Vincent carried Brea back to the parked vehicle. Upon his return to his unclothed human form, his mate had welcomed his attentions. Their joining confirmed her acceptance of his wolf. Her response had been as passionate as the evening before. Nature could not have chosen a better mate for him.

Now, a couple of hours later, he strode through the trees. Eric greeted his alpha and his mate by lowering himself to one knee and bowing his head. Having accepted the alpha's wolf, they would now welcome Brea into the clan as his mate. At Vincent's accepting growl, Eric rose and resumed his role as a driver, opening the rear door.

"Eric too?" Brea whispered as soon as they were ensconced in the back seat again. Scooted close to him, her fingers fastened the buttons of his shirt as he finished restoring his businesslike appearance.

To answer, he leaned forward and kissed her sweet lips again. Once lightly and then with passion, the alpha had claimed his mate. Vincent did not wish his mate to think of any others. She bore his mark. Brea was his.

12

The car slowed and came to a stop. Brea tore her gaze away from the handsome man next to her. "We're here?" she squeaked. Sliding away, Brea brushed her hands over her hair, trying to smooth the brown tresses into a smooth hairstyle. She panicked as her fingers drew a broken twig and leaf from her hair.

"Vincent! You should have warned me we were close to my building. I can't go in like this!" she exclaimed, rattled by the revelations of the morning and now facing what she expected to be an unpleasant encounter. Scrambling for her purse, which lay abandoned on the floor, Brea tried to recapture the professional persona she'd always felt she needed to project at the office.

As she sat up, Vincent's arms wrapped around Brea, pulling her firmly against his warmth. "Shhh! Breathe, my heart. You are all right. I'm here to help." He shifted one hand take the comb from her suddenly still fingers thrust into her purse.

With a shuddering exhale, Brea met his gaze. When he smiled at her reassuringly, she nodded and allowed him to pull the comb from her fingers. She leaned her shoulder against him as he began to stroke the wide plastic teeth through her hair. As a few leaves tumbled to their laps, Brea began to laugh.

"My heart, you will have to learn to shake as my wolf does. You have collected many souvenirs from our brief time in the woods."

"Do I have to go in there?" she whispered.

"Will you be able to sleep knowing that you've discovered something unpleasant?"

Brea thought furiously. Vincent knew her too well. To clear her conscience, she needed to alert someone. "No. I need to at least make sure someone received my report."

"I agree, my heart. You need to close this door. Then, our future will be open without impediments or remorse." Cupping her chin, Vincent warned, "If I enter, that will be considered an attack. As your mate, I want to accompany you inside to ensure your safety. As the alpha, I know that you will not be in danger. A conflict between our clans will be the end for them."

"I have to go in alone?" she asked, shivering as fear swept down her spine with icy fingers.

"I will be outside. You will take the coin inside with you. Do you have it?"

"Here!" Brea scrambled in her purse to find it. The instant her fingers closed around the coin, she could feel it warm. It radiated security. She didn't want to let it go.

"Allow me to help you, my heart." Vincent held out his hand for the coin. When she dropped it reluctantly in his palm, he met her gaze with that red flash of his eyes. "Wear it here, against your skin and near your heart."

His fingers brushed the neckline of her dress and slid under the fabric. Caressing the swell of her generous breasts, Vincent nestled the coin between the heavy globes. Held in place by her lacy bra, the warm metal pressed against her flesh.

"Do not fear. I will know you are safe. If not, I will intercede before harm can befall you." Gliding from the supporting fabric, Vincent cupped one breast and lightly brushed his thumb across her responsive nipple. Just as her breath caught in her throat, the commanding man removed his hand and pressed the button to signal Eric to open the door.

The imposing men escorted her to the front door. To their

surprise, an equally large man met them. He was older, with hair almost entirely silver. "Alpha Woods, my apologies for hiring your mate. I was not aware that she belonged to you."

"Alpha Wilder, meeting Brea has been a recent delight." Vincent acknowledged the older shifter with a polite nod.

"Ahhh, that is why her connection with your clan was not detected." He nodded in response. Turning to Brea, he smiled. "It is unfortunate that your employment will need to end. My personal thanks to you for your brilliant deductions. I received your report. You are very good at what you do."

"Alpha Woods, I stepped down from leading my clan two years ago. After handing the reins to my son, I selfishly retired to live a life without responsibilities. I failed to listen to the urgent warnings from key staff members and from my daughter. When I finally opened my eyes to see the damage to this company, I quietly began to search for the reasons you had affected it so seriously. Brea's sharp mind detected what I could not. Financial fraud had been underway since I'd retired."

He shook his head in clear regret. "My son no longer leads the company. The clan banished him from our lands. Thankfully, my daughter did not abandon her people." The alpha turned to open the door, revealing an attractive woman with raven hair, who stepped through to join the conversation.

"This is Serena Wilder. She now leads the company. I have trust that she will be the future of the business."

Brea felt both men's spines stiffen as Serena extended her hand to Vincent. Smoothly, her mate covered his surprise and shook hands with the newly declared business leader. To Brea's delight, Serena shook hands with her and Eric as well. It appeared that the daughter had developed diplomatic skills that would serve her well in the future.

"Past business deals are finished. My plans are to take this company in a different direction. One that will not compete with yours. There is an opportunity for us to reinvent ourselves and once again become a leader in industry. I could use a mentor as I establish myself," she shared in a tone that signaled her respect for Vincent but her determination to save her father's company.

Once again, Brea felt her lips turn up slightly at the corners. This woman had balls. She'd go far.

"I would welcome the opportunity to talk further with you," Vincent replied.

As the two began to talk business, Alpha Wilder stepped forward slightly toward Brea. "If I may ask you a private question?" he inquired. When she nodded, he continued. "You met your mate recently. May I ask where? My daughter and the clan could use the support of a strong alpha, such as yours. Perhaps she would be as lucky as you were."

Brea turned to point across the street at the quaint Storybook Pub. Its stone exterior and shaded windows beckoned the passersby to enter. "I'd gone there for a drink. A stool was open next to Vincent," she explained.

"Kole O'Shea was the bartender," the older alpha asked with a gleam shining in his eye.

"Yes! Do you know him?"

"He introduced me to my lovely bride, Anabelle. How I miss her. Perhaps you could arrange for their next meeting to be at the Storybook Pub?" he asked quietly, nodding at the two busily talking business.

Must be the original owner's son or grandson? Brea wondered. Pressing the coin against her heart, Brea felt it warm slightly. Instantly, Vincent turned to her. "I'm so hungry, Vincent. Could we go try the special for lunch?" she asked, waving at the pub. Turning to the older man, she asked, "You'll join us, won't you?"

"It will be Serena's and my pleasure to have lunch with you," the silver-haired man replied. When Vincent and Serena nodded their agreement, the foursome crossed the street. Brea's turned back over her shoulder to glance at the older man behind her. She laughed at his wink.

"You are well, my heart?" Vincent asked, looking at her suspiciously.

"Better than I ever expected to be," she answered, threading her fingers between his. The thrill of contact with his skin zinged through her again. It is like a storybook, she thought, smiling at her mate. She welcomed the happily ever after that inevitably would follow.

Learn more about Pepper North:
www.4peppernorth.club

Also by Pepper North:
    Zoey: Dr. Richards Littles 1
    Sharing Shelby
    The Magic of Twelve: Violet

IRISH TWINS

LANE MARTIN

**Two brothers,
one Storybook ending.**

Sub-genre: Contemporary Romance
Relationship: Male/Male/Female

1

MARK

"Why do I feel like I should start with a two cops walk into a bar joke?" The bartender greets us while wiping down the counter in front of the spots my brother and I occupy.

It is pointless to deny it, but I still have to ask, "How did you know?" Mike and I aren't in uniform. Detectives for the Syracuse Police Department only wear blues for ceremonies and funerals.

"I know things. I'm Kole O'Shea, owner of this fine establishment." He places the cloth over his shoulder and shakes our hands as we introduce ourselves. Kole puts two glasses in front of us before turning around to grab a bottle. Mike and I watch him. He hesitates at the bottle of Johnnie Walker but reaches for the Jameson Black instead. *Good choice.* Without asking, he pours us each two fingers.

Impressive. Mike and I raise our glasses and clink them before drinking down the smooth amber liquid. The bar is not what I was expecting. With a name like Storybook Pub, I envisioned some wannabe hipster microbrew. The kind packed with guys in plaid and skinny jeans, and ladies who are trying way too hard. Instead, the pub is low key with well-stocked shelves and no craft beers in sight. Not that we will tell mom she did well by insisting we come here, but she did. Our mom, Tami Madina, would never let us hear the end of it if she thought she was right. We love our mom. She loves us, but she wants something a little more traditional for us than Mike and I do for ourselves. She is itching for grandbabies. We both like kids, but we aren't sure they are in the cards for us. She hasn't hired a matchmaker yet. I'm not sure how we would explain what we are looking for. It isn't exactly conventional.

Our mother is always on us to get out more. She and the rest of the family are sure my brother and I will remain bachelors. Nothing could be further from the truth. Finding what we need in a relationship is a struggle. Our family won't understand. Luckily, our parents live four hours away. Mom's meddling is limited to frequent phone calls and text messages we often dodge.

"Could you do me a favor and take a picture of us so I can send it to our mom?" Mike snorts out a laugh as I explain the need for the photo to our new acquaintance.

"God Mark, you make us seem pathetic? Kole, could you take our picture so we can send it to our mommy?" I have to admit; it does sound pretty pitiful. We are grown-ass men in our thirties, and we both carry guns for a living.

Kole takes my phone from me and steps back to take our picture while I toss my arm over my brother's shoulder.

"Don't be so mean to your brother Mike." Kole offers in a tone that surprisingly mimics our father. We both throw our heads back in laughter as he snaps several photos before handing my cell back to me. Mom will love them.

"Now, would you do something for me?" Mike shrugs at Kole's request.

"What do you need?" I ask skeptically. I need more details before agreeing to anything.

"Do you see that lass on the other side of the bar?" Kole moves aside, revealing a beauty he previously blocked from our vision. I can't take my eyes off of her. The grunt coming from my brother tells me he is as affected as I am. She has a red rose tucked behind her ear, and she taps at the brim of her near-empty glass as she looks around the room. Kole clears his throat to garner our attention.

"She's been waiting for someone for a while. I was hoping you could take her these and offer to buy her a drink." Kole holds out two roses that match hers and hands us each one.

"You want us both to go?" Yes, it is the way Mike and I prefer it, but Kole just met us and has no way of knowing that bit of information.

"Well, yes. Isn't that the way you usually do things?" He raises a brow in question as we look at each other in shock before returning our glances to him. "Remember, I know things." He winks as he once again holds out the flowers we have yet to take. Kole turns his attention to another patron once we relieve him of the roses.

"I don't know if I should worry with the way this night is going," Mike remarks as we both watch the brunette look at her watch. Time is running out. She is about to leave. We don't typically meet random women in bars. Usually, we meet our female companions in groups online. That way we know they share an interest in a particular lifestyle. These women know what they are getting. Walking up to a stranger as a pair is a surefire way to get a drink thrown in your face. We can't let this woman leave looking so sad.

"Kole knows things," I shrug as I stand and begin walking toward her. Watching her walk out the door isn't an option.

"Hold up, bro." Mike is no dummy. He can't do it either. Not without trying to put a smile on her beautiful face.

2

TILLY

I can't believe this is happening to me. Again. I'm an idiot. I thought this time would be different. I don't understand men. Russell Baldwin seemed nice. We chatted for days before he suggested we meet and he never said we should "hang out." He never sent me dick pics. *Shocker.* I thought I finally met someone online who wasn't a complete creep. For a second, I worried I came to the wrong bar or told him I would have a yellow rose instead of red. I triple check, I'm right where we agreed to meet. The rose is definitely supposed to be red. Red, the color of love, or in my case, the color of shame. Shame on me for believing that good men still exist. For all I knew, he was here. Watching me. Laughing at me. It's time for me to go home and delete my dating profile. Tomorrow I'll go and adopt a cat. A cat would love me. A cat wouldn't lie to me. A cat wouldn't laugh at me or send me unwanted penis photos. *A cat can't send pictures, Tilly.* You don't even have a cat yet, and you're already a crazy cat lady. I pull a twenty out of my wallet and leave it on the bar for the friendly bartender before standing to leave.

"Don't go." Followed by a strained, "Please," from someone else catches my attention. I turn to face not one but two handsome strangers. Each holding out a long stem red rose for me. Neither of them are the man I was expecting. My anger at being stood-up by Russell Baldwin is immediately gone. My rage replaced by a heat I have never felt before.

"You're even prettier up close." The first man offers as he extends his rose out to me while the other nods his head in agreement. I take it in my hand and resist the urge to lift it to my nose.

"I couldn't agree more brother. A beautiful flower for a beautiful woman." The second man hands me his rose. I can't help but giggle as I take it. *Brothers. Oh my.*

"I like the sound of that, but you're going to have to tell us what's so funny, beautiful. Please let us buy you a drink." Bachelor number one as I am calling him, for now, smiles. He motions me back toward the seat I just abandoned at the bar. His smile might have caused me to fall on my ass if it weren't for bachelor number two. His hand at my elbow, guides me back to my seat. *Good lord. Is it hot in here?*

I let out another giggle. *Get ahold of yourself, Tilly.* I just can't help it. The idea of either of these gorgeous men calling me beautiful is crazy. I imagine them asking me if I will accept their rose. It's laughable. Are the punking me?

"Whoa, beautiful." My gaze darts around the bar as I remove the rose from behind my ear. Like a fool, I waited far too long with the flower in my hair as a sign for Russell Baldwin that I was the woman he was meeting. When we first agreed upon it, I thought it was romantic. He would be able to find me in the crowd. Now, I think it was what marked me as a target of someone's sick idea of a joke. *It wouldn't be the first time.*

"Take a breath." Bachelor number one looks at me as he takes the seat to my right. He touches my arm gently. His eyes hold no sign of amusement. If anything, he looks concerned. He leans past me and looks at his brother, "Both of you." Bachelor number two sits to my left. He still holds me at my elbow, "And then tell us what's going on in that head of yours." The soothing sound of his voice has a chill running through me. *Everywhere.* It's so confusing. Here I am worrying I'm the brunt of some sick joke, but at the same time, I don't want either of them to stop touching me. *Ever.*

Kole, the bartender I met earlier, appears from nowhere and pours me a cold glass of water. "I'm sorry Tilly. I should have come over and introduced you to Mark and Mike." Kole points to them as he gives their names. Did he send them over? I finally take that breath and proceed to down the entire glass of water. Kole was kind to me when I arrived earlier. He made me feel welcome in his bar. He has no reason to set me up.

"Tilly?" Mike, the brother behind me, echoes my name reverently as he tenderly strokes my arm. My name has never sounded so sweet before.

"Is that short for Matilda?" Brother number one, Mark, asks in awe as he stares at me with eyes the color of creamy hot chocolate. My tongue darts out, and his eyes flare with heat. Never in my life have I felt so consumed. That is, until bachelor number two moves closer to me and whispers in my ear.

"Is it?" His agonized question at the nape of my neck makes me tremble — stunned stupid at my reaction to these men. I nod my head in answer. Kole tosses his bar towel over his shoulder before turning away from us with a wide grin on his face. He mumbles something about Irish eyes smiling down on us.

"Well, I'll be." Mark smiles at my answer. Mike's lips skim the nape of my neck ever so lightly from behind. Another bolt of pleasure goes right through me. What is it about pleasing both of them that make me so hot?

3

MARK

"Mom's never going to let us hear the end of this." What are the odds? *One out of twenty-six dummy.*

"I don't understand." Tilly looks between me and a chuckling Mike behind her. "Are you laughing at me?" She pouts. *Damn, she's cute.*

"Not at you, sweetheart, at the current situation we're in." My brother is enjoying this way too much. Tilly is going to get whiplash if she keeps turning her neck to look back and forth between us the way she is. "I'll tell you what. Why don't we move to a table so you can see both of us at the same time and let us buy you a drink?" I love the way she reacts when I say the word us. From my siblings' groan, I know he sees it too. I know it was a question, but I move and take her hand in mine before I let her answer. I think it will be best if we don't let her overthink this. Now that I'm holding her hand, I don't know how I'll ever let it go. It's small in mine, yet it fits perfectly. It makes me wonder how else we would fit together. Mike moves fluidly with us, never removing his hand from the small of her back.

One look at him and I know we're thinking the same thing. I find a small round table in the corner with three chairs. *Perfect.* I pull out a chair for Tilly before reluctantly letting her go and moving to the other side of the table. Mike sits next to me. Our backs to the wall. Tilly's back to the room. Also good because she won't be able to see anyone looking at us with judgment in their eyes. Kole arrives with a knowing look and a fresh round of drinks in seconds. He gives us a wink before leaving. *Man, he does know things.*

Tilly darts her tongue out and wets her lips before picking up her drink. I want that tongue. Mike and I follow her lead and take our drinks in hand too. "What should we toast to?" Her voice croaks as she looks between us.

"To our meddling mother," Mike offers playfully, lifting his glass. I can't help but chuckle as we clink together.

"You're not twins, but you are close in age." Tilly's voice is as smooth as the whiskey I am drinking. I could listen to her talk forever.

"Exactly nine months," Mike confirms as he leans across the table and smooths an errant strand of hair out of her face. *Lucky hair.* She looks stunned. I can't tell if it's from his answer or from the way he touches her.

"Irish twins," she responds as she subtly leans into his hand that still lingers at the side of her head. *Lucky Mike.* Her eyes flutter shut, and it takes every ounce of restraint I have not to reach out for her too. She's nothing like the women we usually meet. It's like she has no expectations. Like she can't believe she is sitting here having drinks with us. It's refreshing.

"That's what our parents call us. You'd be surprised how many people don't know what Irish twins are." Mike confirms. Irish twins are siblings born within twelve months of each other. We've heard it all our lives. As the story goes, Dad couldn't keep his hands off of mom. Hell, he still can't. Of course, it also doesn't help that Mike and I do everything together. We always have. It's not to say we haven't tried to do things solo. We have. It just doesn't work for us. The only problem is, it's getting tiring being with those women with expectations. We aren't looking for someone who just wants to fuck brothers. Sure, in our late teens and twenties, it was fun, but we're over it now. We want what our parents have. A loving relationship, a bond that will last the test of time. Someone to call ours. Lately, we've thought it just isn't meant to be. We know we've been dubbed the confirmed bachelors of the family. We were beginning to believe it is true. For the first time in a long time, I'm feeling something different when it comes to the hope of finding someone. *Hopeful.* I know Mike feels it too.

Tilly's eyes open as a new song begins to play from the classic jukebox that sits in the corner. The words are out of my mouth without even giving it a second thought, "Would you like to dance with me, Tilly?" I don't dance, but I do love the sound of her name as it rolls off of my tongue. I also love the way she lights up at my questions before looking at Mike, as if for permission. Does she even realize she does it? He nods his head, and we both stand. Mike helps her from her seat and whispers something in her ear before handing her off to me. *Stand down boy.* I lead Tilly to the dance floor if you'd call it that. All I know is that I need this woman in my arms, and now isn't soon enough. If dancing is the excuse I need to make it happen, so be it. I pull Tilly close. It doesn't help with the erection that is screaming at me, but it does soothe the rest of me. Nothing has ever felt so right before.

"What did Mike say to you?" My mouth is positioned next to her ear. I can feel her tremble in my arms. As tempting as it is to put my head down and press my lips to her skin, I need to see her more. Her body may be saying yes, but I need to know what she's thinking.

"He said he was next." Tilly puts her head against my shoulder, and I pull her impossibly closer. "Don't you ever get jealous?" People always ask this question when they find out Mike and I share. Not that we broadcast it, but we don't hide it or deny it when asked. Instead, we try to educate. It's no different than anyone else's sexuality. Some people like raised donuts with maple glaze while others like crawlers. They're both delicious. The bottom line is everyone is entitled to what they want. Who am I to judge? To each his or her own.

"Not like you would think," this is difficult to explain. "I want my brother to be happy." God, I could hold her in my arms like this forever. She smells like vanilla with a dash of cinnamon. "He wants the same for me."

Tilly lifts her head and looks into my eyes. She swallows before asking, "And you share everything?" Our slow sway to the sultry music stops with her question.

I move my hands slowly from her hips, tracing each curve of her body. I swallow hard at the hitch of her breath before I cradle her face in my hands and answer, "Yes, everything." I press my lips to hers, and she melts into the kiss. Her expression is soft when I break the too short for my liking kiss, but I don't want to scare her away. *Not when we just found her.* I lean into her. I stroke the side of her face with the back of my hand as she looks up at me with glossy eyes and a hint of a smile.

"It's my turn, brother." Mike interrupts as the music changes. I step away, knowing this won't work if they don't share the same connection. We exchange a knowing look. Based on the grin he's wearing, I know he feels it too. She's the one. I hate to admit it, but our parents were right. They always said we would know it when the right girl came along. We're still not sure if they know it will be the same girl for both of us. They've never asked, so we've never told. We always figured we would cross that bridge when we came to it. Until tonight it didn't seem like that time would ever arrive. Shit, we wouldn't be here if it weren't for mom and her insistent nagging that we come. On my mental list of things to do tomorrow, I add order mom a muffin assortment from our friend Emily. Our younger brother Matt delivers for her. I'll get points for getting mom a gift. Mom redirects her attention to our little brother. Mike and I get to focus on Tilly. It's a win-win unless you're Matt. *Perfect.*

I can't take my eyes off Mike and Tilly as they dance together. Taking out my phone, I need to capture this moment. I want to remember it forever. I love how at ease they look together. Both of them smiling and relaxed. Their shared laughter makes me feel light. At the end of the song, they return to the table hand in hand.

I want to know more about this woman. Hell, I want to know everything there is to know. I stand and pull out her chair for her. I'm not sure if it bothers me or makes me happy that she acts like a man being a gentleman is so foreign to her. Should Mike and I track down the losers she has dated in the past and kick some ass or thank them. Mike and I are a long way from perfect, but we will always make Tilly feel like the queen she is. I know Mike picks up on her reaction too.

Our understanding of what the other is thinking makes us a great team, both on the job and off.

"What do you do for a living sweet Tilly?" Her skin flushes. I'm not sure if it's from the compliment or embarrassment. Tilly let's go of Mike's hand and tugs at her collar. She answers in a voice so faint we can barely hear her over the music and the noise of the bar.

"I'm a freelance book editor." *Interesting*. What's wrong with that? I'm relieved she didn't say anything dangerous. I couldn't stand the thought of her putting herself in danger on the job.

"What kind of books?" Mike sounds as relieved as I feel.

"Mostly romance, but I've also done some young adult and Dystopian." She shrugs as if it's no big deal. I couldn't do what she does. Hell, if I asked her to edit one of my reports, it would be covered in red. I want to pull her into my arms and tell her she shouldn't be so modest. I resist the urge instead and lift her balled-up fist from the table to my mouth and press a kiss to her soft, warm skin. I love the way she relaxes into each touch. Mike does the same to her other hand. We both watch her reaction with bated breath. She doesn't flinch or back away from being touched by both of us at the same time. Mike offers a soft, "Thank Christ." I couldn't agree with him more.

"What type of romance?" Tilly giggles at Mike's question. I'm glad I'm already sitting down. This woman has the power to bring me to my knees.

"What's so funny, beautiful?" Tilly gasps in surprise. Yeah, she needs to get used to the idea of us thinking she is gorgeous. Again, I find myself wanting to beat down the guys in her past who made her feel like she wasn't as amazing as she is. *Note to self. Don't just tell her with words. Show her with actions.*

Tilly collects herself before redirecting our conversation, "Should I be worried? You mentioned before, your mother would never let you hear the end of this. Now you're asking me about different types of romance." Jesus, Mike and I both double over in laughter. Nothing gets by this woman. *Yep, we are officially screwed.*

Mike retakes her hand, "Oh baby, you have no idea. Mom is going to love you. Romance books are all she and her best friend talk about.

Plus the second she hears your name is Matilda she'll have the wedding invitations printed."

"We kind of have a thing with M names." I indicate to myself, "Mark," before pointing at my brother, "Mike."

"Our dad is Mel, and our little brother is Matt," Mike adds. "Last month, mom and her BFF, Gwen, came to town and dragged us to a book signing with them. We were their 'book bitches.' We carried all their swag, lugged books around all day, and took pictures of them with every single author." Tilly's laughter fills the room. I could listen to her laugh all day.

"Hey, it wasn't funny. Do you have any idea how many times I was slapped on the ass that day? It was mortifying, and mom tried to hook us up with any lady with an M on her nametag. Trust me, we've heard all about Christian, Archer, Gideon, Kellan, and Jesse."

"Well, don't forget Travis, Ridge, Gavin, or Dean," I add. We've heard it all. I love the look of amazement on Tilly's face. "Were you at the signing at the Hilton last month?" It makes me sad to think we missed a month with her, but if Tilly was at that event, I'm sure we would have noticed her. She would have been impossible to miss.

"I was supposed to go, but I got sick and had to cancel my plans at the last minute. I was going to assist one of my authors. I would have gone anyway if I had known such fine-looking and knowledgeable 'book bitches' were attending. I would have been one of the ladies to cop a feel." *I doubt it. Tilly, I wouldn't have minded.*

"Baby, I would have let you have more than just a feel," Mike tells her exactly what I'm thinking.

"Is it hot in here?" Tilly tugs at her shirt. If we weren't out in public, I'd help her take it off.

"I need a distraction. Let's play a round of darts." The last thing I want to do is play a game, but I also don't want this night to end. I refuse to start this thing with Tilly off with us tangled between the sheets. She's not just a fuck for tonight. In our line of work, you need to trust your gut, and my gut is telling me, Tilly is the woman for us. I can feel it.

I retrieve a set of darts from Kole, Tilly admits that she has never played before. The way she listens as I explain the game is endearing.

More often than not, people don't listen, but that's not the case with Tilly at all. It's refreshing. Mike remains seated at the table, watching us closely.

"Okay, I understand the scoring, but I'm still not sure about the throwing part." Tilly watched me, but now it's her turn. Biting her lips as she changes her stance for the third time since I handed her the darts.

"Here, let me help you." I stand behind her and snake an arm around her waist before pulling her against me. I trail my free hand up her side. Her body quakes at my touch as I remind her, "Hold the shaft in the center." My lips ghost the shell of her ear. Her sharp intake of breath proves she is just as affected as I am by our closeness. "Firm but not forced," I coach. "Relax, sweet Tilly." My finger continues its path down her arm until my hand reaches hers. I place my fingers over hers. The thought of instructing her on how I like to be touched enters my head. Her small hand wrapped around my cock. My hand covering hers, encouraging her to grip me like she means it. The image is so clear I close my eyes as she lifts the dart and aims it at the target. She lets go, and it sails at the board, hitting the double twenty.

"Nice shot," Mike whoops from the table where he has been waiting for his time with Tilly.

She turns in my arms and tosses her arms around my neck. "I did it," she beams. The remaining darts in her hand all but forgotten fall to the floor when she moves to kiss me. I pull her closer, loving the way she threads her fingers through the hair at the nape of my neck while I deepen the kiss. I part her lips with my tongue and she doesn't hesitate in reciprocating. *Jesus, could she be any more perfect?* While I would like nothing more than to keep kissing Tilly all night, I know I can't. Tonight isn't just about me. Mike needs his time too.

"I knew you could do it. Good job." I praise her looking into her eyes. Her pupils dilate and her pale skin flushes as she smiles at my compliment. Mike joins us and he turns her around to face him.

"I have a feeling you can do anything you put your mind to, beautiful." Mike is awarded a smile so bright it lights up the room. Mike leans down to kiss her on the cheek. Imagine both of our delight and surprise when she turns her head and plants her lips on his. It's Sunday night, so the bar isn't crowded. I don't particularly care what other people think. Frightening Tilly with public displays of affection with two men isn't something I want to do. *Not yet, anyway.* Tilly is unlike anyone I have ever met before. She is an anomaly, shy yet bold. Inexperienced yet leading the way. The shock on Mike's face at her no holds barred behavior is comical. Hell, I probably have the same stunned expression on my face.

"I think we need to get out of here." Mike looks over Tilly's shoulder, and I nod my agreement. "Tilly, would you be willing to go someplace with us where we can talk?"

"Talk?" Her pout is adorable.

"Yes, talk. Trust me; it's the last thing my body wants to do right now." Mike hasn't let go of her. I'm standing right behind her, forming a Tilly sandwich. The only thing that would make this any better is if we were alone and naked, but Mike is right, we do need to talk.

"I don't want this night to end. It's the best dream I've ever had." Tilly shakes her head as if she can't believe any of this happening either.

"Baby, this is a dream come true, and it has only begun." *Preach brother.*

"Let's go," Tilly confirms her willingness to leave with us by reaching out to take my hand while Mike leads us out of the bar.

4

MARK

Tilly slides into the booth across from us in the diner a short walk down from the pub. The waitress looks like she stepped right out of the fifties. She hands us each a menu and pours three glasses of water before leaving to give us a few minutes to look at the menu. I don't need to look to know what I want. She's sitting right across from us, and I know my brother is on the same page.

The waitress returns, "See anything you like?" Her question directed at Tilly with a snap of her gum.

"I like everything I see." She offers without tearing her eyes off either of us. Mike chokes on his water when the waitress drops an aggravated, "On the menu."

"Oh, I haven't decided. What if I want more than one thing?" She bites her bottom lip, and both of us let out a groan. I swear she's trying to kill us.

"You can have whatever you like, sweetheart," Mike reassures her. The waitress huffs in frustration.

"You go ahead and order first." Our innocent girl requests.

"I'll have the cheesecake." My voice doesn't sound like my own as I say the words. I sound like a prepubescent boy with our mom shaking the door handle while I try to rub one out.

"And I'll have a slice of cherry pie." Mike hands off his menu to the waitress.

"Oh, those both sound good. I'll just share with both of you. Of course, if you don't mind." Mind? As far as we're concerned sharing is the only way to go.

"No. We are good at sharing." Mike confirms his voice off too.

"I'll bet you are." The waitress mumbles while turning away from us. Tilly turns the same shade as the roses we gave her earlier. I clear my throat, hoping to sound like the grown-ass man that I am.

"So, tell us more about your job. How did you get started with editing, and what kinds of books do you edit?"

"Well, I've always loved to read." Her eyes light up as she talks about her passion. I can imagine her in our bay window overlooking the backyard. Tilly's back pressed against my chest. Her feet propped up in Mike's lap while she marks up pages with a red pen, and we watch a game. The thought gives me pause. While we've shared a lot of women, we've never shared our home with any of them. Our house is our sanctuary. Our job as detectives is hectic and stressful. Home is the place we go to recharge and escape the chaos. I've never enjoyed welcoming other people into it. Now that we've met Tilly, I don't look forward to going home without her. The waitress interrupts my crazy thoughts to deliver our desserts.

I turn my plate and push it closer to Tilly's side of the table. Mike follows suit after taking a bite and making an obscene noise. The blush reappears in Tilly's cheeks. She forks a piece of my cheesecake and adds a fork of cherry pie before raising it to her lips and swallowing the bite. *Lord, how I wish I were her fork.* She closes her eyes and hums in appreciation before licking her luscious lips. Her eyes flutter open after a moment passes. Immediately, she covers her mouth and ducks her head in embarrassment.

"Oh, my God. I probably sounded like a porn star." *God knows she'll be starring in all my wet dreams from here on out.*

"That was the hottest thing I've ever heard," Mike tells her as I nod my head in agreement. A sexy woman who has no idea how hot she is just topped my list of favorite things. Tilly has no idea of the things she is doing to us. My dick is so hard right now. I have no idea how I'm going to get up to leave this table.

Attempting to calm myself down, I ask her something I'm curious about, "How did you start editing romance?" Tilly takes another combined bite of our desserts before shrugging.

"It was an accident. My friend asked me to read her first novel. She told me to be brutally honest, and I was. She hit the publish button, and the thing went to the best sellers list like overnight. It's unheard of; we still joke that it must have been a flaw with the algorithm or something." Tilly chuckles before her face falls.

"What's wrong?" She looks so sad, and I want to fix whatever happened to upset her.

"Oh, no, it's nothing like that." Tilly sighs, and I still want to move to her side of the table so that I can be closer to her. Mike relaxes a little in his seat once she assures us nothing happened. "It isn't something Naomi was expecting to happen so fast. She hoped it would do well, but to go to number one and stay there as long as it did caught us both off guard. I was still working at my old job. Then my inbox started filling up. Other would-be authors wanted me to edit for them. I was hesitant at first. Editing a book for a friend is one thing, but doing it for someone you've never met before is another." Tilly got a sad look in her eyes before she continued. "Imagine sending something you've spent countless hours working on off to someone. Only to be picked apart word by word. That first real gig was terrible. With the clients' permission, I gave it to Naomi to review before I sent it back to her. She read the book and my edits. She told me my editing job was crap before she tore off the title page and told me to edit it like she had written it."

"I think I like your friend." Mike forks the last bite of cherry pie and lifts it for her.

"I think she'll like you too — both of you." Dashing her tongue out to lick her luscious lips. I like the way she says 'both of you.'

"Did you?" I ask as she takes the offered bite. The swell of her breasts peeking out as she leans forward to take it. Her body is that of a pin-up model, but she doesn't flaunt those delicious curves she has. If anything, she tries to hide them. When she's ours, we'll remind her daily that she has no reason to be self-conscious. Tilly is stunning, and my brother and I will tell her that until she believes it.

"I did," she beams after swallowing. "It was one of the hardest things I've ever done. I didn't want to hurt the authors' feelings. Being so blunt isn't easy. I worried the word would get out in romancelandia that I was a terrible editor and person. In all honesty, I just wanted to get back to being a reader and working my Monday thru Friday eight to five job."

"But that didn't happen," Mike states the obvious since we already know what she does.

"No, it was a huge success too, and the writer said it was all thanks to me." Her modesty is almost as sexy as her curves.

"So what you're saying is that you have a magic touch." Tilly blushes at my compliment and shakes her head no.

"No, what I'm saying is that sometimes it pays off to say what you are thinking."

Mike nods his head in agreement as I voice, "You're right."

"True. You'll never get answers to questions that go unasked," Mike adds.

"So, I guess I'll ask the question I'm dying to know the answer to and hope you'll be honest with your response." I lean in, wanting to be closer to her.

"Okay, ask away." As confident as she is trying to appear, I can hear hesitancy in her voice.

"Tilly, since this is your story, what does your happily ever after look like?" *Please let it include us.*

5

TILLY

Happily ever after for me? It isn't something that I've given much thought to recently. I'm content with my life as it is. I have a job doing what I love. How many people get to say that? I have a family who loves me and a fantastic network of friends who support me. Okay, they have my back, and they drive me crazy. Naomi is the one that pushed me to go out tonight. I'm satisfied with my book boyfriends and battery-operated toys. She keeps insisting that I need a proper "dicking." *I don't think she meant a two for one special.* I can't help the giggle that escapes me as I look across the table at Mike and Mark. *Yummy.*

"Jesus." Mike shakes his head as he looks from me to his brother. "Are you wondering how you're going to walk out of this place too?"

Mark is stiff in his seat, but never looks away from me. Did I do that? I've read all about smoldering looks, I always thought it was kind of a cliche, but I swear I can feel it. Smoke detectors are about to go off. At least it will be a distraction for us to get out of here.

"What?" I wet my dry lips with my tongue as I shift in my seat. I've never felt so compelled to be with one person before, let alone two people at the same time. I came into tonight prepared to meet Russell. I was ready to have a drink or two with a nice guy. I wouldn't feel a spark for him, and I would go home alone. The date would get my girls off my back about dating for a few months. All would end well. When I decided he wasn't going to show up, I was relieved. Of course, I wouldn't tell my friends that Russell never showed. I would wax poetic about not feeling any connection with him. They would proclaim it to be his loss, and would leave them wanting more for me.

"Tilly?" Mike's smile wavers as he moves his hand slowly across the table toward mine. Mark's eyes lock on me as he rubs at the back of his neck.

His brows pull up as he asks, "Where did you go?"

I dip my chin as the flush creeps across my cheeks. Mike's hold on my hand tightens as Mark scrambles out of the booth and slides in next to me. He tucks his finger under my chin and lifts it. Forcing me to look at him, "This won't work if you don't tell us what is going on in that beautiful head of yours." Mike and Mark share the same eyes. I could look into them forever, and that's what has me feeling so overwhelmed.

I square my shoulders, and another look crosses his face. I'd swear it's pride. He takes a second to look at his brother before he returns his gaze to mine — a knowing grin forms on his handsome face. I sit up straighter, feeling more determined than I should. *Ask for what you want, Tilly.* What's the worst thing they can say? Mark takes my free hand and squeezes it. It's gentle yet reassuring. Mike smooths his thumb across the top of the hand he's holding. *You're not crazy. They feel the connection too.*

"Tonight wasn't supposed to be like this." God, why am I so nervous? "I shape the happily ever afters other people craft. I've never spent a lot of time thinking about my own. After tonight I'm starting to think my story might be a little unorthodox."

"In what way?" Mark questions. Of the two, he is more outspoken. It makes me wonder what it would be like to be with them in bed. Would Mike sit back and watch while Mark dominates the interaction? A shiver runs through my body at the thought.

"Don't stop, Tilly." My eyes dart to Mike. His tone is firmer than he's used with me before. *Zing.* Maybe he won't sit back and watch.

I swallow down the lump that has formed in my throat, "I don't think a traditional relationship is what I'm looking for." I've read every genre of romance. I've always enjoyed a good ménage, but it's nothing I ever pictured for myself. Now I can't get the idea out of my head. I can imagine it, but not with any two men. Mike and Mark are all I can see.

"Tilly, getting arrested is frowned upon in our line of work." Mike groans at my hesitation.

"What would you get arrested for?" I bat my eyelashes feigning innocence. Feeling so sexy is new to me. I try to pull my hands away from them. Neither of them lets me go.

"Do you have any idea what we want to do to you right now?" Mark is so close to me now. My heart is racing.

Mike leans across the table and lowers his voice, "I'd love to bend you over this table and bury myself deep inside your hot tight pussy while you suck my brother off."

"I can see it too, Mike, but after we eat her out like she's that piece of cherry pie." *Oh fuck. Did I just wet myself?* I can't help but squirm in my seat. I've never been this turned on before.

"Well yeah, that's a given," Mike smirks at his brother before licking his lips suggestively.

"So, why don't we get out of here then?" *Is spontaneous combustion a real thing?* We need to leave. *Pronto.* I'm not beyond begging.

"It's not going to happen tonight, babe." Say what? Mark's tone holds no hesitation. I look to Mike for help. Maybe he can change his brother's mind.

"Don't look at me like that, sweetheart. As much as it pains me to say it, he's right." So they aren't playing good cop bad cop. *Boo.* My lip juts out. Mike reaches out and taps my pouty mouth. "That's cute, but it's not going to work on either of us." *Darn it!*

Mark turns my head, forcing me to look at him, "Tilly, if we were after a quick fuck, it would be one thing." The lust that filled his eyes is now gone. A softness I doubt many other people have seen from this intense man fills them.

"But that's not what we want from you," Mike confirms as I look back at him. The way these two communicate without words is a little unnerving. I've never experienced anything like it before. They may not be actual twins, but it's the only thing I can liken it to. The connection they share draws me in. I want more of it.

"What do you want?" I'm both terrified and excited to know the answer.

"Forever," they answer together. I'm not sure forever will be long enough.

6

MARK

"How did you get here tonight?" Tilly didn't run when we told her what we wanted. *Thank God.* As much as I never want this night to end, it's time to get our girl home.

"I took an Uber so I could have a cocktail." *Good girl.* My hand at the small of her back, I guide Tilly out of the diner as Mike pays our bill. I love the way she takes Mike's hand when he catches up to us without shying away from me. I wonder if she even realizes she does it. Considering she's never been with more than one person, she's a natural at it.

I open the passenger door for Tilly, and she hedges for the first time, "You'll have more legroom in the front seat, Mike." While her statement is true, it's not what we need right now. Going forward, we'll drive the truck so she can sit between us where she belongs. Hell, tomorrow, I might trade in this ride for another truck, so bench seats are our only option. Mike crowds Tilly into the opening of the door. I'm already behind it, so I move right behind where she is standing while he pins her to the door. I've never been jealous of my brother. *Until now.* Tilly groans the second Mike's lips touch hers. I lean over the door and inhale her sweet scent. At her neck, I tongue the lobe of her ear with my teeth while Mike continues to kiss her. Like with our touches, she bends her head, giving us each better access to her. I want to taste every part of her.

"Do you feel what you do to him?" I know Mike will take this opportunity to press himself further against her. Her reaction is amusing. If this damn door weren't between us, she would feel how hard I am for her too. "What you need to know is that we will always put you first, Tilly." I flick her tender lobe again before sucking it back into my mouth. I break away when my brother does. Our girl is a limp noodle as Mike drops her into the seat, and I round the hood. Mike chuckles as he belts her in and drops a kiss on the end of her nose before cramming into the back seat. My hand rests on her thigh while he kneads at her shoulders from behind. I'm distracted as I follow her directions to her place.

"It's the gray one on the left." Tilly raises a limp arm and points at a building. She's practically asleep. It's late. She had several drinks at the bar. I'm sure, like me, her adrenaline has been running all night. I'm surprised she hasn't completely crashed. I look forward to carrying her to her door and kissing her goodnight.

Mike and I must realize which building she is pointing to at the same time. We both let out a resounding "fuck no" as I pull away from the curb. Our reaction immediately wakes Tilly up.

"What's wrong? I thought you were taking me home. That was my building." *She doesn't know. She can't.* Taking my hand off her thigh, I grip the steering wheel while I speed away. I look in my review and notice Mike has also removed his hands from Tilly. He shakes his head, and Tilly demands to know what is going on. *That's the million-dollar question.*

7

TILLY

"What the hell is going on?" Mark doesn't answer me as I demand answers. Everything was fine until we got to my place. Other then the Eastwood area of town, I'm not sure where we are now. Mark gets out of the car first. Mike follows him. They have a quick conversation before Mike opens my door and puts out his hand for me. I don't take it at first out of principle. I don't like not knowing what's going on or why the plan to take me home suddenly changed once they saw where I live. It's just an apartment. I haven't lived in the building very long, and I keep pretty much to myself. I'm saving to buy a home. The rent is cheap, and my lease is short term. As soon as I save up a down payment, I'll be moving.

I take Mike's hand with a dramatic sigh, and he helps me out of the car while Mark paces the driveway. With a stomp of my foot, we stop in front of him. Am I being petulant? Maybe, but so is he. "Are you going to tell me what's going on?"

Mark bends and lifts me over his shoulder like I weigh nothing. I squeak out a "Put me down!" as he begins to move up the stairs and into the house — Mike right behind us. Mark pulls out a chair before lowering me into it. Despite his clear anger, he's still gentle with me.

"Now, are you going to tell me what's going on?" The room suits both men. Refinished wood floors and green walls with dark furniture. It's masculine and clean, yet void of a woman's touch. It pisses me off that I want to be the one to add it. "Ugh," I yell to the ceiling. "Is anyone going to tell me what happened?"

Mark leaves the room as he puts his phone to his ear. "We're going to be the ones asking the questions, Tilly." Mike turns a chair around in front of me and sinks into it. Gah, why does he have to be so sexy? I'm mad at him and his caveman brother. Mike crosses his arms over the top of the chair, and I raise a challenging brow. With his sleeves rolled up past his elbows I can't help but admire his muscular arms. It's hard to be mad when I want his hands back on me. Among other things.

"So, start asking." I cross my arms, pushing my boobs up in the process. *Two can play this game.*

"Nice try, baby. Maybe I should get my cuffs." *Yes, please. No. Bad Tilly. Bad girl.* Mike chuckles, no doubt reading my naughty thoughts as Mark comes back into the room, ending his call.

"She's clean." Mark relays to his brother while taking me in. He seems more relaxed now, and Mike seemed relieved.

"I knew it." Mike grins like he knew they had nothing to worry about all along.

"How in the world do the police know I don't have STDs, and why didn't you ask me?" I bolt out of my seat, mad as hell. If the jerks wanted to know, they could have asked me. "Take me home."

"You are home," Mark moves toward me, and I take a step back. He's lost his fucking mind if he thinks I'm staying here. Mike and his sexy arms haven't moved. At least he's no longer smiling.

"That won't do, Tilly. I wasn't talking about diseases. I was talking about your record. I couldn't risk jeopardizing our ongoing investigation by asking you. I had to check things out first." He takes another step closer. I don't move back this time trying to piece together what he said.

"What investigation? I haven't done anything wrong." *I don't even jaywalk.*

"No, you haven't, but the guy who owns your building is not a good guy." I think back to the few times I've met him. He kind of creeps me out. Goosebumps break out all over my arms, and a chill runs through me. Mark takes another step. He slowly raises his hand to my cheek. As mad as I am, I still close my eyes and lean my head into his touch. "We just found you, Tilly. We won't let anything happen to the woman we love?"

My eyes pop open at his use of the "L" word because as crazy as it sounds, I feel the same way. I never knew I could feel something so strong this fast. I think that's why I was so mad. I was afraid that I had been just a fool in love with Mike and Mark.

"You love me?" I ask Mark, who is standing right in front of me, still cradling my face. His hands are warm, and his touch is soft.

"From the moment we saw you," Mike confirms as he wraps his arms around me from behind. How the hell did he get there?

"Just like our parents always said we would." Like before at the car, only this time, Mark is the one kissing me, and Mike is behind me. Only, this time it's better because the door doesn't separate us. We are alone at home, and we have no reason to stop.

EPILOGUE

Mark

Tonight's a big night for us. Mike and I have been ready since the first time we took Tilly to bed with us. The woman was made for us. There is no doubt about it.

"Are you almost ready?" I ask Mike as we enter Tilly's room. We're both a little anxious about tonight. When she moved in, we agreed she should have her own space. For Mike and me, sharing comes naturally. We've done it all our lives. For Tilly, it's new. We weren't sure exactly what the dynamic would be, but we did know that it had to be her choice. With her own space, she holds all the power. She can come to my room, or Mike's, or invite one or both of us to hers.

"Holy shi-" I've never seen a hotter sight. Mike can't even complete his sentence.

"How the hell? No, don't answer that. Forget I asked." When your woman is naked, handcuffed at each wrist with her legs opened with a spreader bar, you don't stop to ask questions. Mike and I thought she was up here getting ready. Obviously, she had help in the shape of Naomi. No way could she have done this alone.

"I seem to have gotten myself into a little trouble officers. Could you give me some assistance?" Tilly bats her eyelashes. Mike doesn't miss a beat and starts stripping. Remember playing shotgun as a kid? Well, we still play it. Only now the stakes are very different. Although, in this case, there isn't a loser sitting in the back seat. Mike and I will take this woman any way we can get her. The first one naked gets to call the shots. Tilly's got us both beat tonight.

"We'll need to take a full report of the situation, ma'am." Mike salutes her as we both stand at full attention naked and ready to report.

"Won't you need a pen and a pad of paper?" Tilly can't get enough sex lately. We can hardly keep up with her.

"I've got everything you need right here, ma'am." I stroke my length as she watches. Her tongue darts out. Mike climbs up on the bed.

"Well, this is a lot to take in. Do you mind if I take a closer look?" He's inches away from her pebbled nipples.

"Not at all, officer. I demand a thorough investigation." Mike cups her tits in his hands and begins sucking her. Tilly's hips rise off the bed, and I grip myself harder. I love the way her body reacts. "Are you going to lend a hand officer?" *Smartass.*

"She's getting a little mouthy partner." I know by now she's soaking wet, and as much as I'd love to keep her cuffed to this bed forever, we do have plans tonight. Mike knows what I'm thinking. He unlocks the cuffs. I pull her to the end of the bed before I flip her over and smack her perfect ass. Mike moves closer to her, his hard length in his hands as he guides it to her greedy mouth while I slide inside of her. Mike grips her hair while I do her hips, and she moans as we begin to move as one. Nothing has ever been so right.

～

Tilly

I don't know why I'm so nervous. I love these men, and they love me. What we have is only going to get better. Nothing they tell me, or

I tell them tonight will change that. The sex we just had together proves how perfect we are for each other.

"Relax, baby." Mark takes my hand as I sit between them in the truck. I have no idea what they have planned, and I'm blindfolded. It's the three month anniversary of the day we met.

"I don't like surprises." That's not true, and they both know it. I love them, but I've had one too many recently. I just want tonight to go well.

The truck stops. Mark kisses me before he gets out. Mike's door opens. "I'm going to carry you inside. I don't want you to trip and fall." I'm pulled out of the truck carefully. I bury my head in Mike's muscular chest. He kisses the top of my head, mumbling something about precious cargo before telling me we don't have far to go.

"I'll get the door," Mark announces. I hear a creak and can tell we are now inside, but I hear nothing but two, "Oh shits" before I'm set down on my feet. I remove the blindfold. It takes a few moments for my eyes to adjust to the light. I recognize the space instantly. It's the Storybook Pub; only it looks nothing like it did the last time we were here. Now it is an empty building. A single table and chair sit in the center of the otherwise empty room. We slowly approach it. On the table are two long stem red roses, a bottle of chilled champagne, three flutes, and a note.

Tilly, Mark, & Mike -

Remember, we all have a story to tell. Tonight is just the beginning of yours. Good luck and enjoy it.

Kole

"Okay, I wasn't expecting this." We're all a little shocked. I sit down in the chair.

"What were you expecting?" Mark asks, kneeling before me and taking my hand. We agreed on brutal honesty in our relationship. I can't do anything other than laugh as Mike takes the same position as his brother.

"Honestly, this. The two of you down on one knee. Crazy, right?" It's absurd because we've known each other for such a short time. Mike and Mark look at each other before looking back at me.

"Hopefully, not too crazy." Mike hesitates before giving his brother another glance.

"Tilly, Kole told us he knew things that night. He was right then. We hope he's right now and that this is just the beginning of our story, will you be our forever?" *I already am Mark.*

"Will you marry us, Tilly?" Mike asks with hope in his eyes. I haven't even met the family yet.

"Is this happening?" Tears cloud my vision as two rings appear.

"Is that a yes?" Mark asks before sliding the first ring on my finger as I nod yes in response before looking at Mike, "Yes to both of you." He slips the other ring in place. They both stand. Mike takes me in his arms as Mark reaches for the champagne.

"I can't have any," I tell him before he opens the bottle.

"Why not?" Mike asks.

"I'm pregnant." Finally, saying the words out loud makes it seem real. I've known for over a week and have been afraid to say anything. Seeing how happy they are at the news confirms how ridiculous I've been. Is it too early to blame the hormones?

Mark pops the cork on the bottle. He laughs hysterically before letting us in on the reason, "I think Kole knew about this too. It's apple juice."

LEARN MORE ABOUT LANE MARTIN:
HTTPS://LINKTR.EE/LANEMARTIN

ALSO BY LANE MARTIN:
FLOURED
SIFTED
EVEN STRENGTH

A MORNING KISS

C. J. CORBIN

You see ghosts?

Sub-genre: Paranormal Romance
Relationship: Male/Female

1

As I rode down in the glass elevator, I could feel the excitement surge through me. I had a new job! Not only did it pay double what I had earned before, but it was with one of the most respected law firms on the West Coast. "Yippee!" I said silently to myself. I didn't want the other passengers to think I was nuts, as so many people already did.

I had a fear of heights too. While the others were commenting on the magnificent view, my back was to the windows of the elevator car. No, I didn't need to see the great scenery. Besides, I lived around San Francisco all of my life, I already knew what the city looked like.

The icy wind blew briskly on this winter's day, but there were no clouds in the sky, and no rain was expected. I hadn't worn a coat to the meeting because I didn't want to deal with carrying it in a warm office building, and now I wished I had. My wool suit was usually warm enough, but I had worn a skirt, and the gusty wind swirled around my legs. The walk to the Bart Station was several blocks ahead of me. Then I would pick up the train to take me home to Oakland.

I checked my watch and realized I could stop for lunch and still beat the commuter traffic home. I spotted what looked like an Irish pub. Well, it did have a big shamrock on the sign… and it was called

Storybook Pub. An unusual name, but this was The City, anything was possible.

The welcomed rush of warm air hit me when I walked in. For a Thursday afternoon, it was surprisingly packed with people. It looked quaint and comfortable inside with tables spread through the large room and green leather booths lining the walls. The bartender, who was behind the massive bar, beckoned me to come in.

"Welcome! We've been expecting you! I saved a place for you," he called out to me.

I almost turned around, thinking that surely someone stood behind me, and he was speaking to them.

He directed my attention to the only free spot in the entire room, an empty booth in the corner.

I waved, nodded, and pointed. Then I turned to look at him again, and I saw her... or it was almost a her ... a translucent figure of a woman. A ghost. Yeah, that was my special superpower and why people, including my family, thought I was weird.

As I headed to the booth. I glanced back, and she was gone. That sort of thing happened to me too.

The spot, as it turned out, was occupied by a man who was buried behind a newspaper reading. He didn't look up when I cleared my throat, hoping to get his attention. Nothing. He just pulled his glass of beer closer to him. I shrugged my shoulders and threw my briefcase onto the bench and sat down.

The bartender who had greeted me walked up with a menu. His smile was broad, and his golden eyes twinkled brightly.

"Welcome to the Storybook Pub, I'm Kole, the owner, and sometime bartender. Sandra will be taking your food order as soon as she's back from her break. We're a bit short-handed today as the winter sniffles have gotten to my crew. What can I get for you on this fine blustery day?" he said with a voice that was rich and melodic and included a heavy Irish brogue. I could hear the rich green rolling hills in it.

His smile was infectious, and I grinned back. Even though it was a weekday, I felt like celebrating. "Do you have Guinness?"

He laughed and waved his arms around him. "She wants to know if we have Guinness?" he roared to everyone seated in the area. They all chuckled as they raised their own mugs. "Cassie, all you have to say is what size you'd like, and it will be here before you can blink!"

"I guess I'll have a large one," I said hesitantly. "And how did you know my name?"

Kole winked and leaned toward me. "That's because I'm a leprechaun, my dear girl," he whispered conspiratorially. "And, yes, I know about the ghost."

I blinked at him in surprise. His was an unusual response.

At this, the man sitting opposite me slowly lowered his paper and peered at the two of us. His face read that he thought both of us were crazy.

"Ahh, Cameron, I see you've decided to give this beautiful blond woman here some of your brilliant attention. I'll get your large G for you," Kole said brightly as he walked away.

I stared directly at the most handsome man I had ever seen. He took my breath away with his square jaw and full lips. His highly chiseled cheekbones were so sharp I thought for sure anyone would cut themselves if they brushed their hand across his face. His wavy black hair and deep blue eyes were the dreams of any romance reader. And then his voice… oh, the angels sang when he was conceived.

"I'm sorry. I was engrossed in an article in the paper. I had to finish it."

"I wouldn't have intruded on your privacy, but there was no other place to sit," I tried to explain.

Then the thought hit me. I knew this man…or at least I thought I did. He was the older brother of a boy I dated in college for a short time. I was sure of it. If only I could remember Todd's last name. Shit!

Sandra, the waitress, interrupted my thoughts as she whisked my drink in front of me. "So, Cameron, another one?"

He looked at his almost empty glass and nodded.

I glanced at the menu and, of course, they had shepherd's pie. After Sandra took my order, I settled back into the booth to enjoy my ale.

By this time, Cameron had folded his paper and set it on the bench next to him. "Is this your first time here?"

I wondered if he meant the pub or in San Francisco? I took a stab and said, "I've never been to this bar. I don't often go into them by myself, but I felt like I was due a celebration this afternoon." Why did I want to explain myself? Something in the deep dark pools of his eyes drew me in.

With his eyebrow raised, he asked, "Celebrating? What is the special occasion?"

"I just accepted a position with Brooks, Fitz, and Dunbar."

He nodded his head. "Ahh, yes, BF&D. Prestigious firm. Are you a trial attorney?"

I grinned. "I am now. I've done mostly corporate work previously. This is a new direction for me."

He lifted his newly placed mug toward me. "Well then, Cassie, congratulations on making it to the big time."

"Thank you," I said and lifted my own beer to meet his.

He cocked his head at me. "I feel like we've met before. I can't remember where though."

"I think we have. I believe I dated your younger brother while I was in college."

His eyebrows raised in surprise. "Todd?"

I nodded my head. "Yes! I just couldn't remember your last name."

He chuckled. "Our last name is Harris."

"Oh! That's right. I lost that one completely. I didn't date him very long. You and I only met that once…" I paused, then my face colored rapidly as I remembered the fateful meeting.

His grin went from ear to ear. "Valentine's weekend. You answered the front door at Todd's apartment, totally naked with just a long stem red rose in your teeth and a can of whipped cream in your hand."

"Don't remind me. I think that was the most embarrassing moment of my entire life! I thought you were Todd."

"So, you said," he teased.

I fanned myself with the cocktail napkin and tried to change the subject. "How is your brother doing?"

Cameron signed heavily, and his mouth grew tight. "Let's say you were a bright spot in his life."

"I'm sorry to hear that. I thought he did well in school."

"It seems he led everyone to believe that. But there are better subjects to talk about, I'm sure."

I looked around the pub and admired the pictures hanging against the dark green wallpaper. "The photographs of Ireland are beautiful."

"They are. Kole told me that he took all of them. He captured the essence of the emerald isle."

"He has a good eye then. They are amazing in their simplicity. It sounds like you know Kole."

"No, I'm just a patron of the pub, like all the rest of the people who come in here. My office is around the corner. It's convenient, and the food is good."

He said that just as Sandra placed a large plate of food in front of me. My eyes grew wide.

"Can I offer you some? There is no way I could eat all this food. Sandra, could you bring us another plate, please?"

"I don't want to eat your lunch, Cassie. I had lunch a couple of hours ago," he replied.

The waitress returned quickly with another place setting. "Help the lady out." She winked at him.

I grinned because I knew I had him. The smell of the food was divine. No one would be able to resist it. I doled out a small amount onto the empty plate and pulled it over to me while I slid the remaining mound of food in front of him.

He chuckled when he saw what I had done. "I'm not winning this one, am I?" When I shook my head, his sapphire eyes sparkled, and he said, "Thank you, then."

The food was "melt in your mouth" good. No wonder the pub was crowded. I definitely would not be brown bagging lunch to work with a place like this down the street from my office. My office… that thought made me feel giddy inside again.

"You said your workplace is in the area?" I asked. "What do you do?"

"I'm an environmental attorney. My corporate offices are here in the city. I try to make it down here several times a month, but otherwise, I work out of my home."

"Oh? Where do you live?"

"It's a small town just north of Sonoma valley called Mintock."

"I know where that is, there is a lake. I've gone waterskiing there. It's quaint."

Cameron smiled. "Yes, it is."

"Have you been there long?" I asked as I stuffed a piece of the delicious soda bread into my mouth. I was never afraid to eat in front of a man.

"I bought the property about fifteen years ago when I first left college. There was a small weekend cabin, and I just recently added several rooms. I've been living there full time for about three years. Video conferencing makes life more manageable. I can work from my home office, which is easier than commuting every day."

I did quick calculations in my head, that put him at about the age of forty. I hadn't realized that Todd's brother was that much older than us. Cameron had ten years on me.

"Do you live here in the city?" he asked.

I shook my head. "No. Over the bridge in Oakland. I have a small concrete box, otherwise known as a townhouse, in a nondescript neighborhood, filled with more concrete boxes."

Cameron's laughter filled the air. It was deep, throaty, and very masculine. It sent chills running through my body. Good chills. The kind that often created a particular pleasant dampness between my legs.

"You do have an artful way of description. You will make a good trial attorney. So, you'll take the train every day?"

I nodded.

"That's a bitch commute. I know the walk to the station isn't too far from here, but I hope you're planning on leaving at a decent hour. This neighborhood can turn rough at night with the crime problem the city has. You can always find a car service."

I ate some of the mashed potatoes from my plate and considered thoughtfully. "You like to solve problems before they happen, don't you?"

"Many problems can be avoided if we just take the time to think things through before they occur. A lot of the ecological accidents are caused by companies who just won't look at the full picture, and then BAM! A major oil spill, then a habitat is destroyed."

"Said the environmental attorney."

He chuckled. "Yes, said the conservationist. Sorry, I get passionate about my work."

"Don't apologize. You are fortunate to work in an area that you love. Not many people can say the same."

"Can you?" he asked.

I took a full breath and tilted my head to the side. "I don't think I have as much passion for my job as you. I'm hoping that being a trial attorney will bring in something new and exciting for me. Don't get me wrong, I truly love the law. Being a lawyer is like solving a puzzle. There is always the excitement of finding a solution using the rules of law."

I pushed my plate away. "I can't eat anymore. It was delicious, but I'm stuffed." I looked at Cameron's plate, and he was finished too. I was glad the food hadn't gone to waste. It was too scrumptious.

He raised his eyebrows and said, "Dessert? They make an outstanding soda bread pudding with an Irish whiskey sauce. Maybe you'd like to share some with me?"

I grinned. "You may be able to talk me into that, but could we wait a bit? I mean… if you have time?"

"I have time," he said smoothly.

His voice hit my dark inner parts, and I felt like squirming on the bench. He was so deliciously handsome. Not in my wildest dreams would I ever have thought that I would meet someone like him today. Okay, maybe I was jumping the gun a little. I didn't even know if he was attached to another person, but he wasn't wearing a ring, so I thought maybe … but then a lot of men didn't wear wedding bands any longer … or perhaps he was gay and just being kind to me… I didn't remember Todd mentioning anything about his brother being gay, but he could be, this was San Francisco after all…

My thoughts continued down this path, and I realized that he was trying to get my attention. How did that happen?

"Earth to Cassie. Cassie, are you still there?" he said as he waved his hands in front of my face.

"Oh, my goodness! I'm sorry." My face colored with embarrassment. "I ... ahh... guess I was thinking about the dessert."

"We *can* order it now if you'd like."

"No... I'm fine. I would really prefer to wait for a little bit. I want to be able to enjoy it."

"Would you like a coffee or another drink?" he asked.

Oh, this was feeling like a date. I liked that. It had been a while since I'd been asked out. Not that I was anti-dating. I wasn't. There just wasn't much opportunity for it with my career.

Then I remembered he had asked a question. "Yes. Yes, coffee would be nice."

He waved Sandra over and ordered two coffees.

"Shall I make that two Irish ones, my dears?" she asked.

I looked blankly at her.

"Yes, Sandra, with Irish whiskey, that sounds good to me. Put a little whipped cream on it too. Would you like a little Irish?" he asked me, and his eyes were twinkling again.

Doh! Irish coffee. Not typically so dense, Cameron had thrown me off my game a bit.

"That sounds good." I used his words. "Whipped cream is fine too."

"Consider it done," she said as she picked up our used plates.

"Do you like whipped cream?" The corner of his luscious mouth was upturned in a half-smirk.

Oh, ...he was flirting. I liked that too.

"Yes, I do. It has many uses."

He leaned forward toward me. "Does it? Would you like to tell me about those uses?"

I pressed my lips together, trying to hide a grin. "It's always good with dessert... and with coffee," I said slowly, drawing out the words.

"Any other less conventional uses? If my memory serves me correctly, the first time I met you was a whipped cream kind of day. What did you do with it that day?"

My laugh had become throaty and deep also. His voice had started a fire deep inside of me. One that I didn't often have, and it felt good.

"Well, after I recovered from my embarrassment and we got rid of you that evening, there was much mischief and merriment to be had with the creamy sweet stuff."

Suddenly Kole was there with two Irish coffees, complete with whipped cream and maraschino cherries. He put both of them on the table in front of me. Before I could slide one over to Cameron, he stopped my hand.

"It looks like the two of you are enjoying yourselves. I always like to see that in my pub. I've asked the cook to set about making a new batch of whiskey sauce for our soda bread pudding. Cassie, I think you'll like it. It will take some time before it's ready. You're not in a hurry, are you?" He peered at me as if he could see through to my soul.

I shook my head slowly. "No… I have time."

"Good," he smiled. "Now Cameron, I think it can get a little drafty over in this corner booth. You need to sit over here next to Cassie, to protect her from the cold air.

Suddenly, I felt a cold draft around my legs, and I shivered. My eyes lifted to Kole. Usually, there was only one instance when that icy coldness would hit me unexpectedly. A ghost.

He smiled broadly and winked at me. "See, what I say is true."

It didn't take Cameron a second. He zipped into my side of the booth without a word. The frosty air left me immediately.

"I'll be back with the pudding as soon as the whiskey sauce is done." His voice faded away as he left us alone.

Cameron was so close I had to actually scoot back on the bench to give him room. He didn't seem to mind. His thighs were in contact with mine, which made my blood heat and my heart race. That was okay with me. There was no problem having a gorgeous man sitting near.

"This is a turn of events. When I woke up this morning to make the long drive to San Francisco, I didn't expect to be sharing lunch with such a beautiful woman. I mean, I remember you from college, but you're even more beautiful now. You have the loveliest eyes, the color … of … honey," he murmured as he drew even closer.

I laughed and looked at him squarely. "I don't actually think you saw my face when we first met."

His eyes shifted down to my breasts, which were thankfully demurely covered with a blouse and suit jacket.

I reached out and tapped him under the chin. "My face is up here."

"Um, yeah," he said as he lifted his head to greet my eyes. "Sorry. Guilty as charged. You have a magnificent body, as I remember too. And I actually think that the vision of you standing at the door is burned into my memory forever. You were so surprised that it took you a while to recover and I took full advantage of that, I'm afraid."

"I don't remember that… all I recall is being mortified." I picked up the maraschino cherry and dangled it for a moment, then I dropped it into my mouth and pulled out the stem very slowly.

He sat there motionless and watched me intently. He plucked the cherry by the stem from his coffee and suspended it just above my lips.

"Could you do that again?" he whispered softly.

I grinned and caught the piece of fruit between my lips and sucked it into my mouth. He didn't let go of the stem, and his soft fingers touched me gently. With my teeth clamped together, he pulled away the stem.

Cameron's tongue licked his lips, and he had a look of awe on his face. He took a long sip of his Irish coffee. I loved how he could recover so quickly. When he pulled his cup away, he had a whipped cream mustache and a dollop on his nose. His sexy tongue licked away the cream on his upper lip, and I swiped my finger over his nose. He caught my finger and sucked it clean. Yes, he created a hot fire inside of me that would soon roar out of control.

I did not know where this would take us. We seemed to get closer and closer together; either that or the bench was shrinking. He hadn't kissed me yet, but I could tell it was on his mind because he kept looking at my lips. The booth was perfect for us since it was in the corner of the bar. It was far more intimate than if we had sat out at one of the tables in the middle of the room.

Our conversation flourished too. Once we had our jobs and homes out of the way, we found things that we had in common.

"Where would you like to visit again?" he asked when he discovered that I loved to travel.

"Oh," I said, "that would have to be Alaska. I've been there twice, actually. The second time I went by myself. It is still so pristine and peaceful."

"Still is the operative word. My firm handles cases in Alaska. In fact, it was the Exxon Valdez oil spill that got me interested in practicing environmental law."

"What? You were only a young boy when that happened."

"True, but I studied the Valdez cases in law school. You must have studied them too. Most schools use the trials to teach that section of the law. And the appeal to the Supreme Court was only about ten years ago."

"Yes, you're right. Wow! I never thought about that during my visit. Where is your favorite place?" I asked.

He sat back and smiled. "I like warm weather trips, so far my favorite has been the Greek Isles. I went with some friends of mine a few years back. We rented a boat and had a blast."

I laughed and clapped my hands. "Opa!"

"Yeah, it was pretty much four weeks of drunkenness. But we had a great time!"

"Did you actually get to see the culture of Greece?"

"Of course, but that boat was fun!"

We had both forgotten about the dessert, and when it finally arrived, we noticed how much the bar had cleared out. I couldn't believe it was already nine-thirty. Where had the time gone?

Kole walked up and set a small box on the table.

"Your dessert is inside. You were having so much fun, I didn't want to interrupt you," he said as he laid the bill discreetly next to Cameron's elbow.

Before I had the chance, Cameron reached into his pocket and pulled out a black American Express card and laid it on top of the bill.

"No!" I exclaimed. "I should be paying for the meal."

Cameron tapped my nose. "You catch it the next time, okay?"

Next time? Oh yay! "Thank you," I answered.

"My car is in the garage next door. I am going to drive you home. It's too late for you to be on the train by yourself," he said, in such a way that it sounded like he wasn't going to hear any arguments about it.

"You know, I will be perfectly okay on the train. I've traveled later than this. Or I can get a car service." But for some reason, maybe from our past history, I felt like I could trust him, so I was glad not to have to take the train so late, and a taxi would be expensive. I was on a tight budget until I started the new job. "But thank you, I know it will take you out of your way. I am grateful," I accepted.

Kole brought the receipt back to the table. His eyes were twinkling again. "It was my pleasure to serve you both tonight. I hope we will see you again."

I smiled and took his offered hand. "Thank you for taking such good care of us."

"No coat?" Cameron asked.

I shook my head. "I wasn't expecting to be out so late."

"Let me get the car, and I'll pick you up outside. Wait in here. I'll honk." Cameron rushed out the door.

Kole stood with me to wait. "So, it's an *us* then?"

I realized that I did refer to Cameron and me as us. "No, not yet. Right now, I've met a nice man."

He nodded his head. "It looked a little more than that from my vantage point."

I shook my head.

"I'm rarely wrong," he said. "Many couples use the Storybook Pub for their beginning."

We stood in silence. I leaned toward him and whispered, "Who is she?"

A shadow of sadness covered his face, and I knew I shouldn't have asked.

"I'm sorry, that was intrusive of me," I murmured hurriedly.

He squeezed my hand, and his eyes looked many years older than his face belied. "No, my dear. I will tell you all about her the next time I see you."

"So, we will see each other again?" I asked. The car horn sounded. "Oh! That must be for me! Thank you, Kole!"

2

Cameron waited for me by the open passenger door of his shiny black Mercedes sports car. I watched him from the passenger seat as he walked around the car and hopped in next to me. He was striking in his black slacks and sweater. Tall and trim, he made a striking figure. I remembered him clearly from the first time we met. After I lived my mortification down, the three of us had spent a lovely weekend together.

I'd never tell him, but seeing him again made me recall that he was the reason I broke up with his brother. Todd couldn't hold a candle to Cameron and, by spending time with both of them, I definitely knew that I did not want Todd in my life. I had a small crush on Cameron back then, and he even popped into my head a few times over the years. It crossed my mind more than once that I wouldn't mind running into him. I didn't expect that ever to happen, yet it did, ten years later…

He pressed a button on the radio, and jazz began to play from the speakers. Good taste in music too.

"Head to the bridge?" he asked.

"Yes."

We were quiet again as the entire evening played in my head.

"A penny for your thoughts," he said as we were stopped at a light.

"Not too many thoughts. I like your car. For being so small, it's surprisingly comfortable. And I love the leather."

"This is my commuter car. It's good on gas and handles the road well. To get to Mintock, you have to drive some mountain roads. It's easier in a small car."

I laughed. "Sounds like a perfect justification to have a sports car."

"What do you drive?"

"Not a sports car. I have a nice safe, and dependable sedan. I didn't make a lot of money as a corporate attorney. I thought environmental attorneys didn't make a fortune either."

He grinned. "We don't. My dad ran his own company. He made a lot of money and invested it wisely. My parents are generous with Todd and me. Though they haven't supported me since I graduated from law school, they do give me gifts once in a while."

"Wow! Are you saying this was a gift?"

"No," he laughed. "I do alright as an attorney. These cars aren't as expensive as they might seem."

"It's still a gorgeous car."

He picked up my hand in his and held it.

"Thank you for letting me drive you home tonight."

"It's me who should be thanking you! This is very kind of you." I didn't know what to say, because my thoughts concentrated on his hand holding mine. I never realized how intimate it was to have someone rub my palm with their thumb. I wondered if he could feel how my pulse accelerated.

"I would have worried about you all night long."

"You would? Why?"

"I like being a knight in shining armor."

"Coming to my rescue? I bet you also like to rescue kittens out of trees too."

"But of course! And I always enjoy kissing fair maidens on the hand too," he said with a contrived English accent while he kissed the back of my hand ever so softly with the barest of touches.

My heart melted at the gesture. "Rescuing distressed women also gets you kissed back." I leaned over and gave him a kiss on the cheek.

He touched his cheek and smiled. "Thank you, my lady."

We were silent as we traveled over the bridge. The view was dark, but the lights of Oakland could be seen in the distance.

"Did you park at the station?" Cameron asked as we hit Oakland.

"No, actually, a neighbor dropped me off this morning. I was just going to grab a cab on the way home. My car is in the shop," I replied.

He grinned. "So, I'll get to see your concrete box?"

"Yes, you will." I laughed and gave him directions.

When we pulled up in front of the block of housing I called home, I turned. "Would you like to come in? For some coffee? You have a long drive home."

"I'm glad you asked!" he said, almost leaping out of the car.

It had been so cozy in the car, and when he opened my car door, the cold air hit me and made me shiver. It felt good when he put his arm around my shoulder and pulled me close. He was warm, and he felt safe to me.

I led him up to the front door and was secretly glad that I had straightened the place before I had left this morning.

"I have a cat, is that okay? I mean, are you allergic?"

"I'm fine with cats."

I opened the door. "She'll probably hide from you. I'd really like to have a dog too, but I'm not home enough. It wouldn't be fair."

I was glad the room was warm and switched on a few lights.

"Your home is inviting," he said, following me in.

I thought of it as a homey kind of place. Comfortable dark brown leather furniture filled the main room. A large-screen television was mounted on the wall opposite the couch. The staircase, which led to the second floor, was against the opposite wall. There was a small desk in the corner by the front door. My dining table sat close to the windows. In the back was the kitchen, and beyond that, I had a small fenced patio. Covering the dark blue accent walls were photos by my favorite wildlife photographer.

"Thank you, it's small. The bedroom is upstairs, and it has a nice little balcony that I like to use in the morning. The view from the back isn't all concrete. It actually overlooks a park. This is the bay area, housing is expensive and difficult to find, especially in a good neighborhood."

Cameron blew out a big breath. "Tell me about it. That's partly the reason I don't live near San Francisco." He looked closely at one of the pictures on the wall... Michael Hoffman ... you know he lives in Mintock. I've met him a couple of times. Nice guy and a terrific talent."

"Really?" I said, "I love his work."

He chuckled. "I can tell."

"So, sit down. Make yourself comfortable. I'll make the coffee."

"Do you need some help?"

I laughed. "I got it. It's pod coffee. I like quick and easy."

I removed my suit jacket and hung it over a chair. I saw him looking at me, appreciatively. That affirmation made all the hours of hard work in the gym worthwhile.

"Slow and hard, is good sometimes too," he murmured.

I could barely hear him and didn't quite know how to respond, so I went into the kitchen to try to recover. When I came back out with the coffee, I was surprised to see that all but one small light had been turned off, and Snowball, my white Persian cat, cuddled up in his lap.

"Oh! She never does that. You're going to get white hair all over your slacks. I'm sorry."

I set the tray on the coffee table. Picking up a cat out of someone's lap can be a delicate maneuver. But, I didn't want to rummage in Cameron's lap, oh ... okay ... yes, I wanted to do that very much! I picked her up by the scruff, which she did not appreciate and let me know by meowing loudly. Snowball scampered up the stairs with what remained of her dignity. Of course, I had a mad urge to try to brush the hair off his lap. Our eyes met, and we both burst out with laughter.

He winked at me and said slyly, "Be my guest." He patted the cushion next to him.

So I slid into the couch next to him. We were both adults, it didn't take a lot of imagination to know what would happen next.

"You don't really want coffee," I said as I turned toward him.

"Not really."

A MORNING KISS

They say the first kiss between two people can tell you everything about them and what they were going to be like together. I suddenly hoped that was true.

Cameron's mouth touched mine softly, and I had never felt anything more natural to me than his lips on mine. The kiss became deeper while his tongue nudged at me, and I welcomed him in. As our mouths explored and delighted, our hands joined in the discovery. The teasing bites against lips and the dancing of tongues stoked the fire that built inside of me.

All night I had yearned to see what was under the clothes he wore and to touch his skin. He obliged me quickly by pulling his sweater over his head. He tossed it, and I didn't care where it landed as long as it was off.

The sweater had hidden it all. The thick muscles across his chest and upper arms. My fingers enjoyed it all, especially the bunching of his muscles while he held me close and caressed my back. I was bold and fluttered my hand just below his belt buckle and was pleasantly greeted with firm hard flesh under the material of his pants.

His mouth moved down along my chin to my throat. Searching fingers lightly touched my breast through my blouse and bra. The thin material of both pieces didn't offer much resistance to his strokes across my nipples. I could feel them hardening in response.

"I want to see you. Bedroom?" he asked.

"Upstairs. Yes. I want more too."

He let me lead him up the steps. My bedroom was large and encompassed the entire second floor.

When Cameron saw the bed, he grinned at me and pulled me close. "That big bed is just for you?"

"It's a big room," I whispered, not really wanting to talk about the room.

"I'll look later. First you. I bet you're even more beautiful than you were ten years ago. Damn, I had a hard-on for you for weeks after we met. The only thing that kept me away from you was the fact that you were Todd's girlfriend," he said as his hands roamed around my bottom to bring us closer together.

"Really? If we're telling the truth, I thought you were much hotter. It was the reason Todd and I broke up."

"Did you ever tell him?"

"Never. I'm not mean. You were just … just more."

He chuckled. "I horned in on you both that weekend. I just couldn't get enough of you. And now, look, I have you after all."

"Now stop talking and back to kissing, please." His erection pressed firmly against my belly, and I wanted more of that, much more.

"I want to take my time because this has been a long time coming."

"Mmmm… there's that word …" I said it slowly, drawing it out, "coming…"

"You're wicked."

"I can be."

I pushed back gently and unbuttoned my blouse.

"Can you do that a little faster?" he said as I slowly exposed my bra. His mouth was on the thin transparent material covering my breasts. He sucked at my nipples, making them wet as they peaked to stiffness. "They are still as beautiful as I remember them." He opened the front closing clasp and pushed the bra to the side.

His lips and tongue were glorious, and he was an expert at using them to their best effect. Cameron's hands tried to mold to my butt, but my pencil-thin skirt impeded his progress because he couldn't get a good grip. His efforts to pull it up failed too.

I giggled and pulled down the back zipper. I had to push at the tight skirt because it wouldn't fall on its own. My blouse and bra landed on the chair behind him. I was glad that I had worn my thong panties today because the look he gave me was gratifying and made me feel incredibly sexy.

He held me at arm's length. His stare made my pulse accelerate, and my blood heat. While I backed up toward the bed, I hooked my fingers into his belt and pulled him along with me.

"I think you have way too many clothes on. I need to see more," I said with a sultry whisper in a voice that surprised even me.

As I sat on the bed, I unbuckled the belt and unzipped his pants.

His bulge poured over the opening of his trousers. Shimmying a bit made them drop to the floor. The material of his briefs was stretched thin by his fully erect cock. It didn't leave much to the imagination. He was so…there.

My own body reflected his. Wetness flooded through my thong, and I felt a delicious ache between my legs. I leaned back against the mattress, spreading my legs on either side of him.

"Want to do the honors?" I suggested as I lifted my hips to make it more convenient for him to slide off the remaining stitch of my clothes.

He leaned over and, before he removed it, ran a finger underneath the thong and brushed through to my core gently. There was a small gasp of delight from both of us. For me, he was so deliciously close to my clit … and for him …

"So wet," he whispered with admiration in his voice. "I need to taste you. I've been thinking of this all night."

He slipped off the thong, and with my legs still spread around him, he knelt and drew close to me.

"Ohhhh…." I murmured as his mouth made contact.

The sheer pleasure of him was incredible. He knew how to please a woman. Oh … seriously. I purred my approval of his skills, but quickly became lost in the sensation that he created in my body. The fire inside built, it incinerated me, and took me over the edge so quickly. All that was left was ash.

Cameron placed his hands on my torso and spread out his fingers. His touch was so electric. It was as if he were transferring energy into me. I leaned up on my elbows and peered at him.

"You have an amazingly talented tongue," I said.

He waggled it at me, and I giggled. "Think so? Glad you like it. I'm gifted in other areas, too," he responded.

His movement up over me was swift and sure. I enjoyed being wrapped in arms. I also couldn't fail to notice that the head of his erection poked out from the top of his briefs. We needed to remedy that, and soon. But first, I reveled in his arms.

My hands stroked the muscles in his back as they slowly inched down to the band of his briefs. My fingers crept between the material and his skin. While moving his shorts down below his ass, I drew my knees up to wrap my legs around him. As he rubbed himself against me, that familiar ache in my core filled me again when I lifted my hips against him. Our motions, I was sure, would make me come again.

He moved against me, and his briefs inched slowly down. When his cock finally sprang free of its bindings, it felt so glorious to have his thick hard flesh being coated with my wetness.

"Damn, Cassie, you feel so good. It's taking everything I have right now not to fuck you like crazy, but I want this to last. Damn, I want it to last." He rolled over off me. "I need to cool down for a moment, or this will be over now."

I now could finally take a long look at him. He kicked off his briefs, and they went sailing to another part of the bedroom. We would find them later. His body was lean, true, but it didn't lack muscles. He had long powerful looking legs. It was evident he was a runner. The muscles that stretched along his chest and upper arms told me he lifted weights too. His body did not have a lot of hair with just the right smattering across his chest, which narrowed down to his waist. And then there was his cock. It was ample, full, and firm.

I shifted down the bed to take a closer look. The vein underneath his shaft was fully visible, and I could help myself. My tongue, with a mind of its own, licked the entire length of his hot swollen flesh.

He roared his groan of pleasure. "Oh, fuck, yes!"

I bent my head further and gave the same treatment to the twin sacs below. It elicited the same reaction as before. Warmed to the task at hand, I took his shaft firmly in hand at the base and drew him into my mouth. I swirled my tongue around the head and could taste his sweet saltiness. I worked at this for only a moment as his hands caressed my head, guiding my rhythm.

"Stop, Cassie." His fingers stilled my movements. "I don't want to come. Wait. Please."

I did as he asked. Secretly, I didn't want him to come either. When it happened, I wanted it to be while he was deep inside of me.

Cameron pulled me up to him. His kisses were fervent as his tongue plundered my mouth and took control. It was a sweet invasion which my tongue and body were all in favor of. Our bodies undulated together. The fire was continually stoked without ceasing. As I rubbed myself against his hip and thigh, I was sure that wetness I felt was not perspiration, but my own silky softness. My core was not being touched but was ready to explode at the slightest pressure.

"Condom?" I whispered. I couldn't wait any longer.

His breathing was labored, it seemed he couldn't wait either. "Yes..." he puffed out. "Pants pocket. Now."

I leaned over the edge of the bed with my butt in the air. While I retrieved his trousers, he took the opportunity and caressed my sex by inserting his finger inside of me. He found my G spot immediately, and I almost collapsed from the pleasure. This would be good. Very good.

I finally found the condom packet and watched him as he rolled it over his magnificent arousal. His wrapped penis stood proudly at attention.

"You better, baby, because I don't think I can control myself. Be easy," he said.

I understood immediately. The question was, could I control myself?

I straddled myself over his waist and held myself above him. He tilted his cock up, and I slid down slowly. Shuddering, I moaned, "Ohhh..." while I threw my head back. The feeling as he filled me was heavenly. He wrapped his hands around my waist and seated me firmly on him. His hard shaft buried deep inside of me. We were finally flesh to flesh, and the pleasure was indescribable.

His hands moved to my breasts, and he held each one separately as his thumbs rubbed against my tender and swollen nipples. I rocked against him, lifted my hips up, and then came down again to fill myself with him over and over.

There was no thought. No speech. Just the sounds made from the ultimate pleasure. Our breathing emerged in gasps as the pressure between our bodies increased. It was evident he strained to hold onto himself.

My cries of ecstasy were the result of the white-hot eruption that set off the frenzied pace that followed. I rode through my orgasm as my body exploded over his. He took control, thrusting upward to meet me as his own wild release flooded through him. He responded with a harsh groan of male satisfaction, and his magnificent body shuddered, which only fed my own pleasure. It kept rippling through me over and over.

I collapsed on him and felt his heart pounding wildly. We both took our ragged breaths of relief and laid together. When his now spent manhood slipped from me, I mourned its loss.

3

We laid together, and the silence enveloped us. When we both finally felt cramped in our positions, we moved slowly.

"I have some wine. Would you like some?" I offered. I wasn't ready for the evening to end.

"That would be great. Can I get it?"

I stood from the bed and slid into the robe that hung in the bathroom. "No. Let me. Would you like some water too?"

"Yeah, that would be great." He sat up. "May I use the towels in the bathroom?" he asked.

"Oh, of course. I'm sorry I didn't offer it. The ones hanging on the rack are fresh. Please help yourself."

I went downstairs and scolded myself. I hated the awkward postcoital moments. I was never sure what to say or do. I didn't want him to leave. It had been such a great day. I was curious how he felt about it too.

I prepared a tray, and before I went up the stairs, I popped into the bathroom located next to the kitchen. I freshened up a bit and then joined Cameron back in the bedroom.

He had already pulled down the bedspread and propped up the

pillows on the bed. Sure enough, Snowball laid across his lap as he leaned back against the headboard. She was purring to her heart's content at the moment and gave me a look that dared me to move her from her comfy location. I gave him a bottle of water, which he downed quickly and then handed him a glass of cabernet.

I pulled back the comforter and settled in next to him. He chuckled as he put his arm around me and pulled me over.

"What's funny?" I asked.

"I thought before you came in that I really need to get a king-sized bed. I forgot how nice it can be."

"I enjoy mine. In fact, I enjoy this entire room. The bedroom sold me on the place."

"I can see why. You don't mind if I stay, do you?" he asked.

"I wouldn't have offered you wine. In fact, I hoped you would."

The comfort level we felt with each other was apparent.

"Now, how did you end up here? No boyfriend in your life?"

"Not really," I answered as I leaned my head against his strong shoulder. My fingers played with his soft chest hair. "Since I decided to change my career direction, I went back to school to brush up on my skills. I knew it would be tough to find a job without trial experience, so I figured it would be wise if I could offer additional education and knowledge on my resume. It worked too because they were looking for someone who they can mold in their image. I'm ready for the molding. I'm looking forward to the challenge."

"It sounds like it."

"What about you? A girlfriend?"

"No, girlfriend. I live alone in Mintock, well, not exactly alone. I have a big black lab called Bear. My neighbors have him right now."

"Oh? Won't they be worried if you don't come home?" I asked with concern in my voice.

"Nah. I often stay the night in San Francisco when I come down. Sometimes there are surprises in my day."

"Like me?"

He chuckled. "Yes, like you. I keep a change of clothes in the trunk and an extra kit."

I raised my eyebrows at him. "Imagine that."

"Are you looking to open your dating calendar?"

"Maybe," I giggled.

"Hmmm… you're going to make this difficult on me."

I giggled again. "Maybe."

He turned over on his side, forgetting that Snowball was on his lap. She let out a loud protest and moved to the bottom of the bed. Cameron pulled me into his arms. I let out a deep sigh.

"What was that for?" he asked.

"I like this."

"So do I."

We both snuggled close and fell asleep.

When I opened my eyes in the morning, it was cloudy and grey outside. Cameron came out of the bathroom with a towel wrap around his hips. He looked adorable and incredibly sexy. Just the way he moved about the room lit a fire deep inside of me.

"Hey, sleepyhead," he said as he sat on the edge of my side of the bed. "I made some coffee for you." He held up the mug. "I hope it didn't get cold. I've got to head home. I have a conference call coming up, and I need to be there. Then I'm heading to the airport. I'm on my way to Wyoming to take some depositions. I'll be gone all week." He slipped back in the bathroom and emerged a few minutes later dressed.

I nodded my head, disappointed that morning sex was not on the agenda. I sat up and reached for my robe.

"No. Stay in bed. You don't need to get up, you're on vacation!" he beamed.

"But I should make you some breakfast. Or something," I replied. I didn't want him to leave.

"Don't worry about me. I'll hit Starbucks on my way up. Listen, I'm going to be back in the city next week. Would you like to meet me at the pub? We could have dinner."

"Um," I paused, that was strange. He didn't want to pick me up? We could go somewhere local and perhaps end up here again. "Yeah. That would be nice."

We made a date, and he insisted that I not walk him out. He gave me a kiss that curled my toes and promised many good things to come.

I threw myself back against the pillows. It had been a glorious night. In fact, I had never had better. He liked to cuddle, which I loved. There hadn't been a moment all night that we parted. My bed could have been a twin for all that it mattered.

4

My notice had already been given at my last job, and they promptly let me go. There were two weeks of vacation to look forward to, and it waited to be put to good use. A quick trip somewhere, maybe to Lake Tahoe, would do me some good.

While I researched some travel plans on the internet, I found myself typing Cameron's name into the search engine and pressed the enter button. It was surprising how much information there was about him. Mainly professional information and about environmental cases, which he had fought and won. There was also a page containing his bio, and since I was interested, I clicked on that.

It listed all the standard items, where he went to school, and wow ... he played baseball in college and was almost drafted into the minor leagues. Todd hadn't mentioned that about himself. It talked about his parents and Todd and ... what the hell? His wife?

I stared hard at the computer. It listed her name, Susan. I quickly typed in her name and found her social media account with a picture. She was a blonde like me, and thankfully that's where the resemblance ended. Her eyes were blue, and mine were brown. She wore her hair cut very short, and mine was long. I think Cameron enjoyed taking my hair out of its bun last night. I loved the way he had splayed it around my shoulders. Her face was stern and severe. I couldn't quite imagine the two of them together. In all of his pictures, he looked like he was having fun. Her, not so much.

But the fact was, he was fucking married. No wonder he had to rush home for a conference call. Shit, he needed to rush back to her. His website didn't mention anything about where he lived, only the address of his office in the city.

I just stared at the computer screen. I shouldn't have felt disappointed, but I was, terribly. I thought I had met someone really nice. It had been my hope that perhaps this would lead somewhere. Then I remembered we had never exchanged telephone numbers. Well, he could always be called at his office. There would be no meeting at the pub. No way. I was definitely not interested in a married man. I had been stupid and done that once before on promises that he would leave his wife for me. I vowed, never again.

Why was a call to Cameron even necessary? He had actually lied to me. Didn't he? Omitting the truth was the same as lying in my book.

This news put a spin on the direction of my day, which was unexpected. I felt used and depressed. I decided not to travel but to throw myself into home projects instead. Over the week, I tackled projects that had waited for attention. Closets, drawers, and the garage were all rearranged. Every time Cameron's face appeared in my thoughts, I dug even further into my projects. However, my mind was ever on the calendar and the quickly approaching meeting date.

I hadn't called Cameron's office to leave a message. Standing him up was a better approach. He didn't deserve anything else. When the day finally arrived, I decided to confront the bastard instead.

I dressed carefully. A short, tight spandex style skirt that was almost indecent with a snug, low-cut sweater on the top would do it. And the five-inch heels that would almost put me at his height would be the cherry on the top of this sundae. I would be the one dessert he'd never enjoy again.

When I arrived early at the Storybook Pub, it was crowded. Kole was busy at the bar with two other bartenders, and he was followed by his ever-present spirit. I hoped he would eventually let me know who she was. I hopped onto the only stool available. The man sitting next to me turned and gave me the eye of approval. Kole saw me immediately, and, in a moment, he stood in front of me.

"She's taken," he said to the man, and the stranger abruptly turned around.

"No, I'm not," I whispered to Kole. I didn't really have any interest in attracting the man's attention again.

"Cameron is already here ... in your spot."

"Well, this won't take long. I'll have a Jameson Bow Street neat."

Kole raised his eyebrows. "That's a strong one, my girl," he said as he poured.

The ghost at Kole's elbow began to swirl around him. I would have blamed it on the whiskey, but I hadn't imbibed...yet.

"She's agitated," I remarked to Kole.

"Yes. What is wrong?"

"Cameron is married."

The puzzlement that covered Kole's face surprised even me. Why would he care? I downed the drink all at once. It burned going down and made me sway on the stool, but I didn't care.

"That cannot be," Kole replied quietly. His ghost quickly vanished.

"He is. I'm going to let him have it. Then I'll be right back."

I hopped off the barstool and stood on wobbly legs. The drink was having more of an effect than I counted on. As I walked away, the vision hit me, and I turned back to him.

"She was your wife, Kole?"

He stared at me, dead on. "Yes."

"Her love for you is immense, which is why she hasn't left this existence. You are soulmates. You've been together for millennia."

"I know," he said as he wiped the bar down.

Sometimes I wished I didn't have the gift. For some people I shared it with, it brought great comfort and for others pain.

Now, I had something important to say. Cameron sat in the same booth in the corner. This time he was facing out, and he was not reading a newspaper. He saw me, and his face lit in delight with a wry smile, which I'm sure, was for my clothes. He moved quickly to stand. When he tried to encircle me with his arms, I raised my hands to press him back. He looked surprised and confused.

"I missed you, Cassie. You look wonderful."

"I'm sure you did."

"Come, sit down. Let's get some drinks."

"I have no intention of sitting with you ... anywhere, you son of a bitch."

"What?" His state of uncertainty rewarded me.

He reached out again for me, and I did something I had never done before. I slapped him across the face. My action caused the patrons around the booth to look up from their conversations.

One man said, "Is he bothering you, miss?"

I turned quickly. "No, I've got this."

When I turned back around, Cameron rubbed his hand on his face.

"What the fuck, Cassie?" he exclaimed.

"You didn't think it was important to tell me you were married? No, you're like all the sleaze buckets around. Good looking men like you are all the same! Get a little action on the side from the single woman. Well, I don't take that type of treatment. How dare you?" While I kept my voice down, it was no less filled with venom.

I turned to leave, but he latched on to my upper arm, and I swung around, ready to punch him.

He caught my hand and hissed, "Do not hit me again."

"Then let go of me!" I spat back.

"Okay." He let go and raised his hands. "But, if you're interested, I do have an explanation."

I rolled my eyes. "Yeah? My wife doesn't understand me? I've heard them all before. I'm sure you can't add anything new."

He slid into the booth. "If you want to hear and can conduct yourself in a civilized manner, I'd like to tell you about it. But, if you're going to do all the talking, then you can leave me out of the conversation. I like you, Cassie, but my patience does have boundaries."

Well, didn't that release some of my piss and vinegar? I stood there for a moment and thought about my options. He just looked at me and was silent.

I took a deep breath. I tried to mask the emotion I felt with one of indifference. "Okay. Say what you have to say." I sat opposite him in the booth.

Sandra approached us, but I waved her off.

He started, "I am not married." I opened my mouth to speak, but he held up his index finger. "Please allow me to continue. I have been separated from my wife for three years. Yes, it was the same time I moved to Mintock. We lived in a beautiful home in Sausalito. We did not divorce right away, because her mother was dying, and I didn't want to put her through both things at the same time." He reached into his briefcase and pulled out a document. He shoved it over to my side of the table. "Read it."

I looked at it. It was a court-filed document stamped with last week's date.

I said with a tiny voice, "Your divorce decree. Your divorce became final on the day we met."

"Yes," he said with his lips firmly pressed together. "I didn't widely advertise my separation or my divorce because that sort of thing never looks good for a lawyer. Especially in the small world that I travel in. So, you wouldn't have found it on the internet unless you did an exhaustive search."

I sat there quietly, embarrassed.

"I am not the type of man who sleeps around. In fact, you were the first woman since my wife…"

I looked at him skeptically. "You had a condom in your pants pocket."

He smiled with amusement. "Yes. My lawyer gave it to me when I left his office after picking up the document. He told me to go out and have fun."

"Well, I'm not the type to sleep around either."

It was his turn to give me a cynical look, which I admit, I deserved.

"I don't," I said softly.

"I believe you," he said.

"Thank you for the explanation. I'm sorry I struck you. I've never done that before." I rose to go.

He caught my hand gently. "Why are you leaving?"

"I apologize. I judged you so poorly, I didn't think you'd want me to stay."

He slid out of the booth and stood next to me. My face was in his hands, and his mouth touched mine so softly at first, and then our kiss became urgent.

When our lips broke apart, all I could see was his smile.

"I want you to stay. Please. I think there is a connection between us that I want to explore. Do you want that too?" he whispered.

"Yes," I answered breathlessly.

I scooted back into the booth, and he joined me.

"Besides," Cameron said as his lips captured mine once again, "morning kisses are my favorites, and we need to have a lot of them."

And we did.

THE END (or is it?)

LEARN MORE ABOUT C. J. CORBIN:
HTTPS://AMZN.TO/2XH8TCX

ALSO BY C. J. CORBIN:
MEETING DESTINY
PROTECTING DESTINY
REVEALING DESTINY

Thank you to all of the contributors involved with this collection for putting your faith in us and being a part of the first book from Love & Devotion Author Services, Inc. You are invaluable and we appreciate your support.

The Partners in Crime,
   Tonya & Naomi

Watch for more and follow us!
   www.lovedevotionevents.com
   lovedevotionevents@gmail.com
   www.facebook.com/lovedevotionevents
   www.facebook.com/groups/lovedevotionevents
   www.instagram.com/lovedevotionevents
   www.twitter.com/lovedevotionae